AF692730

Direct Application of International Criminal Law in National Courts

Direct Application of International Criminal Law in National Courts

by

Ward N. Ferdinandusse

T•M•C• Asser Press
The Hague

Published by T.M.C.ASSER PRESS
P.O.Box 16163, 2500 BD The Hague, The Netherlands

<www.asserpress.nl>

T.M.C.ASSER PRESS' English language books are distributed exclusively by:

Cambridge University Press, The Edinburgh Building, Shaftesbury Road,
Cambridge CB2 2RU, UK,
or
for customers in the USA, Canada and Mexico:
Cambridge University Press, 100 Brook Hill Drive, West Nyack, NY 10994-2133, USA

<www.cambridge.org>

ISBN 10: 90-6704-207-2
ISBN 13: 978-90-6704-207-9

All rights reserved.
© 2006, T.M.C.ASSER PRESS, The Hague, The Netherlands, and the author

No part of the material protected by the copyright notice may be reproduced or utilized in any form or by any means, electronic or mechanical, including photocopying, recording, or by any information storage and retrieval system, without written permission from the copyright owner.

PREFACE

In recent times, following the end of the Cold War, the international community has embarked on a policy of prosecuting those who commit genocide, crimes against humanity and war crimes – known today as "core crimes." It has chosen this course in order to promote international peace, achieve reconciliation and deter future political and military leaders from committing such crimes. International courts have been established to give effect to this policy. The International Criminal Court, the ad hoc tribunals for the former Yugoslavia and Rwanda and the Special Criminal Court for Sierra Leone provide for the prosecution of individuals who have committed core crimes, while accusations that states have committed such crimes increasingly are brought before the International Court of Justice.

However, most opportunities for the prosecution of core crimes arise before national courts. The Statute of the International Criminal Court acknowledges this in its acceptance of the principle of complementarity which gives primary responsibility for trying core crimers to national courts. Some States have enacted legislation empowering their courts to prosecute core crimes, defined in accordance with the definitions of these crimes contained in the Rome Statute of the International Criminal Court. But most States have not done so. Questions arise as to whether the courts of such States will prosecute core crimes and, if so, on what legal basis. Or whether they will refuse to prosecute on the ground that such crimes are unknown to the national legal order.

Issues of this kind are the subject of Ward Ferdinandusse's excellent study.

Ferdinandusse argues that in some cases prosecutions of core crimes have succeeded before national courts without national legislation incorporating such international crimes. Moreover, he claims that there are sound legal arguments in favour of the direct application of international law to enable the prosecution of such crimes – because the law is binding without it being transformed into national law by domestic legislation.

Ferdinandusse accepts that the direct application of international criminal law in such cases presents problems. Domestic courts, unfamiliar with international law, find obstacles in the way of direct application in notions of state sovereignty, the separation of powers and the principle of legality. However, Ferdinandusse maintains that there are competing principles which oblige national courts to prosecute international crimes in the absence of implementing legislation. International humanitarian law obliges national courts to apply core crimes directly; and notions of *jus cogens* do likewise. Moreover, the rule that national courts must interpret national law in accordance with international law – the principle of consistent interpretation – ensures that courts will give direct effect to international criminal law. This is emphasized by the rule of international law that imposes on States a duty to prosecute or extradite serious international crimes. Moreover, Ferdinandusse argues that States should prosecute such crimes as international crimes and not simply as ordinary crimes, such as murder.

Despite international support for the prosecution of core crimes, such prosecutions are rare before national courts. When they do occur they frequently fail as a result of obstructive domestic law institutions and doctrines. To aggravate matters, amnesty laws sometimes block the prosecution of core crimes while the International Court of Justice has held, in the unfortunate Arrest Warrant Case of 2002, that senior government officials enjoy immunity from prosecution for core crimes before national courts. This is a serious problem that threatens the credibility of the international commitment to the prosecution of core crimes. Ward Ferdinandusse's study highlights this problem but at the same time presents compelling legal arguments in favour of the direct application of international core crimes by national courts. He shows convincingly that domestic legal impediments to such prosecutions are not insurmountable and that national law and international law may combine to give effect to the principle of complementarity.

Ward Ferdinandusse has written a book that is rich in international and comparative material, sound on principle and coherent in argument. It deserves the attention of both international and national criminal lawyers as it offers a legal basis for the realization of the commitment to the prosecution of crimes that threaten the welfare of the world.

Leiden, September 2005

John DUGARD
Professor of International Law,
University of Leiden

Member of the International Law Commission

ACKNOWLEDGMENTS

This study is the result of four years of research at the University of Amsterdam. It is embedded in the research project "Interactions between International Law and National Law," directed by Professor André Nollkaemper at the Amsterdam Center for International Law and funded by a Pioneer grant of the Netherlands Organization for Scientific Research (NWO). I wrote parts of it during stays as a Visiting Researcher at New York University and the Irish Centre for Human Rights in Galway. A visit to the Max Planck Institute for Foreign and International Criminal Law in Freiburg am Bresgau was instrumental for the collection of sources. Marjolijn Bastiaans, Jennifer Khurana, Avril McDonald and Philip van Tongeren all contributed to the editing process. I gratefully acknowledge the financial support of the Netherlands Organization for Scientific Research (NWO), the Fulbright Foundation, the Amsterdam University Fund and Dr Hendrik Muller's Vaderlandsch Fonds.

I am grateful to all those colleagues who have kindly responded to my requests for information or comments over the last four years, shared their ideas and sources, or explained the peculiarities of their legal systems to me. I thank the faculties of New York University, the Irish Centre for Human Rights and the Max Planck Institute for Foreign and International Criminal Law for their time and support, in particular Professor Benedict Kingsbury and Professor Cesare Romano in New York and Professor William Schabas in Galway. A special word of thanks goes to Professor John Dugard, Professor Willem van Genugten, Professor Terry Gill, Jann Kleffner, Professor Erika de Wet, Professor Harmen van der Wilt, and, in particular, Professor André Nollkaemper and Professor Bert Swart.

Amsterdam, 20 August 2005 W.F.

TABLE OF CONTENTS

ABBREVIATIONS

AC	Appeal Cases, England and Wales
ACHPR	African Charter on Human and Peoples' Rights
ACHR	American Convention on Human Rights
Acta Jur. Hung.	Acta Juridica Hungarica
AJIL	American Journal of International Law
All ER	All England Law Reports
AP I	First Additional Protocol to the 1949 Geneva Conventions
AP II	Second Additional Protocol to the 1949 Geneva Conventions
Art.	Article
ATCA	(American) Alien Tort Claims Act
AVR	Archiv des Völkerrechts
AZAPO	Azanian Peoples Organization
BGH	Bundesgerichtshof (German Supreme Court)
Bull. crim.	Bulletin criminel (Judgments of the French Supreme Court)
BVerfG	Entscheidungen des Bundesverfassungsgerichts (Judgments of the German Federal Constitutional Court)
BvR	Casenumbers of the Bundesverfassungsgericht
BYIL	British Yearbook of International Law
CA	Court of Appeal
Calif. LR	California Law Review
CAT	Convention against Torture and Other Cruel, Inhuman or Degrading Treatment or Punishment
CCAIL	(German) Code of Crimes against International Law
Cir.	Circuit
CLR	Commonwealth Law Reports
CODICES	Case-law collection of constitutional courts (at http://codices.coe.int)
Columbia LR	Columbia Law Review
CP	Code pénal
CPM	Code pénal militaire
Cr App R	Criminal Appeal Reports
Crim. LR	Criminal Law Review
CUP	Cambridge University Press
Doc.	Document
DPP	Director of Public Prosecutions
Draft Code 1996	Draft Code of Crimes Against the Peace and Security

	of Mankind, 1996 (ILC)
Duke J of Comp. & Int. L	Duke Journal of Comparative & International Law
EC	European Community
ECHR	European Convention of Human Rights
ECJ	European Court of Justice
EComHR	European Commission of Human Rights
ECtHR	European Court of Human Rights
EJIL	European Journal of International Law
Eur. J Crime, Crim. L & Crim. Jus	European Journal of Crime, Criminal Law & Criminal Justice
EWCA Crim.	Court of Appeal, Criminal Division (England & Wales)
EWHC	High Court, Administrative Court (England & Wales)
F.2d	Federal Reporter, Second Series
Fam.	Law Reports: Family Division
FCA	Federal Court of Australia
GAOR	General Assembly Official Records
GATT	General Agreement on Tariffs and Trade
GC	Genocide Convention
GC I	Geneva Convention (I) for the Amelioration of the Condition of the Wounded and Sick in Armed Forces in the Field
GC II	Geneva Convention (II) for the Amelioration of the Condition of Wounded, Sick and Shipwrecked Members of Armed Forces at Sea
GC III	Geneva Convention (III) Relative to the Treatment of Prisoners of War
GC IV	Geneva Convention (IV) Relative to the Protection of Civilian Persons in Time of War
GDR	German Democratic Republic
Harvard ILJ	Harvard International Law Journal
Harvard LR	Harvard Law Review
HR	Hoge Raad (Dutch Supreme Court)
HRC	Human Rights Committee
HRQ	Human Rights Quarterly
HuV	Humanitäres Völkerrecht
IAComHR	Inter-American Commission of Human Rights
IACtHR	Inter-American Court of Human Rights
ICC	International Criminal Court
ICCPR	International Covenant on Civil and Political Rights
ICESCR	International Covenant on Economic, Social and Cultural Rights
ICJ	International Court of Justice
ICL	International criminal law
ICLQ	International and Comparative Law Quarterly

ICRC	International Committee of the Red Cross
ICTR	International Criminal Tribunal for Rwanda
ICTY	International Criminal Tribunal for the former Yugoslavia
ILA	International Law Association
ILC	International Law Commission
ILM	International Legal Materials
ILR	International Law Reports
IMT	International Military Tribunal (Nuremberg Tribunal)
IsraelYBHR	Israel Yearbook on Human Rights
JICJ	Journal of Criminal Justice
LCP	Law and Contemporary Problems
LJIL	Leiden Journal of International Law
Mich. LR	Michigan Law Review
MLR	Military Law Review
MPC	Model Penal Code
MPI	Max Planck Institute
MPYUNL	Max Planck Yearbook of United Nations Law
NATO	North Atlantic Treaty Organization
NGO	Non-governmental organization
NILR	Netherlands International Law Review
NJ	Nederlandse Jurisprudentie
NJB	Nederlands Juristenblad
NJW	Neue Juristische Wochenschrift
No.	Number
NQHR	Netherlands quarterly of human rights
NStZ	Neue Zeitschrift für Strafrecht
NYIL	Netherlands Yearbook of International Law
NZLR	New Zealand Law Reports
OUP	Oxford University Press
p.	page
P.2d	Pacific Reporter, Second Series
para.	paragraph
PC	Privy Council
PCIJ	Permanent Court of International Justice
PKK	Kurdistan Workers' Party
PrepCom	Preparatory Committee
QB/QBD	Law Reports Queen's Bench Division
RdC	Recueil des Cours
RDMDG	Revue de droit militaire et de droit de la guerre
RDPC	Revue de droit pénal et de criminologie

Res.	Resolution
RGDIP	Revue Générale de Droit International Public
RIDC	Revue internationale de droit comparé
RIDP	Revue internationale de droit pénal
RSC	Revue de science criminelle et de droit pénal comparé
SA	South African Law Reports
SACJ	South African Journal of Criminal Justice
SC	Security Council
SCR	Supreme Court Reporter
S.E.	South Eastern Reporter
STC	Simon's Tax Cases
StGB	Strafgesetzbuch (German Penal Code)
Suppl.	Supplement
Texas ILJ.	Texas International Law Journal
UCMJ	(U.S.) Uniform Code of Military Justice
UN	United Nations
UN Doc	United Nations Document
UNTS	United Nations Treaty Series
UNWCC	United Nations War Crimes Commission
US	United States Supreme Court Reports
USC	United States Code
v.	versus
Va. J. Int'l L.	Virginia journal of international law
VCLT	Vienna Convention on the Law of Treaties
Vol.	Volume
WIM	Wet Internationale Misdrijven (Dutch International Crimes Act)
WLR	Weekly Law Reports
WTO	World Trade Organization
WW I	First World War
WW II	Second World War
Yale LJ	The Yale Law Journal
YIHL	Yearbook of International Humanitarian Law
YIL	Yearbook of International Law
YILC	Yearbook of the International Law Commission
ZaöRV	Zeitschrift für ausländisches öffentliches Recht und Völkerrecht

Chapter I
INTRODUCTION

1. Introduction to the Problem

This study will set out the present state of the international legal framework governing direct application in national courts of the international offences of genocide, crimes against humanity and war crimes, the so-called 'core crimes.'[1] On the basis of comparative national and international case law, it will examine the conditions under which international law on the core crimes can or should be applied directly for the prosecution[2] of individuals. I will also explore the underlying considerations for granting or withholding direct application. Direct application in the context of this study means that a national court applies an international rule, without it having been transformed into a rule of national law, because it is binding law for the court.[3]

The problem studied here originates in the fact that national courts are the primary fora for the prosecution of international crimes,[4] including the core crimes.[5] The establishment of the ICC has reinforced rather than weakened their importance, both in principle and in practice. In principle, their primacy has been strengthened because the principle of complementarity underlying the jurisdiction of the ICC confirms the dominant position of national courts.[6] In practice, this primacy is due to the fact that many States are more likely to undertake national prosecutions, stimulated by the heightened attention for international crimes and the prospect of being labelled unwilling or unable by the ICC. Many are also better equipped to do so, as the implementing legislation for the ICC has improved numerous national laws on international crimes.

---

[1] These are the crimes subject to the jurisdiction of the International Criminal Court (ICC). Cf. Art. 20 of the ILC's 1994 Draft Statute of an International Criminal Court (distinguishing genocide, aggression, crimes against humanity and war crimes from selected treaty crimes) and Commentary to Art. 20, in 1994 ILC Yearbook, Vol. II, Part 2, p. 38. Since ICC jurisdiction over the crime of aggression has been postponed for lack of a widely accepted definition, the term core crimes in this study comprises only the other three crimes.

[2] Unless indicated otherwise, the term prosecution in this study refers to the entire process of prosecuting and punishing a defendant. Thus, it denotes a complete trial including any resulting convictions, not solely the work of the prosecution as oppposed to that of the defense and/or the judge(s).

[3] See for a more elaborate definition para. 4 and 5 of this Chapter.

[4] The term international crimes in this study refers solely to crimes of individuals, not of states. See on the latter Pellet 2003; Wyler 2002; Pellet 2001; several articles in 10 EJIL, Issue 2 (1999); Hoogh 1996.

[5] Cf. Arbour 2003, p. 585.

[6] See on the principle of complementarity Kleffner forthcoming 2005; El Zeidy forthcoming 2005.

National prosecutions of international crimes effectively require resort to a combination of national and international law. Most legal systems incorporate (parts of) international law by reference (*renvoi*), also in the field of international criminal law (ICL). For example, several States criminalize violations of "the laws and customs of war," requiring their courts to apply treaties like the Geneva Conventions and customary law in war crimes prosecutions.[7] But even when it is not incorporated, international law has a role to play as it sets standards and provides the basis for national legislation on international crimes. Thus, it is often used by national courts to interpret, correct or supplement national (implementing) legislation.

Intrinsic to the prosecution of international crimes in national courts, the interplay between national and international criminal law raises numerous legal, practical and policy questions. Is ICL subject to the same constitutional scheme as general international law, or are there different conditions for its application? How do courts deal with inconsistencies between national laws and the international rules they are meant to implement? What arguments can be discerned in practice to determine the proper role of international law in national prosecutions?

These and similar questions become all the more important in light of the fact that few, if any, national legal systems regulate the core crimes in full accordance with international law. Many national laws are incomplete, lacking anything from relatively minor provisions to forms of participation to complete crimes. Crimes against humanity, for example, have still not been included in numerous national laws.[8] Furthermore, many national laws diverge from international law in their formulation of the core crimes and corresponding rules. For example, numerous national laws define the groups protected against genocide differently than do the relevant international instruments, which protect national, ethnic, racial and religious groups.[9] Where national laws are incomplete or divergent, the question arises whether direct application of the international law on core crimes itself can (partially) provide the legal basis for a national prosecution.

Doctrine predominantly rejects direct application of international core crimes law in national courts, often in a rather succinct manner.[10] It is a common assump-

---

[7] See e.g. Finnish Penal Code, Chapter 11, Section 1 (enacted 1995):
(1) A person who is in an act of war
1) uses a prohibited means of warfare or weapon;
2) abuses an international symbol designated for the protection of the wounded or the sick; or
3) otherwise violates the provisions of an international agreement on warfare binding on Finland or the generally acknowledged and established rules and customs of war under public international law shall be sentenced for a *war crime* to imprisonment for at least four months and at most six years.
(2) An attempt is punishable.
See further below, Chapter II, para. 3.2.

[8] See Sieber 2004, Vol. I, p. 90, note 65.

[9] See below, Chapter II, para. 2.2.

[10] See Ambos 2003, p. 26 ("En general, el sistema continental o de *civil law* [...] no permite una *aplicacion directa* de normas (penales) internacionales o una transformacion de estas normas a través de una *referencia* al instrumento internacional por las exigencias de los principios *nullum crimen sine lege (certa)* y *nulla poena sine lege*."); Bohlander 2001, p. 12 ("[I] nternational criminal law is still in

tion that "[t]he adoption of implementing legislation is [...] a universal prerequisite for any application of international criminal law principles in the national legal order."[11] However, most commentators provide little or no proof for their views. Rather, they take it for granted that international criminal law differs fundamentally from, for example, human rights law where it concerns direct application. Yet, practice provides a more diverse perspective.

The possible direct application of the international criminalization of the core crimes has received only limited attention in national courts, not least because national prosecutions of international crimes are relatively sparse. Still, it has been examined by the courts of various States, resulting in quite different outcomes.[12] In 1996, the French Court of Cassation held that the Geneva Conventions could not be directly applied for the prosecution of war crimes because their provisions have too general a character, whereas the Hungarian Constitutional Court held in the same year that war crimes can be prosecuted directly on the basis of customary international law, as codified in the Geneva Conventions. In 1999, the Federal Court of Australia held that the prosecution of international crimes can not be based directly on international law or Australian common law, but requires a statutory criminalization. An English Court of Appeal, on the other hand, found in 2004 that the prosecution of international crimes does not require a statute but instead that "international law is capable of being incorporated into English law so as to create a crime punishable in domestic law."[13]

As is apparent from these examples, national courts approach the issue of direct application of the core crimes in very different ways. Even national judgments which share their rejection of direct application can vary considerably in their reasons. It should also be noted that in several States, direct application of international criminal law was accepted without much discussion in previous judgments.[14] These variations in judicial practice call for analysis, especially because the question of direct application can be expected to emerge in numerous national prosecutions to come.[15] After all, deficiencies and incongruities in national implementation law will remain

its formative stages, and it is too early to try and break it down directly to the national level."); Bremer 1999, p. 65-67; Kamminga 1998, p. 569. Cf. Henzelin 2002, p. 78-80; Fichet-Boyle and Mossé 2000, p. 872 ("La répression des infractions internationales définies par les conventions ne peut se faire sans le concours des normes de droit interne."); Sadat Wexler 1994, p. 364 ("Because of the embryonic state of international criminal law, [...] in any modern-day prosecution for crimes against humanity, although the normative aspect is derived from international law and is therefore international in character, the problem of punishment and procedure is necessarily municipal in character."). But compare Wolfrum 1996, p. 235 and 238; Triffterer 1966, p. 85.

[11] Stirling-Zanda 2004, p. 6. See also Gardocki 1989, p. 94: "The direct application of criminal law conventions would, at the present moment be, impossible or would violate the generally accepted standards of the criminal justice. From national reports it is evident, that in no state national courts apply directly international criminal law conventions, although in some of them it is theoretically admissible, on condition that a given convention is sufficiently precise."

[12] All of the following cases are described in more detail in Chapter II, para. 3.3.

[13] See below, note 365.

[14] See below, Chapter II, para. 3.3.b, g and k.

[15] Cf. Swart 2000, p. 204 and Kirby 1995, footnotes 15-21 and accompanying text.

a structural feature of ICL, if only because the important process of progressive criminalization under customary international law resists complete and timely transformation into national law.[16]

Direct application of international criminalization of the core crimes has not only a practical relevance, but also systematic implications for both international criminal law and public international law in general. For international criminal law, these implications can be mapped out in three points.

First, the question of direct application determines in part whether States can fulfill their duty to contribute to the effective enforcement of international criminal law. International law under various circumstances obliges States to prosecute core crimes. Yet States regularly lack adequate national law for such prosecutions. In that case, the possibility of direct application determines whether States can fulfill their duty to prosecute and uphold international criminal law.[17] In the above mentioned Australian case for example, the judges unanimously accepted that Australia is obliged to prosecute genocidal acts committed on its territory while their stance on direct application determined whether or not that obligation could be respected.[18]

Second, direct application provides a valuable litmus test for the quality and development of international criminal law. It is often argued that international criminal law lacks precision and completeness, and should therefore not be directly applied in national prosecutions.[19] That argument has serious implications for the legitimacy of core crimes prosecutions in international courts, and even of ICL itself. If customary and treaty law regarding the core crimes are indeed too unclear and uncertain to form the legal basis for a prosecution in a national court, why would it be acceptable to use that very same law as the basis for a prosecution in an international court? For the legal certainty of the individual, it does not matter so much which court tries him but rather what law it applies. Here, the study of direct application raises fundamental questions about the relationship between national and international courts, the current state of ICL and its possible use as a sanction against individuals. In this regard, the principle of legality takes up a central place in the analysis of direct application.

Third, the choice between direct application of ICL or the use of corresponding national law may have important implications for the coherence and systemization of ICL. While transformation of ICL can have advantages regarding internalization and adaptation to the peculiarities of the national legal system,[20] it brings a risk of distortion of the law. Dissimilarities in the various national laws on core crimes threaten the coherence of ICL. As a practical matter, such variations complicate the

---

[16] Cf. Meron 1996, p. 247.

[17] See e.g. Justice at Risk: War Crimes Trials in Croatia, Bosnia and Herzegovina, and Serbia and Montenegro, 2004, Human Rights Watch, p. 24-27 (plea for direct application of international criminal law in order to allow prosecution of core crimes involving command responsibility, which is not properly regulated in Serbian law).

[18] See below, Chapter II, para. 3.3.d.

[19] See e.g. Bremer 1999, p. 65-67.

[20] See Knop 2000, p. 535.

ascertainment of custom and inhibit the possibilities of different courts to rely on each other's case law. These problems are diminished when all courts apply the very same rules, *id est* international law itself. On the other hand, it should be recognized that unity of law provides no guarantee for unity of adjudication. Divergent interpretation and ignorance of foreign case law (or differing levels of reference to foreign jurisprudence) can lead to very different results based on the same law. Yet, while the risk of distortion of the law should not be overstated, one can query whether direct application of international criminal law can enhance the unity of adjudication and cross-fertilisation between national and international courts.

In a broader context, the study of direct application in the specific field of international criminal law is also relevant for public international law in general, and its role in national legal systems in particular. It requires reconsideration of central concepts, like the maxim that international law leaves States freedom in its implementation, and analysis of relevant developments like the emerging hierarchy of norms, including *jus cogens*.[21] The conditions for direct application of international criminal law examined here will apply at least partly to other fields of international law as well. This study also touches on the question as to what extent the existing framework of public international law can accommodate the peculiarities of an individual-oriented field like international criminal law.

2. Methodology

This study seeks to sketch the dynamics of direct application of the core crimes from the perspective of international law. The description of State practice serves to gain insight to the relevant trends, problems and arguments as well as ascertain the contours of customary international law, but is not a goal in itself. This is not a comparative study. Thus, I will not attempt to be exhaustive in my description of particular crimes or legal systems.

My use of sources follows the generally accepted methodology of international criminal law. This methodology has been described by several authors and need not be repeated in detail here.[22] Like modern international law in general, it recognizes subsidiary means like Draft Codes of the International Law Commission and the work of international bodies like the Human Rights Committee, in addition to the sources mentioned in Art. 38 (1) ICJ Statute.[23] It also departs from the distinction

[21] In doctrine, there is some support for the idea that the *jus cogens* status of an international norm can influence the obligations of the State in implementing it. See generally Wet 2004; Seiderman 2001 and Meron 1986.

[22] See Werle 2003, p. 51-66; Sliedregt 2003, p. 6-9; Bantekas *et al.* 2001, p. 2-4; Paust 2000, p. 3-8

[23] See respectively ICTY, Trial Chamber, *Vasiljevic*, 29 November 2002, para. 200 (subsidiary means like Draft Codes "may reflect legal considerations largely shared by the international community, and they may expertly identify rules of international law, but they do *not* constitute state practice relevant to the determination of a rule of customary international law") and Seibert-Fohr 2002b, p. 308-312.

made in Art. 38 (1) ICJ Statute between primary sources (treaties, custom and general principles) and subsidiary means for the determination of rules of law (judicial decisions and doctrine). This dichotomy between primary sources and subsidiary means does not fully reflect the realities of international criminal law in action. Decisions of both national and international courts are regularly used in other ways than merely as subsidiary means.[24]

3. Limitations

There are many subjects bordering on the topic of this study that can be treated only in passing or not at all. I will not engage in the debate on the desirability of criminal prosecution versus alternative responses to international crimes, like truth commissions, or the sensibility of combining the two.[25] Neither will I compare the (dis)advantages of international and national prosecutions.[26] I readily acknowledge that this study can provide only a limited understanding of the direct application of international criminal law. Some excellent works promote a broader understanding of the role of international law in national courts by focusing less on the formal legal framework and more on factors like the intrinsic value of the rules to be applied and the lines of communications between different courts and other relevant actors.[27] Such studies complement more positivistic ones like the present one in important ways, but cannot replace them.

4. Defining the Framework: International Law in National Courts

The subject at hand, the direct application of international criminal law in national courts, is set in the framework of the role of public international law in national legal systems. The large body of literature on this theme does not share a coherent and consistent definition of relevant concepts.[28] In different writings, terms like "direct application," "domestic validity" and "(non) self-executing" are used in different ways. Therefore, it is necessary to give a concise description of this framework in order to define the key terms of this study. I will provide a more systematic analysis of the framework in Chapter IV.

---

[24] National judgments can provide evidence of *opinio juris* or count as State practice for the ascertainment of customary law. In practice, national and international judgments are also used as independent authorities. See Nollkaemper 2003b; Zegveld 2000, p. 19-21; Lauterpacht 1929, p. 78-94.

[25] See e.g. Sharp 2003, p. 173-177 (arguing that prosecutions of international crimes should avoid a narrow, legalistic strategy but aim for broader benefits to the society affected by the crimes). Cf. Dembour and Haslam 2004.

[26] See e.g. Sands 2003, p. 40-42; Swart 1996, p. 21-34.

[27] See generally Bahdi 2002; Knop 2000; Slaughter 1998; Slaughter 1995 and Slaughter 1994. See also Alford 2003, p. 792; Conforti 2001, p. 18 and below, note 38.

[28] See for an overview of relevant literature Henckaerts 1998.

Broadly speaking, there are two ways for a State to implement international law: incorporation and transformation. **Incorporation** takes place when an international rule is integrated in the national legal order, so that the judiciary can directly apply that rule. This method of incorporation promotes complete implementation of the international rule, as it cannot be modified. **Transformation** denotes the enactment of a national law that mirrors the content of the international rule, thus transforming a rule of international law in a national one. This method of transformation gives the legislature the opportunity to tailor, or even modify, the international rule to fit the peculiarities of the national legal system. Technically speaking, international law is applied not at all after transformation. In these cases, national courts apply national law that reproduces the content of the original international norm.[29]

Incorporation takes place through a **rule of reference**: a rule of national law that makes the international rule itself a part of the national legal order. A rule of reference can be found in the constitution, but also in legislation of a lesser rank. Moreover, it can be a general rule – incorporating an entire source or field of international law, like treaties, customary law, or humanitarian law – but also a specific rule – incorporating only a particular norm or treaty provision. National provisions declaring all treaties to be the law of the land[30] or the crime of apartheid to be regulated by certain paragraphs of the Apartheid Convention,[31] are both rules of reference. A rule of reference can be written as well as unwritten. Thus, when there is a consistent practice of national courts to apply customary international law without an explicit authorization in national law to do so, this practice can be construed to be based on an implicit rule of reference that incorporates customary international law in the domestic legal order of that State.[32]

Incorporation and transformation are two different ways to give effect to a rule of international law, but do not exclude one another.[33] That an international rule has

[29] See Buergenthal 1992, p. 318 and 362; Iwasawa 1986, p. 644. Some scholars assert that international law itself is *never* incorporated in the national legal order or applied in national courts. See e.g. Santulli 2001, p. 88-100 and 105-114 (asserting that international rules integrated and applied in national legal orders amount to "droit étatique d'origine internationale," different in form and content from international law proper). See for a refutation of this argument Lauterpacht 1929, p. 77 and, in the specific context of international criminal law, Lauterpacht 1944, p. 64-67.

[30] See e.g. Art. VI, cl. 2 U.S. Constitution.

[31] See Section 157 of the Hungarian Criminal Code (Btk., in force since 15 June 1996):
"(1) [...]
(2) The person who commits a crime of apartheid shall be punished with imprisonment lasting from 5 to 10 years.
(3) Punishment shall be imprisonment from 10 to 15 years or life imprisonment if the criminal act of apartheid described in subsection (2) has resulted in serious consequences.
(4) For the purposes of subparagraphs (2) and (3), a crime of apartheid shall mean the crime of apartheid defined in paragraphs (a)/(ii), (a)/(iii), (c), (d), (e) and (f) of article II of the International Convention on the Suppression and Punishment of the Crime of Apartheid, adopted on 30 November 1973 by the General Assembly of the United Nations in New York, promulgated by Law Decree No. 27 of 1976."

[32] See Cassese 2001c, p. 172.

[33] Some authors speak of the contrast between transformation and adoption: see e.g. Rack 1979 and Seidl-Hohenveldern 1963. But see Partsch 1992, p. 245; Dijk and Tahzib 1991, p. 417 (distinguishing adoption and incorporation); Iwasawa 1986, p. 638.

been transformed into a rule of national law does not prevent it from being incorporated itself in the national legal order and vice versa. On the contrary, it is often the case that international rules are both themselves part of the legal order, for example through a general rule of reference, and yet are also reflected in corresponding national laws.[34]

When an international rule is incorporated into national law, it acquires **domestic validity**. A rule of international law is domestically valid when it has force of law in the national legal order.[35] It is then binding law, in principle to be applied by the national courts. When this actually happens, I speak of **direct application**.[36] Thus, direct application is a result in a particular situation rather than a test consisting of independent criteria under international law. Application is to be understood in a broad sense here. It is not confined to those cases where rights and duties of individuals are directly derived from international law, but covers every situation where a national court bases (a part of) its decision directly on international law.[37] Accordingly, use of an international norm to refuse application of a national provision is a form of direct application, as is the use of an international norm for the interpretation of national law as long as that international norm is regarded as 'the law of the land.'[38]

For some authors, direct effect refers to use of international law as a rule of decision only, in contrast to its use as a means of interpretation, which is then called indirect effect.[39] Such a distinction is, however, difficult to make in practice and results in an unneccessarily narrow view of the role of international law in national courts.[40] Others do not distinguish between application of binding and non-binding international law, for example between the application of the ECHR by courts of State parties and non-State parties.[41] This lack of distinction eliminates bindingness as an explaining factor in the analysis of international law in national courts altogether, and equates the application of international law with that of foreign law. This is unhelpful. While it should be recognized that a full understanding of the role of international law in national courts requires a broader perspective than the bind-

---

[34] See e.g. O'Keefe 2002, p. 318 and Stuby 1995, p. 449-450.

[35] See Iwasawa 1986, p. 632 and Nollkaemper 2002, p. 159.

[36] Cf. Peyró 2003, p. 81 ("l'applicabilité directe"); Iwasawa 1986, p. 643-645. I refer to direct application rather than direct effect, because the latter's specific position in EC law has made it laden with connotations from that field. For many, the term direct effect signifies questions about the quality of a rule, its substance, *id est* whether it creates rights or duties for individuals, or the standing of individuals to invoke it. See e.g. Nollkaemper 2002, p. 162-163; Santulli 2001, p. 102; Jackson 1992, footnote 1. Such an understanding is too narrow for this study.

[37] Compare Jackson 1992, p. 313 and 321.

[38] See below, p. 148 on the principle of consistent interpretation.

[39] See Betlem and Nollkaemper 2003, p. 571-572; Nollkaemper 2002, p. 158. Compare Wyrozumska 2001, p. 19 (using direct and indirect application in the same sense).

[40] See Knop 2000, p. 501-505 on the pitfalls of defining the direct application of international law in an all-or-nothing fashion.

[41] See e.g. Knop 2000 and below, note 790.

ing/non-binding dichotomy, the factor of bindingness forms an indispensable part of the complete picture.[42]

There can be different reasons why an international rule that is domestically valid may not be directly applied,[43] just as there can be different reasons why a rule of national law may not be applied in a particular case. A restriction on the party invoking the rule, like standing, can prevent its application, or a restriction on the court, like the political questions doctrine. The international rule may be trumped by another legal rule, national or international. It may also be the case that the rule lacks precision or comprehensiveness, and requires supplementation by a national or international action that has not yet been taken. A treaty provision that is deemed unsuitable for direct application, even if domestically valid, is often called **non-self-executing.**[44] The doctrine of self-executing treaties is complex and confused and will be analyzed in Chapter IV, para. 4.

To recapitulate, direct application in the context of this study means that a national court applies an international rule as such because it is binding law, without it being transformed into a rule of national law.[45] Thus, direct application is to be distinguished from the optional use of international law as a non-binding source, which is comparable to the use of foreign law as a source of inspiration. To find that the contents of an international rule are not transformed into national law does not mean that the rule is applied independently of national law. It would be simplistic to interpret direct application of international law as excluding any role for national law. After all, every national legal system has broad rules of reference on the domestic validity of treaties and/or custom. The absence of an *ad hoc* rule of reference incorporating a specific rule of international law normally does not signify complete independence from national law, but rather the presence of a general, perhaps implicit, rule of reference, for example a constitutional provision incorporating treaties or custom. Indeed, it is broadly assumed that the domestic validity of international rules always depends on a rule of national law.[46] Even if that assertion may be questioned, as I will do in Chapter IV,[47] the application of international law in national courts is in practice hardly ever, if at all, fully independent of national law. Of course, some rules of reference are more specific than others. Many of the questions surrounding direct application are most pressing for rules of reference that are general and/or implicit, as they signify the least conscious decision of the legislature to incorporate the specific international rule that is applied.

---

[42] See also above, note 27 and accompanying text.

[43] See Bremer 1999, p. 146 and 150. Cf. Santulli 2001, p. 102-105.

[44] Numerous courts and writers erroneously assert that non-self-executing treaties do not acquire domestic validity. See on this point Iwasawa 1986, p. 644-645.

[45] Cf. Nollkaemper 2002, p. 159.

[46] See Cassese 2001c, p. 168; Knop 2000, p. 521 and Verdross and Simma 1984, p. 539-540. See further below, Chapter IV, para. 3.

[47] See below, p. 140 et seq.

5. Applicable Law: Substantive Criminality for the Core Crimes

In its broadest sense, this study examines the way in which penal rules of international law are implemented and applied in national legal orders. International criminal law in the context of this study refers to 'the accumulation of international legal norms on individual criminal responsibility (without implying that they form a coherent system).'[48] These norms can be found in treaties, custom and general principles.[49] National law is an object of study only where it reflects or implements a rule of international law, not where it regulates national criminal law with international implications. Of the different meanings attributed to ICL in doctrine, this study thus adheres to *droit international pénal* or *Völkerstrafrecht* as opposed to *droit pénal international* and *Internationales Strafrecht*.[50]

More specifically, this study examines the direct application of core crimes law in national prosecutions. Core crimes law is that part of international criminal law which deals with crimes subject to the jurisdiction of the ICC: genocide, crimes against humanity and war crimes. They have also been labelled 'the most serious crimes of concern to the international community as a whole,'[51] crimes against the peace and security of mankind,[52] supranational crimes,[53] international crimes *sensu stricto*, international crimes proper or simply international crimes, as opposed to transnational crimes.[54]

There are several reasons, both practical and systematic, for this focus. First, as a result of the ICC regime – at the time of writing of this study governing almost 100 States parties – national prosecution of the core crimes is now, more than before, a matter of considerable practical importance. Second, the core crimes are all globally punishable under customary international law, also by international courts and for States not party to the ICC. State practice of core crimes prosecutions can be compared both *inter se*, and with the practice of international courts. Third, the core crimes are generally believed to be governed by rules of *jus cogens* status.[55] Fourth, the core crimes generally qualify as the most serious human rights violations, giving rise to additional obligations of the State under international human rights law. All in all, these rules of a customary and peremptory nature apply globally and yield *prima facie* the most stringent international legal demands on States. Therefore, they can reasonably be expected to have the greatest impact on the na-

---

[48] Sunga 1997, p. 7. Cf. Triffterer 1966, p. 30-34.

[49] See below, Chapter IV, para. 5.1.

[50] Schmidt 2002, p. 2-5; Bremer 1999, p. 44-46; Triffterer 1966, p. 25-29 and 173-178; Hettinger 1965, p. 8-10. See for an overview of definitions of international criminal law Hollán 2000; Schwarzenberger 1950.

[51] Fourth preamble and Art. 5 ICC Statute.

[52] See Art. 17, 18 and 20 Draft Code of crimes against the peace and security of mankind 1996. See also Allain and Jones 1997; Bassiouni 1993 and Lukashuk 2001, p. 273.

[53] See Haveman and Kavran 2003; Röling 1979, p. 169.

[54] See on the various definitions of such crimes Triffterer 1989, p. 47 and Hollán 2000.

[55] See below, Chapter V, para. 3.3.

tional level. For these reasons, the core crimes should be distinguished from other international crimes, even though their direct application raises partly the same questions.

It should be noted that this study focuses on the *category of* core crimes, rather than their specific definition in the ICC Statute. Accordingly, the term core crimes in this study refers to the crimes of genocide, crimes against humanity and war crimes under international law generally. These crimes are enumerated in articles 6-8 of the ICC Statute and are further specified in the Elements of Crimes, but are also regulated by various other sources, including custom. While largely similar, there are significant differences in the way these different sources define the core crimes.[56] In the particular case of war crimes, the ICC Statute covers only a part of all war crimes under international law. Again, there is no need at this point to define the crimes in detail, as the divergence between their sources is one of the objects of this study rather than a limiting premise. Instead, I will outline the central elements of each crime, the most important contemporary treaties governing them, and the most obvious points of divergence between different definitions. I will give a more substantial analysis of the category of core crimes in Chapter V.

Genocide concerns the intentional destruction or extermination of a specific group, or part of that group.[57] The primary definition of genocide was included in Art. 2 of the 1948 Genocide Convention and was subsequently reproduced in Art. 4 ICTY Statute, Art. 2 ICTR Statute and Art. 6 ICC Statute. Its central characteristics are (1) the specific intent to destroy a group and (2) the specific character of that group, defined in these treaties as national, ethnical, racial or religious. Genocidal acts include killing as well as several other acts enumerated in the provisions mentioned above and do not require a connection to armed conflict. One of the most important points of possible divergence concerns the character of the group, as both numerous national laws on genocide and the case law of the *ad hoc* tribunals have broadened the definition of protected groups, raising the question whether customary law grants broader protection than do treaties governing genocide.[58]

A crime against humanity requires (1) a widespread or systematic attack (2) against a civilian population. Such an attack must be the result of a plan or policy of a State or organization. Crimes against humanity are defined *inter alia* in Art. 5 ICTY Statute, Art. 3 ICTR Statute and Art. 7 ICC Statute.[59] These provisions list examples of inhumane acts like murder, torture and enslavement. There are several contentious elements in the definition of crimes against humanity, including the open-ended criminalization of "other inhumane acts," the required scale of the crimes

---

[56] Various authors have analyzed the discrepancies between the ICC Statute (and Elements of Crimes) and customary international law. See e.g. Bothe 2001; Cassese 2001b; Cassese 2001a; Fischer 2000.

[57] Cassese 2001b, p. 335.

[58] See below, Chapter II, para. 2.2.b and note 730; Schabas 2001, p. 447-471; Cassese 2001b, p. 341-347. See also Tournaye 2003 (on varying interpretations of genocidal intent). See generally Schabas 2000b.

[59] See Peyró 2003, p. 81.

and the requirement of a nexus to armed conflict.[60] At its conception, the concept of crimes against humanity was connected to armed conflict, but this no longer seems to be the case. Finally, a controversial point concerns the entity behind the attack. Traditionally, crimes against humanity could only be committed by States.[61] Today, certain organizations also qualify as potential perpetrators, but there is no consensus on their required characteristics.[62]

War crimes are connected, obviously, to a state of international or internal armed conflict. Generally speaking, they involve prohibited methods and means of warfare (Hague law) and violations of the law of protected persons (Geneva law).[63] Hague law concerns rights and duties of the military in a conflict, stemming for example from the principle of proportionality and the principle that active combatants and military objectives are the only legitimate targets and are therefore to be distinguished from civilians. Geneva law consists of basic obligations designed to protect victims of armed conflict, namely the wounded, sick, shipwrecked, prisoners of war and civilians. The main treaties regulating war crimes are the Hague Conventions of 1907, the four Geneva Conventions and the First Additional Protocol, Art. 2 and 3 ICTY Statute, Art. 4 ICTR Statute and Art. 8 ICC Statute.[64] Important questions stem *inter alia* from the differences between war crimes committed in international armed conflict, including the particular regime of grave breaches of the Geneva Conventions,[65] and the more recent category of war crimes committed in internal armed conflict.[66]

Several other international crimes can overlap with the three core crimes, even if they are not subject of study in their own right. Apartheid and certain cases of slavery are species of crimes against humanity. Torture can qualify as a war crime or a crime against humanity. Arguably, the same is true for certain attacks commonly labelled as terrorism.[67] While terrorism is a topical issue in ICL, there are good reasons not to add it to the core crimes studied here. First, the definitional unclarity is far greater for terrorism than for the core crimes. International instruments define terrorism in different ways, while numerous States have anti-terrorism laws that are so broad as to cover many crimes that clearly fall outside the scope of ICL.[68] Second, the developments in the regulation of terrorism since 2001

---

[60] See generally Lattanzi 2001 and Cassese 2001a.

[61] See below, note 581.

[62] See below, notes 582 and 583; Lattanzi 2001, p. 485-486 and Cassese 2001a, p. 375-376.

[63] See Sassòli and Bouvier 1999, p. 67-68 and 159. See generally Dörmann 2001; Bothe 2001.

[64] See for an overview of relevant treaties Sassòli and Bouvier 1999, p. 101-104.

[65] See Art. 50 GC I, Art. 51 GC II, Art. 130 GC III, Art. 147 GC IV and Art. 85 AP I.

[66] See Kress 2001; Bothe 1995.

[67] See Keijzer 2003 and Delmas-Marty 2002a, p. 292. Yet, in this regard many commentators, including those asserting that the Al-Qaeda attacks on the U.S. in 2001 amounted to crimes against humanity, ignore the requirement that the attacks must be carried out by an organization with State-like features. See for a critical analysis on this point Schabas 2002b. See also Mexico, Supreme Court, *In re Cavallo (Amparo en Revision 140/2002)*, 10 June 2002 at 911 (concluding that the crime of terrorism can not be subsumed into that of genocide).

[68] See on the definition of terrorism Wilt 2003, p. 57-66. See for an example of national terrorism prosecutions that in no way correspond to international law Pakistan, *Mir Zaman v. Zubair*, 14 January

are so recent as to set it apart from the far more developed core crimes, both concerning its status as an international crime and the development of the resulting interaction between international and national law. The crime of aggression, or crimes against peace,[69] has been excluded for obvious reasons. Not only does its lack of definition in the ICC Statute reflect its unclear status under general international law, there is also an almost complete absence of recent meaningful practice in national legal systems in this regard.[70]

As mentioned above, this study focuses on the international criminalization of, rather than all international rules pertaining to, the core crimes. In other words, the focus is on the situation where the substantive criminality for the prosecution of an individual in a national court is based (in part) directly on international law. The distinction between substance and procedure in criminal law is often unclear and varies in different legal systems.[71] For my definition of direct application, an international criminalization comprises the definition of the crime, forms of participation and rules on jurisdiction. Rules that are of a disputed character but further from the core of substantive criminality, like defenses and statutes of limitations, will not be included.

The inclusion of jurisdiction is imperfect because it straddles the line between substance and procedure. It is necessary, however, because in practice jurisdiction and substantive criminality can be intertwined in complex combinations. In Senegal, for example, an investigating judge in 2000 indicted former Tchadian dictator Hissène Habré for complicity in torture, following the victims' assertion that universal jurisdiction for the national criminalization of torture could be derived directly from the Torture Convention.[72] Such direct application of a treaty cannot be construed as concerning simply the jurisdictional reach of national criminal law, but implicitly derives substantive criminality from international law. Likewise, the trial of Imre Finta in Canada was based on then section 7(3.71) of the Canadian Criminal Code (since repealed), which extended Canadian jurisdiction over ordinary crimes like kidnapping, unlawful confinement, and manslaughter to extraterritorial acts that constitute war crimes or crimes against humanity.[73] It would be mistaken to see this as simply a jurisdictional provision governing manslaughter and other ordinary crimes, where it in fact regulates the substantive criminality of extraterritorial war crimes and crimes against humanity.[74] Of course, the inclusion of jurisdiction at

2003, 36 Pakistan Criminal Law Journal 1086 and Pakistan, *Ata-Ur-Rehman v. State*, 30 October 2002, 36 Pakistan Criminal Law Journal 923 (prosecutions of armed robbery under the Pakistani Anti-terrorism Act 1997).

69 See Art. 6 Nuremberg Charter.

70 See generally Politi 2004; Müller-Schieke 2001 and Antonopolous 2001.

71 See Swart 2002b, p. 583-586 and Fletcher 1998, p. 7-23.

72 This indictment was subsequently annulled by the higher courts, see below, Chapter II, para. 3.3.e.

73 Canada, Supreme Court, *R. v. Imre Finta*, 24 March 1994.

74 Id., para. 58 (Supreme Court confirms holding of the Court of Appeal that "s. 7(3.71) of the *Criminal Code*, is not merely jurisdictional in nature, but rather creates two new offences, a crime against humanity and a war crime, and defines the essential elements of the offences charged."). See also Fletcher 2002, p. 454-458; Cotler 1996, p. 465.

this point is a matter of definition. Throughout the study, jurisdiction will be distinguished from 'pure' substantive criminality where necessary, for example with regard to the principle of legality.

The possible direct application of international criminalization can come up not only in core crimes prosecutions, but also in extradition proceedings, namely to satisfy the double criminality requirement posed by many States. These cases, for example the *Pinochet III* judgment of the English House of Lords, provide valuable information about the topic at hand. However, the legal framework for extradition proceedings is not comparable to that of prosecutions. Unlike the principle of legality, the double criminality rule has no basis in international law where it concerns international crimes.[75] In practice, the two proceedings are treated differently both in international law and in many national legal systems.[76] Therefore, extradition proceedings will serve as useful sources but are not themselves object of study.

I will likewise take into account the practice of the so-called "internationalized" courts[77] where relevant, but not treat it as an independent object of study. Although these courts take up an interesting position on the crossroads of national and international criminal law, their legal framework and the problems they experience in their work are quite unique.[78] In particular, an important part of the law they apply is based on treaties and/or regulations of international interim administrations. Their application of international criminal law can therefore be compared with that by national courts only to a limited extent.

Deriving substantive criminality from international law for a prosecution is in many aspects the 'hard case' that makes questions, for example regarding the principle of legality, most pressing. This limitation thereby allows for a thorough review of the pertinent problems and implications, while at the same time it provides concreteness and a necessary curtailment of the workload. Many considerations on this subject apply, *mutatis mutandis*, to procedural norms of international criminal law, and even to other norms of public international law more generally.

All in all, restricting the scope of the study to the direct application of criminalization of the core crimes will render a homogeneous and rich analysis of the relevant rules of international law without casting the net to wide.Yet, while the subject of this study is quite specific, its general theoretical nature requires attention for the broader context. Therefore, I will focus on substantive criminality for the core crimes, but draw parallels to other international crimes and rules where necessary to describe the relevant legal framework or analyze the underlying issues. Likewise, as the aim here is to sketch the dynamics of direct application of the core crimes rather than give a sharp delineation of their content, I will give specific cases which likely but not conclusively concern core crimes the benefit of the doubt.

---

[75] See Poutiers 2000, p. 945-947. Cf. Lauterpacht 1944, p. 89.

[76] See e.g. U.S., Court of Appeals (First Cir.), *Sabatier v. Dabrowski*, 15 November 1978, 586 F.2d 866 at 869 (extradition is is not considered a criminal proceeding).

[77] See principally Romano *et al.* 2004; Ambos and Othmann 2003.

[78] See below, notes 649-650 and accompanying text.

For example, cases of large-scale torture that may or may not constitute crimes against humanity will be included, insofar as the legal analysis in such cases is relevant for core crimes law.[79]

6. Structure

First, I will give an overview of legislative and judicial State practice regarding the core crimes in Chapter II. This description of practice will show the various ways in which international and national law are used in core crimes prosecutions. In short, core crimes can be prosecuted on the basis of national law, either as ordinary crimes like murder or specifically as international crimes, or directly on the basis of international criminal law. The emphasis in this descriptive part will naturally be on direct application and include legislation as well as resulting national prosecutions or a lack thereof.

Chapter III will examine which policy considerations govern the choice between the different legal bases laid out in Chapter II. I will list the factors that guide legislators, courts and prosecutorial authorities in practice. I will focus mostly on the considerations that are specific to international criminal law and particularly the core crimes, while merely signalling those considerations that apply to the direct application of public international law in general.

Chapter IV constructs the public international law framework of direct application by examining the doctrines and principles that determine the obligations of States in implementing international law in general. It will analyze both the current state of international law and doctrine regarding the role of international law in the national legal order. Topics of analysis include the debate on monism versus dualism, the doctrine of self-executing treaties and the general rule that States are free to implement their international obligations in any way they see fit. I will also set forth the limits of this freedom, most notably the principle of consistent interpretation which obliges national courts to interpret national law in conformity with international law.

Chapter V will focus on the field of international criminal law specifically, in order to identify the characteristics that set it apart from public international law in general. It will analyze the characteristics of the core crimes and their consequences for the implementation of those crimes in the national legal order. Topics of analysis include the obligations under international law to prosecute core crimes and the consequences of the *jus cogens* status of the core crimes.

Chapter VI is devoted entirely to the principle of legality (*nullum crimen, nulla poena sine lege praevia*), as this principle is of great importance for the analysis of direct application of international criminal law in national courts. Focusing on the core crimes, it will examine the application of the principle of legality in national

---

[79] Note that I draw on broader case law in Chapter II in order to give an accurate overview of the situation in different States.

and international practice, its content in international law, and its implications for direct application of core crimes law.

In Chapter VII, I will bring the different strands together and reflect on the international legal framework governing direct application of core crimes law, the future prospects of direct application and its broader implications for international criminal law and public international law in general.

Chapter II
PRACTICE: CORE CRIMES PROSECUTIONS IN NATIONAL COURTS

1. Introduction

This Chapter gives an overview of the different possible legal bases for the national prosecution of core crimes. To this end, I will examine legislative and judicial practice from diverse countries. The aim here is to sketch the dynamics between international and national law and the resulting complications, and therefore I will include relevant jurisprudence and legislation even if they are no longer valid today. The reader who is looking for broader and only up-to-date information on core crimes prosecutions and relevant legislation will find useful references in the footnotes.[80]

While I will focus on the national prosecution of genocide, crimes against humanity and war crimes in the last decades, in order to provide a thorough overview of relevant practice I do not limit myself strictly to these cases. Such a broadening of perspective is necessary, since many countries have no (recent) case law on the specific question of direct application of core crimes law for a national prosecution. Therefore, the question must often be explored with resort to other precedents, for example dealing with other international crimes or extradition instead of prosecution, insofar as relevant for the core crimes.

This Chapter is primarily structured around the different ways national and international law interact as a basis for prosecution. Core crimes can be prosecuted in national courts on the basis of national criminal law (para. 2), or through direct application of international criminal law (para. 3). As to the first, core crimes prosecuted on the basis of national law can be charged both as ordinary crimes (para. 2.1, e.g. murder in a national penal code) or as international crimes (para. 2.2, e.g. genocide in a national penal code). Direct application of international criminalization normally takes place through a rule of reference in national law, which can be very specific (para. 3.2) or more general (para. 3.3).[81]

---

[80] Reports on the legislative and judicial practice of specific States regarding core crimes law can be found *inter alia* in the series *Nationale Strafverfolgung völkerrechtlicher Verbrechen – National Prosecution of International Crimes* (Eser and Kreicker, ed.) and *Strafrecht in Reaktion auf Systemunrecht* (Eser and Arnold, ed.) of the Max Planck Institute for Foreign and International Criminal Law; Neuner 2003; Cassese and Delmas-Marty 2002; Kreß and Lattanzi 2000; 28 RDMDG iss. 1-2 (1989); 60 RIDP iss.1-2 (1989). Information on national legislation in this Chapter has also been derived from the websites and reports of universities and NGOs, in particular Amnesty International, *Report on Universal jurisdiction*, 2001; http://preventgenocide.org/law/domestic; http://www.icrc.org/ihl-nat; http://www.oefre.unibe.ch/law/icl; http://www.legislationline.org and http://www.iccnow.org.

[81] See above, Chapter I, para. 4.

As will become clear, the source of the substantive criminality (national or international law) and the designation of the crime (ordinary v. international crime) yield different possible legal bases for prosecution,[82] but these categories are not easily separable. Many prosecutions derive substantive criminality from a combination of national and international law. For example, direct application of international law may provide the definition of the crime, while national criminal law provides the rules on jurisdiction and forms of participation. Moreover, multiple charges may involve different categories, for example a charge of genocide under national law and of war crimes under international law. Thus, to a certain extent this categorization creates artificial boundaries in a complicated continuum of different combinations of national and international law. Given the complexity of the interaction of international and national law in national prosecutions and the need for an analytical framework, this imperfection is unavoidable. It is important, however, to view the above categorization as one of different techniques to establish substantive criminality that can be combined, rather than as adequate labels for particular prosecutions. Accordingly, some cases will appear in multiple categories.

I will now examine legislative and judicial practice concerning core crimes prosecutions on the basis of national and international law. The part on national law serves mainly to outline the alternatives to direct application and complement the picture of legal bases for national prosecutions, and thus will receive only limited attention. The part on international law will form by far the greatest part of this Chapter. I will pay most attention to direct application of international offences on the basis of a general rule of reference, as it is the most complex and disputed form of direct application. That part, para. 3.3, is subdivided in an overview of different countries to give a thorough description of relevant practice.

2. Prosecution on the Basis of National Law

2.1 Prosecution as an Ordinary Crime

Core crimes concern acts that are generally punishable under various national criminal law provisions, such as murder and assault.[83] Accordingly, core crimes can be,

---

[82] Cf. Kleffner forthcoming 2005, Chapter 7; Bremer 1999, p. 395-399; Kamminga 1998, p. 570 and Wolfrum 1996, p. 242.

[83] See Frände 2003, p. 35-44 (providing a detailed overview of ordinary crimes in Finnish law that correspond to international crimes).
See also Canada, Supreme Court, *R. v. Imre Finta*, 24 March 1994, 28 C.R. (4th) 265 (1994), *La Forest J.* (dissenting), para. 256: "It is evident that compendious expressions like 'murder, extermination, enslavement, deportation, persecution, or any other inhumane act or omission' include acts and omissions that comprise such specific underlying crimes as confinement, kidnapping, robbery and manslaughter under our domestic system of law."
France, Court of Cassation, *Touvier (No. 1)*, 6 February 1975, Bull. crim., no. 42 ("[C]rimes contre l'humanité [...] sont des crimes de droit commun commis dans certaines circonstances et pour certains motifs précisés dans le texte qui les définit").

and often are prosecuted as ordinary crimes. Many national prosecutions in the aftermath of World War II charged the defendants with ordinary rather than international crimes.[84] Defendants that were prosecuted for their involvement in the widespread torture during the Greek Colonel's regime in the period 1967–1974, which arguably amounted to crimes against humanity, were charged with such crimes as repeated abuse of authority, unconstitutional detention and causing serious physical injury.[85] In the United States, Lt. Calley was convicted for his involvement in the infamous My Lai massacre in the Vietnam war on the basis of murder and assault, where he could have been charged with war crimes.[86] International criminal law was likewise ignored in the prosecution of a Russian colonel on the charges of rape and murder of a Chechnyan civilian. This case ended in 2003 in the final confirmation of a 10 year prison sentence.[87] Amidst serious allegations of the widespread use of torture by U.S. forces against Iraqi detainees in 2004, possibly constituting war crimes and/or crimes against humanity,[88] a limited number of military personnel were court-martialled for crimes not of an international nature. Charges included conspiracy, dereliction of duty, cruelty, maltreatment, assault, and indecent acts.[89] These are only a few examples, while the list of prosecutions on the basis of ordinary crimes is long and growing.

Naturally, ordinary crimes are always available as a basis for the prosecution of criminal acts committed within the prosecuting State, since criminal law as a general rule has (at least) territorial application. Ordinary crimes do not normally provide a legal basis for the prosecution of extraterritorial acts amounting to international crimes. Yet, many States declare the provisions of their criminal codes to be applicable to (certain) extraterritorial conduct that constitutes an international crime. Japan, for example, has included Art. 4 (2) in its Penal Code, which supplements the applicability of the Code to crimes committed in Japan, by Japanese or against the Japanese State as follows:

> "In addition to those provided for in the preceding three Articles, this Code shall also apply to every person who has committed outside Japanese territory those crimes mentioned in Book II which are considered to be punishable by a treaty even if committed outside Japanese territory."[90]

---

[84] See numerous examples in Lippman 1999.

[85] See Kritz 1995, Vol. II, p. 270-271 (the Greek Penal Code did not contain a specific prohibition of torture).

[86] See *U.S. v. Calley*, 46 C.M.R. 1131, 1138 (1973) ("[A]ppellant was convicted by general court-martial of three specifications of premeditated murder and one of assault with intent to commit murder in violation of Articles 118 and 134, Uniform Code of Military Justice, 10 USC §§ 918 and 934, respectively. […] Although all charges could have been laid as war crimes, they were prosecuted under the UCMJ").

[87] See Financial Times, 'Colonel jailed for Chechnya killing,' 26 July 2003.

[88] See Paust 2004.

[89] See Murphy 2004, p. 595.

[90] See Tanaka 1995, p. 78-79.

Thus, this provision establishes extraterritorial jurisdiction over treaty crimes, which are then prosecuted as ordinary crimes. Similar provisions can be found in many other legal systems.[91]

Numerous States have given their courts jurisdiction to prosecute specific extra-territorial war crimes, particularly those committed in WW II, as ordinary crimes. For example, the UK's 1991 War Crimes Act provides that proceedings for murder may be brought for certain offences committed in German-held terrritory in WW II, as long as these constituted "a violation of the laws and customs of war."[92] In *R. v. Sawoniuk* (2000), a British Court of Appeal upheld the conviction of the defendant for two counts of murder in Belorussia for his role in the holocaust on the basis of this provision.[93] On the basis of a comparable Canadian statute, the accused in *Regina v. Finta* was charged under the Criminal Code in Canada with (and acquitted of) two counts each of unlawful confinement, robbery, kidnapping and manslaughter in Hungary for his role in the holocaust.[94] As can be seen in these cases, the international character of the core crimes often surfaces in some way during their prosecution, even when they are charged as ordinary crimes.[95] Where a prosecution is based on national provisions like those described above, it must be ascertained that the alleged acts constitute international offences in order to establish extraterritorial jurisdiction.[96] In other cases, international criminal law is applied as a means of interpretation.[97]

Sometimes, the fact that the prosecuted act (allegedly) constitutes an international crime is merely mentioned by a prosecutor or a judge, without practical consequences for the outcome of the case. In *Pius Nwaoga v. The State* (1972), the Nigerian Supreme Court upheld a conviction for a murder during civil war and

---

[91] See below, notes 176-184 and accompanying text.

[92] Section 1:
"(1) Subject to the provisions of this section, proceedings for murder … may be brought against a person in the United Kingdom irrespective of his nationality at the time of the alleged offence if that offence –
(a) was committed during the period beginning with 1 September 1939 and ending with 5 June 1945 in a place which at the time was part of Germany or under German occupation; and
(b) constituted a violation of the laws and customs of war.
(2) No proceedings shall by virtue of this section be brought against any person unless he was on 8 March 1990, or has subsequently become, … resident in the United Kingdom …".

[93] U.K., Court of Appeal, *R. v. Anthony Sawoniuk*, 10 February 2000, [2000] 2 Cr. App. R. 220.

[94] Canada, Supreme Court, *R. v. Imre Finta*, 24 March 1994. See Canadian Criminal Code, R.S.C. 1985, c. C-46, s. 7(3.71).

[95] See also Denmark, Eastern Division of High Court (Third Chamber), *The Prosecution v. Saric*, 25 November 1994 (resort to provisions from GC III and GC IV in order to substantiate charges of causing grievous bodily harm of a grave nature under the Danish penal code).

[96] See Canada, Supreme Court, *R. v. Imre Finta*, 24 March 1994 per Cory J., para. 66-71 and La Forest J. (dissenting), para. 272 and 274.

[97] See e.g. Belgium, Court of Cassation, *Van Beggelaer v. Belgian State*, 27 March 1950, partial English translation in ILR 1950, no. 142 (use of Art. 52 of the Hague Regulations for the interpretation of a national provision criminalizing aid and assistance to the enemy).

stated *obiter* that this killing amounted to a crime against humanity.[98] In the Haitian trial for the Raboteau massacre,[99] in which several members of the Haitian army were convicted for the organized killing of civilians, the defendants were charged and convicted for ordinary crimes but the judgment expressed the view of the court that the acts under consideration amounted to crimes against humanity.[100] This explicitation of the international dimension of the crimes was actively sought by the prosecution with the idea that it might facilitate the extradition of some of the defendants who were absent and had sought refuge in other countries.[101]

In conclusion, international crimes are often prosecuted as ordinary crimes. Their international dimension surfaces in such trials in various ways and to degrees, from direct application of international criminal law in order to establish jurisdiction to merely a reference in passing or not at all.

2.2 Prosecution as an International Crime

2.2.a *International Crimes in National Law*

Many States define and provide for international crimes in their national criminal law. States differ greatly in the extent to which they model these penalizations on international law. Numerous States parties to treaties such as the Genocide Convention and the ICC Statute copy the definitions of (most of) the crimes found in these documents verbatim into their national laws.[102] Others base their penalizations on these treaty provisions, but make minor or more substantive modifications.

Some variations appear minor but may nevertheless bear considerable practical consequences. The French definition of crimes against humanity, for example, requires the constitutive acts to be both widespread *and* systematic,[103] whereas the generally accepted international definition requires them to be "part of a widespread *or* systematic attack."[104] Arguably, this minor textual divergence can considerably raise the threshold for finding a crime against humanity.

---

[98] Nigeria, Supreme Court, *Pius Nwaoga v. The State*, 52 ILR 494-497 at 497: "To our mind, deliberate and intentional killing of an unarmed person living peacefully inside the Federal Territory as in this case is a crime against humanity, and even if committed during a civil war is in violation of the domestic law of the country, and must be punished." Clearly, this qualification is doubtful at the very least.

[99] See Concannon 2001.

[100] Haiti, Gonaïves Tribunal of First Instance, *Raboteau*, 9 November 2000, reported in Concannon 2001.

[101] See e-mail interview of 30 March 2003 with Brian Concannon, one of the lawyers involved in the case on behalf of the Bureau des Avocats Internationaux, on file with the author.

[102] See e.g. the Dutch International Crimes Act (2003).

[103] France, Art. 212 (1) Code Penal: La déportation, la réduction en esclavage ou la pratique massive et systématique d'exécutions sommaires, d'enlèvements de personnes suivis de leur disparition, de la torture ou d'actes inhumains, inspirées par des motifs politiques, philosophiques, raciaux ou religieux et organisées en exécution d'un plan concerté à l'encontre d'un groupe de population civile sont punies de la réclusion criminelle à perpétuité.

[104] See ICC Statute Art. 7 (emphasis added).

On the other hand, some national definitions of international crimes bear only a vague resemblance to relevant international instruments. Art. 448 of the Criminal Law of the People's Republic of China provides that "those mistreating prisoners of war, if the case is serious, are to be sentenced to three years or fewer in prison."[105] In a few cases, the relationship between a national criminalization and its international counterparts is ambiguous. Germany, for example, criminalizes the preparation of a war of aggression.[106] While the German legislature apparently did not intend to implement the crime of aggression under international law, Germany's Chief Federal Prosecutor has later construed this provision in conformity with ICL.[107] Occasionally, national provisions are phrased in such a way that they appear to correspond to international crimes, while they in fact bear no relationship to international criminal law at all. In Islamic law, for instance, homicidal crimes against individual muslims are regarded as crimes against all humanity. Therefore, an "ordinary" murder may be labelled a crime against humanity under Islamic law.[108] It is clear, however, that this designation does in no way correspond to the concept of crimes against humanity under international law. Caution is warranted, therefore, in the analysis and application of international crimes under national law.

A sliding scale is also found between national provisions defining international crimes and rules of reference requiring direct application of international offences. National law may well define a core crime and at the same time refer to its criminalization in international law. For example, the German Code of International Crimes defines as a war crime the killing in connection with an armed conflict of "a person who is to be protected under international humanitarian law."[109] As only the protected status of the victim and not the entire criminalization is taken from international law, it seems this provision defines the international crime rather than incorporates it. This is somewhat more difficult to say for the Canadian provision on genocide, which both defines the essence of the crime and refers to its international criminalization.[110] Finally, the Ethiopian provision on war crimes

---

[105] Compare to Art. 130 GC III: Grave breaches to which the preceding Article relates shall be those involving any of the following acts, if committed against persons or property protected by the Convention: wilful killing, torture or inhuman treatment, including biological experiments, wilfully causing great suffering or serious injury to body or health, compelling a prisoner of war to serve in the forces of the hostile Power, or wilfully depriving a prisoner of war of the rights of fair and regular trial prescribed in this Convention.

[106] See Art. 80 German Criminal Code.

[107] See Kress 2004, p. 246 and 249. See also Alvarez *et al.* 2002, p. 307 (on the unclear relationship between the Argentinean criminalization of murder inspired by racial or religious hatred and the Genocide Convention) and Lenzerini 2000 (on the Italian prohibition of slavery and its ambiguous relationship to corresponding treaties).

[108] See Lambert-Abdelgawad 2002, p. 526-527.

[109] Art. 8 (1) sub 1.

[110] See Canadian Crimes Against Humanity and War Crimes Act, Art. 4 (3): " 'Genocide' means an act or omission committed with intent to destroy, in whole or in part, an identifiable group of persons, as such, that at the time and in the place of its commission, constitutes genocide according to customary international law or conventional international law or by virtue of its being criminal according to the general principles of law recognized by the community of nations...".

clearly combines the two, as it both fully defines the crimes and refers to their international criminalization.[111] A similar combination of definition and referral for the core crimes is found in the Belgian Penal Code.[112]

2.2.b *Case Study: Genocide*

I will further illustrate the spectrum of varying correspondence between international crimes in national law and the underlying international law by examining in some detail national prohibitions of genocide, in particular the protected groups in these national provisions, and some of the resulting prosecutions.

The Genocide Convention limits the concept of genocide to the (intended) destruction of "national, ethnic, religious or racial" groups,[113] and the ICC Statute reproduces this definition.[114] Many States follow this wording in their national legislation.[115] Others, however, have altered the definition of genocide in their na-

---

[111] Art. 282 Ethiopian Penal Code. War crimes against the civilian population: "Whosoever, in time of war, armed conflict or occupation, organizes, orders or engages in, against the civilian population and in violation of the rules of public international law and of international humanitarian conventions:
(a) killings, torture or inhuman treatment, including biological experiments, or any other acts involving dire suffering or bodily harm, or injury to mental or physical health; or
(b) wilful reduction to starvation, destitution or general ruination through the depreciation, counterfeiting or systematic debasement of the currency; or
(c) the compulsory movement or dispersion of the population, its systematic deportation, transfer or detention in concentration camps or forced labour camps; or
(d) forcible enlistment in the enemy's armed forces, intelligence services, or administration; or
(e) denationalization or forcible religious conversion; or
(f) compulsion to acts of prostitution, debauchery or rape; or
(g) measures of intimidation or terror, the taking of hostages or the imposition of collective punishments or reprisals; or
(h) the confiscation of estates, the destruction or appropriation of property, the imposition of unlawful or arbitrary taxes or levies, or of taxes or levies disproportionate to the requirements of strict military necessity, is punishable with rigorous imprisonment from five years to life, or, in cases of exceptional gravity, with death."
See also Art. 283-285 and Mayfield 1995, p. 573.

[112] See Art. 136bis, 136ter and 136quater (inserted by the Law of 5 August 2003).

[113] Genocide Convention Art. 2: "In the present Convention, genocide means any of the following acts committed with intent to destroy, in whole or in part, a national, ethnical, racial or religious group, as such:
(a) Killing members of the group;
(b) Causing serious bodily or mental harm to members of the group;
(c) Deliberately inflicting on the group conditions of life calculated to bring about its physical destruction in whole or in part;
(d) Imposing measures intended to prevent births within the group;
(e) Forcibly transferring children of the group to another group."
See Schabas 2000b, p. 102-150.

[114] See Art. 6 ICC Statute.

[115] See a.o. the national provisions on genocide of Cuba, Albania, Australia, Austria, Azerbaijan, Brazil, Croatia, Denmark, Estonia, Fiji Islands, Hungary, Israel, Italy, Kyrgyzstan, Liechtenstein, Luxembourg, Mali, Mexico, Netherlands, New Zealand, Paraguay, Portugal, Russia, Slovenia, Spain, Sweden, Tajikistan. See also Schabas 2000b, p. 350-351.

tional legislation, making it either overinclusive or underinclusive *vis-à-vis* international law. First, many national provisions extend the category of protected groups to ones that are not included in the Convention, like "political groups,"[116] "social groups"[117] and various other groups.[118] Second, several States broaden the protection against genocidal conduct to the open-ended category of "groups determined by any other arbitrary criterion."[119] Finally, there are also States which have curtailed rather than extended the definition of genocide in their national laws. Bolivia

---

[116] See e.g. Cote d'Ivoire, Code Pénal, Livre II – Titre 1er – Chapitre I: Infractions contre le droit des gens, Art. 137: "Est puni de la peine de mort quiconque, dans le dessein de détruire totalement ou partiellement un groupe national, ethnique, confessionnel ou politique…";
Colombia, Código Penal, Art. 101 (Amended by Law 599 of 24 July 2000): "Genocidio. El que con el propósito de destruir total o parcialmente un grupo nacional, étnico, racial, religioso o político…";
Poland, Penal Code (Kodeks Karny, Amended by Law of 6 June 1997), Art. 118 (1) (Ludobójstwo / Genocide, translation from http://preventgenocide.org/law/domestic): "Any person who, with the intent to destroy, in whole or in part, a national, ethnic, racial, political or religious group or a group of persons with a definite philosophical conviction…";
Ethiopia, Penal Code 1957, Art. 281 (Genocide; Crimes against humanity, translation from http://www.icrc.org/ihl-nat): "Whosoever, with intent to destroy, in whole or in part, a national, ethnic, racial, religious or political group…".
But see below, note 140 on the diverging versions of this provision in Amharic and English.

[117] See Peru, Código Penal, Art. 319o (Amended by Law No. 26926 of 19 February 1998): "Será reprimido con pena privativa de libertad no menor de veinte años el que, con la intención de destruir, total o parcialmente, a un grupo nacional, étnico, social o religioso…";
Latvia, Penal Code, Art. 71: "Par genocīdu, tas ir, par tīšu darbību nolūkā pilnīgi vai daļēji iznīcināt kādu nacionālu, etnisku, rases, sociālu…";
Lithuania, Criminal Code, Art. 99 (translation from http://preventgenocide.org/law/domestic): "Anyone, who with the intent to destroy all or part of people, belonging to any national, ethnical, racial, religious, social or political groups…".

[118] See Austria, Art. 321 (1) Penal Code–Genocide: "Whoever, with the intention to destroy, in whole or in part, a group determined by the belonging to a church or religious community, to a race, an ethnic group, a tribe or a state…"
Costa Rica, Código Penal, Art. 127 (Amended by Law of 14 April 1998): "Quien tome parte en la destrucción total o parcial de un determinado grupo de seres humanos, por razones de raza, nacionalidad, género, edad, opción política, religiosa o sexual, posición social, situación económica o estado civil…";
Estonia, Criminal Code, Art. 90 (Amended by Law of 6 June 2001): "A person who, with the intention to destroy, in whole or in part, a national, ethnical, racial or religious group, a group resisting occupation or any other social group,…";
Rumania, Penal Code 1976, Art. 356 (translation from http://preventgenocide.org/law/domestic): "Genocide: The commission of any of the following acts for the purpose of completely or partially destroying a collectivity or a national, ethnic, racial, or religious group…".

[119] See France, Code Pénal, Article 211-1: "Constitue un génocide le fait, en exécution d'un plan concerté tendant à la destruction totale ou partielle d'un groupe national, ethnique, racial ou religieux, ou d'un groupe déterminé à partir de tout autre critère arbitraire…".
Similar provisions exist in the national laws of Belarus (see Criminal Code, Art. 127), Burkina Faso (see Penal Code, Art. 313) and the Congo (see Law No. 8–98 of 31 October 1998 on the definition and the repression of genocide, war crimes and crimes against humanity, Art. 1). Translations of all these provisions are available at http://www.icrc.org/ihl-nat.
Cf. Finland, Penal Code, Chapter 11, Section 6 (translation from http://preventgenocide.org/law/domestic): "A person who for the purpose of entirely or partially destroying a race or national, ethnic or religious group or another comparable group…".

has omitted racial groups from its prohibition of genocide, El Salvador and the Czech Republic have omitted ethnic groups, and Nicaragua has omitted both racial and national groups.[120]

The variations mentioned so far concern solely the protected groups in the definition of genocide. Further divergence between international law and corresponding national provisions becomes apparent when analyzing the acts that make up genocidal conduct and other elements of the crime. While a comprehensive survey falls outside the scope of this study, I will give some pertinent examples. The United States has copied the definition of the Genocide Convention into its federal criminal law, but has *inter alia* qualified the criterion of intent to destroy in whole or in part a specific group by requiring "*specific* intent to destroy in whole or in *substantial* part."[121] Opinions differ on the extent to which these additional requirements separate the U.S. definition from its international counterpart.[122] France requires acts to be "pursuant to a concerted plan" in order to amount to genocide,[123] whereas the existence of a plan is neither required under the Genocide Convention nor under customary law.[124] Ethiopia has included as a genocidal act "the compulsory movement or dispersion of peoples or children," whereas the Genocide Convention proscribes the forcible transfer of children only.[125]

---

[120] See Bolivia, Código Penal, Art. 138 (omitting racial groups): "El que con propósito de destruir total o parcialmente un grupo nacional, étnico o religioso…";
El Salvador, Código Penal, Art. 361 (omitting ethnic groups): "El que con el propósito de destruir parcial o totalmente un determinado grupo humano, por razón de su nacionalidad, raza o religión…";
Czech Republic, Criminal Code, Part II, Section 259 (1): "Whoever, with intent to annihilate, fully or partially, a national, racial or religious group…";
Nicaragua, Código Penal, Art. 549 (omitting racial and national groups): "Comete el delito de genocidio y será penado con presidio de 15 a 20 años, el que realice actos o dicte medidas tendientes a destruir parcial o totalmente un grupo étnico o religioso…".

[121] See United States Code, Chapter 50A – Section § 1091 (a): "Whoever, whether in time of peace or in time of war, in a circumstance described in subsection (d) and with the specific intent to destroy, in whole or in substantial part, a national, ethnic, racial, or religious group as such…". While the U.S. has made a similar declaration of understanding with regard to the Convention, the effects of that declaration are unclear. No prosecution for genocide has ever been undertaken on the basis of this article.

[122] Compare Bassiouni *et al.* 1989, p. 316-319 with p. 330-331.

[123] See above note 119 ("en exécution d'un plan concerté").

[124] See Kriangsak 2001, p. 76. Cf. ICTR, Trial Chamber, *Kayishema and Ruzindana*, 21 May 1999, para. 94: "It is also the view of the Chamber that although a specific plan to destroy does not constitute an element of genocide, it would appear that it is not easy to carry out a genocide without such a plan, or organisation."

[125] Compare Art. 281 Ethiopian Penal Code with Art. 2 Genocide Convention. That the forcible transfer of adults is not in itself sufficient to constitute genocide is borne out by its explicit rejection during the preparation of the Genocide Convention, its exclusion from the ICC Statute and the fact that considerable discussion arose in the ICC PrepCom over the age limit below which transfer would constitute genocide. However, forcible transfer of adults may form an element of genocide when its genocidal quality is established by context. See Rückert and Witschel 2001, p. 69-70 and Haile 2000, p. 48-49.

Actual prosecutions on the basis of national provisions regarding genocide, and attempts thereto, reflect the variation among these provisions.[126] This will be illustrated by a short review of (attempted) genocide prosecutions in Germany, Spain and Ethiopia.

In Germany, genocide prosecutions have been undertaken on the basis of Art. 220a of the German Penal Code (now repealed but reinstated as Art. 6 German Code of International Crimes).[127] This article copies the definition from the Genocide Convention almost literally, but contains a minor alteration.[128] Where the Convention criminalizes the genocidal act of "deliberately inflicting on the group conditions of life *calculated* to bring about its physical destruction in whole or in part," Art. 220a speaks of "Lebensbedingungen [...] die *geeignet* sind" to bring about that physical destruction (both emphasis added). The word "geeignet" translates back to English as apt, able, or likely, and thus lowers the threshold for finding the infliction of destructive conditions. The conditions no longer need to be calculated to bring about the destruction of the group, but must merely be capable of doing so.

The German courts have in several cases applied the divergent translation in its literal meaning instead of interpreting it in conformity with the Genocide Convention.[129] Some commentators conclude that the courts in doing so have convicted

---

[126] See Schabas 2000b, p. 391-393.

[127] Art. 220a Völkermord:

"(1) Wer in der Absicht, eine nationale, rassische, religiöse oder durch ihr Volkstum bestimmte Gruppe als solche ganz oder teilweise zu zerstören,

1. Mitglieder der Gruppe tötet,
2. Mitgliedern der Gruppe schwere körperliche oder seelische Schäden, insbesondere der in § 226 bezeichneten Art, zufügt,
3. die Gruppe unter Lebensbedingungen stellt, die geeignet sind, deren körperliche Zerstörung ganz oder teilweise herbeizuführen,
4. Maßregeln verhängt, die Geburten innerhalb der Gruppe verhindern sollen,
5. Kinder der Gruppe in eine andere Gruppe gewaltsam überführt,

wird mit lebenslanger Freiheitsstrafe bestraft.

(2) In minder schweren Fällen des Absatzes 1 Nr. 2 bis 5 ist die Strafe Freiheitsstrafe nicht unter fünf Jahren."

[English translation on the ICRC website of Art. 220a Genocide [repealed]:

(1) Whoever, with the intention to destroy, in whole or in part, a national, racial, religious or ethnically distinct group as such,

1. kills members of a group;
2. inflicts serious physical or mental injury, especially of the type described in § 226, on members of a group;
3. subjects the group to conditions of life likely to bring about its physical destruction in whole or in part;
4. imposes measures intended to prevent births within the group;
5. forcibly transfers children from the group to another group, shall be punished by imprisonment for life.

(2) Not less than five years' imprisonment shall be imposed in less serious cases falling under subparagraph (1), numbers 2 to 5.]

[128] See Ambos and Wirth 2001, p. 784-786.

[129] See the prosecutions of Jorgic (Germany, OLG Düsseldorf, *Jorgic*, 26 September 1997, 2 StE 8/96; Germany, Supreme Court (BGH), *Jorgic*, 30 March 1999, 3 StR 215/98, in 19 NStZ (1999), 396-

defendants of genocide on the basis of universal jurisdiction for conduct that did not amount to genocide under international law.[130] It should be noted, however, that the expansive approach taken in these decisions does not result solely from the variation in language. The German courts have also – unconnected to the divergent translation – interpreted the required genocidal intent in a broad manner. Instead of interpreting the specific intent to be the physical destruction of the group, the courts have interpreted the intent to be the destruction of the social existence of the group. While this interpretation was apparently not intended by the drafters of the Convention, it can well be reconciled with the language of Art. 2.[131]

In the Pinochet case, the Spanish indictment which led to his arrest in the United Kingdom included a charge of genocide based on the definition in Art. 137 *bis* of the Spanish Criminal Code.[132] This provision has been changed several times. At its enactment in 1971 it required "the intention of totally or partially destroying a national ethnic, social or religious group." This formulation departed from the language of the Genocide Convention in two respects. First, by deleting the comma between national and ethnic these criteria had been merged, instead of providing two separate ones. Second, the term racial had been replaced by social. These discrepancies were later addressed. In 1983, the word social was replaced by the word racial, and in 1995 the missing comma between national and ethnic was inserted.[133] Thus, the Spanish prohibition of genocide currently mirrors the definition in the Genocide Convention, but this was not the case at the time of Pinochet's alleged crimes.

Immediately after the Investigative Judge issued an arrest warrant against Pinochet, the public prosecutor lodged an appeal before the *Audiencia Nacional*, disputing among other points that the alleged conduct could amount to genocide. The *Audiencia*, however, approved the indictment on the basis that Pinochet's government had targeted "national social groups," namely those that opposed his rule.[134] In doing so, the *Audiencia* gave a very broad interpretation of the term "national groups," including such collectivities as AIDS patients and the elderly.[135] The proceedings against Pinochet were aborted when the United Kingdom judged him unfit to stand trial and let him return to Chile.

404; BGHSt 45, 64-91; Germany, Constitutional Court (BVerfG), *Jorgic*, 12 December 2000, 2 BvR 1290/99, in 54 NJW 2001, 1848-1853), *Kusljic* (Germany, BayObLG, *Kusljic*, 15 December 1999, 6 St 1/99; Germany, BGH, *Kusljic*, 21 February 2001, 3 StR 244/00, in 54 NJW (2001), 2732-2734) and Sokolovic (Germany, OLG Düsseldorf, *Sokolovic*, 29 November 1999, 2 StE 6/97; Germany, BGH, *Sokolovic*, 21 February 2001, 3 StR 372/00; BGHSt 46, 292-307; 54 NJW, 2728-2732). See for an analysis on this point Ambos and Wirth 2001, p. 786-789.

[130] See Ambos and Wirth 2001, p. 788-789.

[131] See Schabas 2003b, p. 58-59; Ambos and Wirth 2001, p. 791-792. Cf. Tournaye 2003, p. 454.

[132] See generally Wilson 1999.

[133] See Spain, Audiencia Nacional, Chilean Genocide Case, 5 November 1998, unreported, para. C (5). See also Wilson 1999, p. 957-961.

[134] See Spain, Audiencia Nacional, Chilean Genocide Case, 5 November 1998, unreported, para. C (5). In addition, the indictment included an allegation of intent to destroy a religious group based on its atheist or agnostic ideology.

[135] Id. See also Wilson 1999, p. 959.

Since 1994, Ethiopia has held large-scale trials for crimes against humanity and genocide allegedly comitted during the Mengistu regime that ruled the country until 1991.[136] There is only limited information available about these "Red Terror" trials, named after the repressive regime of the military council Dergue whose members and accomplices are being prosecuted. So far, more than six thousand defendants[137] have been charged with crimes against humanity and genocide, and alternatively with murder and other crimes against bodily integrity.[138]

The charges of crimes against humanity and genocide are based on Art. 281 of the Ethiopian Penal Code (found in Book III, Title II on Offences Against the Law of Nations).[139] This provision is particular in at least three respects. First, it does not distinguish between crimes against humanity and genocide but blends them together in one crime. Second, the protected groups in the definition of genocide are not restricted to those in the Genocide Convention but include political groups. Third, there is a significant discrepancy between the English and the Amharic version of the provision. While the English version speaks of "a national, ethnic, racial, religious or political group," the Amharic version apparently indicates in relevant part that "whosoever, with the intent to destroy, in whole or in part, a social section of a multinational group having common language and custom (and) be unified by race, religion or political conviction, organizes, orders or engages...."[140] While both the English and the Amharic versions of the Penal Code are authentic, the Amharic version is authoritative in case of discrepancies.[141]

---

[136] See generally Kidane 2003; Ratner and Abrams 2001, p. 173-176; Haile 2000; Gouttes 1998. See for an account of the sort of crimes prosecuted Mayfield 1995, p. 558-562 and (a rather loose description in) Engelschiøn 1995, p. 22-25 or Engelschiøn 1994, p. 42-46.

[137] According to a newsreport in November 2003, some 6426 defendants – including the 106 top officials – were awaiting trial, including almost 3000 in absentia. Meanwhile, more than 1569 decisions have resulted in 1017 convictions. See IRIN, Ethiopia: Defence trial of ex-president begins, 4 November 2003. In 1998, the Special Prosecutor stated that some 5,200 people had been charged with genocide and war crimes. See Wakjira 1998, p. 190. See also Kidane 2003, p. 677 and 690; Haile 2000, p. 7 and Gouttes 1998, p. 702.

[138] See Kidane 2003, p. 676. Cf. Gouttes 1998, p. 702 (stating that in addition 54 defendants have been charged with war crimes). Apparently, some defendants have also been charged with other crimes. See Haile 2000, p. 27 and Gouttes 1998, p. 701-702.

[139] Art. 281. Genocide; Crimes against Humanity

Whosoever, with intent to destroy, in whole or in part, a national, ethnic, racial, religious or political group, organizes, orders or engages in, be it in time of war or in time of peace:

(a) killings, bodily harm or serious injury to the physical or mental health of members of the group, in any way whatsoever; or

(b) measures to prevent the propagation or continued survival of its members or their progeny; or

(c) the compulsory movement or dispersion of peoples or children, or their placing under living conditions calculated to result in their death or disappearance,

is punishable with rigorous imprisonment from five years to life, or, in cases of exceptional gravity, with death.

[140] See Kidane 2003, p. 678, fn 60.

[141] Id.

The charges brought against the first group of defendants in the trials incorporated language from both versions.[142] The first charge alleged genocidal conduct against "members of various political groups whom they arbitrarily designated as anti-people and anti-revolution elements."[143] The second charge alleged "intent to destroy in whole or in part a politically organized multinational social group" followed by the actual killing of "members of the political group."[144] The defendants challenged the charge of genocide on two grounds.[145] First, the defendants pointed to the Amharic version to argue that the Ethiopian legislature had not intended to include political groups as such in the definition of genocide. Second, they argued that Art. 281 was null and void as it conflicted with the definition in the Genocide Convention, which according to Ethiopia's 1955 Constitution has a higher status than national law.[146] The court, however, dismissed these objections, relying at least partly on a French draft of the Penal Code which also contained the reference to political groups.

It seems the inclusion of political groups was decisive for the prosecution of the crimes on the basis of genocide, as the victims could not have been classified under any of the four groups enumerated in the Genocide Convention.[147] Prosecutions are on-going in Ethiopia.

3. Prosecution on the Basis of International Law: Direct Application

3.1 Introduction

For a proper understanding of national practice regarding direct application, it is important to keep in mind the theoretical framework of this study. Direct application in the context of this study means that a national court applies an international rule as such because it is binding law, without it being transformed into a rule of national law.[148] Direct application often involves a rule of reference in national law. As set out above, the different legal bases for prosecution described here (ordinary

---

[142] See Ethiopia, Central High Court, *Indictment of Mengistu and 72 others*, October 1994, Unofficial translation on file with the author.

[143] Id., p. 7.

[144] Id., p. 8.

[145] See Kidane 2003, p. 678-679.

[146] See below, note 442.

[147] See Ethiopia, Central High Court, *Asbete et al.*, 24 March 2002 (Ethiopian Calendar 15-7-1995) (acquittal of five defendants on the facts, after they had earlier been found guilty *inter alia* of "planning and organizing, giving the orders and ultimately engaging in intentionally destroying, in whole or in part a national group with political foundations," charged on the basis of Art. 281 Penal Code). See also Haile 2000, p. 51; Redae 1999, p. 26 (stating that the crimes were committed neither against one of the groups designated under international law, nor with the intent to destroy the group as such). Cf. Kidane 2003, p. 683.

[148] See above, p. 8.

crime, international crime in national law, direct application of international law) are not mutually exclusive, but on the contrary often complement one another. The Canadian *Finta* case provides an appropriate example of a case which combined national and international law. It has been described above as a prosecution on the basis of ordinary crimes. At the same time, it requires direct application of international offences since their fulfilment is a precondition for the exercise of jurisdiction.[149]

Thus, direct application of international offences, including the definition of the crime, jurisdictional provisions and forms of participation,[150] does not rule out a (dominant) role for national law. The interaction of national and international law in national prosecutions takes place in a spectrum of relationships which greatly differ in their distribution of and emphasis on substantive criminality and jurisdiction. I will show the role of direct application in this complicated continuum working from its narrowest and least controversial towards its more disputed forms, namely from specific rules of reference towards general rules of reference, including unwritten ones, as a basis for direct application.

3.2 Specific Rule of Reference

Many countries allow for direct application of international offences through rules of reference to specific norms of international law. In contrast to general rules of reference, specific ones give the individual an explicit indication that international law with a penal content is incorporated into the national legal order. Such specific rules of reference generally refer to international offences either to furnish the substantive criminality for a prosecution or as a condition for establishing jurisdiction.

3.2.a *Rule of Reference for Substantive Criminality*

Numerous national laws contain rules of reference to international offences as a basis for the charges to be laid in national prosecutions. These rules can vary considerably in their specificity. Some rules refer to specific treaty provisions or to particular international crimes, while others refer more generally to all treaty-based or customary offences.

A narrowly tailored provision can derive substantive criminality from a concrete treaty provision. An example can be found in Hungarian law, where the criminal code refers back to specific provisions of the International Convention on the Suppression and Punishment of the Crime of Apartheid to define the crime of apartheid.[151] Several States refer to Art. 2 Genocide Convention.[152] Numerous States

---

[149] See above note 94 and accompanying text.

[150] See above note 71 and accompanying text.

[151] See Hungary, Report to the Committee on the Elimination of Racial Discrimination, 17 May 2002, CERD/C/431/Add.1, para. 33. See also Section 157 of the Hungarian Criminal Code, cited above, note 31.

[152] See Schabas 2000b, p. 351.

Parties to the ICC provide for criminalization of the core crimes in their national law by referring to Art. 6-8 ICC Statute. This is the case, for example, in the United Kingdom.[153] New Zealand allows for direct application not only of the definitions of the crimes, including the Elements of Crimes, but also of the provisions in the ICC Statute on forms of participation and other applicable rules like defences and general principles of criminal law. To achieve this result, New Zealand's implementing legislation specifically lists every article of the ICC Statute that is to be directly applied in national prosecutions.[154]

Many national laws on war crimes criminalize violations of "the laws and customs of war," the content of which is to be found in an extensive collection of both treaty and customary law. In Swiss law, Art. 109 of the Code Pénale Militaire (CPM) penalizes the violation of the laws and customs of war, to be found both in treaties and custom.[155] In 1997, a trial on the basis of this article for war crimes allegedly committed in the conflict in the Former Yugoslavia resulted in an acquittal on the facts.[156] The military prosecutor in the case fleshed out the charges under Art. 109 CPM with the 1949 Geneva Convention relative to the treament of prisoners of war (GC III), the 1949 Geneva Convention relative to the protection of civilian persons in time of war (GC IV), the Protocol Additional to the Geneva Conventions of 12 August 1949, and relating to the protection of victims of international armed conflict (AP I) and the Protocol Additional to the Geneva Conventions of 12 August 1949, and relating to the protection of victims of non-international armed conflict (AP II).[157] A subsequent prosecution of a Rwandan bourgmestre resulted in his imprisonment for 14 years.[158] Again, Art. 109 CPM formed the rule of reference for direct application of the Geneva Conventions. Like in the previous case, the Geneva Conventions were applied as a basis for prosecution themselves, not merely as an indication of customary criminalization.[159] The defendant was convicted of

---

[153] See U.K., International Criminal Court Act 2001, Part 5, Art. 50 and 51.

[154] See Sections 9-12 of New Zealand's International Crimes and International Criminal Court Act 2000. See also Hay 2004, p. 195-199.

[155] Art. 109 CPM, titled Violations of the Laws of War (Violations des lois de la guerre):
(1) Whoever acts contrary to the provisions of any international agreement governing the laws of war or the protection of persons and property, or whoever acts in violation of any other recognized law or custom of war shall be punished with imprisonment except in cases where other provisions involving more severe sanctions are applicable. For offenses of high gravity the penalty is penal servitude.
(2) For offenses of little gravity the punishment can consist of a disciplinary sanction.
Translation from Ziegler 1998. See also Vest 2003, p. 49-50.

[156] Switzerland, Military Tribunal, Division 1 (Tribunal militaire de division I, Lausanne), *In re G.*, 18 April 1997, ICRC website. See Ziegler 1998.

[157] See Switzerland, Military Tribunal, Division 1 (Tribunal militaire de division I, Lausanne), *In re G.*, 18 April 1997, ICRC website, La Cause (charging Art. 3 (1) sub a and c, 13, 14, 12S and 130 GC III; Art. 3 (1) sub a and c, 16, 27, 31, 32, 146 and 147 GC IV; Art. 10, 11, 75, 76, 77 and 85 AP I; Art. 4, 5 and 13 AP II).

[158] See Switzerland, Tribunal militaire, Division 2, Lausanne, *In re N.*, 30 April 1999; Switzerland, Military Court of Appeal, *In re N.*, 26 May 2000, ICRC website and Switzerland, Military Court of Cassation, *In re N.*, 27 April 2001. See also Reydams 2002.

[159] See Roth and Jeanneret 2002b, p. 279.

violating common Art. 3 GC's and Art. 4 AP II.[160] Art. 109 CPM provided the applicable penalties.

Likewise, Art. 8 of the Dutch War Crimes Act (*Wet Oorlogstrafrecht*) criminalized in broad terms all violations of the laws and customs of war.[161] In 1996, a citizen of the Former Yugoslavia was prosecuted on the basis of this provision for his role in the Keratern concentration camp as well as for murder and attempted rape.[162] The District Court endorsed the prosecutor's submissions that the hostilities in Bosnia & Herzegovina amounted to a non-international armed conflict, and that the alleged crimes, if proven, constituted violations of common Art. 3 GC and therefore violations of the laws and customs of war.[163] After that decision, however, a complex appeals process followed, mainly concerning the technical questions whether the War Crimes Act applied to conflicts to which the Netherlands was not a party and whether civil or military courts were competent in ensuing prosecutions. The case reached the Supreme Court twice, which eventually decided that involvement of the Netherlands was not a condition for the exercise of jurisdiction and that the military courts were competent in these prosecutions.[164] Following an earlier negative decision, however, the defendant had been released and by the time the continuation of the prosecution was ordered, he had already fled the country.[165] Art. 8 of the War Crimes Act has since been repealed, but the new International Crimes Act contains a similar provision.[166]

Similar rules of reference to the laws and customs of war can be found in many other States.[167] References to particular crimes can also incorporate far more limited international offences. The Polish Penal Code, for example, threatens with imprisonment anyone "who, against the prohibition by international law or by the provision of law, produces, stockpiles, acquires, sells, retains, transports or sends means of mass destruction or means of combat."[168] Yet, even if the language of this provision refers to a clearly circumscribed set of acts, this rule of reference still,

---

[160] Switzerland, Military Court of Appeal, *In re N.*, 26 May 2000, ICRC website, Chapitre 4 (a).

[161] Art. 8 (1) War Crimes Act: "Anyone who commits a violation of the laws and customs of war shall be liable to a term of imprisonment of not more than ten years or a fine of the fifth category."

[162] Netherlands, Arnhem District Court, Military Division (Chambers), *Knezevic*, 21 February 1996, NJ 1998/463, 30 NYIL 315 (1999).

[163] See Netherlands, Arnhem District Court, Military Division (Chambers), *Knezevic*, 21 February 1996, NJ 1998/463, 30 NYIL 315 (1999), para. 5: "The facts as described and defined in detail in the application entail an act in contravention of the provisions of the common article 3 of the Geneva Conventions and would, if proved, constitute, in the opinion of the court sitting in chambers, a violation of the laws and customs of war, as referred to in section 8 of the War Crimes Act." See also para. 6.3.

[164] Netherlands, Supreme Court, *Knezevic II*, 11 November 1997, NJ 1998/463, para. 5.3, 6.3 and 7.3. The direct application of the Geneva Conventions was not disputed on appeal (see para. 6.1). See also Netherlands, Supreme Court, *Knezevic I*, 22 October 1996, NJ 1998/462.

[165] See on the case generally Elst 1998.

[166] See International Crimes Act 2003, Art. 7.

[167] See above, note 7 and Amnesty International, *Report on Universal jurisdiction*, 2001, Chapter 4.

[168] Art. 121 Polish Penal Code, Law of 6 June 1997. See also Weigend 2003, p. 103-104.

like those to the laws and customs of war, requires an analysis of all sources of international law to find the relevant rules.[169]

An unusually broad rule of reference can be found in Art. 156 (3) of Venezuela's Penal Code, which threatens imprisonment for a period between one and four years to everyone who violates a treaty to which Venezuela is a party "in a manner which entails the responsibility of the State."[170] On its face, this provision appears to criminalize violations of all treaty norms that lead to State responsibility, not just those treaty norms establishing international crimes. Yet, there is reason to adopt a narrower interpretation, since Art. 156 as a whole deals with violations of the laws of war and is placed in Chapter III of Title I of the Penal Code, which regulates crimes against international law. (*De los delitos contra el derecho internacional*). Therefore, it may be thought that this provision refers only to the violation of treaty provisions that entail individual criminal responsibility under international law.[171]

3.2.b *Rule of Reference to Establish Jurisdiction*

There are numerous rules of reference which refer to international offences as a condition to establish jurisdiction, while the acts to be prosecuted are charged on the basis of national criminal law. Such jurisdictional provisions require courts to ascertain whether international offences are fulfilled in order to establish jurisdiction, often extraterritorially. Once this condition is met, the crimes are prosecuted on the basis of national criminal law. Again, these rules of reference vary considerably in the concreteness with which they identify the relevant international law.

Some national provisions refer to all international criminal law regarding a particular crime. Numerous national laws establish jurisdiction for the prosecution of (certain, e.g. only WW II) war crimes, often to be charged as ordinary crimes, on the condition that the acts under consideration constitute violations of the international laws and customs of war.[172] This was the case in the Canadian prosecution of Finta and the British prosecution of Sawoniuk, mentioned above.[173] The extent to which courts actually apply the international offences in such cases can vary considerably. In *Finta*, the analysis and application of international law was extensive.[174] The trial of Sawoniuk, on the other hand, focused predominantly on factual

[169] See also Art. 3 Bangladesh's International Crimes (Tribunals) Act 1973 (Act No. XIX of 19 July 1973) (giving specific national courts the "power to try and punish" the core crimes under reference to international law, as well as "any other crimes under international law"; note, however, that no prosecutions have ever been undertaken on the basis of this act. See Paust and Blaustein 1978).

[170] Art. 156 (3): "Incurren en pena de arresto en Fortaleza o Cárcel Política por tiempo de uno a cuatro años: [...] Los venezolanos o extranjeros que violen las Convenciones o Tratados celebrados por la República, de un modo que comprometa la responsabilidad de ésta. "

[171] Cf. Modolell González 2003, p. 547.

[172] See above para. 2.1.

[173] See above notes 93 and 94.

[174] See Fletcher 2002, p. 455-458.

questions while the qualification of the alleged crimes as war crimes under international law was taken for granted.[175]

In addition, there are those rules which refer to all international offences of a particular source. Many States extend the jurisdiction of their national criminal law to extraterritorial crimes they are permitted or obliged to prosecute under treaty law. Examples can be found in Chinese,[176] Danish,[177] French,[178] German,[179] Greek,[180] Laotian,[181] Spanish,[182] Swiss,[183] and Yemeni[184] law.[185] It should be noted that many of those provisions vest jurisdiction both for international crimes and for conduct that States are obliged to criminalize while international law itself does not do so directly.[186]

Finally, the broadest rules of reference include all international offences, irrespective of their source. Some national laws contain such a broad rule of reference to all sources, but restrict it to criminalization of a mandatory rather than permissive character. Austria, for example, establishes jurisdiction over "punishable acts which Austria is under an obligation to punish even when they were committed abroad."[187] Belgian law contains a similar provision.[188] Some other States have

[175] See U.K., Court of Appeal, *R. v. Anthony Sawoniuk*, 10 February 2000, [2000] 2 Cr. App. R. 220 at 223: "It was not disputed at the trial that the legal conditions for application of this section were met. [...] The victims were civilian members of the Jewish population, and their killing (if committed) was a violation of the laws and customs of war."

[176] See Art. 9 New Chinese Penal Code 1997. See also Yuan and Jianping 2002, p. 350.

[177] See Art. 8, para. 1, Section 5 Danish Penal Code. See also Holdgaard Bukh 1994, p. 341-345.

[178] See Art. 689 French Penal Code.

[179] See Art. 6 (9) German Penal Code.

[180] See Art. 8 Greek Penal Code, translated in Discalopoulou-Livada 2000, p. 120 (providing extraterritorial jurisdiction for specific crimes and "any other crime for which special provisions or international agreements signed and ratified by the Greek State provide the application of Greek penal laws").

[181] See Art. 4 (3) Laotian Criminal Code.

[182] See Art. 23-4 (g) Spanish Ley Orgánica del Poder Judicial. See also Buck 2002, p. 141.

[183] See Art. 6 bis Swiss CP.

[184] See Art. 21 Yemeni Law 21/1998, reported in Lambert-Abdelgawad 2002, p. 530-531.

[185] See also above, para. 2.1.

[186] International obligations to criminalize conduct that is not criminal under international law itself flow *inter alia* from human rights treaties. See below, Chapter V, para. 3.3.a. See also Schmidt 2002, p. 131-132 (distinguishing international offences from "*Externe Strafpflichten mit Umsetzungspflicht*").

[187] See Art. 64 Austrian Penal Code – Acts committed abroad punishable irrespective of the law of the place where they are committed:
(1) The following crimes committed abroad are punished under Austrian criminal law irrespective of the criminal law of the place where they were committed:
[...]
6. other punishable acts which Austria is under an obligation to punish even when they were committed abroad, irrespective of the criminal law of the place where were committed.

[188] Art. 12bis (1) Code of criminal procedure (Code de procédure pénale, modified by Art. 18 of the Law of 5 August 2003): "Hormis les cas visés aux articles 6 à 11, les juridictions belges sont également compétentes pour connaître des infractions commises hors du territoire du Royaume et visées par une règle de droit international conventionnelle ou coutumière liant la Belgique, lorsque cette règle lui impose, de quelque manière que ce soit, de soumettre l'affaire à ses autorités compétentes pour l'exercice des poursuites."

enacted rules of reference that include all international crimes, regardless of the question whether there is a corresponding duty to prosecute.[189]

As is apparent from this overview and that in the preceding paragraph, direct application of international offences on the basis of a specific rule of reference is accepted in different forms by many States all over the world.[190] Few cases question the competence of the legislature to refer to an international criminalization instead of defining it fully in national law. One such case is the judgment of the U.S. Supreme Court in *U.S. v. Smith* (1820).[191] It concerned a prosecution on the basis of a statute providing for the death penalty for "the crime of piracy, as defined by the law of nations."[192] The defendant argued that such a rule of reference was inappropriate since the Constitution required Congress "to define and punish piracies and felonies committed on the high seas, and offences against the law of nations."[193] Since international law did not define piracy with precision and certainty, the defendant contended, it was up to Congress to give "a distinct, intelligible explanation of the nature of the offence in the act itself."[194] The Supreme Court rejected this contention, however, and found that a rule of reference to an international crime was as constitutional as an enumeration of the prohibited acts.[195]

---

[189] See e.g. Ecuador, Code of Criminal Procedure, Art. 18 (6):
"Ámbito de la jurisdicción penal. – Están sujetos a la jurisdicción penal del Ecuador:
6) Los ecuatorianos o extranjeros que cometan delitos contra el Derecho Internacional o previstos en Convenios o Tratados Internacionales vigentes, siempre que no hayan sido juzgados en otro Estado"; Ethiopia, Penal Code, Art. 17 (1) (Offences committed in a foreign country against International Law or Universal Order):
"Any person who has committed in foreign country:
(a) an offence against international law or an international offence specified in Ethiopian legislation, or an international treaty or a convention to which Ethiopia has adhered:
[…]
shall be liable to trial in Ethiopia in accordance with the provisions of this Code and subject to the general conditions mentioned hereinafter (Art. 19 and 20 (2)) unless he has been prosecuted in the foreign country.";
Tajikistan, Art. 15 (2) sub a Criminal Code:
"Foreign nationals and stateless persons who do not permanently reside in the Republic of Tajikistan shall be liable under the present Code for crimes committed outside its boundaries in the following situations:
a) they have committed a crime provided for by the rules of international law recognized by the Republic of Tajikistan or by international treaties and agreements.

[190] See Bridge 1964, p. 1258-1260.

[191] U.S., Supreme Court, *United States v. Smith*, 1820, 18 U.S. 153.

[192] See 18 U.S.C.A. § 481 (*s.* 5.): "That if any person or persons whatsoever, shall, on the high seas, commit the crime of piracy, as defined by the law of nations, and such offender or offenders shall afterwards be brought into, or found in, the United States, every such offender or offenders shall, upon conviction thereof, before the Circuit Court of the United States for the District into which he or they may be brought, or in which he or they shall be found, be punished with death."

[193] See Art. I, Section 8, clause 10 Constitution.

[194] U.S., Supreme Court, *United States v. Smith*, 1820, 18 U.S. 153 at 157.

[195] Id., 158-160.

3.3 General Rule of Reference

3.3.a *Introduction*

The most far-reaching and controversial form of direct application of international criminal law occurs in the absence of a specific rule of reference to an international criminalization. In that case, the question arises whether general rules of reference to international law or a part thereof (treaties, custom or general principles) also incorporate international offences, possibly including rules of jurisdiction, in the national legal order ("general direct application").[196] In other words, is ICL subject to the same constitutional rules on incorporation and transformation as international law in general, or does it take up a special position?

Most States have not explicitly resolved the position of international law in their criminal law either in legislation or practice. Therefore, the question to what extent international criminal law can be directly applied normally requires resort to the general constitutional scheme regarding international law in the national legal order *and* an additional analysis whether international criminal law fits this scheme or encounters additional obstacles. Such an analysis is, however, a complex exercise with an unsure outcome.

It is not enough to examine national provisions on the principle of legality to see whether the text explicitly mentions international law as an accepted legal basis for substantive criminality. If it does, that fact alone does not conclusively determine whether international law can be directly applied or whether a statute is needed to effectuate that substantive criminality. On the other hand, the fact that international law is not explicitly mentioned is by no means the end of the matter. If for example, a national provision requires punishment to be based on national law, it remains to be seen whether national law in that sense includes international law because the latter is incorporated through a general rule of reference.[197] Also, apparently rigid provisions of legality have been interpreted in the light of human rights treaties to include international law, for example in France and Hungary.[198] Thus, national provisions on the principle of legality can not be taken on face value but form only one step in a more elaborate analysis.

Other national, often constitutional provisions can likewise be deceptive in their apparent rejection of international law in criminal matters. In the Netherlands, for example, the Constitution provides that both civil and criminal law "shall be regulated by Act of Parliament in general legal codes."[199] This formulation could be

---

[196] Cf. Komarow 1980, p. 26 ("Application through general rules of incorporation"); Werle 2003, p. 42.

[197] See below, note 204.

[198] See below, para. 3.3.j and 3.3.n.

[199] Art. 107 (1): "Civil law, criminal law and civil and criminal procedure shall be regulated by Act of Parliament in general legal codes without prejudice to the power to regulate certain matters in separate Acts of Parliament."

interpreted to rule out direct application of international criminal law altogether.[200] Yet, it merely expresses the desired codification of national law and has never prevented direct application of international law of any kind.[201]

Ukraine's 1996 Constitution declares that "acts that are crimes, administrative or disciplinary offences, and liability for them are determined exclusively by the laws of Ukraine."[202] The President of Ukraine consequently argued before the Constitutional Court that ratification of the ICC Statute would violate the Constitution, as *inter alia* the Elements of Crimes would amount to foreign legislation imposed in violation of the Constitution. The Constitutional Court rejected this argument on the basis that, pursuant to Art. 9 of the Constitution,[203] treaties "are part of [the] national legislation of Ukraine."[204] From this, one can conclude that direct application of customary international criminal law will be rejected as an unacceptable infringement on the power of the legislature. Despite the robust language on a national legislative monopoly in criminal matters, direct application of treaty-based offences is apparently in conformity with the Constitution of Ukraine.

Russia likewise provides in Art. 3 (1) of its Criminal Code that "criminal activities, their punishability and any other criminal law consequences are governed only by this Code."[205] Yet here also, criminal law may not be so impenetrable to international influences as it may first appear. Russia's Criminal Code aims *inter alia* to "ensure the peace and security of mankind"[206] and is "based upon the Russian Constitution and basic principles and norms of international law."[207] Some observers conclude that criminal law is not singled out from the general constitutional scheme[208] and that international treaties are directly applicable also in criminal

---

[200] See Francisco 2003, p. 134 (while the author merely mentions this provision and does not analyze its consequences, it appears to have contributed to her mistaken conclusion that the Dutch legal order categorically rejects direct application of international criminal law).

[201] See Fleuren 2004, p. 334-336.

[202] Art. 92 (22). See also Art. 92 (14) and 75 ("The sole body of legislative power in Ukraine is the Parliament – the Verkhovna Rada of Ukraine.").

[203] Art. 9: "International treaties that are in force, agreed to be binding by the Verkhovna Rada of Ukraine, are part of the national legislation of Ukraine."

[204] Ukraine, Constitutional Court, *Conformity of the Constitution of Ukraine to the Rome Statute of the International Criminal Court (the Rome Statute case)*, 11 July 2001, para. 2.5 and 2.6 (finding *inter alia* that "agreement for an international agreement to be binding (its ratification) is conducted by Verhovna Rada [Parliament] of Ukraine in the form of a law, which, by its legal nature, does not differ from other laws of Ukraine").

[205] See Lukashuk 2001, p. 267.

[206] See Art. 2 (1) Criminal Code, cited in Lukashuk 2001, p. 267.

[207] See Art. 1 (2) Criminal Code (available on website ICRC): "The present Code is based upon the Constitution of the Russian Federation and basic principles and norms of international law."

[208] See Art. 15 (4) Constitution 1993: "Generally accepted principles and norms of international law and international agreements of the Russian Federation shall be an integral part of its legal system. If an international agreement of the Russian Federation established rules other than those stipulated by law, the rules of the international agreement shall be applicable." See also Art. 5 (3) of the Federal Law on International Treaties of 15 july 1995 and Marie-Schwartzenberg 2002, p. 263

matters.[209] Keeping in mind the Ukrainian example, an authoritative conclusion on the viability of direct application of international offences will have to come from the Russian courts, which have not yet taken up the matter.[210]

These examples demonstrate the difficulties in analyzing direct application of international offences in the absence of judicial pronouncements on the question.[211] For that reason, this section will focus primarily on legal systems where courts have directly addressed the question of whether international offences can be directly applied in the absence of a specific rule of reference. The legal systems described here have been selected principally on the basis of the availability of relevant (recent) judgments, either original or in translation. In addition, a few States have been included which lack recent practice on the precise question of general direct application but merit description for the richness of either their older case law or their doctrine. Care has been taken to include as legally and geographically diverse States as possible, but still Western and European States are decidedly overrepresented. This overrepresentation results at least in part from the fact that their case law is more easily accessible than that of many other States, but may also indicate that the courts of these States are relatively active in the application of international criminal law.

The selected States include ones that reject general direct application altogether, ones that are very open to it, and ones exhibiting various degrees of acceptance between these two extremes. Although the States described here reflect all shades of the spectrum, they are not representative for State practice as a whole, since they have been selected among those States that have most actively confronted the question of direct application of international criminal law.

The country reports vary considerably in length, which is mostly due to the difference in availability and complexity of judicial precedents and other sources for each legal system. Also, well-known judgments are treated in a cursory manner under reference to relevant literature in order to minimize duplication. The following description of national legal systems begins with States that reject direct application of international offences in the absence of a specific rule of reference and

---

[209] See Marie-Schwartzenberg 2002, p. 263. Cf. Lukashuk 2001, p. 268 (concluding that Art. 3 (1) Criminal Code in principle rejects direct application of international criminal law but "cannot be strictly interpreted. For example, as concerns such crimes as aggression, the production and distribution of weapons of mass destruction, and the use of mercenaries, it is unavoidable that the international law norms that provide the definitions of these crimes should be applied directly.") and Komarow 1980, p. 30-32 (on direct application in the Soviet Union).
See also Art. 356 Criminal Code; Russia, Constitutional Court, *On the constitutionality of Presidential Decree No. 2137 of 30 November 1994*, 31 July 1995 and Order No. 75 of the Defence Minister of the USSR on the Announcement of the Geneva Conventions of the 12th of August, 1949 for the Protection of Victims of War and Their Additional Protocols, Moscow 16 February 1990, English translation on ICRC website (on the bindingness of the Geneva Conventions).

[210] See Marie-Schwartzenberg 2002, p. 274.

[211] See also the description of Hungary below, in para. 3.3.n. The "internationalist" interpretation of the principle of legality by the Constitutional Court that allowed direct application of customary offences there was not readily discernible from an analysis of the constitutional framework.

works towards States that are more open to it. To give a thorough outline of national approaches, this overview includes a final paragraph with a brief description of legislation and/or doctrine in other States.

3.3.b *Germany*

In Germany, all international law is incorporated in the national legal order. The German Constitution (*Grundgesetz*) regulates custom in Art. 25, which determines that "the general rules of public international law form part of the Federal law and directly create rights and duties for the inhabitants of the Federal territory."[212] It further states in Art. 59 (2) that "treaties which regulate the political relations of the Federation or relate to matters of Federal legislation require the consent or participation, in the form of a Federal law, of the bodies competent in any specific case for such Federal legislation."[213] Together, Art. 25 and 59 (2) are generally interpreted to affirm or regulate the incorporation of all custom and treaty law in the German legal order.[214]

Before German reunification, there were a few instances of direct application of international criminal law. An example dating back to the 19th century concerned punishment of violations of international shipping regulations for the Danube.[215] After WW I, some of the prosecutions held in Leipzig relied not only on national but also directly on international criminal law.[216] For the prosecution of WW II crimes, West-Germany relied on national criminal law but East-Germany directly applied the Nuremberg Statute for some time.[217] In *Globke* (1963), the East-German Supreme Court (*Oberster Gerichtshof*) held that Art. 6 of the Nuremberg Statute was directly applicable on account of a general rule of reference to international law in the East-German Constitution.[218] In *Fischer* (1966), the prosecution of a

---

[212] Art. 25: "Die allgemeinen Regeln des Völkerrechtes sind Bestandteil des Bundesrechtes. Sie gehen den Gesetzen vor und erzeugen Rechte und Pflichten unmittelbar für die Bewohner des Bundesgebietes."

[213] Art. 59 (2): "Verträge, welche die politischen Beziehungen des Bundes regeln oder sich auf Gegenstände der Bundesgesetzgebung beziehen, bedürfen der Zustimmung oder der Mitwirkung der jeweils für die Bundesgesetzgebung zuständigen Körperschaften in der Form eines Bundesgesetzes. Für Verwaltungsabkommen gelten die Vorschriften über die Bundesverwaltung entsprechend."

[214] In this regard, there is a debate in Germany on the declarative or constitutive character of Arts. 25 and 59 (2). See Bremer 1999, p. 145-151; Pieroth and Jarass 1995, p. 495 and 632. Cf. Roth and Jeanneret 2002a, p. 10; Steiger 2001, p. 68. See for strong recent support for the constitutive theory Germany, Bundesverfassungsgericht, *In re G.*, 14 October 2004, 2 BvR 1481/04, para. 30-45 (but see also para. 46 and 61-62, which are more ambiguous).

[215] See Triffterer 1966, p. 182-188.

[216] See Germany, Reichsgericht in Criminal Matters, Publication of Treaties Case (Germany), 25 September 1920, Partial translation in English in Annual Digest 1923-24, No. 234; Germany, Reichsgericht in Strafsachen, The Llandovery Castle, 16 July 1921, Partial translation in English in Annual Digest 1923-24, No. 235. See also Hankel 2003, p. 66; Schmidt 2002, p. 12-14.

[217] See for an elaborate description of the prosecution of WW II crimes in the GDR Wieland 2002.

[218] German Democratic Republic, Oberster Gerichtshof, *Globke*, 23 July 1963, reproduced in DDR-Justiz und NS-Verbrechen: Sammlung ostdeutscher Strafurteile wegen nationalsozialistischer

medical doctor for crimes committed in Auschwitz, the Supreme Court reiterated the direct applicability of the offences of the Nuremberg Statute and asserted that their direct application was necessary for the proper characterization of the crimes, since ordinary criminal law did not capture all aspects of the acts in question.[219]

In today's reunited Germany, however, the situation is quite different. There is broad consensus in doctrine that modern German law rules out direct application of all international criminal law.[220] The Constitution determines in Art. 103 (2) that "an act may be punished only if it constituted a criminal offence under statutory law before the act was committed."[221] This formulation of the legality principle requires a written basis in national law for all prosecutions.[222] Although the German courts have in certain cases involving particularly serious crimes effectively set aside the principle of legality under application of the so-called Radbruch formula, these appear to be exceptions with little relevance for the direct application of ICL in general.[223] Thus, the principle of legality in German law apparently excludes general direct application of international offences altogether, whether they are contained in custom or treaties.

3.3.c *Switzerland*

Switzerland incorporates both treaty and custom as a general unwritten rule.[224] Swiss legislation also contains a reference to international law for the criminalization of war crimes.[225] Yet, in the absence of such a specific rule of reference, the prin-

Tötungsverbrechen (Demps *et al.*, ed.), Vol. III, p. 182-183 at 183: "Im vorliegenden Verfahren sind die Tatbestände des Art. 6 des IMT-Statuts gemäss Art. 5 der Verfassung der Deutschen Demokratischen Republik als geltendes Recht direkt anzuwenden. Eines besonderen innerstaatlichen Gesetzes bedarf es nicht, weil Art. 5 der Verfassung der Deutschen Demokratischen Republik den allgemein anerkannten Regeln des Völkerrechts im innerstaatlichen Bereich unmittelbar geltung verschafft."

[219] German Democratic Republic, Oberster Gerichtshof, *Fischer*, 25 March 1966, reproduced in DDR-Justiz und NS-Verbrechen: Sammlung ostdeutscher Strafurteile wegen nationalsozialistischer Tötungsverbrechen (Demps *et al.*, ed.), Vol. II, p. 713-714: "Die vom IMT-Statut erfassten völkerrechtlichen Massenverbrechen unterscheiden sich hinsichtlich ihres Charakters, ihrer Begehungsweise als staatlich geplante und organisierte Massenverbrechen und hinsichtlich ihres Ausmasses prinzipiel von allen anderen Straftaten. Ihre vollständige Erfassung und richtige Charakterisierung ist deshalb allein durch unmittelbare Anwendung der einzelnen Tabestandsmerkmale des Art. 6 Buchstaben a, b und c möglich."

[220] See Werle 2003, p. 42; Jessberger 2003, p. 291-292; Schmidt 2002, p. 69-79; Roth and Jeanneret 2002a, p. 10-11; Bremer 1999, p. 151-154; Schilling 1999, p. 399-400; Hettinger 1965, p. 11-12. But see Stuby 1995, p. 449.

[221] Art. 103 (2): "Eine Tat kann nur bestraft werden, wenn die Strafbarkeit gesetzlich bestimmt war, bevor die Tat begangen wurde." See also Art. 1 Criminal Code.

[222] See Pieroth and Jarass 1995, p. 883-885.

[223] See Schmidt 2002, p. 71-78; Rogall 2000, p. 406-418; Schilling 1999, p. 391-392 and 396-399; Arnold and Weigend 1997, p. 89-91.

[224] See Thürer 2001; Bremer 1999, p. 253; Ziegler 1997, p. 565.

[225] See above note 155. See for an elaborate description of relevant provisions Ziegler 1997, p. 567-574.

ciple of legality[226] opposes direct application of international offences for the prosecution of core crimes.[227] The failed attempt to charge a Rwandan bourgmestre with genocide under customary international law demonstrates this state of the law.[228] The Military Tribunal in first instance found that the customary criminalization of genocide and crimes against humanity are not directly applicable in the Swiss legal order and convicted the defendant on the other charges.[229] The Military Court of Appeals agreed on this point, and set out the state of the law in some detail. According to the Court of Appeals, Art. 109 Military Penal Code (CPM)[230] incorporates both customary and treaty-based offences pertaining to war, to be understood as an international armed conflict.[231] Art. 108 (2) expands the direct application of treaty crimes, but not customary offences, to internal armed conflicts. Because the Court of Appeals characterized the conflict in Rwanda as internal, the customary criminalization of genocide could not be applied.[232] In the absence of a governing treaty incorporated through Art. 108 and 109 CPM,[233] the defendant could not be charged with genocide but was convicted only for war crimes.

The different judgments in this case all imply that international offences require a specific rule of reference for direct application.[234] Thus, Swiss law allows general direct application for neither treaty nor custom.[235]

3.3.d *Australia*

The position of public international law in Australia is a matter of some dispute. Roughly speaking, treaties require transformation in national laws but can have limited effects irrespective of such transformation.[236] The position of international

---

226 See Art. 1 Penal Code, Art. 1 Military Penal Code.

227 See Schabas 2003b, p. 48.

228 See above note 158.

229 Switzerland, Tribunal militaire, Division 2, Lausanne, *In re N.*, 30 April 1999. See Reydams 2002, p. 232.

230 See above note 155.

231 Switzerland, Military Court of Appeal, *In re N.*, 26 May 2000, Part. III, Chapitre 1 (b).

232 Switzerland, Military Court of Appeal, *In re N.*, 26 May 2000, Part. III, Chapitre 1 (b): "En l'absence d'une telle convention, il n'est pas possible d'appliquer à un conflit armé interne le droit coutumier prévu à l'art 109 CPM. Dans le cadre du conflit rwandais, de caractère non international [...], la juridiction militaire suisse n'est pas compétente pour juger le cas sous l'angle de la prohibition du génocide découlant du droit coutumier à défaut de ratification de la Convention sur le génocide par la Suisse."

233 Switzerland had at that time not yet ratified the Genocide Convention. Today, Switzerland is a party to the Convention and has introduced a domestic provision on genocide in Art. 264 Penal Code.

234 See also Switzerland, Military Court of Cassation, *In re N.*, 27 April 2001, para. 9a ("la condamnation ne peut être fondée que sur l'Art. 109 CPM").

235 See Bremer 1999, p. 256-258 and Bertossa *et al.* 1993, p. 17. Cf. Roth and Jeanneret 2002b, p. 281 and Cottier 2000.

236 See *Minister for Immigration and Ethnic Affairs v. Teo*h (1995) 183 C.L.R. 273. See also Boas 2004, p. 180-184; Kinley and Martin 2002, p. 467; Daglish 2001, p. 405; Mitchell 2000, p. 28-30; Todres 1998, p. 187-188.

custom is unclear. While custom has been incorporated through the common law in the past, there are contradictory authorities and opinions on its place in the Australian legal order.[237]

The 1999 case of *Nulyarimma* concerning the treatment of aboriginals in Australia answered important questions regarding the direct application of ICL.[238] *Nulyarimma* asked the Federal Court of Australia to pronounce on the applicability of the international crime of genocide in the absence of implementing legislation. The Court ruled with a 2–1 majority that genocide could not be prosecuted under Australian law. In the absence of a relevant statute, the decision turned on the question of whether the customary crime of genocide could be part of the Australian legal order through the common law. Two of the three justices answered that question in the negative in no uncertain terms:

> "[I]t is not enough to say that, **under international law**, an international crime is punishable in a domestic tribunal even in the absence of a domestic law declaring that conduct to be punishable. If genocide is to be regarded as punishable in Australia, on the basis that it is an international crime, it must be shown that **Australian law** permits that result. There being no relevant statute, that means Australian common law."[239]

The majority relied on different arguments to reject direct application of customary offences. Justice Wilcox suggested that international offences could not be equated to non-penal rules as regards their incorporation in the national legal order.[240] Both Justice Wilcox and Justice Whitlam considered the absence of a procedural framework for resulting prosecutions and the principle of legality as obstacles to direct application of international offences.[241] In addition, Justice Whitlam relied on the sovereign character of the administration of criminal justice to reject jurisdiction over international crimes without an explicit national authorization.[242]

---

[237] See Daglish 2001, p. 405-406; Mitchell 2000, p. 31-32.

[238] Australia, Federal Court, *Nulyarimma v. Thompson*, 1 September 1999, [1999] FCA 1192. See Daglish 2001 and Mitchell 2000.

[239] Para. 22, Wilcox J.

[240] Para. 25: "It is one thing, it seems to me, for courts of a particular country to be prepared to treat a civil law rule like the doctrine of foreign sovereign immunity as part of its domestic law, whether because it is accepted by those courts as being 'incorporated' in that law or because it has been 'transformed' by judicial act. It is another thing to say that a norm of international law criminalising conduct that is not made punishable by the domestic law entitles a domestic court to try and punish an offender against that law."

[241] See para. 26, Wilcox J.: "[I]n the realm of criminal law 'the strong presumption *nullum crimen sine lege* (there is no crime unless expressly created by law) applies.' In the case of serious criminal conduct, ground rules are needed. Which courts are to have jurisdiction to try the accused person? What procedures will govern the trial? What punishment may be imposed? These matters need to be resolved before a person is put on trial for an offence as horrendous as genocide." See also Whitlam J. on the rule against common law crimes, para. 54.

[242] Para. 52, Whitlam J.: "Even if it be accepted that customary international law is part of the common law, no one has identified a rule of customary international law to this effect: that courts in common law countries have jurisdiction in respect of those international crimes over which States may

Dissenting Justice Merkel reached a different conclusion, namely that "genocide is an offence under the common law of Australia."[243] In doing so, he relied on the Israeli *Eichmann* case and the reasoning of Lord Millett in *Pinochet*.[244] He rejected arguments that this approach of incorporation via the common law would cause uncertainty or violate the separation of powers.[245] He addressed concerns regarding the principle of legality, in particular the rule against common law crimes, but believed the application of a crime of universal jurisdiction under international law did not entail a violation.[246] Also, Justice Merkel explicitly rejected the argument that the position of international criminal law in the national legal order is different from public international law in general.[247]

Nulyarimma has received broad criticism from commentators as an unclear decision that should be overturned.[248] Yet, it has been followed by several state courts.[249] Thus, it can be concluded that Australian law currently rejects general direct application of international criminal law, both treaty and custom. The statutory requirement formulated in *Nulyarimma* does seem to allow for direct application on the basis of a specific rule of reference.

3.3.e *Senegal*

Attempts to initiate the prosecution of former Tchadian dictator Hissène Habré[250] in Senegal relied heavily on international law.[251] In 1999, several victims of his

exercise universal jurisdiction. That is hardly surprising. Universal jurisdiction conferred by the principles of international law is a component of sovereignty [...], and the way in which sovereignty is exercised will depend on each common law country's peculiar constitutional arrangements."

[243] Para. 186.

[244] Para. 154.

[245] Para. 165-181.

[246] Para. 161 and 178. On the contrary, he emphasized the need for national courts to take account of the developments in international law, see para. 181: "It would be anomalous for the Municipal Courts not to continue their longstanding role of recognising, by adoption, the changes and developments in international law."

[247] Para. 133 and 161: "The authorities to which I have referred do not suggest that the principles governing the adoption of customary international law relate only to international civil law and not to international criminal law. The issue appears to be an open question that has not yet been the subject of authoritative decision although dicta to which I later refer supports the adoption into municipal law of international criminal law in respect of universal crimes. [...] I do not accept that different policy reasons or principles ought to apply to the adoption of customary international criminal law in relation to universal crimes into municipal law." See also para. 139: "[P]iracy is a long recognised example of jurisdiction vesting in a municipal court in respect of international crimes without legislation conferring the jurisdiction."

[248] See above note 238.

[249] See Mitchell 2000, p. 43.

[250] After his fall from power in Tchad in 1990, Habré left behind an estimated 40,000 dead and 200,000 victims of torture to find refuge in Senegal. See Rapport de la Commission d'enquête nationale du ministère tchadien de la Justice (1992), cited in Senegal, *Plainte avec Constitution de Partie Civile Contre Hissène Habré, Présenté au Juge d'Instruction du Tribunal Régional hors classe de Dakar*, 1999, part I (*Informations generales*).

[251] See generally Sharp 2003; Cissé 2002, p. 441-446; Brody and Duffy 2001.

regime filed a "civil party complaint" (*plainte avec constitution de partie civile*) in Senegal, an action requiring a criminal prosecution joined with a civil suit.[252] The complaint accused Habré *inter alia* of crimes against humanity and torture and referred to the ICTR's *Akayesu* judgment, the CAT and the ICC Statute (both ratified by Senegal) as well as national criminal law to substantiate these allegations and Habré's responsibility.[253]

The complaint also relied on international law to argue that the defects in Senegal's national criminal law were no obstacle to the prosecution sought.[254] While Senegal has ratified numerous ICL treaties, it has adopted no provisions on international crimes in its criminal law except for torture.[255] Moreover, criminal jurisdiction of the Senegalese courts is limited to the bases of territoriality, nationality and protection of State interests, while universal jurisdiction is not recognized.[256] Yet, according to then Art. 79 of the Constitution, ratified and published treaties supersede national law.[257]

The victims asserted in their complaint that international law required Senegal to extradite or prosecute Habré. In this regard, they cited the CAT, the Geneva Conventions and general international law.[258] In their view, the lack of a national criminalization of crimes against humanity could be cured by directly applying the criminalization under customary international law.[259] Likewise, universal jurisdiction could be derived directly from general international law, the CAT and the Geneva Conventions, despite the fact that national law suggests otherwise.[260] In support of this view, the complaint cited a non-penal judgment of the Senegalese Supreme

[252] See Sharp 2003, p. 167.

[253] See Senegal, *Plainte avec Constitution de Partie Civile Contre Hissène Habré, Présenté au Juge d'Instruction du Tribunal Régional hors classe de Dakar*, 1999, part IV (Lois applicables).

[254] Id., parts IV and V.

[255] See Cissé 2002, p. 438.

[256] Id., p. 439-441.

[257] Art. 98 of the new Constitution is exactly similar to then Art. 79: "Les traités ou accords régulièrement ratifiés ou approuvés ont, dès leur publication, une autorité supérieure à celle des lois, sous réserve, pour chaque accord ou traité, de son application par l'autre partie."

[258] See Senegal, *Plainte avec Constitution de Partie Civile Contre Hissène Habré, Présenté au Juge d'Instruction du Tribunal Régional hors classe de Dakar*, 1999, parts IV and V.

[259] Id., part IV ("[M]ême si le droit interne du Sénégal n'incrimine pas expressément les crimes contre l'humanité, l'incrimination coutumière de droit international fait normalement partie du droit pénal que le Sénégal peut appliquer;").

[260] Id., part V. Art. 669 of the Code of Criminal Procedure (*Code de procédure pénale*) provides: "Tout étranger qui, hors du territoire de la République, s'est rendu coupable soit comme auteur, soit comme complice, d'un crime ou d'un délit attentatoire à la sûreté de l'Etat ou de contrefaçon du sceau de l'Etat, de monnaies nationales ayant cours, peut être poursuivi et jugé d'après les dispositions des lois sénégalaises ou applicables au Sénégal, s'il est arrêté au Sénégal ou si le Gouvernement obtient son extradition." The plaintiffs acknowledged that this language suggests that *a contrario*, there is no jurisdiction to prosecute other crimes committed outside of Senegal. See Senegal, *Plainte avec Constitution de Partie Civile Contre Hissène Habré, Présenté au Juge d'Instruction du Tribunal Régional hors classe de Dakar*, 1999, part V.

Court which priviliged a treaty over conflicting national law.[261] The victims further referred to the Belgian Pinochet decision and the Furundzija judgment of the ICTY. Lastly, the complaint requested the investigating judge (*juge d'instruction*) to apply Art. 6 (1) of the CAT and detain Habré pending further proceedings.[262]

Following the complaint, the investigating judge of the regional tribunal of Dakar indicted Habré on 3 February 2000 for complicity in torture and placed him under house arrest. Furthermore, the judge opened an investigation against persons to be named for other crimes, including crimes against humanity.[263] But on appeal, the Dakar Court of Appeals quashed the indictment and ruled that the Senegalese courts lacked competence to try Habré for crimes committed abroad.[264] First, the Court held that in the absence of a national criminalization of crimes against humanity, the principle of legality in the criminal code[265] precludes the Senegalese courts to try these crimes.[266] Second, the Court held that Art. 5 CAT orders States to vest jurisdiction over acts of torture, but does not itself establish jurisdiction.[267] Third, the Court considered that criminal law is an autonomous branch of law, uncomparable to other branches and governed by "a certain procedural formalism."[268]

This last statement is an implicit rejection of the suggestion by the victims' lawyers that the CAT could override national criminal law to vest the courts with universal jurisdiction. It seems the Court relied simultaneously on two arguments: first, that the CAT does not itself establish universal jurisdiction and second, that the CAT cannot directly apply to override national criminal law in any case. Therefore, the Court held, it was up to the legislature to modify the Code of criminal procedure and recognize universal jurisidiction for torture. The present state of the law, how-

---

[261] See Brody and Duffy 2001, p. 830-831.

[262] Id., part VI.

[263] See Brody and Duffy 2001, p. 823. But see Cissé 2002, p. 442 (stating that Habré was indicted for torture as well as the other crimes).

[264] See Senegal, Cour d'appel de Dakar, Chambre d'accusation, *Ministère Public et François Diouf Contre Hissène Habré, Arrêt no. 135*, 4 July 2000.

[265] See Art. 4 Code Pénal: "Nulle contravention, nul délit, nul crime ne peuvent être punis de peines qui n'étaient pas prononcées par la loi avant qu'ils fussent commis."

[266] See Senegal, Cour d'appel de Dakar, Chambre d'accusation, *Ministère Public et François Diouf Contre Hissène Habré, Arrêt no. 135*, 4 July 2000, para. 3 (Sur la compétence des juridictions sénégalaises):

"Considérant que le droit positif sénégalais ne renferme à l'heure actuelle aucune incrimination de crimes contre l'humanité, qu'en vertu du principe de la légalité des délits et des peines affirmé à l'article 4 du Code Pénal, les juridictions sénégalaise ne peuvent matériellement connaître de ces faits."

[267] Id.

[268] Id.: "Considérant que la matière qui nous intéresse est relative à la justice pénale; qu'elle est bâtie sur deux grandes règles: d'une part les règles de fond qui définissent les infractions et fixent les peines et d'autres part, les règles de forme qui déterminent la compétence, la saisine et le fonctionnement des juridictions; Elle a toujours manifesté son autonomie par rapport aux autres normes juridiques; que cette particularité est due au caractère sanctionnateur du droit pénal qui tend à la protection des intérêts de la société comme ceux des individus en cause et exige un certain formalisme de procédure; Considérant de ce fait que toute comparaison avec les autres branches du droit est vouée à l'échec..."

ever, excluded it.[269] Thus, Habré could be prosecuted neither for crimes against humanity nor for torture.

On 20 March 2001, the Senegalese *Cour de Cassation* gave the final decision in the case.[270] The judges dismissed all arguments of the *parties civiles* and upheld the judgment of the Court of Appeals, effectively foreclosing any prosecution of Habré in Senegal.[271] Most importantly, the Court of Cassation rejected the arguments that the contested judgment violated the CAT and Art. 79 of the Constitution, which incorporates treaties in the national legal order.[272] The Court did not explicitly endorse the assertion by the Court of Appeals that criminal law is exempted from the general framework which incorporates treaties. Rather, it found that the provisions of the CAT regarding jurisdiction did not fall within the reach of Art. 79 because their execution first required legislative measures.[273] Thus, it it is not entirely clear whether the *Cour de Cassation* embraced the principled exception for criminal law asserted by the Court of Appeals, or merely considered the provisions of the CAT to be non-self-executing without vetoing direct application of treaties with a penal content in general. The proceedings regarding Habré received considerable criticism, both in terms of political interference[274] and on points of law.[275]

In conclusion, the *Habré* case indicates that Senegalese law does not allow direct application of customary offences. The Court of Cassation also rejected direct application of the CAT in this case. Yet, its reasoning leaves open whether treaty-based offences are entirely precluded from direct application, or rather must meet a high burden of self-execution.

3.3.f *Belgium*

The situation in Belgium is symptomatic of the uncertainty regarding general direct application of international criminal law in many States. Case law and doctrine are limited and divided, and the issue has not been conclusively settled in the higher

---

[269] Id.: "Considérant qu'il résulte de ce qui précède que les juridictions sénégalaises ne peuvent connaître des faits de torture commis par un étranger en dehors du territoire sénégalais quelque soit les nationalités des victimes, que le libellé de l'article 669 du Code de Procédure Pénale exclut cette compétence;"

[270] Senegal, Cour de Cassation, *Souleymane Guengueng et autres Contre Hissène Habré, Arrêt no. 14*, 20 March 2001.

[271] Attempts thereafter to initiate prosecutions in Tchad failed. See Sharp 2003, p. 170; Brody and Duffy 2001, p. 825. The proceedings in Tchad did apparently not rely on international criminal law.

[272] Senegal, Cour de Cassation, *Souleymane Guengueng et autres Contre Hissène Habré, Arrêt no. 14*, 20 March 2001, 4th, 6th and 7th *moyens de cassation*, treated together. See Cissé 2002, p. 443-444.

[273] Id.: "[Q]u'il en résulte que l'article 79 de la Constitution ne saurait recevoir application dès lors que l'exécution de la Convention nécessite que soient prises par le Sénégal des mesures législatives préalables."

[274] See Sharp 2003, p. 169-170; Cissé 2002, p. 445; Brody and Duffy 2001, p. 824 (several judicial actors involved in the case were transferred to different positions).

[275] Cissé 2002, p. 444-445 (criticizing in particular the suggested exception to the domestic effect of treaties); Brody and Duffy 2001, p. 834-836.

courts. As a starting point, it may be noted that, like Germany, Belgium incorporates international law in general[276] but also adheres to a strict interpretation of the principle of legality.[277]

Nevertheless, an investigating judge of the Brussels Tribunal of First Instance concluded in *Pinochet* (1998), a case concerning a civil party complaint demanding prosecution *in absentia* of the former Chilean dictator, that the customary criminalization of crimes against humanity was directly applicable in the Belgian legal order, just like other international custom.[278] Judge Vandermeersch derived jurisdiction, the definition of the crime and its imprescriptibility all directly from customary international law, and left no doubt that he felt authorized, and possibly obliged, under international law to prosecute crimes against humanity regardless of the lack of specific implementing legislation in Belgian law at that time.[279] He reasoned that the principle of legality in Belgian law would be satisfied by applying the penalties for relevant ordinary crimes under Belgian law in force at the time the alleged acts were committed.[280] Nonetheless, Judge Vandermeersch denied the request for the immediate issuance of an international arrest warrant as it would be detrimental to the ongoing investigation. When the judge later did issue the warrant, it was not implemented by Great-Britain as Pinochet was returned to Chile on account of his health.

---

[276] See e.g. Panken *et al.* 2004, p. 27-37.

[277] See Art. 12 (2) Constitution: "No one can be prosecuted except in the cases provided for by law, and in the form prescribed by law." ("Nul ne peut etre poursuivi que dans les cas prevus par la loi, et dans les formes qu'elle prescrit.");
Art. 14 Belgian Constitution: "No punishment can be made or given except in pursuance of the law." ("Nulle peine ne peut être établie ni appliquée qu'en vertu de la loi.");
Belgium, Court of Arbitration, 10 July 2002: "By granting Parliament the power (a) to determine in what cases criminal proceedings are possible and what form they should take, and (b) to adopt legislation under which a penalty may be prescribed and applied, Articles 12.2 and 14 of the Constitution assure to all citizens that no action will be punishable and no penalty imposed except under regulations adopted by a democratically elected deliberative assembly."

[278] Belgium, Tribunal of First Instance (District of Brussels), *In re Pinochet Ugarte*, 6 November 1998, YIHL, para. 3.3.

[279] The judge examined the jurisdiction of the Belgian judiciary to prosecute foreigners *in absentia* for crimes committed abroad. Such universal jurisdiction was not established in Belgian law at the time, but the judge derived it directly from international law. Based on the principle "*aut dedere, aut judicare*" and in particular on General Assembly Resolution 3074 of 3 December 1973 (on Principles of international co-operation in the detection, arrest, extradition and punishment of persons guilty of war crimes and crimes against humanity), the judgment established a customary rule granting jurisdiction to national authorities in all circumstances (para. 3.3.3). Finally, he found that crimes against humanity are, as a rule of customary international law which also applies directly, by their nature imprescriptible (para. 4). It should be noted that GA Resolution 3074 is a rather dubious source for universal jurisdiction *in absentia*, as its fifth principle determines that "[p]ersons against whom there is evidence that they have committed war crimes and crimes against humanity shall be subject to trial and, if found guilty, to punishment, as a general rule in the countries in which they committed those crimes."

[280] Id., para. 3.3.2.

In *Sharon and Yaron* (2002), concerning alleged core crimes committed in the infamous Sabra and Chatila massacre in Lebanon, another investigating judge of the Brussels Tribunal of First Instance took a very different stand. The judge rejected the reliance of the civil petitioners on direct application of "customary law and *jus cogens*" to circumvent the restrictions of Belgian statute law.[281] The decision is, however, somewhat confusing in this regard. Art. 12 (2) Constitution determines that prosecutions must be governed by law.[282] In similar language, Art. 4 Penal Code determines that extraterritorial crimes will only be punished in accordance with the law.[283] The judge concluded from these provisions that jurisdiction of Belgian courts to try extraterritorial crimes is "exceptional and strictly limited to cases determined by law."[284] Yet, given the similarity in language of the two provisions, it is hard to see how Art. 4 can raise the bar for extraterritorial prosecutions if *all* prosecutions must already be governed by law. Therefore, it is not entirely clear whether the Brussels Tribunal's rejection of direct application extends to all core crimes prosecutions, or only to extraterritorial ones.

Meanwhile, the situation outside the courtroom is not much clearer. Within weeks of the Pinochet decision, the Belgian Minister of Justice explicitly endorsed general direct application of international core crimes law in a report to the Senate.[285] Some scholars received the Pinochet judgment and its acceptance of direct application of international criminal law wholeheartedly.[286] Others, however, took a very differ-

[281] Belgium, Tribunal of First Instance Brussels (Kamer van Inbeschuldigingstelling), *In re Sharon and Yaron*, 26 June 2002, reproduced in Wouters and Panken 2003, p. 323-339, at 326 and 338.

[282] See above, note 277.

[283] Art. 4 Penal Code: "L'infraction commise hors du territoire du Royaume, par des Belges ou par des etrangers, n'est punie, en Belgique, que dans les cas determines par la loi."

[284] Belgium, Tribunal of First Instance Brussels (Kamer van Inbeschuldigingstelling), *In re Sharon and Yaron*, 26 June 2002, reproduced in Wouters and Panken 2003, p. 323-339, at 327: "Que l'on doit considérer que la compétence des juridictions belges a l'égard des étrangers pour des faits commis hors du territoire de la Belgique est exceptionelle et strictement limitee aux cas determines par la loi."

[285] See Belgium, Law for the punishment of Genocide, Report of the Justice Commission, Belgian Senate, 1 December 1998, No. 1-749/3, para. II B (2):
"Les cours et tribunaux belges peuvent connaître de faits constitutifs de crimes de génocide ou de crimes contre l'humanité commis avant l'entrée en vigueur d'une éventuelle modification de la loi de 1993. Tout d'abord, ces faits sont généralement constitutifs d'infractions de droit commun (meurtres, coups et blessures volontaires, viol, privation illicite de liberté,...) et peuvent être poursuivis sur cette base. Toutefois, des poursuites pourraient être engagées pour crime de droit international, constitutifs de crime de génocide et/ou de crime contre l'humanité en tant que tels.
Dans ce cas, l'incrimination retenue est issue des règles contraignantes de droit international humanitaire et la peine est déterminée en se fondant sur les peines prévues pour l'infraction de droit commun correspondant aux faits considérés." [...] Si des poursuites intervenaient en Belgique pour des faits antérieurs à la modification de la loi de 1993, il n'y aurait donc pas d'entorse aux règles de droit pénal international selon lesquelles le droit pénal ne peut rétroagir au détriment des personnes poursuivies et qu'il n'existe pas d'infraction sans loi qui l'incrimine. L'application de la coûtume internationale en ces matières est d'ailleurs expressément reconnue par les textes internationaux de protection des droits de l'homme. [...] L'introduction d'une incrimination explicite relative aux crimes de génocide et aux crimes contre l'humanité ne constitue donc qu'une confirmation du droit existant..."

[286] See Labrin and Bosly 1999, p. 300 ("Elle mérite d'être approuvée sans réserve.").

ent view and assert that the Belgian legal order rejects general direct application of international offences on account of its principle of legality.[287] To complicate things further, the investigating judge giving the order in Pinochet himself rejected direct application in later scholarly writings.[288]

All in all, it must be concluded that the question of general direct application in Belgium is subject to considerable uncertainty.[289] It should be noted in any case that no such prosecutions have taken place.[290]

3.3.g *United States of America*

In the U.S., it is an unwritten rule that all international law, including treaties, custom and general principles, is incorporated into national law.[291] The Supremacy Clause in the U.S. Constitution, furthermore, declares all treaties to be the supreme law of the land and the judges in every American state to be bound thereby.[292] Yet, it is well-established that treaties, and in fact all international law, are subordinate to the Constitution.[293] Moreover, the actual direct application of international law in American courts is not as far-reaching as one might expect on the basis of the constitutional framework. This is due to the intricacies of national law, which, as in most other States, interpose numerous obstacles between international law's broad domestic validity and its actual application.[294] Among these intricacies are the rank of different international law sources in the American legal system,[295] the question of whether customary international law is state law or federal law,[296] and the use of avoidance doctrines to evade direct application of international law,[297] including the doctrine of self-executing treaties.[298] These matters have been subjected to ex-

---

[287] See Bremer 1999, p. 301-304 and references cited there.

[288] See Vandermeersch 2004, p. 134; Vandermeersch 2002a, p. 70.

[289] See Smet and Naert 2003, p. 50-54 (cautiously concluding that Belgian law may allow direct application of treaty-based offences, but not customary ones); Wyngaert 2003, p. 78-80 and 108-110; Wyngaert 1983, p. 507.

[290] Some prosecutions of WW II crimes have convicted defendants for offences against the laws and customs of war, but done so on the basis of a specific rule of reference to that effect in national law. See e.g. Belgium, Court of Cassation, *In re Köppelmann*, 27 November 1950, partial English translation in ILR 1950, no. 126.

[291] See Restatement 1987 para. 111 and Introductory Note and Henkin 1984, p. 1557. But see Bradley 1999a, p. 539-566.

[292] U.S. Const. Art. VI (2).

[293] See U.S., Supreme Court, *Reid v. Covert*, 10 June 1957, 354 U.S. 1, 354 U.S. 1, at 16: "[N]o agreement with a foreign nation can confer power on the Congress, or on any other branch of Government, which is free from the restraints of the Constitution." See also Bradley 1999a, p. 549-550 and Henkin 1987, p. 869-870.

[294] See generally Rogers 1999; Vázquez 1999; Bradley 1999b; Bradley and Goldsmith 1998; Henkin 1998; Koh 1998; Bradley and Goldsmith 1997; Henkin 1996; Henkin 1987; Lobel 1985; Henkin 1984.

[295] See Henkin 1984, p. 1561-1567.

[296] See for a recent overview of the debate Young 2002.

[297] See Bradley 1999a, p. 555-557.

[298] See principally Vazquez 1995; Buergenthal 1992, p. 370-382; Paust 1988; Iwasawa 1986. See further Yoo 1999b; Yoo 1999a; Sloss 1998; Paust 1993; Riesenfeld 1980. See also below, Chapter IV, para. 4.

tensive and complex analyses, resulting in disputed and sometimes unclear outcomes. There is neither the space nor the need at this stage to delve into all complexities of the position of general international law in the American legal order. Rather, I note the aforementioned uncertainties and focus on the direct applicability of international criminal law.

Direct application of international criminal law on the basis of a specific rule of reference is well accepted in the U.S.[299] Yet, the general direct application of international offences for a criminal prosecution in the U.S. is uncertain at best. Most commentators assume that statutory authority is required for a criminal prosecution,[300] with only a few dissenting voices regarding it as an open question.[301] These commentators base their rejection of general direct application principally on the rule against common law crimes, as formulated early on in *U.S. v. Hudson & Goodwin* (1812).[302] In this case, the Supreme Court in no uncertain terms rejected criminal prosecutions based on common law, finding that "the legislative authority of the Union must first make an act a crime, affix a punishment to it, and declare the Court that shall have jurisdiction of the offence."[303] Most writers take this language to exclude direct application of both treaty and custom in the absence of a specific statutory basis. Some see the *ex post facto* clause of the Constitution[304] as an additional obstacle to direct application of international offences, but this seems a doubtful assertion, taking note of the language of the clause and its application in practice.[305]

Despite the Supreme Court's sweeping language in *Hudson* and the near-unanimous rejection of general direct application in doctrine, the need for a specific statutory basis to give effect to international offences is not all that clear on careful analysis. As a starting point, it is important to realize that general direct application has long been unequivocally accepted in American law. In older cases, both before

[299] See above note 191 and accompanying text.

[300] See Cassel 2001, p. 428-429 ("The fact that international law authorizes states to exercise certain adjudicatory jurisdiction over international crimes does not mean that U.S. courts may, without more, exercise such jurisdiction. Under U.S. law our courts may exercise only such adjudicatory authority as is conferred upon them by U.S. law to prosecute crimes codified in U.S. law."); Cassel 1999, p. 383 (identical); Osofsky 1997, p. 203 and 215; Buergenthal 1992, p. 381 (stating that it "is widely assumed in the United States that a treaty cannot constitutionally create a criminal offence without implementing legislation"); Wise 1989, p. 939-940; Kobrick 1987, p. 1526 ("Although international law is part of the law of the United States, an international crime is not considered a violation of United States law, and the accused cannot be tried in the federal courts, until the United States passes a statute defining and punishing the offense."); Restatement 1987, para. 111, Comment i and Reporters Note 6. Cf. Steinhardt 2004, p. 10-11.

[301] See Paust 2000, p. 249-252; Bassiouni *et al.* 1989, p. 319-320 (remarks of Jordan Paust); Paust 1988, p. 780; Paust 1983, p. 219; Solf and Cummings 1977, p. 211 note 32. See more generally Paust 1991.

[302] U.S., Supreme Court, *United States v. Hudson & Goodwin*, 13 February 1812, 11 U.S. 32 (Mem).

[303] Id., at 34.

[304] U.S. Const. Art. I, § 9, cl. 3: "No Bill of Attainder or ex post facto Law shall be passed."

[305] See Kobrick 1987.

and after *Hudson*, U.S. courts did not hesitate to base criminal proceedings on international law, including both treaty and custom.[306] On the contrary, they regularly asserted a duty to punish crimes against the law of nations.[307] Complete acceptance of direct application of international criminal law is traditionally found in cases concerning war crimes, at least where the U.S. is in some way involved.[308] Section 13 of the so-called Lieber Code, an instruction manual for the U.S. army compiled in 1863, provided that "military offenses which do not come within the statute must be tried and punished under the common law of war."[309] Various cases have since affirmed the permissibility of direct application of international law for war crimes prosecutions, also, or perhaps especially, in the absence of a specific rule of reference.[310]

Thus, the question is when and how this broad acceptance of general direct application was replaced by the strict rejection assumed by contemporary doctrine. There is no recent case law that conclusively settles the question of general direct application in core crimes prosecutions.[311] The reliance on *Hudson* as the main authority for the statute requirement is, however, unconvincing for several reasons.

---

[306] See e.g. U.S., Court of Oyer and Terminer, at Philadelphia, *Respublica v. De Longchamps*, October Sessions, 1784, 1 Dall. 111; U.S., Circuit Court, D. Pennsylvania, *Henfield's Case*, 22 May 1793, 11 F.Cas. 1099. See also Paust 1983, p. 211-213 and 219-220 and references cited there.

[307] See e.g. U.S., Supreme Court, The Antelope, 1825, 23 U.S. 66, 6 L.Ed. 268, 10 Wheat. 66 at 77 (finding that piracy is "a crime against all nations, so as to make it the duty of all to seek out and punish offenders"). Cf. U.S., Supreme Court, *United States v. Klintock*, 1820, 18 U.S. 144 (Mem), 5 L.Ed. 55, 5 Wheat. 144 at 148: "[T]he offence committed on board a piratical vessel, by a pirate, against a subject of Denmark, is an offence against the United States, which the Courts of this country are authorized and bound to punish." See also Steven 1999, p. 443-445 and references cited there.

[308] See 14 U.S. Op. Atty. Gen. 249 at 251.

[309] See Lieber Code (Instructions for the Government of Armies of the United States in the Field, prepared by Francis Lieber, promulgated as General Orders No. 100 by President Lincoln, 24 April 1863), Section 13: "Military jurisdiction is of two kinds: first, that which is conferred and defined by statute; second, that which is derived from the common law of war. Military offenses under the statute-law must be tried in the manner therein directed; but military offenses which do not come within the statute must be tried and punished under the common law of war. The character of the courts which exercise these jurisdictions depends upon the local laws of each particular country."

[310] See Trial of Lothar Eisentrager, 14 L. Rep. Trials of War Crimes 8, 15 (U.S. Mil. Comm'n, Shanghai 1947). Cited in Zaid 2001, fn 41. "A war crime... is not a crime against the law or criminal code of any individual nation, but a crime against the jus gentium. The laws and usages of war are of universal application, and do not depend for their existence upon national laws and frontiers.";
U.S., Supreme Court, *Yamashita v. Styer*, 1946, 327 U.S. 1, at 16: "We do not make the laws of war but we respect them so far as they do not conflict with the commands of Congress or the Constitution."
U.S., Supreme Court, *Ex Parte Quirin*, 1943, 317 U.S. 1, at 27-28: "From the very beginning of its history this Court has recognized and applied the law of war as including that part of the law of nations which prescribes, for the conduct of war, the status, rights and duties of enemy nationals as well as enemy individuals.";
See also Kobrick 1987, p. 1527 and Hyde 1943, p. 88 ("Here is impressive judicial testimony to the effect... that the law of war['s] applicability by the courts in reference to penal matters need not await precise legislative appraisal or definition.").

[311] See Paust 2000, p. 251 and above note 301. Cf. Komarow 1980, p. 26. Judicial practice is limited to several *obiter dicta* and extradition cases of doubtful authority.

First, in *Hudson*, the Supreme Court rejected the prosecution of 'ordinary' common law crimes, not international crimes. Today, it may be an open question whether the rule against common law crimes covers customary international criminal law as well.[312] After all, customary international law is treated like federal common law,[313] but differs from it in important respects.[314] It is clear however, that when *Hudson* was issued, American courts did not interpret it as covering international offences. The Supreme Court found in *U.S. v. Smith* (1820, seven years after *Hudson*) that "the general practice of all nations in punishing all persons, whether natives or foreigners, who have committed [piracy] against any persons whatsoever, with whom they are in amity, is a conclusive proof that [piracy] is supposed to depend, not upon the particular provisions of any municipal code, but upon the law of nations, both for its definition and punishment."[315]

Second, direct application of international offences has taken place regardless of a specific rule of reference long after *Hudson*. Examples include violations of the laws and customs of war as well as other international crimes, based predominantly on custom, but occasionally also on treaty. Several of those cases explicitly rejected the need for a statutory basis.[316] In 1820, like *Smith* seven years after *Hudson*, the Pennsylvania Supreme Court rejected outright the need for a statutory basis and found that the rule against common law crimes did not preclude vesting the jurisdiction for the criminal prosecution of a consul in federal courts solely on the general constitutional provision that "the Supreme Court shall have jurisdiction in all cases affecting a consul."[317] It was fifty years after *Hudson* when Lieber wrote that

---

See e.g. U.S., Court of Appeals (Ninth Circuit), *U.S. v. Matta-Ballesteros*, 1 December 1995, 71 F.3d 754 at 764: "Kidnapping also does not qualify as a *jus cogens* norm, such that its commission would be justiciable in our courts even absent a domestic law. Jus cogens norms, which are nonderogable and peremptory, enjoy the highest status within customary international law, are binding on all nations, and can not be preempted by treaty. [...K]idnapping does not rise to the level of other jus cogens norms, such as torture, murder, genocide, and slavery.";
U.S., Court of Appeals, D.C.Cir., *Demjanjuk v. Meese*, 27 February 1986, 784 F.2d 1114 at 117: "Until the United States and Israel amend the Extradition Treaty to include the crime of genocide and make genocide a crime under their respective domestic laws, genocide does not provide a basis for extradition.";
U.S., District Court, (Cal.), *Matter of Extradition of Artukovic*, 6 February 1986, 628 F.Supp. 1370 at 1377: "'War crimes' are not proscribed in California or the United States. For the same reasons, illusions to 'genocide,' as such, in the requesting papers and evidence, are irrelevant."
Clearly, a general statement that "war crimes are not proscribed in the United States" contravenes longstanding practice.

[312] See Paust 1983, p. 220.

[313] See *Filartiga v. Pena-Irala*, 630 F.2d 876 at 866 (2d Cir. 1980); *Tel-Oren*, 726 F.2d at 810 (Bork, J., concurring).

[314] See U.S., District Court, *Handel v. Artukovic*, 31 January 1985, 601 F.Supp. 1421, at 1426. See also Young 2002, p. 510-511; Henkin 1984, p. 1561.

[315] See U.S., Supreme Court, *United States v. Smith*, 1820, 18 U.S. 153 at 162 (the case itself, however, concerned a specific rule of reference to piracy, see above note 191 and accompanying text).

[316] See above note 310.

[317] See U.S., Supreme Court of Pennsylvania, *Commonwealth v. Kosloff*, 1820, 5 Serg. & Rawle 545, at 5: "The only argument attempted or that can be devised in support of the negative, is that no

"military offenses which do not come within the statute must be tried and punished under the common law of war."[318]

Third, the rationale of the rule against common law crimes is to be found in the separation of powers between the federal government and the American states, not in concerns over legal certainty.[319] That rationale requires federal courts to abstain from formulating new crimes that infringe on the legislative competence of the states. It does not preclude the application of existing international offences on subject matters beyond state competence.[320] This may explain why direct application of the laws of war was left untouched by *Hudson*: the states have no competence in the regulation of war, which is a power of the federal government. It also explains why various other international crimes were directly applied long after *Hudson*: the implementation and enforcement of international criminal law is a federal, not state competence.[321]

Therefore, it can be doubted whether the rule against common law crimes formulated in *Hudson* actually opposes the direct application of international offences.[322] The direct application of the laws of war after *Hudson*, regardless of a specific rule of reference, suggests the opposite. It is unclear why genocide and crimes against humanity should be treated differently. After all, customary international criminal law can not be equated to federal common law, nor do U.S. courts unduly limit state powers in applying it.[323]

---

offence is cognisable in any court of the United States until congress has declared it to be an offence and prescribed the punishment. This is the only consideration which ever had the least weight in my mind. But upon mature reflection I am unable to deny that the courts of the United States can take cognisance, when I find it written in the constitution that the Supreme Court shall have jurisdiction in all cases affecting a consul. Is he not affected in criminal cases much more than in civil? How then can I say that the Supreme Court has no jurisdiction?"

[318] See above note 309.

[319] See U.S., Supreme Court, *United States v. Hudson & Goodwin*, 13 February 1812, 11 U.S. 32 (Mem) at 33-34.

[320] Cf. Henkin 1984, p. 1561-1562.

[321] See Art. I, Section 8, clause 10 Constitution (giving Congress the power "to define and punish piracies and felonies committed on the high seas, and offences against the law of nations."); U.S., District Court (D.C.), *United States v. Yunis*, 12 February 1988, 681 F.Supp. 896 at 903. Cf. U.S., United States Court for China, *U.S. v. Kearny*, 8 October 1923, in Lobingier, Extraterritorial Cases, Vol. II (1928), p. 665-686 at 674 ("The power 'to define and punish piracies and felonies committed on the high seas, and offences against the law of nations' is not made exclusive and it would seem entirely permissible to define and punish 'offenses against the law of nations' by treaty.").

[322] See note to Henfield's Case, 11 F.Cas. 1099, at 1120-1121 ("It is not inconsistent, therefore, with the doctrine discarding the common law as an origin of jurisdiction to the federal courts, to hold that where an express subject matter is ceded to the federal government by the constitution, that subject matter is to be acted upon through the medium of common law forms.").

[323] Cf. Bassiouni *et al.* 1989, p. 319-320, remarks of Jordan Paust: "[A]lthough customary international law has been said to be "part of" the common law, it is not merely "common law" but much more and of a higher transnational status with a recognizable constitutional base. Thus, it is possible that the customary prohibition of genocide is still directly enforceable in our courts despite the lack of relevant domestic legislation…"

It is unclear what obstacles prevent direct application of core crimes law if not the rule against common law crimes. Concerns over legal certainty are an unlikely candidate for several reasons.[324] International law, both written and unwritten, has long been accepted in the U.S. as a "full" source of law, even if its actual application is limited. The Supreme Court suggested in *Smith* that Congress' power to define offences against the law of nations was necessary to shed light on any uncertainties in the law of nations, while well-established crimes like piracy needed no further elaboration in national law.[325] Arguably, the core crimes today are at least as clearly established in international law as piracy in 1820.[326]

As for treaty-based offences, there is some negative but undecisive case law. In *The Over the Top* (1925), a case concerning the smuggling of liquor, a district court held that "[i]t is not the function of treaties to enact the fiscal or criminal law of a nation. For this purpose no treaty is self-executing."[327] However, this judgment was neither consistent in its rejection[328] nor representative of American case law in general. The Supreme Court later found the American-British Treaty in question to be self-executing and held that the treaty did, as to ships of British registry, extend the operation of the criminal laws of the United States to the shifting line designated in the treaty,[329] as had another district court earlier.[330] In *Hopson v. Kreps* (1980) a Court of Appeals stated obiter that "[t]reaty regulations that penalize individuals [...] are generally considered to require domestic legislation before they are given any effect."[331]

[324] Cf. Boot 2002, p. 124-126 and Wagner 1989, p. 910-915. But see Osofsky 1997, p. 201-202. See also U.S., Supreme Court, *Parker v. Levy*, 19 June 1974, 417 U.S. 733 at 756 ("[f]or the reasons which differentiate military society from civilian society, [...] Congress is permitted to legislate both with greater breadth and with greater flexibility when prescribing the rules by which the former shall be governed than it is when prescribing rules for the latter."); U.S., Supreme Court, *Yamashita v. Styer*, 1946, 327 U.S. 1, at 17 ("Obviously charges of violations of the law of war triable before a military tribunal need not be stated with the precision of a common law indictment."). It is open to question, though, which standards apply to core crimes law, even with respect to civilians.

[325] U.S., Supreme Court, *United States v. Smith*, 1820, 18 U.S. 153, at 158-159. See also U.S., Supreme Court, *Sosa v. Alvarez-Machain*, 29 June 2004, 124 S.Ct. 2739, para. IV ("[W]e think courts should require any claim based on the present-day law of nations to rest on a norm of international character accepted by the civilized world and defined with a specificity comparable to the features of the 18th-century paradigms we have recognized [including piracy].").

[326] See on the question of legal certainty in connection to core crimes further below, Chapter VI, para. 5.3.

[327] U.S., District Court (Connecticut), *The Over the Top (Schroeder v. Bissell)*, 26 February 1925, 5 F. 2d 838 at 845.

[328] See id.: "Whether therefore the Senate and the Executive may constitutionally enact criminal legislation by the device of a mere treaty is a question which fortunately we need not discuss. It is sufficient to conclude that the American-British Treaty did not in fact enact new criminal legislation."

[329] U.S., Supreme Court, *Cook v. United States*, 23 January 1933, 288 U.S. 102 at 118-119.

[330] See U.S., District Court (New York), *The Pictonian*, 26 November 1924, 3 F.2d 145 at 148 (reaching the opposite result as *The Over the Top* for the same treaty).

[331] U.S., Court of Appeals, *Hopson v. Kreps*, 14 July 1980, 622 F.2d 1375 at 1380.

The case of *U.S. v. Kearny* (1923), on the other hand, concerned an actual treaty-based prosecution.[332] Decided by the United States Court for China, *Kearny* originated in an unusual setting but nonetheless treated important questions of general American law. The defendant was charged for conspiracy to trade in arms on the basis of several treaties between the U.S. and China that criminalized trading in contraband. The U.S. Court for China rejected both the argument that the treaty provisions were non-self-executing and the contention that it was beyond the treaty-making power to prescribe offenses, which, it was argued, should be done by Congress.[333] In doing so, the court interpreted Supreme Court case law to understand the phrase "offenses against law" as including "those prescribed by treaty equally with those defined by statute."[334] The court also cited examples of other treaty-based offences.[335] In the end, the defendant was sentenced to a fine under direct application of the treaty provisions.

Following *Kearny*, it may be argued that "offenses against the laws of the United States" include those against international criminal law, both custom and treaty, and thus the core crimes. In that case, American courts would have jurisdiction over the core crimes under a general provision like 18 U.S.C para. 3231.[336] It seems this construction would also allow jurisdiction over extraterritorial core crimes. American courts have on numerous occasions assumed extraterritorial jurisdiction in the absence of explicit statutory language to that effect, *inter alia* where extraterritoriality can be inferred from "the nature of the offenses and Congress' other legislative efforts to eliminate the type of crime involved."[337] They have further consistently accepted compliance with international law as a determining factor in interpreting the territorial scope of their jurisdiction.[338] This has most often resulted in a limita-

[332] U.S., United States Court for China, *U.S. v. Kearny*, 8 October 1923, in Lobingier, Extraterritorial Cases, Vol. II (1928), p. 665-686.

[333] Id., at 669-676.

[334] Id., at 671.

[335] Id., at 674-675.

[336] 18 U.S.C para. 3231 ("The district courts of the United States shall have original jurisdiction, exclusive of the courts of the States, of all offenses against the laws of the United States."). See Paust 1971, p. 17-28.

[337] U.S., Court of Appeals (Ninth Circuit), *U.S. v. Vasquez-Velasco*, 25 January 1994, 15 F.3d 833 at 839. See also U.S., Supreme Court, *United States v. Bowman*, 1922, 260 U.S. 94 at 97-98. But see U.S., District Court (D.C.), *United States v. Yunis*, 12 February 1988, 681 F.Supp. 896 at 903 ("Congress has the power to punish crimes committed overseas but it must evince such an intent with clarity"). In any case, it seems such intent can be inferred for international crimes from a general provision like 18 U.S.C para. 3238: "The trial of all offenses begun or committed upon the high seas, or elsewhere out of the jurisdiction of any particular State or district, shall be in the district in which the offender, or any one of two or more joint offenders, is arrested or is first brought; but if such offender or offenders are not so arrested or brought into any district, an indictment or information may be filed in the district of the last known residence of the offender or of any one of two or more joint offenders, or if no such residence is known the indictment or information may be filed in the District of Columbia."

[338] Id., and also U.S., Court of Appeals (Ninth Circuit), *Alvarez-Machain v. U.S.*, 11 June 2001, 331 F.3d 604 at 624-626; U.S., District Court, (Cal.), *U. S. v. Layton*, 6 March 1981, 509 F.Supp. 212 at 222-225; U.S., Court of Appeals (Fifth Circuit), *United States v. Columba-Colella*, 604 F.2d 356 at 358-360.

tion of jurisdiction, but it should logically lead to the acceptance of extraterritorial jurisdiction where international law so requires to comply with an obligation to extradite or prosecute.

Furthermore, although one should be careful to distinguish between different types of cases, it is noteworthy that the direct application of international offences is not categorically rejected in American law. In 1967, Supreme Court Justice Douglas labelled the general direct application of treaty-based offences in the context of a defense to refuse military service in the Vietnam war an undecided and "extremely sensitive and delicate question."[339] Also, civil cases under statutes such as the Alien Tort Claims Act (ATCA)[340] show that U.S. courts today are still willing and able to apply customary international criminal law to the detriment of individuals.[341] In the recent case of *Mehinovic et al. v. Vuckovic*, a district court awarded 140 million dollars in damages, 100 million of which were punitive, for *inter alia* war crimes and crimes against humanity committed in Bosnia-Herzegovina.[342] The CAT, common Art. 3 and the grave breaches provisions of the Geneva Conventions, Art. 2 ICTY Statute, Art. 7 ICC Statute and the Genocide Convention served to ascertain the content of these customary offences. The court explicitly stated that it aimed to "punish the defendant" for his abuses.[343] Of course, in cases such as *Mehinovic* the ATCA provides a specific rule of reference that is limited to civil cases. They are relevant, however, because they demonstrate both that the U.S. courts are capable of handling international offences and the apparent constitutionality of such direct application in proceedings with a (partly) punitive character despite the absence of a statutory criminalization.

In conclusion, the question of direct application of international offences for core crimes prosecutions in the absence of a specific rule of reference cannot be

---

[339] See U.S., Supreme Court, *Mitchell v. United States*, 20 March 1967, 87 S.Ct. 1162 (Mem), 386 U.S. 972, at 972-974 (Dissenting opinion Justice Douglas to denial of certiorari, treating the possible direct application of the crime of aggression as defined in Art. 6 (a) Treaty of London of August 8, 1945 (Nuremberg Statute) on the basis of the constitutional Supremacy Clause as an open question).

[340] See 28 U.S.C. § 1350 (1988): "The district courts shall have original jurisdiction of any civil action by an alien for a tort only, committed in violation of the law of nations or a treaty of the United States."

[341] See U.S., Court of Appeals (2d Cir.), *Filartiga v. Pena-Irala*, 1980, 630 F.2d 876 at 864 ("[T]he objective of the international law making torture punishable as a crime can only be vindicated by imposing punitive damages."). Cf. *Beharry v. Reno*, 183 F.Supp.2d 584 (2002) ("Characterizing a serious penalty as civil rather than criminal does not reduce its sting or make it any less punitive. However bottled, poison is toxic."). See also U.S., Supreme Court, *Sosa v. Alvarez-Machain*, 29 June 2004, 124 S.Ct. 2739 at 2756-2759.

[342] U.S., District Court, *Mehinovic et al. v. Vuckovic*, 2 May 2002, 198 F.Supp.2d 1322, at 1344: "Plaintiffs have shown, as to each of them individually, that defendant Vuckovic committed the following violations of customary international law, which confer jurisdiction, and establish liability, under the ATCA: torture; cruel, inhuman or degrading treatment; arbitrary detention; war crimes; and crimes against humanity."

[343] U.S., District Court, *Mehinovic et al. v. Vuckovic*, 2 May 2002, 198 F.Supp.2d 1322 at 1360: "Punitive damages are designed both to punish and to teach a defendant, and to deter others from committing the same abuses."

answered with certainty. Despite the fact that national law provides only partial jurisdiction over the core crimes, there is no recent case law on the matter.[344] Doctrine generally assumes that only statute can form the basis for a criminal prosecution. Traditionally, however, general direct application has always been accepted, in particular for violations of the laws of war. I have set out what I believe to be strong legal arguments why direct application of all core crimes law is in principle possible under current U.S. law, but acknowledge that this position finds only minimal support in doctrine. In light of the generally sceptical attitude of U.S. courts towards international law today,[345] the chances of continued judicial acceptance of general direct application appear slight.

3.3.h *England and Wales*

This description of English law[346] will not detail the English reception of international law in general[347] or its treatment of international criminal law in particular,[348] since these have all been extensively described already. English law does not allow direct application of treaty provisions but requires their transformation in order to safeguard "parliamentary sovereignty."[349] Thus, due to concerns over the proper separation of powers, direct application of treaty-based offences is altogether excluded.

The position of customary international offences is less clear and was brought to center stage in the *Pinochet* case, which concerned the question of whether the former dictator could be extradited to Spain *inter alia* for acts of torture likely amounting to crimes against humanity committed during his rule in Chile.[350] In *Pinochet III*, Lord Millett expressed his opinion that "the English courts have and always have had extra- territorial jurisdiction in respect of crimes of universal jurisdiction under customary international law" and "did not require the authority of statute to exercise it."[351] He found that international law did not impose this result,

---

[344] See for a detailed analysis of U.S. jurisdiction over the core crimes Cassel 1999, p. 383-387. See also Lee 2002, p. 461-472.

[345] See e.g. U.S., District Court, *Handel v. Artukovic*, 31 January 1985, 601 F.Supp. 1421 at 1427-1428: "While international law may provide the substantive rule of law in a given situation, the enforcement of international law is left to individual states. [...] Until Congress evinces an intent to give effect to international law, either by passing a jurisdictional statute or by incorporating international rights into the statutes of the United States, the Court declines to infer such an intent solely from the United States' membership in the community of nations."

[346] It should be noted that Scotland and the Isle of Man have their own legal system, to be distinguished from that of England and Wales. These legal systems consist in part of law that governs the United Kingdom as a whole. Yet, even when citing legal propositions for the U.K. as a whole, this paragraph concerns solely the law of England and Wales, or in short English law.

[347] See e.g. Shaw 2003, p. 128-143.

[348] See e.g. Turns 2004, p. 341-353; Jones 2002 and Bremer 1999, p. 359-391.

[349] See O'Keefe 2002, p. 319; Jones 2002, p. 35 and Bremer 1999, p. 360-361.

[350] See on the Pinochet case generally Johnson 2002; Woodhouse 2000. For a short insider's account, see Millett 2003.

[351] U.K., House of Lords, *R. v. Bow Street Metropolitan Stipendiary Magistrate & Others, Ex Parte Pinochet Ugarte (No. 3)*, 24 March 1999, [2000] 1 A.C. 147 at 276.

but rather that direct application stemmed from England's incorporation of international custom through the common law.[352] Lord Millett, however, represented a minority opinion. The majority held that extraterritorial torture did not become a crime in the United Kingdom until so provided by the Criminal Justice Act of 1988.[353] While these Law Lords did not specifically discuss the possibility of general direct application of international offences for the prosecution of extraterritorial crimes, their opinions appear to reject it as they assume a statutory basis is required in such cases.[354]

Other authorities, again without explicitly analyzing the matter of general direct application, likewise suggest that prosecutions of extraterrritorial core crimes must find a specific basis in statute.[355] Many commentators assume that the need for a statutory basis applies not only to extraterritorial but to all core crimes prosecutions.[356] They perceive the principle of legality and concerns over the proper separation of powers to be the most important obstacles to general direct application.[357] On the other hand, one scholar shows in an elaborate study how general direct application of customary offences was accepted in the past[358] and in his view still conforms with English law today.

---

[352] Id.: "The jurisdiction of the English criminal courts is usually statutory, but it is supplemented by the common law. Customary international law is part of the common law, and accordingly I consider that the English courts have and always have had extraterritorial criminal jurisdiction in respect of crimes of universal jurisdiction under customary international law." It should be noted, however, that international custom is strictly speaking not part of the common law but "an autonomous non-statutory strand of English law." See O'Keefe 2002, p. 301.

[353] Id., at 148. See further at 189 (Lord Browne-Wilkinson: "I do not consider that torture committed outside the United Kingdom before 29 September 1988 was a crime under U.K. law."); 237 (Lord Hope: "[N]one of these offences, if committed prior to the coming into force of section 134 of the Criminal Justice Act 1988, could be said to be extraterritorial offences against the law of the United Kingdom within the meaning of section 2(2) of the Extradition Act 1989 as there is no basis upon which they could have been tried extraterritorially in this country.") and 290 (Lord Phillips of Worth Matravers: "It is only recently that the criminal courts of this country acquired jurisdiction, pursuant to section 134 of the Criminal Justice Act 1984, to prosecute Senator Pinochet for torture committed outside the territorial jurisdiction."). See also O'Keefe 2002, p. 300-301.

[354] Id., at 276 (Lord Millett: "I understand, however, that your Lordships take a different view, and consider that statutory authority is require[d] before our courts can exercise extraterritorial criminal jurisdiction even in respect of crimes of universal jurisdiction.").

[355] See e.g. U.K., Court of Appeal, *R. v. Anthony Sawoniuk*, 10 February 2000, [2000] 2 Cr. App. R. 220 at 225-226 (English courts can not try extraterritorial, non-homicidal war crimes committed during WW II); U.K., Courts-Martial Appeal Court, *Regina v. Page*, 10 November 1953, [1954] 1 Q.B. 170 at 176 ("Nobody would suggest that an English court could try an alien for an offence not committed on British soil."). See also Gilbert 1993, p. 424-425; Hetherington and Chalmers 1989, p. 95 (War Crimes Inquiry Commission concluding that "under the present law, British courts have no jurisdiction to try an offence of murder, manslaughter or genocide committed abroad by any person who was not a British subject at the time of the alleged offence.") and Lauterpacht 1958, p. 138-139. Cf. Rowe and Meyer 1996, p. 478; Meyer 1983, p. 965-970 and 977-978.

[356] See Jones 2002, p. 35-36, 59 and 66.

[357] See Jones 2002, p. 59 and O'Keefe 2002, p. 311.

[358] See O'Keefe 2002, p. 302.

In *Jones & Milling, Olditch & Pritchard, Richards v. Gloucestershire Crown Prosecution Service* (2004),[359] an English Court of Appeal squarely confronted the question of whether general direct application can provide a legal basis for the prosecution of core crimes committed on English territory. This judgment concerned the joint appeals of three prosecutions for causing criminal damage to military installations. In all three cases, the defendants justified their actions as legitimate opposition to the United Kingdom's participation in the war in Iraq, asserting *inter alia* that their use of force was a reasonable means to prevent the crime of aggression.[360] The court in first instance had rejected this defense, holding that there was no international crime of aggression triable in domestic courts.[361]

The Court of Appeal analyzed the matter in detail. It held that the question of whether the international crime of aggression is triable in English courts depends both on the effect of public international law rules in English law and the principle of certainty:

> "The mere fact that an act can clearly be established to be proscribed by international law, and is described as 'a crime' does not necessarily of itself determine its character in domestic law unless its characteristics are such that it can be translated into domestic law in a way which would entitle domestic courts to impose punishment."[362]

The Court of Appeal concluded that "a rule of international law is capable of being incorporated into English law if it is an established rule derived from one or more of the recognised sources, that is a clear consensus, evidenced by the writings of scholars or otherwise, or by treaty."[363] The Court then examined the Privy Council's decision in *In re Piracy Jure Gentium* (1934),[364] and accepted this case as "authority for the proposition that a rule of international law is capable of being incorporated into domestic law so as to found an indictment which, if proved, can result in punishment. To that extent we accept the submission that international law is capable of being incorporated into English law so as to create a crime punishable in domestic law."[365] The Court distinguished *Pinochet III* for its focus on extraterritorial crimes, thereby limiting its own holding to territorial cases.[366] In the end, the judgment concluded that the lack of international consensus on the elements of the crime of aggression, apparent in the negotiations over the ICC Statute, prevented the finding of "a firmly established rule of international law which establishes a

[359] U.K., Court of Appeal, *Jones & Milling, Olditch & Pritchard, Richards v. Gloucestershire Crown Prosecution Service*, 21 July 2004, [2004] EWCA Crim. 1981.

[360] See Section 3 of the Criminal Law Act 1967 ("A person may use such force as is reasonable in the circumstances in the prevention of crime.").

[361] U.K., Court of Appeal, *Jones & Milling, Olditch & Pritchard, Richards v. Gloucestershire Crown Prosecution Service*, 21 July 2004, [2004] EWCA Crim. 1981, para. 6.

[362] Id., para. 24. See also para. 19.

[363] Id.

[364] U.K., Privy Council, *In re Piracy Jure Gentium*, 26 July 1934, [1934] A.C. 586.

[365] U.K., Court of Appeal, *Jones & Milling, Olditch & Pritchard, Richards v. Gloucestershire Crown Prosecution Service*, 21 July 2004, [2004] EWCA Crim. 1981, para. 30.

[366] Id., para. 37 and 38.

crime of aggression which can be translated into domestic law as a crime in domestic law."[367] More importantly, the Court of Appeal accepted the direct applicability of international offences in general, also in the absence of a specific rule of reference.

In summary, the general direct application of international offences in England and Wales is precluded altogether both for treaty crimes and in extraterritorial cases. The situation is uncertain for customary offences in territorial cases. While the majority of the doctrine reflects an assumption that that statutory authority is also required in these cases, a recent decision of a Court of Appeal explicitly sanctions direct application provided the international criminalization is firmly established. A final verdict on this issue will thus have to await a decision of the House of Lords.

3.3.i *Canada*

In Canada, the Commission of Inquiry on War Criminals (Deschenes Commission) explicitly analyzed the question of general direct application of international offences.[368] The Commission quickly rejected direct application of treaty provisions, as these require transformation under Canadian law.[369] Although custom is incorporated, the rule against common law crimes[370] also precludes direct application of customary international offences, such that the Commission found: "International law as embodied in custom cannot act as a basis for prosecution of war criminals in Canada."[371]

Yet, according to the Deschenes Commission, a different regime applies to acts that are criminal according to the general principles of law recognized by the community of nations. Art. 11 (g) of the 1982 Canadian Charter of Rights and Freedoms, which has constitutional rank and was inspired by Art. 7 (2) ECHR and Art. 15 (2) ICCPR, determines that "any person charged with an offence has the right not to be found guilty on account of any act or omission unless, at the time of the act or omission, it constituted an offence under Canadian or international law or was criminal according to the general principles of law recognized by the community of nations."[372] This interpretation of the principle of legality supersedes any inconsistent legislation.[373] Therefore, the Commission concluded,

> "[i]t follows that, due to this adoption of 'customary' international law *lato sensu* into Canadian law through Art. 11 (g) of the Canadian Charter of Rights and Freedoms,

---

[367] Id., para. 43.

[368] See Report of the Canadian Commission of Inquiry on War Criminals, 1986, Deschenes, p. 127 ("The question is whether war criminals can be prosecuted in Canada by virtue of international law alone.").

[369] Id., p. 127-128.

[370] See Art. 9 (a) Criminal Code: "Notwithstanding anything in this Act or any other Act, no person shall be convicted [...] of an offence at common law."

[371] Id., p. 130.

[372] See also Report of the Canadian Commission of Inquiry on War Criminals, 1986, Deschenes, p. 131.

[373] Id.

war crimes can now form the basis of a criminal prosecution in Canada, notwithstanding the lack of any domestic law, or even any domestic law to the contrary."[374]

However, the Commission qualified its conclusion with the suggestion that "a prosecution under international law appears too esoteric."[375]

It should be noted that the Deschenes Commission's distinction between (general) direct application of custom and general principles of law is illogical. Art. 11 (g) of the Canadian Charter accepts "international law" on an equal footing as general principles for the establishment of individual criminal responsibility. It is hard to see then, why Art. 11 (g) would trump the rule against common law crimes contained in the Criminal Code for general principles, but not for "ordinary" custom.[376] The better position appears to be that both custom and general principles are amenable to general direct application.

In the *Finta* case (1994), the Canadian Supreme Court cautiously endorsed the findings of the Deschenes Commission but did not make the same clear-cut distinction between custom and general principles. Justice Cory stated that "Section 11(g) of the *Charter* allows customary international law to form a basis for the prosecution of war criminals who have violated general principles of law recognized by the community of nations regardless of when or where the criminal act or omission took place. The use of international legal principles to ground jurisdiction for criminal activity committed outside of Canada has thus been constitutionally permissible since 1982."[377] The opinion of dissenting Justice la Forest is somewhat ambiguous, yet appears to accept the reasoning of the Deschenes Commission, save for the prosecution of extraterritorial crimes.[378] For these crimes the situation would be different according to Justice la Forest, both because jurisdiction would be permissive rather than mandatory under international and Canadian law, and because the presumption of territoriality of the criminal law would preclude direct application.

In sum, it appears that the general direct application of international offences in Canada is precluded for treaty crimes, but allowed for custom and general principles. Again, however, the question of general direct application is surrounded by some uncertainty.

3.3.j *France*

French case law on the direct application of international criminal law is rich and complex. Although a simplification, one can say that in general both treaty and custom are incorporated in the French legal order.[379] I will focus first on the posi-

[374] Report of the Canadian Commission of Inquiry on War Criminals, 1986, Deschenes, p. 132.
[375] Id., p. 133.
[376] Id., compare p. 130 and 132.
[377] Canada, Supreme Court, *R. v. Imre Finta*, 24 March 1994, Cory J., para. 64.
[378] See La Forest J. (dissenting), para. 254-256.
[379] See Preamble of the French Constitution of 1946, para. 14 (refered to – and thus incorporated in – the preamble of the Constitution of 1958: "La République française, fidèle à ses traditions, se conforme

tion of treaty-based offences and then come back to custom. Art. 55 Constitution places ratified treaties above national law, but not constitutional law,[380] on the condition of reciprocity.[381] In its 1999 decision on the constitutionality of the ICC Statute, the Constitutional Court found that treaties aiming to protect fundamental human rights, like the ICC Statute, are exempted from the requirement of reciprocal application by other State parties.[382] Thus, it appears that treaties concerning core crimes are not excluded from general incorporation through Art. 55.

French law contains some specific rules of reference to treaty provisions regarding core crimes.[383] Moreover, the French courts have in the past on several occasions directly applied treaty-based offences, in particular concerning crimes against humanity. Klaus Barbie,[384] Paul Touvier[385] and Maurice Papon[386] were all convicted for crimes against humanity committed in WW II, despite the fact that French criminal law contained no statutory criminalization of crimes against humanity as such.[387] These prosecutions relied largely on a law from 1964 that indirectly referred to the Nuremberg Charter and declared crimes against humanity imprescriptible.[388]

---

aux règles du droit public international."). Needless to say, the situation is infinitely more complex than presented here and direct application of international law in France, as elsewhere, is opposed by many obstacles in national law. See for an extensive analysis Oellers-Frahm 2002. For present purposes, however, this simplification suffices.

[380] See France, Court of Cassation, 2 June 2000 ("la suprématie conférée aux engagements internationaux ne s'appliquant pas dans l'ordre interne aux dispositions de valeur constitutionnelle").

[381] Art. 55: "Les traités ou accords régulièrement ratifiés ou approuvés ont, dès leur publication, une autorité supérieure à celle des lois, sous réserve, pour chaque accord ou traité, de son application par l'autre partie." See also Buergenthal 1992, p. 346-348.

[382] France, Conseil Constitutionnel, *Traité portant statut de la Cour pénale internationale*, 22 January 1999: "[L]a France puisse conclure des engagements internationaux en vue de favoriser la paix et la sécurité du monde et d'assurer le respect des principes généraux du droit public international; que les engagements souscrits à cette fin peuvent en particulier prévoir la création d'une juridiction internationale permanente destinée à protéger les droits fondamentaux appartenant à toute personne humaine, en sanctionnant les atteintes les plus graves qui leur seraient portées, et compétente pour juger les responsables de crimes d'une gravité telle qu'ils touchent l'ensemble de la communauté internationale; qu'eu égard à cet objet, les obligations nées de tels engagements s'imposent à chacun des Etats parties indépendamment des conditions de leur exécution par les autres Etats parties; qu'ainsi, la réserve de réciprocité mentionnée à l'article 55 de la Constitution n'a pas lieu de s'appliquer;" See also Oellers-Frahm 2002, p. 868-869.

[383] See in particular Art. 689 French Code of Criminal Procedure.

[384] See France, Court of Cassation, *Barbie (No. 3)*, 3 June 1988, Bull. crim., no. 246; 100 ILR 330; France, Court of Cassation, *Barbie (No. 1)*, 6 October 1983, Bull. crim., no. 239; 78 ILR 125.

[385] France, Court of Cassation, *Touvier*, 1 June 1995, Bull. crim., no. 202; France, Court of Cassation, *Touvier (No. 3)*, 21 October 1993, Bull. crim., no. 307; France, Court of Cassation, *Touvier (No. 2)*, 27 November 1992, Bull. crim. 1992, 1082; 100 ILR 358; France, Court of Appeals of Paris, *Touvier*, 13 April 1992, 100 ILR 337; France, Court of Cassation, *Touvier (No. 1)*, 6 February 1975, Bull. crim., no. 42.

[386] France, Court of Cassation, *Papon*, 23 January 1997, Bull. crim., no. 32.

[387] See Lelieur-Fischer 2004, p. 233; Elliott 2001, p. 131-138 and Sadat Wexler 1994.

[388] See Law No. 64-1326 declaring the imprescriptibility of crimes against humanity: Sole article. Crimes against humanity, as defined by the United Nations' Resolution of February 13, 1946 taking

Importantly, however, the French courts clarified in several judgments that direct application of treaty-based offences did not depend on a specific provision such as the 1964 law but also followed from their general incorporation in French law. In its 1983 judgment in the Barbie case, the Court of Cassation gave its famous statement that "by reason of their nature, the crimes against humanity with which Barbie is indicted do not simply fall within the scope of French municipal criminal law, but are subject to an international criminal order to which the notions of frontiers and extradition rules arising therefrom are completely foreign."[389] The defendant acknowledged that criminal law is subject to the general constitutional framework incorporating international law, but argued that the principle of legality "requires either the ratification of a treaty or a municipal law giving force within the national legal order to declarations, resolutions or undertakings emanating from organizations or international bodies."[390] The Court of Cassation unequivocally rejected this argument, relying both on Art. 15 (2) ICCPR and Art. 7 (2), and on Art. 55 Constitution.[391]

A year later, the Court of Cassation again relied on Art. 15 (2) ICCPR and Art. 7 (2) to reject an appeal to the principle of legality in a subsequent judgment in the same case.[392] Importantly, the court also found that the rule of reference in the 1964 law "limited itself to *confirming* the integration into French law of both the *criminality* of such acts and the fact that they are not subject to statutory limitation."[393] Therefore, the contested judgment "merely confirmed something which was already established under municipal law by the effect of the international agreements [...] to which France had acceded."[394] In the judgment contested before the Court of Cassation, the Court of Appeals had found more specifically that the Nuremberg Charter, being annexed to 1945 London Agreement, had "itself been integrated into the municipal legal order."[395] Thus, the reference to crimes against humanity in the Nuremberg Charter in the 1964 law was found to be declarative rather than constitutive.[396]

At least two later judgments confirmed that treaty-based offences are incorporated into French law through Art. 55 Constitution on the same footing as other

---

account of the definition of crimes against humanity figuring in the Charter of the International Tribunal of August 8, 1945, are imprescriptible by their nature. Translation from Sadat Wexler 1994, p. 320.

389 France, Court of Cassation, *Barbie (No. 1)*, 6 October 1983, Bull. crim., no. 239; 78 ILR 125 at 128 and 130 (citing and confirming the Court of Appeal).

390 Id., at 129.

391 Id., at 131.

392 France, Court de Cassation, *Barbie (No. 2)*, 26 January 1984, Bull. crim., no. 34; 78 ILR 132 at 133 and 135, confirming the holding of the lower court that: "[T]he prosecution of crimes against humanity is in accordance with the general principles of law recognized by civilized nations and, on this account, such crimes are not subject to the operation of the principle of the non-retroactivity of criminal laws."

393 Id., at 135 (emphasis added).

394 Id.

395 Cited by the Court of Cassation, id., at 135.

396 See Lelieur-Fischer 2004, p. 236; Aubert 2000, p. 554.

international law. In its 1992 judgment in *Touvier*, the Paris Court of Appeals held that the definitions of crimes against humanity in the Nuremberg Charter and, remarkably, the UN General Assembly Resolution of 13 February 1946 (affirming the Nuremberg Principles) "have the force of law and even enjoy an authority superior to that of laws by virtue of Article 55 of the Constitution. Consequently, they form part of positive law."[397] In *Boudarel* (1993), concerning French crimes in Indochina, the Court of Cassation held that the criminalization of crimes against humanity stems directly from treaty law, while the French law of 1964 was merely in recognition of this fact.[398] The Court furthermore interpreted the Nuremberg Charter as covering only crimes against humanity committed by the Axis powers in WW II, and concluded that the French crimes in Indochina could be neither designated as crimes against humanity nor prosecuted.

In the WW II cases of *Barbie* and *Touvier*, the interplay between ordinary crimes and the corresponding international offences is rather complex. Several commentators have noted that the language of the different judgments is not consistent, referring to international offences sometimes as "constitutive elements" that complement ordinary crimes and other times as directly applicable "*incriminations*."[399] Yet, even if the precise role of treaty-based offences in these cases may give rise to some confusion, it is beyond doubt that they were directly applicable, even in the absence of a specific rule of reference.[400]

Recent case law, however, has set a high bar for treaty-based offences to be directly applied in practice. In the *Javor* case, Bosnian refugees in France tried to establish universal jurisdiction for the three core crimes and torture on the basis of several international instruments, including the Genocide Convention, the Nuremberg Charter, the CAT, the Geneva Conventions and UN General Assembly Resolution 3074 of 3 December 1973.[401] The investigating judge rejected all but two of these proposed bases, accepting only direct application of the CAT and the Geneva Conventions.[402] The judge found *inter alia* that the Genocide Convention did not provide for extraterritorial jurisdiction and that the Nuremberg Charter as well as GA Resolution 3074 covered only crimes against humanity committed in WW II.

---

[397] France, Court of Appeals of Paris, *Touvier*, 13 April 1992, 100 ILR 337 at 350.

[398] France, Court de Cassation, *Boudarel*, 1 April 1993, Bull. crim., no. 143, p. 353: "que la répression des crimes contre l'humanité trouvant sa source dans des textes de droit international, la loi interne ne peut y déroger; [...the French legislator] a voulu conferer un caractère purement recognitif a la loi du 26 decembre 1964..." See also Lelieur-Fischer 2004, p. 237.

[399] See Aubert 2000, p. 556. Cf. Sadat Wexler 1994, p. 364.

[400] See Elliott 2001, p. 130 ("Progressively the international law on crimes against humanity has been incorporated into French national law, first by the courts relying on the principle of monism, and then by the legislator."); Mattarollo 2001, p. 28; Aubert 2000, p. 552-556 and references cited there, and Zimmermann 1997, p. 281. But see Oellers-Frahm 2002, p. 887.

[401] Note that in this case, Art. 689 French Code of Criminal Procedure provided a specific rule of reference. Yet, the resulting judgments are relevant for general direct application. See Reydams 2003, p. 135-137; Stern 1999; Reydams 1996, p. 41-43 and Maison 1995, p. 263-268.

[402] See France, Tribunal de Grande Instance de Paris, Juge d'Instruction, *In re Javor, Ordonnance*, 6 May 1994, on file with the author.

In 1996, the Court of Cassation rejected also the last two bases.[403] The court found that the CAT established universal jurisdiction only when the accused is present on French territory, which was not the case. As to the Geneva Conventions, the *Cour de Cassation* held that "their provisions have too general a character to be able directly to create rules on extraterritorial jurisdiction in criminal matters."[404] It should be noted that while the net result was the same, namely no legal basis for prosecution, the reason why direct application was rejected in this case was very different for each treaty.[405] That the courts analyzed each treaty on its content affirms that their direct application in a core crimes prosecution is not altogether precluded, even if it was rejected in this specific case. Thus, the reasoning of the different courts involved in *Javor* shows how direct application of core crimes law is (still) in principle accepted in France, but subject to stringent conditions which most ICL treaties do not meet.[406]

Customary offences, on the other hand, are completely barred from general direct application in core crimes prosecutions.[407] The different judgments in the *Barbie* case, in particular the recurrent application of the general principles clauses of the ICCPR and ECHR[408] and the holding of the Court of Cassation that crimes against humanity transcend the scope of French municipal criminal law, might have suggested that customary international offences could be directly applied just like treaty provisions. Yet, the French courts never explicitly sanctioned such direct applica-

[403] France, Court of Cassation, *In re Javor*, 26 March 1996, Bull. crim., no. 132.

[404] Id., at 381: "Ces dispositions revetent un caractere trop general pour creer directement des regles de competence extraterritoriale en matiere penale, lesquelles doivent nécessairement etre rédigées de maniere détaillée et précise." Translation taken from Stern 1999, p. 527. This decision apparently departed from established French case law, which had considered the Geneva Conventions to be self-executing since their ratification by France in 1951. See Reydams 2003, p. 137.

[405] See Stern 1999, p. 526-527. In addition to the treaties already mentioned, direct application of the 1968 Convention on the Non-Applicability of the Statute of Limitations to War Crimes and Crimes against Humanity was rejected for lack of its ratification by France.

[406] See also the similar case of *RSF v. Milles Collines*: France, Tribunal de Grande Instance de Paris, Juge d'Instruction, *Reporters sans Frontières v. Mille Collines, Ordonnance*, 9 February 1995, on file with the author and, in particular, France, Paris Court of Appeals (Cour d'appel de Paris), *Reporters sans Frontières v. Mille Collines*, 6 November 1995, on file with the author:

"[L]a Cour releve, qu'en absence de dispositions de droit interne, la coutume internationale ne saurait avoir pour effet d'étendre la compétence extra-territoriale des juridictions francaises. En ce domaine seules sont applicable dans l'ordre juridique interne les dispositions des traités internationaux a la double condition:

– que ces traités aient été regulierement approuvés ou ratifies par la France;

– et qu'en raison de leur contenu, les dispositions de ces traités comportent en elles-meme un effet direct."

See on this case Reydams 1996, p. 43-44 and on similar cases concerning Rwandan genocide suspects Reydams 2003, p. 137-139.

[407] See Lelieur-Fischer 2004, p. 234-237 and Stern 1999, p, 529. Cf. Benillouche 2002, p. 171-176.

[408] See also France, Court of Cassation, *Glaeser*, 30 June 1976, Bull. crim., no. 236, p. 623: " [Il] convenait d'examiner si l'auteur des crimes dénonces, a les supposer etablis, ne se trouvait pas exclu du benefice de la non-retroactivite de la loi penale, en vertu des dispositions de l'article 7, alinea 2 [ECHR];".

tion of custom, and in later cases unambiguously rejected it. In *Javor*, the investigating judge found that "universal principles defining crimes against humanity as an international crime are not sufficient to establish jurisdiction of the French courts."[409] In *Aussaresses* (2003), the Court of Cassation rejected the prosecution of a French general for self-confessed acts of torture and summary execution of civilians in the Algerian war.[410] The court rejected the argument of the civil petitioner (*partie civile*) that the customary criminalization of crimes against humanity could be directly applied to circumvent the French amnesty law for crimes committed in Algeria, stating that "international customary rules cannot make up for the absence of a provision which criminalizes the acts denounced by the civil petitioner as crimes against humanity."[411]

In conclusion, general direct application of international offences has taken place in French courts but it is open to question whether this might happen again. Recent case law has adopted a more critical approach to direct application, but it is difficult to say whether this reflects a more rigid modern standard or is influenced predominantly by the fact that several of these cases concerned crimes committed by the French army in Algeria rather than WW II crimes committed against the French people. The relevant judgments are rather concise and omit a complete analysis of the matter. As a cautious conclusion, however, one can say that treaty-based offences are domestically valid and in principle directly applicable, but that most ICL treaties, including the Geneva Conventions, do not meet the strict requirements of the French courts to receive direct application in practice. So far, only the Nuremberg Charter has been directly applied in prosecutions of WW II crimes. Customary offences, on the other hand, are precluded from general direct application altogether.

3.3.k *Netherlands*

Following a long-standing customary practice, the Dutch legal order incorporates both treaty and custom.[412] Thus, as a general rule, all international law is domestically valid in the Netherlands. Many writers[413] overlook the fact that Art. 93 and 94

---

[409] France, Tribunal de Grande Instance de Paris, Juge d'Instruction, *In re Javor, Ordonnance*, 6 May 1994, on file with the author, para. 2: "Attendu que si le requérant souligne justement l'existence des principes universels définissant le crime contre l'humanité comme un crime international, ces seuls principes ne sont pas suffisants pour fixer la compétence juridictionelle des Tribunaux Français." (translation by this author). See also France, Paris Court of Appeals (Cour d'appel de Paris), *Reporters sans Frontières v. Mille Collines*, 6 November 1995, on file with the author, cited above, note 406.

[410] France, Court of Cassation, Aussaresses, 17 June 2003, 108 RGDIP 754. See also Lelieur-Fischer 2004.

[411] Id., at 756 ("Qu'enfin, la coutume internationale ne saurait pallier l'absence de texte incriminant, sous la qualification de crimes contre l'humanité, les faits dénoncés par la partie civile"). Translation from Lelieur-Fischer 2004, p. 236.

[412] See Fleuren 2004, p. 18-30. See on the position of custom elaborately Meijers 1985.

[413] See e.g. Strijards 2000, p. 2115.

of the Dutch Constitution[414] do not constitute the necessary rules of reference for this incorporation, but instead form limitations to an unwritten rule of reference that incorporates all international law.[415] Art. 93 requires publication of treaties and decisions of international organisations binding on all persons (self-executing treaties and decisions) before obligations contained therein can bind individuals.[416] Art. 94 determines that only such treaties and instruments supersede national law, including the Constitution itself,[417] thus *a contrario* excluding custom and non-self-executing treaties from superior rank.[418]

International criminal law has never in Dutch legal history been excluded from the general framework of incorporation of international law.[419] Yet, the principle of legality, contained both in Art. 16 Constitution[420] and Art. 1 (1) Penal Code (identical), formulates additional requirements and bars custom, but not treaties, as a basis for criminal prosecution.[421] While there are no recent cases that have fully tested the question of direct application, the above-mentioned state of affairs is well-established in legislative and judicial practice. I will first set out the relevant law for treaties and then for custom.

Treaties have in the past been directly applied as a basis for prosecutions in a few instances. In 1856, the Dutch Supreme Court explicitly affirmed the power of the King to enact treaties with a penal content. In that case, the defendant was sentenced to five years imprisonment under direct application of a treaty prohibiting the solliciting of desertion among foreign servicemen.[422] Since then, the King has lost the treaty-making power and the Constitution has been amended several times,[423] but the position of treaties concerning international criminal law has remained substantially the same. In 1947, the Special Court of Cassation found that jurisdiction to prosecute foreign war criminals required *either* a directly applicable

---

[414] Art. 93: "Provisions of treaties and of resolutions by international institutions, which may be binding on all persons by virtue of their contents shall become binding after they have been published." Art. 94: "Statutory regulations in force within the Kingdom shall not be applicable if such application is in conflict with provisions of treaties that are binding on all persons or of resolutions by international institutions."

[415] See Ferdinandusse 2001, p. 276 and references cited there; Brouwer 1992, p. 267-270.

[416] See Akkermans and Koekkoek 1992, p. 866-870.

[417] See Dijk and Tahzib 1991, p. 422. Significantly, the Constitution explicitly regulates the adoption of conflicting treaties in Art. 91 (3): Any provisions of a treaty that conflict with the Constitution or which lead to conflicts with it may be approved by the Chambers of the Parliament only if at least two-thirds of the votes cast are in favor.

[418] See Netherlands, HR, *Nuygat*, 6 March 1959, NJ 1962/2.

[419] See for an analysis of the position of international criminal law in the Netherlands Ferdinandusse *et al.* 2002; Ferdinandusse 2001. See more generally Knoops 2004; Sluiter 2004; Kleffner 2002 and Swart and Klip 1997.

[420] Article 16: "No offence shall be punishable unless it was an offence under the law at the time it was committed."

[421] See Ferdinandusse *et al.* 2002, p. 343-344.

[422] Netherlands, HR, 3 December 1856, Weekblad van het Regt, No. 1878.

[423] See for a historical overview of the position of treaty law in the Dutch legal order Brouwer 1992.

treaty *or* a statute.[424] When Art. 93 (then Art. 66) was introduced in the Constitution in 1953,[425] the legislature clearly formulated the purpose of that provision, namely to ensure that individuals were familiar with the international obligations binding upon them.[426] In general terms, the Supreme Court held in 1997 that the principle of legality as formulated in Art. 16 Constitution and Art. 1 Penal Code requires a criminalization to be formulated and published in Dutch.[427] This holding reinforces the requirement of publication of treaties, that also follows from Art. 93 Constitution, before their penal provisions can be directly applied.[428] Today, there are few examples of treaty provisions with a penal content being directly applied. Yet, the consistent direct application of Art. 32 of the Treaty of Mannheim for the prosecution of violations of the shipping regulations for the river Rhine shows the continued validity of the principle.[429] It should be noted that the Dutch government has on several occasions denied the possibility of direct application of treaty-based offences.[430] However, these statements clearly contravene established practice.[431]

In most of the few recent Dutch proceedings concerning core crimes, the question of direct application of treaties did not arise.[432] It did to some extent in the *Bouterse* case.[433] Here, the Amsterdam Court of Appeals stated in general terms that Dutch law requires a statute to effect international offences.[434] However, the Court of Appeals made this statement when discussing offences under customary international law, and it contradicts the state of the law regarding direct application

[424] See Netherlands, Bijzondere Raad van Cassatie (Special Court of Cassation), *Ahlbrecht I*, 17 February 1947, NJ 1947/87 ("...dat de Nederlandsche rechter hetzij een met Nederlandsche medewerking tot stand gekomen, daartoe strekkende internationale overeenkomst rechtstreeks kan toepassen, hetzij kan steunen op een Nederlandsche wet").

[425] See on the 1953 amendment of the Constitution generally Panhuys 1964 and Panhuys 1953.

[426] See Akkermans and Koekkoek 1992, p. 866-868. Since neither horizontal effect of human rights obligations nor obligations of individuals under European law were feasible at that time, it can be asked what kind of international obligations for individuals were meant if not those under international criminal law.

[427] HR 24 June 1997, NJ 1998/70, para. 5.6.

[428] See NJ 1998/70, case note para. 2.

[429] See e.g. the following decisions of the Supreme Court: HR 29 juni 1999, NJ 1999/637; HR 9 juni 1998, NJ 1998/858; HR 10 december 1996, NJ 1997/223; HR 9 June 1981, NJ 1981/472. See also Fleuren 2004, p. 330-331; Haak 2000. Another self-executing penal treaty provision is Art. 34 of the 1962 Benelux Treaty on Extradition and Mutual Assistance in Criminal Matters. See Swart and Klip 1997, p. 27. However, there do not appear to be cases of its (direct) application. See for more examples Ferdinandusse 2001, p. 279.

[430] See MvA WIM, EK 28 337, nr. 108b, p. 8 (2003); TK 28337, nr. 6, p. 19; Aanhangsel Handelingen Kamerstukken II 2000/01, 2073-2074 (Kamervragen 995, d.d. 28 March 2001) and the Dutch Initial report to the Committee against Torture, UN Doc CAT/C/9/Add.1, 20 March 1990, at para. 21.

[431] See Ferdinandusse 2001, p. 279. Cf. MvT Uitvoeringswet Genocideverdrag, TK 6613, no. 3, p. 4 (government asserting in 1961 that Art. 7 Genocide Convention is self-executing).

[432] See Netherlands, Supreme Court, *Knezevic II*, 11 November 1997, NJ 1998/463 and Netherlands, Supreme Court, *Knezevic I*, 22 October 1996, NJ 1998/462. See on this case Elst 1998. Cf. Netherlands, Rotterdam District Court, *Nzapali*, 7 April 2004. See on this case Knoops 2004.

[433] See generally Zegveld 2002b; Elst 2002.

[434] Netherlands, Amsterdam Court of Appeals, *Bouterse 2000*, 20 November 2000, NYIL, para. 8.2.

of treaties, as just described. Therefore, one could think this assertion was formulated too broadly and in fact applied only to custom. In any case, this judgment of the Court of Appeals was overruled, and the subsequent 2001 judgment of the Supreme Court clearly endorsed the direct application of penal treaty provisions over the national provisions on the principle of legality.[435] Such direct treaty application did not take place in *Bouterse* itself, though, because the courts assumed there was neither a duty to prosecute *in absentia* nor an applicable criminalization stemming from treaty law for an extraterritorial case of torture and/or crimes against humanity[436] committed in 1982. The later case *In re Zorreguieta et al.* (2002), concerning alleged crimes against humanity and torture committed in Argentina between 1976 and 1983, likewise left the question of direct application aside because the Amsterdam Court of Appeals found it lacked universal jurisdiction in this case.[437]

The *Bouterse* case also offers a recent and explicit formulation of the state of Dutch law regarding direct application of customary offences. While all customary law is incorporated in the Dutch legal order, its direct application as a basis for core crimes prosecutions is blocked by Art. 16 Constitution and Art. 1 Penal Code in combination with custom's lack of a superior position in law.[438] In *Zorreguieta*, the Amsterdam Court of Appeals further reiterated that Dutch courts can not derive jurisdiction from international custom in contravention of Dutch law.[439]

In short, Dutch prosecutions of core crimes can take place under direct application of published, self-executing treaties but not custom. Doctrine overwhelmingly endorses direct application of self-executing treaties for international criminal law in principle, but considers most ICL treaties unfit for direct application.[440]

---

[435] See Netherlands, Supreme Court, *In re Bouterse*, 18 September 2001, English translation in the Netherlands Yearbook of International Law, para. 4.5.

[436] While it is debatable whether the alleged torture and murder of a relatively small group of opposition leaders amounted to crimes against humanity, the Amsterdam Court of Appeals endorsed this qualification, following the advice of Prof. John Dugard. See Netherlands, Amsterdam Court of Appeals, *Bouterse 2000*, 20 November 2000, NYIL, para. 5.1. This holding finds support in case law of the ICTY. See ICTY, Trial Chamber, *Sikirica et al.*, 3 September 2001, Case No. IT-95-8, para. 76-77; ICTY, Trial Chamber, *Jelisic*, 14 December 1999, para. 82.

[437] Netherlands, Amsterdam Court of Appeals, *In re Zorreguieta et al.*, 25 April 2002, para. 5.5: "Het antwoord op de vraag of het delict misdrijven tegen de menselijkheid via verdragen of besluiten van volkenrechtelijke organisaties al dan niet doorwerking heeft in de Nederlandse rechtsorde kan in het midden blijven, omdat te dezen geen aanknoping is te vinden voor (universele) rechtsmacht van Nederland."

[438] See above note 434 and Netherlands, Supreme Court, *In re Bouterse*, 18 September 2001, English translation in the Netherlands Yearbook of International Law, para. 6.4.

[439] Netherlands, Amsterdam Court of Appeals, *In re Zorreguieta et al.*, 25 April 2002, para. 5.5: "Of er een regel van ongeschreven volkenrecht bestaat op grond waarvan Nederland (met terugwerkende kracht) rechtsmacht heeft, kan eveneens in het midden blijven omdat het de rechter niet vrijstaat de nationale rechtsmachtvoorschriften buiten toepassing te laten wegens strijd met ongeschreven volkenrecht."

[440] See Fleuren 2004, p. 329-337; Ferdinandusse *et al.* 2002, p. 343; Ferdinandusse 2001, p. 276-278; Swart and Klip 1997, p. 27 and Bemmelen *et al.* 1995, p. 3-4. Cf. Swart 1996, p. 36-37. But see Francisco 2003, p. 133-138 and Strijards 2000, p. 2115-2117 (Both authors reject all forms of direct application of international criminal law, but ignore the great majority of relevant practice and doctrine

3.3.1 *Ethiopia*

Ethiopia's 1994 Constitution declares that "all international agreements ratified by Ethiopia are an integral part of the law of the land."[441] The rank of treaty law is not definitively set out in the Constitution. While treaties certainly rank below the Constitution, their relationship to other national law is not regulated.[442] For custom, the situation is unclear. The Constitution does not refer explicitly to custom, but that does not rule out its direct applicability.[443]

The constitutional formulation of the principle of legality is quite general and neither includes nor excludes international law as a basis of criminality in an explicit manner.[444] Importantly, the principle of legality must be interpreted in accordance with international law.[445] As is well known, the principle of legality in international instruments includes custom and general principles as a basis for criminality.[446] But on the other hand, Art. 28 (1) Constitution determines that "criminal liability of persons who commit crimes against humanity, so defined by international agreements ratified by Ethiopia and by other laws of Ethiopia, such as genocide, summary executions, forcible disappearances or torture shall not be barred by statute of limitation" (emphasis added). This formulation could be read as limiting the legal basis for criminal liability of crimes that can not be subject to a statute of limitations to "international agreements and other laws of Ethiopia," thus excluding unwritten international law.

Partly due to a lack of readily accessible authoritative sources, it is difficult to draw firm conclusions on the possibility of general direct application in Ethiopia. Several commentators have reported that ICL is directly applicable in Ethiopia and that the Special Prosecutor's Office decided to apply customary humanitarian law in the Red Terror trials[447] for cases that are not covered by the Penal Code.[448]

---

and misinterpret the few cases they discuss. To reject the direct application of penal treaty provisions, Francisco promotes the principle of legality to the status of a "protolegal" principle (p. 138), a form of natural law unknown in Dutch legal practice, without citing a single case to support this proposition. Strijards rejects the superior status of self-executing treaties in the field of criminal law under reference to a case from 1950 (p. 2117). Both assertions contravene practice and are clearly ruled out by the 2001 *Bouterse* judgment of the Supreme Court, cited above note 435).

[441] See Art. 9 (4).

[442] See Art. 9 (1) Constitution: "The Constitution is the supreme law of the land. Any law, customary practice or a decision of an organ of state or a public official which contravenes this Constitution shall be of no effect." See also Scholler 1997, p. 171.

[443] See Haile 2000, p. 47.

[444] See Art. 22 Constitution: (1) No one shall be held guilty of any criminal offence on account of any act or omission which did not constitute a criminal offence at the time when it was committed. Nor shall a heavier penalty be imposed on any person than the one that was applicable at the time when the criminal offence was committed.

[445] See Art. 13 (2): "The fundamental rights and freedoms specified in this Chapter shall be interpreted in a manner conforming to the principles of the Universal Declaration of Human Rights, International Covenants on Human Rights and International instruments adopted by Ethiopia."

[446] See below, Chapter VI, para. 5.1.

[447] See above, para. 2.2.b (iii).

[448] See Mayfield 1995, p. 572-574; Engelschiøn 1994, p. 48-51. Cf. Ratner and Abrams 2001, p. 174.

Another writer is more cautious in this regard.[449] It seems that there is no judicial practice on this matter, as the national Penal Code has so far provided sufficient legal basis for the prosecution of international crimes.[450]

In the end, there is not enough material to confirm the rather brief reports on general direct application of core crimes law in Ethiopia. None of the writers mentioned earlier provides a full analysis of the question of direct application, and there is no readily accessible judicial practice on the matter. As such, no definitive conclusions can be drawn.

3.3.m *Argentina*

In Argentina, deference to international law dates back to the Constitution of 1853.[451] It is, however, particularly the case law of the Argentinean Supreme Court (*Corte Suprema de Justicia de la Nación*) in the 1990s that has firmly established the direct applicability and effectiveness of international law.[452] Several constitutional revisions have cemented this trend, so that the Constitution now clearly expresses not only the direct applicability of treaty law,[453] but also its higher rank than that of statute law and even the constitutional rank of selected human rights treaties.[454] It is further settled case law that customary international law is also directly appli-

---

[449] See Haile 2000, p. 53 (stating that the application of crimes against humanity "should be limited to specific acts that are criminal under the Ethiopian penal code [...] in order to avoid ambiguity and obviate the legality challenge.").

[450] See above, para. 2.2.b (iii). See also report in 4 YIHL 499 (2001).

[451] See Art. 102 Constitution 1853, now Art. 118 Constitution, cited below, note 458. See also Alvarez *et al.* 2002, p. 302-303.

[452] See in particular Argentina, Supreme Court, *Ekmekdjian v. Sofovich*, 7 July 1992, described below, Chapter IV, para. 5.1. See also Alvarez *et al.* 2002, p. 302-305; Buergenthal 1992, p. 357-359.

[453] See Art. 31 Constitution 1998 ("This Constitution, the laws of the Nation enacted by Congress in pursuance thereof, and treaties with foreign powers, are the supreme law of the Nation...").

[454] Art. 75:

"Congress is empowered:

[...]

22. To approve or reject treaties concluded with other nations and international organizations, and concordats with the Holy See. Treaties and concordats have a higher hierarchy than laws.

The American Declaration of the Rights and Duties of Man; the Universal Declaration of Human Rights; the American Convention on Human Rights; the International Pact on Economic, Social and Cultural Rights; the International Pact on Civil and Political Rights and its empowering Protocol; the Convention on the Prevention and Punishment of Genocide; the International Convention on the Elimination of all Forms of Racial Discrimination; the Convention on the Elimination of all Forms of Discrimination against Woman; the Convention against Torture and other Cruel, Inhuman or Degrading Treatments or Punishments; the Convention on the Rights of the Child; in the full force of their provisions, they have constitutional hierarchy, do no repeal any section of the First Part of this Constitution and are to be understood as complementing the rights and guarantees recognized herein. [...]"

See also Raimondo 2003, p. 118-120; Alvarez *et al.* 2002, p. 329 (asserting that this provision has created "un bloc de constitutionnalité ou le droit interne et le droit international sont pratiquement confondus."); Sancinetti and Ferrante 2002, p. 352-357; Mattarollo 2001, p. 13.

cable,[455] and that treaties must be interpreted in accordance with the case law of international courts.[456]

Whether this direct applicability extends to international criminal law is a matter of debate.[457] A relevant provision in this regard is Art. 118 of the Constitution, which provides that the trials for crimes "committed outside the territory of the Nation against international law" shall be held "at such place as Congress may determine by a special law."[458] Several commentators interpret this provision as a recognition of the direct applicability of international criminal law in the Argentinean legal order.[459] Others are, however, more cautious[460] or dispute this interpretation of Art. 118, pointing *inter alia* to the principle of legality in Art. 18 Constitution[461] and the fact that the required special jurisdictional law has never been passed.[462] It is noteworthy, furthermore, that Argentina has entered a reservation with regard to Art. 15 (2) ICCPR, declaring that "the application of the second part of article 15 of the International Covenant on Civil and Political Rights shall be subject to the principle laid down in article 18 of the Argentine National Constitution."[463] The effects of this reservation, however, are disputed. A few decisions of federal courts have

---

[455] See Alvarez *et al.* 2002, p. 326-327; Mattarollo 2001, p. 13 and 35-36. See also Art. 21 of Law 48: "Los Tribunales y Jueces Nacionales en el ejercicio de susfunciones procederán aplicando la Constitución como ley suprema dela Nación, las leyes que haya sancionado o sancione el Congreso,los Tratados con Naciones extranjeras, las leyes particulares delas Provincias, las leyes generales que han regido anteriormente ala Nación y los principios del derecho de gentes, según lo exijan respectivamente los casos que se sujeten a su conocimiento en elorden de prelación que va establecido."

[456] See Alvarez *et al.* 2002, p. 304-305 and 329.

[457] Compare Alvarez *et al.* 2002, p. 309, 311, 319-320, 327, 329 and Mattarollo 2001, p. 34-35 (accepting direct application of international criminal law) with Malarino 2003, p. 38 and 61; Ambos 2002b, p. 479-483, 492 and 495-496 (rejecting it). See also Sancinetti and Ferrante 2002, p. 376-380, 385 and 392; Sancinetti and Ferrante 1999, p. 432-451 (concluding it is an open question).

[458] Art. 118 Constitution: "Todos los juicios criminales ordinarios, que no se deriven del despacho de acusación concedido en la Cámara de Diputados se terminarán por jurados, luego que se establezca en la República esta institución. La actuación de estos juicios se hará en la misma provincia donde se hubiera cometido el delito; pero cuando éste se cometa fuera de los límites de la Nación, contra el derecho de gentes, el Congreso determinará por una ley especial el lugar en que haya de seguirse el juicio."

[459] See Schiffrin 2003, p. 151; Alvarez *et al.* 2002, p. 321 and 326-327; Sancinetti and Ferrante 2002, p. 378; Mattarollo 2001, p. 34 and 42.

[460] See Raimondo 2003, p. 120 (stating that Art. 118 "implies the recognition of a customary international rule that authorizes Argentina to prosecute international crimes committed outside its territory.").

[461] Art. 18 Constitution: "Ningún habitante de la Nación puede ser penado sin juicio previo fundado en ley anterior al hecho del proceso, ni juzgado por comisiones especiales, o sacado de los jueces designados por la ley antes del hecho de la causa." ("No inhabitant of the Nation may be punished without previous trial based on a law enacted before the act that gives rise to the process, nor tried by special committees, nor removed from the judges appointed by law before the act for which he is tried. [...]").

[462] See Malarino 2003, p. 56-58; Ambos 2002b, p. 480-482.

[463] See Sancinetti and Ferrante 2002, p. 382-385; Sancinetti and Ferrante 1999, p. 439-443.

noted that the reservation to the ICCPR can not alter the similar principle of legality under customary international law or even *jus cogens*.[464]

The question of whether genocide, crimes against humanity and war crimes can be prosecuted directly on the basis of international law has not been conclusively settled in Argentinean case law. But while no actual prosecutions on the basis of direct application have taken place, precedents regarding the extradition of war criminals[465] and certain amnesty laws[466] appear to support a positive answer to the question of direct application. In *Schwammberger*, a case from 1989 concerning the extradition to Germany of a suspect of crimes against humanity committed in WW II, the question arose whether direct application of international criminal law could secure imprescriptibility of the crimes in question. A federal court held unequivocally that the Constitution recognized the primacy of international law also in criminal matters, and that the principle of legality does not apply in a strict sense to international crimes.[467] The Argentinean Supreme Court subsequently confirmed this judgment.[468]

In the extradition proceedings concerning Erich Priebke (1995), suspected of war crimes and crimes against humanity committed in Italy during WW II, the Argentinean Supreme Court applied customary international law and found that the proceedings were governed by principles of *jus cogens* status that cannot be altered by the States involved.[469] One of the judges found that the Geneva Conventions and the Genocide Convention enjoy a "presumption of operationality," and that at least the majority of their provisions are directly applicable.[470] Significantly, one of the dissenting judges accepted the direct applicability of international criminal law

---

[464] See below, note 477 and accompanying text; Mattarollo 2001, p. 17, 20-22 and 35. Cf. Sancinetti and Ferrante 2002, p. 382-385.

[465] See for an overview and analysis of relevant extradition proceedings Schiffrin 2003.

[466] See Law No. 23.521 of 9 June 1987 ("Obediencia Debida") and Law No. 23.492 of 29 December 1986 ("Ley de Punto Final"). Technically speaking, these laws did not proclaim amnesties but merely regulated the availability of the defense of superior orders and a timeline for criminal prosecutions. However, they had the aim and effect of amnesty laws and are generally designated as such in doctrine. Therefore, I will follow this terminology. While these laws have been abrogated in Argentina's 2003 Law nullifying Obediencia Debida and Punto Final ("declaranse insanablemente nulas las leyes 23.492 y 23.521."), the value of this step appears to be mostly symbolic. See Alvarez *et al.* 2002, p. 318.

[467] Argentina, Federal Court of La Plata, *Extradition Josef Franz Leo Schwammberger*, 30 August 1989, per Judge Leopoldo Schiffrin, para. 50, cited in Alvarez *et al.* 2002, p. 320. See also Malarino 2003, p. 52-53; Schiffrin 2003, p. 141-145; Sancinetti and Ferrante 2002, p. 386-387.

[468] Argentina, Supreme Court, *Extradition Josef Franz Leo Schwammberger*, 20 March 1990, 313 Fallos de la Corte Suprema de Justicia de la Nacion 256.

[469] Argentina, Supreme Court, *Extradition of Erich Priebke*, 2 November 1995, 1996-I Jurisprudencia Argentina 324 at 331, per Judges Boggiano, López and Fayt, para. 4: ("...la calificación de los delitos contra la humanidad no depende de la voluntad de los Estados requirente o requerido en el proceso de extradición sino de los principios del ius cogens del Derecho Internacional"). See also Sancinetti and Ferrante 2002, p. 387-390; Mattarollo 2001, p. 35-36; Consigli 1998.

[470] Id. at 353, per Judge Bossert, para. 53 (finding that "sus cláusulas gozan de la presunción de operatividad [...] por ser, en su mayoría, claras y completas para su directa aplicación por los Estados partes e individuos sin necesidad de una implementación directa"). See also Alvarez *et al.* 2002, p. 309.

in principle, but regarded the lack of a specified penalty for war crimes and crimes against humanity as a decisive obstacle.[471] The majority of the Supreme Court, however, did not share this objection and accepted in general terms direct applicability of international criminal law.[472] Accordingly, the Court relied directly on international law to find the crimes under consideration imprescriptible and punishable in Argentina, thus satisfying the double criminality requirement in the extradition treaty between Argentina and Italy.[473]

In a 1999 decision regarding the pre-trial detention of former head of the *junta* Jorge Videla,[474] a federal court explicitly addressed the import of the principle of legality, including Argentina's reservation to Art. 15 (2) ICCPR for the prosecution of crimes against humanity.[475] The federal court held that crimes against humanity are not subject to statutes of limitations, regardless of any national provisions to the contrary.[476] It pointed out that the principle of legality as laid down in Art. 15 ICCPR was binding on Argentina also on the basis of other international sources, such as the ACHR.[477] As such, the federal court found that it could not disregard laws established by the international legal system which take precedence over internal laws, "even if this implies assigning a significance to the principle of legality distinct from that which has traditionally been accorded it by internal courts and by the Argentine government, whose reserves in the matter can in no way modify the international regulations and the weight of the obligations arising from the other sources of international legal norms."[478] Moreover, the federal court asserted that "[t]he constitutional mandate of article 118, [...] establishing a kind of universal jurisdiction for the prosecution of crimes against international law and fully empowering the Argentine courts to carry out such trials would not be coherent if at the same time a sort of deconstructed law were allowed to be applied to every case which implied restrictions or exceptions to the normative framework which would

---

[471] Id., at 361-362, per Judge Petracchi (dissenting), para. 2-5. See also Mattarollo 2001, p. 36-37.

[472] Id., per Judges Nazareno and Moliné O'Connor, para. 39 and Judge Bossert, para. 51: "Que a diferencia de otros sistemas constitucionales como el de los Estados Unidos de América en el que el constituyente le atribuyó al Congreso la facultad de 'definir y castigar' las 'ofensas contra la ley de las naciones' (Art. I secc. 8), su par argentino al no conceder similar prerrogativa al Congreso Nacional para esa formulación receptó directamente los postulados del derecho internacional sobre el tema en las condiciones de su vigencia y, por tal motivo, resulta obligatoria la aplicación del Derecho de Gentes en la jurisdicción nacional – que así integra el orden jurídico general – deconformidad con lo dispuesto por el Art. 21 ley 48 ya citado."

[473] See Consigli 1998, p. 342-343.

[474] The crimes of the military dictatorship between 1976 and 1983, the early attempts to prosecute these crimes and the subsequent legal and political obstacles are well-known and will not be detailed here. See e.g. Alvarez *et al.* 2002, p. 299-301 and 312-316; Brown 2002, p. 203-215; Ratner and Abrams 2001, p. 169-171; Latcham 1989, p. 355-364; Meyer 1983, p. 948-954.

[475] Argentina, Federal Court of Buenos Aires, *Videla, Ruling on Pre-trial Detention*, 9 September 1999, cited in Mattarollo 2001, p. 39-41.

[476] See Mattarollo 2001, p. 39.

[477] Id., p. 40.

[478] Id., p. 39-40.

be applicable at the international level."[479] Several other judgments of federal courts contain similar or even identical holdings.[480]

Of particular interest is the case of *Julio Simon* (2001), in which an Argentinean federal judge nullified two amnesty laws[481] to allow prosecution for the alleged kidnapping and disappearance of several victims, including a child who was subsequently raised by a military couple.[482] After a lengthy analysis of relevant Argentinean legislation and case law, the judgment concluded that Art. 118 Constitution indeed provided for the direct application of international criminal law.[483] It further concluded that such direct application was not obligatory if the crimes in question could also be prosecuted on the basis of ordinary criminal law.[484] The judgment was upheld both on appeal (2001)[485] and by the Argentinean Supreme Court (2005).[486]

In *Arancibia Clavel* (2004), the Argentinean Supreme Court confirmed the internationalist approach to core crimes found in the cases recited above.[487] The suspect had been convicted by an Argentine federal court of homicide through the use of explosives and for participation in a criminal association, namely a Chilean intelligence unit which operated both in Chile and Argentina and targeted opponents of the Pinochet regime.[488] On appeal, the Argentinean Criminal Court of Appeals (*la Cámara Nacional de Casación Penal*) reversed the decision and held that the charge of participation in a criminal association was barred by statutory limitations.[489] Yet, by a narrow 5-3 majority the Supreme Court held that crimes against

---

[479] Id., p. 41.

[480] See Argentina, Federal Court of Buenos Aires, *In re Massera s/ Excepciones*, 9 September 1999, para. III: "No resultaría coherente, por otro lado, el mandato constitucional del artículo 118 en el sentido de establecer una suerte de jurisdicción universal para el juzgamiento de estos delitos contra el derecho de gentes y la plena facultad de los tribunales argentinos para efectuar tales procesos, si se admitiera a la vez la aplicación a cada caso de una suerte de derecho deconstruido que implicara recortes o excepciones a la normatividad que sería aplicable en el ámbito internacional." See further Mattarollo 2001, p. 41, note 63.

[481] See above, note 466.

[482] Argentina, Judge Gabriel Cavallo of the Buenos Aires Federal Court, *Julio Simon (Case no. 8686/2000, "Simon, Julio, Del Cerro, Juan Antonio s/sustracción de menores de 10 años")*, 6 March 2001, 2000/B Nueva Doctrina Penal 527. See on this case Malarino 2003, p. 73-74; Alvarez *et al.* 2002, p. 322-324; Brown 2002, p. 203-210 and also below, Chapter V, para. 5.

[483] Id., at 587 (para. IV A).

[484] Id., at 590 (para. IV B): "[L]a punibilidad de las conductas con base exclusiva en el derecho de gentes no es una exigencia del derecho penal internacional sino una regla que cobra sentido, mas bien, en casos donde la ley penal de un estado no considera punibles a esas conductas."

[485] Argentina, Federal Chamber of Appeals, *Incidente de Apelacion de Julio Simon*, 9 November 2001.

[486] Argentina, Supreme Court, *Julio Simon*, 14 June 2005.

[487] Argentina, Supreme Court, *Arancibia Clavel, Enrique Lautaro s/ homicidio calificado y asociación ilícita y otros*, 24 August 2004. See also below, Chapter V, para. 5.

[488] Id., para. 1-3.

[489] Id., para. 2.

humanity, including genocide, torture, executions and forced disappearances, are not subject to statutes of limitation.[490]

In its reasoning, the Supreme Court relied extensively on international instruments and the case law of the IACtHR regarding the duty to prosecute serious human rights violations.[491] The Court reiterated the importance of Art. 118 Constitution for international crimes and the finding in *Priebke* that the provisions of modern treaties enjoy a "presumption of operationality."[492] The Court interpreted the principle of legality in an internationalist manner, refusing to find a violation since at the time of the acts in question customary international law regulated both the criminality of the acts and the prohibition of statutes of limitations.[493] The three dissenting judges, on the other hand, rejected such an internationalist interpretation and asserted that the principle of legality provides a decisive obstacle against direct application of international criminal law.[494]

In conclusion, Argentinean doctrine is divided and actual prosecutions directly on the basis of international offences are lacking. Yet, judicial practice predominantly supports the conclusion that all international offences, both treaty and custom, can constitute a basis for core crimes prosecutions. Thus, one can cautiously conclude that Argentinean law in principle accepts general direct application of all core crimes law. The principle of legality is not a likely obstacle against direct application, as recent case law has interpreted it in an internationalist manner.

3.3.n *Hungary*

In post-communist Hungary, attempts to punish serious crimes of the former regime brought the question of direct application of international offences to the fore.[495] The crimes under consideration included the use of deadly force against demonstrating civilians and the extra-judicial execution of dissidents. Committed during the 1956 invasion by the Soviet Union, many of these particular crimes were believed to constitute crimes against humanity and/or war crimes. National criminal law offered no basis for prosecution, because the statute of limitations for the relevant crimes had run out.[496] To overcome this obstacle, the legislature first tried to adopt a new statute of limitations with retroactive effect and then to interpret the existing statute of limitations as having been interrupted by the political unwill of the communist regime to prosecute the crimes under consideration.[497] These at-

[490] Id., para. 16-23.
[491] Id., para. 13 and 35-36, and all separate votes.
[492] Id., para. 16 and 30.
[493] Id., para. 22, 23, 28 and 33. See also vote of Judge Boggiano, para. 32 and 40.
[494] Id., separate votes of Judges Belluscio, Fayt and Vazquez.
[495] See generally Correspondents' Reports by Peter Kovacs in 3 YIHL 518-519 (2000); 2 YIHL 375-377 (1999); 1 YIHL 451-455 (1998); Wiener 1997; Trang 1994.
[496] See for a short general description of Hungarian criminal law Udvaros 2002, p. 211-220.
[497] See for an overview of this legislative process Udvaros 2002, p. 227-241; Sonnevend 1997, p. 196-202; Halmai and Scheppele 1996, p. 158-165; Brunner and Halmai 1995, p. 25-30.

tempts, however, stranded on the veto of the Constitutional Court.[498] The Court interpreted the principle of legality in the Hungarian Constitution[499] to cover not only the definition of the crime but "every aspect of criminal liability."[500] Therefore, any modification or reinstatement of a statute of limitations already expired would violate the principle of legality and thus be unconstitutional.[501]

Thus, the prospects for prosecution did not look good. The Constitutional Court had made it clear that it would not bend the principle of legality, holding *inter alia* that the Constitution "required offences and their punishment and that [*sic*] the declaration of criminality of an act be regulated only by statute" and that "conviction and punishment could only proceed according to the law in force at the time of the commission of the crime."[502] Nonetheless, the legislature adopted a statute in 1993 that retroactively exempted certain crimes, ordinary ones but also war crimes and crimes against humanity, from the statute of limitations altogether.[503] In line with its earlier decisions, the Constitutional Court declared this statute unconstitutional insofar as it concerned ordinary crimes.[504] The situation for war crimes and crimes against humanity, however, was quite different and prompted the Court to analyze the direct applicability of international offences *in extenso*.

In its seminal decision of 1993, the Constitutional Court first analyzed the position of international law in general under the Hungarian Constitution.[505] In short, custom is incorporated through a rule of reference in the Constitution, while treaties are incorporated through their promulgation or publication.[506] Importantly, Art.

---

[498] See principally Hungary, Constitutional Court, *Decision No. 11/1992, On retroactive criminal legislation*, 5 March 1992, English translation in Sólyom/Brunner 2000, p. 214-228 (hereinafter *Decision No. 11/1992*) and Hungary, Constitutional Court, *Decision No. 53/1993, On War Crimes and Crimes against Humanity*, 13 October 1993, English translation in Sólyom/Brunner 2000, p. 273-283 (hereinafter *Decision No. 53/1993*). See also Sonnevend 1997, p. 202-206.

[499] See Art. 57 (4) Hungarian Constitution 1949: "No one shall be declared guilty and subjected to punishment for an offense that was not a criminal offense under Hungarian law at the time such offense was committed."

[500] See *Decision No. 11/1992*, para. 5: "[L]egal certainty cannot be limited to the determination of the elements of a crime and the punishment. The same constitutional requirements are imposed on every aspect of criminal liability – from the conditions of punishability to the regulation of sentencing." Cf. Barreto 2002, p. 13.

[501] See *Decision No. 11/1992*, para. 5: "The principle of reliance requires that once a reason for the termination of punishability is realized there may be no new statute making the same offence punishable once again."

[502] *Decision No. 11/1992*, at 215. See also p. 222-226.

[503] Law of 16 February 1993, English translation reproduced in *Decision No. 53/1993* on website ICRC. See Sonnevend 1997, p. 206-207; Halmai and Scheppele 1996, p. 165.

[504] Hungary, Constitutional Court, *Decision No. 53/1993, On War Crimes and Crimes against Humanity*, 13 October 1993, English translation in Sólyom/Brunner 2000, p. 273-283, at 275 and 277.

[505] Id., at 276-277. See for an analysis of the judgment Zimmermann 1997, p. 288-295; Mohácsi and Polt 1996. See also Sonnevend 1997.

[506] Note, however, that in Hungarian doctrine and practice, a different terminology is used than in this study. It is often said that a constitutional rule of reference to custom amounts to its "general transformation," and that "promulgation or publication in the Official Gazette" of a treaty amounts to its "specific transformation." Both custom and treaty themselves become part of the legal order, how-

7 (1) Constitution determines that "the legal system of the Republic of Hungary accepts the generally recognized rules of international law, and shall harmonize the country's domestic law with the obligations assumed under international law." While this provision incorporates only unwritten international law,[507] the duty to harmonize the national law with international obligations extends to all international law, including treaties.[508] Furthermore, the Constitutional Court explained that this provision "absolutely does not preclude certain 'generally recognized rules' from being defined by other agreements (as well)... [...] The United Nations Charter and the Geneva Conventions, for instance, may contain such rules."[509] Thus, to the extent that treaty provisions reflect customary law, their content is directly applicable in the Hungarian legal order regardless of their ratification or publication.

The Constitutional Court then set out to analyze the international law on war crimes and crimes against humanity. It found that "the norms on war crimes and crimes against humanity are undoubtedly part of customary international law" as well as general principles recognized by the community of nations, and therefore directly applicable in the Hungarian legal order.[510] Thus, even though their content had not been published in the Official Gazette,[511] the Geneva Conventions "may be applied constitutionally in the criminal courts,"[512] as a reflection of customary law.[513] With these words, the Constitutional Court effectively advocated general direct application of customary offences. In so doing, the Court pointed out an alternative legal basis for prosecution of the communist crimes, because it again struck down the statute under consideration. Although it agreed with the legislature's choice to rely on international criminal law, the Court pointed out that the statute was inconsistent with international law and therefore in violation of Art. 7 (1) Constitution. In referring to the Geneva Conventions, the statute "conflate[d] several regulations of

---

ever, and are thus, in the terminology of this study, incorporated and directly applied. See Hungary, *Report to the Committee on the Elimination of Racial Discrimination*, 17 May 2002, CERD/C/431/Add.1, para. 3 and Hungary, Constitutional Court, *Decision No. 53/1993, On War Crimes and Crimes against Humanity*, 13 October 1993, English translation in Sólyom/Brunner 2000, p. 273-283, p. 274. See elaborately Küpper 1998.

[507] There is some unclarity as to the exact body of unwritten law incorporated through Art. 7 (1). Compare Udvaros 2002, p. 282 and Küpper 1998, p. 243 ("die allgemein anerkannten Regeln des Völkerrechts"); Sólyom and Brunner 2000, p. 276-277 ("the generally recognized rules of international law") with the translation of the ICRC ("the generally recognized principles of international law") and Mohácsi and Polt 1996, p. 334 ("the universally recognized rules and regulations of international law"). Yet, it can safely be assumed that Art. 7 (1) in fact incorporates both (universal, not regional) custom and general principles. See Küpper 1998, p. 243-248; Sonnevend 1997, p. 210.

[508] *Decision No. 53/1993*, para. 3b: "[A]rticle 7 § (1) of the Constitution requires the harmony of the Constitution and the obligations derived from international law – assumed directly under the Constitution or undertaken in treaties – as well as domestic law;" See also Trang 1995, p. 15-17.

[509] *Decision No. 53/1993* at 277, para. 3a.

[510] Id., at 281.

[511] See Sonnevend 1997, p. 214.

[512] *Decision No. 53/1993* at 283.

[513] See Udvaros 2002, p. 237-240; Sonnevend 1997, p. 214 and 225; Mohácsi and Polt 1996, p. 336-337.

the Geneva Conventions addressing different subject matters and categories of protected persons and create[d] a connection among them which does not appear in the Conventions."[514] The statute *inter alia* declared that grave breaches of the Geneva Conventions apply in a situation of internal armed conflict.

How then, did the Constitutional Court reconcile its approval of direct application of customary international offences with its earlier, rather strict holdings on the principle of legality? Here, the Court relied heavily on the binding force of international law. It pointed to the gravity of war crimes and crimes against humanity, their *jus cogens* status, and the fact that international law imposes a duty to prosecute these crimes.[515] It rigorously separated international criminal law from its national counterpart, and emphasized that the two could not be fused.[516] The Court stated inter alia that "the significance of [war crimes and crimes against humanity] is too great to permit their punishment to be made dependent upon the acquiescence or general penal law policy of individual nation states."[517] Therefore the Court, with reference to Art. 7 (2) ECHR and Art. 15 (2) ICCPR, held that the prosecution of core crimes is governed only by the principle of legality under international law, and not by its Hungarian counterpart.[518] What effectively happens in these prosecutions is that, pursuant to the incorporation of international custom through the Constitution, in Hungarian courts "alongside with the domestic law, another legal system, certain rules of international law, must concurrently be given effect."[519]

Remarkably, the legislature failed again in its next attempt to provide a legal basis for prosecution of past crimes. It solely eliminated the section on ordinary crimes and renumbered the other provisions, and then re-enacted the 1993 statute without addressing the Constitutional Court's concerns over its erroneous references to the Geneva Conventions. Not surprisingly, therefore, the Constitutional

---

[514] *Decision No. 53/1993* at 283.

[515] Id., at 277-279 and 281. See for a fuller discussion of this part of the judgment below, Chapter V, para. 5.

[516] Id., at 279 and 282: "The gravity of war crimes and crimes against humanity, the fact that by their commission international peace, security and, indeed, humanity itself was placed in danger, cannot be reconciled with making their punishment subject to domestic law. [...] Through the penal power of the Hungarian state it is, in fact, the penal power of the international community which is given effect within the framework of conditions and guarantees provided by international law. Domestic substantive law may be applied only to the extent international law expressly commands it (for instance, as is the case with imposition of sentencing)."

[517] Id., at 278.

[518] Id., at 278-282: "[I]nternational guarantees cannot be replaced or substituted by the legal guarantees of domestic law. International law applies the guarantee of *nullum crimen sine lege* to itself, and not to the domestic law. [...] The international legal regulation of war crimes and crimes against humanity pays no heed to the principle of *nullum crimen* given effect by domestic law when it makes the punishment of these offenses independent of the fact whether or not they constituted a criminal offense in the domestic penal law at the time of their commission. [...W]hat occurs in this case is not the abandonment or destruction of the principle of *nullum crimen* but its limitation to the sphere of domestic law."

[519] Id., p. 281-282.

Court in 1996 struck down the re-enacted statute.[520] Perhaps concerned over the ability of the legislature to ever get it right, the Court in even clearer terms pointed to the possibility to prosecute under general direct application of customary international offences.[521]

Following the Constitutional Court's suggestion, the prosecutorial authorities have since 1993 initiated more than 40 prosecutions under direct application of customary international law as codified in the Geneva Conventions.[522] In many cases, these prosecutions were halted for lack of evidence, because the suspect was not available to stand trial, or for similar practical reasons.[523] In other cases, the various elements of the international offences were deemed not to be present.[524] Several proceedings, however, led to convictions.[525] In the *Sálgotarján* case (1994), concerning the shooting and killing of unarmed, demonstrating civilians, the court applied Art. 2 and Art. 3 (a) GC IV. The court explicitly found that national rules of reference, including Art. 7 (1) Constitution have only a declaratory character, while international offences are directly applicable *per se*.[526] Moreover, it held that the lack of publication of the Geneva Conventions in Hungary did not bar their direct application in the case.[527] Two defendants were sentenced to five years imprisonment for crimes against humanity, while ten others were acquitted.[528] The Appeals Court, however, applied only Art. 2 and not 3, labelling the 1956 conflict as an international rather than an internal armed conflict, and consequently, the killings as grave breaches under Art. 147 GC IV. The judges followed the reasoning of the Constitutional Court in finding no violation of the principle of legality, and derived the applicable penalties from comparable ordinary crimes.[529] The Appeals Court acquitted one of the two defendants, but raised the sentence of the other and also sentenced two of the suspects acquitted in first instance to two years imprisonment.[530]

In the *Kecskemét* case (1995), concerning summary executions of several prisoners, the court applied Art. 3 (1a) GC IV. Two defendants were convicted for crimes against humanity and sentenced to two years imprisonment on probation.[531]

---

[520] Hungary, Constitutional Court, *Decision No. 36/1996*, 4 November 1996, para. II (1). See also Sonnevend 1997, p. 222-224.

[521] Id., para. II (2): "Toutefois, la Cour constitutionnelle attire l'attention sur le fait que le doit international définit lui-même tous les crimes poursuivis et punissables et toutes les conditions de leur punissabilité."

[522] Udvaros 2002, p. 267.

[523] Id., p. 268, 271-274 and 277-278.

[524] Id., p. 269-270 and 277 (in particular the elements of intent, and protected status of the victims under the Geneva Conventions were found absent in numerous cases).

[525] See 3 YIHL 518-519 (2000).

[526] Udvaros 2002, p. 282-283.

[527] Id.

[528] Id., p. 276-277 and 281-283.

[529] Id., p. 299.

[530] Id., p. 278-279 and 287-288.

[531] Id., p. 277 and 283-284.

On appeal, however, the judgment was vacated and the appellant was remanded for trial.[532] Several comparable cases equally accepted the direct application of GC IV, but were halted due to practical complications.[533] Others are apparently on-going,[534] but information on these proceedings is very limited.

In conclusion, both customary and (promulgated) treaty-based offences of core crimes are directly applicable in Hungary.[535] In the last ten years, several prosecutions for war crimes and crimes against humanity have taken place under general direct application of their international offences. The Hungarian courts have explicitly found that a specific rule of reference is not necessary in this regard. The Geneva Conventions have been applied in these proceedings as evidence of customary criminalization rather than in their own right, which allowed the courts to avoid complications regarding their (lack of) publication in Hungary. The principle of legality in Hungarian law has been interpreted to apply only to national, not international crimes, while the principle of legality under international law sanctions custom as a basis for prosecution.

3.3.o *Other States*

I will now give a cursory overview of legislation and doctrine regarding general direct application in other States. The reader should keep in mind, though, that not all of the conclusions cited here are the result of thorough study of this particular topic. Some information stems from government reports to human rights bodies, which on occasion contain an overly optimistic outlook on one's own legal system. Information has also been (indirectly) derived from some NGO reports, which are generally thorough and accurate but do not always provide an entirely neutral assessment of the law. In the end, given the complexity of the matter only authoritative pronouncements of national courts on precisely the question at hand yield a conclusive answer, as set out at the beginning of this paragraph. As in the more elaborate description of a limited group of States above, four different groups of national legal systems can be distinguished where it concerns general direct application.

First, numerous legal systems reject direct application in the absence of a specific rule of reference both for treaty and custom, like Australia does. This may be

---

[532] Id., p. 279.

[533] Id., p. 284-287.

[534] See Hungary, *Report to the Human Rights Committee*, 13 March 2001, CCPR/C/HUN/2000/4, para. 299.

[535] See also Hungary, *Report to the Committee against Torture*, 17 June 1998, CAT/C/34/Add.10, para. 2 and 21: "As the [Torture] Convention has been fully integrated into the Hungarian legal system, the provisions of the Convention have the legal status of a sui generis law and consequently are directly enforceable. [...] In cases where the Convention contains provisions for the jurisdiction of the courts, as well as penalties for persons who are guilty of practising torture and other cruel, inhuman or degrading treatment or punishment, the implementation of the Convention is within the normal competence of the courts."

due to a general rejection of direct application for all international law, as in **Denmark**[536] and **many Islamic States.**[537] It can also result from a strict formulation of the principle of legality in national law, as described above in the case of Germany and Switzerland. Other States that have been reported to reject general direct application completely are **Botswana**[538] and **Tanzania.**[539]

Second, there are those States that reject general direct application of treaty-based offences but accept it for customary ones, at least in principle. In **South Africa**, international customary law is directly applicable and the principle of legality explicitly recognizes international law as a basis for prosecution.[540] Still, doctrine is divided, with some writers accepting direct application while others reject it, often without specifying the perceived obstacles that would preclude it.[541] The Supreme Court of **Zimbabwe** stated in 1985, in a case concerning extraterritorial theft committed by a Zimbabwean diplomat, that "the permissibility under international law for a State to exercise jurisdiction is not a sufficient basis for the exercise of jurisdiction by a municipal court of that State."[542] Yet, the language of the decision suggests that criminal law is not exempted from the general incorporation of international custom, and that a mandatory international customary criminalization rather than a permissive rule may be directly applicable.[543]

Third, many States follow the reverse constitutional scheme for the incorporation of international law, and, like France, allow general direct application of treaty-based, but not customary offences. In **Haiti**, for example, the *Ordonnance* (indictment) of the Raboteau trial,[544] suggested that war crimes could be prosecuted directly on the basis of the Geneva Conventions.[545] However, in the end all defen-

---

[536] See Holdgaard Bukh 1994, p. 341.

[537] See Lambert-Abdelgawad 2002, p. 529 and 535-536.

[538] See Nsereko 2000, p. 178.

[539] See Kamanga 1998, p. 77 ("[G]enocide, strictly speaking, is yet to be proclaimed a crime under Tanzanian laws, and logically, not penally sanctionable.").

[540] See Section 232 and 35 (3) (1) Constitution.

[541] Compare Jessberger and Powell 2002, p. 349-350 (noting the direct applicability of international customary offences, but a general reluctance among the courts to apply them) and Maqungo 2000, p. 186 with Erasmus and Kemp 2002, p. 77 and Dugard 2000, p. 141-142.

[542] See Zimbabwe, Supreme Court, *S v. Mharapara*, 17 October 1985, 1986 (1) SA 556 at 559.

[543] Id., at 559 ("Thus the fact that customary international law is part of the municipal law of a State does not assist [for a basis of prosecution], because there is only a permissive principle involved and not a mandatory rule.").

[544] See above note 99 and accompanying text.

[545] Haiti, Juge d'Instruction Jean Senat Fleury of the Gonaïves Tribunal of First Instance, *Ordonnance Raboteau Massacre*, 27 August 1999, On file with the author, p. 52 and 159:

"Attendu que les actes accomplis par ces militaires et civils armés les 18 et 22 avril 1994 à Raboteau, sont manifestement illégaux, contraires aux Conventions et Traités internationaux ratifiés par Haïti… Attendu qu'aux termes de l'article 42-3 de la dite Constitution, les violences exercées et les crimes perpétrés par des militaires, rendent ces derniers justiciables des tribunaux de Droit Commun.

[…]

Attendu que les infractions graves à l'article 3 commun des quatre Conventions de Genève sont assimilables aux 'crimes de guerre.' Il n'y a donc que deux possibilités:

dants were charged with ordinary crimes. General direct application of treaty-based offences appears to be possible also in **Austria**,[546] **Chile**,[547] **Greece**,[548] **Russia**,[549] **Spain**,[550] and **Ukraine**.[551] As is true for the incorporation of public international law in general, there is often a significant gap between the constitutional rules on general direct application of treaty-based offences and their actual effect in judicial practice. In numerous States, treaty-based offences are domestically valid and can in principle be directly applied. Yet, courts simply refuse to do so, for example because they regard the relevant treaties as non-self-executing or because they show a hostile attitude to international law in general. Such divergence between the constitutional framework and actual practice has been noted e.g. for **Brazil**[552] and **Iran**.[553]

Fourth, a few States appear to sanction the general direct application of all international offences, like Hungary and Argentina. This situation is primarily the case where the national formulation of the principle of legality explicitly includes international law as a legal basis for punishment. Such is the case for example in **Poland**. Despite the fact that the Polish Constitution lists treaties, but not custom among the Polish sources of law,[554] some writers conclude that the constitutional

a) Il n'y a pas eu de conflit armé interne. Dans ce cas, les infractions perpétrées constituent des crimes de droit commun punis par le Code pénal.
b) Il y a eu un conflit armé interne. Dans ce cas les infractions perpétrées constituent des 'crimes de guerre,' réprimées par les Conventions de Genève ratifiées par Haïti."
Art. 42 (3) Constitution reads:
"Les cas de conflit entre civils et militaires, les abus, violences et crimes perpétrés contre un civil par un militaire dans l'exercice de ses fonctions, relèvent exclusivement des tribunaux de droit commun."
See also Art. 276 (2) Constitution:
"Les Traités ou Accord Internationaux, une fois sanctionnés et ratifiés dans les formes prévues par la Constitution, font partie de la Législation du Pays et abrogent toutes les Lois qui leur sont contraires."

546 See Gartner 2000, p. 52.

547 See Ambos 2002b, p. 500-502.

548 See Discalopoulou-Livada 2000, p. 118. See more generally Kareklás and Papacharalambous 2001, part C and Spirakos 1990, especially p. 76 and 135-137.

549 See above note 205 and accompanying text.

550 See Buck 2002, p. 146-149. Cf. Yánez-Barnuevo and Roldán 2000, p. 203-206.

551 See above note 204 and accompanying text.

552 See Choukr 2002, p. 334. Compare further Choukr 2002, p. 336 with Ambos 2002b, p. 493 and 499-500. General direct application has apparently been accepted in the past, as suggested by a 1905 judgment of the Brazilian Supreme Court that in directly applying a treaty in an extradition case interpreted the 1891 Constitution as granting federal courts jurisdiction to "direct the procedures and judge matters of international criminal law." See Dolinger 1993, p. 1080.

553 See Beigzadeh and Nadjafi 2002, p. 400-401 and 416.

554 Art. 87 (1) Constitution 1997: "The sources of universally binding law of the Republic of Poland shall be: the Constitution, statutes, ratified international agreements, and regulations." See generally Wyrozumska 2001.

formulation of the principle of legality[555] signifies an acceptance of general direct application for all international offences.[556]

As a conclusion to this overview of national legal systems, some States can be mentioned where the situation is especially uncertain. In **Angola**, a 1976 trial of mercenaries was partly based on charges of crimes against peace and the crime of mercenarism, both based on such international instruments as the Nuremberg Statute and numerous U.N. Resolutions. The defendants were convicted for mercenarism under customary international law. The many legal flaws and the political character of this trial, however, seriously impede its authoritative value.[557] Finally, the state of the law on general direct application in **China**,[558] **Croatia**,[559] **Egypt**,[560] **Finland**,[561] **Italy**,[562] **Morocco**,[563] **Portugal**,[564] is diffuse, disputed or unclear, at least for this author.

4. Conclusion

The overview of legislative and judicial practice in this Chapter allows us to draw some inferences that provide a better understanding of the concept of direct application of international offences.

First, the different legal bases for the prosecution of core crimes distinguished in this Chapter (national or international law, ordinary or international crime) do not exclude but complement one another. Most, if not all, States do not rely on the same technique to criminalize all core crimes, but instead utilize different ones, often all three. Perhaps the most common combination before the drafting of the ICC Statute was the criminalization of genocide as an international crime under national law and a rule of reference ensuring direct application of international law for war crimes, while the criminalization of crimes against humanity was left to ordinary criminal law.[565] This can possibly be explained by the complexity and breadth of the inter-

[555] See Art. 42 (1) Constitution 1997: "Only a person who has committed an act prohibited by a statute in force at the moment of commission thereof, and which is subject to a penalty, shall be held criminally responsible. This principle shall not prevent punishment of any act which, at the moment of its commission, constituted an offence within the meaning of international law." See also Weigend 2003, p. 143.

[556] See Pomorski 2001, p. 316. There appears to be no relevant practice in this regard. Cf. Weigend and Zoll 2002, p. 127.

[557] See Lockwood 1977.

[558] See Yuan and Jianping 2002, p. 355-356.

[559] See Art. 31 and 134 Croation Constitution. See also Josipovic *et al.* 2001, p. 95 and 121.

[560] See Abdelgawad 2002, p. 379-383, 390 and 393.

[561] See Frände 2003, p. 71 (principle of legality excludes general direct application of customary offences but the situation for treaty-based offences is not reported).

[562] See Zappala 2002, p. 211 and Benvenuti 2000, p. 125-127.

[563] See Ayat 2002, p. 431-435.

[564] See Escarameia 2000, p. 151-155 and 166-167.

[565] Cf. Amnesty International, *Report on Universal jurisdiction*, 2001, Chapters 4, 6 and 8.

national law on war crimes and the (pre-ICC) absence of a treaty-based general definition of crimes against humanity, while the Genocide Convention provided both an incentive to criminalize genocide in national law and an easily transposable definition.[566] Combinations of the different legal bases are also prevalent in actual national prosecutions. It is not uncommon to find defendants being charged with a combination of ordinary and international crimes, the latter drawn either from national or international law, or from both.[567]

Second, direct application of international offences for the punishment of core crimes is not a foreign concept that lacks application in practice. It is not even exceptional. Most, if not all, States have enacted specific rules of reference in national law that require direct application of (specific rules or parts of) international criminal law in national prosecutions. Decidedly less common, but still accepted in numerous States, is general direct application of international offences in the absence of a specific rule of reference.

Third, there is no clear dividing line between the universally accepted direct application on the basis of a specific rule of reference and the often rejected general direct application of international offences. National legal systems show a diverse and complex range of rules of reference that defy clear-cut categorization. Some rules refer to particular treaty provisions, some to particular international crimes, some to a source of international law, and some to a combination of crimes and sources. Some rules refer to international law for the definition of the crime and some to establish jurisdiction. Consequently, substantive criminality is often derived from a combination of national and international rules that is not easily disentangled. In short, the difference between direct application on the basis of a specific rule of reference and general direct application can be difficult to ascertain and is often smaller than one might think. One may ask whether the difference between a specific rule of reference establishing extraterritorial jurisdiction for crimes "which are considered to be punishable by a treaty,"[568] and a general rule of reference incorporating all treaties is all that fundamental.

Fourth, general direct application of international offences is not a novel concept. Individual criminal responsibility under international law has a long history, not only for piracy and war crimes but also for other crimes such as offenses against internationally protected persons like consuls.[569] Direct application of international criminal law, both treaty and custom, has occurred in numerous prosecutions in the courts of different nations over the last centuries, also in the absence of a specific

[566] Cf. Peyró 2003, p. 76-77. See for a fuller analysis of the reasons behind this legislative practice below, Chapter III.

[567] See e.g. the cases cited above, notes 129 and 229.

[568] See above note 90 and accompanying text.

[569] See Panken 2003; Schmidt 2002, p. 6-24; Amnesty International, *Report on Universal jurisdiction*, 2001, Chapter 2; Komarow 1980, p. 22-23; Triffterer 1966, p. 4-15.

rule of reference.[570] Yet, it should be noted that numerous States where ICL was directly applied in the past appear more hesitant to do so today.

Fifth, contemporary national practice regarding general direct application of international core crimes law is varied, and more often than not shrouded in uncertainty. Numerous States, like Australia and Germany, reject it both for treaty and custom. Others, like France, accept it for treaty law but not for custom. In States like Canada, the reverse situation is found. Finally, a few States, among them Hungary and Argentina, accept general direct application of all international law for core crimes prosecutions. Yet, in most States that accept it, general direct application is seldomly or never used in core crimes prosecutions. It appears that prosecutors and courts prefer to use other legal bases wherever possible.[571]

Sixth, the States that have thus far rejected general direct application of treaty-based offences have done so for different reasons. As a result, the prospects for general direct application in the future are very different in these legal systems. States that require transformation of treaty provisions, like the United Kingdom, or completely reject direct application of international criminal law in the absence of a specific rule of reference, like Australia and Switzerland, will not see a change of judicial practice any time soon. On the other hand, States that have so far rejected direct application of treaties like the Geneva Conventions for lack of precision or completeness rather than on principle, like Senegal and France, might allow future prosecutions under direct application of more developed treaties, such as the ICC Statute.

Seventh, as one might expect, national courts look primarily to national law in determining the viability of general direct application of international core crimes law. In national law, the two pivotal determining factors are the constitutional rules on the transformation or incorporation of public international law in general and the principle of legality. The great majority of States allow for the incorporation of at least one of the sources of international law.[572] In order to receive general direct application, international law must then either be recognized as a source of criminality by the national formulation of the principle of legality or be assigned a superior rank in the national legal system so as to supersede it. The latter option is exceptional though, since the principle of legality often has constitutional rank in national legal systems.

Eighth, while national courts look primarily to national law, their attitude in doing so is of great importance. The legal framework determinative for the viability of general direct application has many variables that allow for different accents in analysis and corresponding differing outcomes. Courts with an internationalist inclination may draw different conclusions from the same legal framework than courts

[570] See in particular the paragraphs on the U.S., Germany and the Netherlands. See also Poland, Voivodship Court of Warsaw, *In re Koch*, 9 March 1959, 30 ILR 496 at 504 and 506-507, cited below, notes 1257-1260; Triffterer 1966, p. 7-8 and 182-188.

[571] Cf. Cassese 2003a, p. 303-305.

[572] Cf. Cassese 1985, p. 441.

that are more focused on national law. The French and Hungarian courts, for example, both sanctioned direct application by interpreting their national formulations of the principle of legality in light of the broader provisions of the ECHR and the ICCPR. Other national courts have analyzed comparable legal frameworks as excluding direct application by adhering to a strict view of the principle of legality. Thus, general direct application is not determined solely by the state of national law, but also by the extent to which national courts feel compelled to enforce international criminal law.

Chapter III
UNDERLYING CONSIDERATIONS: WHAT CRIME, WHAT LAW?

1. Introduction

The previous Chapter presented an overview of national legislative and judicial practice focusing on the legal basis for core crimes prosecutions in national courts. A distinction was made between direct application of international offences and prosecution based on national criminal law. A further distinction was made in national law between ordinary crimes and international crimes. Thus, core crimes can be prosecuted as ordinary crimes, as international crimes defined in national law, and by direct application of international offences. The dividing lines between these categories are not always clear. Often, prosecutions are based on a combination of the three. In addition, it has become clear that numerous States allow direct application of (certain) international offences in principle but lack a corresponding practice.

The aim of this Chapter is to present the considerations that influence the actual occurrence or non-occurrence of direct application of the international criminalization of the core crimes. These underlying considerations affect the choices both between different legal bases for prosecution, and between granting and withholding direct application in the absence of an alternative basis for prosecution. At the national level, these choices are made, first, by the legislature and executive when they shape the national legal framework, second, by the prosecuting authorities when they select the legal basis on which to press charges, and, third, by the courts when they decide whether or not to uphold these charges. Of course, the degree of freedom to act enjoyed by each of these categories of actors in making these choices varies considerably. The choices of the legislature and executive largely determine the possibilities of the prosecutor, while the courts are constrained by the choices of all these actors. Nevertheless, even though they fulfill different roles, the considerations these actors entertain regarding direct application largely overlap. In analyzing these considerations I will therefore distinguish between the different actors only where relevant.

In this Chapter I shall primarily be looking at policy considerations, for example concerning practical complications and political concerns. I will analyze arguments of a legal nature, including those concerning the specificity of the law, in the following three chapters. The description of national judicial practice in the previous Chapter demonstrates that the principle of legality is intimately connected with the question of direct application of international offences. Courts confront appeals to the principle of legality in various ways, and with different results.[573] Doctrine

[573] Compare e.g. Germany and Senegal to France and Hungary in Chapter II.

generally points to the principle of legality as the greatest, if not decisive, obstacle to direct application of ICL.[574] In light of the importance and complexity of this subject, the principle of legality and related issues such as the accessibility and foreseeability of core crimes law will be analyzed separately, in Chapter VI.

However, this Chapter includes some legal analysis where necessary for a full understanding of the policy considerations. Moreover, it is not always possible to separate legal arguments and policy considerations when analyzing legislative and judicial practice.[575] For example, when a legislature or court refers to arguments regarding legal certainty to justify a particular legislative or judicial decision, it is not always clear whether it is referring to legal rules regarding the principle of legality *requiring* that particular outcome or solely to policy considerations that justify the outcome as the exercise of a certain discretion. This overview therefore focuses on policy considerations but prefers a more complete analysis of related points over a rigid separation of law and policy.

The considerations set out here vary greatly in relevance, specificity and the extent to which they are explicitly expressed in practice. Some are so central that they appear in almost every decision and debate on direct application, others are apparently less important. In the appraisal of the different considerations, there are significant differences between different States and legal systems,[576] as well as between practitioners and academics of different backgrounds. Some considerations pertain to direct application of all international rules, while others are relevant only for the offences studied here. Some are explicitly discussed in judgments and legislative debates, while others can be deduced only from a broader analysis of national practice and doctrine.

All these considerations, however, have a significant bearing on the question of direct application of international core crimes law. Reviewing them together will shed more light on the relevance and the practical consequences of direct application in core crimes prosecutions. It will also contribute to a better understanding of the practice set out in Chapter II, in particular the noted gap between potential and actual direct application. Finally, this review will show that international law is not neutral in its assessment of the different possible legal bases for core crimes prosecutions and will thereby provide the broader background to the legal analysis in the following chapters. The differences between the various considerations, for example in relevance and specificity, will be indicated in their descriptions.

From here on, I will first describe the minimalism and selectivity that govern the approach of national actors towards core crimes prosecutions. These are general characteristics of national practice rather than considerations that directly govern direct application. Yet, they constitute key features of national practice regarding the core crimes which must be discussed in order to arrive at a full understanding of

---

[574] See e.g. Ambos 2002b, p. 492-493; Benillouche 2002, p. 174; Strijards 2000, p. 2115; Bremer 1999, p. 396; Triffterer 1966, p. 10 and 38.

[575] Cf. Mundis 2004, p. 4; Dupuy 1999, p. 118.

[576] Compare the different country reports above, Chapter II, para. 3.3.

that practice. Also, as will be shown shortly, minimalism and selectivity do in practice influence the acceptance or rejection of direct application of core crimes law. After this, I will set out the partially overlapping underlying considerations, working from broader and more fundamental considerations such as State sovereignty and the democratic legitimacy of the law towards more practical ones such as the penalties attached to the different legal bases for prosecution.

2. Minimalism and Selectivity in Core Crimes Prosecution

An important characteristic of national practice regarding the core crimes is the persistent lack of prosecutions.[577] While recent years have seen a notable increase in the activity of national courts, the level of national core crimes prosecutions is still minimal.[578] As will be explained more fully below, this reality brings questions concerning direct application to the fore.[579] The global lack of prosecutions has much to do with the fact that many core crimes are "system crimes."[580] Such crimes are not simply the result of the criminal impulses of individuals on the loose, but rather the product of State machineries at work. Genocide and numerous war crimes can by their very nature only be committed with either active or passive involvement of the State or, at the very least, an armed group with a significant degree of organization. Crimes against humanity, as originally conceived during WW II, could only be committed with active or passive State involvement.[581] Today, customary international law broadens the category of possible perpetrators to include organi-

---

[577] See e.g. Kamminga 1998, p. 564 ("[O]nly a small proportion of those who commit genocide, crimes against humanity or war crimes are ever brought to justice."); Wolfrum 1996, p. 245 ("[I]n practice, the rules of the four Geneva Conventions have been applied very rarely to the prosecution of grave breaches."); Cohen 1995, p. 20 ("There has probably been no historical instance where anything remotely like a full policy of criminal accountability has been implemented.").

[578] See e.g. ICJ, International Court of Justice, *Case concerning the Arrest Warrant of 11 April 2000 (Democratic Republic of the Congo v. Belgium)*, 14 February 2002, Joint Separate Opinion of Judges Higgins, Kooijmans and Buergenthal, para. 32 ("[T]here has been a remarkably modest corpus of national case law emanating from the jurisdictional possibilities provided in the Geneva Conventions or in Additional Protocol I."). A significant factor in the recent increase of (attempted) core crimes prosecutions appears to be the increased activity of victims with standing to initiate criminal prosecutions in particular legal systems (*parties civiles*). See Wible 2002, p. 282-283.

[579] See below, p. 96 *et seq.*

[580] See Cassese 2003a, p. 295-298; Swart 2002c, p. 244; Jäger 1995, p. 327; Röling 1979, p. 164-166. Cf. Nollkaemper 2003a, p. 624; Nollkaemper 2000, p. 18. For a short time after WW II, the ILC expressed this characteristic by referring to "offences which contain a political element." In light of its obvious definitional complications, however, this term was quickly abandoned. See Triffterer 1966, p. 201-210.

[581] See Schabas 2002b, p. 257. In Art. 2 (11) of its 1954 Draft Code of Offences against the Peace and Security of Mankind, the ILC labelled as crimes against humanity only inhuman acts committed "by the authorities of a State or by private individuals acting at the instigation or with toleration of such authorities," but it later abandoned this requirement. See Boot 2002, p. 464-465.

zations,[582] but it appears these must have certain State-like features.[583] Most often, crimes against humanity are characterized by at least passive State involvement.[584] To be sure, there certainly are core crimes of an individual rather than systemic nature, in particular isolated war crimes.[585] But on the whole, support or acquiescence of State institutions is an important characteristic of the core crimes.[586]

Core crimes prosecutions are an unpopular undertaking for several reasons. First, core crimes prosecutions are often controversial because they involve State officials and implicate State institutions like armies or governments. Although core crimes prosecutions formally have no bearing on questions of State responsibility,[587] it is true at least to some extent that a "judgment against an individual perpetrator can be considered as a (partial) remedy against the state."[588] Second, their character as system crimes also means that core crimes are seldomly committed in isolation. Therefore, a succesful prosecution may pave the way for an unwanted influx of related cases, leading to an overburdening of the legal system.[589] Third,

---

[582] Cf. Art. 7 para. 2 (a) ICC Statute, which requires the attack to be "pursuant to or in furtherance of a State *or organizational* policy."

[583] See ICTY, Trial Chamber, *Kupreskic*, 14 January 2000, para. 551-555, in particular at 552: "The need for crimes against humanity to have been at least tolerated by a State, Government or entity is also stressed in national and international case-law. The crimes at issue may also be State-sponsored or at any rate may be part of a governmental policy or of an entity holding *de facto* authority over a territory."
But see ICTY, Trial Chamber, *Tadic*, 7 May 1997, para. 645-648 and 654-655, in particular at 654: "The Prosecution in its pre-trial brief argues that under international law crimes against humanity can be committed on behalf of entities exercising de facto control over a particular territory but without international recognition or formal status of a *de jure* state, or by a terrorist group or organization. The Defence does not challenge this assertion, which conforms with recent statements regarding crimes against humanity."
It is thus open to debate whether entities like ETA and Al-Quaeda can commit crimes against humanity. See Schabas 2002b, p. 257-259.

[584] See Schabas 2002b, p. 259 ("The very reason why the concept of crimes against humanity was originally developed, at Nuremberg, was so that atrocities that went unpunished by the judicial authorities of the State in question would not escape prosecution."); Cassese 2001a, 356-360.

[585] This may occur on a larger scale when every form of effective State authority is absent. However, even in failed States there usually are some entities that claim institutional authority.

[586] It should be noted that often, States put the blame for their war crimes entirely on the individuals who physically committed them, while they themselves in fact bear responsibility for, at the very least, contributing factors like a lack of adequate training and supervision, unclear combat instructions and/or a failure to adequately punish such crimes.

[587] See e.g. Art. 25 (4) ICC Statute.

[588] Nollkaemper 2003a, p. 638.

[589] See Wolfrum 1996, p. 245 (explaining the divergence between the numerous national prosecutions for [pre-2001] terrorism and the scarcity of such prosecutions for war crimes by the fact that "[w]hereas the prosecution of war crimes would require dealing with several or many cases, terrorist attacks can be regarded as isolated cases where the prosecution of one does not necessarily result in the prosecution of other similar cases."). Furthermore, the global lack of core crimes prosecutions may lead to an influx of cases in the few States that actively pursue prosecutions, especially when they have large immigrant communities and grant victims the competence to initiate proceedings. See e.g. Wouters and Panken 2003, p. 2-4 and 26 (on the extensive list of proceedings concerning core crimes in Belgium before the adaptation of the law on international crimes in 2003, and the resulting financial and organizational consequences).

prosecutions of core crimes are complicated, costly and time-consuming. In most core crimes prosecutions, both the law to be applied and the facts of the case are extensive and complex, requiring considerable expertise and time of the actors involved. Prosecutions involving foreign victims or perpetrators, which is regularly the case for core crimes, add many complications. Already difficult assessments of law and facts become even more complex due to cultural and linguistic barriers.[590] Foreign defendants, victims or witnesses may require expensive translation services and visits to foreign sites, both with uncertain outcomes.[591]

All in all, the many complexities involved make core crimes prosecutions daunting tasks with unsure results, and States therefore generally avoid rather than welcome them.[592] Some of the legal and practical complications, which will be discussed more fully below, may justify a cautious approach.[593] Yet, others are of a more dubious nature. In particular, States are not only minimalist but also selective when it comes to the prosecution of core crimes. Prosecution of a State's own nationals often requires judging the wars and crimes of one's own government, which is not a popular task.[594] The prosecution of foreign citizens, let alone State officials, or even the prospect of such prosecutions, can lead to serious political tensions between the different States involved.[595]

As a result, practice shows that States adequately prosecute mostly core crimes committed by other or past regimes, not those of their own officials and citizens, and tend to ignore core crimes involving allies and powerful States.[596] Prosecutions

[590] See e.g. Switzerland, Military Court of Cassation, *In re N.*, 27 April 2001, para. 6b and 8c: "Se référant au jugement de première instance, le Tribunal d'appel a tenu compte de la situation particulière des témoins qui ont vécu les événements sanglants du printemps 1994 au Rwanda, qui ont souvent perdu des proches, qui ont subi des traumatismes, qui sont parfois illettrés ou ne connaissent pas le calendrier. Ces circonstances ne sont pas usuelles pour les tribunaux suisses. [...] Il est à l'évidence délicat pour un tribunal d'un pays étranger d'apprécier, plusieurs années après les faits, l'étendue des pouvoirs d'un magistrat de l'administration civile du Rwanda pendant une période de quelques semaines dans des circonstances dramatiques."

[591] See for an instructive overview of the efforts and complications involved in the prosecution of a Rwandese genocide suspect in France ECtHR, *Mutimura v. France*, 8 June 2004, para. 8-59 and 61. See also Hetherington and Chalmers 1989, p. 102: "We would not wish the difficulties of prosecution [of extraterritorial WW II crimes] in this country to be understimated. It is undoubtedly true that when trying a case of murder, a British jury will be most impressed by material witnesses whom they have seen in the flesh and whom they have seen cross-examined. [...] How impressed a jury would be with evidence received via a satellite link, which would also be extremely expensive, when cross-examination is through an interpreter, is difficult to predict."

[592] See Kirby 2004, p. 250; Justice at Risk: War Crimes Trials in Croatia, Bosnia and Herzegovina, and Serbia and Montenegro, 2004, Human Rights Watch; Wouters and Panken 2003, p. 25-26; Kamminga 1998, p. 574. See for documented instances of reluctance to prosecute extraterritorial core crimes when the suspect was present on State territory e.g. Schabas 2003a, p. 35-36; Posner 2002, p. 416.

[593] See in particular para. 6 on manageability of the law.

[594] See e.g. Sadat 2003, p. 161 (on the opposition in France to prosecution of collaborators in WW II out of fear of dividing French society).

[595] See e.g. Kirby 2004, p. 253; Zeidy 2003, p. 860-861; Röling 1979, p. 184.

[596] See Justice at Risk: War Crimes Trials in Croatia, Bosnia and Herzegovina, and Serbia and Montenegro, 2004, Human Rights Watch, p. 9-10 (on ethnic bias in national war crimes prosecutions in the States of the Former Yugoslavia);

of core crimes in the courts of the State involved while the regime responsible is still in power are few at best, and mostly symbolic.[597] Such prosecutions normally charge the defendants with ordinary crimes, which negates the broader context of the core crimes,[598] and result in low sentences.[599] Despite occasional suggestions to the contrary,[600] democracies have no better track record in the prosecution of their own core crimes than other States.[601]

The States that are most willing to prosecute their own nationals, namely societies emerging from the rule of an oppressive regime, are usually overburdened with cases, defendants and evidence to be processed. At the same time, their governmental institutions are destabilized and ill-equipped. Consequently, they have to select

ICJ, International Court of Justice, *Case concerning the Arrest Warrant of 11 April 2000 (Democratic Republic of the Congo v. Belgium)*, 14 February 2002, Joint Separate Opinion of Judges Higgins, Kooijmans and Buergenthal, para. 32: "The chance that a Minister for Foreign Affairs will be tried in his own country in accordance with the relevant rules of domestic law or that his immunity will be waived by his own State is not high as long as there has been no change of power…";
Germany, Supreme Court (BGH), Jorgic, 30 March 1999, 3 StR 215/98, in 19 NStZ (1999), 396-404; BGHSt 45, 64-91, para. I (aa): "Da die besonders schwer wiegenden Fälle des Völkermords häufig durch den Heimatstaat der Opfer oder wenigstens mit dessen Duldung begangen werden, ist in der Regel eine effektive Strafverfolgung im Tatortstaat nicht zu erwarten.";
U.K., *House of Lords, R. v. Bow Street Metropolitan Stipendiary Magistrate & Others, Ex Parte Pinochet Ugarte (No. 3)*, 24 March 1999, [2000] 1 A.C. 147 at 199, per Lord Browne-Wilkinson: "[T]he fact that the local court had jurisdiction to deal with the international crime of torture was nothing to the point so long as the totalitarian regime remained in power: a totalitarian regime will not permit adjudication by its own courts on its own shortcomings. Hence the demand for some international machinery to repress state torture which is not dependent upon the local courts where the torture was committed.";
Canada, Supreme Court, *R. v. Imre Finta*, 24 March 1994, per La Forest J. (dissenting), para. 253: "It would be pointless to rely solely on the state where such a crime has been committed, since that state will often be implicated in the crime, particularly crimes against humanity."
See also Steinhardt 2004, p. 21; Jessberger 2003, p. 285; Schabas 2003b, p. 43 and 60; Seiderman 2001, p. 209; Bassiouni 1998, p. 141-142; Swart 1996, p. 6-7.

[597] See Cassese 2002, p. 565. Cf. Steinhardt 2004, p. 14; Rowe and Meyer 1996, p. 480.

[598] See on the context and international dimension of the core crimes below, para. 8.

[599] See for examples of such cases above, Chapter II, para. 2.1 and Lauterpacht 1944, p. 84. Cf. Indonesia, Ad Hoc Human Rights Tribunal at the Human Rights Court of Justice of Central Jakarta, *Abilio Soares*, 14 August 2002; Bertodano 2004, p. 922-925 and Bertodano 2003, p. 234-236. (Indonesia prosecutes its former Governor of East-Timor for crimes against humanity, but in an inadequate manner leading to a sentence of a mere three years imprisonment which was annulled by the Indonesian Supreme Court on 4 November 2004.)

[600] See e.g. Cassel 2001, p. 440-441.

[601] Western democracies, for example, have not adequately prosecuted the many war crimes and/or crimes against humanity they have committed in the last fifty years alone against their indigenous peoples, in WW II, in colonial wars, and in numerous armed conflicts in the last decades. See e.g. Eftekhari 2003 and Lelieur-Fischer 2004 (on French war crimes and crimes against humanity committed in Algeria and their impunity); Barrett 2001 (on the indiscriminate U.S. bombing of Cambodia and Laos, likely constituting war crimes and/or crimes against humanity); Australia, Federal Court, *Nulyarimma v. Thompson*, 1 September 1999, [1999] FCA 1192, para. 5-17 (on Australia's policies towards its indigenous population, arguably constituting at least crimes against humanity well into the 1960s); Waters 2003 and Cottier 2001 (on alleged NATO war crimes during the Kosovo conflict), Röling 1979, p. 196-197 and Rüter 1973, p. 149-165 (on the lack of adequate prosecutions for Dutch war crimes committed in WW II and Indonesia).

cases and forego many core crimes prosecutions, if only to avoid serious fair trial problems.[602]

In short, States for various reasons tend to curtail (the prospect of) core crimes prosecutions in general and are selective in the ones they enable and undertake. Minimalism and selectivity can be found in all governmental institutions concerned, even if they are seldom formulated. National legislation on core crimes is often delayed, incomplete and restrictive, and falls well short of what is permitted or required under international law.[603] Most legislatures prefer to formulate narrow bases of jurisdiction and criminalization over broader ones.[604] Some of them also add procedural barriers for core crimes prosecutions to take place. Several States, for example, require consent of certain State authorities for the institution of core crimes prosecutions, while such consent is not required for ordinary prosecutions.[605] Sometimes, legislatures simply have other priorities.[606]

Prosecutorial and judicial authorities are no different. Of course, there are notable exceptions like Belgian Judge Vandermeersch[607] and Spanish Judge Garzon.[608]

[602] The case of Rwanda is well-described, but not the only one. After the fall of Mengistu's regime, for example, Ethiopia was faced with more than 5000 defendants of serious crimes, many of which apparently core crimes, as well as thousands of witnesses, and more than 300,000 pieces of documentary evidence. The resulting workload for the authorities, who lacked both resources and expertise, was formidable and included more than 1300 *habeas corpus* petitions alone. See Kidane 2003, p. 671-672 and 690-693; Haile 2000, p. 35-36; Gouttes 1998, p. 697. See generally Redae 1999; Mayfield 1995.

[603] See Kamminga 1998, p. 570; Osofsky 1997, p. 218; Reydams 1996, p. 28; Komarow 1980, p. 34-35. Even a far-going national law like the Belgian law on international crimes, it should be remembered, was still a severely delayed piece of implementing legislation. See Wouters and Panken 2003, p. 10-14.

[604] See e.g. Bassiouni *et al.* 1989, p. 320-321, remarks Bassiouni: "Somehow it seems that legislation like the [U.S.] implementing legislation on the Genocide Convention and the Canadian statute on prosecuting war crimes and crimes against humanity is focused toward the past and reflects more of a political statement on the part of legislative bodies referring to past experiences than a genuine effort to develop a legal instrument reflecting the present and, one hopes, applying to the future. [...] It also seems to me that there is a more insidious purpose in this type of legislation, whether it is the U.S. legislation or the Canadian legislation. The insidious purpose is to pass the legislation so that politicians can say we have it, but in fact to draft it in such a way that it is totally impossible to carry out." And p. 324-325, remarks Steven Lubet: "In sum, the [U.S.] Genocide Implementation Act appears to have been drafted in such a manner as to make it inapplicable in any practical sense. [...] It transcends irony that the legislative debate concerning the Implementation Act only discussed crimes that the Act cannot reach. [...] The Genocide Implementation Act must be seen as a conscious decision not to pursue genocide where and when it is most likely to occur."

[605] See Section 53 (3) of the U.K.'s International Criminal Court Act 2001 (providing that proceedings for core crimes shall not be instituted except by or with the consent of the Attorney General). Various other States require consent of higher State officials for the prosecution of extraterritorial core crimes, also when the suspect is present on State territory and there is a duty to prosecute. See e.g. Vandermeersch 2004, p. 145; Wyngaert 2003, p. 673-674 and 1120-1121; Holdgaard Bukh 1994, p. 348.

[606] See Ayat 2002, p. 429 and Discalopoulou-Livada 2000, p. 121 (noting instances where national governments have stated that enacting legislation on core crimes was postponed because there were other priorities).

[607] See above, note 278 and accompanying text.

[608] See above, notes 132-134 and references cited there.

Generally, however, both prosecutors and courts tend to minimize and carefully select their involvement in core crimes prosecutions.[609] Prosecutorial authorities are hesitant to use their available options to prosecute.[610] In many countries, foreign suspects of core crimes are confronted by civil claims, exclusion from refugee status, denaturalization and/or deportation rather than by criminal prosecution.[611] Judges exert their influence through their generally restrictive interpretation and application of the law in core crimes prosecutions.[612] Here also selectivity can play a role. The French courts, for example, have been noticeably stricter in their application of the principle of legality for core crimes committed by the French military in former colonies than for Axis crimes committed in WW II.[613]

Minimalism and selectivity affect all core crimes prosecutions, or lack thereof, no matter what their legal basis. They are important factors for a full understanding of national practice regarding core crimes prosecutions. At the same time, they also have their bearing on the specific question of direct application in several ways. First, minimalism of the legislature[614] explains both why the question of general direct application comes up regularly in national courts and why its answer is of great practical importance. It is generally the imperfect state of national legislation on core crimes that prompts the question whether general direct application can provide an alternative basis for a prosecution that can not otherwise take place. The description in Chapter II of national proceedings, for example in Australia, Senegal and Hungary, attests to this fact.

Second, considerations of minimalism and selectivity influence national authorities on all levels to be critical of, and sometimes outright hostile to, direct application of international offences.[615] As will be discussed in more detail below, this

---

[609] See Belgium, Tribunal of First Instance (District of Brussels), *In re Pinochet Ugarte*, 6 November 1998, para. 3.3.3: "Now, in humanitarian law, the risk does not seem to lie as much in the fact that the national authorities exceed their competence but rather in the reflex with which they look for pretexts to justify their lack of competence, leaving the door wide open to the impunity of the most serious crimes (which is definitely contrary to the *raison d'etre* of the rules of international law)."

[610] See e.g. Ziegler 1997, p. 583 ("Switzerland's political authorities have mentioned on several occasions that they prefer extraditing war criminals over prosecuting them domestically.").

[611] See Aceves 2000, p. 141-149. See also Handmaker 2003, p. 688-689 (on the disparity in the Netherlands between the exclusion from refugee protection of several hundreds of suspects of international crimes and the lack of subsequent criminal prosecutions); Schabas 2003b, p. 50-51; Elst 2000, p. 816; Schabas 1999, p. 531 ("[T]he lack of success of the Justice Department in prosecuting Nazi war criminals has resulted in a policy decision to remove war criminals from Canada under the Immigration Act rather than prosecute them in Canada."); Reydams 1996, p. 39-41; Hetherington and Chalmers 1989, p. 70-72 (on the U.S. policy to deport rather than prosecute war crimes suspects).

[612] See Cassese 2003a, p. 306 ("[N]ational courts have developed in their judicial practice a *restrictive tendency* to limit as much as possible the impact of international rules on the exercise of jurisdiction by national courts over international crimes.").

[613] See Lelieur-Fischer 2004, p. 236.

[614] See e.g. O'Keefe 2004, p. 758 (describing how political and practical considerations guided the Scottish and English legislatures in limiting the jurisdictional reach of their ICC implementing legislation).

[615] See Abdelgawad 2002, p. 393; Choukr 2002, p. 334.

critical attitude is motivated in part by the complexities of international criminal law. Yet often legislators, prosecutors and courts also entertain a desire to exert maximal control over the applicable law so as to be able to curtail and select the resulting prosecutions. Direct application, especially general but also on the basis of a specific rule of reference, does not afford maximal control. The international offences that are directly applied can not be changed as easily as those in a statute, nor be sidelined with measures like amnesty laws. Moreover, it is generally not readily apparent to what extent international law is incorporated in the national legal order and this extent may be subject to (rapid) change.[616]

National authorities hardly ever openly express their desire to control, curtail and select core crimes prosecutions. It is therefore impossible to say to what extent it influences their approach to direct application. Only occasionally do national authorities reveal that they are (also) guided by considerations of minimalism and selectivity in their approach to core crimes law. In *Tel-Oren v. Libyan Arab Republic* (1984), an American Circuit Court rejected direct application of the 1907 Hague Convention, relying heavily on the practical problems direct application would cause.[617] In *Handel v. Artukovic* (1985), an American District Court expressed even more clearly that it found the same treaty to be non-self-executing, not for legal reasons but because its direct application would "create insurmountable problems."[618] While these cases concerned civil rather than criminal proceedings, they are relevant for the question of direct application in core crimes prosecutions both as precedents on the non-self-executingness of the 1907 Hague Convention and because the considerations expressed by the courts largely pertain to criminal prosecutions as well.

There are other examples of courts openly expressing that practical considerations lead them to adopt a restrictive interpretation of the law under consideration.

---

[616] See Kirby 2004, p. 250; Röling 1979, p. 186.

[617] U.S., Circuit Court (D.C.Cir.), *Tel-Oren v. Libyan Arab Republic*, 1984, 726 F.2d 774 at 810 (Bork, J., concurring): "[T]he code of behavior the Conventions set out could create perhaps hundreds of thousands or millions of lawsuits by the many individuals, including prisoners of war, who might think their rights under the [1907] Hague Convention violated in the course of any large-scale war. Those lawsuits might be far beyond the capacity of any legal system to resolve at all, much less accurately and fairly; and the courts of a victorious nation might well be less hospitable to such suits against that nation or the members of its armed forces than the courts of a defeated nation might, perforce, have to be. Finally, the prospect of innumerable private suits at the end of a war might be an obstacle to the negotiation of peace and the resumption of normal relations between nations."

[618] U.S., District Court, *Handel v. Artukovic*, 31 January 1985, 601 F.Supp. 1421, at 1425:
"Unlike the Geneva Convention, there is no provision in the [1907] Hague Convention for implementation by the party states. However, the consequences of implying self-execution compel the conclusion that the treaty is not a source of rights enforceable by an individual litigant in a domestic court. Recognition of a private remedy under the Convention would create insurmountable problems for the legal system that attempted it; would potentially interfere with foreign relations; and would pose serious problems of fairness in enforcement.
[...Citing the practical considerations of Judge Bork in *Tel-Oren*]
For the reasons that Judge Bork outlined, this Court agrees that non-self-execution is the appropriate result."

In *Al-Adsani* (1996), an English Court of Appeals declined to set aside the immunity of the State of Kuwait in order to allow a claim for civil damages for torture. Lord Justice Stuart-Smith made it clear that his position was influenced by the practical consequences a contrary decision would entail, noting *inter alia* that a "vast number of people come to this country each year seeking refuge and asylum, and many of these allege that they have been tortured in the country whence they came."[619] A subsequent judgment of the ECtHR in this case accepted that the prohibition of torture has *jus cogens* status, but refused to find that the immunity of Kuwait violated the right of access to court of the applicant.[620] At least two of the judges conveyed that they had been influenced to a considerable extent by the practical implications of the matter. In a separate opinion, they noted that "there is much wisdom" in the considerations of Lord Justice Stuart-Smith and added that another outcome of the case would have as a result "that precisely those States which so far have been most liberal in accepting refugees and asylum seekers, would have had imposed upon them the additional burden of guaranteeing access to court for the determination of perhaps hundreds of refugees' civil claims for compensation for alleged torture."[621] Again, this example concerns civil rather than criminal proceedings. Still, it is not difficult to see how similar considerations may lead courts to reject direct application of international criminal law, which would at the very least complicate numerous States' policies of deportation instead of prosecution of foreign suspects of core crimes. All in all, a negative attitude towards core crimes prosecutions is not at all uncommon among national prosecutors and courts.[622] As

[619] U.K., Court of Appeal, *Al-Adsani v. Al-Sabah and Kuwait*, 12 March 1996, Lord Justice Stuart-Smith: "... A moment's reflection is enough to show that the practical consequences of the Plaintiff's submission would be dire. The courts in the United Kingdom are open to all who seek their help, whether they are British citizens or not. A vast number of people come to this country each year seeking refuge and asylum, and many of these allege that they have been tortured in the country whence they came. Some of these claims are no doubt justified, others are more doubtful. Those who are presently charged with the responsibility for deciding whether applicants are genuine refugees have a difficult enough task, but at least they know much of the background and surrounding circumstances against which the claim is made. The court would be in no such position. The foreign States would be unlikely to submit to the jurisdiction of the United Kingdom court, and in its absence the court would have no means of testing the claim or making a just determination...." Cited in ECtHR, *Al-Adsani v. United Kingdom*, 21 November 2001, para. 18.

[620] ECtHR, *Al-Adsani v. United Kingdom*, 21 November 2001.

[621] Id., Concurring Opinion of Judge Pellonpaa, joined by Judge Bratza.

[622] See e.g. Netherlands, Amsterdam Court of Appeals, *In re Pinochet*, 4 January 1995, 28 NYIL 363 (1997) at 364-365. In proceedings challenging the decision of the Public Prosecutor not to prosecute retired Chilean dictator Pinochet for torture upon his visit to the Netherlands in 1994, the Prosecutions Department asserted that such a prosecution would not only be "illusory," given practical problems such as the collection of evidence, but also "disproportionate and presumptuous." The Prosecutions Department even asserted that Pinochet's presence in the Netherlands, which was a fact of public knowledge, had not been established with certainty. The Amsterdam Court of Appeals upheld the decision of the Prosecutor, calling the complaint against it "manifestly ill-founded" and holding that "prosecution of Pinochet by the Dutch Public Prosecutions Department would encounter so many legal and practical problems that the Public Prosecutor was perfectly within his rights to decide not to prosecute." See on this decision Ingelse and Wilt 1996.

a result, the possibility of direct application is regularly ignored, or treated with a negative bias.

3. Sovereignty

The prosecution of core crimes regularly gives rise to considerations about State sovereignty.[623] The administration of criminal justice has always been and still is one of the most fundamental tasks of the State and is a core component of its sovereignty. General direct application of core crimes law, *id est* in the absence of a specific rule of reference, thus may be thought to infringe at least to some extent on the sovereign right of the State to shape its criminal law process to its liking. Appeals to sovereignty in the context of core crimes law fit within the broader discussion on the concept of sovereignty in contemporary international law.[624]

Practice provides some support for the argument that national courts should prosecute only crimes that have received explicit recognition in national law, either through transformation or a specific rule of reference, to safeguard the sovereignty of the State in its administration of criminal justice. In *Nulyarimma v. Thompson* (1999), for example, the Federal Court of Australia relied not only on the absence of a procedural framework and the principle of legality, but also on the sovereign character of the administration of criminal justice to reject jurisdiction over international crimes without an explicit national authorization.[625] It is hard to say to what extent sovereignty related considerations play a role in practice, but it can safely be assumed that *Nulyarimma* is not unique in this respect.[626]

---

[623] See Ferdinandusse 2004, p. 1050 and references cited there (on sovereignty based arguments in core crimes law).

[624] See Rubenfeld 2003; Kälin 2000, p. 118-128. Note in this regard that numerous writers have criticized the contemporary use of the notion of sovereignty as imprecise and confused. See Henkin 1999; Koskenniemi 1997, p. 225; Lauterpacht 1997; Henkin 1994. Cf. Koskenniemi 1989, p. 192-263.

[625] Australia, Federal Court, *Nulyarimma v. Thompson*, 1 September 1999, [1999] FCA 1192, para. 52, per Whitlam J., cited above, note 242.

[626] See e.g. Spain, Tribunal Supremo, *Guatemalan Genocide* Case, 25 February 2003, 42 ILM 686, para. II sub 1: "La jurisdicción es una de las expresiones de la soberanía del Estado. Es entendida como la facultad o potestad de juzgar, es decir, de ejercer sobre determinadas personas y en relación a determinados hechos, uno de los poderes del Estado, sometiéndolas, en el caso del derecho penal, al ius puniendi que la ley le atribuye."

Cf. Luxembourg, Court of Appeal, *Pinochet*, 11 February 1999, 119 ILR 360 at 363: "[T]he Luxembourg courts do not [...] become competent to exercise jurisdiction, in the absence of a legal provision establishing international jurisdiction consequent upon the accession of Luxembourg to the Torture Convention of 1984, having due regard to the significance of jurisdiction as a matter of public policy.";

Ukraine, Constitutional Court, *Conformity of the Constitution of Ukraine to the Rome Statute of the International Criminal Court (the Rome Statute case)*, 11 July 2001, para. 2.4; U.S., District Court, *Handel v. Artukovic*, 31 January 1985, 601 F.Supp. 1421 at 1428: "Unlike violations of federal statutes or the United States Constitution, no American legislative body has acted in any way with respect to customary international law. To imply a cause of action from the law of nations would completely defeat the critical right of the sovereign to determine whether and how international rights should be enforced in that municipality."

However, it should be noted that States' powers to shape their criminal laws are restricted primarily by the very fact that international law contains obligations for both States and individuals regarding the core crimes, rather than by the direct application of that body of law. After all, implementing legislation may give the State some opportunity to adapt core crimes law, but the substantial choices have already been made at the international level. Therefore, the extent to which State sovereignty can be protected by rejecting direct application and requiring implementing legislation is rather limited.[627]

4. Democratic Legitimacy

In democratic States, sovereignty-based considerations are partly tied to the democratic legitimacy of the criminal justice system.[628] International (criminal) law is not enacted by an elected legislature, and therefore its direct application injects democratic legal orders with a collection of norms that lack the democratic legitimacy of national law.[629] However, here also several caveats must be issued. First, like sovereignty, democratic legitimacy is not substantially furthered by requiring implementing legislation that does not leave any substantial choices. If one wants to enhance the quality of the law-making process, that improvement must take place where the law is actually made, which is on the international level.[630]

Second, the very assumption that all criminal law must be made on the national level through a democratic law-making process may be questioned. After all, the international dimension of core crimes law removes its legislative process at least partly from the sovereign prerogatives of individual States.[631] It is doubtful then

---

See also Cassese 2001c, p. 168: "States consider [...] the translation of international commands into domestic legal standards [as a] part and parcel of their sovereignty, and are unwilling to surrender it to international control. National self-interest stands in the way of a sensible regulation of this crucial area. As a consequence each State decides, on its own, how to make international law binding on State agencies and individuals and what status and rank to assign to it in the hierarchy of municipal sources of law.";
Perkins 1997, p. 483. Compare the 2001 Princeton Principles on Universal Jurisdiction, no. 3 (available at http://www1.umn.edu/humanrts/instree/princeton.html: "With respect to serious crimes under international law as specified in Principle 2 (1), national judicial organs may rely on universal jurisdiction even if their national legislation does not specifically provide for it.").

[627] Cf. Wouters 2004, p. 30-31; Ferdinandusse 2003, p. 123-125.

[628] See e.g. Belgium, Court of Arbitration, 10 July 2002: "By granting Parliament the power (a) to determine in what cases criminal proceedings are possible and what form they should take, and (b) to adopt legislation under which a penalty may be prescribed and applied, Articles 12.2 and 14 of the Constitution assure to all citizens that no action will be punishable and no penalty imposed except under regulations adopted by a democratically elected deliberative assembly." See also Henzelin 2002, p. 80. See for a more general discussion of democratic accountability and ICL Morris 2001.

[629] Cf. Kirby 2004, p. 243-246 and 248-249.

[630] See Pescatore 1987, p. 276.

[631] See Australia, Federal Court, *Nulyarimma v. Thompson*, 1 September 1999, [1999] FCA 1192, per Merkel J., dissenting, para. 136 ("[U]niversal crimes directly impact upon and attack "the interna-

whether this body of law can be measured by the same standards as national law. Moreover, democratic legitimacy is not the only benchmark of the rule of law.[632] In short, it is mistaken to apply the notions of sovereignty and democratic legitimacy to international core crimes law in the same way as they are applied to national criminal law.

Third, the opposition between a democratically sound national law and an undemocratic international law is at least partly an oversimplification. The different State organs that shape national law also play a role in the formation of international law.[633] Elected executives and legislatures are involved in the making of both custom and treaty through various actions, including negotiating and approving treaties, crafting national legislation and making statements on issues of international law.[634] Furthermore, they also have considerable powers to override the judiciary's contributions to international law, *inter alia* through legislation.[635] The balance between those organs is decidedly different on the national and international plane, and the democratic legitimacy of international law may be less than that of many national laws or at least more indirect, but it is not entirely absent.

All in all, considerations of democratic legitimacy do have their bearing on direct application of core crimes law in practice. Yet, as is the case for sovereignty, both the weight of and the optimal solutions for concerns over democratic legitimacy are doubftul in the case of core crimes law. In fact, it is a central feature of core crimes law that it bypasses the national legislature in order to directly regulate the behavior of individuals. One could think therefore that these concerns suggest a limitation of the scope of core crimes law and a strengthening of the democratic quality of the international law-making process rather than advocate against direct application.

5. Separation of Powers

Closely linked to the issues of sovereignty and democratic legitimacy are considerations about the separation of powers. Direct application of international offences in the absence of a specific rule of reference in national law can distort the balance between the different national actors involved in the making and application of criminal law.[636] It reduces the influence of the legislature and gives more power to

tional legal order" and cannot be considered purely internal matters of sovereign States."). See for a discussion of the characteristics of core crimes law below, Chapter V, para. 3.

[632] See for a particularly strong analysis Zakaria 2003, p. 239-256. Cf. Wouters 2004, p. 29-30.

[633] See Wouters 2004, p. 31.

[634] See e.g. Labrin and Bosly 1999, p. 292-293 (on the various legislative steps concerning core crimes in Belgium).

[635] See Boas 2004, p. 182-183 and Todres 1998, p. 187–88 (on the Australian legislature's, ultimately negative, consideration of legislation to reverse the doctrine of legitimate expectations derived from unincorporated treaties in the Australian *Teoh* case) and below, note 647.

[636] Cf. Kirby 2004, p. 243-246 and 248-249.

the executive to regulate penal matters through treaty law, as well as more discretion to the judiciary through the application of customary law.[637] In federal States, it may allow the federal government to regulate through treaties penal matters that are otherwise reserved for the states.[638]

In practice, separation of powers considerations appear to play a significant role in the rejection of direct application of various international offences. Particularly in common law States, the rejection of direct application of treaty law and the requirement of statutory authorization of extraterritorial jurisdiction are inspired considerably by the desire to preserve the position of the legislature.[639] Other States, predominantly civil law ones, with the same goal in mind ban custom rather than treaty from direct application.[640] However, while separations of powers considerations and their implications in practice take various forms in different States, as Chapter II indicates, it is apparent that they have their bearing on practice.

Meanwhile, by and large the same caveats apply as just set out for the related issues of sovereignty and democratic legitimacy. Distortion of the default separation of powers results primarily from the very existence of core crimes law, not just from its direct application. Rejecting direct application of core crimes law does not substantially enhance the position of the legislature, since its legitimate influence through implementing legislation is very limited. Furthermore, the distorting effect of direct application is real and significant, but should not be overstated. Most national legislatures have approved various steps in the development of core crimes law directly through legislation, e.g. on specific crimes and the cooperation with the *ad hoc* tribunals, and indirectly through control over the executive. Of course, this is only a limited form of control over this body of law. Yet, one can not say that the development of core crimes law has bypassed national legislatures entirely.

Nulyarimma v. Thompson (1999) provides a vivid illustration of the different possible approaches to separation of powers concerns. In this case, the Australian government successfully urged its Federal Court to reject direct application of the customary international criminalization of genocide, arguing *inter alia* that "the creation of new crimes is a matter of policy for the legislature, rather than the courts, to determine."[641] Therefore, the government contended, "the extent to which international criminal law is to be incorporated into domestic law and also whether Australia's international obligations are to be implemented domestically, is for the

[637] See Rogers 1999, p. 215 ("To say that the courts have an additional body of 'higher law' to apply, to be found in the whole amorphous body of customary international law, is to inject an enormously distorting overdose of additional power into the Judicial Branch.").

[638] An alteration of the division of competences between the federal government and the individual states can also take place through implementing legislation. See on this point Australia, High Court, *Polyukhovich v. The Commonwealth of Australia and Another*, 14 August 1991.

[639] See the paragraphs on England and Wales, the United States and Australia in ChapterII. See also Kirby 2004, p. 245-246; Collins 2002, p. 493.

[640] See e.g. Ferdinandusse *et al.* 2002, p. 344.

[641] Australia, Federal Court, *Nulyarimma v. Thompson*, 1 September 1999, [1999] FCA 1192, para. 166.

legislature alone to determine."[642] While the impact of this argument on the outcome of the case is unclear, the majority seemed to endorse it.[643] Dissenting Justice Merkel, however, firmly rejected the argument that a proper separation of powers required the courts to ignore the crime of genocide in the absence of implementing legislation. He accepted the contention that Australian courts can no longer create offences, as used to be the case under the common law.[644] Yet, he posited that the incorporation of existing international crimes in municipal law must be distinguished from the creation of new crimes, and is within the proper ambit of the courts' functions.[645]

The arguments and counter arguments in *Nulyarimma* neatly capture both the essence of the problem and its limits where it concerns core crimes law. The creation of new crimes without involvement of the legislature is indeed fundamentally problematic. This provides a solid argument against the direct application of treaty-based offences that neither reflect customary law nor have received the endorsement of the legislature, either through legislative approval of the treaty itself or through a rule of reference in national law. However, the judicial recognition of genocide, crimes against humanity and war crimes can hardly be said to amount to the creation of new offences, even if direct application may well contribute to their further development. States, including Australia, have consistently rejected the argument that they were making new crimes when adopting retrospective war crimes legislation and setting up the *ad hoc* tribunals.[646] It is not easy to see why that would be different for national courts, as long as they apply core crimes law within its international boundaries. Where courts go beyond those boundaries, the legislature can issue overriding legislation to correct them.[647]

But while direct application of core crimes law does not provide national courts with unchecked powers to create new crimes, it can give them considerable leeway to shape the legal framework for the prosecution of existing ones. Prosecutions under direct application of international criminal law often allow national courts flexibility in combining national and international rules.[648] Also, direct application of customary offences allows courts a certain measure of discretion in formulating the precise elements of those crimes. In this regard, it should be noted that there are significant differences between national and international courts when it comes to their discretion in the prosecution of international crimes. First, international courts

---

[642] Id.

[643] Id, para. 57.

[644] Id., para. 176.

[645] Id., para. 177-179.

[646] See below, note 1305 and Belgium, Law for the punishment of Genocide, Report of the Justice Commission, Belgian Senate, 1 December 1998, No. 1-749/3, para. II (B) sub 2. See also Turns 2004, p. 354.

[647] Cf. e.g. Art. 14 Canada's Crimes against Humanity and War Crimes Act 2000 (correcting the Canadian Supreme Court's holding in *Finta* that superior orders defense is available if no moral choice is possible even when orders are manifestly illegal). See also Stahn 2000, p. 206.

[648] See on this point below, notes 708-714 and accompanying text.

have a legal framework in their Statutes and rules that is more coherent and less flexible than the hodgepodge of national and international law from which national courts can choose. Second, international courts generally have greater expertise and are therefore less likely too err in their exercise of discretion. For national courts, which often lack a thorough grasp of the international law they apply, more flexibility suggests a greater likelihood of mistakes.[649] Finally, international courts arguably have more legitimacy to develop international criminal law. Supported by at least a large part of the international community, international courts may have a better claim to the inevitable law making function that comes with the exercise of judicial discretion than national courts do. Then again, it may be argued that the development of core crimes law requires the concerted efforts of the national and international judiciary alike, not either one by itself.

In summary, separation of powers considerations have considerable relevance for the question of direct application. The prominence and practical consequences of these considerations differ for various States, depending *inter alia* on their constitutional framework and the quality of their judiciary. Again, however, both the weight and implications of these considerations deserve critical scrutiny in particular cases.

6. Manageability of the Law

Once national authorities have decided to take action regarding the core crimes, an important consideration is the manageability of the law they are going to enact or apply. National law-makers and prosecutors often appear to favor national law as a basis for core crimes prosecutions over direct application of international criminal law because the former is more straightforward, accessible and familiar, and thus more "manageable," than the latter.[650] Simply put, the different actors involved in the enforcement of international core crimes law on the national level have good reasons to keep the law, and thereby their work, as simple as possible. This facilitates both the making of the law and its enforcement, prevents complications in its application and thereby enhances the chances for succesful prosecutions.

A preference for national law finds expression both on a practical and a more systematic level. As a practical matter, many national authorities have long regarded, and to a lesser extent still regard, international criminal law as a foreign enterprise full of hazards. This may encourage them, if only instinctively, to favor national law over international law as a basis for the prosecution of core crimes, and ordinary crimes over international crimes. In more systematic terms, there are good reasons in the making and application of law to choose the most simple solution, in order to minimize the risk of error and resulting flaws in the legal system. This consideration may prompt the same choices in a more reasoned manner. The trans-

[649] See below notes 660 and 676 for examples of such mistakes.

[650] See Lambert-Abdelgawad 2003, p. 569; Rowe 1991, p. 226.

formation of international offences into national law gives the legislature the welcome chance to clarify and supplement any points it finds unclear.[651]

Within national law, ordinary crimes may be preferred over specific international offences. It takes more time and effort to legislate on the core crimes with all their complications than simply extend jurisdiction for existing ordinary crimes like murder. For most prosecutors and courts, ordinary crimes are more familiar and easier to handle than international crimes.[652] They are normally better developed and yield more precedents to rely on.[653] Also, they are easier to prove. It is more difficult to establish genocidal intent, the existence of an armed conflict for war crimes or the context necessary for crimes against humanity, than to prove multiple counts of murder.[654] Therefore, it is generally more efficient and successful to prosecute on the basis of ordinary rather than international crimes where a choice is available.[655]

The difference in manageability of national and international law may weigh in heavily on the choices of legislatures and prosecutors alike. This is particularly, but not exclusively, so for States with a legal system of limited means and expertise in international law. International law is a complex and dynamic field, the proper understanding of which requires lengthy study. Most national actors in core crimes prosecutions, including courts, are not thoroughly trained in international law and can not fully grasp all its complexities in the limited time they can devote to its

---

[651] See Yuan and Jianping 2002, p. 356.

[652] See Nollkaemper 2003b, p. 292; Lukashuk 2001, p. 275.

[653] See Kirby 2004, p. 255-256; Haile 2000, p. 35.

[654] See e.g. Germany, Bavarian Higher Court (BayObLG), *Djajic*, 23 May 1997, 3 St 20/06, in 51 NJW (1998), 392-395, where the defendant was convicted on counts of murder and attempted murder but cleared from the charge of complicity in genocide since genocidal intent could not be proven. Cf. Colombia, Corte Constitucional, Sala Plena, *Sentencia C-578 (In re Corte Penal Internacional)*, 30 July 2002, 31 Jurisprudencia y Doctrina 2231 at 2273 (finding that Art. 20 (2) ICC Statute leaves States the possibility to prosecute suspects who have been acquitted by the ICC on the basis of ordinary crimes, implying that ordinary crimes may be proven where core crimes can not). See also Bremer 240-242.

[655] See Schabas 2002b, p. 260. Yet, this may not always be the case. It appears that a prosecution for genocide or war crimes rather than murder may have certain advantages, for example in cases where the body of the victim is missing or his identity can not be established. Cf. Switzerland, Military Court of Cassation, *In re N.*, 27 April 2001, para. 4b ("Une poursuite pénale pour violations des lois de la guerre n'implique pas en soi la mention précise de l'identité des victimes."). According to one commentator, the prosecution in the Ethiopian "Red Terror" trials preferred to charge the defendants with genocide rather than homicide because the latter charge would require each murder to be linked to the defendants whereas charges of genocide did not require such concrete linkage between every murder and every defendant. See Kidane 2003, p. 679 and 684. It is, however, unclear on which ground Kidane bases this assumption and it is likewise uncertain how this strategy has played out in the trials. Still, the difference in this regard may be highly dependent on the circumstances of the case and the form of responsibility to be charged, but it is indeed plausible that for example the ordering or inducing of genocide would be difficult to prosecute on the basis of separate charges of homicide where a concrete link between the defendant and these homicides could not be proved but his involvement in a general genocidal plan could.

examination. The intricacies of custom constitute a prime example,[656] but international law is complex in many other aspects.

International criminal law is no exception in this regard.[657] The recent experiences of the internationalized courts in Kosovo, Sierra Leone and East-Timor show that national judges who lack expertise may have great difficulties in handling international criminal law. Several commentators have detailed how numerous judgments in those courts have failed to properly apply different elements and concepts of core crimes law.[658] In part, this problem is one of adequate staffing, funding and support.[659] But those judgments from Kosovo, Sierra Leone and East-Timor also serve as a reminder that direct application of international criminal law is a very complex task. There are more cases that show how national courts struggle with international criminal law,[660] possibly leading to a general preference for national law over international law and ordinary crimes over international crimes.

---

[656] See numerous contributions on the application of international custom in national courts in 4 Non-State Actors and International Law, issue 1 (2004) and Wouters and Eeckhoutte 2002, p. 229-232.

[657] See Stahn 2000, p. 201.

[658] See Bertodano 2004, p. 99-920; Bertodano 2003, p. 232 and 239-241; Dickinson 2003, p. 305; Bohlander 2001 and various critical assessments of the case law of the Special Court for Sierra Leone in 2 Journal of International Criminal Justice iss. 4 (2004).

[659] See Bertodano 2003, p. 241; Dickinson 2003, p. 307.

[660] In the curious case of *Ex parte Thring* (2000), a British Court of Appeal held in no uncertain terms that the notion of an indiscriminate attack was too complicated for judicial review. See U.K., Court of Appeal (Civil Division), *R. v. Secretary of State ex parte Thring*, 20 July 2000, ICRC website, Clarke L.J.: "The court would face what seems to me to be an almost insuperable problem. In order to determine whether an attack was indiscriminate within art 51 (5)(b) of the Geneva Convention, it would be necessary to consider whether an attack or attacks might be expected to cause: '... incidental loss of civilian life, injury to civilians, damage to civilian objects, or a combination thereof, which would be excessive in relation to the concrete and direct military advantage anticipated.' This would involve a consideration of the military advantages concerned. For my part, while I see the force of the submissions made by the applicant, I do not think that the court could sensibly carry out an analysis of such a military advantages or disadvantages, which would involve a consideration of the activities of United Kingdom military operations over Iraq."
Bennett J.: "The fact that the courts are ill-equipped in these matters is graphically shown by the terms of para (5) of art 51 of the Geneva Convention, now in the Geneva Conventions (Amendment) Act 1995, [...I]t would be necessary to go into what happened on the occasions upon which the Royal Air Force used either missiles or bombs. It would then be necessary for the court to have evidence about the 'concrete and direct military advantage anticipated'; and, having had that, it would then be necessary for the court to exercise its judgment, as I read the paragraph, as to whether or not that advantage was excessive in relation to the incidental loss of civilian life, injury to civilians or damage to civilian objects, or a combination thereof. In my judgment, the resolution of such issues is not susceptible to judicial review."
While this concerned a civil case regarding an injunction to carry out military operations in Iraq, the language broadly disqualifies the ability of the judiciary to judge the notion of an indiscriminate attack, which is an element of certain war crimes, and shows the complexities national courts may encounter in enforcing humanitarian law. See also U.S., Court of Appeals, Ninth Circuit (Cal.), *Quinn v. Robinson*, 26 August 1997, 783 F.2d 776 at 799: "In Artukovic we erroneously assumed that 'crimes against humanity' was synonymous with 'war crimes,' and then concluded in a somewhat irrelevant fashion that not all war crimes automatically fall outside the ambit of the political offense exception. See 247 F.2d at 204. Our analysis was less than persuasive."
See also Kirby 2004, p. 251.

Some of the more active national authorities tacitly acknowledge the complexity of international core crimes law through the different measures they take to facilitate prosecutions. Several legislatures take measures to concentrate core crimes prosecutions in specific courts or districts, and install special prosecutorial units, both in order to foster expertise.[661] National courts often hear expert-witnesses to inform them on the requirements of international law when dealing with the core crimes.[662] Occasionally, they analyze the differences among the various possible legal bases explicitly. In the Canadian *Finta* case, one of the justices paid considerable attention to the manageability of the law underlying the prosecution. Justice La Forest considered the prosecution of war crimes and crimes against humanity on the basis of ordinary crimes to yield "obvious advantages."[663] Especially for the jury, which consists of lay men, the familiarity of national law was to be preferred over the complexities of international law, Justice La Forest found.[664]

It should be noted that for the legislature, the desire to keep its task as simple as possible may conflict with the aspiration to enact the best manageable legal basis for core crimes prosecutions. Together with a jurisdictional extension for ordinary crimes, a reference to international law is probably the most straightforward form of criminalization, especially for complex crimes. Thus, many States proscribe war

---

661 In the Netherlands, for example, core crimes prosecutions are brought by a special prosecutorial unit and held in the district court of The Hague. See Art. 15 WIM.

662 See e.g. Netherlands, Amsterdam Court of Appeals, In re Bouterse, 3 March 2000, NJ 2000/266, para. 5.4; Canada, Supreme Court, *R. v. Imre Finta*, 24 March 1994, para. 19 and 106; Poland, Voivodship Court of Warsaw, In re Koch, 9 March 1959, 30 ILR 496 at 503 and 509-510.

663 Canada, Supreme Court, *R. v. Imre Finta*, 24 March 1994, La Forest J. (dissenting), para. 261: "There are obvious advantages to the second approach [prosecuting on the basis of national ordinary crimes]. The judge and especially the jury are able to function largely pursuant to a system of law which, being our own, is more familiar to us and more precise. As much as possible, the intricacies of what constitutes international law and how it functions (with which even the judge is often unfamiliar) are avoided. The judge is able to instruct the jury secure in his or her knowledge of Canadian law. With the exception of international defences, which are available to the accused, the jury can then perform its function pursuant to Canadian law which demands proof beyond a reasonable doubt that the accused committed the offence – a Canadian offence – with which he or she is charged."

664 Id. See also para. 322-323: "[E]ven among the authorities, much confusion exists as to the distillation of the contents of international law. No clear articulation of the physical and mental elements of the international offences of war crimes and crimes against humanity and their defences is found among scholars in this area. This confusion is understandable and unavoidable in our system of international law among sovereign nations. Although some aspect of these offences are delineated in conventions, this is not the case for all; another important source of international law is custom. To establish custom, an extensive survey of the practices of nations is required. It is, of course, not an answer to this complicated task to say that the contents of international offences are too difficult to distill and, therefore, that the accused cannot be found guilty; the confusion is the reality of the international law which Canada has obliged itself to observe and apply. This abandonment of international obligation, however, is likely to occur where the jury is called upon to determine the contents of the international offences. The necessary confusion could mislead the jury into believing that international norms are not really law and opens the door to manipulative lawyering."

crimes by reference to "the laws and customs of war," and/or specific treaties.[665] Such rules of reference facilitate the work of the legislature, but leave it the judicial authorities to sort out the hard questions of ascertaining and applying the relevant international rules. Hence, there may be a certain conflict of interest in workload between the various national actors involved.

Three caveats regarding the manageability of the law are in order at this point. First, although core crimes law is complex and contains many open questions, there are various instruments that make it more manageable, also for non-experts. The legal instruments of the various international tribunals provide authoritative codifications of customary law. The case law of those tribunals provides further guidance on numerous important principles and questions. Finally, there are many doctrinal works that offer reliable and comprehensive support. These different sources certainly do not address all areas of confusion, and sometimes contradict each other. Also, national courts may have problems locating and accessing the most authoritative ones and distinguishing those from the ones that are partisan, parochial or otherwise of lesser value.[666] Yet, the abundance of codification, case law and doctrine in core crimes law does mitigate its complexity to a considerable extent.

Second, the extent to which national law can remedy the complexities of core crimes law is limited. National law can only clarify or replace international offences within the boundaries set by international law. Whatever legal basis one chooses for a core crimes prosecution, questions about the content of the relevant international rules will often come up in one way or another. The *Finta* case provides a suitable illustration.[667] The choice to prosecute WW II war crimes and crimes against humanity on the basis of ordinary crimes like robbery, kidnapping and manslaughter did not relieve the prosecutor and court from confronting difficult questions of international criminal law, with fatal consequences in this particular case.[668] The usefulness of interposing rules of national law to mitigate the hard questions of international law may therefore be questioned.

Third, the argument that international core crimes law is too complex to form the basis for national prosecutions is put in perspective by the fact that national courts regularly apply it in other contexts. National courts of various, but certainly not all, States are quite comfortable directly applying complex concepts of international criminal law in many cases concerning the exclusion of asylum seekers from

---

[665] The reason that many States choose an open-ended rule of reference for war crimes is probably practical and connected to the extensive, complex and until recently uncodified body of humanitarian law. Unlike genocide, the definition of war crimes is no easy task for a legislator. Now that the ICC Statute provides an elaboration of (most) war crimes, many national laws refer to that Statute. See above, Chapter II, para. 3.2.

[666] See Mendelson 2004, p. 80; Burke-White 2002, p. 67-68.

[667] See above, note 73 and accompanying text.

[668] In short, the Canadian Supreme Court required proof of the *actus reus* and *mens rea* of both the ordinary crimes under Canadian criminal law and the underlying international crimes. The high requirements of proof of the knowledge of the defendant that he was committing international crimes, as well as the broad acceptance of defences like superior orders and mistake of fact, led to the acquittal of the defendant. See Turns 2004, p. 356-358; Fletcher 2002, p. 455-458; Cotler 1996.

refugee status,[669] civil damage claims for core crimes,[670] various forms of civil disobedience against the military[671] and even the occasional libel case.[672] Quite a few of those cases apply core crimes law in detail in a manner that is not fundamentally different from their application in a criminal proceeding.[673]

Criminal proceedings generally require higher standards than non-criminal ones, but in practice the difference is not always obvious.[674] Also, procedural variations like those in the standard of proof do not touch on the question whether the law is sufficiently clear for direct application. These non-criminal cases show that national courts regularly consider core crimes law to be sufficiently manageable to form the legal basis for judgments that stigmatize individuals as core crimes perpetrators and attach practical consequences that can be as severe as criminal penalties.[675] Still, the import of such non-criminal proceedings should not be overstated. Several of those administrative and civil proceedings apply core crimes law in a cursory or incorrect manner and thus lend support to the argument that international law is complex, rather than contradict it.[676]

In conclusion, considerations of manageability and effectiveness may well argue in favor of using national law and ordinary crimes rather than international law

---

[669] See Handmaker 2003; Schabas 2003b, p. 50-51; Zegveld 2001.

[670] See numerous cases under the U.S. Alien Tort Claims Act, e.g. U.S., District Court (Cal.), *Sarei v. Rio Tinto PLC*, 9 July 2002, 221 F.Supp.2d 1116 (finding that Papua New Guinea residents provided *prima facie* evidence of war crimes and crimes against humanity, including genocide, against international mining group) and U.S., Court of Appeals (Second Circuit), *Kadic v. Karadzic*, 13 October 1995, 70 F.3d 232. See also Japan, Tokyo District Court, *Shimoda et al. v. The State*, 7 December 1963 (examining at length the legality of the atomic bombing of Hiroshima and Nagasaki under international humanitarian law).

[671] See e.g. U.K., Court of Appeal, *Jones & Milling, Olditch & Pritchard, Richards v. Gloucestershire Crown Prosecution Service*, 21 July 2004, [2004] EWCA Crim 1981; Scotland, High Court of Justiciary Appeal Court, *Angela Zelter v. Bodil Ulla Roder, Ellen Moxley*, 30 March 2001, para, 65-99; U.K., Queens Bench Division, Hipperson v. DPP, 3 July 1996, [1996] C.L.Y. 1445.

[672] See U.K., High Court of Justice Queen's Bench Division, *Ken Lukowiak v. Unidad Editorial SA*, 6 July 2001, para. 30-38 (libel case for accusation of war crime committed in the Anglo-Argentinean war over the Falkland/Malvinas Islands).

[673] See e.g. U.S., District Court, *Mehinovic et al. v. Vuckovic*, 2 May 2002, 198 F.Supp.2d 1322, described above, Chapter II, para. 3.3.g. Cf. Netherlands, HR, *In re Kesbir*, 7 May 2004 (In this case concerning the extradition of an alleged PKK-leader to Turkey, both the Attorney-General and the defense argued extensively on the applicability of the humanitarian law of internal armed conflicts to the situation in Turkey as well as the question whether the Turkish military could be a legitimate target under that body of law, but the Supreme Court did not reach a decision on these points.)

[674] Cf. Wagner 1989, p. 895-897 (concluding that denaturalization and deportation proceedings in the U.S. often require the government to prove that the individual actually committed a war crime or crime against humanity while the U.S. Supreme Court has determined that the burden of proof in these proceedings is "substantially identical with that required in criminal cases").

[675] See above, notes 341 and 343.

[676] For example, Dutch proceedings regarding the exclusion of refugees on the basis of Art. 1F Refugee Convention regularly conflate crimes against humanity with human rights violations, or summarily and questionably assume that the latter amount to the former. See e.g. Netherlands, The Hague District Court, 29 August 2003; Netherlands, The Hague District Court, 11 July 2002; Zegveld 2001. See also above, note 660.

and international crimes as a basis for prosecution. Yet although there are good reasons to choose the most simple option available, the case for national law is not clear-cut. National courts will generally have to delve into questions of international law regardless of the legal basis of the charges. While there are various national judgments that illustrate the errors and complications that can result from direct application of core crimes law, other cases demonstrate that national courts are not as a general rule incapable of performing that task.

7. Development and Coherence of Core Crimes Law

The legal basis enacted and applied for national prosecutions has implications for the development and coherence of core crimes law. After all, the formation and development of legal rules take place through their formulation, interpretation and application.[677] These are more fundamental considerations that do not often seem to play a role in practice. Yet, occasionally they may figure directly or indirectly in the decision making processes of the different actors involved.[678] Also, with the continuing development of ICL these more fundamental systemic considerations may gain significance. They will therefore be treated here.

First, it may be asked how the legal basis for core crimes prosecutions affects their contributing value for the development of ICL. Formulating specific national legislation regarding the core crimes gives the legislature not only the power to control the implementation of core crimes law on the national level but also a voice in its development on the international level. It leads to State practice and contributes to the development of customary ICL. The broadening of protected groups in many national definitions of genocide, for example, fuels a corresponding trend in customary international law that would not otherwise take place, or at least not with the same force.[679]

Prosecuting core crimes directly on the basis of their international offences leaves more power to interpret and develop core crimes law for the judiciary, at the expense of the legislature's influence. The flexible nature of judicial development can prove an advantage in a rapidly changing field like ICL. On the other hand, the shift of influence from the legislature to the judiciary may imply a diminution of the clarity and authoritativeness of State practice, at least when the law in question is applied only seldomly or in an incoherent fashion, as is the case for core crimes law in many States. In such circumstances, legislation may carry more weight than case

---

[677] While this process is inherent in the very nature of customary international law, it is also of obvious importance for the clarification and development of treaty law.

[678] See e.g. Canada, Supreme Court, *R. v. Imre Finta*, 24 March 1994, La Forest J. (dissenting), para. 323 ("Not only is the judge better trained than the jury in evaluating international law, but, in fact, his or her interpretation of international law bears some force internationally.").

[679] See above, Chapter II, para. 2.2.b and, on the current status of this trend in contemporary international law below, note 730.

law due to its general scope, the authority and democratic legitimacy of its source, and its (at least relative) clarity.

However, an important factor in the development of international law is the judicial dialogue that takes place when different courts interpret the same concepts and take into account each other's case law.[680] The more the law applied in national prosecutions diverges from the corresponding international law, the more this exchange is distorted. Therefore, direct application of international criminal law may have the advantage of fostering a more direct dialogue between different courts that apply the same law, and expounding the international law itself rather than a national reproduction of it.[681] The value for other courts of core crimes prosecutions on the basis of ordinary criminal law will often be rather limited, while prosecutions on the basis of national law that specifically deals with the core crimes probably occupies the middle ground, depending *inter alia* on the extent to which this national law diverges from the underlying international rules.

A recent study of the various ways the ICTY has used national judgments as sources of international criminal law illustrates that the legal basis for national core crimes prosecutions may well influence their value for other courts.[682] The ICTY has on several occasions qualified the value as a precedent of core crimes prosecutions on the basis of national law. In *Tadic*, the Trial Chamber commented on the judgment of the French Cour de Cassation in *Barbie*:

> "While instructive, it should be noted that the court in the *Barbie* case was applying national legislation that declared crimes against humanity not subject to statutory limitation, although the national legislation defined crimes against humanity by reference to the United Nations resolution of 13 February 1946, which referred back to the Nürnberg Charter…."[683]

In *Furundzija*, the Trial Chamber warned that "for a correct appraisal of [the] case law, it is important to bear in mind, with each of the cases to be examined, the forum in which the case was heard, as well as the law applied, as these factors determine its authoritative value."[684] It then commented on the case law of British military courts that "the law applied was domestic, thus rendering the pronouncements of the British courts less helpful in establishing rules of international law on this issue. However, there is sufficient similarity between the law applied in the

---

[680] See Schabas 2003b, p. 63 ("More diversity and debate as the [national and international] levels of jurisdiction interact can only stimulate legal clarity."); Burke-White 2002, p. 90-95; Crawford 2001, p. 30; note 2001, p. 2061-2062; Buergenthal 1992, p. 394. But see for criticism of the international judicial dialogue in general Rosenkrantz 2003.

[681] Cf. Criddle 2004, p. 497-498.

[682] See Nollkaemper 2003b.

[683] ICTY, Trial Chamber, *Tadic*, 7 May 1997, para. 642. Note that this reading ignores the declarative rather than constitutive nature of the reference to the Nuremberg Charter in French law. See above, Chapter II, para. 3.3.j.

[684] ICTY, Trial Chamber, *Furundzija*, 10 December 1998, para. 194.

British cases and under Control Council Law No. 10 for these cases to merit consideration."[685]

So, there are signs that the legal basis of national prosecutions indeed makes up a significant determining factor for their value as a legal precedent for other courts, and thus for their contribution to the development of core crimes law. Then again, the differences in this regard should not be overstated as the reliance by international and other national courts on national judgments depends on many other factors besides their legal basis.[686] Also, a desire to strengthen the national rule of law rather than worry about the development of international criminal law may result in a conscious decision to prosecute on the basis of ordinary crimes, especially for States with an underdeveloped or threatened legal system.[687]

Second, there is the question how the legal basis for national prosecutions affects the coherence of core crimes law. The multitude of national and international voices, both legislative and judicial, involved in the development of core crimes law can easily lead to a lack of harmony. This is only a particular variant of the classical tension between the development and coherence of (customary) international law. Yet, the penal character of core crimes law makes this tension decidedly intense, and heightens the need for coherence.[688] After all, coherence of the law partly determines the legal certainty of the individual, which is a fundamental concern in criminal law.[689] Therefore, both the development of core crimes law and the legal certainty of the individual require at least a minimal measure of coherence of the law used in national prosecutions.[690]

Obviously, unity of law does not guarantuee harmony in its application by different courts. ICL is replete with examples where courts have interpreted and applied the same law in different ways.[691] The ICTY and the ICTR, for example, have developed significantly diverging case law on issues like the definition of rape,

---

685 ICTY, Trial Chamber, *Furundzija*, 10 December 1998, para. 196. See also ICTY, Appeals Chamber, *Erdemovic*, 7 October 1997, para. 52-55.

686 See Dickinson 2003, p. 304-308. Obviously, the accessibility of the judgment concerned is an important factor, which in turn depends *inter alia* on its language and source of publication. Cf. Stirling-Zanda 2000, p. 260-274. Moreover, courts often seem to be guided by other considerations in their use of case law than methodological concerns over the law applied. See for an analysis of other factors that determine the extent and significance of the international judicial dialogue Helfer and Slaughter 1997; Slaughter 1994.

687 See e-mail interview of 30 March 2003 with Brian Concannon, on file with the author (stating that the Bureau des Avocats Internationaux preferred to prosecute human rights violations in Haiti on the basis of national rather than international law in order to strengthen the rule of Haitian law).

688 See ICTY, Appeals Chamber, *Aleksovski*, 24 March 2000, para. 113: "The need for coherence is particularly acute in the context in which the Tribunal operates, where the norms of international humanitarian law and international criminal law are developing, and where, therefore, the need for those appearing before the Tribunal, the accused and the Prosecution, to be certain of the regime in which cases are tried is even more pronounced."

689 See further below, Chapter VI, para. 5.3 (on the foreseeability of core crimes law).

690 Cf. Delmas-Marty 2003, p. 21.

691 See e.g. Ziegler 1998, p. 81 (on the divergent interpretation of the international or non-international nature of the armed conflict in the former Yugoslavia by the Swiss courts and the ICTY).

cumulative charging, the existence of a hierarchy of international crimes and the question of whether the *mens rea* of murder as a crime against humanity requires premeditation.[692] Between the criminal courts of various States, different national conceptions of relevant elements may lead to divergent interpretation and application of identical offences.[693] Still, unity of law may not solve all problems, but it provides a better chance on a more or less coherent body of case law regarding the core crimes than a situation in which national courts all apply their own divergent laws.

The need for coherence of core crimes law finds clear recognition in practice. There is no principle of *stare decisis* in international criminal law.[694] Judgments of international criminal tribunals do not form binding precedents even for their own subsequent proceedings, let alone for national courts.[695] Yet, the different actors involved in the enforcement of core crimes law strive for coherence of the law and its application in various ways. Several recent national laws regarding core crimes not only refer to the offences in the ICC Statute, or copy them, but also require or allow their courts to take into account the way these offences are interpreted in the Elements of Crimes and/or applied by the ICC.[696] Other legislatures have expressed

---

[692] See respectively Chinkin 2003, p. 144-149; Haveman 2003b and Dörmann 2001, p. 131 (rape); Stuckenberg 2001, p. 573-585 (cumulative charging); Nemitz 2001, p. 615 and Seiderman 2001, p. 230-232 (hierarchy of crimes) and Cumes 2003, p. 53-55 (premeditation).

[693] See Netherlands, Bijzondere Raad van Cassatie, *Ahlbrecht II*, 11 April 1949, NJ 1949/425; Partial English translation in Annual Digest 1949, No. 141, at p. 396-397 (on the different forms of homicide in national laws and their consequences for the interpretation of murder as a crime against humanity).

[694] See ICTY, Trial Chamber, *Kupreskic*, 14 January 2000, para. 540. See also Ferdinandusse 2004, p. 1048-1051.

[695] See Art. 21(2) ICC Statute ("The Court *may* apply principles and rules of law as interpreted in its previous decisions." – emphasis added). The *ne bis in idem* rule requires acceptance of specific judgments as final, but does not make them legal precedents in a wider sense. See Art. 20 ICC Statute, Art. 10 ICTY Statute and Art. 9 ICTR Statute.

[696] See e.g. UK, Art. 50 International Criminal Court Act 2001:
"(1) In this Part:
'genocide' means an act of genocide as defined in article 6 [ICC Statute],
'crime against humanity' means a crime against humanity as defined in article 7, and
'war crime' means a war crime as defined in article 8.2.
(2) In interpreting and applying the provisions of those articles the court shall take into account:
(a) any relevant Elements of Crimes adopted in accordance with article 9
[...]
(5) In interpreting and applying the provisions of the articles referred to in subsection (1) the court shall take into account any relevant judgment or decision of the ICC. Account may also be taken of any other relevant international jurisprudence."
See likewise Art. 65 (5) and 66 (4). See also New Zealand, Art. 12 International Crimes and International Criminal Court Act 2000 (General principles of criminal law):
"[...]
(4) For the purposes of interpreting and applying articles 6 to 8 of the Statute in proceedings for an offence against section 9 or section 10 or section 11, ---
(a) the New Zealand Court exercising jurisdiction in the proceedings may have regard to any elements of crimes adopted or amended in accordance with article 9 of the Statute."

their expectation that national law will be interpreted in conformity with the case law of the ICC and other international courts during the drafting process rather than in the implementing legislation itself.[697] National courts occasionally correct the legislature in order to safeguard harmony in core crimes law.[698] In general, both national and international courts foster coherence of the law where possible and even recognize an informal hierarchy of precedents, topped by the international courts that carry most authority and expertise.[699]

Coherence of the law is a relevant consideration, but it does not unambiguously plead for national or international law as a basis for core crimes prosecutions.[700] On the one hand, direct application of ICL ensures that national and international courts apply the same law and facilitates the judicial dialogue.[701] At this point, it is pertinent to note the subtle difference between a rule of reference to an international criminalization and a seemingly identical national criminalization of an international crime. It may be thought that it makes no difference whether a national law refers to an international criminalization like Art. 2 Genocide Convention or contains a verbatim reproduction of it, and often this will be true. Still, there can be a significant difference in the way national courts interpret these offences.[702] In many States, provisions of national law are interpreted according to national rules of in-

[697] See e.g. Werle 2003, p. 232-234. But compare Boas 2004, p. 186-189 (on the Australian declaration accompanying its ratification of the ICC Statute that the core crimes "will be interpreted and applied in a way that accords with the way they are implemented in Australian domestic law").

[698] See e.g. the repeated invalidations of national laws implementing provisions from the Geneva Conventions in a flawed manner by the Hungarian Constitutional Court, above, Chapter II, para. 3.3.n. See particularly Hungary, Constitutional Court, *Decision No. 36/1996*, 4 November 1996, para. 1: "En effet, la Loi rapproche les différentes dispositions concernant les champs d'application matériel et personnel des Conventions de Genève et de ce fait elle crée des rapports inexistants dans les Conventions. Ainsi, elle modifie le contenu des Conventions de Genève, viole l'harmonie entre le droit international et le droit interne, empêche l'application des principes généralement reconnus du droit international." Unofficial translation from website ICRC.

[699] See e.g. ICTR, Appeals Chamber, *Semanza, Decision*, 31 May 2000, Separate Opinion of Judge Shahabuddeen, in particular para. 25-32; ICTY, Appeals Chamber, *Aleksovski*, 24 March 2000, para. 107 and 113. See also Ferdinandusse 2004, p. 1051; Jones and Powles 2003, p. 370-371. But see Switzerland, Military Court of Cassation, *In re N.*, 27 April 2001, para. 9d (finding that there is no need to analyze certain differences in interpretation of the law between the Swiss Court of Appeal and the ICTR: "Il n'y a donc pas lieu d'analyser de façon plus approfondie cette prétendue divergence dans l'interprétation des normes du droit international humanitaire. En revanche, il convient de vérifier si, dans l'application de ces critères sur la base des faits constatés de manière non arbitraire, le Tribunal d'appel a considéré à juste titre que les éléments constitutifs du délit de l'Art. 109 CPM étaient réunis.").

[700] Cf. Bridge 1964, p. 1260.

[701] See Wible 2002, p. 266 and 295: "Domestic courts should incorporate as much international law, including both substantive and procedural standards, as possible into prosecutions for international crimes. [...] Because the crimes at issue are violations of universal norms, it is essential that national prosecutions maintain an international character and that there be formal mechanisms to prevent divergence from certain core universal touchstones. Harmonizing international criminal law will lead to a more coherent body of law, will better protect defendants from deficient prosecutions, and will act as a restraint on unjust exercise of extraterritoriality." Cf. Wouters and Panken 2003, p. 13-14 and 37. But see Delmas-Marty 2003, p. 23.

[702] Cf. Criddle 2004, p. 449-463.

terpretation, while directly applicable treaty provisions are interpreted according to international rules of treaty interpretation as codified in the VCLT.[703] While it is not self-evident that the general rules of treaty interpretation are suitable for ICL,[704] national courts may look primarily to international sources to decide questions of interpretation for directly applicable international offences, but turn to national sources like the drafting process of the national law to interpret homonymous national provisions.[705] Therefore, incorporation of international provisions may provide greater coherence of international law than transformation.

On the other hand, the coherence stemming from direct application should not be idealized. National courts can render very divergent interpretations of international law, particularly custom. Where this is the case, national legislatures may lay down a more authoritative interpretation of international rules in national law. Although legislatures can also differ in their reading of the law, they will often bring unity to diverging case law and thus provide a welcome increase of coherence, at least within the national legal order. Plus, the difference between national and international rules of interpretation set out above will in practice often be minimal or even none. After all, when interpreting national implementing laws courts often resort to international law in order to ascertain either the intent of the legislature, which is normally to give effect to the underlying international law, or the spirit or purpose of the law.[706] Conversely, national courts regularly pay lip-service to the international rules of treaty interpretation while they do not in fact follow them, adopting a more nationalist interpretation instead.[707] Thus, whether national or international law as a basis for core crimes prosecutions brings greater coherence in

---

[703] See e.g. Argentina, Supreme Court, 23 December 1997, CODICES ARG-1998-1-002 (International treaties must be interpreted in accordance with Art. 31 and 32 VCLT). See also Ferdinandusse 2001, p. 281; Bremer 1999, p. 362; Buergenthal 1992, p. 362-363; Partsch 1992, p. 250-251. Cf. Criddle 2004 (analyzing how U.S. courts have traditionally adhered to international rules of treaty interpretation but are currently divided); Zemanek 1998, p. 191.

[704] See Tournaye 2003, p. 454; Schabas 2002a, p. 167-171; Schabas 2000a, p. 541-543. See also ICTY, Trial Chamber, *Vasiljevic*, 29 November 2002, para. 193-204. See for criticism of this decision Cassese 2004b and Weckel and Chaouch Helel 2003, p. 751-759.

[705] Cf. Partsch 1992, p. 246; Sinclair 1984, p. 274-275.

[706] Resort to international law may therefore be required by quite general provisions on interpretation. See e.g. Art. 2 (3) Ethiopian Penal Code: "In cases of doubt the court shall interpret the law according to its spirit, in accordance with the meaning intended by the legislature so as to achieve the purpose it has in view." See Haile 2000, p. 48-49. Likewise, the classification of national provisions, for example in a title of the penal code concerning offenses against the law of nations, may indicate recourse to underlying international law. See Haile 2000, p. 53. See also U.K., House of Lords, *R. v. Bow Street Metropolitan Stipendiary Magistrate & Others, Ex Parte Pinochet Ugarte (No. 3)*, 24 March 1999, [2000] 1 A.C. 147 at 163: "Section 134 refers without qualification to 'public officials' or persons acting in an official capacity. A former head of state cannot be excluded from its ambit. The ordinary meaning of the words does not support limitation, and, as a provision giving effect to the United Kingdom's obligations under a Convention it should, where possible, be construed compatibly with those obligations."

[707] See Lambert-Abdelgawad 2003, p. 566-567 ("[L]es interprétations nationalisées du droit international sont la règle courante").

practice depends on different factors, *inter alia* the clarity of the international norms and national courts' practice of interpretation.

The need for coherence plays out not only for core crimes law in general, but also in individual cases. A case in point is the prosecution of the Rwandan *bourgmestre* N. in Switzerland.[708] The different courts in this case frequently referred to the international character of the prosecution and the practice of the ICTR, also when deciding points that were regulated by Swiss law. A leading principle in striking the balance between Swiss and international law, however, seemed to be lacking, as can be seen in the judgment of the Military Court of Cassation (2001). In ruling that the defendant could be charged with the murder of unnamed victims, the Court stated that whatever the procedure of the ICTR may be on that point, the Swiss courts would follow their own.[709] Yet, when the credibility of the testimony of traumatized and illiterate survivors was contested, the Court relied heavily on the practice of the ICTR to justify the use of partly inaccurate statements.[710] Similarly, the Court treated the findings of the ICTR as decisive for the question whether the situation in Rwanda amounted to a non-international armed conflict, but subsequently dismissed its authority when analyzing the nexus between the crimes and the armed conflict.[711] Unlike the Court of Appeal, however, the Court of Cassation considered it convenient to apply the criteria of the ICTR on this point.[712] Finally, the Court of Cassation ignored the practice of the ICTR again when judging the suitability of the sentence, stating *inter alia* that the national sentencing criteria might be different from those of the ICTR.[713] In short, it is unclear why national

---

[708] See above, Chapter II, para. 3.3.c.

[709] Switzerland, Military Court of Cassation, *In re N.*, 27 April 2001, para. 4b: "Une poursuite pénale pour violations des lois de la guerre n'implique pas en soi la mention précise de l'identité des victimes. [...] L'accusé se prévaut encore d'une règle prétendument applicable devant le TPIR, selon laquelle, en cas d'accusation de violation de l'Art. 3 commun, les victimes devraient être nommément visées. Dans sa motivation, l'accusé ne renvoie à aucune norme du Statut ou du règlement de procédure de ce Tribunal, ni à aucun élément précis de sa jurisprudence. Quoi qu'il en soit, les juridictions suisses n'ont pas à appliquer les règles de procédure étrangères ou internationales. Quant à celles du droit suisse (Art. 147 PPM), elles ont été respectées dans le cas particulier. Ce motif de cassation est en conséquence mal fondé."

[710] Id., para. 6b.

[711] Id., para. 3d and 9d: "Le TPIR a en effet admis, dans les jugements de ses Chambres de première instance où la question devait être résolue, que les événements ou les massacres de population au Rwanda entre avril et juillet 1994 s'inscrivaient dans le contexte d'un conflit armé interne [...] Le Tribunal militaire de cassation, en tant que Cour suprême, interprète de façon autonome l'Art. 109 CPM. [...] Les critères utilisés par les Chambres de première instance du TPIR pour déterminer si l'Art. 3 commun et le Protocole II ont été violés ne doivent pas nécessairement être repris dans la jurisprudence nationale suisse."

[712] Id., para. 9d: "Dans le cas particulier, il convient donc de reprendre [the ICTR] critères et de les interpréter en fonction de la situation concrète de l'accusé. C'est maladroitement que le Tribunal d'appel a affirmé s'écarter de l'actuelle jurisprudence du TPIR dès lors que, ce nonobstant, il a en définitive appliqué au cas particulier des critères correspondant à ceux que l'on vient d'exposer."

[713] Id., para. 13b: "Il est vrai que les Chambres de première instance du TPIR ont prononcé des peines plus sévères à l'encontre de responsables du génocide ou des massacres au Rwanda, notamment à l'encontre du bourgmestre de Taba, Jean-Paul Akayesu, mais cet élément n'est pas déterminant. Il

law prevailed over international practice on some issues, but not on others. Such selective reliance on international law is not uncommon in national prosecutions of core crimes.[714] One could think that a more principled and explicit procedure for balancing the relevant national and international rules would be desirable, if only to eliminate the appearance of what could be called "law shopping" by national judges. This consideration does not so much favor any particular legal basis but rather requires a clear and consistent choice in this respect.

All in all, considerations regarding the development and coherence of core crimes law do not clearly point to national or international law as the preferred basis for core crimes prosecutions. While national criminalization of the core crimes makes a stronger legislative contribution to the development of ICL, direct application of international offences bears more judicial influence and stimulates the international judicial dialogue. Likewise, the coherence of core crimes law may benefit both from direct application of international norms and from their codification and clarification in national law. Prosecutions on the basis of ordinary crimes, however, constitute the least preferred option when considering the development and coherence of core crimes law.

8. Underinclusion and Overinclusion

The possible legal bases for core crimes prosecutions vary considerably in the acts they criminalize. It has been noted time and again that essentially every single national law shows lacunae in the criminalization of the core crimes.[715] But simultaneously, national definitions regularly cover acts which can not properly be characterized as core crimes. In other words, national criminal law is often both underinclusive and overinclusive at the same time. Thus, the choice between national and international law as a basis for the prosecution of core crimes can have significant consequences for the ability of States to fulfill their obligations under international law. Therefore, underinclusion and overinclusion of the different potential legal bases are noteworthy considerations for the decision which law to enact or apply.

A lack of congruence with the underlying international law characterizes both ordinary and international offences in national law. Ordinary offences are often underinclusive. Leaving aside for now the international dimension and contextual element of the core crimes, discussed above, national law regarding ordinary crimes simply does not cover numerous specific acts that make up core crimes. This is

n'est pas certain d'une part que les critères adoptés dans le Statut de ce Tribunal international pour la fixation de la peine correspondent à ceux de l'Art. 44 CPM…"

[714] See Bridge 1964, p. 1260.

[715] See Schabas 2003b, p. 62; Jessberger 2003, p. 283; Cassese 2002, p. 561; Swart 2002b, p. 569; Wolfrum 1996, p. 242; Fugard 1989, p. 43-44. See on the situation in particular States e.g. Benillouche 2002, p. 173 (France); Lambert-Abdelgawad 2002, p. 529 and 535 (Islamic States); Hettinger 1965, p. 123 (Germany). Cf. Ambos 2002b, p. 499 (Latin-American States).

often the case for non-homicidal acts that amount to war crimes or crimes against humanity.[716] Pertinent examples include unjustifiable delay in the repatriation of prisoners of war, which constitutes a grave breach under AP I,[717] and certain acts of persecution.[718] Perhaps focusing too much on the most obvious and violent core crimes, which correspond to ordinary crimes like murder and rape, States easily overestimate the extent to which their ordinary criminal law covers the core crimes.[719]

At the same time, ordinary offences are generally also overinclusive. The broad definitions of ordinary criminal law cast the net far wider than the more specific ones in international core crimes law. For example, if one prosecutes a killing in war as murder or manslaughter, the question of military necessity is left out of the definition of the crime. As a result, killings that are justified under the laws of war may fulfill the definition of murder. In some States, their legitimacy under humanitarian law will then serve as a ground of justification, leading the defendant to be classified as a "*gerechtfertigter Straftäter,*" whereas the killing should not have been classified as a crime at all.[720]

Likewise, national definitions of international crimes are often underinclusive, overinclusive or both. The above description of national provisions on genocide illustrates how variations in formulation regularly add elements to the core crimes, or omit them.[721] Such discrepancies are also found abundantly in national definitions of the other core crimes,[722] and in ancillary isues like command responsibil-

---

[716] See Vandermeersch 2004, p. 135 and 137; Segall 2003, p. 267; Wouters and Panken 2003, p. 10-11; Stahn 2000, p. 202; Holdgaard Bukh 1994, p. 349; Lauterpacht 1958, p. 137-139.

[717] See Art. 85 (4) sub b AP I.

[718] See Art. 7 (1) sub h ICC Statute.

[719] See Malarino 2003, p. 61-63 (on the limited extent to which ordinary Argentinean criminal law covers core crimes); Schabas 2000b, p. 352-353; Bremer 1999, p. 159-249 (showing in a detailed analysis how the reliance of Germany on ordinary crimes prior to the adoption of the 2003 Code on International Crimes failed to ensure the effective prosecution of all war crimes); Bothe 1996, p. 294-295; Wolfrum 1996, p. 243; Bothe 1995, p. 242-243. Cf. numerous recommendations of the Committee against Torture, noting that parties to the CAT have failed to enact torture as a specific crime while their ordinary criminal law does not cover all acts of torture. See e.g. Lambert-Abdelgawad 2002, p. 533 and United Nations Committee against Torture and Holmström 2000, p. 4 (Country Report on Algeria, 1996); 30 (Colombia, 1995) and 42 (Cuba, 1997: "The failure to establish a specific crime of torture as required by the Convention leaves a gap in the application of its provisions that is not filled by any of the existing offences directed against violations of the bodily integrity or the dignity of the individual.").

[720] See Wyngaert 2003, p. 211; Bremer 1999, p. 246; Bothe 1996, p. 295. Cf. Rowe and Meyer 1996, p. 479.

[721] See above, Chapter II, para. 2.2.b.

[722] See e.g. Vandermeersch 2004, p. 138-141 (on the discrepancies between the ICC Statute and corresponding Belgian law); Elst 1998, p. 1587-1593 (on the discrepancies between the Geneva Conventions and corresponding offences in Dutch criminal law before the Code on International Crimes 2003); Komarow 1980, p. 32-33. Cf. Modolell González 2003, p. 537 (on the Venezuelan criminalization of "condititions analogous to slavery"); Abdelgawad 2002, p. 374-375 (Egyptian criminalization of torture more restrictive than CAT definition); Lenzerini 2000 (on the Italian criminalization of "condititions analogous to slavery" interpreted in light of the 1926 Slavery Convention and the 1956 Supplementary Convention on the Abolition of Slavery, the Slave Trade and Institutions and Practices Similar to Slavery).

ity.[723] Generally, these discrepancies are a conscious choice of the legislature,[724] but occasionally they are simply the result of oversight.[725] Whatever the reason, many national provisions on genocide, crimes against humanity and war crimes do not criminalize these offences exhaustively, or on the contrary expand their scope. A very common example of overinclusion concerns the choice of numerous legislatures to proscribe war crimes by a general rule of reference to violations of the laws and customs of war.[726] After all, not all violations of humanitarian law amount to war crimes.[727]

The disparities between national legislation and corresponding international law can lead to different problems. Underinclusion can obviously thwart or at least complicate core crimes prosecutions that a State wants to conduct.[728] It can also lead to a violation of the State's international obligations to criminalize the core crimes in its national legislation and to prosecute them.[729] Overinclusion, on the other hand, can cause a State to prosecute acts as core crimes that cannot be categorized as such under international law. The proceedings in Spain, Germany and Ethiopia described above, for example, all appear to have charged defendants with genocide for acts that did not amount to genocide under international law.[730] This is

---

[723] Compare e.g. Section 5 of Canada's Crimes against Humanity and War Crimes Act and Art. 13 and 14 of Germany's Code of International Crimes to Art. 28 ICC Statute.

[724] See e.g. Schabas 2000b, p. 351 (citing a Candadian legislative committee as stating that "we believe that the definition of genocide should be drawn somewhat more narrowly than in the international Convention so as to include only killing and its substantial equivalents").

[725] See Vandermeersch 2004, p. 136 (Belgian law copying Art. 7 ICC Statute on crimes against humanity omitted several constituting acts by oversight. This gap was later repaired).

[726] See above, Chapter II, para. 3.2.a.

[727] See ICTY, Appeals Chamber, *Tadic, Decision on the Defence Motion for Interlocutory Appeal on Jurisdiction*, 2 October 1995 para. 86-94 and 134-135. See also Dinstein 2004, p. 229; Cassese 2003a, p. 50-51. However, it may be argued that "violations of the laws and customs of war" has become a term of art, referring only to those violations giving rise to individual criminal responsibility, as a result of its inclusion in numerous national criminal laws and the ICTY Statute. See Australia, High Court, *Polyukhovich v. The Commonwealth of Australia and Another*, 14 August 1991, per Brennan J., para. 4 ("A war crime in international law is a violation of the laws and customs of war.").

[728] Note, however, that it can also make such prosecutions easier by requiring less elements to be proven.

[729] See on the legal basis and extent of the duty to proscribe and prosecute core crimes below, note 1038 and Chapter V, para. 3.3.d.

[730] See above, Chapter II, para. 2.2.b. While most of the acts in question fall outside the scope of the Genocide Convention, it is open to debate whether customary international law nowadays recognizes a broader definition of genocide which would encompass, *inter alia*, political groups as possible victims. On the one hand, the recognition of political groups is reflected in various national laws and judgments and goes back to GA Resolution 96-1 of 1946:

"Affirms that genocide is a crime under international law which the civilized world condemns, and for the commission of which principals and accomplices – whether private individuals, public officials or statesmen, and whether the crime is committed on religious, racial, political or any other grounds – are punishable."

On the other hand, political groups were consciously excluded from the Genocide Convention and attempts to expand the definition of genocide along these lines have been unambiguously rejected in the drafting of the ICC Statute. See respectively Heintze 2000, p. 227 and Rückert and Witschel 2001,

not necessarily problematic. Ethiopia, for example, is permitted under international law to prosecute crimes committed by its nationals on its territory, even if these crimes do probably not fall within the definition of genocide under international law. Yet there are several ways in which prosecutions on the basis of overinclusive national law can violate international law.

First, prosecutions of acts committed in international armed conflict on the basis of overinclusive national law may violate international humanitarian law. The complexity of this question requires a broader discussion of the relationship between national criminal law and core crimes law. As a general rule, States are free to shape their criminal laws to their preferences and thus to prohibit acts that international law does not criminalize.[731] The international criminalization of genocide, crimes against humanity and war crimes in internal armed conflict constitutes only minimum norms.[732] They do not have a legitimizing function, which would mean that relevant acts not prohibited by these norms must be considered to be permissible. Therefore, within the normal limits of jurisdiction imposed by international law, States are free to proscribe and prosecute acts that fall outside these international offences, such as "genocidal" acts against political groups. Arguably, this freedom includes the competence to label such acts as genocide, crimes against humanity or war crimes in national criminal law.[733] Practice shows both that several States do so, and that other States fail to object to this practice.

In *Kesbir* (2004), the Dutch Supreme Court analyzed the relationship between national criminal law and international humanitarian law governing internal armed conflicts in some detail.[734] The petitioner in this case appealed to the Supreme

---

p. 66. Moreover, the *ad hoc* tribunals have, questionably, interpreted the protected groups to extend to other stable ones, but not to political groups. See ICTR, Trial Chamber, *Akayesu*, 2 September 1998, para. 511 and 516 and ICTY, Trial Chamber, *Jelisic*, 14 December 1999, para. 69. Thus, while there may be a nascent trend in this respect, it appears that the crime of genocide under customary international law does not currrently include acts committed against political groups. See Mexico, Supreme Court, *In re Cavallo (Amparo en Revision 140/2002)*, 10 June 2002 at 892-896. See also Reydams 2003, p. 187; Schabas 2000b, p. 150. But see Schaack 1997, p. 2280-2281.

[731] Numerous treaties with a penal content expressly preserve the freedom of States Parties to legislate in excess of the treaty. Such provisions are merely confirmations of the general rule. See e.g. Art. 1 (2) and 5 (3) CAT. See for a list of further examples O'Keefe 2004, p. 751.

[732] Cf. ICTY, Trial Chamber, *Tadic, Decision on the Defence Motion on Jurisdiction*, 10 August 1995, para. 67-74 and ICJ, *Case Concerning Military and Paramilitary Activities in and against Nicaragua (Nicaragua v. United States of America)*, 27 June 1986, para. 218-219.

[733] See Colombia, Corte Constitucional, Sala Plena, *Genocidio, Sentencia C-177*, 14 February 2001, 30 Jurisprudencia y Doctrina 707 at 710: "Esta Corte encuentra que ningún reparo puede formularse a la ampliación que de la protección del genocidio a los grupos políticos, hace la norma cuestionada, pues es sabido que la regulación contenida en los tratados y pactos internacionales consagra un parámetro mínimo de protección, de modo que nada se opone a que los Estados, en sus legislaciones internas consagren un mayor ámbito de protección. Así, pues, no hay óbice para que las legislaciones nacionales adopten un concepto más amplio de genocidio, siempre y cuando se conserve la esencia de este crimen, que consiste en la destrucción sustemática y deliberada de un grupo humano, que tenga una identidad definida. Y es indudable que un grupo político la tiene." See also Kleffner 2003, p. 100; Green 2000, p. 293.

[734] Netherlands, HR, *In re Kesbir*, 7 May 2004.

Court to block her extradition to Turkey, where she was suspected of various crimes connected to her alleged involvement in the Kurdish organization PKK. She argued that several of the accusations against her concerned acts committed in an internal armed conflict which did not constitute crimes under international humanitarian law, and therefore not under Dutch law either.[735] The desired outcome of this argument was the rejection of Turkey's extradition request for lack of double criminality of the acts in question, which was required by Dutch law.[736] The broader claim underlying it was that the application of humanitarian law to internal armed conflicts is exclusive and rules out more extensive criminalization in national criminal law.[737] The Supreme Court rejected the argument in careful language, limiting its findings to situations of internal armed conflict. The Court held that the application of international humanitarian law to internal armed conflicts is not exclusive and that Common Art. 3 of the Geneva Conventions contains only minimum standards.[738] As Common Art. 3 does not "legitimize" the alleged violent acts in question the Court found that the State retains the competence to punish these acts on the basis of its ordinary criminal law.[739] In other words, overinclusion of national criminal law does not violate international law where it concerns acts committed in internal armed conflict.

However, it seems that the situation is different where it concerns humanitarian law governing international armed conflicts. In internal armed conflicts, international humanitarian law merely provides a minimum standard that complements national criminal law.[740] In international armed conflicts, on the other hand, international humanitarian law constitutes the *lex specialis*. It holds this position of *lex specialis* in relation to international human rights law,[741] and arguably also *vis-à-vis* national criminal law. States may of course proscribe acts connected to international armed conflict for their own citizens, for example aiding the enemy,[742] as well as acts that are not regulated by humanitarian law. But they may not unilater-

[735] Dutch law regarding war crimes refers in general terms to the laws and customs of war. See above, note 161.

[736] Netherlands, HR, *In re Kesbir*, 7 May 2004, para. 3.3.

[737] Id., para. 3.3.3.

[738] Id., para. 3.3.6 and 3.3.7.

[739] Id., para. 3.3.7: "De omstandigheid dat [Common Art. 3 GC's…] van toepassing is, doet niet af aan de bevoegdheid van de betrokken Staat om strafbare feiten, begaan door leden van een gewapende oppositionele groep in verband met een intern gewapend conflict volgens zijn commune strafrecht te vervolgen en te bestraffen. Uit Art. 3 vloeit naar zijn aard dus niet voort dat anderen dan de niet aan de strijd deelnemende personen geen bescherming toekomt tegen aanslagen op hun leven of tegen lichamelijke geweldpleging. Dit artikel legitimeert zodanige handelingen niet."

[740] See Green 2000, p. 319.

[741] See ICJ, *Legality of the Threat or Use of Nuclear Weapons, Advisory Opinion*, 8 July 1996, para. 25 ("In principle, the right not arbitrarily to be deprived of one's life applies also in hostilities. The test of what is an arbitrary deprivation of life, however, then falls to be determined by the applicable *lex specialis*, namely, the law applicable in armed conflict which is designed to regulate the conduct of hostilities."). Cf. ICJ, *Legal Consequences of the Construction of a Wall in the Occupied Palestinian Territory, Advisory Opinion*, 9 July 2004, para. 105-106.

[742] See above, note 97.

ally impose stricter rules of warfare on their adversaries by prosecuting acts under national criminal law that are considered to be legitimate acts of warfare under international humanitarian law. In this sense, international humanitarian law does have a legitimizing function for lawful combatants.[743] If a pilot on a bombing mission in an international armed conflict adheres to international humanitarian law's demands, such as the principles of proportionality and distinction, her prosecution on charges of manslaughter and criminal damage would violate international humanitarian law.[744]

Several judgments of national courts show that the question of the admissibility of an overinclusive national criminal law governing acts committed in international armed conflict is not without controversy. In *Public Prosecutor v. Koi* (1967), a divided Privy Council quashed the conviction of several Indonesian soldiers who had been found guilty of the possession of explosives in Malaysia on the basis of Malaysia's Internal Security Act 1960. The soldiers were captured during an armed conflict between Indonesia and Malaysia. The majority found that "members of regular forces fighting in enemy country [...] are not subject to domestic criminal law."[745] Two dissenting Lords, on the other hand, stated that they knew "of no rule of international law which suggests that the national laws may not be applied to the armed forces of an enemy which invade the national territory."[746] In *Polyukhovich* (1991), dissenting judge Brennan of the Australian High Court rejected the idea that international humanitarian law has a legitimizing function, yet seemed to accept its quality of *lex specialis.*[747]

As such, the relationship between national criminal law and international humanitarian law outlined above is not beyond debate. In addition, there is a tension between the current tendency to relativize the distinctions between the legal regimes applicable to international and internal armed conflict[748] and the difference in the legitimizing function of those regimes mentioned above. Yet, it appears that this trend has so far not led to a recognition of armed opposition groups in internal

[743] See Art. 43 (2) AP I ("Members of the armed forces of a Party to a conflict [...] are combatants, that is to say, they have the right to participate directly in hostilities."). See also Dinstein 2004, p. 27-28 and 234 Green 2000, p. 112; Rowe 1991, p. 219 and 222. But see Baxter 1973, p. 73.

[744] See Rowe 1991, p. 226. Cf. Wyngaert 2003, p. 661.

[745] Malaysia, Privy Council, *Public Prosecutor v. Koi*, 4 December 1967, [1968] A.C. 829 at 860, per Lord Hodson.

[746] Id., at 867, per Lord Guest and Sir Garfield Barwick.

[747] Australia, High Court, *Polyukhovich v. The Commonwealth of Australia and Another*, 14 August 1991, per Brennan J. dissenting, para. 4-5 and 45: "[The laws and customs of war] limit the belligerents' choice of means of injuring enemy forces, controlling enemy prisoners of war and treating enemy civilians, but are silent as to acts which do not contravene those limitations. [...I]t is clear that the draftsman misunderstood the effect of the laws, customs and usages of war, for they give no permission for acts which would otherwise be forbidden; they simply forbid particular means of injuring enemy forces, controlling enemy prisoners of war or treating enemy civilians. [...] The real objection to the validity of the [Australian War Crimes Amendment Act 1988] is that the Act rejects international law as the governing law for the trial of persons allegedly guilty of war crimes and adopts a municipal law definition which operates retrospectively."

[748] Cf. Sassòli *et al.* 2003, p. 152-153; Nollkaemper and Zegveld 2002, p. 411-415.

armed conflict as lawful combatants, with a corresponding right to participate in hostilities.[749] Therefore, the conclusion is warranted that with regard to international, but not internal armed conflict, prosecutions on the basis of overinclusive national criminal law can violate international law, even if they take place on the basis of territorial jurisdiction.

Second, when overcharging takes place in a prosecution on the basis of universal jurisdiction, it may well exceed international law's limitations on the exercise of extraterritorial jurisdiction.[750] Whether a particular case indeed amounts to a violation depends principally on the availability of an alternative basis of jurisdiction for prosecution. Even if Spanish courts are wrong to classify certain political murders in Latin-American States as genocide, they may still have universal jurisdiction to prosecute those murders if these do in fact constitute other international crimes such as crimes against humanity. It is important to also note that a violation can stem not only from overinclusive national law, but also from the wrongful application of international offences to acts that do not amount to the crimes charged. Both points are illustrated by the French case *MC Ruby* (1995), in which the French *Cour de Cassation* based jurisdiction over acts of assault committed on a ship on the high seas on a provision providing for universal jurisdiction for torture as defined by the CAT.[751] The acts in question clearly did not fit that definition of torture, since they were neither perpetrated or condoned by a public official, nor committed for one of the goals enumerated in the CAT.[752] Yet, this prosecution arguably did not violate international law, since jurisdiction could also be based, as the Court of Appeals in this case had done, on the concept of an indivisible link between the acts committed on the high seas and acts committed in French territorial seas.[753] Of course, avoiding overinclusion of national law will not prevent all cases of overcharging, but it certainly provides an important step in that direction.

In practice, inconsistencies and lack of clarity in national law regarding core crimes often do not have direct consequences. Even where resulting prosecutions depart from international law, as likely was the case in Germany, Spain and Ethiopia,[754] this does not necessarily affect their outcomes in a practical sense. On occasion, however, the discrepancies between national offences and their international counterparts inhibit or delay the prosecution of core crimes. In Hungary, the Constitutional Court more than once annulled legislation which erratically formulated definitions of war crimes to be applied to crimes committed during the communist

---

[749] Cf. Art. 8 (3) ICC Statute ("Nothing in paragraph 2 (c) and (e) [governing war crimes in internal armed conflict] shall affect the responsibility of a Government to maintain or re-establish law and order in the State or to defend the unity and territorial integrity of the State, by all legitimate means."). Prosecutions on the basis of national criminal law would seem to constitute a legitimate means to re-establish law and order in the sense of this provision.

[750] See below, note 1204 and O'Keefe 2004, p. 759.

[751] France, Court of Cassation, MC Ruby, 3 May 1995, Bull. crim., no. 161.

[752] See Art. 1 (1) CAT. See also Koering-Joulin 1997, p. 146-150.

[753] See Koering-Joulin 1997, p. 144 and 152-153.

[754] See above, note 730.

era for being inconsistent with international law. With considerable delay, the intended prosecutions later took place based directly on international offences.[755] In Estonia, a prosecution for genocide and crimes against humanity was annulled and referred back to the courts of first instance, because the result reached on the basis of the national criminalization of these crimes was deemed inconsistent with international law.[756]

In conclusion, the fact that national provisions regarding the core crimes are often underinclusive, overinclusive or both complicates their enforcement and may lead to violations of international law. The intrinsic under- and overinclusiveness of ordinary crimes makes them singularly unfit as a basis for the prosecution of core crimes. However direct application of international law may also have advantages over national provisions regarding genocide, crimes against humanity and war crimes. Theoretically, such national provisions could perfectly mirror core crimes law and avoid all disparities, but the reality is otherwise. Of course, the minimalistic approach of many national authorities noted above may in fact cause them to favor national law for its underinclusiveness.

9. Rank and Effects of the Crime and the Law

A next, rather practical, consideration to take into account concerns the rank and effects of the different legal bases for core crimes prosecutions. First, directly applicable international law may have a different rank in the national legal order than statutory law.[757] The rank of the different sources of international (criminal) law differs in various States, depending on the hierarchy set by national law.[758] Thus, whether substantive criminality is based on national law, treaty law or customary international law may have implications for its hierarchical position *vis-à-vis* other relevant norms, such as amnesty laws and the principle of legality.[759]

Second, the core crimes, whether defined in national or international law, are often credited with particular effects that ordinary crimes lack. For example, there

[755] See above, Chapter II, para. 3.3.n.

[756] See Saar and Sootak 2003, p. 269-274.

[757] It should be noted that the considerations regarding the rank of international law set out here principally concern general direct application. International law that is directly applied on the basis of a specific rule of reference generally has the same rank in the national legal order as the national provision that refers to it.

[758] See above, Chapter II, para. 3.3. Cf. Cassese 1985.

[759] See e.g. the position of the Dutch Supreme Court on this point, above, Chapter II, para. 3.3.k. Compare the practice of the Special Court for Sierra Leone, which has jurisdiction both over certain international crimes and ordinary crimes under the national criminal law of Sierra Leone. The Prosecutor of the Special Court decided early on to charge only international crimes in his indictments as this, in his view, would minimize both successful challenges to the jurisdiction of the Court on the basis of the amnesty provision in the Lome Peace Accord and complications stemming from Sierra Leonean criminal jurisprudence. Interview with Mr. David Crane, Prosecutor of the Special Court for Sierra Leone, held in The Hague, 9 December 2003.

is significant support for the proposition that genocide, crimes against humanity and war crimes cannot constitute political crimes,[760] and are not subject to statutes of limitations and the *ne bis in idem* rule.[761] There is also authority for the proposition that these crimes trump official immunities,[762] as well as double criminality requirements and other obstacles to extradition,[763] but these effects are more contested. Apart from the legal effects, the designation of certain acts as international rather than as ordinary crimes may in practice put more political pressure on other States to render cooperation where needed.

Thus, the choice of the legal basis for the charges can have practical implications for the outcome of a core crimes prosecution.[764] It should be noted, however, that the derogation of obstacles in national law is not entirely dependent on the rank of and effects ascribed to the offences in question. National obstacles like amnesty laws have been overcome in numerous cases where core crimes have been charged as ordinary crimes.[765] Yet, even if they are not always decisive, the rank and effects of the different offences certainly make up a relevant consideration, in particular for legislators and prosecutorial authorities.

10. Penalties

A final consideration of a practical nature concerns the available penalties. Within national law, the choice between international and ordinary crimes as a basis for prosecution can have significant consequences in this regard. A recent study on the punishment of serious crimes in the States making up the Former Yugoslavia and 23 other countries from all over the world paints the following picture.[766] Regarding homicidal crimes, the applicable penalties do not differ substantially for ordinary and international crimes.[767] This can be explained by the fact that most legal

[760] See Mexico, Supreme Court, *In re Cavallo (Amparo en Revision 140/2002)*, 10 June 2002 at 892-896; Austria, Supreme Court (Oberster Gerichtshof), Cvjetkovic, 13 July 1994, available at http://www.ris.bka.gv.at/; Italy, Tribunale Supremo Militare, General Wagener and others, 13 March 1950, Rivista Penale, 1059-II, 745-764 at 753: "Crimes against the laws and customs of war cannot be considered political offences, as they do not harm a political interest of a particular State, nor a political right of a particular citizen. They are, instead, crimes of *lèse-humanité (reati di lesa umanità)* and, as previously demonstrated, the norms prohibiting them have a universal character, not simply a territorial one. Such crimes, therefore, due to their very subject matter and particular nature are precisely of a different and opposite kind from political offences." (Unofficial translation cited in ICTY, Appeals Chamber, *Tadic, Decision on the Defence Motion for Interlocutory Appeal on Jurisdiction*, 2 October 1995 para. 57). But compare Lauterpacht 1944, p. 91.

[761] See Cassese 2003a, p. 316-320; Alvarez *et al.* 2002, p. 319-320; Mattarollo 2001, p. 33 and 38-39.

[762] See Cassese 2003a, p. 264-274.

[763] See below, Chapter V, para. 5. See also Swart 2002b, p. 580-581.

[764] Cf. Schabas 2003b, p. 62.

[765] See below, Chapter V, para. 5. See also Alvarez *et al.* 2002, p. 329.

[766] Sieber 2004. The report was requested by the ICTY for sentencing in the *Nikolic* case.

[767] See Sieber 2004, Vol. I, p. 91-97.

systems already reserve their highest penalties for ordinary homicidal crimes such as murder. For non-homicidal crimes, however, the differences can be considerable. In general, penalties for crimes such as torture and rape are substantially higher when these are criminalized specifically as an international rather than an ordinary crime.[768] The differences are especially significant for international crimes that have no real counterpart in national law, such as persecution.[769] While different elements of these crimes may be covered by ordinary offences, these do not reflect their grave context and as a result allow only penalties that do not compare to those of international crimes.[770]

The choice between national law and general direct application of international offences is more complicated, since most international offences are not accompanied by specified penalties. This point will be discussed extensively below, in Chapter VI, paragraph 5.4. At this point, however, it can already be noted that the specification of penalties in national criminal law provides a clear advantage.

11. Conclusion

The choice between national and international law as a basis for core crimes prosecutions is often framed as a choice between well-known but rigid law and a body of largely unfamiliar rules which is more flexible in its adaptation to new circumstances.[771] The above analysis shows that the picture is both more complex and more refined than that. There are many different considerations to be balanced in the comparison of national and international law, practical as well as principled ones. These considerations in part explain the limited occurrence of direct application in practice, due primarily to the minimalist and selective attitude of national actors involved and the complexity of international criminal law. They also show that international law neither categorically prohibits or proscribes any particular legal basis for core crimes prosecutions, nor is completely neutral in its assessment of these different possible legal bases.

Leaving aside the principle of legality for closer analysis, the considerations analyzed in this Chapter point in different directions. National provisions that specifically criminalize genocide, crimes against humanity and war crimes may be appreciated for their manageability, the close scrutiny they have received from the national legislature and their significant contribution to State practice and thus the development of core crimes law. Direct application of international offences, on the

[768] Id., p. 98-113.

[769] Id., p. 114-124.

[770] Cf. ICTY, Appeals Chamber, *Mucic et al.*, 20 February 2001 para. 758: "The offences which the Tribunal tries are of such a nature that there is little assistance to be gained from sentencing patterns in relation to often fundamentally different offences in domestic jurisdictions, beyond that which the Tribunal gains from the courts of the former Yugoslavia in accordance with Article 24 of the Tribunal's Statute."

[771] See e.g. Kamminga 1998, p. 570.

other hand, avoids the problem of underinclusion and overinclusion, stimulates the judicial dialogue and thus coherence of core crimes law, and may also have certain practical advantages such as imprescriptibility. Charging core crimes as ordinary crimes in national law may be an effective prosecutorial strategy, particularly in legal systems of limited means. Yet, it has serious drawbacks, in particular its failure to cover all relevant acts and to express the international character of the crimes, and therefore provides, it is submitted here, no more than a second-best solution.

Chapter IV
THE PUBLIC INTERNATIONAL LAW FRAMEWORK OF IMPLEMENTATION

1. Introduction

This Chapter analyzes the international legal framework that governs the implementation of public international law in the national legal order. The analysis, while setting out this framework in general terms, will focus primarily on national courts. It will thus form a basis for the more specific analysis of the international legal framework governing the direct application of international offences in national courts. The lay-out of this Chapter is as follows. First, it will give a short comment on the theories of monism and dualism and their (limited) relevance for today's practice (para. 2). Second, it will set forth the general rule that States are free to shape the implementation of their international obligations as they see fit, as well as its practical implications (para. 3). Third, it will show how the doctrine of self-executing treaties can be seen as a manifestation of the freedom rule (para. 4). Fourth, it will analyze the limits and qualifications of the freedom rule (para. 5). Particular attention will be paid to the tension between freedom of implementation and the principle of *pacta sunt servanda* (5.1), as well as the fact that national courts interpret national law in conformity with international law with considerable consistency (5.2). I will also analyze whether a specific qualification of the freedom rule is required for the particular fields of international law of a humanitarian character and peremptory norms, or *jus cogens* (5.3).

2. Theory: Monism–Dualism

Academic writing regarding the relationship between national and international law has long been dominated by the dichotomy between monism and dualism. Taken literally, these terms postulate that national and international law are part of one and the same legal order (monism), or that they constitute separate legal orders (dualism).[772] In this basic form, the dichotomy between monism and dualism establishes a starting point for the analysis of the effects of international law in the national legal order. It brings to the fore the fundamental question of whether international law is actually part of, and thus presumptively valid in, the national legal order.

[772] A variant of dualism is pluralism, expressing the plurality of national legal orders. See Partsch 1992, p. 238. See for recent analysis of the monism-dualism debate and copious references to older literature Arangio-Ruiz 2003; Gaja 2003; Wasilkowski 1996; Heiskanen 1992, p. 1-10; Partsch 1992, p. 238-242.

How and to what extent States can alter that presumption of domestic validity (monism) or non-validity (dualism), and do so in practice, is then a topic for further analysis.

However, the monism-dualism dichotomy is the starting point for a highly complicated discourse that requires a thorough separation of theory and practice and clarifies State practice only to a limited extent. Many instances of State practice can be explained both under monist and dualist theories. National rules of reference to international law, for example, may be evidence of a monist attitude when they are declarative, but of a dualist attitude when they are constitutive.[773] In the Netherlands, the legislature in its 1953 revision of the Constitution expressed the standpoint that the new constitutional provisions on the domestic validity of treaties were only declaratory of the legal situation that was dictated by international law.[774] This position finds some support in the fact that traditionally, all international law is incorporated in the Dutch legal order by way of an unwritten rule rather than constitutional provisions.[775] However, in 1956 the legislature abandoned this view when it only slightly altered the provisions on the domestic validity of treaties, but declared them to be constitutive rather than declaratory.[776] The same ambiguity extends to many other aspects of the role of international law in national legal orders. Even the fact that many national courts do not in principle apply treaties as a source of law can be conceptualized either as a limitation of national origin permitted by international law (fitting monism) or as international law's lack of authority in this sphere (fitting dualism).[777] Since State practice seldom reveals the doctrinal positions underlying the practical results, let alone in a conclusive manner,[778] the explanatory power of monism and dualism is limited.[779]

Moreover, many writings on monism and dualism take these notions far beyond their literal meaning, which merely questions the existence of one or two legal orders. First, most scholars include the question of hierarchy in their definition of monism. They assert that monism stands not only for the proposition that international and national law make up one legal order, but also that one, most often international law, is superior in rank to the other.[780] These are, however, separate questions

[773] See above, note 214. See also Tomuschat 2001, p. 367. Cf. Lauterpacht 1970, p. 216-230.

[774] See Fleuren 2004, p. 188; Brouwer 1992, p. 138.

[775] See above, note 415 and accompanying text.

[776] See Brouwer 1992, p. 252.

[777] Cf. Fleuren 2004, p. 15.

[778] That legislatures are not always firmly decided in their doctrinal stand on international law is evidenced not only by the Dutch and German examples, but also by the preparatory work on Art. 4 of the Constitution of the Weimar Republic, in which the legislature quickly meandered between different conceptions of the obligatory nature of international law for inter-state relations. See Simma 1995, p. 41-43.

[779] Cf. Denza 2003, p. 421; Partsch 1992, p. 246. But see for a notable analysis of the constitutive rather than declaratory nature of the rule of reference to international law in the Venezuelan constitution Venezuela, Tribunal Supremo de Justicia, Sala de Casación Penal, 21 November 2000.

[780] See e.g. Arangio-Ruiz 2003, p. 917; Heiskanen 1992, p. 3-4.

and treating them as one distorts the analysis of both.[781] A second complication in the monist-dualist debate concerns its "ideological and political overtones."[782] Some writers defend monism or dualism as an article of faith rather than as a tool for legal analysis.[783] Third, others use monism and dualism as labels for particular legal systems, asserting that certain States are monist and others dualist.[784] Generally, this use of the terms focuses on the direct applicability of international law, or even only treaty law, in practice rather than on the doctrinal position of the State.[785] All in all, the variance in meaning ascribed to the terms monism and dualism has confused the debate and further undermined the usefulness of these terms for the analysis of the relationship between national and international law.[786]

Doctrine has by now mostly abandoned the monism-dualism debate, making a move to pragmatism.[787] Scholarship regarding the interaction of national and international law has predominantly moved away from conceptual analysis of the legal framework to focus on practical results.[788] As some scholars have noted, the lack of attention for a unifying theory has serious drawbacks.[789] Lack of a proper theoretical grounding, to name but one example, likely contributes to the unfortunate tendency of various scholars to equate the application of international law in national courts to that of foreign law, ignoring the obvious and important differences between the two.[790] Yet a rejuvenation of the theoretical discourse does not necessarily imply a resurrection of the monism-dualism debate, in fact far from it.

An attempt to classify this study as either "monist" or "dualist" will quickly illustrate the problems with these terms. This study examines the requirements of international law regarding the direct application of core crimes law in national

[781] See Ferdinandusse 2003, p. 60-61. Cf. Santulli 2001, p. II-III; Jackson 1992, p. 318-319; Lauterpacht 1970, p. 227-228; Lauterpacht 1929, p. 77.

[782] Partsch 1992, p. 238.

[783] See Partsch 1992, p. 241-242. Even a prominent and thorough scholar like Hans Kelsen included decidedly normative elements in his account of monism. See Kelsen 1934, p. 129-154. See for a description of his scholarship Gattini 2004 and the different contributions in 9 European Journal of International Law, iss. 2 (1998).

[784] See e.g. Aust 2000, p. 146-156; Buergenthal 1992, p. 316-317.

[785] See Fleuren 2004, p. 10-11 and 16-17; Arangio-Ruiz 2003, p. 915.

[786] Cf. Heiskanen 1992, p. 12 ("The monist-dualist debate lacks technical specificity.").

[787] See Santulli 2001, p. 281; Heiskanen 1992, p. 5-42.

[788] Cf. Santulli 2001, p. 105-106.

[789] See e.g. Arangio-Ruiz 2003, p. 914-915. Not also that the need for a renewed theoretical understanding of the relationship between national and international law is a central premise of the Amsterdam Center for International Law's research project on "Interactions between International Law and National Law," of which this study is a part.

[790] To be sure, there are certainly parallels to be drawn between the judicial application of foreign and international law, and valuable lessons to be learned by doing so. See above, p. 8-9. Yet, to equate the two disregards crucial differences in bindingness and authoritativeness and misconstrues their respective positions in the national legal order. See e.g. The International Judicial Dialogue: When Domestic Constitutional Courts Join the Conversation 2001, 114 Harvard LR 2049 at 2051 (2001) (contending "that [national] courts' willingness to analyze and then either to follow or disregard foreign and supranational precedents suggests that they do not view domestic law as subordinate to international law.").

courts. It thus assumes that international law can, at least partly, regulate its own application in national courts, a premise that will strike some as irremediably monist. Some observations on the role of international law in national courts, in particular the principle of consistent interpretation in para. 5.2, likewise reflect a belief that national and international law do not constitute fundamentally separate legal orders. On the other hand, I do acknowledge that in many States so many obstacles in national law impede the effective application of international law such that the practical result amounts to a *de facto* separation of national and international law. Commentators who use monism and dualism in a practical, result oriented rather than doctrinal sense may regard such observations as "dualist." Thus, I will not use the terms monism and dualism in this study, because of their limited explanatory power and diffuse meaning.

3. The General Rule: Freedom of Implementation

As a general rule, international law leaves States free to implement and fulfill their international obligations in any way they see fit. For some time, a body of extensive scholarly debate questioned the applicability of the freedom of implementation to human rights law.[791] Still today, the holdings of several international bodies leave the door open to an appeal to the principle of effectiveness to argue that the nature of human rights treaties requires their direct application in national courts.[792] Yet, it is commonly accepted that human rights treaties, like international law in general, are not directly applicable *per se*.[793] Thus, the oft-noted general rule remains that "international law does not itself prescribe how it should be applied or enforced at the national level."[794] Also, the case law of international courts reflects a deference to actors on the national level in the margin of appreciation. Both human rights courts[795] and the ICJ[796] consistently give States substantial leeway to choose the means of implementation of their international obligations.

---

791 See Nollkaemper 2002, p. 164-165; Buergenthal 1992, p. 335-340.

792 See below, notes 974-983 and accompanying text.

793 See ECtHR, *Swedish Engine Drivers' Union v. Sweden*, 6 February 1976, para. 50 (stating that the ECHR does not lay down "for the Contracting States any given manner for ensuring within their internal law the effective implementation of any of the provisions of the Convention."). See also Germany, Bundesverfassungsgericht, *In re G.*, 14 October 2004, 2 BvR 1481/04, para. 31 and 45; above, note 791.

794 Denza 2003, p. 415. See also Lambert-Abdelgawad 2003, p. 541; Santulli 2001, p. v; Tomuschat 2001, p. 359-360; Stein 1994, p. 431; Heiskanen 1992, p. 20-21.

795 See e.g. IACtHR, Proposed Amendments of the Naturalization Provisions of the Constitution of Costa Rica, 19 January 1984, Advisory Opinion OC-4/84, (Ser. A) No. 4, para. 58-62. See also Benvenisti 1999 and on the ECtHR Hutchinson 1999; Yourow 1995 and various articles in 19 Human Rights Law Journal, iss. 1 (1998).

796 See e.g. ICJ, *Germany v. United States (LaGrand case)*, 27 June 2001, para. 125. But compare below, note 1030.

In doctrine, far-reaching freedom of implementation is often regarded as beneficial for both individual States and international law. First, the most traditional argument postulates that this freedom is a pivotal aspect of State sovereignty.[797] According to this view, a more intrusive regime of implementation would infringe on the internal separation of powers and/or the democratic legitimacy of the law, the shaping of both of which is a prerogative of the State.[798]

Second, the bottom-up approach of having States regulate the implementation of their international obligations themselves is generally thought to be more effective than a top-down regime detailed by international law. Since the intricacies of their national legal orders are best known to States themselves, freedom of implementation allows them to choose the most effective way of implementing their international obligations.[799] It also allows them to mitigate some of the complexities of international law. A mediating role of national law may be valued in particular to alleviate the vagueness and uncertainty of (customary) international law for national courts.[800]

It may be countered, however, that a more intrusive framework of implementation could reduce and prevent inequalities in the effectuation of international law by imposing the same standards on all States. More rigid and precise international rules on implementation could, for example, prevent the situation that the courts of one State hold their executive branch strictly to its treaty obligations while the courts of another State party refuse to remedy comparable violations. Since national courts may hesitate to enforce various rules of international law in order to avoid imposing limitations on other branches of government which do not constrain foreign counterparts,[801] a more intrusive regime of implementation may also have positive effects on the effectuation of international law.

Freedom of implementation itself is uncontroversial.[802] International legal scholarship commonly understands freedom of implementation as giving States the liberty to separate[803] national and international law,[804] to choose which State organs

---

[797] See above, note 626.

[798] See above, Chapter III, para. 3, 4 and 5.

[799] See Kamminga 1998, p. 569-570. Cf. McFadden 1995, p. 47; Buergenthal 1992, p. 320.

[800] See above Chapter III, para. 6; Jackson 1992, p. 324-325.

[801] See below, note 991. See also Slaughter 1994, p. 116-117; Buergenthal 1992, p. 335; Jackson 1992, p. 326. Cf. Tomuschat 2001, p. 365-366.

[802] But see below, para. 5.3 for an analysis of the question whether the freedom of implementation fully applies to all categories of international norms.

[803] Or keep separated, depending on one's doctrinal viewpoint regarding the unity or separateness of national and international law.

[804] See Betlem and Nollkaemper 2003, p. 573; Reydams 2003, p. 137, note 40 ("Whether an international convention can be directly applicable in the domestic legal order is [...] purely a matter of national law."); Partsch 1992, p. 242 and Jacobs 1987, p. xxiv:

"[T]he effect of international law generally, and of treaties in particular, within the legal order of a State will always depend on a rule of domestic law. The fundamental principle is that the application of treaties is governed by domestic constitutional law. It is true that domestic law may, under certain conditions, require or permit the application of treaties, which are binding on the State, even if they have not been incorporated into domestic law. But this application of treaties "as such" is prescribed by

will enforce international obligations, to order other organs to ignore those obligations,[805] and to make the judicial application of international law subject to various demands such as the principle of reciprocity and the doctrine of self-executing treaties,[806] or to limit it altogether.[807]

Yet, the conditions and limits of freedom of implementation are a matter of debate. Both courts and scholars frequently overestimate the extent of this freedom, invoking it to defend courses of action that (potentially) violate international obligations.[808] They especially overestimate the extent to which international law allows States to keep international obligations separated from and subordinated to national law. An extreme view in this regard, notably expressed in a Separate Opinion of a Judge of the ICJ, is Sir Percy Spender's assertion that "assuming the constitutionality and validity of the Act within the domestic legal system of the State concerned, it is competent for a State party to any treaty or convention to pass a law binding on its own authorities to the effect that, notwithstanding anything in the treaty or convention, certain provisions thereof binding on that State shall not apply, or to legislate in terms clearly inconsistent with, and intending to override, the terms of an existing treaty. [...] But that in no way would be relevant to the question whether that legislation-or an act done pursuant to it-is or is not in breach of or

---

a rule of domestic constitutional law. It is not a situation reached by the application of a rule of international law, since such a rule, to have effect, itself depends upon recognition by domestic law."; Fitzmaurice 1958, p. 68-69 ("When it is said that international law in a number of ways prescribes what States must do or not do in their own territory, this does not mean that international law has, as such, direct and immediate application in State territory."). But see Pescatore 1987, p. 281-282 (arguing that requiring the transformation of international obligations allows States to abstain from internal execution and deprives treaties from their contractual and international character; as a result "incorporation procedures and methods based on 'transformation' are ... by their very essence incompatible with good faith in international relations.").

[805] See e.g. Verdross and Simma 1984, p. 539-540: "[International law] überträgt seine Durchführung den verpflichteten Staatten, die es durch ihre Organen zur Anwendung zu bringen haben.... Bezweckt eine Völkerrechtsnorm Rechtswirkungen im innerstaatlichen Bereich, so muß ihr Inhalt in die innerstaatliche Rechtsordnung eingeführt ('inkorporiert') werden, um durch die staatlichen Organe erfüllt werden zu können." [International law delegates its effectuation to the obliged States, which are to execute it through their organs.... If a norm of international law has the purpose of taking legal effect within the State, its content must be introduced (incorporated) in the national legal order to enable State organs to comply with it. – translation by this author];
Fitzmaurice 1958, p. 90-91. But see Conforti 2001, p. 18 and 21–23; Danilenko 1999, p. 54; Lauterpacht 1970, p. 280 ("To say that the State – and the State only – is the subject of international duties is to say ... that international duties bind no one; it is to interpose a screen of irresponsibility between the rule of international law and the agency expected to give effect to it."). See for an elaborate problematization of the international obligations of State organs, or lack thereof, Ferdinandusse 2003.

[806] See Partsch 1992, p. 245.

[807] See Tomuschat 2001, p. 363; Henkin 1993, p. 149 and 153: "The international obligation is upon the state, not upon any particular branch, institution, or individual member of its government [...]. Since a state's responsibility to give effect to international obligations does not fall upon any particular institution of its government, international law does not require that domestic courts apply and give effect to international obligations."

[808] See below, notes 817-819 and 869-870.

incompatible with obligations binding upon the State by virtue of a treaty or convention."[809]

Sir Spender's statement, it is submitted here, does not correctly reflect the demands of international law.[810] All liberties flowing from the freedom of implementation are subject to the condition of effective compliance with international law. States are allowed to separate national and international law and to order certain State organs to ignore international obligations only if they fulfill these obligations in another way. International law does not allow States to violate their obligations and accept State responsibility as a suitable price to pay.[811] In a general institutional sense, international law may accept the need for exceptional cases of violation and adaptation,[812] but in concrete situations these remain violations and thus prohibited until they gather enough weight to change the rule in question. States are obviously in a practical sense *able* to legislate in contravention of their international obligations, but international law does not allow them to do so. Sir Percy Spender admits so himself when he states earlier in the same separate opinion that "[a] State, party to the Convention, may not, whatever the subject-matter of the law under which it acts, do anything which contravenes the provisions of the Convention."[813] This rather straightforward statement is hard to reconcile with the one quoted above.

When the general rule of freedom comes into conflict with the basic principle that States must perform their international obligations in good faith (*pacta sunt servanda)*,[814] the latter must prevail.[815] This is perhaps a trite observation, but in practice national courts show considerable divergence in their appreciation of the limits of the freedom of implementation.[816] National courts look predominantly, sometimes even exclusively, to national law in order to decide whether and to what extent to give effect to international law.[817] They regularly allow the executive and

---

[809] ICJ, *Case concerning the application of the Convention of 1902 governing the Guardianship of Infants (Netherlands v. Sweden)*, 28 November 1958, 1958 I.C.J. 55 at 125-126, Separate Opinion of Judge Spender.

[810] Unless one interprets the word "competent" as denoting mere factual possibility rather than international legality. Such an interpretation seems stretched, however, given the place of this citation in a separate opinion of a judge of the ICJ.

[811] See in this regard Jackson 2004 and Jackson 1997.

[812] See D'Amato 1987, p. 376-377.

[813] Id., at 119.

[814] See Art. 26 VCLT; ICJ, *Border and Transborder Armed Actions (Nicaragua v. Honduras), Jurisdiction and Admissibility*, 1988, 1988 ICJ 69, para. 94; ICJ, *Nuclear Tests (Australia v. France)*, 20 December 1974, para. 46.

[815] Cf. Rosenne 1989, p. 39 ("It is axiomatic that a treaty, made between States, is binding upon each State as a whole, upon each one of its organs. This is implicit in the lapidary formulation of the *pacta sunt servanda* rule in article 26 of the Vienna Conventions.");

[816] See Stirling-Zanda 2004, p. 11-20; Nollkaemper 2002, p. 167-179; Aust 2000, p. 143-161; Buergenthal 1992, p. 359-360; Cassese 1985. Cf. Ferdinandusse 2003, p. 56-60.

[817] See e.g. U.K., *Blackburn v. Attorney-General*, 1971, 2 All ER 1380, 1 WLR 1037, 52 ILR 414: "Even if a treaty is signed, it is elementary that these courts take no notice of treaties as such. We take no notice of treaties until they are embodied in laws enacted by Parliament, and then only to the extent that Parliament tells us."; U.S., Supreme Court, *Rainey v. United States*, 1914, 232 U.S. 310 at 316

the legislature to violate international obligations.[818] It is not at all uncommon for a national court to assert that "[i]nternational practice is law only in so far as we adopt it, and like all common or statute law it bends to the will of the Congress,"[819] or words to that effect. It is especially telling that even initiatives for reform that aim at more effective enforcement of international obligations at the national level often focus on national law's endorsement of international law.[820] On the other hand, numerous national judgments are notably stricter in their adherence to international obligations, even if that requires a limitation of the freedom of implementation.[821]

For this thesis, the limits of the freedom of implementation, imposed *inter alia* by the principle of *pacta sunt servanda*, are very relevant. Clearly, the freedom rule is not compatible with a general international obligation of States to directly apply international norms. Still, the question remains if, and under what conditions, national courts should directly apply international norms where necessary to prevent violations of these norms. Such situations normally result from a failure of the government to take appropriate steps to fulfill its international obligations, such as the drafting of implementing legislation. As shown above, this is not at all uncommon in core crimes law.[822] Therefore, the remainder of this Chapter will further explore the manifestations and limits of the freedom rule, as well as possible qualifications of the rule for specific categories of international norms.

4. The Doctrine of Self-Executing Treaties

States' freedom of implementation finds visible expression in the doctrine of self-executing treaties. Many States incorporate treaties in their domestic law, but differentiate between treaty provisions that are directly applicable in national courts, or self-executing, and those that are not. The doctrine of self-executing treaties, a

("Treaties are contracts between nations, and by the Constitution are made the law of the land."). But compare U.S., Supreme Court, *Breard v. Greene*, 14 April 1998, 523 U.S. 371 at 375 ("[I]t has been recognized in international law that, *absent a clear and express statement to the contrary*, the procedural rules of the forum State govern the implementation of the treaty in that State." – emphasis added). See also Denza 2003, p. 420-421.

[818] See e.g. Germany, Bundesverfassungsgericht, *In re G.*, 14 October 2004, 2 BvR 1481/04, para. 35; South-Africa, South African Constitutional Court, *Azanian Peoples Organization (AZAPO) and Others v. President of the Republic of South Africa and Others*, 25 July 1996, para. 27; Australia, High Court, *Horta v. The Commonwealth*, 18 August 1994, 181 CLR 183 at 195 (all holding that their respective constitutions allow the legislature to violate international law).

[819] U.S., District Court (Connecticut), *The Over the Top (Schroeder v. Bissell)*, 26 February 1925, 5 F. 2d 838 at 843.

[820] See *Resolution of the Institut de Droit International* (1993 Milan), 65 Annuaire De L'Institut De Droit International 321, Art. 1 ("National courts should be empowered by their domestic legal order to interpret and apply international law with full independence").

[821] See cases cited below, para. 5.1.

[822] See above, Chapter II, para. 2 and Chapter III, para. 2 and 8.

term originating in American law,[823] is found in some form or another in many different States.[824] It is a limitation on the enforceability of treaties in national courts imposed by national law,[825] and thus a clear manifestation of the freedom of implementation in State practice.

What makes a treaty provision self-executing or non-self-executing is not readily definable, due to the confused state of national practice in various States.[826] National courts have applied many different tests in this regard, employing both objective and subjective criteria. Under the most common objective test, courts will find a treaty provision non-self-executing when its subject is not amenable to adjudication in national courts or when its effectuation requires legislative action. The former is often assumed for foreign affairs matters like the peaceful settlement of disputes.[827] The latter is generally the case when the provision regulates a subject that falls under the exclusive competence of the legislature,[828] lacks precision[829] or contains an explicit reference to envisaged legislation, for example to "such conditions as the law may establish."[830] In this sense, the doctrine of self-executing treaties merely requires national courts to leave aside treaty provisions that are incomplete, imprecise or otherwise unfit for national judicial application. While the intent of the parties to the treaty may be taken into account as an additional factor, the primary criterion is the content and language of the treaty provision in question.

A subjective test gives far greater weight to the intent of the parties, considering treaty provisions non-self-executing whenever the parties intended to prevent these provisions from being enforced in national courts.[831] In this way, the doctrine of self-executing treaties no longer hinges on the content of the treaty, but provides a "switch" for the treaty makers to turn judicial review in national courts off at will. This can be done by a clause to that effect in the treaty[832] or, when courts accept the intent of their own executive or legislature as sufficient regardless of the view of

---

[823] The seminal judgment in this regard is U.S., Supreme Court, *Foster & Elam v. Neilson*, January Term, 1829, 27 U.S. (2 Pet.) 253. See Vazquez 1995, p. 700-704; Buergenthal 1992, p. 371-376; Paust 1988, p. 766-769.

[824] See Iwasawa 1998, p. 44-49; Buergenthal 1992; Iwasawa 1986, p. 628-629 and 640-642. See for an extensive overview of the literature Henckaerts 1998. See for a recent and thorough study of the Dutch doctrine of self-executing treaties or "een ieder verbindende verdragen" Fleuren 2004.

[825] See Fleuren 2004, p. 253-254; Iwasawa 1998, p. 48; Buergenthal 1992, p. 317-321; Iwasawa 1986, p. 650-652.

[826] See on the lack of clarity in the practice of different States Fleuren 2004, p. 391 and references cited there; Bremer 1999, p. 150; Heringa 1989, p. 231-260. Cf. Iwasawa 1998, p. 44-77.

[827] See Iwasawa 1986, p. 679-684.

[828] See Vazquez 1995, p. 718-719. Cf. Fleuren 2004, p. 37-38; Paust 1988, p. 775-781.

[829] See Fleuren 2004, p. 287-298; Paust 1988, p. 767-768.

[830] See e.g. Art. 14 (1) ACHR: "Anyone injured by inaccurate or offensive statements or ideas disseminated to the public in general by a legally regulated medium of communication has the right to reply or to make a correction using the same communications outlet, under such conditions as the law may establish." But see Fleuren 2004, p. 268-286; Iwasawa 1986, p. 661 and below, p. 144.

[831] See Fleuren 2004, p. 245-259; Vazquez 1995, p. 705-710; Buergenthal 1992, p. 384; Iwasawa 1986, p. 654-657 and 665-670

[832] See Nollkaemper 2002, p. 171.

the other parties, by a unilateral declaration at any stage in the conclusion and implementation of the treaty.[833] Some national courts presume that treaties are as a rule non-self-executing, requiring an indication that the parties intended to make them self-executing rather than the other way round.[834] Others have (mis)interpreted provisions calling for domestic implementation of the treaty as a sign that the treaty as a whole is intended to be non-self-executing.[835]

Yet the contrast between objective and subjective tests[836] is only the beginning of the differences and complications in practice. Courts have applied complex and confused combinations of objective and subjective tests as well as others that, even if they do not violate international law, have no apparent legal basis. Some courts, echoing European Community law, have characterized only treaty provisions creating rights for individuals as self-executing.[837] Some national judgments have held treaty provisions to be non-self-executing simply because their direct application would bring unwelcome practical implications.[838] Thus, self-execution is effectively a multifaceted concept that allows courts to put aside treaty provisions for very different reasons.[839]

On closer scrutiny, it appears that the doctrine of self-executing treaties functions primarily as a stand-in for other avoidance doctrines, predominantly those that flow from separation of powers concerns.[840] The objective test as to whether treaty provisions are precise and complete enough actually has little or no independent meaning and national courts have subordinated it to institutional concerns from the very beginning of the doctrine of self-executing treaties.[841] After all, there are no technical standards which establish an objective minimum threshold for provisions of law to be applicable by the courts. Courts can apply even vague or incomplete rules in a meaningful way, be it that the effects of such rules will often be more limited than those of "mature" rules. In fact, imprecision and incompleteness can amount to a (possibly intentional[842]) strengthening of the powers of the courts. Both national and international courts regularly apply international provisions which

[833] See Redgwell 2003; Sloss 1998; Buergenthal 1997, p. 220-223.

[834] See Vazquez 1995, p. 705; Iwasawa 1986, p. 656

[835] See Iwasawa 1998, p. 53-54; Vazquez 1995, p. 709; Iwasawa 1986, p. 658-660.

[836] Compare Nollkaemper 2002, p. 161 (distinguishing subjective and objective direct effect of international law, whereby the first denotes the right of the individual to invoke a provision rather than the intent of the parties to the treaty to make it self-executing, and the second corresponds to the content based test set out here).

[837] See Fleuren 2004, p. 305; Vazquez 1995, p. 719-722; Iwasawa 1986, p. 629-631 and 646-649. Cf. Buergenthal 1992, p. 325-335.

[838] See above, notes 617 and 618. See also Vazquez 1995, p. 711 and 715-716.

[839] See Vazquez 1995, p. 715-716. Cf. Nollkaemper 2002, p. 179; Buergenthal 1992, p. 370.

[840] See for an overview of various avoidance doctrines employed by national courts Collins 2002; Benvenisti 1993, para. II C.

[841] See Buergenthal 1992, p. 374-380.

[842] See U.K., Family Division, *In re N. (Child Abduction: Jurisdiction)*, 31 August 1994, [1995] Fam 96 at 100, per Wilson J.:

"The terminology [of Art. 7, 8 and 11 of the Hague Convention on the Civil Aspects of International Child Abduction 1980] is noticeably wide. I consider myself to be under a duty, as the judicial authority

(other) national courts consider non-self-executing. The relativity of the precision and completeness test also shows in the fact that national courts often employ different standards of precision and completeness depending on the rank and character of the law involved, for example applying constitutional provisions that are far less detailed than treaty provisions they consider non-self-executing.[843]

All of this is not to say that the entire doctrine of self-executing treaties is superfluous or wrong. There are legitimate separation of powers concerns involved in the direct application of treaty provisions, especially when these are broad or imprecise. A limited test of self-execution can provide a useful tool to maintain a proper institutional balance. The point is rather that the precision and completeness test is not actually of a technical or objective nature, but rather a step in a separation of powers inquiry that allows courts to set aside treaty provisions where their application would bring the courts into (unwanted) conflict with other branches of government.[844] This partly explains why courts apply such different standards in ascertaining precision and completeness: these vary with the institutional balance in the cases concerned.

Scholars have vigorously criticized the doctrine of self-executing treaties. Commentators in different States have called the practice of their courts in this regard confused and unpredictable,[845] even unconstitutional.[846] One scholar has criticized the tendency of some national courts "to engage in an open-ended inquiry to determine on a case-by-case basis whether judicial enforcement of a particular treaty is a good idea" as "incompatible with our society's conceptions about what it means for a norm to have the status of "law," and, in particular, about the judiciary's role in enforcing norms having such status."[847] Others have implored courts to use narrower avoidance doctrines instead.[848]

---

of a contracting state, to act expeditiously, [...], in proceedings for the return of this child. I interpret the language both of the Articles of the Convention and of the text of the [British implementing] Act as being deliberately wide in its instruction to this court to co-operate with all other Contracting States in making orders which will secure the return of wrongfully taken children."

See also U.K., Family Division, *In re C. (Abduction: Interim Directions: Accomodation by Local Authority)*, 12 December 2003, [2003] EWHC 3065 (Fam), [2004] 1 FLR 653 (similarly endorsing and using the discretion stemming from the broad language of Art. 7 Hague Convention on the Civil Aspects of International Child Abduction 1980, which reads:

"Central Authorities shall co-operate with each other and promote co-operation amongst the competent authorities in their respective States to secure the prompt return of children and to achieve the other objects of this Convention.

In particular, either directly or through any intermediary, they shall take all appropriate measures-

[...]

(b) to prevent further harm to the child or prejudice to interested parties by taking or causing to be taken provisional measures;").

[843] See Tomuschat 2001, p. 365; Buergenthal 1997, p. 219 ("The precision and detail required in Austria to make ordinary treaty provisions self-executing do not apply to treaties that have constitutional status"). Cf. Buergenthal 1992, p. 392.

[844] See Tomuschat 2001, p. 365; Buergenthal 1992, p. 382.

[845] See above, note 826.

[846] See Paust 1988, p. 760.

[847] Vazquez 1995, p. 715-716.

[848] See Fleuren 2004, p. 423-454.

Significantly, however, none of these commentators asserts that the doctrine of self-executing treaties in itself violates international law. For it is generally accepted, that if States are at liberty to preclude their courts from applying treaties entirely, they must also be free to employ any limitation that falls short of a complete bar.[849] Yet certain applications and consequences of the doctrine do in fact violate international law. The refusal by some courts to find certain treaty provisions self-executing because their direct application would lead to unwelcome consequences directly leads to a violation of those treaty norms. Likewise, States which deny self-execution to certain provisions or entire treaties while at the same time failing to ensure their effectuation through implementing legislation violate the principle of *pacta sunt servanda*.[850]

5. Limits and Qualifications of the General Rule

Practice shows diverse legal phenomena that call into question the limits of the freedom of implementation, as well as possible qualifications of the freedom rule for specific categories of international norms. This paragraph will discuss the limits of the freedom rule (5.1), focus on the practice of national courts to interpret national law in conformity with international obligations (5.2), and analyze whether the ground rule of State freedom is valid in its entirety for the specific categories of international law of a humanitarian character and peremptory norms (5.3).

5.1 Limits of the Freedom of Implementation

Both scholars and national courts easily overestimate the extent of freedom of implementation. They regularly assume that the freedom rule implies that international law is silent on its effects in the national legal order, and consequently that "the effect of international law [...] within the legal order of a State will always depend on a rule of domestic law."[851] While numerous national courts have adopted this view,[852] there are good reasons to doubt it.

First, in most States, courts take international obligations into account in their interpretation of national law. More often than not, they do so without a clear obligation to that effect in national legislation. Numerous national judgments assert or suggest that international, not national law requires this practice of consistent interpretation. In light of its importance, this practice will be analyzed separately, in para. 5.2 below.

Second, a historical analysis of the reception of international law in various legal orders suggests otherwise. The fact that the courts of many States gave effect to

---

[849] Cf. Iwasawa 1986, p. 651, particularly note 103.
[850] See Kälin 2000, p. 117.
[851] See above, note 804.
[852] See above, note 817-819.

international law before their national laws contained any provisions requiring them to do so suggests that, at least originally, they perceived the domestic validity of international law as flowing from international law itself, rather than from national law.[853] In the U.S., for example, the domestic validity and direct applicability of international law was silently accepted in the early days of the Republic.[854] While the historical understanding of the reception of international law in the U.S. is complex and disputed,[855] there are clear indications that traditionally, the direct applicability of international law did not depend on a rule of national law.[856] The same is true for numerous other States, in particular for custom but also for treaty law.[857] The shift in position of the Dutch legislature described above[858] shows that national rules of reference to international law can be interpreted as declarative or constitutive. Thus, one cannot, as some scholars do,[859] without further analysis take national rules of reference as evidence of international law's silence on its effects in the national legal order.[860]

Third, an analysis of the role of various international norms of a procedural character in national legal orders also casts doubt on the notion that international obligations only take effect in the national legal order to the extent that national law so determines. For example, a moderating role of national law is hardly feasible for the duty to refrain from defeating the object and purpose of a treaty before its entry into force.[861] After all, this obligation serves a preliminary and temporary role –

---

[853] Cf. Nollkaemper 2002, p. 167.

[854] See Criddle 2004, p. 473; Paust 1988, p. 763; Henkin 1987, p. 866-869 and 886.

[855] See e.g. Flaherty 1999 and Yoo 1999a.

[856] See Perkins 1997, p. 485-489 ("In the understanding of the founders of the republic, the law of nations was applicable in our courts because it was binding on the United States. [...] The Constitution reflected their understanding of a binding law of nations that stood on its own authority."); Wright 1916, p. 223-227. See also U.S., Supreme Court, *Chisholm v. Georgia*, February Term, 1793, 2 U.S. 419 at 474: "Prior [to the enactment of the Constitution], the United States had, by taking a place among the nations of the earth, become amenable to the laws of nations; and it was their interest as well as their duty to provide, that those laws should be respected and obeyed."

[857] See Stirling-Zanda 2000, p. 120-125; Danilenko 1999, p. 61 ("Judicial practice also indicates that some CIS judges embrace international law even in situations where neither the constitutional provisions nor the general political environment favours the direct application of international standards."); Buergenthal 1997, p. 214 ("[I]n some states where the constitution failed to deal expressly with the question of the domestic status of treaties, the courts have on their own adopted the article VI [of the U.S. Constitution] solution, provided always that the national parliament had a role in the ratification process," citing the example of Uruguay); Buergenthal 1992, p. 348 (quoting judgment of 27 May 1971 (*Le Ski*) of the Belgium Court of Cassation, which held that in case of conflict treaties prevail over national law and, crucially, that their supremacy "is attributable to the very nature of international law").

[858] See above, notes 774 and 776 and accompanying text.

[859] See e.g. Arangio-Ruiz 2003, p. 937-939; Rogers 1999, p. 31 ("The very application of [different authorizations in national law to apply international law] by United States domestic courts is an inherent rejection of the idea that international law is *ipso facto* binding in United States courts *without an independent basis for reference to it in domestic law*." (italics in original)).

[860] See Nollkaemper 2002, p. 168; Simma 1995, p. 43.

[861] See Art. 18 VCLT. See also Klabbers 2001a.

one meant to precede the treaty's operation and implementation through national law. It seems unrealistic to argue that State organs are only bound by the duty to refrain from defeating the object and purpose of a treaty if national law contains an explicit rule to that effect. In fact, the more general understanding of the duty in the few national judgments employing it suggests otherwise.[862]

In practice, national courts do not subject all rules of international law to the same tests and standards. They frequently apply international rules of a predominantly procedural character, such as those on immunities and treaty interpretation, as a matter of routine, but subject more substantive ones, especially those governing the rights and duties of individuals, to rather rigid justiciability tests like the doctrine of self-executing treaties.[863] Thus, the need for a national "trigger" to effectuate international obligations in the national legal order may be less clear-cut than often thought.

Varying interpretations of the extent of the freedom of implementation can be seen in particular cases where there is a tension between the freedom rule and the principle of *pacta sunt servanda*. When the legislature and executive have failed to take adequate implementing measures, national courts often refrain from upholding international law through direct application, finding that they cannot substitute for the political organs in choosing the mode of compliance with international obligations. In such cases, the freedom to choose *how* to implement in practice extends to a freedom to choose *whether* to implement at all.[864]

An apt illustration is the Belgian *Vermeire* case.[865] In a 1979 judgment, the ECtHR had found the different inheritance rights of legitimate and illegitimate children in Belgium discriminatory and in violation of the ECHR.[866] The Belgian legislature acknowledged the problem but was rather slow in its reform of the legislation in question. So it could happen that in 1983 Mrs. Vermeire, an illegitimate child, presented an inheritance claim to a Brussels Court of First Instance which was ruled out by the still unchanged Belgian law, but clearly warranted under the ECHR.[867]

---

[862] See Botswana, Court of Appeal, *Unity Dow v. Attorney-General of Botswana*, 3 July 1992, 1994 (6) Butterworths Constitutional Law Reports 1 at 137–140 (per Aguda J., striking down discriminatory legislation on the basis of unincorporated treaties, noting *inter alia* that if a treaty "has merely been signed but not incorporated into domestic law, a domestic court must accept the position that the Legislature or the Executive will not act contrary to the undertaken given on behalf of the country by the Executive in the convention, agreement, treaty, protocol or other obligation" and that it was "bound to accept the position that this country will not deliberately enact laws in contravention of its international undertakings and obligations."). See also Argentina, Judge Gabriel Cavallo of the Buenos Aires Federal Court, *Julio Simon (Case no. 8686/2000, "Simon, Julio, Del Cerro, Juan Antonio s/sustracción de menores de 10 años")*, 6 March 2001, 2000/B Nueva Doctrina Penal 527 (striking down several amnesty laws, *inter alia* on the basis that they are incompatible with the object and purpose of the CAT) and Klabbers 2001a, p. 319-322.

[863] See Nollkaemper 2002, p. 169.

[864] See e.g. above, text preceding note 642.

[865] See on this case Ferdinandusse 2003, p. 83-85 and Polakiewicz 1991.

[866] ECtHR, *Marckx v. Belgium*, 13 June 1979.

[867] See ECtHR, *Vermeire v. Belgium*, 29 November 1991, para. 8-10.

In these circumstances, the Court of First Instance adhered to the terms of the ECHR and granted Mrs. Vermeire the same inheritance rights as legitimate children, in contravention of the Belgian law.[868]

On appeal, however, the Brussels Court of Appeal quashed the judgment in first instance and denied Mrs. Vermeire her right of inheritance. The Court of Appeal followed the Belgian law rather than the ECHR, because there were various ways to comply with Belgium's obligations under the ECHR and, the Court of Appeal held, those choices should be made by the legislature and not the courts.[869] The Belgian Court of Cassation upheld this decision.[870] Thus, the higher Belgian courts in this particular case sanctioned a breach of an international obligation in order to uphold the freedom of implementation. The ECtHR did not agree with this approach, finding that "[t]he freedom of choice allowed to a State as to the means of fulfilling its obligation under Article 53 [(now Article 46 ECHR)] cannot allow it to suspend the application of the Convention while waiting for such a reform to be completed…."[871]

As can be seen in the Vermeire case, it is not uncommon for national courts to uphold the freedom of implementation to the point of violating international obligations because the legislature and/or executive have not decided on a means to effectuate those obligations. But there is also contrary practice.[872] National courts have rendered many judgments that uphold the principle of *pacta sunt servanda* over the freedom of implementation. Nowadays, such contrary practice is especially strong in human rights law,[873] but it is not limited to that field. In the last decades, both national[874] and international courts[875] have delivered judgments in various fields of law that place more emphasis on an effective enforcement of international law than on the State's freedom of implementation. It should be noted that

---

[868] Id. at para. 10, citing the Court of First Instance: "[T]he prohibition on discrimination between legitimate and illegitimate children as regards inheritance rights [was] formulated in the [1979 ECHR] judgment sufficiently clearly and precisely to allow a domestic court to apply it directly in the cases brought before it."

[869] Id. at para. 11, citing the Court of Appeal: "[I]n so far as Article 8 (Art. 8) entails negative obligations prohibiting arbitrary interference by the State in the private or family life of persons residing within its territory, it lays down a rule which is sufficiently precise and comprehensive and is directly applicable, but this is not the case in so far as Article 8 (Art. 8) imposes a positive obligation on the Belgian State to create a legal status in conformity with the principles stated in the said provision of the Convention; (...) given that on this point the Belgian State has various means to choose from for fulfilling this obligation, the provision is no longer sufficiently precise and comprehensive and must be interpreted as an obligation to act, responsibility for which is on the legislature, not the judiciary."

[870] Id., para. 12.

[871] Id. at para. 25–26.

[872] See older examples in Morgenstern 1950. Cf. Lauterpacht 1929, p. 67-75.

[873] See for examples and a separate analysis of international law concerning the rights and duties of individuals below, para. 5.3.a.

[874] See generally Bahdi 2002; Conforti 2001; Higgins 2001; Higgins 2000; Danilenko 1999; Kirby 1998; Franck and Fox 1996; Buergenthal 1995; Benvenisti 1994; Conforti 1993; Cassese 1990, p. 228-231.

[875] See Ferdinandusse 2003, p. 65-100; Denza 2003, p. 419-420.

much of this contrary case law is inconsistent and contains the proverbial exceptions to the rule. National courts regularly curtail the State's freedom of implementation in exceptional cases only to revert to more conservative positions in subsequent cases of a similar nature.

However, some of this contrary practice is of considerable authority and consistency. A particularly interesting example in this regard, both because of its consistency and its far-reaching consequences, is a quite recent group of cases in predominantly Latin-American courts that use Art. 27 of the Vienna Convention of the Law of Treaties to establish supremacy of international law over national law. The import of Art. 27 VCLT, which establishes that "a party may not invoke the provisions of its internal law as justification for its failure to perform a treaty," is on its face limited to inter-State relationships, to be settled on the international plane. Yet, several national judgments have credited Art. 27 with far-reaching effects in the national legal order.

In *Ekmekdjian v. Sofovich* (1992),[876] a case concerning the right of reply under Art. 14 (1) ACHR,[877] the Argentinean Supreme Court ascribed far-reaching effects to the incorporation of the VCLT in the national legal order, concluding that Art. 27 effectively required all State organs "to accord normative priority to treaties and imposed on them the obligation to emit the necessary regulations to ensure that treaty provisions be fully implemented."[878] Indeed, in *Ekmekdjian* the Supreme Court regulated the right of reply by judicial decree to make it effective, despite the fact that the Argentinean legislature had failed to establish by law the conditions under which the right could be exercised as envisaged in Art. 14 ACHR. Of broader importance was its holding that Art. 27 VCLT requires State organs to give primacy to treaty obligations and ensure their effective application even in the face of contrary national law or gaps therein.[879]

Furthermore, the Supreme Court explicitly rejected the proposition that States are at liberty to keep international law out of their national courts, stating that "it

---

[876] Argentina, Supreme Court, *Ekmekdjian v. Sofovich*, 7 July 1992. See on this case Ferdinandusse 2003, p. 113-116; Sancinetti and Ferrante 2002, p. 354-356; Buergenthal 1995, p. 695-699.

[877] Art. 14 (1) ACHR: "Anyone injured by inaccurate or offensive statements or ideas disseminated to the public in general by a legally regulated medium of communication has the right to reply or to make a correction using the same communications outlet, under such conditions as the law may establish."

[878] Buergenthal 1995, p. 697-698. See also Argentina, Supreme Court, *Arancibia Clavel, Enrique Lautaro s/ homicidio calificado y asociación ilícita y otros*, 24 August 2004, per Judge Fayt, para. 22-25.

[879] Argentina, Supreme Court, *Ekmekdjian v. Sofovich*, 7 July 1992, para. 19: "Que la necesaria aplicación del Art. 27 de la Convención de Viena impone a los órganos del Estado argentino asignar primacía al tratado ante un eventual conflicto con cualquier norma interna contraria o con la omisión de dictar disposiciones que, en sus efectos, equivalgan al incumplimiento del tratado internacional en los términos del citado Art. 27." [That the necessary application of article 27 of the Vienna Convention places an obligation upon the organs of the Argentine State to give primacy to the treaty in the event that a conflict arises with any contrary provision of domestic law or in the event it has omitted to enact provisions and that such omission, in its effects, is tantamount to non observance of the international treaty under the terms set out in article 27. – unofficial translation]

should be borne in mind that when the Nation ratifies a treaty which it has signed with another State, it is making an international commitment that its administrative and jurisdictional bodies will apply that treaty to the cases covered thereby, provided that it contains sufficiently specific descriptions of such cases to permit its immediate application."[880] Argentinean courts have adhered to the interpretation of Art. 27 VCLT in *Ekmekdjian* in several later cases.[881]

The Peruvian *Consejo Supremo de Justicio Militar* followed the interpretation of Art. 27 VCLT of the Argentinean Supreme Court in the *Barrios Altos* case (2001).[882] Confronted with a judgment of the IACtHR demanding prosecutions of members of the military for certain crimes on the one hand, and two amnesty laws impeding those prosecutions on the other, the Peruvian military court relied *inter alia* on Art. 27 VCLT to give effect to the international judgment. It ordered investigation and prosecution of the crimes, stating:

> "That Peru is a party to the Vienna Convention on the Law of Treaties, which establishes by its twenty-seventh article that '[a] party may not invoke the provisions of its internal law as justification for its failure to perform a treaty,' in the spirit of which, the Consejo Supremo de Justicia Militar, as an integral part of the Peruvian State, must comply with the international ruling in accordance with its terms and in such manner as to implement the decision it contains in its entirety, vesting it with full effect and eliminating any obstacle presented by substantive or procedural internal law that might stand in the way of its due execution and full performance...."[883]

In Spain, both the *Tribunal Supremo* and the *Audiencia Nacional* have in a more cursory manner invoked Art. 27 VCLT simultaneously with Art. 96 of the Spanish

---

880 Id., para. 20: "Que en el mismo orden de ideas, debe tenerse presente que cuando la Nación ratifica un tratado que firmó con otro Estado, se obliga internacionalmente a que sus órganos administrativos y jurisdiccionales lo apliquen a los supuestos que ese tratado contemple, siempre que contenga descripciones lo suficientemente concretas de tales supuestos de hechos que hagan posible su aplicación inmediata. "

881 See case law cited in Argentina, Supreme Court, *Arancibia Clavel, Enrique Lautaro s/ homicidio calificado y asociación ilícita y otros*, 24 August 2004, per Judge Fayt, para. 23-25; Argentina, Federal Chamber of Appeals, *Incidente de Apelacion de Julio Simon*, 9 November 2001, para. XI; Argentina, Judge Gabriel Cavallo of the Buenos Aires Federal Court, *Julio Simon (Case no. 8686/2000, "Simon, Julio, Del Cerro, Juan Antonio s/sustracción de menores de 10 años")*, 6 March 2001, 2000/B Nueva Doctrina Penal 527, para. VI (A).

882 Peru, Consejo Supremo de Justicio Militar, *In re Barrios Altos*, 4 June 2001, Case No. 494-V-94, on file with the author. See for a description in some detail below, Chapter V, para. 5.

883 Unofficial translation by Mason Weisz. Peru, Consejo Supremo de Justicio Militar, *In re Barrios Altos*, 4 June 2001, Case No. 494-V-94, on file with the author, unnumbered paragraph: "Que, el Perú es parte de la Convención de Viena sobre Derecho de los Tratados, la misma que establece en su artículo veintisiete que '*no se puede invocar disposiciones de derecho interno como justificación del incumplimiento de un Tratado,*' en tal sentido, el Consejo Supremo de Justicia Militar, como parte integrante del Estado Peruano, debe dar cumplimiento a la sentencia internacional en sus propios términos y de modo que haga efectiva en todos sus extremos la decisión que ella contiene, otorgándole plenitud de efectos y levantado todo obstacúlo de derecho material y procesal propios del derecho interno que impida su debida ejecución y su cumplimiento en forma integral."

Constitution to require national law's conformity with international treaties.[884] Chilean courts have likewise relied on a combination of national law and Art. 27 VCLT to substantiate the supremacy of treaties in the national legal order.[885]

In these cases, one could say that the national courts involved use Art. 27 VCLT to import the supremacy of international law through the back door. A more traditional approach, which can be seen in other national courts, limits the import of Art. 27 to the international plane in order to preserve the freedom of the State to decide how and when to give effect to its international obligations.[886] For example, an appeal to Art. 27 VCLT before the Senegalese Court of Cassation in order to overcome lacunae in Senegalese law and ensure the prosecution of Hissene Habré failed.[887] The Court of Cassation did not explicitly address the argument but clearly refused to vest Art. 27 VCLT with the same far-reaching effects as its Latin-American counterparts did.[888]

The contrast between *Vermeire* and *Ekmekdjian*, both cases concerning the position of national courts where the legislature has failed to act in order to ensure the effective enjoyment of human rights, is notable. Unlike the higher Belgian courts in *Vermeire*, the Latin-American and Spanish courts in the cases just described place an effective enforcement of international obligations above prolonged freedom of implementation of the State. These courts assume that international law may in general be silent as to *how* it is to be effectuated in the national legal order, but not *that* it is to be effectuated there. The same assumption underlies the practice of most national courts to interpret national law in conformity with international law, to which I now turn.

5.2 The Principle of Consistent Interpretation

National courts all over the world interpret national law in conformity with international law to the greatest extent possible. This principle of consistent interpretation has a long history, and is also called the rule of presumptive conformity[889] or

---

[884] See Spain, Tribunal Supremo, *Guatemalan Genocide Case*, 25 February 2003, 42 ILM 686, para. II (10); Spain, Audiencia Nacional, *Argentinean Genocide Case*, 4 November 1998, unreported, para. C (2).

[885] See Chile, Court of Appeals (Santiago), *In re Fernando Laureani Maturana y Miguel Krassnoff Marchenko*, 5 January 2004 para. 51-52. Confirmed in Chile, Supreme Court, *In re Miguel Angel Sandoval Rodríguez*, 17 November 2004.

[886] See e.g. U.K., Chancery Division, *NEC Semi-Conductors Ltd and other test claimants v. Inland Revenue Commissioners*, 24 November 2003, para. 50 (rejecting an appeal to Art. 26 and 27 VCLT as "codification of public law principles"): "[Arts. 26 and 27 VCLT] are concerned with the obligations in international law between the states which are the parties to international treaties, not with issues of how private parties may or may not be able to rely against a state on the contents of a treaty."

[887] Senegal, Cour de Cassation, *Souleymane Guengueng et autres Contre Hissène Habré, Arrêt no. 14*, 20 March 2001, 7th *moyen de cassation*.

[888] See above, Chapter II, para. 3.3.e.

[889] See Conforti 1997, p. 11 (calling the presumption of conformity of domestic law to international law "the most common criterion" in case-law of national courts regarding human rights); Lauterpacht 1970, p. 157.

interprétation conforme.[890] It is found in Argentina,[891] Botswana,[892] Germany,[893] Japan,[894] the Netherlands,[895] Switzerland,[896] the U.K.,[897] the U.S.,[898] and many other States on all continents.[899] Some commentators have judged State practice sufficiently consistent to infer "an international duty of [national] courts to interpret, within their constitutional mandates, national law in the light of international law."[900] Indeed, it appears that the principle of consistent interpretation is a general principle of law in the sense of Art. 38 (1) sub c ICJ Statute.[901] Even if national

---

[890] See Stirling-Zanda 2004, p. 7.

[891] See Alvarez *et al.* 2002, p. 329.

[892] See Botswana, Court of Appeal, *Unity Dow v. Attorney-General of Botswana*, 3 July 1992, 1994 (6) Butterworths Constitutional Law Reports 1 at 139-140: "[I]t is the clear duty of this court when faced with the difficult task of the construction of provisions of the Constitution to keep in mind the international obligation. If the Constitutional provisions are such as can be construed to ensure the compliance of the State with its international obligations then they must be so construed. It may be otherwise, if fully aware of its international obligations under a regime creating treaty, convention, agreement or protocol, a State deliberately and in clear language enacts a law in contravention of such treaty, convention, agreement, or protocol."

[893] See Germany, Bundesverfassungsgericht, *In re G.*, 14 October 2004, 2 BvR 1481/04, in particular para. 29-33 and 60-61. See also Bernhardt 2002, p. 392-397.

[894] See Iwasawa 1998, p. 85-89.

[895] See Fleuren 2004, p. 372-382; Betlem and Nollkaemper 2003, in particular p. 574-576.

[896] See Thürer 2001, p. 191; Wildhaber 1974.

[897] See U.K., House of Lords, *Attorney General v. British Broadcasting Corporation*, 12 June 1980, 3 All E.R. 161, (1981) AC 303 at 354, per Lord Scarman: "[T]here is a presumption, albeit rebuttable, that our municipal law will be consistent with our international obligations [...]I do not doubt that, in considering how far we should extend the application of contempt of court, we must bear in mind the impact of whatever decision we may be minded to make upon the international obligations assumed by the United Kingdom under the [ECHR]." See also Denza 2003, p. 433; Cassese 1985, p. 356; Buergenthal 1992, p. 360-361.

[898] In the U.S., the principle is generally called the Charming Betsy canon, after the 1804 Supreme Court case that stated that "an act of Congress ought never to be construed to violate the law of nations if any other possible construction remains." U.S., Supreme Court, *Murray v. The Schooner Charming Betsy*, 1804, 6 U.S. (2 Cranch) 64 at 118. See for a recent application U.S., United States Court of International Trade, *The Timken Company v. U.S.*, 5 September 2002, 240 F.Supp.2d 1228 at 1238-1239 ("While an unambiguous statute will prevail over a conflicting international obligation, an ambiguous statute should be interpreted so as to avoid conflict with international obligations."). See also Rogers 1999, p. 36-73; Bradley 1998; Rogers 1998.

[899] See Betlem and Nollkaemper 2003, p. 575 (citing examples from Australia, Israel and the U.K.); Stirling-Zanda 2000, p. 127-129 (Italy, Portugal, Germany and Greece); Benvenisti 1994, notes 28 and 29 (Canada, Israel, Namibia and Zimbabwe); Jacobs 1987, p. xxvi (mentioning "the principle common to many systems that [domestic] legislation should wherever possible be so construed as not to conflict with the international obligations of the State," followed by country reports describing the canon of construction a.o. in Denmark (p. 33), France (p. 60), then Federal Republic of Germany (p. 69), Italy (p. 100) and United Kingdom (p. 135 and 137)); Cassese 1985, p. 398 (*inter alia* Poland and India); Meijers 1985, p. 117-129 (*inter alia* Austria and Pakistan). Cf. Bangalore Principle 4, *reported in* 14 Commonwealth Law Bulletin 1196 at 1197 (1988): "[T]here is a growing tendency for national courts to have regard to these international norms for the purpose of deciding cases where the domestic law – whether constitutional, statute or common law – is uncertain or incomplete..."

[900] Betlem and Nollkaemper 2003, p. 574.

[901] See Benvenisti 1994, p. 428 ("[It] may well be considered a general principle of law, that domestic law is *prima facie* compatible with international law."); Committee on Economic, Social and

courts regularly fail to interpret their laws in such a way as to heed relevant international obligations, they seldom if ever dispute the existence of the principle.[902]

Numerous States have embodied the principle of consistent interpretation in their national laws, either explicitly[903] or implicitly.[904] That does not mean, however, that in those States the principle is of national origin. In many of these cases the legislature followed the courts, rather than the other way round. Both in South Africa and Russia, for example, the courts adhered to the principle of consistent interpretation before their constitutions instructed them to do so.[905] Likewise, the English courts accepted an obligation to interpret national law in conformity with the ECHR long before Section 3 of the Human Rights Act[906] codified it.[907]

Cultural Rights, *General comment 9*, 3 December 1998, UN Doc E/C.12/1998/24, para 15: "It is generally accepted that domestic law should be interpreted as far as possible in a way which conforms to a State's international legal obligations. Thus, when a domestic decision maker is faced with a choice between an interpretation of domestic law that would place the State in breach of the [International Covenant on Economic, Social and Cultural Rights] and one that would enable the State to comply with the Covenant, international law requires the choice of the latter.";
HRC, *Concluding Observations on Ireland, Doc. CCPR/C/79/Add.21*, 3 August 1993, para. 18 ("Notwithstanding that the [ICCPR] cannot be directly invoked in the [Irish] courts, the need to comply with the international obligations should be taken fully into account by the judiciary."). Cf. Iwasawa 1998, p. 83 ("In most states, the principle is established that courts must interpret domestic laws in conformity with international law.")

[902] See e.g. Barak-Erez 2004, p. 615.

[903] See Section 233 of South-Africa's 1996 Constitution: "When interpreting any legislation, every court must prefer any reasonable interpretation of the legislation that is consistent with international law over any alternative interpretation that is inconsistent with international law."
See also Section 39 (1); Art. 13 (2) Ethiopia's 1994 Constitution: "The fundamental rights and freedoms specified in this Chapter shall be interpreted in a manner conforming to the principles of the Universal Declaration of Human Rights, International Covenants on Human Rights and International instruments adopted by Ethiopia."

[904] See Art. 17 (1) of Russia's 1993 Constitution: "The basic rights and liberties in conformity with the commonly recognized principles and norms of the international law shall be recognized and guaranteed in the Russian Federation and under this Constitution."
See also Art. 7 (1) of Hungary's Constitution, cited above, text preceding note 507 and Hungary, Constitutional Court, *Decision No. 53/1993, On War Crimes and Crimes against Humanity*, 13 October 1993, English translation in Sólyom/Brunner 2000, p. 273-283 at 277: "Article 7 § (1) of the Constitution also means that by the Constitution's order, the Republic of Hungary participates in the community of nations; this participation, therefore, is a constitutional command for domestic law. It follows therefrom [that] the Constitution and domestic law must be interpreted in a manner whereby the generally recognized international rules are truly given effect."

[905] See respectively Dugard 1997, p. 84-86; Danilenko 1999, p. 56.

[906] Section 3 (1) 1998 Human Rights Act, available at www.legislation.hmso.gov.uk ("So far as it is possible to do so, primary legislation and subordinate legislation must be read and given effect in a way which is compatible with the [European] Convention rights.").

[907] See e.g. U.K., Court of Appeal, *Schering Chemicals Ltd v. Falkman Ltd*, 27 January 1981, [1982] Q.B. 1 at 18, per Lord Denning ("I take it that our law should conform so far as possible with the provisions of the European Convention on Human Rights."); U.K., House of Lords, *Derbyshire County Council v. Times Newspapers Limited*, 1992, (1992) 1 QB 770 at 830, per Lord Butler-Sloss: "[T]he principles governing the duty of the English court to take account of article 10 [ECHR] appear to be as follows: where the law is clear and unambiguous, either stated as the common law or enacted by Parliament, recourse to article 10 is unnecessary and inappropriate. [...] But where there is an ambigu-

National courts approach the principle of consistent interpretation from two different angles.[908] First, courts may concentrate on the intent of the legislature and strive to respect it. In doing so, they consider internationalist interpretation to be the most accurate way to ascertain the meaning of the national law. According to this theory, the legislature would only violate international law after explicit deliberation and motivation. If such explicit intent to violate can not be found, the law must have been meant to conform to international law. While the result is international law friendly, the motivation behind it is to respect national rather than international law.

Second, courts may be focused more on honoring international obligations than on finding the most accurate interpretation of national law.[909] In such cases, the reasoning of the courts often evinces a strong urge to uphold international law.[910] A historic example is the British case *Le Louis* (1817), where Lord Stowell stated that "no nation can privilege itself to commit a crime against the law of nations by a mere municipal regulation of its own… the Legislature must be understood to have contemplated all that was within its power, and no more."[911] Some modern cases take such an internationalist approach to the principle that they effectively transform it into a mandate to uphold international obligations rather than use it as a tool to resolve ambiguities in national law.[912]

---

ity, or the law is otherwise unclear or so far undeclared by an appellate court, the English court is not only entitled but, in my judgment, obliged to consider the implications of article 10." See also Meron 1989, p. 116-117.

[908] See Rogers 1998, p. 640; Gulmann 1987, p. 32-33 (describing consistent interpretation in Danish law and distinguishing the rule of interpretation, that focuses on compliance with international obligations, and the rule of presumption, that focuses on the intent of the legislature).

[909] See Betlem and Nollkaemper 2003, p. 576.

[910] See e.g. Australia, High Court, *Newcrest Mining (WA) Ltd v. The Commonwealth*, 14 August 1997, 190 CLR 513 at 657-658, per Kirby J.: "[T]he inter-relationship of national and international law, including in relation to fundamental rights, is "undergoing evolution." […] To the full extent that its text permits, Australia's Constitution, as the fundamental law of government in this country, accommodates itself to international law, including in so far as that law expresses basic rights." – footnotes omitted;
Australia, High Court, *Minister for Immigration and Ethnic Affairs v. Teoh*, 7 April 1995, 183 CLR 273 at 287, per Mason C.J. and Deane J.: "It is accepted that a statute is to be interpreted and applied, as far as its language permits, so that it is in conformity and not in conflict with the established rules of international law.[…] In this context, there are strong reasons for rejecting a narrow conception of ambiguity. If the language of the legislation is susceptible of a construction which is consistent with the terms of the international instrument and the obligations which it imposes on Australia, then that construction should prevail.";
U.S., Court of Appeals (D.C. Circuit), *Finzer v. Barry*, 1986, 798 F.2d 1450 at 1460 ("It would be quite improper for the judiciary to disregard international obligations that are inseparable from our nationhood."); U.S., District Court (Connecticut), *The Over the Top (Schroeder v. Bissell)*, 26 February 1925, 5 F. 2d 838 at 842.

[911] U.K., *Le Louis*, 2 Dods. 210 at 251 and 254, cited in Lauterpacht 1970, p. 157.

[912] See India, Supreme Court, *Apparel Export Promotion Council v. A. K. Chopra*, 1999, (1999) A.I.R. 625 at 634-635: "This Court has in numerous cases emphasised that while discussing constitutional requirements, court and counsel must never forget the core principle embodied in the International Conventions and Instruments and as far as possible give effect to the principles contained in

While the results of these two approaches can differ considerably,[913] in practice the two categories can not always be adequately separated. Many national judgments silently adhere to the principle of consistent interpretation without clear motivation.[914] Other judgments fuse the two approaches with varying emphasis on one or the other.[915] For example, courts may sanction a breach of international law by an ambiguous national law only if the legislature clearly intended to bring about that factual situation *and* explicitly stated its intent to breach the international obligation by doing so.[916] In the absence of an explicit intention to breach, the intent of the legislature to bring about the specific result is not enough and will be overruled by the court in favour of an internationalist interpretation.[917]

It is also not uncommon to see national courts pay lip-service to the goal of ascertaining legislative intent, but go to such lengths to avoid violations of international law that the resulting judgments really belong to the second, internationally-oriented category. These cases generally involve national laws that are in conflict with international law rather than ambiguous on their face,[918] and the resulting judgments hardly disguise their dedication to the enforcement of international law.[919] In *Sharon and Yaron* (2003), the Belgian Court of Cassation first acknowledged that Art. 5 (3) of Belgium's 1993 Law relating to the suppression of grave viola-

---

those international instruments. The Courts are under an obligation to give due regard to International Conventions and Norms for construing domestic laws more so when there is no inconsistency between them and there is a void in domestic law."

[913] Cf. Betlem and Nollkaemper 2003, p. 585.

[914] See The International Judicial Dialogue: When Domestic Constitutional Courts Join the Conversation 2001, 114 Harvard LR 2049 at 2062-2063 (2001).

[915] Compare e.g. in Germany, Bundesverfassungsgericht, *In re G.*, 14 October 2004, 2 BvR 1481/04, para. 30-33 to 46. See also Rogers 1998, p. 640-645.

[916] See Conforti 1997, p. 12 (stating that this rule is followed mostly by American and Swiss courts).

[917] See Italy, Court of Cassation, *Ministero Finanze v. Societa Compagnia di Navigazione Marsud*, 20 October 1976, 3 Italian Yearbook of International Law 361 at 364: "[I]t is difficult to imagine that the State would wish to break an agreement which it had just recognized. Use must, therefore, be made of the principle of interpretation which requires that, failing written provision to the contrary, the State must, when enacting a provision, be presumed to have intended to honour rather than to breach international commitments. The fact that, as the preparatory work on the provision makes clear, the legislature (wrongly) considered the introduction of the new charge to be compatible with the agreement and on that account intended it to apply to GATT-originated goods as well, is in no sense a conclusive reason for the adoption of an interpretation consonant with that intent." See also U.S., Court of Appeals (Fifth Circuit), *Spiess v. C. Itoh & Co. (America)*, 1981, 643 F.2d 355 at 362.

[918] See Benvenisti 1994, p. 428 (calling the principle "a potent tool that judges in a great number of jurisdictions use to apply international norms despite apparent conflicts with domestic law").

[919] See e.g. U.S., Court of Appeals (Fifth Circuit), *United States v. Columba-Colella*, 604 F.2d 356 at 360-361 (federal court avoided extraterritorial application of very general but not ambiguous criminal statute in violation of international law by deciding "that because the defendant's act in this case is beyond its competence to proscribe, Congress did not intend to assert jurisdiction here under 18 U.S.C. para. 2313," and ended its judgment with the statement that "[t]he result we reach is part of the price a nation must pay to support mutuality of comity between sovereign nations."). But see for a different reading of this case Rogers 1999, p. 46-48.

tions of international humanitarian law ruled out a defense of immunity.[920] However, it then "interpreted" this provision in such a way as to avoid a violation of the international obligation to grant immunity that had just been affirmed by the ICJ in *Congo v. Belgium*.[921] The Court of Cassation held that "if this provision of Belgian domestic law were interpreted as setting aside the immunity principle of customary international criminal law, this provision would contravene the aforementioned principle; that the aforementioned rule cannot therefore be considered to have such a meaning, but instead must be understood as only excluding the official capacity of a person as a basis for penal non-accountability for the crimes enumerated in this statute."[922] Thus, in order to avoid a violation of international law, Belgium's highest court effectively overruled the clear intent of the legislature[923] to set aside immunity for core crimes prosecutions under the guise of interpretation.

Another rather extreme example of the fictitious construction of intent in order to observe an international obligation is the famous *PLO Mission* case.[924] In 1987, the U.S. Congress passed an Anti-Terrorism Act that *inter alia* banned all PLO offices within the jurisdiction of the United States. Closing the PLO′s Observer Mission in New York would violate the Headquarters Agreement with the United Nations, but it was clear from the text and drafting history of the Act that Congress intended to do so.[925] Accordingly, the Justice Department filed suit in the Federal District Court of the Southern District Court of New York to secure closure of the PLO Mission. Faced with this conflict between the Act and a treaty, Judge Palmieri, writing for the District Court, first affirmed Congress' competence to violate a treaty and stated that other branches of government were bound to implement such a

---

[920] Belgium, Court of Cassation, *In re Sharon and Yaron*, 12 February 2003, para. IV: "Attendu que, sans doute, aux termes de l'article 5,,§ 3, de la loi du 16 juin 1993 relative à la répression des violations graves du droit international humanitaire, l'immunité attachée à la qualité officielle d'une personne n'empêche pas l'application de ladite loi;" ("Whereas, without doubt, in pursuance of Article 5, § 3 of the statute of June 16 1993, relating to the suppression of grave violations of international humanitarian law, immunity attaching to a person's official status does not prevent application of the aforementioned statute.")

[921] ICJ, International Court of Justice, *Case concerning the Arrest Warrant of 11 April 2000 (Democratic Republic of the Congo v. Belgium)*, 14 February 2002.

[922] Belgium, Court of Cassation, *In re Sharon and Yaron*, 12 February 2003, para. IV: "Attendu que, toutefois, cette règle de droit interne contreviendrait au principe de droit pénal coutumier international précité si elle était interprétée comme ayant pour objet d'écarter l'immunité que ce principe consacre; que ladite règle ne peut donc avoir cet objet mais doit être comprise comme excluant seulement que la qualité officielle d'une personne puisse entraîner son irresponsabilité pénale à raison des crimes de droit international énumérés par la loi;"

[923] See Belgium, Law for the punishment of Genocide, Report of the Justice Commission, Belgian Senate, 1 December 1998, No. 1-749/3, para. II (B) sub 2 ("l'amendement gouvernemental vise à confirmer explicitement la règle de la non-pertinence des immunités de juridiction et d'exécution dans la cadre de l'application de la loi"). See also Panken *et al.* 2004, p. 27-31; Wouters 2004, p. 34.

[924] U.S., District Court (New York), *United States v. Palestine Liberation Organization*, 1988, 695 F. Supp. 1456. See Higgins 2001, p. 552-554 and Reisman 1989.

[925] See Reisman 1989, p. 415-17 ("It was of little concern to its drafters that the legislation would have violated an international agreement. Despite Judge Palmieri's opinion, there was no question that such was its intention and consequence").

violation when Congress' intent was sufficiently clear.[926] In a surprising move, he then ruled that the intention to violate the Headquarters Agreement was not manifest in the Act, which declared it unlawful "notwithstanding any provision of law to the contrary" to establish or maintain PLO facilities or establishments within U.S. jurisdiction.[927] Therefore, he "interpreted" the Act in conformity with the Headquarters Agreement, with the result that it did not apply to the PLO Mission in New York. Since the Justice Department decided not to appeal, this was the final word in the case and the PLO Mission remained open.

It should be noted that cases like *In re Sharon and Yaron* and the *PLO Mission* case give a good idea of the strong potential of the principle of consistent interpretation,[928] but are not representative for its application in national courts. Most national courts do no more than what the principle requires: to interpret national law in conformity with international obligations, not to effectively overrule it. The principle of consistent interpretation under international law does not require *contra legem* interpretation as found in these more extreme cases.

The important role of the principle of consistent interpretation in national courts constitutes a limit to the freedom of interpretation in two ways. First, it disproves the theory that international law needs a "trigger" in national law in order to take effect on the national level. The fact that international law obliges national courts to heed international obligations in interpreting national law means that it is not silent on its effects in the national legal order, nor allows States to keep international norms out of their courts entirely.

Second, as a more practical effect, the principle of consistent interpretation may bypass certain obstacles raised by national law to the application and effectuation of international law in national courts. For example, the case of *Timken Co. v. U.S.* (2002) demonstrates how the principle can be used by litigants to overcome limitations on standing.[929] The *Timken* court held that a private party can not challenge government action on the ground that it violates the World Trade Organization agreement because national law explicitly precludes such an action.[930] However, the court held that a litigant is free to claim that the government's application and interpretation of United States antidumping law is contrary to congressional intent on the ground that it violates the WTO agreement which Congress intended to implement.[931] Obviously, the result is by and large the same. Thus, in this case the prin-

[926] U.S., District Court (New York), *United States v. Palestine Liberation Organization*, 1988, 695 F.Supp. 1456 at 1463-1465.

[927] Id., at 1471.

[928] See also Germany, Bundesverfassungsgericht, *In re G.*, 14 October 2004, 2 BvR 1481/04, para. 51: "Hat der [ECtHR] eine innerstaatliche Vorschrift für konventionswidrig erklärt, so kann diese Vorschrift entweder in der Rechtsanwendungspraxis völkerrechtskonform ausgelegt werden, oder der Gesetzgeber hat die Möglichkeit, diese mit der Konvention unvereinbare innerstaatliche Vorschrift zu ändern."

[929] U.S., United States Court of International Trade, *The Timken Company v. U.S.*, 5 September 2002, 240 F.Supp.2d 1228.

[930] Id., at 1238.

[931] Id.

ciple was used to indirectly challenge rather than interpret national law on the basis of a treaty, where national law would normally rule out such a challenge. Such effects of the principle of consistent interpretation can significantly curtail the freedom of implementation in practice by limiting a State's ability to control the justiciability of rules of international law and the standing of private parties to invoke them.[932]

5.3 **Separate Regimes for Specific Categories?**

The previous two sub-paragraphs have discussed the limits of the freedom of implementation in general. It may also be asked whether this freedom of the State applies equally to all international law, or requires qualification for particular categories of international norms. In contemporary international law, this question appears most pertinent for international norms of a humanitarian character, as well as those of *jus cogens* status.[933]

5.3.a *International Law of a Humanitarian Character*

Numerous commentators have noted that international law's increased focus on and direct ties to the individual call into question the continued viability of the freedom of implementation as a general rule.[934] Conceptually, the fact that international law is to a lesser and lesser extent exclusively inter-State law erodes the rationale for complete State control over its implementation at least to a certain degree.[935] Where international law governs the rights and duties of individuals, it

---

[932] See Betlem and Nollkaemper 2003, p. 577-578; Iwasawa 1986, p. 689-690. Cf. Fleuren 2004, p. 377-382.

[933] Note in this regard that a recent study on the implementation of Security Council resolutions concludes that "despite the proliferation of sanctions, the quasi-constitutional nature of Security Council resolutions contrasts with the place and formal ranking given to these resolutions in domestic law" and "[d]espite the importance of these resolutions, at the domestic level, even in monist states they are assimilated to non self-executing treaty obligations and do not have immediate legal effects for individuals in member states." Gowlland-Debbas 2003, p. 69-70. See elaborately Gowlland Debbas and Tehindrazanarivelo 2004. Therefore, Security Council resolutions will not be studied as a separate category of international norms here.

[934] See Stein 1994, p. 450: "Despite the pervasive mutation in the international system, the state is not about to 'whither away.' Yet, because of this mutation, one may question the continued functionality of the rule that a state is free, subject only to the broad international 'good faith' standard, to choose the ways and means of implementing a treaty to which it is a party, and specifically to determine whether a treaty should or should not directly apply in its internal legal order. Unfettered discretion in the hands of national political institutions is particularly problematic in the case of treaties aimed at granting rights to, and imposing obligations upon, individuals."; Cf. Ferdinandusse 2003, p. 102-109; Nollkaemper 2000, p. 6-7, 13, 20 and 27; Bothe 1996, p. 302; Pescatore 1987, p. 274; Buergenthal 1985, p. 20 ("A legal system developed over centuries to regulate relations between states must make considerable conceptual adjustments to accommodate the extension of its normative reach to individuals.").

[935] Cf. Gaja 2003, p. 7 ("Should one accept the view that international law confers rights and obligations on individuals, it seems reasonable to hold that international law may also impose obligations on specific State organs.").

may not require the same freedom of implementation as where it functions primarily as a contract between States.[936]

The question of whether the general freedom rule applies to international law governing individuals is particularly pertinent for international law of a humanitarian character.[937] This category of international law has been loosely, and somewhat circularly, defined as those norms "that uphold and promote humanitarian principles and the human dignity of individuals."[938] These norms are found in the closely related bodies of human rights law, international criminal law and international humanitarian law. There are strong indications that this field of international law has particular characteristics, which set it apart from public international law in general and have practical consequences for its creation and application. It may be asked whether these characteristics also have their bearing on the implementation regime for this field of law, possibly resulting in a modification of the freedom rule.

The first characteristic that distinguishes international law of a humanitarian character from general international law is its largely non-reciprocal nature.[939] While this category of international law undoubtedly creates (often *erga omnes*) obligations between States, it is not simply State-to-State law. The ICJ held long ago that the Genocide Convention "was manifestly adopted for a purely humanitarian and civilizing purpose. [...] Consequently, in a convention of this type one cannot speak of individual advantages or disadvantages to States, nor of the maintenance of a perfect contractual balance between rights and duties."[940] The authoritative commentary on the Geneva Conventions asserts that the obligation "to respect and to ensure respect for the present Convention in all circumstances" in common Art. 1 "is not an engagement concluded on a basis of reciprocity, binding each party to the contract only in so far as the other party observes its obligations. It is rather a series of unilateral engagements solemnly contracted before the world [...] so universally recognized as an imperative call of civilization."[941]

Human rights bodies have adopted the same line of reasoning. The IACtHR has emphasized that "modern human rights treaties in general, and the American Convention in particular, are not multilateral treaties of the traditional type concluded

---

[936] Cf. Kelsen 1942, p. 89-97.

[937] See Rasulov 2003, p. 151-152; Craven 2000, p. 492-493. Cf. Provost 1995, p. 383.

[938] See Rasulov 2003, p. 144 (drawing on the term "treaties of a humanitarian character" in Art. 60 (5) VCLT, which is generally understood to comprise human rights law as well as international humanitarian law). See also Provost 1995, p. 402-403.

[939] See e.g. Common Art. 1 GI/IV; Art. 1(1) AP I; Art. 4(1) AP II. See also Meron 1989, p. 246.

[940] ICJ, *Reservations to the Convention on the Prevention and Punishment of Genocide (Advisory Opinion)*, 19511951 ICJ 23.

[941] Pictet *et al.* 1960, Vol. IV, p. 15. Cf. Art. 63 GC I, Art. 62 GC II, Art. 142 GC III, Art. 158 GC IV, Art. 1 (2) AP I and Preamble, para. 4 AP II; ICJ, *Case Concerning Military and Paramilitary Activities in and against Nicaragua (Nicaragua v. United States of America)*, 27 June 1986, para. 220: "[T]here is an obligation on the United States Government, in the terms of Article 1 of the Geneva Conventions, to 'respect' the Conventions and even 'to ensure respect' for them 'in all circumstances,' since such an obligation does not derive only from the Conventions themselves, but from the general principles of humanitarian law to which the Conventions merely give specific expression."

to accomplish the reciprocal exchange of rights for the mutual benefit of the contracting States," but rather that the ACHR is a "multilateral legal instrument or framework enabling States to make binding unilateral commitments not to violate the human rights of individuals within their jurisdiction."[942] Similar observations have been made by other human rights bodies.[943]

That international obligations of a humanitarian character are not subject to a condition of reciprocity to the same extent as general international law has various concrete consequences. It means obligations of this kind may not be affected by countermeasures,[944] while relevant treaty provisions can not be terminated or suspended in case of a material breach by another contracting party.[945]

Second, the practice of international bodies shows a trend to limit not only the principle of reciprocity, but also the principle of consent for (at least certain) international obligations of a humanitarian character. The HRC has repeatedly asserted that "human rights treaties devolve with territory, and that States continue to be bound by the obligations under the [ICCPR] entered into by the predecessor State. Once the people living in a territory find themselves under the protection of the International Covenant on Civil and Political Rights, they cannot be stripped of that protection on account of a change in sovereignty."[946] This position thus denies States the choice to be bound by the ICCPR or not in respect of territories which they have acquired from States Parties to the Covenant. It further implies "that international law does not permit a State which has ratified or acceded or succeeded to the Covenant to denounce it or withdraw from it."[947] There is also support for the assertion that treaties of a humanitarian character are subject to automatic succession for new States[948] and a strong presumption against the admissibility of reservations, which, however, falls short of a total ban.[949]

---

[942] IACtHR, The Effect of Reservations on the Entry Into Force of the American Convention on Human Rights (Art. 74 and 75), 24 September 1982, Advisory Opinion OC-2/82, (Ser. A) No. 2, para. 29 and 33.

[943] See Craven 2000, p. 498-510; Schabas 2000b, p. 529-531; Provost 1995, p. 387-388.

[944] See Art. 50 (1) sub b and c Articles on State Responsibility (2001) (excluding "obligations for the protection of fundamental human rights" and "obligations of a humanitarian character prohibiting reprisals" from obligations that can be affected by countermeasures). Note that in this article, obligations of a humanitarian character refer to humanitarian law only, while human rights law is mentioned separately. See Commentary to Art. 50, p. 336.

[945] See Art. 60 (5) VCLT (prohibiting the termination or suspension of "provisions relating to the protection of the human person contained in treaties of a humanitarian character" in case of the material breach of a treaty).

[946] HRC, *Concluding Observations on Portugal (Macau)*, 4 November 1999, Doc. CCPR/C/79/Add.108, para. 3. See also HRC, *Concluding Observations on Portugal*, 5 May 1997, Doc. CCPR/C/79/Add.77, para. 4 and references cited there.

[947] HRC, *General Comment 26 (Continuity of obligations)*, 8 December 1997, para. 5.

[948] See ICJ, *Case Concerning Application of the Convention on the Prevention and Punishment of the Crime of Genocide (Bosnia-Herzegovina v. Yugoslavia), preliminary objections*, 11 July 1996, Separate Opinions of Judges Shahabuddeen and Weeramantry.

[949] See principally ECtHR, *Loizidou v. Turkey, Preliminary Objections*, 23 March 1995, para. 95; IACtHR, The Effect of Reservations on the Entry Into Force of the American Convention on Human

Likewise, the ICJ has observed on different occasions that "a great many rules" of humanitarian law are "fundamental to the respect of the human person" as well as "elementary considerations of humanity," and "are to be observed by all States whether or not they have ratified the conventions that contain them, because they constitute intransgressible principles of international customary law."[950] Of course, *all* customary international obligations must be observed also by States that have not ratified treaties containing identical norms. This is not particular for international law of a humanitarian character. However, the language quoted in the paragraphs above suggests that something more is at stake than just the familiar situation of parallel sources of international obligations. Terms like "an imperative call of civilization," "elementary considerations of humanity" and "intransgressible principles," suggest that these norms are always binding, at least partly *because* of their humanitarian character.[951]

Third, it appears that the formation of new customary rules of a humanitarian character is subject to more lenient demands than those for customary international law in general. This method of ascertaining custom essentially puts more emphasis on the requirement of *opinio juris*, and less on that of State practice.[952] Courts and commentators speak in this regard of an "enlightened analysis" of customary law,[953] the utilization of *opinio necessitatis*[954] or modern positivism.[955] The *ad hoc* tribunals have relied on it for important findings, such as the existence of individual criminal responsibility for acts committed in internal armed conflicts.[956] Recently, the Ethiopia-Eritrea Arbitration Commission observed that there are "important modern authorities [...] for the proposition that rules that commend themselves to the international community in general, such as rules of international humanitarian

Rights (Art. 74 and 75), 24 September 1982, Advisory Opinion OC-2/82, (Ser. A) No. 2; ICJ, *Reservations to the Convention on the Prevention and Punishment of Genocide (Advisory Opinion)*, 1951. See also Redgwell 2003, p. 395-404; Craven 2000, p. 494-497 and 507-510; Schabas 2000b, p. 530-531; Lijnzaad 1995.

950 ICJ, *Legality of the Threat or Use of Nuclear Weapons, Advisory Opinion*, 8 July 1996, para. 79 (quoting *Corfu Channel* 1949, 1949 ICJ 22).

951 See ICJ, *Reservations to the Convention on the Prevention and Punishment of Genocide (Advisory Opinion)*, 19511951 ICJ 23: "The origins of the Convention show that it was the intention of the United Nations to condemn and punish genocide as 'a crime under international law' involving a denial of the right of existence of entire human groups, a denial which shocks the conscience of mankind and results in great losses to humanity, and which is contrary to moral law and to the spirit and aims of the United Nations (Resolution 96 (I) of the General Assembly, December 11th 1946). The first consequence *arising from this conception* is that the principles underlying the Convention are principles which are recognized by civilized nations as binding on States, even without any conventional obligation." (emphasis added)

952 See Meron 1998, p. 28. See also Sliedregt 2003, p. 7-8; Zegveld 2002a, p. 22-24 and Meron 1996. Some scholars argue that instead of differentiating the threshold for custom, certain fields, like human rights law, should be regarded as embodying general principles of law rather than customary norms. See Safferling 2001, p. 26-27.

953 Meron 1998, p. 26.

954 See ICTY, Trial Chamber, *Kupreskic*, 14 January 2000, para. 527.

955 See Heinegg 2003, p. 34; Roberts 2001; Simma and Paulus 1999. See also Reydams 2003, p. 7-8; Koskenniemi 1990; Meron 1989, p. 42, 74 and 246-247.

956 See below, Chapter V, para. 3.1.

law, can more quickly become part of customary international law than other types of rules found in treaties."[957] While this particular method is closely tied to the limited direct and public interaction between States in this field of law,[958] the humanitarian character of the norms in question also plays a role.

Yet the law is more complex than many of the statements above suggest. An elaborate study on the principle of reciprocity in human rights and humanitarian law published in 1995 concludes that "reciprocity permeates both bodies of law without constituting a fundamental principle of either."[959] Humanitarian law may contain a strong presumption against reprisals, but various States have explicitly asserted their right to resort to reprisals under certain circumstances as recently as their ratification of the ICC Statute.[960] Also, two recent studies conclude that State practice does not on the whole reflect a principle of automatic succession for treaties of a humanitarian character.[961]

Thus, it would be an overstatement to say that the principles of reciprocity and consent play no role at all in international law of a humanitarian character. In this regard, it is important to realize that international law of a humanitarian character is, and long has been, the subject of continuous efforts by various actors to enhance its efficacy, *inter alia* through a diminution of the role of reciprocity and consent. Humanitarian law in particular was traditionally a fully contractual and reciprocal field of law, but has developed more and more towards a model of unconditional and universal application.[962] This development explains why law of a humanitarian character and its constitutive instruments contain both reciprocal and non-reciprocal elements, sometimes in awkward combinations.[963]

International courts and bodies, as well as NGOs, play a leading role in the quest for a more effective international law of a humanitarian character and the corresponding curtailment of the principles of reciprocity and consent. There is, therefore, good reason for a critical assessment of their findings on the particular nature of this field of law, as these may well be more progressive than existing law. A certain skepticism is in order especially when particular effects, such as unconditional and universal application, are grounded not on legal arguments but on normative appeals to notions such as an "imperative call of civilization" or "elementary considerations of humanity." Such normative claims can also be characterized as

[957] Eritrea-Ethiopia Claims Commission, *Partial Awards on Prisoners of War between the State of Eritrea and the Federal Democratic Republic of Ethiopia*, 1 July 2003 Eritrea's Claim 17, para. 40. See also Roht-Arriaza 1990, p. 490-492.

[958] See Steiner and Alston 2000, p. 227-232; Meron 1989, p. 44.

[959] Provost 1995, p. 453.

[960] See Kleffner 2003, p. 102; Rowe and Meyer 1996, p. 480; Rowe 1991, p. 223; Röling 1979, p. 190. See also Moir 2002, p. 237-243 (on the presumed illegality of reprisals in internal armed conflict); Greenwood 2001.

[961] See Rasulov 2003, p. 157-167 and International Law Association, *Rapport final sur la succession en matière de traités*, April 2002, p. 28.

[962] See Abi-Saab 1984, p. 266-270. Cf. Provost 1995, p. 384-385.

[963] Compare e.g. common Art. 1 and 2 Geneva Conventions.

techniques in a hegemonic struggle for greater control between different actors in international law, and there may indeed be some truth in the oft-cited notion that "whoever invokes humanity wants to cheat."[964]

Even when leaving aside the institutional interests of the actors involved, appeals to the tenets of humanity and civilization may be criticized as indeterminate and therefore unworkable. This indeterminacy calls into question exactly which rule and principles of a humanitarian character are subject to particular regimes such as a limitation of the principles of reciprocity and consent. After all, the obligation to refrain from genocide can be more convincingly characterized as an "imperative call of civilization" than, say, the obligation to guarantee the right of reply.[965] In general, the imperative character of legal rules is more often than not debatable. For example, some people would characterize bull-fighting as "a violation of the plain dictates of the law of humanity,"[966] whereas others would certainly disagree.

Still, it seems there is sufficient consensus on at least the limited core of standards of humanity and civilization necessary to attach tangible legal consequences to such notions. Few people would deny that acts of genocide or crimes against humanity are incompatible with basic notions of humanity and civilization.[967] This core, however, is very limited indeed. Developments in recent years shed doubt even on the long-established[968] characterization of the prohibition of torture as a common minimal standard. In some States that have long condemned torture as inhumane, there is a public debate on the (il)legitimacy of the use of torture against suspects of terrorism.[969] There are indications that at least one such State actually engages in institutionalized torture of terrorism suspects.[970] Moreover, some national courts in other liberal States have explicitly found that under certain circumstances extradition of individuals facing torture may be justified[971] or that evidence

---

[964] See Koskenniemi 2003, p. 97 and 108-110.

[965] See on the right of reply as embodied in the ACHR above, note 877.

[966] U.S., Supreme Judicial Court of Massachusetts, *Commonwealth v. Tilton*, October Term, 1844, 49 Mass. 232 at 234-235: "[T]he game or sport of cock- fighting is unlawful, because it is a violation alike of the prohibitions of a statute, and of the plain dictates of the law of humanity [...] As being barbarous and cruel, leading to disorder and danger, and tending to deaden the feelings of humanity, both in those who participate in it, and those who witness it, it appears to us to stand on the same footing with bull-fighting..."

[967] See Koskenniemi 1990, p. 1946-1947: "It is inherently difficult to accept the notion that states are legally bound not to engage in genocide [...] only if they have ratified and not formally denounced the 1948 Genocide Convention. Some norms seem so basic, so important, that it is more than slightly artificial to argue that states are legally bound to comply with them simply because there exists an agreement between them to that effect..."; Lauterpacht 1944, p. 65.

[968] See Hope 2004, p. 823-826.

[969] See e.g. McCarthy 2004.

[970] See Hope 2004, p. 827-832; *The United States' 'Disappeared': The CIA's Long-Term 'Ghost Detainees,'* Human Rights Watch Briefing Paper, October 2004, p. 10-13, available at http://www.humanrightswatch.org/backgrounder/usa/us1004/index.htm. Cf. Cassese 2004a (on the attempts of the U.S. Government to relativize the impact of the international prohibition of torture on its officials).

[971] See below, note 1015.

resulting from torture may be admissible in court.[972] Regrettable as these developments may be, they do not seriously challenge the international prohibition of torture. Yet, they illustrate that appeals to self-evident standards of humanity and civilization are credible only for a very limited category of norms.

The question then arises whether the particular position of international law of a humanitarian character extends to its implementation. Human rights bodies, in particular the HRC, have argued that a specific legal regime for this field of law is necessary to ensure its effective enforcement. According to this line of reasoning, the effectuation of international law which regulates the rights and duties of individuals, as international law of a humanitarian character largely does, can not be left to the standard enforcement mechanisms on the international level but must primarily take place in the national legal order.[973] Thus, while the importance or natural law character of the rules involved may also play a role, this argument is grounded in essence on an appeal to effectiveness. This argument implies a significant restriction of States' freedom of implementation, in its strongest form amounting to mandatory direct applicability of the international rules.

Most human rights bodies have advanced this argument in a merely aspirational formulation.[974] The UN Committee on Economic, Social and Cultural Rights, for example, first acknowledged that the ICESCR does not formally command its incorporation in domestic law, but then stated that such incorporation was nevertheless "desirable" and that "[i]n general, legally binding international human rights standards should operate directly and immediately within the domestic legal system of each State party, thereby enabling individuals to seek enforcement of their rights before national courts and tribunals."[975] The ECtHR has similarly endorsed the advantages of incorporation while upholding its optional character.[976]

---

[972] See U.K., Court of Appeal, *A, B, C, D, E, F, G, H, Mahmoud Abu Rideh, Jamal Ajouaou v. Secretary of State*, 11 August 2004, in particular para. 125-138, 253, 423, 438 and 506.

[973] See Committee on Economic, *General comment 9*, 3 December 1998, UN Doc E/C.12/1998/24, para. 4 ("The existence and further development of international procedures for the pursuit of individual [human rights] claims is important, but such procedures are ultimately only supplementary to effective national remedies."). See also the effective remedy clauses in the human rights treaties, below note 1109. Cf. Seibert-Fohr 2001, p. 426-429.

[974] See Seibert-Fohr 2001, p. 422-423; Tomuschat 2001, p. 360-364; Buergenthal 1992, p. 336.

[975] See Committee on Economic, *General comment 9*, 3 December 1998, UN Doc E/C.12/1998/24, para. 4 and 8: "In general, legally binding international human rights standards should operate directly and immediately within the domestic legal system of each State party, thereby enabling individuals to seek enforcement of their rights before national courts and tribunals. [...] While the [International Covenant on Economic, Social and Cultural Rights] does not formally oblige States to incorporate its provisions in domestic law, such an approach is desirable. Direct incorporation avoids problems that might arise in the translation of treaty obligations into national law, and provides a basis for the direct invocation of the Covenant rights by individuals in national courts. For these reasons, the Committee strongly encourages formal adoption or incorporation of the Covenant in national law."

[976] See ECtHR, *Ireland v. UK*, 18 January 1978, para. 239: "[T]he drafters of the Convention [...] intended to make it clear that the rights and freedoms set out in Section I would be directly secured to anyone within the jurisdiction of the Contracting States [...]. That intention finds a particularly faithful reflection in those instances where the Convention has been incorporated into domestic law." See also above, note 793.

The HRC likewise started out cautiously and has long adhered to the position that "article 2 of the Covenant generally leaves it to the States parties concerned to choose their method of implementation in their territories within the framework set out in that article."[977] In recent years, however, the HRC has substantially increased its demands on States.[978] It has found that States may not rely on unwritten law but must codify human rights law,[979] and that "the need to comply with the international obligations [under the ICCPR] should be taken fully into account by the judiciary."[980] Moreover, the HRC recommends and requires incorporation and direct application of the ICCPR with increasing forcefulness.[981] In its 1994 concluding observations on Nepal, for example, the Committee emphasized "the need for the provisions of the Covenant to be fully incorporated into domestic law and made enforceable by domestic courts."[982] Thus, the HRC assumes considerable restrictions on the freedom of implementation and is edging closer and closer towards mandatory direct applicability of the ICCPR.[983]

State practice reveals some noteworthy trends regarding the implementation of international law of a humanitarian character. Numerous States have vested (parts of) international human rights law with constitutional status which differs from the position of international law in general, thereby limiting their own ability to shape or limit the effectuation of human rights law through national law.[984] Conceptually, this choice of the legislature is an exercise rather than a negation of the freedom of implementation. Also, it appears this trend is prompted largely by practical developments.[985] Still, it amounts to a practical restriction of the freedom of implemen-

[977] HRC, *General Comment 3 (Article 2: Implementation at the national level)*, 29 July 1981, para. 1. See for an overview of the HRC's jurisprudence to this effect Seibert-Fohr 2001, p. 429-430.

[978] See Seibert-Fohr 2001, p. 430-438.

[979] See HRC, *Concluding Observations on the United Kingdom of Great Britain and Northern Ireland, Doc. CCPR/C/79/Add.55*, 21 July 1995, para. 9 and 20; HRC, *Concluding Observations on Iceland, Doc. CCPR/C/79/Add.26*, 3 November 1993, para. 6.

[980] See above, note 901. See also Seibert-Fohr 2001, p. 434-435.

[981] See e.g. HRC, *Concluding Observations on Denmark, Doc. CCPR/C/79/Add.68*, 18 November 1996, para. 17 ("The Committee recommends that the State party take appropriate measures to ensure the direct application of the provisions of the Covenant into domestic law."); HRC, *Concluding Observations on Gabon, Doc. CCPR/C/79/Add.71*, 18 November 1996, para. 18 ("The Committee recommends that the Covenant be incorporated in the domestic legal order and that its provisions be made directly applicable before the courts."). See also Seibert-Fohr 2001, p. 433-436

[982] HRC, *Concluding Observations on Nepal, Doc. CCPR/C/79/Add.41*, 10 November 1994, para. 12.

[983] See Seibert-Fohr 2001, p. 436. See for a finding of mandatory direct applicability of the Covenant in the limited context of detention review HRC, *A. v. Australia*, 30 April 1997, CCPR/C/59/D/560/1993, para. 9.5: "By stipulating that the [national] court must have the power to order release 'if the detention is not lawful,' article 9, paragraph 4, [ICCPR] requires that the court be empowered to order release, if the detention is incompatible with the requirements in article 9, paragraph 1, or in other provisions of the Covenant."

[984] See Vereshchetin 1996, p. 32-33; Stein 1994, p. 435-442; Buergenthal 1992, p. 350-355.

[985] See Buergenthal 1997, p. 214 (identifying the institutional dynamics of international human rights courts and the emergence from non-democratic rule as important incentives for States to elevate human rights norms to constitutional rank).

tation as well as a recognition of the tension between far-reaching freedom of the State on the one hand and the effectuation of international law of a humanitarian character on the other.

Furthermore, several national courts have enforced international norms of a humanitarian character in ways that coincide with the HRC's stricter views on the need for effective application at the national level.[986] In *Tavita v. Minister of Immigration* (1994), for example, a Court of Appeals in New Zealand dismissed the suggestion that the Minister of Immigration and his Department were at liberty to ignore the (unincorporated) ICCPR and the Convention on the Rights of the Child as "an unattractive argument, apparently implying that New Zealand's adherence to the international instruments has been at least partly window-dressing."[987] The court avoided a ruling on this point by granting a stay to allow the Minister to reconsider his decision in this case, but warned that "[t]he law as to the bearing on domestic law of international human rights and instruments declaring them is undergoing evolution."[988]

Various national courts have acknowledged the non-reciprocal nature of international obligations of a humanitarian character. In the *Oubeid* case (2003), the Israeli Supreme Court rejected the argument of the Israeli Attorney General that two Lebanese prisoners could be denied visits of ICRC delegates on account of Hezbollah's

---

[986] See e.g. India, Supreme Court, *Vishaka v. State of Rajasthan*, 13 August 1997, (1999) Butterworths H.R.C. 261: "There is no reason why [certain unincorporated] international conventions and norms cannot, therefore, be used for construing the fundamental rights expressly guaranteed in the Constitution of India which embody the basic concept of gender equality in all spheres of human activity.
In view of the above, and the absence of enacted law to provide for the effective enforcement of the basic human right of gender equality and guarantee against sexual harassment and abuse, more particularly against sexual harassment at work places, we lay down the guidelines and norms specified hereinafter for due observance at all work places or other institutions, until a legislation is enacted for the purpose."
Australia, High Court, *Minister for Immigration and Ethnic Affairs v. Teoh*, 7 April 1995, 183 CLR 273 at 291, per Justices Mason and Deane: "Ratification by Australia of an international convention is not to be dismissed as a merely platitudinous or ineffectual act, particularly when the instrument evidences internationally accepted standards to be applied by courts and administrative authorities in dealing with basic human rights affecting the family and children. Rather, ratification of a convention is a positive statement by the executive government of this country to the world and to the Australian people that the executive government and its agencies will act in accordance with the convention. That positive statement is an adequate foundation for a legitimate expectation, absent statutory or executive indications to the contrary, that administrative decision-makers will act in conformity with the Convention."
Cf. Jamaica, Privy Council, *Lewis v. Attorney General*, (2001) 2 AC 50 at 84-85; Trinidad and Tobago, Privy Council, *Briggs v. Baptiste*, 28 October 1999, [2000] 2 AC 40, dissenting judgment Lord Nicholls of Birkenhead; Trinidad and Tobago, Privy Council, *Thomas and Hilaire v. Baptiste*, 23 March 1999, (1999) 3 W.L.R. 249. See on these cases also Collins 2002, p. 494-496. See further examples in the literature cited above, note 874.

[987] New-Zealand, Court of Appeals, *Tavita v. Minister of Immigration*, 17 December 1993, [1994] 2 NZLR 257 at 265.

[988] Id.

refusal to allow such visits to kidnapped Israeli soldiers.[989] Some courts have accordingly set aside limitations of national law based on the principle of reciprocity. The French Constitutional Court held in 1999 that treaties aiming to protect fundamental human rights are exempted from the constitutional requirement of reciprocal application of treaties by other States parties.[990] However not all national courts follow this line. In *Hamdi v. Rumsfeld* (2003), a U.S. court of appeals held the Third Geneva Convention to be non-self-executing in order to avoid "creating disparity among nations," thus ignoring the non-reciprocal nature of the Geneva Conventions.[991]

However, it should be noted that these cases are generally stronger in language than in consistency, and thus not representative of national judicial practice. Judgments denying in clear terms the ability of the State to reject the direct applicability of humanitarian treaties are matched by at least as many judgments holding such treaties to be non-self-executing.[992] Thus, it may be asked to what extent the views of the HRC reflect current international law, and more generally whether State practice indicates a more stringent regime of implementation for international law of a humanitarian character. As noted earlier, it is generally assumed that international law, including that of a humanitarian character, is not directly applicable *per se*.[993] State practice reveals broad acceptance of the HRC's demand that national courts should take relevant international obligations into account,[994] but not of mandatory direct application of the ICCPR or international law of a humanitarian character more generally. As is apparent from the observations of the HRC itself, many States do not allow for direct application of (specific parts of) the ICCPR.[995] In light of the absence of a clear textual basis in the ICCPR and the HRC's own earlier find-

---

[989] Israel, Supreme Court, *Oubeid and al-Dirani v. Minister of Defence et al.*, 23 August 2001. See in particular 32 Israel YBHR 352. See also Israel, Supreme Court, *Society of Physicians for Human Rights v. IDF Commander in the West Bank*, 8 April 2002 (abuse of ambulances in combat situations by Palestinians does not constitute a justification for the Israeli army to violate rules of humanitarian law).

[990] See above, note 382.

[991] U.S., Court of Appeals (Fourth Circuit), *Hamdi v. Rumsfeld*, 8 January 2003, 316 F.3d 450 at 469: "[W]e would have thereby imposed on the United States a mechanism of enforceability that might not find an analogue in any other nation. This is not to say, of course, that the Geneva Convention is meaningless. Rather, its values are vindicated by diplomatic means and reciprocity, as specifically contemplated by Article 132." Reversed on other grounds in U.S., Supreme Court, *Hamdi v. Rumsfeld*, 28 June 2004, 124 S.Ct. 2633.

[992] See e.g. Switzerland, Military Court of Cassation, *In re N.*, 27 April 2001, para. 9 (a): "Quant aux Art. 146 et 147 de la Convention (IV) de Genève relative à la protection des personnes civiles en temps de guerre, il s'agit de dispositions énonçant des obligations mises à la charge des Parties contractantes (promulguer une législation spéciale pour les sanctions pénales à appliquer aux personnes ayant commis des infractions graves à cette Convention; rechercher toute personne prévenue d'une violation de la Convention; juger une telle personne ou la remettre pour jugement à un autre Etat intéressé); elles ne contiennent donc pas de règles directement applicables à la conduite des hostilités."; U.S., Court of Appeals, D.C.Cir., *Demjanjuk v. Meese*, 27 February 1986, 784 F.2d 1114 (finding the Genocide Convention non-self-executing).

[993] See above, note 793.

[994] See above, para. 5.2.

[995] See Seibert-Fohr 2001, p. 429-436.

ings to the contrary, it thus appears that the Committee's cautious move towards mandatory direct application does not currently represent positive international law. Still, cases such as *Tavita* demonstrate that national courts, like the HRC, can be particularly uncomfortable with the room that unfettered freedom of implementation leaves for States to distort or negate the effects of international law where it concerns obligations of a humanitarian character.

In conclusion, there is a notable difference between the potential of the idea to subject international law of a humanitarian character to a more stringent regime of implementation and its acceptance in current international law. Conceptually, it is not difficult to see the logic of a more stringent regime. If some international norms are so fundamental that they bind States *per se* regardless of their consent, while proceedings on the national level provide the most, or even only, effective means of enforcement, it is difficult to accept that the applicability of those norms in national courts is subject to the discretion of the State.

On balance, however, State practice shows a certain tendency to limit the freedom of implementation for international obligations of a humanitarian character, yet is far from conclusive in this regard. National courts have on various occasions limited the principle of reciprocity or the State's freedom to disregard signed but unratified treaties, but in many other cases treated norms of a humanitarian character no differently than general international law. Thus, the special position of international law of a humanitarian character appears to be in development, but should not be overstated.

5.3.b *Jus Cogens*

The idea that States are governed by a category of "peremptory norms of international law," or *jus cogens*, has gained significant support both in practice and doctrine over the last fifty years.[996] The concept of *jus cogens* was developed within the law of treaties, but there is considerable support nowadays for its broader application beyond that field of law.[997] According to the Vienna Convention on the Law of Treaties, "a peremptory norm of general international law is a norm accepted and recognized by the international community of States as a whole as a norm from which no derogation is permitted and which can be modified only by a subsequent norm of general international law having the same character."[998] The concept of *jus cogens* is puzzling in literally all its aspects. It is unclear exactly how a norm is elevated to or demoted from *jus cogens* status, what are the consequences of that status, and which norms currently fit into the category of peremptory norms.[999] In 1990, a commentator aired his bewilderment in this regard in the aptly titled article

[996] See principally Seiderman 2001, p. 35-121; Hannikainen 1988; Alexidze 1981; Gaja 1981; Robledo 1981.

[997] See Wet 2004, p. 98-100; Seiderman 2001, p. 56-59; Weisburd 1995, p. 18-19; Gaja 1981, p. 290-301.

[998] Art. 53 VCLT. See also Art. 64 and 71.

[999] See Weisburd 1995, p. 10-40. Cf. Nieto-Navia 2003, p. 610-622 and 627-640.

"It's a bird, it's a plane, it's *jus cogens*."[1000] Since then, writings and judgments of all sorts have prolifically invoked the concept of *jus cogens*, but the confusion remains.[1001]

Leaving aside the many other intricacies of *jus cogens*, this section focuses solely on its possible consequences for the implementation of international obligations in national legal systems.[1002] Although the concept of *jus cogens* principally elevates norms to a higher status on the international plane, it has been suggested that it may also affect their status and application in national legal orders.[1003] Indeed, there is both international and national practice to suggest that the effectuation of *jus cogens* norms in the national legal order is governed by a particular regime that is more demanding than that of international norms in general. On the international plane, the ICTY found in its *Furundzija* judgment that the *jus cogens* nature of the prohibition against torture has certain effects at "the inter- state *and* individual levels."[1004]

On the national plane, numerous courts have embraced the idea that the peremptory character of international norms is relevant for their effects in the national legal order.[1005] National courts have suggested, *inter alia*, that the consequences of *jus cogens* status might include domestic validity in the absence of a corresponding rule of national law,[1006] supremacy over national rules, e.g. those on immunities,[1007] and strengthened enforcement differing from the normal separation of powers.[1008] Numerous national judgments concerning the core crimes refer to their *jus cogens* status as a significant factor.[1009] In a rare case of legislative practice, the 1999

[1000] D'Amato 1990.

[1001] See Salcedo 1997, p. 590. While there are some excellent studies on this subject, see above note 996, these face formidable obstacles. The complexity of the concept, its minimal regulation in written international law and the tendency of many courts and writers to invoke *jus cogens* in diverse ways without substantial analysis together perpetuate the existing confusion.

[1002] See for a specific analysis of the *jus cogens* status of the core crimes and its consequences for their prosecution below, Chapter V, para. 3.2.

[1003] See generally Wet 2004; Perkins 1997, p. 483-485.

[1004] ICTY, Trial Chamber, *Furundzija*, 10 December 1998, para. 155 (emphasis added). See for an analysis of this holding below, p. 166 *et seq*. See also ECtHR, *Al-Adsani v. United Kingdom*, 21 November 2001, in particular the separate and dissenting opinions.

[1005] See Stirling-Zanda 2000, p. 211-212.

[1006] See U.S., Court of Appeals (Ninth Circuit), *U.S. v. Matta-Ballesteros*, 1 December 1995, 71 F.3d 754 at 764 ("Kidnapping also does not qualify as a *jus cogens* norm, such that its commission would be justiciable in our courts even absent a domestic law.").

[1007] See Wet 2004, 105-112; Seiderman 2001, p. 111-115.

[1008] See *Committee of U.S. Citizens Living in Nicaragua v. Reagan*, 859 F.2d 929, 935 (1988): "When our government's two political branches, acting together, contravene an international legal norm, does this court have any authority to remedy the violation? The answer is "no" if the type of international obligation that Congress and the President violate is either a treaty or a rule of customary international law. If, on the other hand, Congress and the President violate a peremptory norm (or *jus cogens*), the domestic legal consequences are unclear."

[1009] See below, Chapter V, para. 5.

Swiss Constitution explicitly recognizes *jus cogens* as a limitation to the national legislative process.[1010]

However, it appears that neither international nor national practice regarding the domestic effects of *jus cogens* norms in general carries enough weight to carry a corresponding rule of customary international law. There is considerable contrary practice that treats *jus cogens* norms with less deference. The suggestion that the *jus cogens* status of international norms overrides immunities, whether contained in national or international rules, has ultimately been rejected by national[1011] and international[1012] courts alike. Numerous decisions of national courts reject the proposition that peremptory rules are exempt from the general national framework of implementation in any way.[1013] Some national courts have held that *jus cogens* status does not remove all discretion in the application of international law.[1014] In *Suresh v. Canada* (2002), for example, the Canadian Supreme Court cautiously accepted that the prohibition of torture might have *jus cogens* status, yet found that "in exceptional circumstances, deportation [of refugees who] face torture might be justified."[1015]

[1010] See Art. 139 (3) (Volksinitiative auf Teilrevision der Bundesverfassung): "Verletzt die Initiative die Einheit der Form, die Einheit der Materie oder zwingendes Völkerrecht, so erklärt die Bundesverfassung sie für ganz oder teilweise ungültig."
Art. 193 (4) (Totalrevision) "Die zwingenden Bestimmungen des Völkerrechts dürfen nicht verletzt werden."
Art. 194 (2) (Teilrevision) "Die Teilrevision muss die Einheit der Materie wahren und darf die zwingenden Bestimmungen des Völkerrechts nicht verletzen."
See Wet 2004, p. 101-105; Thürer 2001, p. 183-185.

[1011] See e.g. Germany, Bundesgerichtshof, *Distomo Massacre Case*, 26 June 2003, BGH – III ZR 245/98, para. I sub b (holding that international law does not deny State immunity for violations of *jus cogens*); See also Gattini 2003, p. 354 (stating that all superior domestic courts which have pronounced on the matter have declined to make an exception to State immunity for grave violations of fundamental human rights); Working Group of the International Law Commission, *Report on Jurisdictional Immunities of States and their Property*, 1999 (concluding that national case law predominantly upholds immunity claims in civil suits regarding *jus cogens* violations); Bergen 1999, p. 169 (observing that in U.S. case law, immunities apply also in cases concerning violations of *jus cogens* norms).

[1012] ICJ, International Court of Justice, *Case concerning the Arrest Warrant of 11 April 2000 (Democratic Republic of the Congo v. Belgium)*, 14 February 2002; ECtHR, *Kalogeropoulou v. Greece and Germany, Decision on Admissibility*, 12 December 2002, para. D1a (id.); ECtHR, *Al-Adsani v. United Kingdom*, 21 November 2001 (note however that the ECtHR decided Al-Adsani with a narrow 9-8 majority).

[1013] See e.g. U.S., Court of Appeals (Ninth Circuit), *Siderman de Blake v. Argentina*, 22 May 1992, 965 F.2d 699 (holding that the *jus cogens* character of a violated norm does not obviate the need to establish jurisdiction on the basis of the Foreign Sovereign Immunities Act).

[1014] See e.g. U.S., District Court (Cal.), *Sarei v. Rio Tinto PLC*, 9 July 2002, 221 F.Supp.2d 1116 at 1152-1153 and 1207 (rejecting racial discrimination as a basis for the civil claim of Papua New Guinea residents against international mining group "on international comity grounds," despite finding that racial discrimination constitutes a violation of a *jus cogens* norm and comity is a discretionary doctrine).

[1015] Canada, Supreme Court, *Suresh v. Canada (Minister of Citizenship and Immigration)*, 22 May 2002, 2002 SCC 1, para. 65 and 78:
"Although this Court is not being asked to pronounce on the status of the prohibition on torture in

Furthermore, the great majority of judgments, national or international, that privilege *jus cogens* norms is of limited authority. This case law consists to a significant extent of *obiter dicta* and decisions that have subsequently been overruled. Also, in many cases it is unclear whether an appeal to *jus cogens* status actually determines the outcome or merely serves to affirm a conclusion reached on other grounds. In addition, it can be unclear whether State practice actually says anything about the international rules regarding *jus cogens* or merely reflects a policy choice of the State. The value of the constitutional provisions in Switzerland, for example, is open to doubt. Does international law not prohibit national legislatures to contravene *any* international obligation, rather than just peremptory norms? From the viewpoint of international law, it is unclear whether these Swiss provisions express anything more than a partial reproduction of the well-established rule that States may not alter or contravene their international obligations through national legislation.[1016]

An additional problem that limits the authority of many relevant judgments is the quality of their reasoning.[1017] Many national courts declare international norms to be peremptory and to have far-reaching consequences without any analysis or substantiation. Often, it is clear from their holdings that they do not master the relevant law. This, obviously, undermines the authoritative value of their judgments. The assertion that a violation of a "*jus cogens* norm [is] justiciable in [national] courts even absent a domestic law," is an interesting and defensible proposition, but what is it worth coming from a court which believes that "murder" is a *jus cogens* norm?[1018]

International judges may be more knowledgeable about the concept of *jus cogens*, but their holdings are not necessarily clearer or better substantiated. The ICTY's dictum on the consequences of the *jus cogens* status of torture in *Furundzija*, for example, is rather ambiguous. In light of its broad recognition as an authoritative

---

international law, the fact that such a principle is included in numerous multilateral instruments, that it does not form part of any known domestic administrative practice, and that it is considered by many academics to be an emerging, if not established peremptory norm, suggests that it cannot be easily derogated from.

[...]

We do not exclude the possibility that in exceptional circumstances, deportation to face torture might be justified..."

See also Zambia, High Court, *The People v. Davies Mumeno, No HPR/79*, 10 July 1990, 1990-1992 Zambia Law Reports 13 (while *jus cogens* is not explicitly addressed, the court cites and follows the Zambian Supreme Court's holding that "corporal punishment is a form of inhuman and degrading punishment which should be imposed sparingly and only in most serious circumstances.").

1016 Cf. Wet 2004, p. 104-105.

1017 See Seiderman 2001, p. 93.

1018 U.S., Court of Appeals (Ninth Circuit), *U.S. v. Matta-Ballesteros*, 1 December 1995, 71 F.3d 754 at 764: "Kidnapping also does not qualify as a *jus cogens* norm, such that its commission would be justiciable in our courts even absent a domestic law. [...K]idnapping does not rise to the level of other jus cogens norms, such as torture, murder, genocide, and slavery."

precedent both in practice[1019] and doctrine,[1020] it will be analyzed here in some detail. The tribunal speaks of "effects at the inter- state *and* individual levels" which include international de-legitimization of national acts authorising torture and, consequently, criminal responsibility of torturers notwithstanding any national measure to the contrary.[1021] Furthermore, the Trial chamber holds that the peremptory character of the norm entitles every State to prosecute and punish torturers present on its territory and disallows the application of statutes of limitations and the political offence exemption to cases of torture.[1022]

[1019] It has been widely cited by national and international courts alike. See e.g. ECtHR, *Al-Adsani v. United Kingdom*, 21 November 2001, para. 30 and U.K., House of Lords, *R. v. Bow Street Metropolitan Stipendiary Magistrate & Others, Ex Parte Pinochet Ugarte (No. 3)*, 24 March 1999, [2000] 1 A.C. 147 at 198.

[1020] See e.g. Gitti 1999, p. 81-82; Wilson 1999, p. 955-956 and below, notes 1023 and 1024.

[1021] ICTY, Trial Chamber, *Furundzija*, 10 December 1998, para. 154-155:

"154. Clearly, the jus cogens nature of the prohibition against torture articulates the notion that the prohibition has now become one of the most fundamental standards of the international community. Furthermore, this prohibition is designed to produce a deterrent effect, in that it signals to all members of the international community and the individuals over whom they wield authority that the prohibition of torture is an absolute value from which nobody must deviate.

155. The fact that torture is prohibited by a peremptory norm of international law has other effects at the inter- state and individual levels. At the inter-state level, it serves to internationally de-legitimise any legislative, administrative or judicial act authorising torture. It would be senseless to argue, on the one hand, that on account of the jus cogens value of the prohibition against torture, treaties or customary rules providing for torture would be null and void ab initio, and then be unmindful of a State say, taking national measures authorising or condoning torture or absolving its perpetrators through an amnesty law. If such a situation were to arise, the national measures, violating the general principle and any relevant treaty provision, would produce the legal effects discussed above and in addition would not be accorded international legal recognition. Proceedings could be initiated by potential victims if they had locus standi before a competent international or national judicial body with a view to asking it to hold the national measure to be internationally unlawful; or the victim could bring a civil suit for damage in a foreign court, which would therefore be asked inter alia to disregard the legal value of the national authorising act. What is even more important is that perpetrators of torture acting upon or benefiting from those national measures may nevertheless be held criminally responsible for torture, whether in a foreign State, or in their own State under a subsequent regime. In short, in spite of possible national authorisation by legislative or judicial bodies to violate the principle banning torture, individuals remain bound to comply with that principle. As the International Military Tribunal at Nuremberg put it: 'individuals have international duties which transcend the national obligations of obedience imposed by the individual State'."

[1022] ICTY, Trial Chamber, *Furundzija*, 10 December 1998, para. 156-157:

"156. Furthermore, at the individual level, that is, that of criminal liability, it would seem that one of the consequences of the jus cogens character bestowed by the international community upon the prohibition of torture is that every State is entitled to investigate, prosecute and punish or extradite individuals accused of torture, who are present in a territory under its jurisdiction. Indeed, it would be inconsistent on the one hand to prohibit torture to such an extent as to restrict the normally unfettered treaty- making power of sovereign States, and on the other hand bar States from prosecuting and punishing those torturers who have engaged in this odious practice abroad. This legal basis for States' universal jurisdiction over torture bears out and strengthens the legal foundation for such jurisdiction found by other courts in the inherently universal character of the crime. It has been held that international crimes being universally condemned wherever they occur, every State has the right to prosecute and punish the authors of such crimes. As stated in general terms by the Supreme Court of Israel in Eichmann, and

One of the judges in the case has later asserted that this holding stands for the proposition that "peremptory norms may produce legal effects at the municipal law level."[1023] Several writers have drawn similar conclusions.[1024] On close reading, however, this interpretation is questionable. First, it should be noted that the language of the decision is often ambiguous. The "inter- state and individual levels" constitute a false dichotomy, since the individual level obviously does not represent the national legal order. After all, the Tribunal finds that at the individual level, "every State is entitled to investigate, prosecute and punish torture,"[1025] which can only be an entitlement under international law. The term "de-legitimise" in para. 155 is colloquial and has no clear-cut meaning in international law. In para. 156, the Tribunal first concludes that a right to prosecute torturers present in one's territory is "one of the consequences" of *jus cogens* status, but subsequently states that this legal basis "bears out and strengthens" the established legal foundation for universal jurisdiction, thus leaving unclear to what extent *jus cogens* status is either necessary or sufficient for the exercise of universal jurisdiction.

Second, the holding mentions various effects that are not particular for *jus cogens*. The maxim that international law pays no heed to contrary national law, either in international proceedings or for the determination of individual criminal responsibility, applies to all rules of international law, not only peremptory norms. The proposition that international law grants States universal jurisdiction over all *jus cogens* crimes while prohibiting them to apply statutes of limitations or the political offence exemption is interesting. Yet nothing in the judgment suggests that these effects are limited to *jus cogens* crimes only or take place directly on the municipal law level.

In conclusion, then, the *Furundzija* dictum says nothing new about the national implementation of *jus cogens* norms. The only other possible outcome requires an interpretation of para. 155 as envisaging the automatic invalidation of national acts contravening *jus cogens* directly in the national legal order rather than under international law. This interpretation is left open by the ambiguity of the relevant sentence, as it is unclear whether the finding that "the national measures [...] would produce the legal effects discussed above" refers back to being "null and void ab initio" or to international de-legitimisation. For the interpretation of automatic invalidation pleads that "international de-legitimisation" and "not being accorded international legal recognition" would amount to the same thing, for which reason

---

echoed by a USA court in Demjanjuk, 'it is the universal character of the crimes in question i.e. international crimes which vests in every State the authority to try and punish those who participated in their commission'."

157. It would seem that other consequences include the fact that torture may not be covered by a statute of limitations, and must not be excluded from extradition under any political offence exemption."

[1023] See Cassese 2001c, p. 145.

[1024] See De Wet 2003, p. 100 (speaking of a proposal to apply *jus cogens* in national law) and Seiderman 2001, p. 59 (concluding that "the jus cogens character of norms carries direct legal effects vis-à-vis the legal character of all official domestic actions").

[1025] ICTY, Trial Chamber, *Furundzija*, 10 December 1998, para. 156.

"the legal effects discussed above" must refer back to being "null and void ab initio." This interpretation is squarely contradicted, however, by the fact that the paragraph sets out to discuss effects at "the inter-state level." Moreover, in para. 150, the Trial Chamber found that "the mere fact of keeping in force or passing legislation contrary to the international prohibition of torture generates international State responsibility," suggesting a more cautious approach than automatic invalidation.

The commentators who interpret the *Furundzija* dictum as a progressive holding on the effects of *jus cogens* norms are equally ambiguous in specifying its precise meaning. The judge cited earlier, for example, states that "as the ICTY held in Furundzija, peremptory norms may produce legal effects at the municipal law level: they de-legitimize any legislative or administrative act authorizing the prohibited conduct. Consequently, national measures [...] may not be accorded international legal recognition or at any rate are not opposable to other States."[1026] This comment hardly makes things clearer. De-legitimization is not a legal effect, and a lack of international legal recognition and opposability to other States are neither "legal effects at the municipal law level" nor exclusive for *jus cogens* norms. Rather, they can be the fate of each and every national measure that violates international law. All in all, the holding in *Furundzija* is too unclear and contradictory to serve as firm evidence for the statement that the *jus cogens* character of a norm determines its effects in national law.

In conclusion, national and international practice regarding the domestic legal consequences of peremptory norms of international law is divided at best, and often unclear or poorly reasoned.[1027] The lack of analysis and obvious mistakes in many judgments, especially of national courts, notably undercut their authoritative value. A cautious tendency can be discerned to accept a privileged position for *jus cogens* norms in the national legal order, but in the absence of firm State practice a corresponding rule of customary international law currently appears to be only in the (early) formative stages.[1028]

The prospects for future development of a privileged position of *jus cogens* norms in the national legal order are uncertain, and plagued by two fundamental problems. First, many of the suggested consequences of *jus cogens* status in the national legal order rest on the assumption that the rank of a norm is in itself enough to eliminate procedural barriers to its effectuation. This assumption is problematic. If one accepts that national courts lack the authority to judge the conduct of other States or their officials, then no characteristic of any given norm, whether it is its superior rank, intrinsic value or any other feature, can cure that omission. The argument that the *jus cogens* status of torture in itself gives national courts a competence to judge foreign States and officials which they would otherwise lack, is not far off from the argument that murder is such a serious crime that everybody should be allowed to punish its perpetrators. Both rest on an overly simplistic connection between char-

---

[1026] Cassese 2001c, p. 145. Cf. Art. 41 of the ILC's 2001 Articles on State Responsibility.

[1027] See Seiderman 2001, p. 35 and 121.

[1028] See Wet 2004, p. 119-120; Seiderman 2001, p. 121.

acteristics of the norm and the procedure for its effectuation. Of course, States may well decide that it is no longer desirable to exempt their acts from scrutiny in foreign courts where peremptory norms are at stake. Importantly though, such a step primarily requires a rethinking of the concept of sovereign immunity, rather than *jus cogens*. Courts and scholars often fail to broaden their analysis accordingly when analyzing the continued viability of immunities for *jus cogens* norms.

Second, any enhancement of the position of *jus cogens* norms risks limiting the impact of non-peremptory norms of international law (*jus dispositivum)* by implication. As set out above, the constitutional reference to *jus cogens* in Switzerland may be interpreted as a licence for the Swiss legislature to ignore *jus dispositivum* at will. This problem of relative normativity has figured in the academic debate of *jus cogens* and its implications for a long time, but is still very much with us today.[1029]

However, as the case law of national and international courts indicates despite its uncertainties and imperfections, the concept of *jus cogens* is certainly not devoid of potential in the national legal order. One could think that in an optimal scenario, the manoeuvring space of States would be differentiated in such a way as to allow maximum freedom of implementation, including the capability to adapt and in exceptional cases violate international obligations, but to limit violations of international law that flow from negligence or the desire to seek a unilateral exemption from international obligations that are otherwise left intact. A strengthened implementation and/or enforcement of *jus cogens* norms could provide a first step for such a differentiation, as States have virtually no possibility to adjust or need to mitigate the effects of their peremptory obligations in any case.[1030]

6. Conclusion

States have the freedom to implement their international obligations in any way they see fit as long as they give full effect to those obligations. Yet the consequences of this general rule are easily and often overestimated. For national courts, taking the freedom of the State as a starting point logically leads to a predominant focus on the national rules relevant for the implementation and application of international law in the national legal order. Numerous courts and scholars even go so far as to focus exclusively on what national law has to say on the matter. This is, however, erroneous.

International law grants States great freedom, but does not allow national courts to ignore international obligations altogether. The principle of consistent interpreta-

---

[1029] See principally Weil 1983. See also Wet 2004, p. 104 and 118-121.

[1030] Cf. ICJ, *Oil Platforms (Islamic Republic of Iran v. United States of America)*, 6 November 2003, para. 73 and Separate Opinion Judge Kooimans, para. 46: "[The United States] opted for means the use of which must be subjected to strict legal norms, since the prohibition of force is considered to have a peremptory character. The measure of discretion to which the United States is entitled is therefore considerably more limited than if it had chosen, for instance, the use of economic measures."

tion requires national courts to take international obligations into account in their construction of national law. It also follows both from a historical analysis of the reception of international law in national courts and a review of contemporary practice that international law is not silent on its own implementation and enforcement on the national level. Therefore, the international legality of certain modern variants of the doctrine of self-executing treaties is at least doubtful. While national law may impose far-going limitations on the application of international law by national courts, the practice of some courts to declare treaties non-self-executing solely or predominantly because they perceive the practical effects of their application as unwelcome violates their duty to give effect to international obligations where national law allows it.

Finally, practice shows a certain tendency towards a limitation of the freedom of implementation for international obligations of a humanitarian character and peremptory norms. For the first category, this tendency is limited but real. In the case of *jus cogens*, practice is diffuse and mostly aspirational.

Chapter V
THE FRAMEWORK OF IMPLEMENTATION FOR THE CORE CRIMES

1. Introduction

The previous Chapter set forth the general demands of international law for the implementation of international obligations in the national legal order. It noted that international law, as a default rule, leaves States free to implement their international obligations in the way they see fit. It also noted that, despite significant practice of national courts to this effect, the freedom of implementation does not extend to a freedom to violate international obligations. All liberties of States flowing from the freedom of implementation, such as the limitation of the judicial application of international law in national courts, are subject to the condition that the State ultimately adheres to its international obligations. Chapter IV further showed that there is practice to suggest that the general international framework of implementation is subject to modification for certain kinds of international law, in particular that of a humanitarian character and/or *jus cogens* status. Yet it concluded that State practice is mostly aspirational, and at best divided, on the question of whether international law subjects those particular categories of international law to a more stringent regime of implementation and application.

The question then arises whether the general framework of implementation applies in its entirety to international core crimes law. Core crimes law is not only of a humanitarian character and *jus cogens* status, but has additional characteristics that have been interpreted in practice and doctrine to influence its implementation.[1031] In this Chapter, I will analyze whether international law imposes different demands on States for the implementation of core crimes law than the general framework outlined in Chapter IV. To this end, I will analyze the relevant characteristics of core crimes law[1032] and the way national courts treat the particularities of core crimes law in practice.

[1031] Cf. ICTY, Appeals Chamber, *Erdemovic*, 7 October 1997, Joint Separate Opinion of Judges McDonald and Vohrah, para. 78: "It is clear to us that whatever is the distinction between the international legal order and municipal legal orders in general, the distinction is imperfect in respect of the criminal law which, both at the international and the municipal level, is directed towards consistent aims." See also Stein 1994, p. 450 (cited above, note 934) and Lauterpacht 1944, p. 64 ("In no other sphere does the view that international law is binding only upon States and not upon individuals lead to more paradoxical consequences and nowhere has it in practice been rejected more emphatically than in the domain of the laws of war.").

[1032] It should be noted at the outset that none of the characteristics to be mentioned here is *in itself* unique for core crimes law. The goal here is to analyze whether and to what extent the framework of implementation of core crimes law differs from international law's general framework, not to what

Taking a broad approach, I will explore the characteristics of both international criminal law in general (para. 2) and the core crimes in particular (para. 3), insofar as these are relevant for the question of implementation. I will examine in some detail the particularly grave character of the core crimes (para. 3.1), their *jus cogens* status (para. 3.2) and the mandatory character of their prosecution, which flows not only from international criminal law, but also from human rights law and the law on State responsibility (para. 3.3). This part continues the analysis of paragraph 5.3 of the previous Chapter on the more specific level of core crimes law. Next, I will ask whether international law requires States to reflect the international character of the core crimes in national prosecutions or allows them to prosecute core crimes as if they are ordinary crimes like murder (para. 4). Having thus examined the particularities of core crimes law, I will analyze to what extent national courts in practice adhere to or deviate from the general framework of implementation for international law where it concerns the core crimes (para. 5). Finally, I will describe the influence of the ICC Statute on the implementation of core crimes law (para. 6), before making up the balance of the current international framework of implementation for core crimes law (para. 7).

2. Characteristics of International Criminal Law

What then, are the characteristics of international criminal law that influence its implementation in the national legal order? Chapter I defined international criminal law as 'the accumulation of international legal norms on individual criminal responsibility,' in other words: the penal aspects of international law.[1033] This definition indicates a first characteristic that, even if it is obvious, requires mentioning: ICL primarily focuses on and addresses individuals.[1034]

Second, and logically following from the first, the intended effects of ICL take place primarily within States and not between States. Therefore, ICL explicitly employs the national legal orders, and is essentially dependent on them, for its effectuation. The fact that ICL aims to stop individuals from performing certain acts does not mean it addresses *only* individuals. To regulate individual behavior, ICL issues a dual set of rules.[1035] One addresses the individual and attaches criminal responsibility directly to certain acts. Another set of rules addresses States and authorizes or obliges them to prosecute infractions of certain norms.[1036] The utili-

extent core crimes law can be distinguished from other particular fields of international law. Certainly, there are other fields for which the viability of the general framework of implementation may be questioned, in part for similar reasons as those set out here.

[1033] See above, p. 10.

[1034] See on the implications of this point, above, Chapter IV, para. 5.3.a.

[1035] See Burke-White 2002, p. 76-77; Triffterer 1966, p. 180-181.

[1036] The norms of the first and the second set do overlap only partially. ICL also addresses the responsibility of States to react to certain infractions for which it does not impose criminal responsibility directly on individuals, as for example in the case of environmental crimes. See also above, note 186.

zation of States, and thus their national courts, to prosecute international crimes is known as the *indirect model* of enforcement, as opposed to the *direct model* which employs international courts.[1037] Importantly, the obligations of States are not limited to ensuring the effectuation of individual criminal responsibility, but often include separate obligations to enact necessary legislation.[1038] Therefore, lacunae in the national legal system that obstruct core crimes prosecutions can be internationally wrongful in and of themselves, not solely in connection to an actual instance of impunity in practice.[1039]

Third, it is generally accepted that States are, as a default rule, free to implement and effectuate their obligations under ICL in any way they see fit, as is the case for public international law in general.[1040] ICL articulates relatively clearly which crimes must be prosecuted, but is far less detailed on the manner in which these prosecutions should take place. There is, for example, no general international rule that obligates States to prosecute international crimes directly on the basis of international law, or on the basis of any particular ground of jurisdiction.[1041] In theory, this freedom allows States to choose the most effective way of implementing their international obligations.[1042] In practice, the lack of specific implementing obligations often results in incomplete or otherwise imperfect implementation of the law, contributing to the widespread impunity for international crimes.

The fact that ICL leaves States considerable freedom of implementation should not obscure the fact that international offences themselves are relatively precise. From the perspective of a national (penal) lawyer, international offences may be ambiguous and confusing. From an international law perspective, however, they are among the international norms which articulate the clearest standards.[1043] They do not, for example, require States to "establish an international regime, including appropriate procedures, to govern the exploitation of the natural resources of the

---

[1037] See Mantovani 2003, p. 27; Werle 2003, p. 78-79; Bassiouni 1999b, p. 110.

[1038] See e.g. Art. 5 GC; Art. 49 (1) GC I; Art. 50 (1) GC II; Art. 129 (1) GC III; Art. 146 (1) GC IV; Art. 4 1973 International Convention on the Suppression and Punishment of the Crime of Apartheid; Art. 5 CAT. See also Fichet-Boyle and Mossé 2000.

[1039] See ICTY, Trial Chamber, *Furundzija*, 10 December 1998, para. 149. Cf. IACtHR, Certain Attributes of the Inter-American Commission on Human Rights (Art. 41, 42, 44, 46, 47, 50 and 51 of the American Convention on Human Rights), 16 July 1993, Advisory Opinion OC-13/93, (Ser. A) No. 13, para. 26 ("A State may violate an international treaty and, specifically, the Convention, in many ways. It may do so in the latter case, for example, by failing to establish the norms required by Article 2."); Harris *et al.* 1995, p. 19-20.

[1040] See Lambert-Abdelgawad 2003, p. 541. See on the freedom of implementation in general international law above, Chapter IV, para. 3.

[1041] See Cassese 2003a, p. 301. See on the question whether core crimes may be charged as ordinary rather than international crimes below, para. 4.

[1042] See above, p. 133.

[1043] Cf. Paust 1991, p. 368 (who may be slightly overstating the point in asserting that "it is difficult to imagine a more mandatory, controlling, detailed, definable, universal, and useful set of treaty standards" than those contained in the Geneva Conventions).

moon as such exploitation is about to become feasible,"[1044] but straightforwardly prohibit certain acts, threaten punishment to transgressors and oblige States to enforce these norms. There is only limited room for interpretation.

Human rights law specifies further demands, determining *inter alia* that prosecution may take place only in independent courts.[1045] The combination of ICL and human rights law gives a clear indication of the State organs which are responsible for the implementation of these treaty obligations, and sets limits on the way they may do so. Although numerous choices in the implementation process remain, such as which courts are to apply what law, the interplay of different international obligations significantly curtails the freedom of States in practice. Also, ICL is becoming more and more detailed and comprehensive. It increasingly regulates defences, forms of participation, general principles governing prosecutions and related matters.[1046]

Moreover, international law requires States to give full effect to their international obligations.[1047] In interpreting these obligations, States must take into account their object and purpose.[1048] The object and purpose of ICL, or at least a pivotal aspect of it, is to prevent these crimes and, in order to achieve that goal, to punish international crimes when they occur.[1049] States have, in treaties, other international instruments and declarations of various kinds, consistently maintained that punishment of international crimes is an essential and necessary step for their prevention.[1050] International courts take the same view.[1051] Therefore, States must

---

[1044] Art. 11 (5) Agreement Governing the Activities of States on the Moon and Other Celestial Bodies (5 December 1979).

[1045] See e.g. Cassese 2003a, p. 309-310.

[1046] See e.g. Mantovani 2003; Safferling 2001. Note, however, that ICL's regulation of such matters is still far from complete. See Sassoli 2002, p. 121-123.

[1047] Cf. Art. 26 VCLT, widely believed to reflect customary law.

[1048] Cf. Art. 31 VCLT, widely believed to reflect customary law.

[1049] See Sadat 2003, p. 164; Wouters and Panken 2003, p. 12; Bothe 1996, p. 293.

[1050] See e.g. Preamble Rome Statute, para. 5 ("Determined to put an end to impunity for the perpetrators of these crimes and thus to contribute to the prevention of such crimes"); Preamble 1968 Convention on the Non-Applicability of Statutory Limitations to War Crimes and Crimes Against Humanity, para. 5: "Convinced that the effective punishment of war crimes and crimes against humanity is an important element in the prevention of such crimes, the protection of human rights and fundamental freedoms, the encouragement of confidence, the furtherance of co-operation among peoples and the promotion of international peace and security." See also Bothe 1995, p. 241.

[1051] See e.g. ICTR, Trial Chamber, *Niyitegeka*, 16 May 2003, para. 484: "In reaching its decision on an appropriate sentence to be imposed on the Accused, the Chamber has taken due consideration of the well-established principles of retribution, deterrence, and protection of society. Specific emphasis is placed on general deterrence, so as to demonstrate 'that the international community [is] not ready to tolerate serious violations of international humanitarian law and human rights.' " (footnote omitted); ICTR, Trial Chamber, *Akayesu, Sentencing Judgment*, 2 October 1998, unnumbered para.: "[T]he establishment of the Tribunal was to prosecute and punish the perpetrators of the atrocities in Rwanda in such a way as to put an end to impunity and thereby to promote national reconciliation and the restoration of peace. It is therefore clear that the penalties imposed on accused persons found guilty by the Tribunal must be directed on the one hand attri - - attribution (sic) of said accused who must see their crime punished and on the other hand as deterrence, namely dissuading for good those who will be

take into account the goal of punishing core crimes perpetrators in every step of implementation they take. Where choices are to be made, be it in the interpretation of international law and national law or in legislative action, States are required to choose the option which best guarantees punishment of core crimes perpetrators.

Fourth, ICL is a strongly normative body of international law. Like human rights law, international criminal law differs from the traditional Westphalian conception of public international law in that it sets a normative standard as opposed to the "agnostic, procedural international law whose merit consisted in its refraining from imposing any external normative ideal on the international society."[1052] ICL is, in a sense, a set of values rather than a language for participants. Even stronger than human rights law, the very act of criminalization expresses a powerful, negative judgment.[1053] Its normative character may influence ICL's enforcement in national courts. After all, the notion that the intrinsic value of the rule to be applied or the issue at stake can alter the balance between conflicting rules is not foreign to international law.[1054]

3. Characteristics of the Core Crimes

3.1 The Grave Character of the Core Crimes

It will not be easy to find a text dealing with core crimes law that fails to mention their exceptional gravity. Legal instruments and judgments regarding these crimes are replete with references to their odious nature. The core crimes concern acts which threaten the peace and security of mankind.[1055] They are of a particularly

---

tempted in future to perpetrate such atrocities by showing them that the International community was no longer ready to tolerate serious violations of International humanitarian law and human rights."; ICTY, Trial Chamber, *Erdemovic, Sentencing Judgment*, 29 November 1996, para. 64-65, cited below, note 1220. Cf. ICJ, *Case Concerning Application of the Convention on the Prevention and Punishment of the Crime of Genocide (Bosnia-Herzegovina v. Yugoslavia), preliminary objections*, 11 July 1996, para. 31; ICTY, Trial Chamber, *Tadic, Decision on the Prosecutor's Motion Requesting Protective Measures for Victims and Witnesses*, 10 August 1995, para. 18 ("The object and purpose of the [ICTY] is evident in the Security Council resolutions establishing the International Tribunal and has been described as threefold: to do justice, to deter further crimes and to contribute to the restoration and maintenance of peace.").

[1052] Koskenniemi 2003, p. 90.

[1053] See Safferling 2001, p. 58 (stating that "only the gravest acts against the international community can be criminalized at the international level"). Cf. Seiderman 2001, p. 187 and 202.

[1054] See Nollkaemper 2003a, p. 630-631 (analyzing how international courts vary the standard of proof according to the gravity of the matter under consideration). Cf. Santulli 2001, p. 113-114, note 211. But see Eritrea-Ethiopia Claims Commission, *Partial Awards on Prisoners of War between the State of Eritrea and the Federal Democratic Republic of Ethiopia*, 1 July 2003, Eritrea's Claim 17, para. 45-47.

[1055] See Art. 17, 18 and 20 Draft Code 1996. Cf. preamble ICC Statute, para. 3 ("Recognizing that such grave crimes threaten the peace, security and well-being of the world"). See also Triffterer 1966, p. 195-217. Historically, international criminal law was strongly focused on protecting the international community, i.e. ensuring the unimpeded functioning of States. The goal of protecting civilians

heinous character, indeed, even "inhumane"[1056] and "shocking for the conscience of humanity."[1057] It is widely accepted that core crimes law, in this sense including the crime of aggression, tops the normative hierarchy of international law.[1058]

Many of these statements effectively declare the criminalization of the core crimes to consist of norms of natural law. Qualifications such as "inhumane" and "shocking for the conscience of humanity" exude the idea that the law on core crimes is not simply a choice of the relevant actors in international law, but rather an objective standard which imposes itself on everyone who wishes to partake in civilized society.[1059] That they are "crimes against the peace and security of mankind" suggests that their prevention and punishment is not just desirable but necessary to ensure the continued survival of mankind.[1060]

The criticism of appeals to natural law notions like "the conscience of humanity," relayed in Chapter IV, also applies in the context of core crimes law.[1061] There

---

from grave suffering has emerged more recently with the advent of human rights law. See Zoller and Reshetov 1990, p. 100 ("There was no offense against the law of nations when – however serious the offense committed by the individual – states could conduct their regular affairs along orderly and predictable lines.").

[1056] See e.g. ICC Statute Art. 7 (1) sub k. Cf. Kritz 1996, 151 ("There will be cases of crimes so horrific that the international community will be obliged, for its own sake and for the preservation of fundamental universal principles, to hold the key planners or perpetrators accountable to all of humanity.").

[1057] See e.g. Preamble ICC Statute, para. 2.

[1058] See Congo (the), Supreme Court, *Projet de loi portant définition et répression des crimes contre l'Humanite*, 24 March 1998, Au fond ("[N]ul ne peut valablement prétendre ignorer que le génocide et les autres crimes contre l'Humanité sont la forme la plus grave et la plus intolérable des atteintes contre la personne humaine et qu'ils sont naturellement interdits,"). Cf. Swart 1996, p. 6-7; Bassiouni 1996, p. 141-142; Triffterer 1966, p. 178. But see below, notes 1280 to 1282.

[1059] See preamble Genocide Convention, para. 1 and 3 (stating that genocide is "condemned by the civilized world" and "an odious scourge"). Cf. ICJ, *Reservations to the Convention on the Prevention and Punishment of Genocide (Advisory Opinion)*, 1951, 1951 ICJ 23, reiterated in ICJ, *Case Concerning Application of the Convention on the Prevention and Punishment of the Crime of Genocide (Bosnia-Herzegovina v. Yugoslavia), preliminary objections*, 11 July 1996, para. 31: "The origins of the Convention show that it was the intention of the United Nations to condemn and punish genocide as 'a crime under international law' involving a denial of the right of existence of entire human groups, a denial which shocks the conscience of mankind and results in great losses to humanity, and which is *contrary to moral law* and to the spirit and aims of the United Nations (Resolution 96 (I) of the General Assembly, December 11th 1946)." (emphasis added); Israel, Supreme Court, *Attorney General of Israel v. Eichmann*, 29 May 1962, 36 ILR 277, at 291, 293 ("Those crimes entail individual criminal responsibility because they [...] affront the conscience of civilized nations.").

[1060] See ICTY, Trial Chamber, *Erdemovic, Sentencing Judgment*, 29 November 1996, para. 28: "Crimes against humanity [...] are inhumane acts that by their extent and gravity go beyond the limits tolerable to the international community, which must perforce demand their punishment. But crimes against humanity also transcend the individual because when the individual is assaulted, humanity comes under attack and is negated. It is therefore the concept of humanity as victim which essentially characterises crimes against humanity." See also Schwarzenberger 1950, p. 272-273 ("In any social group in which a criminal law exists the highest values and interests are protected by rules of criminal law. International crimes would, therefore, be in all likelihood only acts of subjects or objects of international law which strike at the very roots of international society.").

[1061] See above, p. 157-158.

are many acts which – hardly anyone will dispute – are incompatible with basic notions of humanity. Yet, our failure to apply such standards in a consistent manner undermines the authority of their invocation. The application of double standards to different core crimes surpasses simple factual denials of, or popular support for, particular crimes in situations of conflict. It also takes the shape of more reasoned positions. An eminent modern philosopher has argued that there is a "supreme emergency exception" which "allows us to set aside – in certain special circumstances – the strict status of civilians that normally prevents their being directly attacked in war."[1062] Therefore, he posits, the British bombing of German cities in WW II was justifiable in the period that Great-Britain alone opposed Germany and "had no other means to break Germany's superior power."[1063]

Clearly, core crimes law categorically excludes such means-ends reasoning, regardless of how important or noble the end may be. To introduce it, no matter in how limited a manner, relativizes the inhumane character of the core crimes. If one accepts that Allied violations of humanitarian law in WW II may have been justified by a supreme emergency exception, one opens the door to a similar means-end defence for other core crimes. Even though such a defence will generally fail, its very possibility severely undermines the notion that some acts are so odious that they can never be permitted.

Still, such criticism amounts to a relevant qualification of appeals to natural law notions, but not a repudiation of the grave character of the core crimes. Courts and scholars have conceptualized the grave nature of core crimes law not only as a claim to natural law status, but also as merely a particularly strong normative content,[1064] or as an alternative articulation of its non-consensualist character expressed in more positivistic terms by reference to its customary and peremptory status.[1065] Whatever the label one attaches to it, the implications are substantially the same.[1066] The grave character of genocide, crimes against humanity and war crimes are frequently invoked as a justification to interpret or even adapt procedural and other

[1062] Rawls 1999, p. 98.

[1063] Id.

[1064] See Triffterer 1989, 42-44; Röling 1979, p. 163: "The underdeveloped international legal order obviously needs a criminal law for those carrying out certain acts within that order. Such a need will arise if the standards of the legal community are of such cogency that other and lesser sanctions, such as reparations, are not considered sufficient."

[1065] Cf. Spain, Tribunal Supremo, Guatemalan Genocide Case, 25 February 2003, 42 ILM 686, para II sub 5.

[1066] Cf. Hungary, Constitutional Court, Decision No. 53/1993, On War Crimes and Crimes against Humanity, 13 October 1993, English translation in Sólyom/Brunner 2000, p. 273-283 at 277: "[The] international status [of war crimes and crimes against humanity] derives from their definition on a supra-national level, either on the basis of natural law (invocation of basic principles above and beyond positive law within international law is also a guarantee against arbitrary international agreements), or by reference to the protection of the 'foundations of the international community,' or by citing the threat posed by these activities for all of humanity: its commissioners are 'enemies of the human race.' Thus, the significance of these offenses is too great to permit their punishment to be made dependent upon the acquiescence or general penal law policy of individual nation states."

relevant rules in such a way as to ensure their prevention and punishment to the fullest extent possible.

First, the exceptional character of the core crimes has been invoked to defend a method of ascertaining the content of customary law which stresses the element of *opinio juris* over that of consistent state practice. This method has been applied to law of a humanitarian character more generally, and is conceptualized partly as a necessary consequence of the prevailing complications in the analysis of State practice.[1067] Yet considerable emphasis has also been put on the character of the norms involved, particularly in the specific context of core crimes law. The underlying idea appears to be that the importance and necessity of the norm, when accepted by the international community, can remedy deficiencies in state practice that would normally bar it from becoming a rule of customary international law.[1068]

The *ad hoc* tribunals have frequently referred to the gravity of war crimes in internal armed conflicts to supplement the questionable legal foundation of their conclusion that these acts incur individual criminal responsibility under customary law.[1069] None of these references suggests that the gravity of these crimes obviates the need to establish their criminality under customary law altogether. However, they can reasonably be interpreted as a justification for the application of an "enlightened" ascertainment of customary law to the core crimes. While this proposition raises serious methodological concerns,[1070] it has garnered considerable support. The fact that a great number of States embraced the concept of war crimes in internal armed conflicts in the ICC Statute, which was to contain only crimes with customary status, provides significant support for the reasoning in *Tadic* and similar cases.[1071]

Second, the character of the core crimes implies a restriction of the element of reciprocity in this body of law.[1072] Violation by one State cannot excuse another's non-compliance.[1073] Third, the character of the core crimes is regularly invoked as an argument to decide other questions of law in their prosecution. Numerous na-

[1067] See above, Chapter IV, para. 5.3.a.

[1068] Cf. Meron 1989, p. 42.

[1069] See e.g. ICTY, Appeals Chamber, *Delalic et al.,* 20 February 2001, para. 173 ("It is universally acknowledged that the acts enumerated in common Article 3 [Geneva Conventions] are wrongful and shock the conscience of civilised people, and thus are, in the language of Article 15 (2) of the ICCPR, "criminal according to the general principles of law recognised by civilised nations."); ICTR, Trial Chamber, *Akayesu*, 2 September 1998, para. 616 ("[I]t is clear that the authors of such egregious violations must incur individual criminal responsibility for their deeds."); ICTY, Appeals Chamber, *Tadic, Decision on the Defence Motion for Interlocutory Appeal on Jurisdiction*, 2 October 1995, para. 129 ("Principles and rules of humanitarian law reflect 'elementary considerations of humanity' widely recognized as the mandatory minimum for conduct in armed conflicts of any kind. No one can doubt the gravity of the acts at issue, nor the interest of the international community in their prohibition.").

[1070] See for a critical analysis Heinegg 2003.

[1071] Cf. Robinson and Hebel 1999, p. 194.

[1072] See ICTY, Trial Chamber, *Kupreskic*, 14 January 2000, para. 511 ("The Trial Chamber wishes to stress, in this regard, the irrelevance of reciprocity, particularly in relation to obligations found within international humanitarian law which have an absolute and non-derogable character.").

[1073] But see above, note 11.

tional courts have posited that it is the grave nature of the core crimes which makes them subject to universal jurisdiction, a departure from the principle that criminal law jurisdiction is as a general rule territorial.[1074] Such assertions find support in doctrine.[1075] International courts and bodies have appealed to the particularities of core crimes law to justify modifications of defences and due process rights.[1076] Most important in the context of this study, various national courts have invoked the nature of the core crimes to exempt their prosecution from particular rules and limitations in the national legal order. These cases will be discussed below, in paragraph 4.

3.2 The *Jus Cogens* Status of the Core Crimes

A further factor to be taken into account when analyzing the implementation, in particular the direct application, of core crimes law is its *jus cogens* status. Although I have concluded in Chapter IV that international law does not at present

[1074] See e.g. Belgium, Tribunal of First Instance (District of Brussels), *In re Pinochet Ugarte*, 6 November 1998, para. 3.3.3: "It has got to be one thing or the other: either crimes of humanity are just incriminations among many other ones that do not transcend borders and their suppression is left to the discretion of each state, or these crimes are of an unspeakable and unacceptable nature and the responsibility for their repression is shared by all.";
Australia, High Court, *Polyukhovich v. The Commonwealth of Australia and Another*, 14 August 1991, para. 34 (Toohey, J.: "Where conduct, because of its magnitude, affects the moral interests of humanity and thus assumes the status of a crime in international law, the principle of universality must, almost inevitably, prevail..."); U.S., District Court (D.C.), *United States v. Yunis*, 12 February 1988, 681 F.Supp. 896 at 900 ("The Universal principle recognizes that certain offenses are so heinous and so widely condemned that [any State that captures the offender may prosecute]"); U.S., Court of Appeals (Sixth Circuit), *Demjanjuk v. Petrovsky*, 1985, 776 F.2d 571 at 582 ("This universality principle is based on the assumption that some crimes are so universally condemned that the perpetrators are the enemies of all people."); Israel, Supreme Court, *Attorney General of Israel v. Eichmann*, 29 May 1962, 36 ILR 277 at 299: "Not only do all the crimes attributed to the appellant bear an international character, but their harmful and murderous effects were so embracing and widespread as to shake the international community to its very foundations. The State of Israel therefore was entitled, pursuant to the principle of universal jurisdiction and in the capacity of a guardian of international law and an agent for its enforcement, to try the appellant."

[1075] See e.g. El Zeidy 2003, p. 838-839.

[1076] See e.g. ICTY, Appeals Chamber, *Erdemovic*, 7 October 1997, Joint Separate Opinion of Judge McDonald and Judge Vohrah, para. 75 (rejecting duress as a defense for crimes against humanity and war crimes with an appeal to the grave character of those crimes) and below, Chapter VI, para. 5.3 (nature of the core crimes as an argument in the discussion on the principle of legality). See also ICTY, Appeals Chamber, *Kovacevic*, 2 July 1998, Separate Opinion of Judge Shahabuddeen; ICTY, Trial Chamber, *Tadic, Decision on the Prosecutor's Motion Requesting Protective Measures for Victims and Witnesses*, 10 August 1995, para. 28-30 (finding that the interpretations of due process rights by other international judicial bodies in the context of proceedings regarding ordinary crimes are relevant but not decisive for the proceedings regarding international crimes before the ICTY); EComHR, *X. v. Federal Republic of Germany*, 6 July 1976, Application/Requete No. 6946/75, p. 115: "[T]he exceptional character of criminal proceedings involving war crimes committed during World War II renders, in the Commission's opinion, inapplicable the principles [regarding Art. 6 ECHR] developed in the case-law of the Commission and the Court of Human Rights in connection with cases involving other criminal offences." See further Schabas 2002a, p. 172-174.

impose a stricter implementation regime for all *jus cogens* norms, the peremptory status of core crimes law can still be a relevant factor for its implementation.

Immediately, however, it must be noted that the uncertainty surrounding *jus cogens* in general[1077] certainly extends to the core crimes. In this regard, it is pertinent at this stage to reiterate the conclusion that the *Furundzija* dictum of the ICTY does not actually ascribe unique effects to the peremptory character of the prohibition of torture in an unequivocal manner.[1078] More generally, it is often reiterated that genocide, crimes against humanity and war crimes are "*jus cogens* crimes,"[1079] but is less common to find an analysis of the precise scope and consequences of this status.[1080] Yet such an analysis is indispensable because a statement that genocide or torture is a *jus cogens* crime is too general to be meaningful. International law imposes different obligations regarding the core crimes on States and individuals. These obligations can not automatically be lumped together and all branded *jus cogens*.[1081] In particular, the fact that the *jus cogens* status of the prohibition of genocide, crimes against humanity and war crimes may bring about a duty to prosecute those crimes, does not mean that this duty to prosecute is itself also a peremptory norm.

In practice and doctrine, at least three different obligations can be distinguished. First, the obligation not to contribute to core crimes, be it by act or omission, surely has *jus cogens* status.[1082] In other words, both the prohibition for States to actively participate in, or allow core crimes in any way and the individual criminal responsibility for core crimes under international law are peremptory norms.[1083] These norms make up the core of the international prohibition of these crimes. For individuals, it seems this *jus cogens* status has no *direct* consequences. They cannot themselves contract out of any of their international obligations or alter them in any way, so the peremptory character of those obligations does not actually change anything in this respect. Yet, there are *indirect* consequences for individuals, in particular the fact that States cannot agree to repeal individual criminal responsibility for the core crimes.

[1077] See above, Chapter IV, para. 5.3.b.

[1078] See above, p. 169.

[1079] Bassiouni 1998 and Bassiouni 1996. See also e.g. El Zeidy 2002, p. 947-949; Mattarollo 2001, p. 19-22.

[1080] See Meron 1986, p. 22.

[1081] Cf. Henzelin 2000, p. 434: "La seule qualification de *jus cogens* de l'interdiction des crimes d'agression, d'apartheid, de génocide ou d'esclavage ne donne pas forcément le droit et n'oblige certainement pas, *en soi*, un Etat qui ne pratique pas lui-même l'agression, l'apartheid, le génocide ou l'esclavage, de poursuivre et de juger, selon le principe de l'universalité, un responsable d'un autre Etat agresseur, génocidaire, esclavagiste ou pratiquant l'apartheid." See also below, note 1278 and accompanying text.

[1082] See Dupuy 2000, p. 79.

[1083] See Gil Gil 1999, p. 53-54.

Second, States are under a customary obligation to prosecute core crimes.[1084] Whether this obligation is a peremptory norm or not is an open question. On the one hand, there is considerable force in, and widespread recognition for, the argument that punishment of the core crimes is an intrinsic and necessary part of their prevention.[1085] If that is the case, the duty to prosecute must enjoy the same peremptory character as the duty to prevent.[1086] On the other hand, State practice suggests otherwise. It is generally accepted that the doctrine of immunity for (certain) State officials overrides the duty to prosecute, also in the case of *jus cogens* crimes.[1087] Since States can derogate from the rules on immunity by treaty,[1088] these rules cannot be *jus cogens* norms. It follows logically that the duty to prosecute can not be a peremptory norm either, since those norms can only be trumped by other peremptory norms.[1089] Thus, the peremptory or non-peremptory character of the duty to prosecute the core crimes is uncertain. Yet, in light of current State practice and its numerous exceptions to the duty to prosecute – immunities, amnesties and prosecutorial discretion – the better view seems to be that the duty does not have *jus cogens* status.

Third, under different human rights treaties and possibly under customary international law, States are under an obligation to provide civil remedies for core crimes victims.[1090] Yet, there are no signs that the right to a remedy for core crimes victims has been accepted "by the international community of States as a whole as a norm from which no derogation is permitted."[1091] In proceedings before national and international courts, victims have invoked the *jus cogens* status of the core crimes to attack the immunities that generally preclude the adjudication or enforcement of civil claims against foreign States and their officials. This line of reasoning, however, has been widely rejected in national and international courts.[1092] Moreover, it can be doubted whether civil remedies are, like criminal prosecutions, an integral and necessary part of the prevention of core crimes.[1093] Like the rules on immunity for State officials, the rules on State immunity are not (trumping) *jus cogens*

[1084] See below, para. 3.4.

[1085] Both ICL and human rights law base the need for punishment precisely on this rationale. See above, notes 1050 and 1051 and below, para. 3.3.a.

[1086] See Seiderman 2001, p. 106 and 110. See also Mexico, Supreme Court, *In re Cavallo (Amparo en Revision 140/2002)*, 10 June 2002, p. 493-494 and below, note 1267 and accompanying text.

[1087] See ICJ, International Court of Justice, *Case concerning the Arrest Warrant of 11 April 2000 (Democratic Republic of the Congo v. Belgium)*, 14 February 2002.

[1088] See e.g. Art. 27 (2) ICC Statute.

[1089] Cf. Art. 53 VCLT.

[1090] See below, note 1109. See e.g. IACtHR, *Bulacio v. Argentina*, 18 September 2003, para. 70-73; ECtHR, *Aktas v. Turkey*, 24 April 2003, para. 329. See also Shirey 2004 (arguing that customary law imposes a duty to compensate victims of torture committed both in and outside armed conflict, while many of the sources she cites support a duty to provide civil remedies for core crimes more generally).

[1091] Art. 53 VCLT.

[1092] See above, notes 1011 and 1012 and accompanying text.

[1093] Cf. below, notes 1130 and 1131. But see Schaack 2001, p. 155-159.

norms.[1094] Accordingly, the obligation to provide civil remedies for core crimes is probably not of a peremptory character.[1095]

Thus, the *jus cogens* status of the core crimes does not automatically extend to all international obligations regarding those crimes. While the prohibition for States and individuals to commit core crimes is of a peremptory character, the obligation to provide civil remedies for those crimes is not. The status of the duty to prosecute core crimes is uncertain. This uncertainty is fed by a decided lack of rigor of national and international courts in their analysis of the *jus cogens* status of core crimes law. Like is the case for peremptory norms in general,[1096] national courts often invoke the *jus cogens* status of the core crimes, but seldom substantiate it or specify its implications. One commentator has observed that many national judgments of genocide contain "a purely gratuitous claim that [relevant] customary norms are also peremptory or *jus cogens* principles, [...] without explanation."[1097] This lack of substantiation is relatively unproblematic when it concerns the basic prohibitions of genocide, crimes against humanity and war crimes, given that their peremptory character is not seriously disputed. However, both national and international courts too often fail to distinguish between the different international obligations relevant to core crimes, and also leave unclear exactly what conclusions they draw from the *jus cogens* status of the core crimes. On the other hand, some attempts to address these matters in more detail result in conclusions that are difficult to comprehend.[1098]

[1094] See ECtHR, *Al-Adsani v. United Kingdom*, 21 November 2001, dissenting opinion Judges Rozakis and Caflisch, joined by Judges Wildhaber, Costa, Cabral Barreto and Vajic, para. 2: "The Court's majority do not seem, on the other hand, to deny that the rules on State immunity; customary or conventional, do not belong to the category of *jus cogens*; and rightly so, because it is clear that the rules of State immunity, deriving from both customary and conventional international law, have never been considered by the international community as rules with a hierarchically higher status."

[1095] See ECtHR, *Al-Adsani v. United Kingdom*, 21 November 2001, para. 61 and Concurring Opinion of Judge Zupancic (distinguishing criminal and civil liability for torture when discussing the effects of its peremptory character). But compare the dissenting opinion of Judges Rozakis and Caflisch, joined by Judges Wildhaber, Costa, Cabral Barreto and Vajic, in particular para. 4.

[1096] See above, Chapter IV, para. 5.3.b.

[1097] Schabas 2003b, p. 61.

[1098] See e.g. ECtHR, *Al-Adsani v. United Kingdom*, 21 November 2001, dissenting opinion of Judge Ferrari Bravo (asserting that as a consequence of the *jus cogens* status of torture, States must allow claims for civil damages in extraterritorial cases of torture because they are under "a duty to *contribute* to the punishment of torture," but are "not, obviously, [under a duty] to punish, [such cases] since it was clear that the acts of torture had not taken place in the United Kingdom but elsewhere, in a State over which the Court did not have jurisdiction."); U.K., House of Lords, *R. v. Bow Street Metropolitan Stipendiary Magistrate & Others, Ex Parte Pinochet Ugarte (No. 3)*, 24 March 1999, [2000] 1 A.C. 147 at 198 and 204-205, where Lord Browne-Wilkinson contradicted himself in stating that: "The jus cogens nature of the international crime of torture justifies states in taking universal jurisdiction over torture wherever committed. [...] I have doubts whether, before the coming into force of the Torture Convention, the existence of the international crime of torture as jus cogens was enough to justify the conclusion that the organisation of state torture could not rank for immunity purposes as performance of an official function. At that stage there was no international tribunal to punish torture and no general jurisdiction to permit or require its punishment in domestic courts. Not until there was

While it is important to take note of the persisting lack of clarity surrounding *jus cogens* norms in general, there is neither place nor necessity for their full analysis at this stage. Rather, I limit myself in this study to the import of *jus cogens* status for the enforcement of these rules in national courts. In this context, the lack of clarity just noted do not render the *jus cogens* status of core crimes law immaterial. The fact that this *jus cogens* status is regularly invoked in national prosecutions is in itself significant. It shows that national courts consider it a relevant factor, despite the fact that it is usually not regulated or even mentioned in their national law. Moreover, numerous judgments do ascribe clear effects to the peremptory character of the core crimes. These effects include, for example, a duty to prosecute[1099] and imprescriptibility.[1100] Most importantly in the context of this study, various national courts have found that the peremptory character of the core crimes alters the normal balance between national and international law in their practice. These judgments will be discussed below, in paragraph 4.

3.3 The Duty to Prosecute Core Crimes

Over the last few decades, international law has significantly increased its demands on States to prosecute perpetrators of core crimes. International legal practice, in particular that of the human rights bodies, and corresponding academic work on the duty to prosecute have proliferated.[1101] At the same time, various commentators question the extent to which the work of the human rights bodies and doctrine reflect an actual duty to prosecute in positive international law.[1102] Therefore, this paragraph will first outline the basis and (alleged) content of the duty to prosecute in international law, particularly as derived from treaties and the practice of the human rights bodies (para. 3.3.a), and then describe to what extent the duty has

---

some form of universal jurisdiction for punishment of the crime of torture could it really be talked about as a fully constituted international crime. What the Torture Convention did provide what was missing: a worldwide universal jurisdiction." See also above, Chapter IV, para. 5.3.b, on the ICTY's obiter dictum in *Furundzija* regarding the consequences of the peremptory character of torture.

[1099] See e.g. below, note 1149. Cf. Congo (the), Supreme Court, *Projet de loi portant définition et répression des crimes contre l'Humanite*, 24 March 1998, *Au fond*:

"Considérant que la République du Congo est également Partie à la Convention du 9 Décembre 1948 relative à la prévention et à la répression du crime de génocide en vertu de la théorie de la succession d'état d'une part et d'autre part en vertu de ce que les normes contenues dans ladite convention du 9 Décembre 1948 sont de nos jours considérées comme l'expression du droit des gens c'est-à-dire comme des normes impératives et obligatoires pour tous et auxquelles nul état ne peut valablement se soustraire…".

[1100] See e.g. Argentina, Supreme Court, *Arancibia Clavel, Enrique Lautaro s/ homicidio calificado y asociación ilícita y otros*, 24 August 2004, in particular para. 29 and vote of J. Boggiano, para. 30-32 and 40; above, notes 467-476 and several other cases cited in Cassese 2003a, p. 318.

[1101] See e.g. Aldana-Pindell 2002, p. 1412-1436; Tomuschat 2002; Seibert-Fohr 2002b; Kleffner 2000; Ambos 1999; Schilling 1999; Scharf 1996a; Roht-Arriaza 1995. See for an extensive overview of pre-1999 literature Penrose 1999. See for an interesting jurisprudential analysis of the duty to prosecute Pedain 2002.

[1102] See below, notes 1147 and 1151.

been accepted in State practice (para. 3.3.b). It will deal with the specific issue of amnesty laws (para. 3.3.c) before drawing conclusions on the current status of the duty to prosecute (para. 3.3.d).

It should be noted at the outset that the following analysis will distinguish the duty to prosecute in general from the admissibility of amnesty laws under international law.[1103] While these two questions are closely connected, they cannot be fused. International law may well oblige States to prosecute as a general rule, though this rule may be deviated from in extreme circumstances. Simply said: that Rwandese courts may feel entitled at some point to sanction an amnesty law to save their criminal justice system from drowning can hardly justify the conclusion that prosecutors in the Netherlands are at liberty to begin or forego core crimes prosecutions as they see fit. Of course, State practice in the field of amnesty laws is relevant for the determination of the duty to prosecute, especially where legislatures or courts discuss that duty in general terms. Exclusion of amnesties for core crimes is a clear indication of a duty to prosecute. Yet permission for such amnesties may well evidence an exception to rather than a full-scale negation of the duty to prosecute. Thus, a proper conceptual approach requires a distinction between a duty to prosecute in general and the permissibility of amnesty laws. Accordingly, sub-paragraph 3.3.b will examine State practice regarding the duty to prosecute core crimes in general, while sub-paragraph 3.3.c will appraise the implications of State practice regarding amnesty laws.

3.3.a *Basis of the Duty to Prosecute in International Law*

The duty to prosecute has three distinct bases in positive international law that differ in their territorial scope and with regard to the crimes they cover.[1104] First, human rights law requires States to prosecute all serious human rights violations, including but not limited to most core crimes, committed in their jurisdiction.[1105] This duty to prosecute finds its basis both in States' general obligation to respect

---

[1103] See on the specific question of amnesties e.g. Sadat 2004; Robinson 2003; Seibert-Fohr 2003; Delmas-Marty 2002b, p. 626-637; O'Shea 2002; Wyngaert and Ongena 2001; Dugard 1999; Scharf 1996b; Hammel 1993.

[1104] Additional indications for a duty to prosecute certain crimes can be found in international obligations to legislate for those crimes, not to apply statutes of limitations, pardons and immunities and, indeed, the very fact that international law criminalizes them. See above, note 307. See also Wise 1989, p. 933. These are, however, generally seen as additional support, but not a firm legal basis for a duty to prosecute. See Kleffner 2000, p. 16.

[1105] In this regard, the term human rights violations broadly refers to acts of both State agents and private individuals, in accordance with the views of the human rights bodies that the duty to prosecute extends to crimes committed by private individuals. See e.g. ECtHR, *M.C. v. Bulgaria*, 4 December 2003, para. 149-151; IACtHR, *Velasquez Rodriguez*, 29 July 1988, para. 173 ("What is decisive is whether a violation of the rights recognized by the Convention has occurred with the support or the acquiescence of the government, *or* whether the State has allowed the act to take place without taking measures to prevent it or to punish those responsible." – emphasis added). See also Seibert-Fohr 2002a, p. 326-327.

and ensure[1106] human rights like the right to life[1107] and the right to be free from torture,[1108] and in the procedural rights of victims, such as the right to an effective remedy and access to court.[1109] It has been developed primarily in the case law of the international human rights bodies.

The IACtHR was at the forefront of the development of a duty to prosecute serious human rights violations. The seminal case in this regard is *Velasquez Rodriguez* (1988), where the Court held that "States must prevent, investigate and punish any violation of the rights recognized by the [Inter-American] Convention."[1110] Since then, the IACtHR has developed this line of reasoning in various cases.[1111]

Unlike the IACtHR, the ECtHR cannot order prosecution as a *remedy*.[1112] Yet like its Inter-American counterpart, it has nonetheless developed a line of cases which reads a duty to prosecute in the Convention. In *M.C. v. Bulgaria* (2003), the Court held that "effective deterrence against grave acts such as rape, where fundamental values and essential aspects of private life are at stake, requires efficient criminal-law provisions."[1113] Therefore, the Court found, "States have a positive obligation inherent in Articles 3 and 8 of the Convention to enact criminal-law provisions effectively punishing rape and to apply them in practice through effective investigation and prosecution."[1114] The ECtHR has taken this approach in numer-

[1106] See Art. 2 ICCPR; Art. 1 ECHR; Art. 1 ACHR; Art. 1 ACHPR.

[1107] See Art. 6 ICCPR; Art. 2 ECHR; Art. 4 ACHR; Art. 4 ACHPR.

[1108] See Art. 7 ICCPR; Art. 3 ECHR; Art. 5 ACHR (right to personal security and integrity); Art. 4 and 5 ACHPR (right to life and physical and moral integrity, respectively the prohibition of all forms of exploitation and degradation of man).

[1109] See Art. 13 ECHR (right to an effective remedy); Art. 8 ACHR (right to due process); Art. 25 ACHR (right to due judicial protection). The human rights bodies differ somewhat in their appreciation of the different legal bases and have rejected several attempts to broaden the foundation of the duty to prosecute. For example, it has been argued unsuccessfully in cases before the HRC that a duty to prosecute also flows from the right to a fair trial (Art. 14 para. 1 ICCPR) and the qualification of the principle of legality (Art. 15 para. 2 ICCPR). See Seibert-Fohr 2002b, p. 313-314.

[1110] IACtHR, *Velasquez Rodriguez*, 29 July 1988, Series C No. 4 and 95 I.L.R. 232, para. 166.

[1111] See e.g IACtHR, *Bulacio v. Argentina*, 18 September 2003, para. 38 and 110-121; IACtHR, *Barrios Altos* case 2001, below notes 1249-1251; IACtHR, Giraldo Cardona, Order of the Court of September 30, 1999, 30 September 1999, Ser. E, No. 2 (imposing a duty to prosecute as a necessary provisional measure in the sense of Art. 63 (2) IACHR to safeguard the wellbeing of witnesses). See also IAComHR, *Mendoza et al. v. Uruguay*, 2 October 1992, Report No. 29/92, 82nd session, OEA/LV/11.82Doc.25, para. 40: "What is denounced as incompatible with the [American] Convention are the legal consequences of the law with respect to the right to a fair trial. One of the law's effects was to deny the victim or his rightful claimant the opportunity to participate in the criminal proceedings, which is the appropriate means to investigate the commission of the crimes denounced [*inter alia* disappearances of persons and abduction of minors], determine criminal liability and impose punishment on those responsible, their accomplices and accessories after the fact."

[1112] See ECtHR, *Ireland v. UK*, 13 December 1977, para. 187 ("the Court finds that the sanctions available to it do not include the power to direct one of those States to institute criminal or disciplinary proceedings in accordance with its domestic law."). See also Harris *et al.* 1995, p. 683-684.

[1113] ECtHR, *M.C. v. Bulgaria*, 4 December 2003, para. 150.

[1114] Id., para. 153.

ous other cases and read a duty to prosecute in various provisions of the ECHR.[1115]

The HRC follows a similar path in its communications.[1116] The Committee has for example denounced certain amnesty laws as "an obstacle to the investigation and punishment of the persons responsible for offences committed in the past, contrary to article 2 of the Covenant."[1117] The African Commission on Human and Peoples' Rights has taken only cautious steps in the same direction.[1118]

The great majority of this case law concerns torture and homicidal acts. Since core crimes are by definition serious offences and involve "fundamental values,"[1119] it can reasonably be assumed that the duty to prosecute flowing from human rights law extends to all of them, with the possible exception of a few war crimes that do not involve bodily harm.[1120] In keeping with its normal scope, human rights law obliges States to prosecute serious violations committed in their jurisdiction.[1121] Thus, with only limited exceptions,[1122] this duty to prosecute encompasses territorial, but not extraterritorial core crimes.

However, a possible widening of the duty to prosecute with broad implications lies in interpreting victims' right of access to court in their State of residence to extend to core crimes committed elsewhere. In *Al-Adsani* (2001), the ECtHR found the right of access to court in the United Kingdom applicable in a case regarding

---

[1115] See e.g. ECtHR, *Aktas v. Turkey*, 24 April 2003, para. 329; ECtHR, *Kiliç v. Turkey*, 28 March 2000, para. 93: "[N]o effective criminal investigation can be considered to have been conducted in accordance with Article 13 [ECHR, right to an effective remedy] […] The Court finds therefore that the applicant has been denied an effective remedy in respect of the death of his brother."; ECtHR, *Assenov and Others v. Bulgaria*, 28 October 1998, para. 102 and 114-118. See also Mowbray 2002; Chiavario 2001.

[1116] See elaborately Seibert-Fohr 2002b and Seibert-Fohr 2002a.

[1117] HRC, Comments on Peru, Doc. CCPR/CO/70/PER, para. 9.

[1118] See AfrComHPR, *Commission Nationale des Droits de l'Homme et des Libertés v. Chad*, October, 1995, Communication No. 74/92, para. 22 ("Even where it cannot be proved that violations were committed by government agents, the government had a responsibility to secure the safety and the liberty of its citizens, and to conduct investigations into murders. Chad therefore is responsible for the violations of the African Charter."). See also Murray 2000, p. 74 and 82.

[1119] See ECtHR, *X and Y v. The Netherlands*, 27 February 1985, para. 27 ("The Court finds that the protection afforded by the civil law in the case of [a sexual offence against a minor] is insufficient. This is a case where fundamental values and essential aspects of private life are at stake. Effective deterrence is indispensable in this area and it can be achieved only by criminal-law provisions.").

[1120] The question how far the duty to prosecute human rights violations extends beyond the core crimes is not relevant here and must be left aside.

[1121] Cf. ECtHR, *Kalogeropoulou v. Greece and Germany, Decision on Admissibility*, 12 December 2002, available in French only, para. D2; ECtHR, *Al-Adsani v. United Kingdom*, 21 November 2001, para. 37-41.

[1122] See ICJ, *Legal Consequences of the Construction of a Wall in the Occupied Palestinian Territory, Advisory Opinion*, 9 July 2004para. 107-113; ECtHR, *Ilascu and Others v. Moldova and Russia*, 7 May 2004, para. 310-335; ECtHR, *Bankovic and others v. Belgium and others*, 12 December 2001, para. 59-73; ECtHR, *Loizidou v. Turkey, Preliminary Objections*, 23 March 1995, para. 62. See also Coomans and Kamminga 2004; Cassese 2004a, p. 874; Cassese 2003a, p. 11-14.

torture committed in Kuwait.[1123] The ECtHR made a principled distinction between violations inside and outside the forum State to reject the applicability of the right to a remedy.[1124] However, the Court did not accept the United Kingdom's argument that the right of access to court could not extend to matters outside the State's jurisdiction.[1125] Thus, *Al-Adsani* suggests that victims of core crimes violations abroad might have a right to see their attackers prosecuted on the basis of extraterritorial jurisdiction if the legal obstacles to such prosecutions are regarded as arbitrary or serving no legitimate aim.

More recently, the ECtHR continued this line of reasoning in *Mutimura v. France* (2004), concerning the right of Rwandan genocide victims to see a *genocidaire* living in France prosecuted.[1126] In this case, the ECtHR found a violation of Art. 6 (1) and 13 ECHR for an unreasonable delay in the handling of both the civil party complaint filed by the victims and the resulting prosecution. Significantly, neither the Court nor respondent France questioned the applicability of the right of access to court and right to a remedy to extraterritorial crimes. Several cases in national courts provide further support.[1127] Note, however, that in this construction the duty to prosecute extraterritorial core crimes is not independent and general but attached to the presence (and legal participation) of victims of those crimes.

Commentators have long doubted whether the initially cautious language of the human rights bodies in fact required criminal punishment. Expressions like the need to "bring perpetrators to justice" or to "hold them responsible" appeared to leave room for other remedies than criminal prosecution, like civil damages, disciplinary measures and lustration.[1128] Such language also suggested that an investigation alone may suffice, for example through a truth commission, with no further need for sanctions of any kind.[1129] However, the human rights bodies have substantially expanded and clarified their outlook on these points in recent years, and it appears that both suggestions must now in principle be rejected. The duty to inves-

---

[1123] See ECtHR, *Al-Adsani v. United Kingdom*, 21 November 2001, para. 46-49 and 52-67. It is to be noted that this case concerned a civil remedy rather than a criminal prosecution. However, the judgment suggests in para. 61 that its reading of the law applies *a fortiori* to the obligation to prosecute.

[1124] Id., para. 40: "The applicant does not contend that the alleged torture took place within the jurisdiction of the United Kingdom or that the United Kingdom authorities had any causal connection with its occurrence. In these circumstances, it cannot be said that the High Contracting Party was under a duty to provide a civil remedy to the applicant in respect of torture allegedly carried out by the Kuwaiti authorities."

[1125] Id., para. 44 and 46-49.

[1126] ECtHR, *Mutimura v. France*, 8 June 2004.

[1127] See Luxembourg, Court of Appeal, *Pinochet*, 11 February 1999, 119 ILR 360 at 362 ("It is not disputed that the offences allegedly committed by Augusto Pinochet Ugarte, a Chilean national, were committed in Chile against persons of Chilean nationality. Those persons of Chilean nationality, resident in Luxembourg with the status of political refugees, are entitled in Luxembourg to the same treatment as nationals in relation to access to the courts."). See also the Dutch cases *Bouterse*, above note 434, and *Zorreguieta*, above note 439, concerning victims' access to court for extraterritorial crimes.

[1128] See e.g. Scharf 1996a, p. 50-52; Roht-Arriaza 1990, p. 509-510.

[1129] See Provost 2002, p. 112-115.

tigate is clearly distinct from the additional duty to prosecute.[1130] Punishment of serious human rights violations must be effective and proportionate, which requires, certainly for the core crimes, criminal sanctions.[1131]

Second, States have in several treaty regimes accepted obligations to prosecute particular core crimes.[1132] The 1948 Genocide Convention obliges States to prosecute genocide, at least when committed on their territory.[1133] For crimes against humanity, several treaties governing specific crimes like slavery and apartheid im-

---

[1130] See IACtHR, *Godínez Cruz, Compensatory Damages*, 21 July 1989, para. 30 ("The duty to investigate is in addition to the duties to prevent involuntary disappearances and to punish those directly responsible."); ECtHR, *Hugh Jordan v. the United Kingdom*, 4 May 2001, para. 130: "Notwithstanding the useful fact finding function that an inquest may provide in some cases, the Court considers that in this case it could play no effective role in the identification or prosecution of any criminal offences which may have occurred and, in that respect, falls short of the requirements of Article 2." Cf. HRC, *Comments on Cambodia, Doc. CCPR/C/79/Add.108*, 1999, para. 6 ("The State party should take steps without delay to ensure that the alleged perpetrators of gross human rights violations and crimes against humanity are brought to trial before properly constituted independent courts ..."). See also Aldana-Pindell 2002, p. 1437-1456; Alvarez *et al.* 2002, p. 329-330; Mowbray 2002.

[1131] See ECtHR, *McShane v. the United Kingdom*, 28 May 2002 para. 125:
"While, civil proceedings would provide a judicial fact finding forum, with the attendant safeguards and the ability to reach findings of unlawfulness, with the possibility of an award of damages, it is however a procedure undertaken on the initiative of the applicant, not the authorities, and it does not involve the identification or punishment of any alleged perpetrator. As such, it cannot be taken into account in the assessment of the State's compliance with its procedural obligations under Article 2 of the Convention.";
IACtHR, Barrios Altos Case, (*Chimbipuma Aguierre v. Peru*), Merits, 14 May 2001, (Ser. C) No. 75 (2001) and 41 ILM 93 (2002) at 118, para. 13 (Ramirez, Sergio Garcia, J., concurring and noting that "certain very serious human rights violations must be punished surely and effectively at the national and international level"); HRC, *Bautista de Arellana v. Colombia*, 27 October 1995, Doc. CCPR/C/55/D/563/1993, para. 8.2 and 8.6:
"[P]urely disciplinary and administrative remedies cannot be deemed to constitute adequate and effective remedies within the meaning of article 2, paragraph 3, of the Covenant, in the event of particularly serious violations of human rights, notably in the event of an alleged violation of the right to life.
[...]
[T]he State party is under a duty to investigate thoroughly alleged violations of human rights, and in particular forced disappearances of persons and violations of the right to life, and to prosecute criminally, try and punish those held responsible for such violations. This duty applies a fortiori in cases in which the perpetrators of such violations have been identified.";
Contrary to what has been suggested, the specific requirement of criminal sanctions does not contravene the drafting history of the ICCPR. Compare Seibert-Fohr 2002a, p. 321-322 with Scharf 1996, p.49.
But see HRC, *Thomas v. Jamaica*, 1993, Doc. CCPR/C/49/D/321/1988, para. 11 (finding an obligation to investigate allegations of torture "with a view to instituting as appropriate criminal *or other* procedures against those found responsible," emphasis added).

[1132] See O'Shea 2002, p. 141-151; Kleffner 2000, p. 17-37.

[1133] Art. 1, 4 and 6. See also ICJ, *Case Concerning Application of the Convention on the Prevention and Punishment of the Crime of Genocide (Bosnia-Herzegovina v. Yugoslavia), preliminary objections*, 11 July 1996, para. 31 ("the obligation [...] to prevent and to punish the crime of genocide is not territorially limited by the Convention"); ICJ, *Reservations to the Convention on the Prevention and Punishment of Genocide (Advisory Opinion)*, 1951 I.C.J. Reports 1951, p. 23 (noting "the universal character both of the condemnation of genocide and of the co-operation required 'in order to liberate mankind from such an odious scourge' ").

pose affirmative obligations.[1134] The Geneva Conventions require States to either extradite or prosecute perpetrators of grave breaches.[1135] Other treaties establish additional obligations to prosecute war crimes.[1136]

The ICC Statute in its preamble "recall[s] that it is the duty of every State to exercise its criminal jurisdiction over those responsible for international crimes."[1137] Thus, the Statute in a general sense recognizes an obligation for States to prosecute core crimes perpetrators. The term "recalling" indicates that this duty was already established under general international law and merely affirmed, not created, by the Statute. Yet, the wording of the preamble leaves open to doubt the scope of this duty.[1138] In addition, a duty to prosecute core crimes flows from Security Council resolutions,[1139] for example from Resolution 1373 (2001) to the extent that core crimes overlap with terrorist acts.[1140]

[1134] See Art. 4 1973 International Convention on the Suppression and Punishment of the Crime of Apartheid; Art. 2 and 6 1926 Slavery Convention; Art. 1, 3, 5 and 6 1956 Supplementary Convention on the Abolition of Slavery, the Slave Trade and Institutions and Practices Similar to Slavery; Art. 1-4 Convention for the Suppression of the Traffic in Persons and of the Exploitation of the Prostitution of Others; Art. 4, 6 and 7 CAT; Art. 1 and 6 1985 Inter-American Convention to Prevent and Punish Torture.

[1135] See Art. 49 GC I; Art. 50 GC II; Art. 129 GC III; Art. 146 GC IV; Art. 85 and 87 AP I. Compare further Reydams 1996, p. 34 (asserting also a duty to search, arrest and prosecute persons responsible for violations of common Article 3 Geneva Conventions) with Meron 1998, p. 23: "The fact that the Geneva Conventions created the obligation of *aut dedere aut judicare* only with regard to grave breaches does not mean that significant other breaches of the Geneva Conventions may not be punished by any state party to the Convention, or by international criminal tribunals, provided that they reflect significant obligations and customary law. In my view, any third state has the right, although probably not the duty, to prosecute serious violations of the Geneva Conventions, including those of common Article 3, even when it has no special nexus with either the offender or the victim."

[1136] See e.g. Art. 28 1954 Hague Convention for the Protection of Cultural Property in the Event of Armed Conflict (obliging States Parties "to take, within the framework of their ordinary criminal jurisdiction, all necessary steps to prosecute and impose penal or disciplinary sanctions upon those persons, of whatever nationality, who commit or order to be committed a breach of the present Convention").

[1137] ICC Statute, preamble, para. 6: "Affirming that the most serious crimes of concern to the international community as a whole must not go unpunished and that their effective prosecution must be ensured by taking measures at the national level and by enhancing international cooperation, [...] Recalling that it is the duty of every State to exercise its criminal jurisdiction over those responsible for international crimes,"

[1138] See Arbour 2003, p. 586-587. It can be questioned whether the preamble recognizes a duty to enact any legislation necessary to prosecute core crimes, or merely to utilize the legislation already in place ("*its* jurisdiction"). See on this question Cassese 2003a, p. 302; Kleffner 2003, p. 92.

[1139] See Swart 2002a, p. 1-2; Scharf 1996a, p. 59-60.

[1140] See SC Resolution 1373 (28 September 2001), para. 1 and 2:
"1. *Decides* that all States shall:
(a) Prevent and suppress the financing of terrorist acts;
(b) Criminalize the wilful provision or collection, by any means, directly or indirectly, of funds by their nationals or in their territories with the intention that the funds should be used, or in the knowledge that they are to be used, in order to carry out terrorist acts;
[...]
2. *Decides also* that all States shall:
[...]
(e) Ensure that any person who participates in the financing, planning, preparation or perpetration of

Third, the law of State responsibility may in specific cases require punishment of perpetrators of crimes that violate international law, *inter alia* as part of the satisfaction to be given by the violating State.[1141] This obligation can extend to all crimes everywhere, as long as they constitute international wrongful acts attributable to the State, either directly or on the basis of due diligence.[1142]

These three different sources of the duty to prosecute share the same core. They establish the obligatory rather than discretionary character of the punishment of core crimes for States. Yet, there are two noteworthy differences between them. First, they have a different territorial scope. Human rights law principally requires States to prosecute core crimes committed within their territory. The treaties on specific crimes generally impose either a duty to prosecute territorial crimes, or a duty to prosecute or extradite. The law of State responsibility may require States to prosecute certain core crimes committed both within their jurisdiction and by their officials abroad.

Second, not all of these sources represent rules of customary law. The relevant rules of the law of State responsibility do. The relevant provisions of the general human rights treaties as well as treaties like the Genocide Convention, the Geneva Conventions and the CAT may also be thought to reflect custom on account of the broad ratification of these treaties and subsequent consistent State practice.[1143] The 1973 International Convention on the Suppression and Punishment of the Crime of Apartheid, on the other hand, with only twenty States Parties can not easily be assumed to codify customary law.

The question then arises to what extent these three different sources give rise to a duty to prosecute the core crimes under customary international law. Doctrine is divided on this point. Nonetheless, some base lines can be drawn. First, there is no general obligation to extradite or prosecute for *all* extraterritorial crimes.[1144] Sec-

---

terrorist acts or in supporting terrorist acts is brought to justice and ensure that, in addition to any other measures against them, such terrorist acts are established as serious criminal offences in domestic laws and regulations and that the punishment duly reflects the seriousness of such terrorist acts."
But compare ICTY, Trial Chamber, *Delalic et al.,* 16 November 1998, para. 418 ("[T]he Security Council, not being a legislative body, cannot create offences."). See on the relationship between core crimes and terrorism, above, note 67.

[1141] See Art. 37 (2) of the ILC's 2001 Articles on State Responsibility ("Satisfaction may consist in an acknowledgement of the breach, an expression of regret, a formal apology or another appropriate modality."). See als Commentary No. 5 to Art. 37 (stating that "disciplinary or penal action against the individuals whose conduct caused the internationally wrongful act" may be one of the appropriate modalities).

[1142] See Nollkaemper 2003a, p. 636-638; O'Shea 2002, p. 209-213; Nollkaemper 2000, p. 22-23; Wilt 2000, p. 326-331; Rosenne 1998, p. 163-164; Hoogh 1996, p. 163-166; Roht-Arriaza 1990, p. 501-505; Triffterer 1966, p. 179-180.

[1143] See Cassese 2003b, p. 591-592; O'Shea 2002, p. 229 and 238; Roht-Arriaza 1990, p. 490-492. See on the role of multilateral treaties in the formation of customary rules Scott and Carr 1996.

[1144] See ICJ, Lockerbie Case (*Libya v. United Kingdom*), Provisional Measures, Joint Declaration of Judges Evensen, Tarassov, Guillaume and Aguilar, 9 April 1992, 1992 ICJ 24, para. 2: "In so far as general international law is concerned, extradition is a sovereign decision of the requested State, which is never under an obligation to carry it out. Moreover, in general international law there is no obligation

ond, there is a clear consensus that States are not under an obligation to prosecute extraterritorial core crimes in the absence of *any* link to the crime, such as nationality or presence of the offender.[1145]

Commentators further agree that international law is moving towards a general obligation on States to prosecute all core crimes perpetrators present in their jurisdiction.[1146] Yet, they mostly concur that this development is on-going and has not yet resulted in a rule of positive law.[1147] Although the duty to prosecute or extradite is included in many treaties on specific crimes,[1148] both current State practice[1149]

---

to prosecute in default of extradition. Although since the days of Covarruvias and Grotius such a formula has been advocated by some legal scholars, it has never been part of positive law. This being so, every State is at liberty to request extradition and every State is free to refuse it. Should it refuse, a State is not obliged to prosecute." Yet, the declaration subsequently notes that numerous treaties have modified this situation for the States Parties thereto. Thus, despite the categorical language of this statement, it clearly represents the default rule rather than the state of the law for each and every crime. See also Cassese 2003a, p. 301.

[1145] Rather, it is a matter of some debate whether there is even a right to prosecute in the absence of any link. Compare e.g. Belgium, Tribunal of First Instance Brussels (Kamer van Inbeschuldigingstelling), *In re Sharon and Yaron*, 26 June 2002, reproduced in Wouters and Panken 2003, p. 323-339 at 334 ("Qu'un droit qui consisterait a juger 'in absentia' ne releve donc pas du ius cogens, car il est contraire aux [the Geneva Conventions, the Genocide Convention and the ICC Statute].") and Netherlands, Amsterdam Court of Appeals, *In re Pinochet*, 4 January 1995, 28 NYIL 363 (1997) at 364 to Belgium, Tribunal of First Instance (District of Brussels), *In re Pinochet Ugarte*, 6 November 1998, para. 3.3.3: "[N]ational authorities have the right and even under certain circumstances the obligation to prosecute the authors of such crimes irrespective of where they are found. The fight against impunity of authors of crimes under international law falls [...] within the responsibility of all states of which the national authorities have the obligation or, at the very least, the right to take all measures in order to assure the prosecution and the repression of crimes against humanity." See for further analysis of this question O'Keefe 2004; Reydams 2003, p. 38-42 and 223-224; El Zeidy 2003; Vandermeersch 2002b, p. 600-607; Henzelin 2000, p. 381-447.

[1146] See Sadat 2003, p. 163; Cassese 2003a, p. 302; Delmas-Marty 2002b, p. 632-634; Ratner and Abrams 2001, p. 337 ("[R]ecent actions by states suggest that a general norm requiring investigation and punishment of gross abusers is gradually emerging."); Dugard 2001, p. 698; Kleffner 2000, p. 27; Dugard 1999, p. 1004. See also Art. 9 Draft Code 1996 (containing an obligation to extradite or prosecute the core crimes).

[1147] See Cassese 2003a, p. 301-303 (asserting that there is no customary obligation to prosecute the core crimes, but only a "general obligation of international cooperation for their prevention and punishment); Tomuschat 2002, p. 342-343 (asserting that States have a customary duty to prosecute "grave crimes against the life, physical integrity and freedom of human beings committed in their respective territories," but not for extraterritorial crimes); Swart 2000, p. 202. Bassiouni makes a strong case for a duty to prosecute all *jus cogens* crimes in sweeping terms, but at the same time acknowledges it is of an aspirational nature and lacks firm State practice. See Bassiouni 1999a, p. 219 and 574; Bassiouni 1996, p. 63 and 66.

[1148] See Bassiouni and Wise 1995, p. 73-302.

[1149] Only a few national judgments provide support for a general duty to prosecute or extradite core crimes perpetrators. See e.g. Australia, Federal Court, *Nulyarimma v. Thompson*, 1 September 1999, [1999] FCA 1192, Whitlam J., para. 57: "The emergence after the Second World War of the international crime of genocide no doubt imposes non-derogable obligations on Australia under the law of nations. The exercise of universal jurisdiction to prosecute such an offence is a matter for the Commonwealth...");
Merkel J., para. 81 and 141: "It was also common ground between the parties, correctly in my view, that [...] the prohibition of genocide is a peremptory norm of customary international law (*jus cogens*)

and the cautious language of the ICC Statute call into question its current viability as a general customary rule for all core crimes.[1150] The work of the ICC and the corresponding practice of States may well bring more clarity to this matter in the years to come.

Some scholars also deny a general customary obligation to prosecute territorial core crimes and thus appear to recognize only the specific obligations contained in ICL treaties.[1151] They assert that the duty to prosecute formulated in the work of the human rights bodies exists only on paper, while States do not actually accept it in their legislation and judicial practice.[1152] In the absence of firm State practice, the argument goes, there can be no customary duty to prosecute, no matter how many international judgments, communications, declarations, UN resolutions, draft codes and principles assert the contrary.

However, State practice regarding the duty to prosecute has to a significant extent followed the development of international bodies and instruments. Therefore, I will analyze this practice in order to ascertain whether international law imposes a positive duty on States to prosecute all core crimes committed within their jurisdiction. The following analysis will take into account only individual declarations of States, legislation, and judgments of national courts, these being generally perceived as the "make-or-break" element of State practice regarding the duty to prosecute. Without in any way doubting their significance, joint declarations and other international instruments and practice will be left aside, as they have been elaborately described elsewhere.[1153]

3.3.b *Acceptance of the Duty to Prosecute in State Practice*

Recent years have seen a growing number of States explicitly acknowledging a duty to prosecute core crimes committed within their jurisdiction. They have done so in different ways.

First, many States have accepted the duty to prosecute territorial core crimes in declarations to this effect, particularly communications to human rights bodies.[1154]

---

giving rise to non derogable obligations *erga omnes* that is, enforcement obligations owed by each nation State to the international community as a whole. [...] As explained earlier it is not in dispute that the acceptance under international law of a universal crime which has attained the status of *jus cogens* obliges a nation state to punish an offender or to extradite that offender, who is within its territory, to a state that will punish the offender."
Cf. Mexico, Supreme Court, *In re Cavallo (Amparo en Revision 140/2002)*, 10 June 2002, p. 493-497 and the Belgian and Australian cases cited above, note 1074.

[1150] See Eser and Kreicker 2003, p. 440-443; Henzelin 2000, p. 376; Wilt 2000, p. 331-334.

[1151] See e.g. Scharf 1996a, p. 61. Presenting at a conference in Galway, Ireland, in 2004, Professor Scharf asserted that the duty to prosecute had still not matured in customary international law and adhered to the conclusions of his earlier writings. Cf. Ratner and Abrams 2001, p. 337.

[1152] See e.g. Gitti 1999, p. 75; Dugard 1999, p. 1003; Scharf 1996a, p. 56-59.

[1153] See the literature mentioned above, note 1101.

[1154] See e.g. Hungary, Report to the Human Rights Committee, 13 March 2001, CCPR/C/HUN/2000/4, para. 288 (explaining that action was taken "partly in response to obligations arising from the [ICCPR], which requires states to bring to justice the perpetrators of human rights violations"). See also Gitti 1999, p. 76-80; Roht-Arriaza 1990, p. 496-498.

This includes many States that have a poor human rights record, such as Paraguay,[1155] Peru,[1156] and various other Latin-American States.[1157] These States do not adequately prosecute core crimes in practice, but implicitly or explicitly recognize a duty to do so while disputing the factual extent of their violations or citing practical problems as an excuse.[1158] Apart from reports to human rights bodies, States have acknowledged a duty to prosecute in various other statements and communications. In Ethiopia, for example, the Special Prosecutor's Office stated in a 1994 report on the ambitious and complex nature of its undertaking to prosecute thousands of suspects of international crimes committed under the Mengistu regime that the Transitional Government of Ethiopia accepted "their international legal obligations to investigate and bring to justice those involved in human rights crimes."[1159]

Second, the duty to prosecute territorial core crimes is reflected in national legislation. Various kinds of national laws embody the principle that core crimes must

---

[1155] See Paraguay, *Reply to the Inter-American Commission of Human Rights*, March 2002, Chapter III on Impunity: "Los principales logros del actual sistema penal, y específicamente, en materia procesal son, 1) la eficiencia punitiva (no a la impunidad) [...] En ésta oportunidad, se reitera a la Comisión que la justicia paraguaya conforme con sus atribuciones, facultades y deberes constitucionales y legales está obligada a investigar y sancionar a los culpables de hechos punibles tipificados en el ordenamiento interno y más aun de los crímenes contra los derechos humanos. [...] Como podrá apreciar la Comisión de la información suministrada por el Estado con respecto a la obligación de investigar y sancionar las violaciones de los derechos humanos cometidas durante la dictadura 1954-1989 queda de manifiesto que *"A la presente fecha la mayoría de tales violaciones han sido investigadas y castigadas"* y por ende, demostrado el cumplimiento efectivo por parte de la justicia paraguaya de los mandatos de la Constitución, de las obligaciones internacionales contraídas libremente y las leyes penales vigentes."; HRC, *Comments on Paraguay, Doc. CCPR/C/79/Add. 48*, 1995, para. 9 ("The Committee appreciates the declaration made by the delegation according to which the Government will not enact any amnesty law, and that, on the contrary, concrete steps have already or are being taken to make accountable perpetrators of human rights abuses under the past dictatorial regime.").

[1156] In the *Barrios Altos* case, Peru submitted a communication of aquiescence to the IACtHR and explicitly recognized "its international responsibility for the violation of the right to a fair trial and to judicial guarantees embodied in Articles 8 and 25 of the American Convention on Human Rights, because it had failed to conduct a thorough investigation of the facts and had not duly punished those responsible for the crimes." See IACtHR, Barrios Altos Case, (*Chimbipuma Aguierre v. Peru*), Merits, 14 May 2001, (Ser. C) No. 75 (2001) and 41 ILM 93 (2002), para. 35 and 39.

[1157] See e.g. HRC, *Concluding Observations on Guatemala*, 27 August 2001, Doc. CCPR/CO/72/GTM, para. 8.

[1158] See e.g. IAComHR, *Lincoleo v. Chile*, 16 April 2001, para. 10-18; HRC, *Periodic Report of Guatemala to the HRC, Doc. CCPR/C/GTM/99/2*, 5 April 2000, para. 35-40 and 78-91 ("Measures against Impunity" and "Public Prosecutor's Department"); HRC, *Periodic Report of Chile to the HRC*, 3 December 1998, Doc. CCPR/C/95/Add.11, para. 80 ("Exceptionally, deaths which have been reported as possible instances of excessive use of force by law enforcement officials have immediately been referred to the courts for investigation.") and generally the Annual Reports of the Inter-American Commission on Human Rights, especially the chapters on "Follow-up on the compliance with recommendations of the IAComHR" and "Follow-up of the recommendations formulated by the IAComHR in its reports on the situation of human rights in member states." See also Ambos 1999, p. 354.

[1159] See Ethiopia, Office of the Special Prosecutor, Report on The Special Prosecution Process of War Criminals and Human Rights Violators in Ethiopia, February 1994, Reproduced in Kritz 1995, Vol. III, p. 559-575, p. 559.

be punished. On the highest level of legislation, this principle finds expression in the constitutions of several States, particularly those that have recently emerged from totalitarian rule. Among the States that include a duty to prosecute core crimes in their constitution are Ecuador,[1160] Ethiopia,[1161] and Venezuela.[1162] Various States

---

[1160] See Art. 23 (2) Constitution 1998:
"[...]
El Estado adoptará las medidas necesarias para prevenir, eliminar y sancionar, en especial, la violencia contra los niños, adolescentes, las mujeres y personas de la tercera edad.
Las acciones y penas por genocidio, tortura, desaparición forzada de personas, secuestro y homicidio por razones políticas o de conciencia, serán imprescriptibles. Estos delitos no serán susceptibles de indulto o amnistía. En estos casos, la obediencia a órdenes superiores no eximirá de responsabilidad."

[1161] See Article 28 (1) Constitution 1994 (Crimes Against Humanity): "Criminal liability of persons who commit crimes against humanity, so defined by international agreements ratified by Ethiopia and by other laws of Ethiopia, such as genocide, summary executions, forcible disappearances or torture shall not be barred by statute of limitation. Such offences may not be commuted by amnesty or pardon of the legislature or any other state organ."

[1162] See Art. 29 Constitution:
"El Estado estará obligado a investigar y sancionar legalmente los delitos contra los derechos humanos cometidos por sus autoridades.
Las acciones para sancionar los delitos de lesa humanidad, violaciones graves a los derechos humanos y los crímenes de guerra son imprescriptibles. Las violaciones de derechos humanos y los delitos de lesa humanidad serán investigados y juzgados por los tribunales ordinarios. Dichos delitos quedan excluidos de los beneficios que puedan conllevar su impunidad, incluidos el indulto y la amnistía"
("The State will be obliged to investigate and legally sanction crimes against humanity perpetrated by its authorities.
The legal actions to prosecute crimes against humanity, grave human rights violations and war crimes will be without statute of limitation. Human rights violations and crimes against humanity will be investigated and judged by regular tribunals. Those crimes are excluded from any benefit that could lead to their impunity, including pardon and amnesty" – Translation by Zandra Valenzuela Delgado).
See for an elaborate interpretation of this provision Venezuela, Tribunal Supremo de Justicia, Sala Constitucional, 9 december 2002. Cf. Art. 10 of the 2002 Constitution of the Congo:
"[...]
Tout individu, tout agent de l'État, toute autorité publique qui se rendrait coupable d'acte de torture ou de traitement cruel et inhumain, soit de sa propre initiative, soit sur instruction *est puni* conformément à la loi." (emphasis added);
Art. 29 Constitution of Argentina:
"El Congreso no puede conceder al Ejecutivo nacional, ni las legislaturas provinciales a los gobernadores de provincia, facultades extraordinarias, ni la suma del poder público, ni otorgarles sumisiones o supremacías por las que la vida, el honor o las fortunas de los argentinos queden a merced de gobiernos o persona alguna. Actos de esta naturaleza llevan consigo una nulidad insanable, y sujetarán a los que los formulen, consientan o firmen, a la responsabilidad y pena de los infames traidores a la Patria"
("Congress may not vest on the National Executive Power – nor may the provincial legislatures vest on the provincial governors – extraordinary powers or the total public authority; it may not grant acts of submission or supremacy whereby the life, honor, or wealth of the Argentine people will be at the mercy of governments or any person whatsoever. Acts of this nature shall be utterly void, and shall render those who formulate them, consent to them or sign them, liable to be condemned as infamous traitors to their fatherland.")
This article has been interpreted on numerous occasions by the Argentinean courts, including the Supreme Court, to prohibit amnesties for "acts involving the usurpation of public power or state terrorism." See Brown 2002, p. 208-209. See also Coria 2003, p. 481 (on current constitutional reform in Peru which includes the proposal to rule out impunity for war crimes and crimes against humanity in the Constitution).

have adopted amnesty laws but explicitly excluded the core crimes from their scope, which points to the mandatory character of the prosecution of these crimes.[1163] Further recognition of the duty to prosecute can be found in many national criminal laws, some specific,[1164] other general. Many States have enacted provisions in their criminal codes that establish jurisdiction over all acts for which international law (or only treaties) demands prosecution.[1165] In so doing, States recognize that there is an international duty to prosecute, but the extent of this duty remains unclear. It also deserves mention that numerous legal systems impose an obligation to prosecute all, or certain categories of crimes within their jurisdiction. This is the situation, for example, in most Latin-American States[1166] and Switzerland.[1167] Although such long-standing national practice did not originate in a belief that it was obligatory under international law, it may be taken into account in when assessing whether more recent expressions of a State's *opinio juris* on the international duty to prosecute are matched by corresponding legislative and judicial practice.

Third, the duty to prosecute territorial core crimes has been accepted by numerous national courts.[1168] Often, courts rely on treaties covering specific core crimes

---

[1163] See e.g. Cote d'Ivoire, Art. 4 Amnesty Law No. 2003-309 of 8 August 2003 (excluding from amnesty "infractions constitutives de violations graves des droits de l'homme et du droit international humanitaire" as well as "infractions qualifiées par le code pénal ivoirien de crimes et délits contre le droit des gens"). Art. 8 of the 1996 National Reconciliation Act of Guatemala explicitly excludes from amnesty "crimes of genocide, torture and forced disappearance, as well as those violations that do not have a statute of limitations or which do not permit the extinction of criminal responsibility, in accordance with the domestic law and the international treaties ratified by Guatemala." See Aldana-Pindell 2002, p. 1480; HRC, *Concluding Observations on Guatemala*, 27 August 2001, Doc. CCPR/CO/72/GTM, para. 12 (2001). Croatia has enacted several amnesty laws in the last decade which all exclude core crimes from their scope. See Konjecic 1998.

[1164] See e.g. Colombia, Art. 14 Law 589 of 6 July 2000 defining genocide, forced disappearance, forced displacement and torture, and making certain other provisions ("Los delitos que tipifica la presente ley no son amnistiables ni indultables."). Cf. preamble to the Rwandese Organic Law No. 40/2000 of January 26, 2001 setting up 'Gacaca Jurisdictions' and organising prosecutions for offences constituting the crime of genocide or crimes against humanity, committed between October 1, 1990 and December 31, 1994 ("Given the necessity to achieve reconciliation and justice in Rwanda, to eradicate forever the culture of impunity and enact laws allowing for the prosecution and sentencing of perpetrators").

[1165] See above, Chapter II, para. 3.2.b.

[1166] See e.g. Art. 71 Argentinean Penal Code:

"Deberán iniciarse de oficio todas las acciones penales, con excepción de las siguientes:
1) las que dependieren de instancia privada;
2) las acciones privadas. "

See also Art. 5 Argentinean Code of Criminal Procedure. See further the different country reports in Ambos and Malarino 2003.

[1167] See Art. 103 and 114 Swiss Code of Military Criminal Procedure (requiring the investigation and prosecution of all criminal acts under the Military Criminal Code). See also Ziegler 1997, p. 575-576.

[1168] See e.g. Indonesia, Ad Hoc Human Rights Tribunal at the Human Rights Court of Justice of Central Jakarta, *Abilio Soares*, 14 August 2002, p. 65 of 82 ("Punishment of the perpetrators of [serious human rights violations covering genocide and crimes against humanity] is recognized as an obligation to the entire international community (erga omnes obligation).") and below, note 1267 (Hungary) and 1252 (Peru). See also Cassese 2003a, p. 314 (on Spanish cases).

to substantiate this duty.[1169] But human right treaties are increasingly recognized as an additional or alternative basis. The Venezuelan Supreme Court held in 2002, under referral to the case law of the IACtHR, that amnesty provisions are inadmissible in the case of grave violations of human rights because they contravene non-derogable rights recognized by international human rights law.[1170] "This is to say," the *Tribunal Supremo de Justicia* explained, "that there is a material impossibility to apply [such norms], with the intention to impede or hinder the clarification of such facts, identify and prosecute those responsible for it, and prevent relatives and victims from knowing the truth and receive reparations."[1171] Several other national courts, including those in Argentina,[1172] Bolivia,[1173] Chile[1174] Colombia[1175] and Mexico,[1176] have similarly recognized the duty to prosecute under international human rights law, and relied on it to set aside obstacles in national law that would otherwise block prosecution. In its first judgment in the *Bouterse* case (2000), the Amsterdam Court of Appeals found that prosecution of human rights violations is an obligation for the territorial State under the ICCPR, in this case Surinam, while prosecution in the Netherlands would, in the absence of the suspect, be merely "opportune."[1177] In Haiti, the 1999 indictment of the Raboteau trial referred to the

---

[1169] See e.g. Ukraine, Constitutional Court, *Conformity of the Constitution of Ukraine to the Rome Statute of the International Criminal Court (the Rome Statute case)*, 11 July 2001, para. 2.2 (finding that the duty to prosecute the core crimes had been established by numerous treaties before the entry into force of the ICC Statute, including but not limited to the Geneva Conventions, the Apartheid Convention and the CAT).

[1170] Venezuela, Tribunal Supremo de Justicia, Sala Constitucional, 9 december 2002, para. III: "Recientemente la Corte Interamericana de Derechos Humanos sostuvo que son inadmisibles las disposiciones de amnistía, las disposiciones de prescripción y el establecimiento de excluyentes de responsabilidad que pretendan impedir la investigación y sanción de los responsables de las violaciones graves de los derechos humanos tales como la tortura, las ejecuciones sumarias, extralegales o arbitrarias y las desapariciones forzadas, todas ellas prohibidas por contravenir derechos inderogables reconocidos por el Derecho Internacional de los Derechos Humanos (Caso *Barrios Altos*, sentencia de 14 de marzo de 2001). Es decir, existe imposibilidad material en la aplicación de aquellas normas dictadas con posterioridad a la ocurrencia de hechos de esta naturaleza, con la intención de vedar u obstaculizar su esclarecimiento, identificar y juzgar a sus responsables e impedir a las víctimas y familiares conocer la verdad y recibir la reparación, si a ello hubiere lugar."

[1171] Id., translation by Zandra Valenzuela-Delgado.

[1172] See Argentina, Supreme Court, *Arancibia Clavel, Enrique Lautaro s/ homicidio calificado y asociación ilícita y otros*, 24 August 2004, in particular para. 13, and other cases below, para. 4.

[1173] See Bolivia, Tribunal Constitucional, *Resolución 1190/2001-R (Trujillo Oroza)*, 12 November 2001. See also Santalla Vargas 2003, p. 105-106.

[1174] See Chile, Court of Appeals (Santiago), *In re Fernando Laureani Maturana y Miguel Krassnoff Marchenko*, 5 January 2004, in particular para. 49 and 84 (referring *inter alia* to case law of the IACtHR). Confirmed in Chile, Supreme Court, *In re Miguel Angel Sandoval Rodríguez*, 17 November 2004.

[1175] See Colombia, Corte Constitucional, Sala Plena, *Sentencia C-578 (In re Corte Penal Internacional)*, 30 July 2002, 31 Jurisprudencia y Doctrina 2231, in particular at 2265, 2268-2269 and 2275-2277.

[1176] See Mexico, Supreme Court, *In re Cavallo (Amparo en Revision 140/2002)*, 10 June 2002 at 909.

[1177] Netherlands, Amsterdam Court of Appeals, *In re Bouterse*, 3 March 2000, NJ 2000/266, para. 4.2: "Het hof stelt voorop dat het instellen van een strafrechtelijk onderzoek ter zake van de op het

ACHR and the ICCPR before mentioning national law, and subsequently concluded that the perpetrators must be prosecuted.[1178]

What then is the contrary practice that casts doubt on the customary status of a duty to prosecute? Of course, the sad fact remains that most core crimes still go unpunished.[1179] Yet blatant violations, even on a broad scale, do not by themselves alter international rules. On the contrary, violations often reinforce the rule, because the State involved tries to justify an exception to the rule rather than its very existence.[1180] As noted above, States defend their lack of core crimes prosecutions generally with denials of the crimes or practical excuses rather than with legal arguments.[1181] Thus, most violations of the duty to prosecute core crimes reinforce the legal norm rather than contradict it. Explicit denials in national case law of the very existence of a duty to prosecute core crimes are scarce.[1182]

It should also be noted that the question of whether general human rights law imposes a duty to prosecute territorial core crimes is primarily one of interpretation of existing customary rights and obligations, rather than an assessment of a brand new customary rule. Due to the widespread ratification and implementation of human rights instruments, primarily the ICCPR, ACHR and ECHR, there is little doubt that States are under a customary obligation to respect and ensure fundamental human rights such as the right to life, freedom from torture and access to court. If States and human right bodies alike interpret those rights as encompassing a duty for the State to prosecute territorial core crimes, which they generally do, violations

---

eigen grondgebied mogelijk gepleegde strafbare feiten, die schendingen van mensenrechten opleverden, in beginsel een verplichting is die voor de Republiek Suriname voortvloeit uit het Internationaal Verdrag inzake burgerrechten en politieke rechten, waarbij het sinds 1977 partij is. [...] Vervolging in Nederland zou [...] opportuun zijn."

[1178] See Haiti, Juge d'Instruction Jean Senat Fleury of the Gonaïves Tribunal of First Instance, Ordonnance Raboteau Massacre, 27 August 1999, On file with the author, Conclusion, p. 159-160: "Vu: les traités et conventions internationaux ratifiés par Haïti, notamment la **Déclaration Universelle des droits de l'homme** adopté le 10 décembre 1948; **la Convention Américaine relative aux droits de l'homme** adopté le 22 novembre 1969 et entrée en vigueurs le 18 juillet 1978; **le Pacte International relatif aux droits civils et politiques** adopté le 16 décembre 1966 et ratifié par Haïti en 1991 et, éventuellement l'article 3 commun aux **quatre conventions de Genève de 1949** ratifiées par la République d'Haïti,

[...]

Considérant que les actes arbitraires, attentoires à la vie et à l'intégrité physique de la personne humaine perpétrés les 18 et 22 avril 1994 contre la population civile de Raboteau (Gonaïves) constituent des crimes graves et les auteurs doivent être poursuivis." (emphasis in original)

[1179] See above, Chapter III, para. 2; Pasqualucci 2003, p. 339-340 (concluding that States in the Inter-American system have often failed to live up to their duty to prosecute); Jayawickrama 2002, p. 489-491. See for a detailed account of impunity in Guatemala Aldana-Pindell 2002, p. 1480-1498.

[1180] See ICJ, *Case Concerning Military and Paramilitary Activities in and against Nicaragua (Nicaragua v. United States of America)*, 27 June 1986, para. 186: "If a State acts in a way prima facie incompatible with a recognized rule, but defends its conduct by appealing to exceptions or justifications contained within the rule itself, then whether or not the State's conduct is in fact justifiable on that basis, the significance of that attitude is to confirm rather than to weaken the rule."

[1181] See above, notes 1154 to 1158.

[1182] See below, note 1186.

of that duty cannot easily change that conclusion. In other words, the customary status of the broader international norms that give rise to the duty to prosecute – such as the right of access to court and the right to life – is not dependent on the practice of actual prosecutions, but is already well-established. It seems numerous commentators fail to take this point into account in their assessment of State practice.

3.3.c *Amnesty Laws*

Just as national judgments denying a duty to prosecute the core crimes in general are scarce, national laws granting broad amnesties after situations of conflict or war are numerous.[1183] Many of these amnesty laws extend the impunity they grant to core crimes perpetrators. Consequently, commentators often view these laws as being decisively contrary State practice which precludes the finding of a general duty to prosecute the core crimes.[1184] However, this assertion is, certainly today, questionable for several reasons.

First, as set out above, in light of the specific and exigent circumstances that generate them, amnesties should be seen as possible exceptions to a duty to prosecute, rather than as wholesale denials of that duty.[1185] Indeed, the South African Constitutional Court in the famous *Azapo* case (1996) did not take a position against a duty to prosecute serious human rights violations in general, but instead accepted the South African amnesty law in light of the exceptional character of both the situation of transition and the conditions for amnesty.[1186]

Thus, while their non-application or prohibition certainly reinforces a duty to prosecute, phenomena like amnesty laws, and also prosecutorial discretion for that matter, do not collide head-on with such a duty. More likely, they are indicative of an exception to that duty. As one commentator notes, amnesties may well be reconciled with a general duty to prosecute, provided the circumstances require such a step and the conditions of the amnesty reflect a proper balance between the differ-

[1183] See Cassese 2003a, p. 312.

[1184] See Sadat 2004, p. 203; Ratner and Abrams 2001, p. 153; Dugard 1999, p. 1003-1004; Scharf 1996a, p. 57-58.

[1185] Cf. Sadat 2003, p. 188; Tomuschat 2002, p. 343-348; Schabas 2000b, p. 399-400.

[1186] See South-Africa, South African Constitutional Court, *Azanian Peoples Organization (AZAPO) and Others v. President of the Republic of South Africa and Others*, 25 July 1996, para. 28-36, in particular 31: "It is one thing to allow the officers of a hostile power which has invaded a foreign state to remain unpunished for gross violations of human rights perpetrated against others during the course of such conflict. It is another thing to compel such punishment in circumstances where such violations have substantially occurred in consequence of conflict between different formations within the same state in respect of the permissible political direction which that state should take with regard to the structures of the state and the parameters of its political policies and where it becomes necessary after the cessation of such conflict for the society traumatised by such a conflict to reconstruct itself." Note also that the Constitutional Court did not deny an international duty to prosecute serious human rights violations committed outside armed conflicts *in general*, but only that such a duty would flow from the Geneva Conventions. Apparently, the applicants in the case did not invoke human rights law as a basis for the duty to prosecute. See para. 25, 30 and 32.

ent interests involved.[1187] This fact is aptly demonstrated by the ICC Statute, which in a general sense recognizes the necessity to prosecute but at the same time allows for prosecutorial discretion, and is silent on the legality and effects of amnesties because the negotiating States could not reach agreement on that point.[1188]

Second, it seems that many commentators overestimate the actual weight of existing amnesty laws in their assessment of State practice. Simply listing all amnesties in different States obscures the fact that they are very different in their scope and application. Various amnesty laws explicitly exclude the core crimes from their scope,[1189] while others are ambiguous in this respect but have not prevented core crimes prosecutions in practice.[1190] Some amnesty laws that are regularly cited as contrary practice are contested more than ever in the States that have adopted them.[1191] For example, the amnesty laws in Argentina have both been set aside by the courts and revoked by the legislature.[1192] In many States which have adopted amnesty laws, the complicated political situation delays the dialectical process between amnesties and prosecutions. We might therefore have to wait some time be-

---

[1187] See Harris *et al.* 1995, p. 39-40: "The duty to enforce the law to protect life also requires the proper investigation of all suspicious deaths [...] and the prosecution of both public and private offenders, subject to the normal rules as to prosecutorial discretion. [...] An amnesty for persons convicted or suspected of homicide is not inconsistent with Article 2 [ECHR] provided that it reflects a proper balance between the interests of the state in the particular circumstances in which the amnesty is declared and the general need to enforce the law to protect the right to life." See also Holdgaard Bukh 1994, p. 348.

[1188] See preamble, para. 6 and Art. 53 (1) sub c ICC Statute. See also Robinson 2003, p. 483; Seibert-Fohr 2003.

[1189] See above, note 1163.

[1190] Haiti's 1994 amnesty law, for example, applied only to "political matters" and not to the serious crimes that followed. Apparently, it has never been invoked by a defendant in a coup-era human rights trial while several perpetrators of international crimes have been prosecuted and punished. See Concannon 2000, note 54. Cf. Scharf 1996b, p. 15-18. Note also that the French Court of Cassation has on several occasions upheld amnesty laws for French crimes committed in Algeria and Indochina on the basis that these crimes did not amount to crimes against humanity. See Lelieur-Fischer 2004, p. 241-242. In particular the Court's holding in *Aussaresses* (17 June 2003) that "since the alleged acts cannot be prosecuted as crimes against humanity, they are subject to the provisions of the amnesty law," suggests that crimes against humanity can not be amnistied but must be prosecuted. See Lelieur-Fischer 2004, p. 242. Compare to France, Cour de Cassation, Ely Ould Dha, 23 October 2002, Bull. crim., no. 195 (refusing to apply a Mauritanian amnesty law in the prosecution of alleged acts of torture, holding *inter alia* that French prosecutions on the basis of universal jurisdiction are governed by French, not foreign law, and that application of foreign amnesty laws would cancel the purpose of universal jurisdiction); France, Conseil Constitutionnel, *Traité portant statut de la Cour pénale internationale*, 22 January 1999, para. 34 (holding that France's obligation to arrest and hand over to the ICC anyone responsible for acts which, under French law, are covered by an amnesty or a time-limit infringed the essential conditions for the exercise of national sovereignty as articulated in the Constitution, thus implying that the core crimes could be the subject of amnesties and statutes of limitations). Note, however, that a subsequent revision of the Constitution changed this situation to ensure its compatibility with the ICC Statute and thus ruled out the possibility of an amnesty for the core crimes. See Cassese 2003a, p. 315.

[1191] See e.g. Artucio 2001 (on proceedings contesting amnesty laws in Chile).

[1192] See above, Chapter II, para. 3.3.m.

fore we can pass final judgment on the authoritative value of many amnesty laws for core crimes.

The international legality of amnesty laws covering core crimes is highly complicated, not least because of the great diversity of amnesty regimes. There is considerable uncertainty of the law on this point, as can be seen in the lack of consensus on the implications of amnesty laws in the negotiation of the ICC Statute. International law is in rapid development in this area and corresponding academic work is rich and proliferating.[1193] No attempt will be made here to address the more intricate issues of amnesty laws for core crimes. Clearly, current international law contains a strong presumption against amnesties for core crimes, but probably no more than that.[1194] In practice, a rigid ban of all amnesties seems simply unrealistic, given the practical exigencies in a State such as Rwanda. In any case, amnesty laws do not generally constitute contrary practice to the very existence of a duty to prosecute the core crimes.

3.3.d *Conclusion: Current Status of the Duty to Prosecute*

A customary duty to prosecute core crimes finds its basis in human rights law, treaties concerning specific crimes, the law of State responsibility and corresponding State practice. While international law appears to be moving towards a more comprehensive duty to prosecute serious crimes, at present a general duty to prosecute or extradite all core crimes perpetrators is not firmly established. Of course, such a duty does exist for specific core crimes such as grave breaches of the Geneva Conventions and torture as a crime against humanity, taking into account the relevant treaties and their status as evidence of customary law.

However, customary international law today does impose a duty on States to prosecute all core crimes committed within their jurisdiction.[1195] The preceding analysis reveals that State practice has developed significantly in the last decades, and especially in recent years.[1196] While actual prosecutions are still limited, many States have recognized their duty to prosecute in a broad sense in the preamble of the ICC Statute and more specifically in national legislation, communications to human rights bodies and judicial practice. It can no longer be said that the duty to prosecute is limited to "paper practice." A proper assessment of the duty to prosecute under human rights law as a matter of interpretation of existing customary norms rather than the ascertainment of brand new ones, reveals a duty to prosecute

---

[1193] See above, note 1103.

[1194] See Special Court for Sierra Leone, Appeals Chamber, *Prosecutor against Kallon and Kamara, Decision on Challenge to Jurisdiction (Lomé Accord Amnesty)*, 13 March 2004, para. 66-71.

[1195] See Ambos 1999, p. 353-354.

[1196] Compare e.g. the imperative language of recent national laws and judgments with the preamble to Bangladesh's International Crimes (Tribunals) Act 1973 (Act No. XIX of 19 July 1973) ("Whereas it is *expedient* to provide for the detention, prosecution and punishment of the persons for genocide, crimes against humanity, war crimes and other crimes under international law…" – emphasis added).

all territorial core crimes. Amnesty laws constitute evidence of a possible exception rather than a negation of the duty to prosecute in general.

As paragraph 5 of this Chapter will show, the duty to prosecute the core crimes can have substantial implications for the direct application of their international criminalization in national courts. The breadth and diversity of the international law involved makes the duty to prosecute hard to ignore. In fact, such disregard is realistic only in national legal systems which exclude international law from the national judicial process altogether. This, however, would be contrary to the principle of consistent interpretation, as I will set out in some detail in Chapter VII.

4. The International Character of Core Crimes Prosecutions

Given the characteristics of the core crimes just explored, it may be asked whether or not international law allows States to prosecute core crimes as if they are ordinary crimes. On the one hand, core crimes prosecutions must take place in conformity with international law.[1197] Notably, Art. 75 (7) AP I dictates that "in order to avoid any doubt concerning the prosecution and trial of persons accused of war crimes and crimes against humanity [...] persons who are accused of such crimes should be submitted for the purpose of prosecution and trial in accordance with the applicable rules of international law." It appears that this provision does not lay down the mandatory application of international law, but it does require that the law applied "must be strictly in conformity with the respective rules of international law."[1198] Generally, ordinary criminal law does not reflect all relevant international rules on core crimes prosecutions and will thus not fulfill this requirement.

Accordingly, practice provides some indication that core crimes prosecutions may not take place on the basis of ordinary criminal law.[1199] In 2001, the Colombian Constitutional Court unambiguously rejected the ordinary crimes approach,[1200] as did the Belgian government in amending its legislation on core crimes in 1998.[1201]

[1197] Cf. Australia, High Court, *Polyukhovich v. The Commonwealth of Australia and Another*, 14 August 1991 (containing an elaborate discussion of and divergent opinions on the need for conformity of national provisions regarding international crimes and the underlying international law). See on this case Burmester 2004.

[1198] Pilloud *et al.* 1987, p. 887 and 889.

[1199] See above, note 219.

[1200] See Colombia, Corte Constitucional, Sala Plena, *Genocidio, Sentencia C-177*, 14 February 2001, 30 Jurisprudencia y Doctrina 707 at 713-714: "Ciertamente, esta Corte considera inadmisible la tesis según la cual las conductas de aniquilacion de los grupos que actúan al margen de la ley, podrian recriminarse acudiendo a otros tipos penales, verbigracia el homicidio, pues ella desconoce la especificidad del genocidio y la importancia de incriminar las conductas constitutivas de crimenes de lesa humanidad [...] En efecto, esta tesis degrada la importancia del bien juridico que se busca proteger al penalizar el genocidio, que no es tan sólo la vida e integridad sino el derecho a la existencia misma de los grupos humanos..."

[1201] See Belgium, Law for the punishment of Genocide, Report of the Justice Commission, Belgian Senate, 1 December 1998, No. 1-749/3, para. II (A) and (B) sub 2: "[L]e grand intérêt qu'elle [the

The *ad hoc* tribunals do not take into account national prosecutions on the basis of ordinary crimes in their application of the *ne bis in idem* principle, suggesting that they do not regard such prosecutions as satisfactory responses to core crimes.[1202] Taking a similar stand, the ILC has in its Draft Codes and Statute for an International Criminal Court long favored a *ne bis in idem* rule similar to those of the *ad hoc* tribunals.[1203]

The case against ordinary crimes charging is particularly strong for prosecutions on the basis of universal jurisdiction. After all, it is generally assumed that international law grants States universal jurisdiction to prosecute the core crimes, but not ordinary crimes such as murder and assault.[1204] Regarding core crimes prosecutions involving non-nationals more generally, one may note the assertion of the Dutch Special Court of Cassation in *Ahlbrecht I* (1947) that "[i]t would be unreasonable to apply to members of the military and civil services of the enemy the provisions of Dutch criminal law which had never been intended to govern their conduct, instead of applying to them the international rules of war which were intended to govern it."[1205] This point may have broader significance than just for the laws of war. One could think that it is "unreasonable" more generally to judge

---

inclusion of a criminalization of genocide in national criminal law] présente tient à sa valeur symbolique, en ce sens que les auteurs d'un génocide pourront être punis sur la base de cette incrimination spécifique, sans que le juge pénal doive se baser, pour les condamner, sur d'autres qualifications pénales telles que l'homicide intentionnel ou le meurtre. L'effet d'une condamnation pour génocide et son caractère préventif s'en trouveront renforcés. [...] L'introduction d'une incrimination explicite relative aux crimes de génocide et aux crimes contre l'humanité ne constitue donc qu'une confirmation du droit existant, en en assurant une meilleure visibilité, attirant l'attention sur la spécificité de ces faits et la nécessité, d'une part, de les poursuivre et, d'autre part, de les poursuivre en tant que tels."

1202 See Statute ICTY Art. 10 (2) and Statute ICTR Art. 9 (2). See also ICTY, Appeals Chamber, *Tadic, Decision on the Defence Motion for Interlocutory Appeal on Jurisdiction*, 2 October 1995, Separate Opinion of Judge Sidhwa on the Defence Motion for Interlocutory Appeal on Jurisdiction, para. 83: "[The ICTY's jurisdictional primacy over national courts] recognises the right of all nations to ensure the prevention of such violations by establishing international criminal tribunals appropriately empowered to deal with these matters, or else international crimes would be dealt with as ordinary crimes and the guilty would not be adequately punished."

1203 See Art. 42 (2) ILC Draft Statute for an International Criminal Court 1994; Art. 9 (3) ILC Draft Code 1991; Art. 12 (2) ILC Draft Code 1996; Commentary no. 10 to Art. 12 Draft Code 1996 (stating that if an "individual was tried by a national court for an 'ordinary' crime rather than one of the more serious crimes under the Code [...] the individual has not been tried or punished for the same crime but for a 'lesser crime' that does not encompass the full extent of his criminal conduct."). See also Zappala 2002, p. 196; Wouters and Panken 2003, p. 7.

1204 Cf. Reydams 2003, p. 21 (pointing out that prosecution on the basis of universal jurisdiction *prima facie* infringes on the non-intervention principle and therefore requires a permissive rule of international law, which international law grants for certain crimes only). See also below, note 1145.

1205 See Netherlands, Bijzondere Raad van Cassatie (Special Court of Cassation), *Ahlbrecht I*, 17 February 1947, Annual Digest 1947, p. 198 (NJ 1947/87, p. 188: "[D]at het ook onredelijk zou zijn, vreemde militairen en ambtenaren te berechten naar Nederlandsche normen die niet voor hen geschreven zijn, in plaats van hen te berechten naar de wèl voor hen geschreven normen die de oorlogsvoering beheerschen..."). Cf. Australia, High Court, *Polyukhovich v. The Commonwealth of Australia and Another*, 14 August 1991, per Brennan J., para. 3 ("[I]t is artificial to apply a municipal system of law designed for the preservation of the King's peace to acts done by or on behalf of belligerents in war.").

defendants of extraterritorial core crimes on the basis of national norms that were not known to them and not written for international crimes, instead of applying the international norms that govern these offences.

Yet there is considerable practice to the contrary. In practice, full descriptive power of the charges must often be sacrificed to the demands of time, evidence and competing priorities,[1206] and prosecutions that charge genocide, crimes against humanity and war crimes as ordinary crimes like murder and assault are not at all uncommon.[1207] In 2001, an Argentinean court ruled explicitly that core crimes may be charged as ordinary crimes.[1208] Several States have explicitly stated that they regarded their ordinary criminal law as a sufficient basis for the prosecution of war crimes, and many others appear to follow this approach.[1209] Unlike the Statutes of the ICTY and the ICTR, the ICC Statute blocks a second prosecution if the accused has effectively been prosecuted by another court "for conduct also proscribed under" the Statute, thus leaving the characterization of the crime open to national courts.[1210] Numerous States have expressed their opposition to the more stringent *ne bis in idem* proposals of the ILC and their wish to preserve the freedom to prosecute on the basis of ordinary crimes.[1211] Hence, it appears that the *ne bis in idem* principle in general international law prohibits repeated prosecution and punishment regardless of the law applied for the first prosecution.[1212]

[1206] See Special Court for Sierra Leone, Trial Chamber, *Majority Decision on the Prosecution's Application for Leave to File an Interlocutory Appeal against the Decision's Request for Leave to Amend the Indictment against Samuel Hinga Norman, Moinini Fofana and Allieu Kondewa*, 2 August 2004, para. 29.

[1207] See Argentina, Judge Gabriel Cavallo of the Buenos Aires Federal Court, *Julio Simon (Case no. 8686/2000, "Simon, Julio, Del Cerro, Juan Antonio s/sustracción de menores de 10 años")*, 6 March 2001, 2000/B Nueva Doctrina Penal 527, at 590, para. IV B ("En efecto, en la mayoría de los procesos seguidos ante cortes de diversos países que juzgaron crímenes de esta naturaleza [crimes against humanity] se han aplicado tipos penales creados por la ley de ese país."). See also above, Chapter II, para. 2.1.

[1208] Id.: "Esta subsunción en tipos penales locales de ningún modo contraría ni elimina el carácter de crímenes contra la humanidad de las conductas en análisis (cuestión que establece el derecho de gentes a través de normas ius cogens) ni impide aplicarles las reglas y las consecuencias jurídicas que les cabe por tratarse de crímenes contra el derecho de gentes." "[Prosecution on the basis] of local criminal offenses, would not in anyway contradict, nor eliminate the nature of the crimes against humanity of the conduct analyzed in this case (this as established in international law, throughout the peremptory norms of *jus cogens*) nor impede the application of the rules, and the correlating legal consequences related with its nature, being crimes against international law." – unofficial translation by Zandra Valenzuela-Delgado.

[1209] See Elst 2000, p. 827-828.

[1210] See Statute ICC, Art. 20 (3). See also Kleffner 2003, p. 95-96; Wyngaert and Ongena 2001, p. 724-728. But see El Zeidy 2002, p. 832-835.

[1211] See Bassiouni 1993, p. 181-185.

[1212] See Bassiouni and Manikas 1996, p. 335 ("It can be said ... that a general principle of law exists that prohibits repeated punishment and repeated prosecution for the same facts irrespective of the specific criminal charges."). Note however that the *ne bis in idem* principle in general international law does not prohibit repeated prosecution in different States. See Kleffner and Nollkaemper 2004, p. 374.

For core crimes prosecutions on the basis of universal jurisdiction, practice is not much different. Numerous such prosecutions have charged core crimes as ordinary crimes.[1213] In some instances, national courts have disallowed such charges, but done so solely on the basis of obstacles in national law.[1214] Most national courts do not regard the prosecution of core crimes as ordinary crimes to be prohibited *per se* by international law, whether on the basis of universal jurisdiction or not. Neither have States publicly protested against this form of charging. Thus, while there are sound reasons to believe that ordinary crimes do not meet all requirements of international law when it comes to core crimes prosecutions, practice does not on the whole reflect the premise that international law prohibits the prosecution of core crimes as ordinary crimes.

Still, even if international law allows it, to prosecute a core crime as an ordinary crime is quite unsatisfactory. It ignores important aspects of the prosecuted act, like its broader context and the particular intent of the perpetrator. To prosecute a genocidal killing as murder is at least as wide of the mark as prosecuting a carefully planned murder as manslaughter.[1215] Ordinary offences do simply not express the criminality of the conduct to be prosecuted in an adequate manner.[1216] Rather, it is often said that the prosecution of core crimes as ordinary crimes banalizes them to a certain degree.[1217] This can be unsatisfying, particularly for the victims, as one of the goals of these prosecutions is to expose the crimes for what they are in the context that made them possible,[1218] not simply to impose punishment on the de-

---

[1213] See *inter alia* the *Finta* and *Sawoniuk* cases above, Chapter II, para. 2.1; Germany, BGH, *Kusljic*, 21 February 2001, 3 StR 244/00, in 54 NJW (2001), 2732-2734 and Germany, BayObLG, *Kusljic*, 15 December 1999, 6 St 1/99 (conviction for both genocide and murder); *Djajic*, above, note 654. In *Finta*, the Canadian courts extensively analyzed the manner in which ordinary crimes would form the basis for a prosecution on the basis of universal jurisdiction, yet never even considered the possibility that international law would disallow this practice. See also Baxter 1973, p. 67-69.

[1214] In the Swiss prosecution of *Niyonteze*, a Rwandan bourgmestre was convicted for both the ordinary crimes of murder and instigation of murder, and war crimes. See Switzerland, Tribunal militaire, Division 2, Lausanne, *In re N.*, 30 April 1999. The military court of appeal, however, found that as a matter of Swiss law military courts have no jurisdiction over ordinary crimes committed by civilians, and upheld only the conviction for war crimes. See Switzerland, Military Court of Appeal, *In re N.*, 26 May 2000, Chapitre 1 (c). See also Reydams 2002, p. 234.

[1215] See for a non-legal but apt explanation Gourevitch 1998, p. 201 ("What distinguishes genocide from murder, and even from acts of political murder that claim as many victims, is the intent. The crime is wanting to make a people extinct. The idea is the crime.").

[1216] See Abi-Saab 2003, p. 598; Dickinson 2003, p. 305; Stahn 2000, p. 201. Cf. Canada, Supreme Court, *R. v. Imre Finta*, 24 March 1994, Cory J., para. 72 ("[A] war crime or a crime against humanity is not the same as a domestic offence. […] There are fundamentally important additional elements involved in a war crime or a crime against humanity.").

[1217] See Klabbers 2003, p. 59 ("To reduce genocide or crimes against humanity to multiple murder or multiple assault and battery cases is to somehow misconstrue them and turn them into banalities."); Sadat Wexler 1994, p. 326-327 ("To state that a crime against humanity is just like any other crime, but with something extra added, banalizes it."). Cf. Fletcher 1998, p. 11; Koering-Joulin 1997, p. 150.

[1218] Note that the goal of exposition meant here is limited to the broader context *insofar* as relevant for the crimes under consideration. It does not extend to the fundamentally problematic and oft-criticized proposition that criminal trials should aim to establish a complete historical record of an entire conflict or era. See on the latter point Special Court for Sierra Leone, Trial Chamber, *Majority Decision*

fendants.[1219] It may also undercut the deterrent value of core crimes prosecutions. As these crimes are generally instigated or condoned by the State or committed in the absence of effective State authority, the deterrent effect of prosecutions hinges in part on their ability to convey the message that it is the international community, not just national authorities, that will not tolerate these crimes.[1220] This, in turn, requires an adequate reflection of their international character.

Of course, the deterrent effects of international criminal law are unclear and disputed.[1221] In part, the scepticism of the academic community in this regard appears tied to an overly simplistic notion of deterrence as being dependent on an explicit cost-benefit analysis of prospective offenders on their way to the scene of the crime.[1222] A more refined conception which focuses on the effect of international criminal justice on the structures and patterns that facilitate core crimes may lead to a more optimistic assessment.[1223] However, regardless of the doubts and misgivings of many scholars, courts and other actors in international criminal law firmly adhere to the idea of prosecutions as a deterring mechanism.[1224] In this regard, there is a significant gap between practice and (at least a part of) academia.

In summary, international law probably does not prevent States from trying the core crimes as ordinary crimes. Yet, there are both principled and practical reasons to reject ordinary offences like murder as a basis for core crimes prosecutions for their failure to capture the international character of the crimes. Of course, practical constraints often count heavily, and any prosecution is better than none whatsoever. Also, it should be noted that the international character of a prosecution does not

---

on the Prosecution's Application for Leave to File an Interlocutory Appeal against the Decision's Request for Leave to Amend the Indictment against Samuel Hinga Norman, Moinini Fofana and Allieu Kondewa, 2 August 2004, para. 31. See also Aldana-Pindell 2002, p. 1473-1474; Koskenniemi 2002, p. 3-5; Crocker 1999, p. 51-52; Arendt 1963, p. 205 and 232.

[1219] Cf. Chinkin 2003, p. 138 ("The cases before the ad hoc Tribunals [...] confirm that rape and sexual abuse of the civilian population are public crimes of violence inherent to the aims of the warring parties. They are not the random, private or personal acts of individual fighters that can somehow be distanced from the broader picture."). See also ICTR, Trial Chamber, *Akayesu*, 2 September 1998, para. 731-732.

[1220] Cf. ICTY, Trial Chamber, *Erdemovic, Sentencing Judgment*, 29 November 1996, para. 64-65: "One of the purposes of punishment for a crime against humanity lies precisely in stigmatising criminal conduct which has infringed a value fundamental not merely to a given society, but to humanity as a whole. [...T]he International Tribunal sees public reprobation and stigmatisation by the international community, which would thereby express its indignation over heinous crimes and denounce the perpetrators, as one of the essential functions of a prison sentence for a crime against humanity."; ICTY, Trial Chamber, *Blaskic*, 3 March 2000, para. 761-764. See also Jørgensen 2000, p. 98 ("It cannot be denied that hierarchical terms or quality labels serve a deterrent function by sending out a warning signal that the international community will not accept violations of certain 'higher' obligations.").

[1221] See Sadat 2004, p. 206; Klabbers 2001b, p. 253 and 265;, p. 461-462. But see Kamminga 1998, p. 564 and 577.

[1222] See e.g. Zimmerman 2003, p. 203 (remarks Jan Klabbers); Tallgren 2002, p. 567 and 584; Brierly 1927, p. 84.

[1223] See e.g. Aldana-Pindell 2002, p. 1470-1476; Ambos 2002c, p. 320-321. Cf. Röling 1979, p. 190.

[1224] See above, notes 1050 and 1051.

depend entirely on the particular charges, but can be expressed through other means, like references to the case law of international tribunals. Still, the charges laid are an important factor in this regard.

5. The Characteristics of Core Crimes in the Practice of National Courts

Having examined the various characteristics of the core crimes, what remains is an appraisal of their relevance for the balance between national and international law in the practice of national courts. The courts of different States have invoked various of the characteristics examined above as determining factors in national prosecutions of core crimes. They have attached tangible consequences in particular to the grave and international character of the core crimes, their *jus cogens* status and the international obligation to prosecute them. To a significant degree, this practice can be explained as an interpretation of core crimes law in light of its object and purpose.[1225] However, in several cases this "interpretation" in practice amounts to a modification or rejection of established rules of national and international law and raises the question of whether the particular characteristics of the core crimes require the direct application of their international criminalization.

It is difficult, if not impossible, to determine the weight attached in national judgments to each individual characteristic that distinguishes core crimes prosecutions from other (criminal) proceedings. National courts generally reiterate characteristics like the grave character and *jus cogens* status of core crimes without specifying which they see as determinative for their conclusions and which constitute merely additional factors. Apparently, it is often the combination of different characteristics that leads courts to carve out a special position for core crimes law. They have done so in different ways.

Some national courts have asserted that particular rules of national (criminal) law do not apply at all to core crimes prosecutions. The French Court of Cassation, for example, stated in its 1983 judgment in the Barbie case that "*by reason of their nature*, the crimes against humanity with which Barbie is indicted do not simply fall within the scope of French municipal criminal law, but are subject to an international criminal order to which the notions of frontiers and extradition rules arising therefrom are completely foreign."[1226] Likewise, one of the judges of the Argentinean Supreme Court asserted in *Schwammberger* (1990) that "neither time, borders nor the law of any particular State" could impede the punishment of crimes against

---

[1225] See above, note 1048 and accompanying text.

[1226] France, Court of Cassation, *Barbie (No. 1)*, 6 October 1983, Bull. crim., no. 239; 78 I.L.R. 125 at 128 and 130 (citing and confirming the Court of Appeal, emphasis added).

humanity.[1227] Such holdings evince what one commentator has called a "radical cosmopolitan view on international criminal justice."[1228]

Somewhat more cautiously, the Supreme Court of Costa Rica found in 2000 that the core crimes are at least to some extent exempted from the general regime of criminal law.[1229] In judging the compatibility of the ICC Statute with the Costa Rican Constitution, the Supreme Court determined that the constitutional provisions on the non-extradition of nationals[1230] and the immunities of members of parliament[1231] did not apply to proceedings before the ICC. It held that those constitutional guarantees are not absolute but compatible with the development of human rights law and that the Constitution does not oppose new developments in this regard but rather promotes them.[1232] The Court referred, *inter alia*, to the nature of the core crimes in denying the applicability of these constitutional provisions to proceedings involving the ICC.[1233] Comparable progressive interpretations of constitutional provisions in light of the nature of the core crimes have been endorsed by the courts and governments of several other States Parties to the ICC Statute.[1234] This line of reasoning has also been employed to set aside constitutional obstacles to direct application such as the principle of legality, for example in Hungary.[1235]

Other national courts have found that the particular characteristics of core crimes law elevate it to a superior rank, sometimes in deviation from the normal status of international norms in the national legal order. Thus, even if the ordinary rules of national (criminal) law do generally apply, they cannot obstruct core crimes prosecutions.

In Argentina, various judgments of federal courts have upheld the supremacy of international criminal law in core crimes proceedings.[1236] Particularly noteworthy

---

[1227] Argentina, Supreme Court, Extradition Josef Franz Leo Schwammberger, 20 March 1990, 313 Fallos de la Corte Suprema de Justicia de la Nacion 256 at 265-266, per Judge Roger ("Ni el tiempo, las fronteras o la ley de determinado pais, pueden impedir esta razonable avance del Derecho punitivo ante actitudes tan repudiables y que tan hondamente degradan al hombre y socavan la convivencia civilizada.").

[1228] Reydams 2003, p. 137.

[1229] Costa Rica, Supreme Court of Justice (Constitutional Chamber), *Advisory Opinion on the constitutionality of the draft law of approbation of the Rome Statute on the International Criminal Court*, 1 November 2000. See Lambert-Abdelgawad 2003, p. 545.

[1230] See Art. 32 of Costa Rica's 1949 Constitution ("Ningún costarricense podrá ser compelido a abandonar el territorio nacional.").

[1231] See Art. 110 and 121 (9) of Costa Rica's 1949 Constitution.

[1232] Costa Rica, Supreme Court of Justice (Constitutional Chamber), *Advisory Opinion on the constitutionality of the draft law of approbation of the Rome Statute on the International Criminal Court*, 1 November 2000, para. 11.

[1233] Costa Rica, Supreme Court of Justice (Constitutional Chamber), *Advisory Opinion on the constitutionality of the draft law of approbation of the Rome Statute on the International Criminal Court*, 1 November 2000, para. 12.

[1234] See Lambert-Abdelgawad 2003, p. 545-548, 555-556 and 566.

[1235] See above, Chapter II, para. 3.3.n.

[1236] See above, Chapter II, para. 3.3.m.

is the case of *Julio Simon* (2001).[1237] In the *Simon* case, federal judge Gabriel Cavallo found that the crimes of kidnapping and forced disappearance in question constituted crimes against humanity, the criminality and punishability of which are determined by the international community and not left to the discretion of individual States.[1238] In his decision of more than 100 pages, the judge dwelled extensively on the *jus cogens* status of the norms involved, the grave character of crimes against humanity and the duty to prosecute the crimes under consideration.[1239] In regard of the latter, Judge Cavallo cited *inter alia* the CAT, the ACHR and the ICCPR, as well as relevant case law of the IACtHR and other human rights bodies.[1240] Throughout the entire opinion, the judge referred repeatedly to numerous sources of international law, including the ICC Statute.[1241] Judge Cavallo asserted that the recognition of crimes against humanity and the conditions of their prosecution follow not only from Art. 118 of the Argentinean Constitution, but also, *inter alia*, from Argentina's role in the international community, and its recognition of *jus cogens* through the VCLT.[1242] Finally, he declared two Argentinean amnesty laws incompatible with Art. 1, 2, 8 and 25 ACHR, Art. 2 and 9 ICCPR, the object and purpose of the CAT, as well as national law.[1243]

On appeal, the Federal Chamber of Appeals upheld the decision of Judge Cavallo, following his reasoning closely and relying equally on a breadth of international sources and case law.[1244] The Court of Appeals reiterated *inter alia* that the qualification and punishability of the crimes was not up to the State, but governed by international principles of a peremptory character.[1245] The appeals judgment also discussed the duty to prosecute under human rights law at length, and concluded that there was no alternative for the invalidation of the amnesty laws.[1246] Like Judge Cavallo, the Federal Chamber of Appeals relied both on national and international law in reaching its decision.[1247]

1237 Argentina, Judge Gabriel Cavallo of the Buenos Aires Federal Court, Julio Simon (Case no. 8686/2000, "Simon, Julio, Del Cerro, Juan Antonio s/sustracción de menores de 10 años"), 6 March 2001, 2000/B Nueva Doctrina Penal 527. See above, p. 75.

1238 Id., para. II (C) and III (J).

1239 Id., *inter alia* para. III (E) and (I), as well as IV (B).

1240 Id., para. III (E), (F) and (I).

1241 Id., e.g. para. III (I).

1242 Id., at 598: "Entonces, el reconocimiento de los crímenes contra la humanidad así como las condiciones para su juzgamiento que impone el derecho de gentes a través de sus normas más encumbradas, no sólo se deriva de la recepción que realiza el Art. 118 de la Constitución Nacional, tal como se ha expresado más arriba, sino, además, del hecho de formar parte de la comunidad internacional, de aceptar sus normas, de formar parte de la Convención de Viena sobre el Derecho de los Tratados (que consagra una de las funciones del *ius cogens*) y el hecho de haber contribuido a la consolidación del derecho penal internacional."

1243 Id., operative paragraph ("Resuelvo").

1244 Argentina, Federal Chamber of Appeals, *Incidente de Apelacion de Julio Simon*, 9 November 2001.

1245 Id., *inter alia* para. XVIII (2).

1246 Id., *inter alia* para. XV and XVIII.

1247 It is to be noted that numerous human rights treaties are incorporated in the Argentinean Constitution. See above, note 454.

On 14 June 2005, the Argentinean Supreme Court issued a lengthy judgment in the *Simon* case which is very much in line with the lower court judgments. With a 7-1 vote and one abstention, the Supreme Court declared that the amnesty laws violated international obligations and are therefore unconstitutional. The Court held that forced disappearance is a crime against humanity, in violation of *jus cogens* norms and for that reason cannot be subject to any statutes of limitation. Within its reasoning, the Supreme Court referred frequently to the duty to prosecute under international law, the case law of the IACtHR and other human rights bodies, the grave character of the crimes under consideration and the concept of *jus cogens*.

The highest military court of Peru reached an outcome comparable to that of the Argentinean courts in *Simon*, relying primarily on a combination of the duty to prosecute, national law and the Vienna Convention of the Law of Treaties. The *Barrios Altos* case (2001) arguably concerned crimes against humanity.[1248] In 1991, six members of the Peruvian army attacked a group of civilians in a neighborhood in Lima known as Barrios Altos, killing fifteen civilians. Two amnesty laws subsequently deterred investigation and prosecution of the matter.[1249] Yet, when the case reached the IACtHR, Peru recognized its international responsibility in the case and declared its willingness to reach a friendly settlement with the petitioners.[1250] The IACtHR decided unanimously that Amnesty Laws No. 26479 and No. 26492 were "incompatible with the American Convention on Human Rights and, consequently, lack[ed] legal effect."[1251]

Just weeks after the judgment of the Inter-American Court, the Peruvian *Consejo Supremo de Justicio Militar* ordered the military courts to give effect to the judgment, "which resulted in the reopening of the Barrios Altos case at the national level and the rendering of the amnesty laws without effect."[1252] In doing so, the highest military court relied both on the authorization in Peruvian law to execute international court judgments,[1253] and the Vienna Convention of the Law of Treaties.[1254] This Peruvian judgment uses several of the same arguments as the Argentinean judgments in the *Simon* case, including the duty to prosecute, but lacks

---

1248 See on this case generally Ferdinandusse 2003, p. 89-93 and Cerna 2002.

1249 IACtHR, Barrios Altos Case, (*Chimbipuma Aguierre v. Peru*), Merits, 14 May 2001, (Ser. C) No. 75 (2001) and 41 ILM 93 (2002), para. 4–19.

1250 Id., para. 37-39.

1251 Id. at para. 51(4). See for an analysis of the scope of this holding Ferdinandusse 2003, p. 90-91.

1252 Cerna 2002, p. 92. See Peru, Consejo Supremo de Justicio Militar, *In re Barrios Altos*, 4 June 2001, Case No. 494-V-94, on file with the author. See also Alvarez *et al.* 2002, p. 325.

1253 See Texto Unico de la Ley Organica del Poder Judicial, Art. 151 (available at http://www.Minjus.gob.pe, last visited Sept. 2, 2003): "Las sentencias expedidas por los Tribunales Internacionales, constituídos según Tratados de los que es parte el Perú, son transcritas por el Ministerio de Relaciones Exteriores al Presidente de la Corte Suprema, quien las remite a la Sala en que se agotó la jurisdicción interna y dispone la ejecución de la sentencia supranacional por el Juez Especializado o Mixto competente."

1254 See above, p. 145.

any discussion of the *jus cogens* status and the grave character of the core crimes.[1255] Their outcomes are, however, substantially the same.

Other judgments, on the other hand, rely emphatically on the *jus cogens* status of core crimes law. A relatively early example dates back to 1959,[1256] when the Polish Voivodship Court of Warsaw directly applied the Fourth Hague Convention of 1907 and the Nuremberg Charter for the prosecution of crimes against humanity, war crimes and crimes against peace committed during WW II.[1257] The Polish Court held *inter alia* that the Fourth Hague Convention "constitutes *jus cogens*, i.e., it contains rules the application of which does not depend on the free discretion of any State."[1258] The Supreme Court of Poland affirmed this judgment, holding that "[t]he basis of responsibility for war crimes rests on two international instruments," namely the Moscow Declaration of 30 October 1943 and the London Agreement of 8 August 1945, including the annexed Nuremberg Charter.[1259] The Supreme Court further distinguished extradition of common criminals from extradition of war criminals, stating that "[t]he above international treaties regulate in a different way from our own law of extradition the procedure of punishing war criminals, and they provide for responsibility for all war crimes and crimes against humanity."[1260]

In Argentina, various penal judgments on different levels before the *Simon* case have asserted that no national law, not even the Constitution, can prevent the effectuation of international norms of *jus cogens* status.[1261] In several other States, precedents of limited authority also credit peremptory norms with an enhanced status in the national legal order in rather general terms. In the *Bouterse* case, the Dutch Attorney-General suggested in 2001 that all *jus cogens* norms might supersede national law in deviation of the normal implementation framework in the Netherlands, which gives supremacy only to treaties but not to custom.[1262] However, this

---

[1255] Note that the Argentinean judgments also relied on Art. 27 VCLT, albeit it gave them less emphasis. See Argentina, Federal Chamber of Appeals, *Incidente de Apelacion de Julio Simon*, 9 November 2001, para. XI; Argentina, Judge Gabriel Cavallo of the Buenos Aires Federal Court, Julio Simon (Case no. 8686/2000, "Simon, Julio, Del Cerro, Juan Antonio s/sustracción de menores de 10 años"), 6 March 2001, 2000/B Nueva Doctrina Penal 527, para. VI (A).

[1256] Although the notion of *jus cogens* was not codified in a treaty until the VCLT of 1969, it appeared in doctrine, and to a lesser extent practice, before that date. See Hannikainen 1988, p. 23-156; Robledo 1981, p. 17-36; Kunz 1945, p. 187-193.

[1257] Poland, Voivodship Court of Warsaw, *In re Koch*, 9 March 1959, 30 ILR 496. See in particular 504: "The [London Agreement of 8 August 1945 and the annexed Nuremberg Charter] are obligatory in Polish municipal law, while at the same time they define the content of war crimes and crimes against humanity, and also fix the sanctions therefore; as multilateral international treaties, they have legal force in many States." Note, however, that the accused was found guilty of crimes summarily set out in a Polish decree of 1944, while the international instruments were apparently applied to furnish the definitions of those crimes. Id., p. 497 and 509.

[1258] Id., p. 503.

[1259] Poland, Supreme Court, *In re Koch*, 10 November 1959, 30 ILR 509 at 510.

[1260] Id.

[1261] Examples are cited in the *Simon* case in both instances. See also Mattarollo 2001, p. 21-22, 35-36 and 40.

[1262] Netherlands, Attorney-General to the Supreme Court, *Voordracht en vordering tot cassatie in het belang der wet door de Procureur-Generaal (Petition for Cassation in re Bouterse)*, 8 May 2001,

assumption did not affect the outcome of the case since the Attorney-General did not believe that the prohibition of prescription of torture constitutes a *jus cogens* norm[1263] and the Supreme Court did not reach a holding on this point. A similar but more ambiguous holding is found in the Belgian *Pinochet* ruling of 1998.[1264]

In one of the most detailed and elaborately motivated examples, the Hungarian Constitutional Court by and large exempted war crimes and crimes against humanity from the regular framework of national criminal law in its 1993 decision that allowed direct application of international criminal law for the prosecution of these crimes.[1265] In doing so, the Constitutional Court relied extensively on their particular characteristics. It noted that "these crimes threaten the foundations of humanity and international coexistence" and that "the rules of non-applicability of statutory limitations are closely related to the nature of war crimes and crimes against humanity"[1266] It reiterated that both specific treaties and human rights law require their prosecution.[1267]

The Hungarian Constitutional Court also found that "the regulations on the punishment of war crimes and crimes against humanity" are peremptory norms of general international law and "those states which refuse to assume these obligations cannot participate in the community of nations."[1268] Furthermore, it held that in the context of national prosecutions of international crimes "[n]o domestic law confronted with a conflicting and express peremptory rule of international law (*jus cogens*) may be given effect."[1269] After all, "[t]he gravity of war crimes and crimes against humanity, the fact that by their commission international peace, security and, indeed, humanity itself was placed in danger, cannot be reconciled with making their punishment subject to domestic law."[1270]

NJ 2002/559, para. 94: "Bij het hierna volgende wordt er van uitgegaan dat ook ongeschreven ius cogens bij onverenigbaarheid met de wet deze laatste verdringt, zulks in afwijking van wat overigens naar gangbare opvatting voortvloeit uit Art. 94 Grondwet."

[1263] Id., para. 105: "[G]een regel van ongeschreven volkenrecht, laat staan van ius cogens, [verbiedt] verjaring van het recht tot strafvordering inzake foltering [...]."

[1264] Belgium, Tribunal of First Instance (District of Brussels), *In re Pinochet Ugarte*, 6 November 1998, para. 3.3.2: "[T]here are grounds to consider that before being codified into treaties or acts, crimes against humanity were sanctioned by international custom and are, as such, part of the international *jus cogens* which imposes itself on the internal legal order with restrictive effect 'erga omnes'."

[1265] See generally above, Chapter II, para. 3.3.n.

[1266] See Hungary, Constitutional Court, Decision No. 53/1993, On War Crimes and Crimes against Humanity, 13 October 1993, English translation in Sólyom/Brunner 2000, p. 273-283, at 281 and 283.

[1267] Id. at 278: "The states committed themselves by international agreements to the punishing of such crimes. During the past ten to fifteen years, the activities of international organizations (committees and tribunals) established to monitor and ensure compliance with the comprehensive human rights conventions have come to articulate with increasing vigor the condemnation of those states which in their domestic law fail to comply with their international obligations. (It is primarily the decisions and resolutions of the Inter-American Court of Human Rights and the Inter-American Commission of Human Rights which developed the international law based duty of states to initiate criminal prosecution which may not be avoided even by amnesty)."

[1268] Id., at 281.

[1269] Id., at 282.

[1270] Id., at 279.

Therefore, the Hungarian Constitutional Court concluded, the core crimes are "*sui generis* criminal offenses" that can be punished "even by those member states whose domestic system of law does not recognize the definition or does not punish that action or omission," namely under direct application of their international criminalization.[1271] This decision effectively exempted core crimes law from the general national framework governing criminal proceedings altogether, authorizing instead its application in parallel with national criminal law. Its basic argument is that in core crimes prosecutions, national courts must function as organs of the international community rather than as enforcers of national criminal law.[1272]

These judgments of national courts all point in a similar direction. They differ somewhat in their reasoning and the characteristics they ascribe to the core crimes. They also draw slightly varying conclusions from their analysis of core crimes law. But they share the conviction that core crimes must be effectively prosecuted in national courts, where necessary through an alteration of the normal balance between national and international law in favor of the latter.

However, the picture drawn so far requires qualification. First, there is significant practice to the contrary. Numerous national judgments reject the idea that the particular characteristics of the core crimes affect their justiciability in the national legal order. Several judgments do so implicitly. For example, legal opinions on the constitutionality of the ICC Statute in Belgium, Luxembourg and France have found the absence of immunity incompatible with their constitutional provisions on the inviolability of high State officials, thus rejecting the approach of Costa Rica and Ukraine which makes an exception for the core crimes in this regard.[1273] Other national judgments refuse to apply a different test to establish jurisdiction for the core crimes than for crimes of a non-peremptory character.[1274] An illuminating implicit rejection of the particular character of core crimes law is found in the decision on the constitutionality of Australian war crimes legislation in *Polyukhovich* (1991). Dissenting Judge Brennan of the Australian High Court considered the legislation under scrutiny to be unconstitutional for exceeding the foreign affairs power of parliament. Ignoring appeals to the grave and international character of war crimes, Judge Brennan issued a lengthy and technical analysis on the separation of powers involved, culminating in the question of whether a law would be "properly characterized as a law with respect to external affairs if it imposed a criminal penalty on a person who, being a citizen and resident of France, had dropped litter in a Parisian street forty years ago?"[1275]

[1271] Id., at 279.

[1272] Cf. id., at 278: "[T]he state which prosecutes and punishes crimes against humanity and war crimes, acts upon the mandate given to it by the community of nations, according to the conditions imposed by international law."

[1273] See Lambert-Abdelgawad 2003, p. 544 and 546. See also Correa 2003 (on the 2002 judgment of the Chilean Constitutional Court declaring the ICC Statute unconstitutional).

[1274] See for examples of such case law Chapter II.

[1275] Australia, High Court, *Polyukhovich v. The Commonwealth of Australia and Another*, 14 August 1991, Brennan J., dissenting, para. 13.

Some national judgments state explicitly that traits of the core crimes like their *jus cogens* status and grave nature have no special consequences on the municipal law level. In *Nulyarimma* (1999), for example, the Federal Court of Australia held that in the absence of implementing legislation, Australian courts cannot punish genocide "simply because it has now become recognised as an international crime with the status of *jus cogens* under customary international law."[1276] One of the justices first accepted both the peremptory character of the international prohibition of genocide and the fact that international law commands its prosecution, and subsequently described the choice to enforce the international criminalization of genocide as "a policy issue" which should be decided in the negative.[1277] Similarly, in *Pinochet III*, the House of Lords accepted that torture is a *jus cogens* crime, but found that this status could not remedy a lack of implementing legislation, holding *inter alia* that *jus cogens* "is not a rule of jurisdiction."[1278]

Some judgments and dissenting opinions reject outright the assertion that the grave and international character of the core crimes makes them fundamentally different from ordinary crimes. These include judgments from the very same courts that in other cases ascribed a far-going autonomy to core crimes law. The French *Cour de Cassation* had, just eight years before finding in *Barbie* (1983) that "crimes against humanity do not simply fall within the scope of French municipal criminal law but are subject to an international criminal order,"[1279] asserted in *Touvier* (1975) that "crimes against humanity are ordinary crimes committed under certain circumstances and for certain motives specified in the text that defines them."[1280] Also, in several later decisions the *Cour de Cassation* adhered more to its line of reasoning in *Touvier* than to its bold statement in *Barbie* about an international criminal order.[1281] In Canada, a dissenting judge in the *Finta* case (1994) issued an opinion of the same tenor as the holding in *Touvier*.[1282]

[1276] Australia, Federal Court, *Nulyarimma v. Thompson*, 1 September 1999, [1999] FCA 1192, para. 57, Whitlam J.: "The courts of the States and the Territories can have no authority for themselves to proscribe conduct as criminal under the common law simply because it has now become recognised as an international crime with the status of *jus cogens* under customary international law." See also para. 53

[1277] Australia, Federal Court, *Nulyarimma v. Thompson,* 1 September 1999, [1999] FCA 1192, para. 18 and 26, Wilcox J.

[1278] U.K., House of Lords, *R. v. Bow Street Metropolitan Stipendiary Magistrate & Others, Ex Parte Pinochet Ugarte (No. 3)*, 24 March 1999, [2000] 1 A.C. 147 at 175. See also at 148, 174, 247, 261, and 275.

[1279] See above note 1226.

[1280] France, Court of Cassation, *Touvier (No. 1)*, 6 February 1975, Bull. crim., no. 42, p. 117 ("[C]rimes contre l'humanité [...] sont des crimes de droit commun commis dans certaines circonstances et pour certains motifs précisés dans le texte qui les définit."). Translation taken from Sadat Wexler 1994, p. 326.

[1281] See above, Chapter II, para. 3.3.j.

[1282] Canada, Supreme Court, *R. v. Imre Finta*, 24 March 1994, La Forest J. (dissenting), para. 258 and 290: "[T]he acts comprised in war crimes and crimes against humanity are in this country in essence crimes that fall under the familiar rubrics of our law such as confinement, kidnapping, and the like. They would be equally blameworthy if done by private individuals or criminal groups for other

Second, it should be noted that most of the judgments which assert an enhanced position for the core crimes in the national legal order rely not only on the particular characteristics of core crimes law, but also, simultaneously, on their State's constitutional framework regarding the incorporation of international law. The judgment of the Hungarian Constitutional Court relied to a great extent on a constitutional clause which requires harmonization of national and *all* international law, not only core crimes law.[1283] The Argentinean cases mentioned above, including the *Simon* case, likewise relied heavily on constitutional provisions.[1284] Both in *Nulyarimma* and *Pinochet III*, the dissenting judges who accepted direct application of the customary offences of genocide and torture respectively, based their minority views on incorporation through the common law rather than the *jus cogens* status or heinous nature of these crimes.[1285]

Then again, the fact that these judgments do not rely *solely* on the particular characteristics of the core crimes does not diminish the authoritative value of their holdings, which in explicit language assert a special position for the core crimes. In addition, a relativization of the contrary practice is also in order. Many judgments do neither embrace an autonomous position for the core crimes nor reject it explicitly. While such judgments do amount to implicit contrary practice, they do not carry the same weight as judgments which explicitly discuss and decide the matter, especially if the position of the core crimes has not been brought up or (adequately) argued in the case. Some of the judgments that explicitly reject a special position for the core crimes, such as *Nulyarimma*, clearly violate international law.[1286]

---

similar vile motives. The additional circumstances are added to crimes against humanity to tie them to the international norm and permit extraterritorial prosecution by all states. […] More serious was that the trial judge at several points referred to the accused's actions having 'risen up' to the quality of a war crime or crime against humanity. This is not strictly accurate; there may be different considerations for the offences under international law, and they may have some additional requirements to those for domestic offences, but these are not always higher and may not be related to *individual culpability*. To use language that suggests that somehow there is a higher degree of culpability required in relation to the international crimes is misleading."

[1283] See Hungary, Constitutional Court, Decision No. 53/1993, On War Crimes and Crimes against Humanity, 13 October 1993, English translation in Sólyom/Brunner 2000, p. 273-283 at 274-275. See above, Chapter II, para. 3.3.n.

[1284] See above, Chapter II, para. 3.3.m.

[1285] See Australia, Federal Court, *Nulyarimma v. Thompson*, 1 September 1999, [1999] FCA 1192, para. 183-186 (While Justice Merkel loosely suggests in para. 183 that the *jus cogens* character of genocide is an additional reason to endorse this form of incorporation, stating that "genocide is an *a fortiori* example of where a rule of international law is to be adopted as part of municipal law," his elaborate analysis of the criminal aspects of the Australian common law makes clear that the peremptory character of the norm is not in itself enough to override the national implementation framework); U.K., House of Lords, *R. v. Bow Street Metropolitan Stipendiary Magistrate & Others, Ex Parte Pinochet Ugarte (No. 3)*, 24 March 1999, [2000] 1 A.C. 147 at 276. See further above, Chapter II, para. 3.3.d and 3.3.h.

[1286] Apart from the actual result of such cases, it should be acknowledged that national courts themselves violate their duty to interpret national law in conformity with international obligations when they recognize an international obligation, characterize the decision to adhere to that obligation or not as a "policy choice" and then decline to adhere to it. See on the principle of consistent interpretation above, Chapter IV, para. 5.2.

Finally, it should be noted that several of the precedents mentioned above, both *pro* and *contra* a special position, are strong in language but limited in authority. Dissenting opinions, *obiter dicta* and older precedents of courts that have since then changed their stance do not carry the same weight as recent decisions that turn on the very question discussed here. Of course, the place of the courts involved in their national judicial hierarchy also counts.

On balance, the stance of national courts is divided. Various national courts have directly applied core crimes law in order to exempt the core crimes from (at least part of) the national legal framework governing ordinary criminal proceedings,[1287] but others explicitly or implicitly reject this line of reasoning. While the involvement of the highest courts of different States gives some momentum to the tendency to exempt core crimes law from national limitations that would ordinarily prevent its enforcement in national courts, practice is too limited and inconsistent to support a corresponding rule of positive international law in this regard. Still, this tendency is a noteworthy development, and finds additional support in the enactment of the ICC Statute and the resulting implementing practice of several nations, to which I now turn.

6. Implications of the ICC Statute and its Implementation

The coming into force of the ICC Statute provides additional support for the tendency of some national courts to enforce international core crimes law regardless of shortcomings in relevant national law. First, the Statute contains a detailed and very complete regulation of core crimes law which many States have incorporated into their national legal orders. The Statute sets out definitions of the crimes and forms of participation, as well as applicable penalties, and predominantly reflects international customary law.[1288] Therefore, the ability of many national courts to rely on international law for the prosecution of core crimes has greatly improved. Moreover, since the Statute in a general sense confirms the customary duty to prosecute core crimes perpetrators, it also brings an (additional) source of explicit recognition of this duty into many national laws.[1289]

[1287] Note that the use of a rule of internationale law in order to refuse application of a rule of national law meets the definition of direct application as set out above, p. 8.

[1288] See above, note 56.

[1289] Some national judgments have accordingly recognized a duty to prosecute flowing from the ICC Statute. See Belgium, Tribunal of First Instance Brussels (Kamer van Inbeschuldigingstelling), *In re Sharon and Yaron*, 26 June 2002, reproduced in Wouters and Panken 2003, p. 323-339 at 332 ("[Q]ue le Statut de Rome comporte ainsi des obligations a caractere juridictionel" – The implications of this rather terse statement are unclear, but it is noteworthy that the Belgian court referred to jurisdictional obligations flowing from the ICC Statute in proceedings concerning alleged extraterritorial core crimes.); France, Paris Court of Appeals (Cour d'appel de Paris), In re Gadaffi, 20 October 2000, 105 RGDIP 475-476 at 476: "Qu'au demeurant, la convention portant statut de la Cour pénale internationale, [...] indique dans son préeambule, 'qu'il est du devoir de chaque Etat de soumettre à sa juridiction criminelle les responsables de crimes internationaux', [...] Qu'il est ainsi reconnu par cette convention qu'il est

Second, the way some States have implemented the ICC Statute in their domestic law, or are in the process of doing so, provides support for an autonomous position of core crimes law. As set out above, several constitutional courts have carved out an exception for core crimes law in the constitutional framework governing criminal proceedings.[1290] Other States have explicitly made exceptions for the ICC Statute through amendments to their constitutions. Generally, the purpose of these amendments was merely to allow quick ratification of the ICC Statute without having to do a thorough revision of the entire constitution.[1291] The result, however, is a distinction between core crimes law and other criminal law. For example, Luxembourg has explicitly placed its obligations under the ICC Statute above constitutional requirements by providing in its Constitution that "the provisions of the Constitution do not hinder the approval of the Statute of the International Criminal Court, done in Rome on 17 July 1998, and the performance of the obligations arising from the Statute according to the conditions provided therein."[1292] France has expressed in its Constitution that it may recognize the ICC under the conditions stipulated in the Statute.[1293] Other States have adopted similar constitutional provisions regarding the ICC.[1294] The practice of various States to exempt the ICC Stat-

du devoir pour les Etats l'ayant ratifié de juger les crimes internationaux, lesquels ne sauraient, aux termes de l'article 22 [ICC Statute] susvisé, être limités aux crimes contre l'humanité, de génocide, d'apartheid et de guerre, ce quand bien-même la personne poursuivie aurait la qualité officielle de chef d'Etat ou de gouvernement. " ("Moreover, the preamble to the convention constituting the Statute of the International Criminal Court, [...] says that "it is the duty of every State to exercise its criminal jurisdiction over those responsible for international crimes." [...] That convention recognizes a duty on the part of ratifying states to try defendants for international crimes, as Article 22 [ICC Statute] provides, including but not limited to crimes against humanity, genocide, apartheid and war crimes, even if the accused is an official head of state or government"). Overruled on other points in France, Court of Cassation, *In re Gadaffi*, 13 March 2001, 105 RGDIP 473-474.

[1290] See above, notes 1229-1234.

[1291] See Lambert-Abdelgawad 2003, p. 563-564.

[1292] Art. 118 Constitution, modified by the Law of 8 August 2000 (Loi du 8 août 2000 portant révision de l'article 118 de la Constitution, *Mém.*, A-No 83, 25 août 2000): "Les dispositions de la Constitution ne font pas obstacle à l'approbation du Statut de la Cour Pénale Internationale, fait à Rome, le 17 juillet 1998, et à l'exécution des obligations en découlant dans les conditions prévues par ledit Statut." (Unofficial translation ICRC.)

[1293] France, Art. 53-2 Constitution, modified by Decision 98-408 DC of 22 January 1999: "La République peut reconnaître la juridiction de la Cour pénale internationale dans les conditions prévues par le traité signé le 18 juillet 1998."

[1294] See Colombia, Art. 93 Constitution: "[...] El Estado Colombiano puede reconocer la jurisdicción de la Corte Penal Internacional en los términos previstos en el Estatuto de Roma adoptado el 17 de julio de 1998 por la Conferencia de Plenipotenciarios de las Naciones Unidas y, consecuentemente, ratificar este tratado de conformidad con el procedimiento establecido en esta Constitución. La admisión de un tratamiento diferente en materias sustanciales por parte del Estatuto de Roma con respecto a las garantías contenidas en la Constitución tendrá efectos exclusivamente dentro del ámbito de la materia regulada en él."
Ireland, Art. 29 (9) Constitution: "The State may ratify the Rome Statute of the International Criminal Court done at Rome on the 17th day of July, 1998.";
Portugal, Art. 7 (7) Constitution: "Portugal pode, tendo em vista a realização de uma justiça internacional que promova o respeito pelos direitos da pessoa humana e dos povos, aceitar a jurisdição do Tribunal

ute from the normal constitutional framework governing criminal proceedings, both through judicial interpretation and legislation, provides support for an autonomous position of core crimes law.

7. Conclusion

Several characteristics of international criminal law in general, and the core crimes in particular, sit uncomfortably with international law's general framework of implementation. It may be questioned to what extent (the combination of) the *jus cogens* status of core crimes law, its disqualification of contrary national law, its focus on individuals, the grave nature of the core crimes, the duty to prosecute them and their character as system crimes can be reconciled with the freedom of States to block judicial enforcement of international law in the national legal order, make that enforcement dependent on national implementing law, or subject it to the principle of reciprocity.

Various national courts have exempted core crimes law from different rules and principles that normally govern the judicial application of international law. Together, these cases suggest that core crimes law, on account of the characteristics mentioned above, takes up a particular position in the national legal order. This suggestion of a more or less autonomous position reflects the international character of the core crimes in a heightened focus on the relevant international rules and a corresponding limitation of the extent to which national law can constrain their effectuation. It finds support in the significant but divided case law of national and international courts on the particular position of *all* international law of a humanitarian character.[1295] The practice in various States to exempt the ICC Statute from certain constitutional provisions may add further momentum to this development.

However, there are also numerous national judgments that refuse to give full effect to international core crimes law through an internationalist approach to obstacles in national law. Some of these contrary judgments constitute clear violations of international law and serve principally as a reminder that national courts are too often unaware of their international obligations, or are unwilling to heed them. International law demands to be given full effect, where necessary through direct application. Nonetheless, the practice of national courts in core crimes prosecutions is divided, so that it cannot be concluded that international law subjects core crimes law to a more stringent regime than other international norms. Still, it is

---

Penal Internacional, nas condições de complementaridade e demais termos estabelecidos no Estatuto de Roma."
Although most of these provisions do not explicitly single out the obligations flowing from the ICC Statute from normal constitutional limitations, they were all adopted with this goal in mind. See Lambert-Abdelgawad 2003, p. 562-563 (also reporting similar initiatives in Cameroon and Brasil) and Duffy 2001, p. 9-10.

[1295] See above, Chapter IV, para. 5.3.a.

noteworthy that numerous national courts have taken a decidedly internationalist stance on the implementation and effectuation of core crimes law.

Chapter VI
THE PRINCIPLE OF LEGALITY AND DIRECT APPLICATION OF CORE CRIMES

1. Introduction

In this Chapter, I will analyze the tension between the principle of legality (*nullum crimen, nulla poena sine lege praevia*) and direct application of international core crimes law in national courts. As established in Chapter V, States are under a duty to prosecute at least core crimes committed on their territory, regardless of the state of their national law in this respect. As shown in Chapter II, several national courts have confronted the question of whether core crimes can be prosecuted directly on the basis of international law where relevant national law is absent or defective. In various cases, these courts denied direct application. Of the many different (including practical) considerations that play a role in decisions on direct application, described in Chapter III, a key legal obstacle appears to be the principle of legality. Learned writers also point to the principle of legality as a cardinal obstacle to direct application.[1296]

I will now analyze the demands of the principle of legality under international law regarding national prosecutions of core crimes. This analysis concerns solely those requirements of the international principle of legality that are potentially decisive for the question of direct application of core crimes law in national courts.[1297] Accordingly, I will leave aside the question of whether the international principle prohibits analogy and extensive interpretation,[1298] as it exceeds the scope of this study. Where appropriate, I will distinguish between treaty-based and customary offences, as these raise different concerns with regard to the principle of legality.

Analyzing the role of the international principle of legality in national core crime prosecutions is no easy task. There are many dichotomies that influence the content ascribed to *nullum crimen*: national law – international law, national courts – international courts, ordinary crimes – core crimes. Most judgments do not elaborate on the way in which these factors determine their interpretation of the principle of legality. Therefore, it is not always clear which precedents are determinative for the international rules applicable to core crimes prosecutions in national courts and which ones are less relevant. Moreover, as soon will become clear, there are consid-

---

[1296] See above, notes 10-11.

[1297] Note, however, that the principle of legality certainly affects direct application of core crimes law as the basis for a national prosecution, but not necessarily other instances like direct application in order to refuse application of national statutes of limitations. See below, p. 223.

[1298] Compare Schmidt 2002, p. 54-55; Lamb 2001, p. 734 (assuming a prohibition of extensive interpretation and analogy) with Bremer 1999, p. 62; Bassiouni 1996, p. 289-290.

erable disagreements among States on this topic. Due to these factors, the law set forth here is subject to some uncertainty.

The following analysis requires several steps. First, I will map the purpose and legal basis of the principle of legality under international law (para. 2). Second, I will consider whether the core crimes are in a special position or are subject to the principle of legality in the same way as are ordinary crimes (para. 3). Third, I will scrutinize the relationship between the international principle and the principle of legality in national legal systems (para. 4). Fourth, I will discuss in turn the demands of the principle in customary international law on the specific points of applicable law (para. 5.1), its accessibility (para. 5.2), its foreseeability (para. 5.3), and the applicable penalties (para. 5.4). Fifth, I will apply these general demands to specific international offences (para. 6). Sixth, I will discuss what role international law leaves for national principles of legality in core crimes prosecutions in national courts (para. 7). Finally, I will summarize the conclusions of this Chapter (para. 8).

2. Legal Basis and Purpose of the Principle of Legality

The principle of legality is found both in national law[1299] (hereinafter national principle of legality) and international law (hereinafter international principle of legality), the latter including custom[1300] as well as treaties.[1301] An early recognition of the principle of legality by an international court appears in the PCIJ's Advisory Opinion in the *Danzig* case.[1302] The national and international principles share the same two essential goals. The first is to guarantuee the legal certainty of the individual. Legal certainty requires offences to be specific and forbids their retroactive application. These are essential conditions for individuals to know in advance both the "moral quality" (acceptable or unacceptable) and the legal consequences of their behavior.[1303]

Second, the principle of legality delimits and separates the powers of the institutional actors involved in the (international) criminal justice system.[1304] It prevents the legislature from punishing past acts by legislation, instead of criminalizing fu-

[1299] See Bassiouni 1996, p. 270-280; Boot 2002, p. 81-126.

[1300] See Werle 2003, p. 38; Barboza 2000, p. 148.

[1301] See Art. 22 and 23 ICC Statute; Art. 15 ICCPR; Art. 7 ECHR; Art. 9 ACHR; Art. 7 (2) African Charter on Human and People's Rights; Art. 99 GC III; Art. 65, 67 GC IV; Art. 75 (4) (c) AP I; Art. 6 (2) (c) AP II. See also Art. 11(2) Universal Declaration of Human Rights; Art. 49 Charter of Fundamental Rights of the European Union, 7 December 2000.

[1302] PCIJ, Consistency of Certain Danzig Legislative Decrees with the Constitution of the Free City, Advisory Opinion, 1935, Series A/B, No. 65, 3, PCIJ, Series A/B, No. 65, 3 at 514. Reproduced in Bassiouni 1999a, p. 138-140.

[1303] Cf. Fletcher 1998, p. 10-13. See also Arnold and Weigend 1997, p. 87; Wilt 1994, p. 11-16.

[1304] See Cassese 2003a, p. 141-142; Boot 2002, p. 125 and 307; Haveman 2003, p. 265. Cf. Klabbers 2003, p. 67.

ture conduct.[1305] It also stops the judiciary, national or international, from imposing arbitrary punishment and effectively drawing up new offences. In international criminal law, the principle has the added function of ensuring that the law is specific enough for States to fulfill their obligations regarding the enforcement of ICL and the cooperation with international tribunals.[1306] Thus, it prevents international criminal courts from demanding transferal of, or cooperation in, prosecutions where States have no obligation to do so under international law. These institutional ramifications, like the legal certainty of the individual, require core crimes law to clearly distinguish criminal from non-criminal conduct.[1307]

The demands of specificity and non-retroactivity make up the core of the principle of legality. Doctrine generally assumes that the principle of legality requires prosecution and punishment of individuals to be based on a legal norm that (1) existed at the time of the offense (*nullum crimen sine lege praevia*) (2) is accessible to the individuals it addresses and (3) is so clear as to make the possibility of prosecution and punishment foreseeable (the requirement of *lex certa*).[1308] In addition, the requirement of an indication of the applicable penalties is often seen as an intrinsic part of the principle (*nulla poena sine lege*), but, as will be shown below, its scope in international law is uncertain.[1309]

The legal basis and foreseeability of a prosecution should be judged for the time the crime was committed. Between the commission of the crime and its prosecution, the scope of the criminalization may not be expanded, nor may the penalty be increased. However, other conditions of the prosecution that are not material for the determination of the "moral quality" of the act, such as statutes of limitation and rules on jurisdiction, are not subject to the international principle of legality. Thus, they can be determined and changed after the commission of the crime. While some States extend the principle of legality to cover such conditions, neither treaty law nor State practice provides a basis for a corresponding international rule.[1310] There is ample evidence, furthermore, that the international principle of legality is substantially different from the standards in many national laws, and far more

[1305] Cf. Australia, High Court, *Polyukhovich v. The Commonwealth of Australia and Another*, 14 August 1991, per Mason, CJ, para. 23-41 (discussing and dismissing the argument that the retroactive character of Australian war crimes legislation amounts to punishment by legislation and therefore infringes on the judicial powers of the courts).

[1306] See Dixon *et al.* 2003, p. 456; Broomhall 1999, p. 451.

[1307] See on the topic of separation of powers further above, Chapter III, para. 5.

[1308] Cf. Cassese 2003a, p. 141-142; Jones and Powles 2003, p. 401.

[1309] See below, para. 5.4.

[1310] See e.g. Poland, Constitutional Tribunal, *Case of 6 July 1999*, 6 July 1999, para. II (2): "[The principle of legality] does not encompass situations when that act was prohibited at the moment of commitment and then due to different reasons it stopped being punishable. The moment of commitment of the act is the point of reference for that principle. Everything what happens later is off the range of its application." See also Swart 2002b, p. 584-586. Cf. Fletcher 1998, p. 10-23. But see Safferling 2001, p. 87-88 (contending that the international principle of legality requires the existence of the court that will judge the crime before it occurs).

minimalistic.[1311] Before setting out to map the different requirements of the international principle of legality for core crimes prosecutions, I will inquire whether the core crimes are treated different from or similar to ordinary crimes in this regard.

3. A Special Position for the Core Crimes?

Are prosecutions of the core crimes, including those in national courts, subject to the international principle of legality in the same way as prosecutions of ordinary crimes, or are they governed by different standards? The answer to this question determines to what extent State practice on the principle of legality in general, including cases of ordinary crimes, is relevant for the particular category of core crimes prosecutions.

Some older authors have maintained that the principle of legality does not apply to international crimes at all because it is not compatible with the structure of international criminal law.[1312] They supported the negation of an international principle of legality generally by reference to post WW II prosecutions. Indeed, the language of some of those judgments suggests a complete disregard of the principle of legality. In *United States v. Altstötter* (1947), a U.S. Military Tribunal stated that "[i]t would be sheer absurdity to suggest that the *ex post facto* rule, as known to constitutional states, could be applied to a treaty, a custom, or a common law decision of an international tribunal, or to the international acquiescence which follows the event. To have attempted to apply the *ex post facto* principle to judicial decisions of common international law would have been to strangle that law at birth."[1313] However, despite this categorical language, the Tribunal ultimately opted for a restrictive interpretation of the principle of legality rather than its non-application.[1314]

On closer scrutiny, post-WW II prosecutions generally rejected a rigid reading of the *nullum crimen* principle, rather than the principle in its entirety. In *United States v. Von List* (1947), for example, the Tribunal found that "it is not essential that a crime be specifically defined and charged in accordance with a particular ordinance, statute, or treaty if it is made a crime by international convention, recognized customs and usages of war, or the general principles of criminal justice com-

---

[1311] See Kittichaisaree 2001, p. 269-272; Paust 2000, p. 8; Vyver 1999, p. 316 ("[T]he same standard of specificity required for the circumscription of criminal offences by some criminal justice systems does not apply in international law").

[1312] See Woetzel 1960, p. 112-116 and references cited there.

[1313] U.S., Military Tribunal at Nuremberg, *United States v. Altstötter et al.* (Justice case), 3-4 December 1947, III Trials of War Criminals Before the Nuremberg Military Tribunals Under Control Council Law No. 10, 1946-1949 at 975.

[1314] Id., at 977-978: "As a principle of justice and fair play, the rule in question will be given full effect. As applied in the field of international law that principle requires proof before conviction that the accused knew or should have known that in matters of international concern he was guilty of participation in a nationally organized system of injustice and persecution shocking to the moral sense of mankind, and that he knew or should have known that he would be subject to punishment if caught."

mon to civilized nations generally."[1315] Clearly, the condition that the crime be recognized under international law signifies a recognition of the principle.[1316] Similarly, in many post-WW II prosecutions the principle of legality was interpreted in a restrictive manner, but still treated with considerable deference.[1317] On balance, therefore, it seems more accurate to say that these prosecutions reflect a recognition of at least a minimal core of the principle, rather than not at all.[1318]

A similar picture emerges from various more recent judgments of national courts. Several of those judgments suggest that the principle of legality does not apply at all to particular crimes or situations. Examples include the German *Borderguards* cases, in which both German courts and the ECtHR effectively set aside the principle of legality, in a manner which arguably amounts to a violation of international law.[1319] An explicit departure from the principle of legality is also found in the jurisprudence of the Indonesian Ad hoc Human Rights Tribunal. In the case of *Abilio Soares* (2002), the Tribunal first reiterated the international origin and non-derogability of the principle of legality.[1320] However, the Tribunal then referred to the jurisdictional scheme of the ICTY and ICTR and concluded "that the legality principle is not absolutely valid and there may be exceptions to this principle."[1321] In the case of *Domingos Mendonca* (2003), East-Timor's Special Panel for Serious Crimes held that "under customary international law crimes against humanity are criminal under general principles of law recognized by the community of nations, and thus constitute an exception to the principle of retroactivity."[1322] While again sweeping in language, these judgments all make sure to establish the criminality of

---

[1315] U.S., Military Tribunal at Nuremberg, *United States v. Von List et al.* (Hostages case), 1948, Annual Digest 1948, No. 215, p. 634-635.

[1316] Id., p. 635; "If the acts charged were in fact crimes under international law when committed, they cannot be said to be *ex post facto* acts or retroactive pronouncements."

[1317] See Boot 2002, p. 179-222; Zimmermann 1997, p. 11-12.

[1318] Compare Boot 2002, p. 219 ("In war crimes trials conducted after the Second World War, the *nullum crimen sine lege* principle has been interpreted and applied in a more liberal way than in current national criminal laws.") with Paust 1997a, p. 666 (concluding that "it is doubtful, then, that either the IMT at Nuremberg or the subsequent Tribunal under Control Law. No. 10 considered nullum crimen sine lege to be a principle of international law"). See also Triffterer 1966, p. 40-41.

[1319] See below, note 1440 and accompanying text. See also note 1461 (on the question whether the borderguards cases involved core crimes).

[1320] Indonesia, Ad Hoc Human Rights Tribunal at the Human Rights Court of Justice of Central Jakarta, *Abilio Soares*, 14 August 2002, unnumbered paragraph, p. 64 of 82: "In considering, that the prohibition of retroactive law (ex facto) is a basic right that is a non derogable right, as stipulated in Article 28 (i) 2nd Amendment 1945 Constitution and Article 4 Law No. 39 year 1999 concerning Human Rights, is universal and is derived from Article 11 of the Universal Declaration of Human Rights." (The Tribunal made further references to the ICCPR and ECHR.)

[1321] Id., p. 65: "Therefore the retroactive principle may also be valid to examine and try serious human rights violations cases in the prescribed periods, in particular as in the Penjelasan Undang-undang [commentary accompanying the law] it is clearly stated that: 'in other words the retroactive principle may be applied to protect human rights itself under Article 28 jo verse (2) Undang-undang Dasar 1945 [i.e. the 1945 Constitution]'."

[1322] East-Timor, Special Panel for Serious Crimes, *Domingos Mendonca, Decision on the defense motion for the Court to order the Public Prosecutor to amend the indictment*, 24 July 2003, para. 20.

the conduct under international law, or at the very least verify the foreseeability of its punishment.[1323] Thus, they do not set aside the principle of legality but rather adopt more flexible standards for international crimes.

A differentiation in the standards of the principle of legality for ordinary crimes and international crimes has been adopted also by various other national courts. Argentinean case law to this effect has been described above.[1324] The Colombian Constitutional Court found in its 2002 judgment on the constitutionality of the ICC Statute that the standards of the principle of legality are not identical for international and national criminal law.[1325] Various national courts have relied on Art. 15 (2) ICCPR and Art. 7 (2) ECHR to adopt this differentiation.[1326] In *Barbie* (1984), the French courts rejected appeals to the principle of legality by reference to these provisions of the ECHR and the ICCPR, finding that crimes against humanity are exempted from the principle of legality as formulated in French law.[1327] A similar reasoning was applied by the Slovenian Constitutional Court in several cases in the 1990s.[1328] The Court struck down certain *ex post facto* criminalization of acts committed during WW II for violating the principle of legality in the Slovenian Constitution.[1329] With reference to Art. 15 (2) ICCPR and Art. 7 (2) ECHR, however, the Court made an exception for all acts which "attract a penalty by the general legal principles recognized by civilised nations.[1330]

[1323] See on the Borderguards cases below, notes 1444, 1460 and accompanying text; Indonesia, Ad Hoc Human Rights Tribunal at the Human Rights Court of Justice of Central Jakarta, *Abilio Soares*, 14 August 2002, p. 59 (stating that the "crime against humanity has become part of general legal principles recognized by a community of nations, [so] that violence by commission or ommission may be charged retroactively"); East-Timor, Special Panel for Serious Crimes, *Domingos Mendonca, Decision on the defense motion for the Court to order the Public Prosecutor to amend the indictment*, 24 July 2003, para. 22-30.

[1324] See above, Chapter II, para. 3.3.m.

[1325] See Colombia, Corte Constitucional, Sala Plena, *Sentencia C-578 (In re Corte Penal Internacional)*, 30 July 2002, 31 Jurisprudencia y Doctrina 2231 at 2292 (speaking of "un estándar diferente del principio de legalidad que orienta el derecho penal tanto en el ámbito nacional como en el contexto internacional").

[1326] See on these provisions also below, para. 5.1.

[1327] France, Court de Cassation, *Barbie (No. 2)*, 26 January 1984, Bull. crim., no. 34; 78 I.L.R. 132, at Bull. crim., no. 34, p. 92 (Cour de Cassation citing and affirming the Court of Appeals): "[Q]u'en définitive, l'incrimination de crimes contre l'humanité est conforme aux principes généraux de droit reconnus par les nations civilisées; qu'a ce titre ces crimes échappent au principe de la non-rétroactivité des lois de répression..."

[1328] See Slovenia, Constitutional Court, *U-I-248/96*, 30 September 1998 and Slovenia, Constitutional Court, *U-I-6/93*, 13 January 1994.

[1329] See Art. 28 Constitution: "No person may be punished for an offence which was unknown to the criminal law, or which attracted no penalty, at the time the offence was allegedly committed."

[1330] Slovenia, Constitutional Court, *U-I-6/93*, 13 January 1994, para. 20. See also Slovenia, Constitutional Court, *U-I-248/96*, 30 September 1998, para. 14: "The Constitutional Court already in the cited decision No. U-I-6/93 found the retroactive application of the Decree on Military Courts allowed insofar as consistent with the general legal principles recognized by civilized nations. It compared the Decree's retroactivity with the retroactive effect of the London Agreement reached on 8 August 1945, on the basis of which Nuremberg trials for war crimes had been carried out. The retroactivity of that time was legitimate due to the fact that during World War II such delicta were committed which could

In Hungary, in 1993 the Constitutional Court also found that prosecutions for crimes against humanity and war crimes are not governed by the national principle of legality, again with reference to the aforementioned articles of the ICCPR and the ECHR. The Constitutional Court held that the general principles exception in these treaties "makes possible the prosecution of the aforenoted and described *sui generis* criminal offenses defined by international law even by those member states whose domestic system of law does not recognize the definition or does not punish that action or omission." [1331] For, the Court found, "such acts must be prosecuted and punished in accordance with the conditions and requirements imposed by international law. The second section of both (International and European) Conventions evidently break through the penal law guarantees of domestic law."[1332]

Some States, following the language of the ECHR and the ICCPR, have included an exception for international crimes in their formulation of the principle of legality in national law. An example can be found in Art. 42 (1) of the Polish Constitution of 1997 which determines that the principle of legality "shall not prevent punishment of any act which, at the moment of its commission, constituted an offence within the meaning of international law."[1333] Similar provisions are found in the Criminal Code of Bosnia and Herzegovina[1334] and the Canadian Constitution.[1335] On the basis of the latter provision, the Canadian Commission of Inquiry on War Criminals concluded that general principles of law recognized by the community of nations can form the basis for war crimes prosecutions.[1336]

The gist of these national decisions and provisions is that prosecutions of core crimes, also in national courts, are governed by the standards of the international principle of legality, which are more lenient than the standards of their national criminal law.[1337] This approach appears to be in line with the position of contempo-

not have been imagined, nor even envisaged, by previous legislatures. For these very reasons the departure from the prohibition of the retroactive effect of criminal laws should be allowed and legitimate also in [this] case..."

[1331] See above, note 1271.

[1332] Id.

[1333] See above, note 555.

[1334] Art. 3 (2): "No punishment or other criminal sanction may be imposed on any person for an act which, prior to being perpetrated, has not been defined as a criminal offence by law or international law, and for which a punishment has not been prescribed by law."; Draft Art. 4a: "Articles 3 and 4 of this Code [containing the principle of legality] shall not prejudice the trial and punishment of any person for any act or omission which, at the time when it was commited, was criminal according to the general principles of international law."

[1335] See above, text preceding note 372.

[1336] See above, Chapter II, para. 3.3.i.

[1337] See also *Australia, High Court, Polyukhovich v. The Commonwealth of Australia and Another,* 14 August 1991, Justice Dawson, para. 18: "[T]he *ex post facto* creation of war crimes may be seen as justifiable in a way that is not possible with other *ex post facto* criminal laws [... T]he wrongful nature of the conduct ought to have been apparent to those who engaged in it even if, because of the circumstances in which the conduct took place, there was no offence against domestic law. [... T]his justification for a different approach with respect to war crimes is reflected in [Article 15 of] the International Covenant on Civil and Political Rights [...] War crimes [...] simply could not, in any civilized community, have been described as innocent or blameless conduct merely because of the absence of proscription by law."

rary human rights law. While the ICCPR and the ECHR declare the principle of legality to be non-derogable,[1338] they also contain an exception clause for acts that are "criminal according to the general principles of law."[1339] The ECtHR relied on this exception in *Naletilic v. Croatia* (2000) to find a complaint based on Art. 7 ECHR inadmissible.[1340] The applicant complained against his transferal to the ICTY, where he was accused of crimes against humanity and war crimes, asserting *inter alia* a violation of Art. 7 ECHR on the ground that he might be sentenced to a heavier penalty by the ICTY than by the domestic courts.[1341] The European Court noted concisely:

> "As to the applicant's contention that he might receive a heavier punishment by the ICTY than he might have received by domestic courts if the latter exercised their jurisdiction to finalise the proceedings against him, the Court notes that, even assuming Article 7 of the Convention to apply to the present case, the specific provision that could be applicable to it would be paragraph 2 rather than paragraph 1 of Article 7 of the Convention. This means that the second sentence of Article 7 § 1 of the Convention invoked by the applicant could not apply."[1342]

Thus, like the national courts cited above, the ECtHR makes a clear distinction between core crimes and ordinary crimes with regard to the principle of legality.[1343]

Yet there is also practice to the contrary. Many national laws do not make an explicit exception for the prosecution of international crimes in their formulation of the principle of legality. Instead, a few States have made reservations to the exception clauses in the ECHR and the ICCPR in order to object to the prosecution of acts that were criminal according to general principles of law. When ratifying the ECHR, then West-Germany declared that it would only apply Art. 7 (2) within the limits of its national law.[1344] Since that national law contained a strict principle of

---

[1338] See Art. 4 (2) ICCPR and Art. 15 ECHR. See also Art. 27 (1) ACHR.

[1339] See Art. 15 (2) ICCPR:

Nothing in this article shall prejudice the trial and punishment of any person for any act or omission which, at the time when it was committed, was criminal according to the general principles of law recognized by the community of nations.

and Art. 7 (2) ECHR:

"This article shall not prejudice the trial and punishment of any person for any act or omission which, at the time when it was committed, was criminal according to the general principles of law recognised by civilised nations."

[1340] ECtHR, *Naletilic v. Croatia, Admissibility decision*, 4 May 2000.

[1341] Id., para. 2.

[1342] Id.

[1343] This position is in line with earlier findings of the EComHR that standards of due process developed for prosecutions of ordinary crimes can not automatically be transposed to war crimes prosecutions. See above, note 1076.

[1344] See Reservation to Art. 7 ECHR contained in the instrument of ratification, deposited on 5 December 1952 (Original English: "The German Federal Republic makes the reservation that it will only apply the provisions of Article 7 paragraph 2 of the Convention within the limits of Article 103 paragraph 2 of the Basic Law of the German Federal Republic. This provides that any act is only punishable if it was so by law before the offence was committed."). Cf. Boot 2002, p. 159.

legality, this statement essentially amounted to non-acceptance of Art. 7 (2).[1345] In a similar manner, Argentina made a reservation to Art. 15 (2) ICCPR, but this reservation has effectively been set aside by subsequent case law of the Argentinean courts.[1346]

In *Armando dos Santos*, East-Timor's Court of Appeal held that "even though the acts committed by the defendant in 1999 include the crime against humanity provided for under Section 5.1 (a) of UNTAET Regulation 2000/15, the defendant may not be tried and convicted based on this criminal law, which did not exist upon the date on which these acts were committed and, as such, may not be applied retroactively."[1347] In cases like *Bouterse* (2001), and *Habré* (2001), the core crimes are not treated differently than ordinary crimes where it concerns the demands of the principle of legality.[1348] In *Habré*, the Senegalese Court of Appeals found that in the absence of a criminalization of crimes against humanity in national law, the principle of legality in the Penal Code precludes the prosecution of those crimes in Senegalese courts.[1349] In *Bouterse*, the Dutch Supreme Court found that the principle of legality as formulated in Dutch law does not make an exception for international crimes, but constitutes an "unreserved prohibition" of prosecutions that are not based on Dutch law.[1350] Numerous other judgments do not contain such explicit statements on the role of the principle of legality, but appear to adhere to the same line of reasoning in a more implicit manner.[1351] They see no reason to treat international crimes differently than ordinary crimes where it concerns the principle of legality.

In sum, the picture that emerges from State practice is divided. Despite sweeping language to the contrary in some judgments, the principle of legality does apply to the core crimes at least in some form. While there are strong legislative and judicial precedents for applying only a minimal *nullum crimen* standard to the core crimes, also in national courts, practice is divided on this point. It is beyond doubt, however, that the precedents mentioned indicate that there can be significant differences between the national and the international principle of legality.

[1345] Note, however, that the reservation has since been withdrawn. See Note Verbale from the Permanent Representation of the Federal Republic of Germany, dated 1 October 2001, registered at the Secretariat General on 5 October 2001.

[1346] See above, Chapter II, para. 3.3.m.

[1347] East-Timor, Court of Appeal, *Armando dos Santos, Applicable Subsidiary Law decision*, 15 July 2003, p. 14. Note, however, that this decision departs from several other judgments of the Court of Appeal and that the Special Panel for Serious Crimes has openly refused to adhere to it. See e.g. East-Timor, Special Panel for Serious Crimes, *Domingos Mendonca, Decision on the defense motion for the Court to order the Public Prosecutor to amend the indictment*, 24 July 2003.

[1348] See above, Chapter II, para. 3.3.e and 3.3.k.

[1349] See above, note 266.

[1350] See above, note 435 and accompanying text.

[1351] See above, Chapter II, in particular the paragraphs on Australia and Switzerland.

4. The International and the National Principle of Legality

National prosecutions are governed simultaneously by national and international law. Therefore, the question arises as to how the demands of the principle of legality under these two bodies of law relate to one another. Are the standards they postulate on the basis of their common core of specificity and non-retroactivity comparable? Should we distinguish the international principle of legality from its national counterparts as imposing fundamentally different standards? For direct application of ICL in prosecutions of the core crimes, this is a crucial question. After all, it is a fundamental rule of international law that obligations under national law cannot excuse violations of international obligations. Thus, a national principle of legality that goes beyond the requirements of international law is not a valid reason to forego a mandatory prosecution of a core crime.

Practice indicates that States regard the international principle of legality as a minimal standard which differs considerably from the stricter standards many set in their national laws. First, this is reflected in the overwhelming support exhibited by states for the *ad hoc* tribunals. If States demanding a written definition of both the crime and the penalty under their national law had viewed these conditions as satisfying an international obligation, they could not have supported the *ad hoc* tribunals in their present form. The great majority of States accepts prosecutions for crimes in Rwanda and Yugoslavia on the basis that these crimes were well established in customary international law at the time of commission, which shows that even States with strict national principles of legality interpret the international principle as being more lenient.

Second, the lack of congruence between the national and international principles of legality can be discerned in national legislative and judicial practice, as described in the preceding paragraph. In the Netherlands, for example, the Supreme Court acknowledged in *Bouterse* that the national principle of legality did not match the principle as formulated in Art. 7 ECHR.[1352] Also, the West-German reservation to Art. 7 (2) ECHR and the Argentinean one to Art. 15 (2) ICCPR show that these States perceived their national principles of legality as more demanding than and thus distinct from the formulations of the principle in the human rights treaties. Meanwhile, national judgments refusing prosecution of core crimes generally refer only to national principles of legality without elaborating on the relationship between the national and the international principle.[1353]

Thus, there are good reasons to distinguish the international principle of legality from its national counterparts.[1354] Even if they share a common core, the discrep-

---

[1352] See Netherlands, HR, *In re Bouterse*, 18 September 2001, para. 4. See also Dutch legislative history acknowledging different standards of national principle of legality and Art. 7 ECHR, cited in para. 4.3.2.

[1353] See above, Chapter II, e.g. para. 3.3.c and 3.3.d.

[1354] See Cassese 2003a, p. 139-158; Werle 2003, p. 38; Mattarollo 2001, p. 25; Bremer 1999, p. 153 and elaborately Triffterer 1966, p. 38-139.

ancies between the national and the international formulations of the principle are considerable and of substantial effect. As the ICTY noted in *Delalic*, these discrepancies reflect differences between national and international law, *inter alia* in their nature, legislative policies and standards, and drafting process.[1355]

It follows that in the analysis of the demands of international law regarding the *nullum crimen* principle for national prosecutions of core crimes, care should be taken to distinguish rules ascribed to national law from those ascribed to international law. This is a complex task. The simultaneous application of the international and stricter national principles of legality leads to the situation that much of State practice is relevant to ascertain what is *allowed* by the international principle of legality, but not what is *required* by it, unless expressly indicated otherwise. The finding of the Hungarian Courts that prosecution of core crimes on the basis of customary international law is permissible indicates that they interpret the principle of legality under international law as allowing this practice. On the other hand, there is no indication that the Dutch Supreme Court understands its stricter interpretation of the principle of legality as required by international law. On the contrary, the Supreme Court expressly indicated that it based its decision on the Dutch principle of legality and not on the more lenient international principle.[1356]

Meanwhile, it should be noted that various States espoused a more rigid view of the international principle of legality during the establishment of the *ad hoc* tribunals and the ICC.[1357] In this regard, there is a clear desire among certain States to elevate the international principle of legality to a stricter level, comparable to their national principles.[1358] This tendency could reduce the divergence between the international principle and stricter national principles in the future. At present, however, it seems that the push for a stricter principle has not resulted in an adaptation of the principle of legality under general international law.

Notably, the ICC Statute contains a strict principle of legality in Arts. 22 and 23.[1359] However, the import of these provisions is not clear-cut, since the Statute

---

[1355] See ICTY, Trial Chamber, *Delalic et al.,* 16 November 1998, para. 403-405.

[1356] The Court declined to analyze whether the international principle would allow the prosecution of Bouterse where the national principle did not, as it could not discern a duty to prosecute in the case. See Netherlands, HR, *In re Bouterse*, 18 September 2001, para. 4.5-4.8.

[1357] See Lamb 2001, p. 762-765; Peglau 2001b; Schabas 2000c, p. 524-528 and 536-538; Broomhall 1999, p. 448-450.

[1358] Cf. Cassese 2003a, p. 142-145.

[1359] Art. 22:

" 1. A person shall not be criminally responsible under this Statute unless the conduct in question constitutes, at the time it takes place, a crime within the jurisdiction of the Court.
2. The definition of a crime shall be strictly construed and shall not be extended by analogy. In case of ambiguity, the definition shall be interpreted in favour of the person being investigated, prosecuted or convicted.
3. This article shall not affect the characterization of any conduct as criminal under international law independently of this Statute."

Art. 23:

"A person convicted by the Court may be punished only in accordance with this Statute."

does not fully correspond to customary law. The ICC's lack of jurisdiction over core crimes committed before the entry into force of the Statute is not a consequence of the principle of legality, but a political choice.[1360] In fact, the Statute recognizes explicitly that neither its formulation of the principle of legality nor its sentencing provisions reflect the demands of general international law.[1361] Of course, the Statute's provisions may contribute to a more rigid interpretation of the principle of legality under general international law in the future. Yet, it appears that they currently neither reflect customary international law nor have a bearing on the prosecution of core crimes in national courts.[1362]

Finally, it should be emphasized that the distinction between principles of legality in national and international law does not correspond to a separation between national and international courts. The international principle of legality governs proceedings in all courts, also national ones. Its focus is primarily on the individual who is to benefit from the principle, as can be readily seen in the formulations in different treaties. Thus, the interpretation by international courts of the required legal certainty could be relevant for the demands put upon national courts and will be included in the following analysis.

5. The Principle of Legality under Customary International Law

This paragraph will analyze the requirements of the principle of legality under customary international law with regard to the legal basis for the prosecution of core crimes, the accessibility of that law, its foreseeability, and the provision of applicable penalties. I will pay substantial attention to Art. 7 (2) ECHR and Art. 15 (2) ICCPR, as these provisions and their application in practice are generally seen as important indications for the principle of legality under customary international law.

5.1 International Criminal Law as *Lex*

The traditional sources of international criminal law are treaties, custom and general principles.[1363] Security Council resolutions constitute an additional source.[1364] As some authors contend that the principle of legality requires a written law, it is occasionally doubted whether custom and general principles constitute law in the

---

[1360] See Jessberger 2003, p. 283-284. See also Art. 124, which allows States parties to postpone the Court's jurisdiction for war crimes for a period of seven years.

[1361] See Art. 22 (3) and Art. 80: "Nothing in this Part affects the application by States of penalties prescribed by their national law, nor the law of States which do not provide for penalties prescribed in this Part."

[1362] See Broomhall 1999, p. 448, 451 and 459; Fife 1999, p. 1010.

[1363] See Bassiouni 1999a, p. 4.

[1364] See above, notes 1139-1140.

sense of *nullum crimen sine lege.*[1365] Consequently, transformation into written national law would be necessary. This doubt is unwarranted.

The international principle of legality, whether under customary law or as defined in human rights treaties,[1366] does not exclude unwritten law from the notion of *lex.*[1367] Civil law states generally formulate a stricter national principle requiring written law, and frequently exclude international law as an independent basis for prosecution altogether,[1368] but this practice does not likely reflect customary law or a general principle of that nature.[1369] Various formulations of the principle of legality in international treaties to which many civil law states are parties, as well as the practice of the *ad hoc* tribunals, accept that customary law can provide a basis for substantive criminality.[1370] Moreover, the fact that many States in their national laws simply refer to international criminal law in general terms, e.g. "the laws and customs of war," suggests that they do not altogether exclude international offences, including customary ones, as a legal basis for prosecution.[1371]

Likewise, it can safely be assumed that the *nullum crimen* principle allows general principles to serve as a source of substantive criminality. Several authors have argued that the reference to general principles in Art. 7 (2) ECHR and Art. 15 (2) ICCPR cover only the admissibility of post-WW II prosecutions[1372] or the Nuremberg Principles,[1373] and have no broader relevance in modern international law. Both a correct interpretation of these treaties and subsequent State practice, however, require a firm rejection of this assertion.[1374] First, it is an elementary rule of treaty interpretation that the *travaux preparatoires* cannot alter the ordinary meaning of the text of a treaty.[1375] A normal contextual analysis of these provisions obviates the need to resort to the drafting history altogether, especially when taking into account the character of these human rights treaties as "living instruments."

Even if they are to be consulted, the *travaux preparatoires* of the ICCPR indicate that Art. 15 (2) was indeed inspired by the wish to safeguard the legitimacy of

---

[1365] See Lamb 2001, p. 734 and 749. Cf. Mattarollo 2001, p. 25-26 (asserting that the international principle of legality "requires the existence of a text, but only vis-à-vis a given norm of conduct," not necessarily to lay down the "norm of repression"); Rubin 1998, p. 391-392.

[1366] Cf. Boot 2002, p. 127-178.

[1367] See Bassiouni 1996, p. 289 ("International criminal law currently requires the existence of a legal prohibition arising under conventional or customary international law"). See also ECtHR, *C.R. v. the United Kingdom*, 27 October 1995, para. 33; ECtHR, *Sunday Times v. UK*, 26 April 1979, para. 47.

[1368] See Triffterer 1989, p. 60.

[1369] See e.g. Sassoli 2002, p. 123; Dressler 1995, p. 19-22 (on the still significant role of unwritten rules in the criminal law of common law States).

[1370] See Boot 2002, p. 307 and Lamb 2001, p. 742-746.

[1371] See Ziegler 1997, p. 573. See also above, Chapter II, para. 3.2.

[1372] See Boot 2002, p. 628 ("The exception clauses in the European Convention and the International Covenant must be limited to the war crimes trials conducted after the Second World War." See more generally p. 137-141, 158-161 and 177-178); Schmidt 2002, p. 65.

[1373] See Dutertre 2003, p. 240 and Simma and Paulus 2000, p. 64.

[1374] See Peyró 2003, p. 81-83.

[1375] Cf. VCLT Art. 31 and 32, widely believed to reflect customary law.

post-WW II prosecutions,[1376] but they do not warrant the conclusion that the effect of this provision is limited to those proceedings. On the contrary, while some States understood the second paragraph to cover only post-WW II prosecutions, numerous parties expressed their view that it should cover future cases.[1377] The representative of Yugoslavia, for example, stated that Art. 15 (2) "provided that crimes against humanity should always be punished, whenever and wherever they had been committed."[1378] According to Ghana it "represented a saving clause introduced in the interest of the States parties to the Covenant, enabling them, despite paragraph 1, to convict or acquit defendants and fix penalties for offences in accordance with their own legislation."[1379] Thus, the parties clearly did not agree to give a "special meaning"[1380] to the term general principles which restricted its scope to post-WW II prosecutions.[1381] The same can be concluded for Art. 7 (2) ECHR, for example from the German reservation to that provision, which pertains to its future application.[1382]

Moreover, the general applicability of Art. 7 (2) ECHR and Art. 15 (2) ICCPR has been accepted in practice. Resort to these provisions is limited but consistent. Some national laws explicitly recognize general principles as a source of substan-

[1376] See Weissbrodt 2001, p. 75-91.

[1377] See e.g. U.N. Doc. E/CN.4/SR.159 (1950) at 12-13 (Representative of the United Kingdom stated that: "It was important to emphasize in the covenant that acts which might not so far be the subject of express provisions in international law, could nevertheless be contrary to the general principles of law recognized implicitly in both national and international legislation." This position was explicitly supported by Lebanon, Greece, France and Yugoslavia.); U.N. Doc. A/C.3/SR.1008 (1960) at 133-134 (Representative of Poland stated that "she could not agree with [those] who had attempted to deny the existence of the general principles of international law…the Polish delegation wished to declare publicly that if war crimes like those which had been punished at Nürnberg should be perpetrated in the future, they must be judged with the same severity and in accordance with the same principles of international law." (para. 2-3), support for the applicability of Art. 15 (2) to future situations was expressed by India and Cuba).

[1378] U.N. Doc. A/C.3/SR.1008 (1960), at 135: "Thus article 15, paragraph 2, of the draft Covenant merely strengthened and confirmed the fundamental principles of the United Nations. He was firmly opposed to its deletion and to any amendment which might weaken it. Such a provision should be included in the Covenants, and should form an integral part of an international instrument; that might perhaps prevent a repetition of past events and deprive war criminals of any opportunity of escaping justice on the ground that their offences were not provided for under the laws of their country or under international law." Support for this position was expressed by the Philippines and the USSR (p. 136-137). Saudi-Arabia stated that it "saw no reason for basing paragraph 2 of Article 15 on the Nürnberg and Tokyo trials alone. […] Dictatorial regimes and colonial wars had been and still were the occasion for crimes similar to those referred to in paragraph 2 of the article under discussion." (p. 137, para. 30)

[1379] U.N. Doc. A/C.3/SR.1010 (1960) at 145, para. 17. Similar views were expressed by Czechoslovakia, Afghanistan and Romania (p. 146-147).

[1380] Cf. VCLT Art. 31 (4).

[1381] See Report of the Canadian Commission of Inquiry on War Criminals, 1986, Deschenes, p. 143 ("It is true that some delegations had expressed a deep concern for the protection of the past…[…] But many more had taken into consideration both the past and the future.")

[1382] See above, note 1344. Cf. Harris *et al.* 1995, p. 281-282; Report of the Canadian Commission of Inquiry on War Criminals, 1986, Deschenes, p. 137-139 and Triffterer 1966, p. 73-74.

tive criminality and various national courts have applied them in recent cases.[1383] The ECtHR has relied on Art. 7 (2) ECHR in *Naletilic v. Croatia*,[1384] and several separate opinions in other cases have also interpreted this provision as meaning just what it says, rather than as an obsolete reference to past WW II prosecutions.[1385] In the *Borderguards* case (2001) for example, Judge Pellonpää considered as one of the relevant questions whether the killing of a fugitive in Berlin in the 1970s "constituted an offence under international law (paragraph 1 of Article 7) or was "criminal according to the general principles of law recognised by civilised nations" (paragraph 2)."[1386] Likewise, the ICTY in *Delalic* rejected an alleged violation of the principle of legality under referral to Art. 15 (2) ICCPR, thus confirming its general applicability.[1387] In *Furundzija*, the ICTY even posited that the principle of legality does not rule out resort to general principles as a source of criminality but on the contrary may require their consideration.[1388]

In conclusion, customary law and general principles are both law as required by the maxim *nullum crimen sine lege*.[1389] Their application might raise issues with respect to accessibility and foreseeability, but their quality as a source of interna-

[1383] See above, para. 3 of this Chapter.

[1384] See above, note 1340.

[1385] See Barreto 2002, p. 16. Cf. Report of the Canadian Commission of Inquiry on War Criminals, 1986, Deschenes, p. 139-141.

[1386] ECtHR, *K. – H. W. v. Germany*, 22 March 2001, Partly Dissenting Opinion of Judge Pellonpää, joined by Judge Zupancic. See also Partly Dissenting Opinion of Judge Cabral Barreto, para. 4. Cf. EComHR, *S.W. v. the United Kingdom*, 27 June 1994, Dissenting Opinion of Judge Loucaides, joined by Judge Trechsel, Judge Nowicki and Judge Cabral Barreto: "The *travaux préparatoires* indicate that [Art. 7 (2) ECHR] was intended to cover prosecution of crimes against humanity in the context of the post-second world war Nuremberg trials. While it cannot be excluded that other conduct might fall within the ambit of the paragraph, I am of the opinion that there is insufficient general consensus as regards marital rape…"

[1387] ICTY, Trial Chamber, *Delalic et al.*, 16 November 1998, para. 313 ("[T]he caveat contained in Article 15, paragraph 2, of the ICCPR should be taken into account when considering the application of the principle of *nullum crimen sine lege* in the present case."); affirmed in ICTY, Appeals Chamber, *Delalic et al.*, 20 February 2001, para. 173: "It is universally acknowledged that the acts enumerated in common Article 3 [Geneva Conventions] are wrongful and shock the conscience of civilised people, and thus are, in the language of Article 15(2) of the ICCPR, 'criminal according to the general principles of law recognised by civilised nations'."

[1388] ICTY, Trial Chamber, *Furundzija*, 10 December 1998, para. 177: "The Trial Chamber […] considers that, to arrive at an accurate definition of rape based on the criminal law principle of specificity (*Bestimmtheitgrundsatz*, also referred to by the maxim '*nullum crimen sine lege stricta*'), it is necessary to look for principles of criminal law common to the major legal systems of the world. These principles may be derived, with all due caution, from national laws." See also ICTY, Appeals Chamber, *Tadic, Decision on the Defence Motion for Interlocutory Appeal on Jurisdiction*, 2 October 1995, para. 128-134.

[1389] In this context, it should also be noted that uncertainties about the state of development of international criminal law were raised as an argument against inclusion of an explicit reference to international law in Article 15 (1) of the ICCPR, but were rejected. See Bossuyt 1987, p. 324.

tional criminal law is well established in general international law, as indicated by the provisions of the ICCPR and ECHR and the practice of a variety of States.[1390]

5.2 Accessibility

The principle of legality requires not only that criminalisations are based on law, but also that this law is readily accessible.[1391] Accessibility presupposes that the legal rules making the acts in question punishable must be available to the person concerned. The accessibility of the law on core crimes constitutes a somewhat abstract if not fictitious test and is problematic in two respects. These are, first, the dependence on States to make international criminal law accessible to individuals, and second, the particularly poor accessibility of unwritten sources of international law.

The first problem follows from the fact that international law largely depends on national governments for its dissemination. It is up to States to make international law accessible to their citizens by translating and publishing treaties and other material sources of international law. Consequently, many States allow the direct application of treaty provisions against individuals only after the treaty has been published.[1392] Some national courts prosecuting foreign suspects for core crimes ascertain that the relevant treaties were in force in the State of the crime, and thus accessible to the defendants.[1393]

[1390] See Shahabuddeen 2004; Pellet 2002, p. 1057-1058 ("Custom is a source of international law to the same extent as treaties and is just as apt to constitute the indispensable *lex*."); Barreto 2002, p. 3; Bremer 1999, p. 60-61; Morris and Scharf 1998, p. 124 ("The binding force of the relevant customary law on all States would ensure respect for the *nullum crimen sine lege* principle since there would be no question as to whether the particular conduct was prohibited in the State where the crime was committed."); Triffterer 1966, p. 139. Cf. Schmidt 2001, p. 48-50 and 64-66. But see Boot 2002, p. 628 ("At present, consensus among states about the criminality of conduct under international law beyond existing treaties is still absent." However, this conclusion is hard to reconcile with the authors earlier observations that unwritten sources of criminality are accepted in various international treaties and in the practice of national and international courts. See p. 124-125, 176 and 626-627).

[1391] See ECtHR, *C.R. v. the United Kingdom*, 27 October 1995, para. 33 ("[W]hen speaking of 'law' Article 7 (Art. 7) alludes to the very same concept as that to which the Convention refers elsewhere when using that term, a concept which comprises written as well as unwritten law and implies qualitative requirements, notably those of accessibility and foreseeability.").

[1392] See e.g. Art. 93 Dutch Constitution; Belgium, Court of Cassation, *Publication of Treaties Case (Belgium)*, 25 November 1993; Germany, Reichsgericht in Strafsachen, *Publication of Treaties Case (Germany)*, 25 September 1920, Partial translation in English in Annual Digest 1919-1922, No. 234, p. 323.

[1393] See e.g. Swiss *Tribunal Militaire de Division I*, 18 April 1997, para. En Droit, Compétence; Swiss *Tribunal Militaire D'appel 1A*, Niyonteze 2000, Chapitre 3 sub A; Swiss Tribunal Militaire de Cassation, Niyonteze 2001, para. II sub b (all establishing that the territorial States of the crimes were bound by the relevant Geneva Conventions and Protocols). Although these courts do not specify the relevance of their findings, it seems plausible that accessibility of the law is an important reason to establish the status of the treaties in the territorial State. After all, it is not relevant for the scope of the duty to extradite or prosecute under the Geneva Conventions, which extends to all alleged perpetrators, not only nationals of the Contracting parties.

The advent of the information age has to some extent diminished the central role of the State in disseminating the content of international law. Today, there is a growing body of information that makes international law accessible independent of State action. Using the internet and other means of mass communication, international organizations like the U.N. and the Red Cross, as well as educational institutions and NGO's disseminate international law to a large audience. However, for groups that are hampered by lack of access to modern means of communication and/or language barriers, the State still plays a particularly crucial role in the dissemination of international law. This dependence is problematic, since the applicability of core crimes law should as a matter of principle be independent from the efforts of the national government.[1394]

The second problem concerns the accessibility of offences based on customary law and general principles. As these are unwritten sources, they can not simply be published as are treaties or statutes. As a result, they are less accessible to the general public. Of course, expressions of the customary norm are generally accessible. Individuals can inform themselves of customary rules through judgments of national and international courts, declarations and communications of States, as well as treaties, legislation and other sources.

For the core crimes in particular, an indication of the law can be derived from numerous readily available sources, such as treaties, relevant international documents, the widespread condemnation of crimes under international law, reports about proceedings against (alleged) perpetrators in national and international courts and the work of academics, governmental and non-governmental organisations. However, the fact that the ascertainment of a customary rule often requires the analysis of many sources combined, and the fact that most of these sources are not comprehensive, clearly diminishes the accessibility of customary rules. For example, the ICTY has relied upon many and diverse sources to ascertain certain customary rules – including case law, military manuals and legislation of numerous countries – which are not readily accessible to the average individual.

While the dependence on the State for dissemination and the poor accessibility of unwritten international law are real problems, they are greatly mitigated by the fundamental character of many of the core crimes. Whether one believes that the core crimes constitute a modern form of natural law or not, a successful plea of lack of accessibility of the law is hard to imagine for a crime like genocide. Still, one can conclude that proper concerns over accessibility plead for the codification of ICL in treaties or authoritative studies of customary law.[1395]

[1394] Cf. Art. 27 (2) and 33 ICC Statute (irrelevance of official capacity and superior orders); Nuremberg Principles II (fact that internal law does not impose a penalty does not relieve perpetrator from responsibility under international law) and IV (no defense of superior orders provided a moral choice was possible). See also Argentina, Judge Gabriel Cavallo of the Buenos Aires Federal Court, Julio Simon (Case no. 8686/2000, "Simon, Julio, Del Cerro, Juan Antonio s/sustracción de menores de 10 años"), 6 March 2001, 2000/B Nueva Doctrina Penal 527, para. III (J).

[1395] See for an impressive example of the latter Henckaerts 2005.

In the practice of both national and international courts, claims about a lack of knowledge of the applicable law are relatively scarce and consistently denied.[1396] It appears that ultimately, accessibility of the law is not an independent requirement of the principle of legality, but rather a step in the scrutiny of the foreseeability of the norm. The legal certainty of the individual is safeguarded where she is aware of the rules to be followed, no matter how she has learned of them. In spite of the wording of some judgments of the ECtHR, which suggests that accessibility and foreseeability are two different coexisting demands,[1397] accessibility is not explicitly included in the various treaty provisions and seems relevant only in the context of the question of foreseeability.[1398] It is inconceivable that the principle of legality would preclude the prosecution of a perpetrator who was aware of the illegality of his conduct but unable to access the relevant law. Therefore, the following analysis of the requirement of foreseeability will further clarify the relevance of the principle of legality for the direct application of the core crimes.

5.3 Foreseeability

The essence of the principle of legality, that an individual may not be prosecuted for conduct she could not know was punishable, requires the law to be so clear as to make its consequences foreseeable.[1399] In this respect, the prosecution of core crimes gives rise to several problems, especially when the international offences are directly applied.[1400] The old warning that criminal proceedings before national courts are "a questionable method of removing outstanding doubts and laying down authoritatively the existing law on subjects of controversy"[1401] has not lost its cogency. The rudimentary state of ICL negatively impacts its foreseeability in numerous ways. Both international offences themselves and the system of ICL in which they are enforced share a number of characteristics that negatively influence their foreseeability. In addition, the interplay between ICL and national law can lead to divergent or even conflicting demands on individuals.

[1396] See below notes 1415-1418.

[1397] See above note 1391 ("accessibility *and* foreseeability").

[1398] In other instances, the ECtHR has treated foreseeability as the only requirement to be satisfied. See e.g. ECtHR, *C.R. v. the United Kingdom*, 27 October 1995, para. 42-44.

[1399] See e.g. ECtHR, *G. v. France*, 27 September 1995, para. 24-25; ECtHR, *Sunday Times v. UK*, 26 April 1979, para. 48-49.

[1400] See e.g., p. 559; Yuan and Jianping 2002, p. 356; Hullu 2000, p. 334. Cf. Bassiouni *et al.* 1989, p. 326-327, remarks by Benjamin Ferencz: "Those who have criticized the [Genocide] Convention for vagueness are absolutely correct. Any prosecutor would face formidable, if not insurmountable, obstacles: was there requisite 'intent,' was the elimination of the target group 'substantial,' was it an 'act of state' or 'military necessity' or 'putative military necessity,' is it applicable in civil wars, and would prosecution be an illegal interference in internal affairs? [...] The international community has not yet reached the point of civilization where offenses are unambiguously and unequivocally condemned."

[1401] Lauterpacht 1944, p. 74.

First, most international offences, including the core crimes, are not formulated as "classic prohibitions." As relevant treaties are generally addressed to States and not individuals, the difference between a direct international criminalization and an order for States to do so is not always evident.[1402] Further, the need to compromise in international law-making often inhibits the formulation of clear, unambiguous offences. Consequently, many international offences lack a detailed description of the prohibited conduct,[1403] applicable penalties,[1404] and even references to its character as a crime or its intended prosecution.[1405] A pertinent example of an international crime which lacks a clear definition is aggression.

Second, as stated above when discussing accessibility, even when leaving aside the matter of national implementation, the law on the core crimes is contained in a plurality of formal sources. These sources complement one another, but at times they are at variance or even contradictory. For the foreseeability of customary rules, a plurality of material sources poses further problems. Custom is ascertained by the synthesis of many diverse material sources, most of which are not readily accessible for the average individual.[1406] These sources, both national and international, often differ to a certain extent, which can lead to confusion about the precise content of the rule. A pertinent example is torture as a war crime or crime against humanity. In *Delalic*, the ICTY resorted *inter alia* to the Geneva Conventions and Protocols, CAT, 1975 Declaration on Torture, Universal Declaration of Human Rights, ICCPR, ECHR, ACHR, Inter-American Convention to Prevent and Punish Torture, African Charter on Human and Peoples' Rights, 1907 Hague Convention (IV), as well as to the jurisprudence of several international and regional judicial bodies, to arrive at a definition of torture.[1407] Taking into account the ICTY's elaborate treatment of these divergent provisions, it cannot be said that the elements of torture must have been crystal clear to the defendants at the time of their acts. Moreover, custom can be formed and adapted by digressing from established rules. The gradual process whereby violations of existing customary rules gain enough support to change the law and establish a new rule, with all uncertainties of a transitional period, is not exactly beneficial for the legal certainty of the individual.

Third, an important distinction between national and international criminal law is the lack of a supreme judicial authority in the latter system. A coherent body of case-law can remedy vagueness in the law to a large extent.[1408] International crimi-

[1402] That ICL predominantly relies on the indirect enforcement model is reflected in its limited content specificity. See Bassiouni 1999a, p. 5. See further below, para. 6.

[1403] See e.g. Rückert and Witschel 2001, p. 75 (on the lack of a definition of extermination as a crime against humanity prior to the ICC Statute).

[1404] See below para. 5.4.

[1405] See Paust 1997a, p. 664.

[1406] See above para. 5.2.

[1407] ICTY, Trial Chamber, *Delalic et al.*, 16 November 1998, para. 452-497.

[1408] See ECtHR, *Kokkinakis v. Greece*, 25 May 1993, para. 40 ("In this instance there existed a body of settled national case-law [...]. This case-law, which had been published and was accessible, supplemented the letter of [the law] and was such as to enable Mr Kokkinakis to regulate his conduct in the matter.").

nal law lacks a judicial body with the competence of authoritative interpretation. The various national and international courts influence each other to a significant extent, but are not formally bound to follow each other's precedents. Thus, they sometimes give different interpretations of the same customary rules.[1409] The lack of a coherent body of case-law negatively affects the foreseeability of the core crimes.[1410]

The fourth problem concerns the interplay between national law and international offences. This can transpire in two different forms. National law can serve to implement international offences, but it can also issue contradictory demands. While national implementing law spelling out the international crimes to be prosecuted will generally enhance foreseeability,[1411] both forms of interplay can actually diminish the foreseeability for the individual.

For all criminal law with an international component, rules of national law that are meant to clarify international norms, to complement them, or to enable their national enforcement, may well result in complex referrals to different bodies of law, doing little to enhance the individual's legal certainty.[1412] In the particular case of core crimes law, such national rules can obscure the fact that it is ultimately international law that must determine the content of the rule. Regardless of the content of national law, core crimes law always binds the individual on the international level. Thus, when an international criminalization is transformed into a national law that is incomplete or that differs from its international equivalent, reliance on that national law might lead individuals to erroneously assume that their conduct conforms to international law.[1413]

Likewise, a focus on the legal framework that determines the national enforcement of core crimes can distract attention from the fact that enforcement of these crimes can also take place in other States or by international tribunals and is not dependent on any particular implementation regime.[1414] Thus, even the most thor-

[1409] See above, notes 691-693.

[1410] See ECtHR, *Kokkinakis v. Greece*, 25 May 1993, para. 52 ("An offence must be clearly defined in the law. This condition is satisfied where the individual can know from the wording of the relevant provision and, if need be, with the assistance of the courts' interpretation of it, what acts and omissions will make him liable"). Cf. Wasilkowski 1996, p. 335 (stating that the case-law of the European Court of Justice is what gives European law the character of a system).

[1411] See Stahn 2000, p. 202.

[1412] See for an instructive example Belgium, Court of Cassation, 2 June 1993 (endorsing a prosecution for illegal hunting of deer on the basis of "l'arrêté de l'Exécution régional wallon du 18 avril 1991 fixant l'ouverture et la fermeture de la chasse [...] pris en exécution de la loi du 20 avril 1982 portant approbation du Protocole signé à Luxembourg le 20 juin 1977 modifiant la Convention Benelux en matière de chasse et de protection des oiseaux signée à Bruxelles le 10 juin 1970 et approuvée par la loi du 29 juillet 1971," even though the mentioned 1982 law refers to a no longer existing hunting law from 1882 for the conditions of prosecution). See also Hullu 2000, p. 337-339.

[1413] See Stahn 2000, p. 201.

[1414] Cf. ICTY, Trial Chamber, *Furundzija*, 10 December 1998, para. 155: "Perpetrators of torture acting upon or benefiting from ... national measures may nevertheless be held criminally responsible for torture, whether in a foreign State, or in their own State under a subsequent regime. In short, in spite of possible national authorisation by legislative or judicial bodies to violate the principle banning

ough study of one's own legal system is of limited value when one is later prosecuted in other States or by an international tribunal, as some citizens of the former Yugoslavia and Rwanda have learned.

In addition, national law can impose demands on individuals that contradict those of international criminal law. In fact, as many core crimes are State-sponsored, this might happen more often than not. When soldiers under a legal obligation to follow orders are ordered to commit war crimes, this clearly raises doubts about the foreseeability of the consequences of their conduct. This is especially the case when they are younger and at the bottom of the hierarchy.

However, in recent practice, arguments about a lack of foreseeability have systematically been dismissed, predominantly on the basis of the manifest illegality of the core crimes in question.[1415] In *Delalic*, the ICTY found that "it strains credibility to contend that the accused would not recognise the criminal nature of the acts alleged in the Indictment."[1416] In the *Finta* case (1994), Justice Cory stated that "war crimes or crimes against humanity are so repulsive, so reprehensible, and so well understood that it simply cannot be argued that the definition of crimes against humanity and war crimes are vague or uncertain."[1417] The Italian courts have rejected defenses of ignorance and mistake of law in several contemporary prosecutions of slavery, finding that slavery constitutes a "natural crime."[1418]

These cases show how national and international courts generally see appeals to a lack of foreseeability as incompatible with the gravity of many of the core crimes. They signal that the prohibition of genocide and crimes against humanity under international law can be found as much in positive sources as in their very nature as universal crimes.[1419] At least since Nuremberg and Tokyo, the international community has assumed that the prohibition of these crimes is common knowledge. This assumption is strengthened by the fact that the conduct that constitutes these crimes is criminalized by all legal systems in the world (as murder, assault, etc.). Because genocide, crimes against humanity and the more obvious war crimes are universally condemned, their prohibition can also be presumed to be known to everyone.

---

torture, individuals remain bound to comply with that principle. As the International Military Tribunal at Nuremberg put it: 'individuals have international duties which transcend the national obligations of obedience imposed by the individual State'."

[1415] See Sliedregt 2003, p. 314-315 and 326-331; David 2002, p. 734-738; Mattarollo 2001, p. 27.

[1416] ICTY, Trial Chamber, *Delalic et al.,* 16 November 1998, para. 313. Affirmed in ICTY, Appeals Chamber, *Delalic et al.,* 20 February 2001, para. 179.

[1417] Canada, Supreme Court, *R. v. Imre Finta*, 24 March 1994, Cory J., para. 215: "The definitions of crimes against humanity and war crimes include the gravest, cruellest, most serious and heinous acts that can be perpetrated upon human beings. These crimes, which violate fundamental human values, are vehemently condemned by the citizens of all civilized nations." *See id.*, para. 212.

[1418] See Lenzerini 2000, p. 275 and 277 (citing *inter alia* cases from 1989 and 1993).

[1419] See Canada, Supreme Court, *R. v. Imre Finta*, 24 March 1994, La Forest J. (dissenting), para. 347 ("much of this conduct is illegal under international law because it is considered so obviously morally culpable that it verges on being mala in se").

Consequentially, foreseeability may not necessarily require knowledge of the exact definition of the crime. As one commentator rightly states, the negotiations on the ICC Statute show that the precise content of war crimes and crimes against humanity is not so well known and agreed as is often claimed.[1420] Yet, the differences are generally technical rather than fundamental and more likely to exculpate suspects whose conduct is widely regarded as criminal than to incriminate individuals who are generally seen as innocent. Simply put, the foreseeability of the criminalization of offences such as rape and murder in a non-international armed conflict does not in the first place depend on their precise definition under international law. In *Kunarac*, the ICTY affirmed its earlier holding in *Furundzija* that international law prohibited torture as war crime without defining the specific content of that prohibition.[1421] The assumption that the core crimes need not be defined in detail finds implicit support in various national laws that contain open rules of reference, for example to the laws and customs of war, and has been adopted in several national prosecutions.[1422] Such cases often rely on the manifest illegality of the crimes in question as a more important factor for establishing the foreseeability of their prosecution.

An exception should be made for various war crimes, since not all war crimes are manifestly illegal. Some war crimes can hardly be said to be of a self-evident nature, for example certain acts that do not involve bodily harm.[1423] It seems over-optimistic to assume that the general public recognizes the manifest illegality of e.g. the abuse of the Red Cross signs, which constitutes a grave breach of the Geneva Conventions.[1424] Other war crimes concern choices of a rather technical nature in large military campaigns, for example in the selection of targets. The line between permissible and forbidden belligerent action is not always clear.[1425] Even well-trained armies can face complex questions with debatable outcomes regarding the legality of their operational choices. The fact that war crimes are not of the same status as the other core crimes in this regard finds expression in the ICC Statute,

[1420] See Haveman 2003a, p. 60.

[1421] ICTY, Trial Chamber, *Kunarac, Kovac and Vukovic*, 22 February 2001, para. 468-469.

[1422] See e.g. U.S., Supreme Court, Ex Parte Quirin, 1943, 317 U.S. 1 at 29-30: "It is no objection that Congress in providing for the trial of such offenses has not itself undertaken to codify that branch of international law or to mark its precise boundaries, or to enumerate or define by statute all the acts which that law condemns. […] Congress had the choice of crystallizing in permanent form and in minute detail every offense against the law of war, or of adopting the system of common law applied by military tribunals so far as it should be recognized and deemed applicable by the courts. It chose the latter course."

[1423] Note however that in this regard one cannot make a categorical distinction between crimes involving bodily harm and those that do not, but should judge the manifest illegality of war crimes in the context of specific situations. See Lauterpacht 1944, p. 79 (warning that it is not helpful "to establish a rigid distinction between offences against life and limb and those against property. Pillage, plunder and arbitrary destruction of private and public property may, in their effects be no less cruel and deserving of punishment than acts of personal violence.").

[1424] See Art. 85 (3) sub f AP I.

[1425] See Röling 1979, p. 197 (noting that the destruction of houses may be either a lawful act of war or a war crime, depending on the circumstances); Lauterpacht 1944, p. 74-80.

which designates genocide and crimes against humanity, but not war crimes, as "manifestly unlawful" for the defense of superior orders.[1426] This represents a regression from customary law for those war crimes that are manifestly illegal and may well complicate their prosecution.[1427] Yet, this approach seems appropriate for those war crimes of a less self-evident nature.

In addition to manifest illegality, there is a second notion which mitigates problems of foreseeability for core crimes law. Where defendants perform public functions, often after expert training, they may be held to a higher standard of conduct than the average individual. This is the notion of *Garantenstellung*.[1428] Military personnel can be expected to familiarize themselves with the laws of war, and State officials can be expected to have more knowledge of international law than private citizens.[1429] After all, law may still satisfy the requirement of foreseeability if the person concerned has to take appropriate legal advice to assess, to a degree that is reasonable in the circumstances, the consequences which a given action may entail.[1430] If that can be expected from a private person,[1431] it can *a fortiori* be expected from individuals responsible for the conduct of public affairs, who generally have the opportunity to consult legal advisors prior to the implementation of a given policy. Having the possibility to do so also implies a higher degree of foreseeability. At least to some extent, the same can be said with regard to individuals who exercise *de facto* authority and thereby are in a position to order and commit crimes under international law.[1432] They can be expected to take special care in assessing the risks that such activity entails.

Together, the manifest illegality of many core crimes and the heightened standard of knowledge required from military personnel and civilians in a position of authority leave little room for a succesful defense on the basis of a lack of foreseeability. After all, these two notions complement each other. War crimes that are not manifestly illegal are often committed by military personnel who may be assumed to know the laws of war. Choices in target selection for military campaigns may be complex, but the people making those choices are expected to go to lengths in studying the relevant law in order to make the right decisions.

[1426] See Art. 33 (2) ICC Statute.

[1427] See Cassese 1999, p. 155-157. The lack of manifest illegality opens a way for a limited ground excluding criminal responsibility on the basis of mistake of law or superior orders. See Art. 32 (2) and 33 ICC Statute. See for an elaborate analysis Sliedregt 2003, p. 301-341.

[1428] See Sliedregt 2003, p. 237-238

[1429] See Art. 83 and 87 (2) AP I. See also Sliedregt 2003, p. 304.

[1430] See, among other authorities, ECtHR, *Tolstoy Miloslavsky v. the United Kingdom*, 13 July 1995, para. 37.

[1431] Cf. ECtHR, *Cantoni v. France*, 15 November 1996, para. 35, (supermarket owner was held to have had the duty to seek legal advice in order to establish whether the sale of a given product was allowed). But compare ECJ, *Kolpinghuis Nijmegen BV*, 8 October 1987 (principle of legal certainty precludes reliance on unimplemented EC directive regarding the sale of mineral water for prosecution of café owner).

[1432] See Art. 28 ICC Statute and Zegveld 2002a, p. 121-131.

Still, the manifestly illegal character of the core crimes may be a pivotal factor in determining the foreseeability of their criminal prosecution, but should not be used as a standard answer to routinely deny all appeals to the principle of legality.[1433] Care should be taken to address each *nullum crimen* defense on its merits, taking into account the international nature and special characteristics of the core crimes. This requires an analysis that is not overly narrow, but at the same time respects the line between moral indignation and legal prohibition.[1434] While the former feeds the latter, the grave character of the conduct is not in itself enough to reject a *nullum crimen* defense but can only support the legal analysis. In short, moral blame, criminality under national law and criminality under international law are three different qualifications of human behavior and should be distinguished as such. Admittedly, this is easier said than done.

The fact that complete reliance on manifest illegality can yield problematic results is demonstrated by the German Borderguards case (2001) before the ECtHR.[1435] It should be noted that the following account concerns only the prosecution of the borderguard himself. The prosecution of policy makers responsible for the border regime is not comparable where it concerns the question of foreseeability and should thus be distinguished.[1436]

The applicant had been convicted of intentional homicide in Germany for shooting and killing a fugitive in 1972, when he served as a 20 year old borderguard in former East Germany. At that time, there was a clear gap between East German law and policy. The law demanded proportionality and respect for the right to life and criminalized homicide even if committed pursuant to statute or orders, while State policy required the borderguard to act as he did: borderguards were instructed to shoot fugitives and non-compliance with these orders was punished as negligence of duty.[1437] After the shooting, the borderguard was decorated and rewarded with a financial bonus. Some twenty years later, however, the regime changed and the borderguard was prosecuted for the killing. The German courts differed slightly in their reasoning but predominantly relied on Radbruch's formula, which essentially posits that positive law should not be applied if this will lead to intolerable injustice.[1438] In all instances, the German courts found the shooting to be manifestly illegal and therefore punishment of the borderguard to be justified.[1439]

[1433] See e.g. Klabbers 2003, p. 67 ("[The] very impossibility of defining [the core crimes] comprehensively [...] dictates that the *nullum crimen sine lege* defense need not be taken too seriously.").

[1434] See Boot 2002, p. 177 ("[A[n arbitrary punishment cannot be atoned by moral judgment about the conduct concerned, as the principle of *nullum crimen sine lege* exactly protects against such weighing of interests.").

[1435] ECtHR, *K. – H. W. v. Germany*, 22 March 2001 (hereinafter *KHW. v. Germany*). See Rytter 2003 and Boot 2002, p. 161-170.

[1436] See ECtHR, *Krenz et al. v. Germany*, 22 March 2001.

[1437] *KHW. v. Germany*, para. 71.

[1438] Id., para. 20. See elaborately Hassemer 2002.

[1439] See for the facts, the relevant national law and the proceedings in the German courts *KHW. v. Germany*, para. 10-33 and Rytter 2003, p. 41-45; Schmidt 2002, p. 73-78; Gropp 1996. References to German literature can be found in Arnold *et al.* 2003.

The ECtHR found that the prosecution of the borderguard was not in violation of the principle of legality embodied in Art. 7 ECHR. In a confused and unclear judgment, the Court effectively suggested that the principle of legality can be interpreted more leniently where the most fundamental human rights are at stake[1440] and that individual criminal responsibility can be derived solely from human rights law.[1441] The Court grounded the permissibility of the prosecution on the illegality of the conduct both in national and international law, but at the same time seemed to perform a balancing act between the principle of legality and the right to life. It did not make a clear choice for any of these options, however, and thereby undermined the persuasiveness of all of them.[1442]

In answering the question of whether the prosecution was foreseeable at the time of the shooting, the ECtHR relied on the manifest illegality of East Germany's border control policy. The Court took the view that "even a private soldier could not show total, blind obedience to orders which flagrantly infringed not only the GDR's own legal principles but also internationally recognised human rights."[1443] It cited approvingly the German *Bundesverfassungsgericht* as stating:

> "The decisive factor is that the killing of an unarmed fugitive by sustained fire was, in the circumstances of the case, such a dreadful act, not justifiable by any defence whatsoever, that it must have been immediately apparent and obvious even to an indoctrinated person that it breached the proportionality principle and the elementary prohibition on the taking of human life"[1444]

It is submitted here that the finding that the borderguard could have foreseen the illegality of killing an unarmed fugitive in 1972 is, like the Court's suggestion that individual criminal responsibility can be based solely on human rights instruments, mistaken. National law, which must always be assessed in its totality, including administrative regulations and relevant orders,[1445] did evidently not provide suffi-

---

[1440] See para. 88-90: "[R]egard being had to the pre-eminence of the right to life in all international instruments on the protection of human rights [...] the Court considers that the German courts' strict interpretation of the GDR's legislation in the present case was compatible with Article 7 § 1 of the Convention. [...] The Court considers that a State practice such as the GDR's border-policing policy, which flagrantly infringes human rights and above all the right to life, the supreme value in the international hierarchy of human rights, cannot be covered by the protection of Article 7 § 1 of the Convention. That practice, which emptied of its substance the legislation on which it was supposed to be based, and which was imposed on all organs of the GDR, including its judicial bodies, cannot be described as 'law' within the meaning of Art. 7 of the Convention."

[1441] See para. 103 ("Even supposing that [individual criminal] responsibility cannot be inferred from the above-mentioned international instruments on the protection of human rights, it may be deduced from those instruments when they are read together with Article 95 of the GDR's Criminal Code").

[1442] See for a lucid analysis on this point Rytter 2003, p. 43-59.

[1443] *KHW. v. Germany*, para. 76.

[1444] Id., para. 80. See also Bothe 1996, p. 296.

[1445] In assessing the foreseeability of the law, regard should be had to all relevant sources, including e.g. administrative practice. Cf. ECtHR, *Leander v. Sweden*, 25 February 1987, para. 51 and ECtHR, *Silver and others v. United Kingdom*, 25 February 1983, para. 88-89.

cient notice. On the contrary: it provided notice that disobedience of the order to shoot would be punished. As for international law, the Court found that the human rights to life and freedom of movement sufficiently established the illegality of the shooting.[1446] This argument fails for two reasons.

First, East Germany was a party neither to the ECHR nor to the ICCPR at the material time. The Court therefore needed to take a two-step approach: it derived foreseeability from international human rights law, which should have been known by the borderguard because national law referred to it.[1447] Of course, this selective reliance on national law is unfair, as it disregards the fact that anyone looking to the *totality* of East-German law in 1972 would conclude that apparently the human rights law referred to did not preclude the border control policy under dispute.[1448]

Second, and more importantly, the assertion that the international rights to life and freedom of movement in 1972 unambiguously precluded the border control policy is questionable at the very least. Under the human rights conventions, both rights are subject to exceptions regulated by law[1449] and East Germany was not the only State to provide such exceptions. Certainly at that time, but still today, several States restricted the right of their citizens to leave the country.[1450] The suggested international consensus on the illegality of the use of deadly force against an unarmed fugitive in 1972 is even more doubtful. This can be aptly demonstrated by reference to the American case *Tennessee v. Garner* (1985).[1451] It should be noted in this regard that both *Garner* and *KHW. v. Germany* concerned the killing of fleeing suspects of non-violent crimes: whatever one may think of the GDR legal system at that time, it is undisputed that by crossing the border, fugitives committed an offence against GDR law.

In *Garner*, the U.S. Supreme Court judged the constitutionality of a statute which provided that after giving notice of an intent to arrest, a police officer "may use all the necessary means to effect the arrest."[1452] The specific case concerned the shooting and killing of a burglary suspect in 1974, two years after the shooting that gave rise to the borderguards case. While the lower courts were divided on the matter, the Supreme Court ruled that the use of deadly force against an apparantly unarmed, non-dangerous fleeing suspect violated the U.S. Constitution.[1453] Three

---

1446 *KHW. v. Germany*, para. 92-101 and 105.

1447 Id., para. 104-105: "[A]lthough the event in issue took place in 1972, and therefore before ratification of the International Covenant, he should have known, as an ordinary citizen, that firing on unarmed persons who were merely trying to leave their country infringed fundamental and human rights, as he could not have been unaware of the legislation of his own country. In the light of all of the above considerations, the Court considers that at the time when it was committed the applicant's act constituted an offence defined with sufficient accessibility and foreseeability by the rules of international law on the protection of human rights."

1448 Cf. Pieroth and Jarass 1995, p. 888-889.

1449 See ECHR Art. 2 (2) and Protocol 4, Art. 2 (2); ICCPR Art. 6 (1) and 12 (3).

1450 See generally Jayawickrama 2002, p. 451-457.

1451 U.S., Supreme Court, *Tennessee v. Garner*, 27 March 1985, 105 S.Ct. 1694.

1452 Id., at 1696.

1453 Id., at 1701.

judges dissented, placing the public interest of law enforcement above that of the individual, and finding that "the legitimate interests of the suspect in these circumstances are adequately accommodated by the Tennessee statute: to avoid the use of deadly force and the consequent risk to his life, the suspect need merely obey the valid order to halt."[1454] At that time, numerous American states entertained a similar rule on the use of deadly force as Tennessee.[1455]

Although the U.S. Supreme Court in *Garner* found the use of deadly force to be unreasonable, that conclusion was controversial. This can be seen in the lack of unity in the findings of the different courts and judges involved, the fact that a similar rule on the use of deadly force was in operation in many American states and the way the judgment was received in the legal community.[1456] Moreover, *Garner* was concerned with the constitutionality of the shooting and not the individual criminal responsibility of the police officer. Also, the holding in *Garner* is a narrow one. Even today, it is interpreted in the USA as ruling out the use of deadly force to prevent the escape of an unarmed, non-dangerous *suspect*, but not of an unarmed, non-dangerous *detainee*.[1457] Likewise, in South Africa the killing of an unarmed, non-dangerous suspect of a minor crime was under certain circumstances regarded as justifiable homicide well into the 1990's and its (il)legality is still a matter of some controversy.[1458] Although the situation might be different today,[1459] these examples indicate that in 1972 the illegality under international law of the killing of an unarmed, non-dangerous fugitive was questionable at best.

While the circumstances of the cases were very different, both the Borderguards case and *Garner* turned essentially on the legitimacy of killing an unarmed, non-dangerous fugitive to prevent his escape.[1460] It took the American judiciary more

---

[1454] Id., at 1710-1711: "Against the strong public interests justifying the conduct at issue here must be weighed the individual interests implicated in the use of deadly force by police officers. […] A proper balancing of the interests involved suggests that use of deadly force as a last resort to apprehend a criminal suspect fleeing from the scene of a nighttime burglary is not unreasonable…"

[1455] See id., at 1703-1704.

[1456] See e.g. Allen *et al.* 1995, p. 882 (one of the questions following *Garner* asks "if a person who chooses to communicate by telephone in effect forfeits any privacy interest in the identity of the number dialed, […] why should a person who chooses to be a fleeing burglar not forfeit the right to personal safety?").

[1457] See U.S., Court of Appeals (Fifth Circuit), *Brothers v. Klevenhagen*, 1 August 1994, 28 F.3d 452 (killing of an unarmed, non-dangerous pretrial detainee to prevent his escape is not constitutionally unreasonable). See on this case White III 1995.

[1458] See Burchell 2000, p. 212.

[1459] See ECtHR, *Nachova and others v. Bulgaria*, 26 February 2004, para. 103: "[B]alanced against the imperative need to preserve life as a fundamental value, the legitimate aim of effecting a lawful arrest cannot justify putting human life at risk where the fugitive has committed a non-violent offence and does not pose a threat to anyone. Any other approach would be incompatible with the basic principles of democratic societies, as universally accepted today…"

[1460] See *KHW. v. Germany*, para. 17 ("[T]he [German] Regional Court held that, even for a private soldier, it should have been obvious that firing at an unarmed person infringed the duty of humanity.") and Concurring Opinion of Judge Bratza, joined by Judge Vajic ("I can find no reason to depart from the considered opinion of the national courts that opening fire on a defenceless person, who was attempting to swim away from East-Berlin and who posed no threat to life or limb, so clearly breached

than ten years to reach a final decision in that specific case, without once having mentioned the individual criminal responsibility of the police officer involved or the imperatives of international human rights law. In this light, it seems rather unreasonable to expect a 20-year old borderguard, at the bottom of the hierarchy and subject to disciplinary proceedings, to conclude that the border control policy regulated by national law evidently fell outside the legitimate exeptions to the right to life and freedom of movement and should therefore not be executed.

In sum, the borderguards case illustrates how anger over an immoral act or regime can tempt us to blur the line between moral indignation and legal prohibition under the guise of manifest illegality. At the same time, it is open to discussion whether his conduct can be classified as a crime against humanity.[1461] This should warn us that even for core crimes, arguments concerning a lack of foreseeability cannot be rejected out of hand.[1462]

But while the borderguards case cautions against automatic reliance on the manifest illegality of core crimes, it is not a reason to discard the notion altogether. The circumstances of the case – in particular its highly institutionalized setting, the law enforcement character of the act and the fact that comparable use of deadly force is not uncommon in other situations – set it apart from the great majority of core crimes. Most core crimes involve acts of cruelty, discriminatory acts against particular groups, or other acts that are criminalized everywhere. Their manifest illegality is therefore a very different matter, as suggested by the fact that they are generally concealed rather than celebrated in public after the fact.[1463] It is hard to disagree with the finding of the ICTR in judging the discriminatory acts of sexual violence, beatings and murders in *Akayesu* that "it is clear that the authors of such egregious violations must incur individual criminal responsibility for their deeds."[1464] The same is true for most core crimes.

5.4 Penalties

The principle *nulla poena sine lege* prohibits retroactive penalties. It is undisputed that the principle forbids the imposition of heavier punishment then the one applicable at the time of the crime.[1465] The status of another requirement commonly

any principle of proportionality that it was foreseeable that it violated the legal prohibition on killing.").

[1461] The ECtHR did not reach a decision on this point. See *KHW. v. Germany*, para. 106. The judges were divided on this question in their individual opinions. Compare Concurring Opinion Judge Loucaides (concluding that the killing constituted a crime against humanity) with Partly Dissenting Opinion of Judge Cabral Barreto and Partly Dissenting Opinion of Judge Pellonpää, joined by Judge Zupancic.

[1462] See Osiel 1999. Cf. Stirling-Zanda 2001, p. 91-94.

[1463] Although core crimes perpetrators, particularly those in the military, are regularly praised and rewarded in their own States, such public appraisal is normally confined to the individuals involved and not the specific crimes they have committed.

[1464] ICTR, Trial Chamber, *Akayesu*, 2 September 1998, para. 616.

[1465] See Universal Declaration of Human Rights, Art. 11 (2); ECHR Art. 7 (1); ICCPR Art. 15 (1); IACHR Art. 9. See also e.g. HRC, *Casafranca v. Peru*, Views of the Human Rights Committee under

attributed to the *nulla poena* principle[1466] is less clear under international law: the mandatory indication of the applicable penalties in law. Most human rights instruments do not formulate any demands regarding specificity or form of the determination of the penalty. The relevant provisions require a definition of the crime in law, but their demands regarding penalties are generally limited to the prohibition of heavier penalties than those applicable at the time of the crime.[1467] Since doctrine generally perceives the *nulla poena* principle as a major obstacle to direct application of international criminal law,[1468] I will treat it in some detail.

In practice, roughly four approaches can be discerned regarding the requirement of an indication of the penalty for core crimes. First, a strict approach to the *nulla poena* principle sees a clear indication in law of the penalty as being a prerequisite for prosecution, also for the core crimes. As an example of this approach, the preamble to Rwanda's law on the national prosecution of the international crimes committed in the 1990's states that prosecutions must be based on the national penal code because the relevant international conventions lack corresponding penalties.[1469] However, it should be noted that the sources referred to before reaching that conclusion include the national principle of legality in Rwanda's 1991 Constitution, but not the international principle of legality.[1470]

---

the Optional Protocol to the International Covenant on Civil and Political Rights, (Communication No. 981/2001) (September 19, 2003), para. 7.4; ECtHR, *Jamil v. France*, 25 May 1995, para. 34-36. But see ICTY, Trial Chamber, *Delalic et al.*, 16 November 1998, para. 1210-1212. The prohibition of heavier penalties should not be confused with the mandatory application of lighter penalties enacted after the crime, the *lex mitior* principle. While the two are often grouped together, for example in Art. 15 (1) ICCPR, the *lex mitior* principle is distinct from the *nulla poena* principle.

1466 See Werle 2003, p. 89; Kittichaisaree 2001, p. 14.

1467 See provisions cited above, note 1465.

1468 See e.g. Peyró 2003, p. 83; Choukr 2002, p. 336; Massé 1998, p. 839-840. But see Cassese 2003a, p. 157.

1469 See Organic Law No. 40/2000 of January 26, 2001 setting up "Gacaca Jurisdictions" and organising prosecutions for offences constituting the crime of genocide or crimes against humanity, committed between October 1, 1990 and December 31, 1994, Preamble:
"Given that the acts committed are offenses provided for and punished by the Penal Code as well as the crime of genocide or crimes against humanity;
Given that the December 9, 1948 Convention on the Prevention and Suppression of the Crime of Genocide, the August 12, 1949 Geneva Convention, relative to the Protection of Civilian Persons in Time of War and its additional protocols, and the November 26, 1968 Convention on the Non-Applicability of Statutory Limitations to War Crimes and Crimes against Humanity;
Given that Rwanda has ratified those three conventions and published them in the Official Gazette of the Republic of Rwanda without having provided penalties for these crimes;
Whereas, consequently, prosecutions must be based on the Penal Code;"
See also Organic Law No. 08/96 of August 30, 1996 on the organisation of prosecutions for offences constituting the crime of genocide or crimes against humanity, committed between 1 October 1990 and 31 December 1994, preamble. Cited in Schabas 2003b, footnote 42.

1470 Id., referring to Rwanda's 1991 Constitution, Art. 12, which reads in relevant part:
"[...]
(2) The liberty of the human being shall be inviolable; no one may be prosecuted, arrested, imprisoned, or convicted other than in the cases prescribed by the law in effect at the time of the perpetrated act and within the forms prescribed by that law.
(3) No infraction may be punished by penalties which were not prescribed by law before it was committed."

The second approach to the *nulla poena* principle requires a clear indication of the penalty, but allows recourse to relevant ordinary crimes in force at the time of the offence to "borrow" such an indication.[1471] Thus, it allows punishment for the core crimes under application of the penalties proscribed for ordinary crimes such as murder and assault. The drafters of the statutes of the ICTY and the ICTR, although divided on this question,[1472] ultimately decided to demand both tribunals to "have recourse to the general practice regarding prison sentences" in the courts of the countries concerned.[1473] While the language of these provisions leaves open the question of whether this recourse to national penalties is binding or merely a policy choice, the drafting history indicates that the aim of the proposers was to satisfy the *nulla poena* principle.[1474]

Yet both *ad hoc* tribunals squarely rejected the notion that the *nulla poena* principle requires recourse to national penalties.[1475] In *Erdemovic*, the ICTY stated that:

> "It might be argued that the reference to the general practice regarding prison sentences is required by the principle *nullum crimen nulla poena sine lege.* Justifying the reference to this practice by that principle, however, would mean not recognising the criminal nature universally attached to crimes against humanity or, at best, would render such a reference superfluous. The Trial Chamber has, in fact, demonstrated that crimes against humanity are a well established part of the international legal order and have incurred the severest penalties. It would therefore be a mistake to interpret this reference by the principle of legality…."[1476]

In contravention of the intentions of the proposers of the provision, both the ICTY[1477] and the ICTR[1478] have consistently held that the recourse to national sentencing practice is not required by the *nulla poena* principle, but rather only constitutes a non-binding guideline.[1479]

Other indications for support or opposition of the second approach are ambiguous. No recourse to national penalties is required under the ICC Statute. However, the Statute contains a general provision on penalties[1480] and has no retroactive application. Therefore, the *nulla poena* question does not arise as was the case for the *ad hoc* tribunals. Some national judgments assert that the *nulla poena* principle

---

[1471] See Mattarollo 2001, p. 27-28. Cf. O'Keefe 2002, p. 327-333.

[1472] See Schabas 1997, p. 469-473.

[1473] See Statute ICTY, Art. 24 (1) and Statute ICTR, Art. 23 (1).

[1474] See Schabas 1997, p. 469-473 and 482.

[1475] See Schabas 2000c, p. 528-536.

[1476] ICTY, Trial Chamber I, *Erdemovic* Sentencing Judgment, 29 November 1996, para. 38.

[1477] See ICTY, *Delalic et al.*, Appeal, 20 february 2001, para. 813; ICTY, Trial Chamber I, *Erdemovic* Sentencing Judgment, 29 November 1996, para. 40.

[1478] See *Prosecutor v. Serushago,* Case No. ICTR-98-39-A (Appeals Chamber), April 6, 2000, para. 30.

[1479] See Lamb 2001, p. 758-762.

[1480] See Art. 77 ICC Statute.

may be satisfied by application of the penalty provisions of national criminal law. Yet the value of most of these findings for international law is limited, as explained above, due to the convergence of national and international principles of legality. For example, the Belgian *Pinochet* judgment (1998) suggested recourse to the penalties provided for corresponding offences in national law, but explicitly based that requirement on the national principle of legality.[1481] It thus provides an indication of the content of the Belgian, but not necessarily the international formulation of the *nulla poena* principle.

The third approach minimizes the required indication of the penalty for the core crimes, sometimes to the point of discarding it altogether. What the principle requires, the argument essentially posits, is a warning that there will be a penalty, or perhaps a broad indication of its form or severity, but not a precise description.[1482] Thus, in its strongest form this approach effectively discards the strict condition of an indication of the penalty and merely requires an indication of criminality. After all, conduct can be criminalized without specification of a corresponding penalty.[1483] The ILC has in its work on the Draft Codes of Crimes Against the Peace and Security of Mankind adhered to the view that an indication of criminality, rather than a precise penalty, suffices for international crimes. Accordingly, the different Draft Codes contain only minimal penalty provisions.[1484] In its commentary on the 1996 Draft Code, the ILC asserted that "it is, in any event, not necessary for an individual to know in advance the precise punishment so long as the actions constitute a crime of extreme gravity for which there will be severe punishment."[1485] Various States, however, objected to this position.[1486]

Traditionally, many different States accepted a minimal indication of penalties, or even a lack thereof, for all crimes. Common law systems have long accepted the power of the courts to determine the applicable penalties where the law was si-

---

[1481] See Belgian *Pinochet*, para. 3.3.2.

[1482] See Paust 1997a, p. 664 and Paust 1997b, p. 321; Triffterer 1966, p. 139. Cf. Schabas 2000c, p. 538-539.

[1483] See ICTY, Appeals Chamber, *Delalic et al.,* 20 February 2001, para. 162-163; ICTY, Appeals Chamber, *Tadic, Decision on the Defence Motion for Interlocutory Appeal on Jurisdiction*, 2 October 1995, para. 128. See also Massé 1998, p. 839.

[1484] See Art. 3 Draft Code 1996: "An individual who is responsible for a crime against the peace and security of mankind shall be liable to punishment. The punishment shall be commensurate with the character and gravity of the crime."
Art. 3 (1) Draft Code 1991: "An individual who commits a crime against the peace and security of mankind is responsible therefor and is liable to punishment."
Art. 5 Draft Code 1951: "The penalty for any offence in this Code shall be determined by the tribunal exercising jurisdiction over the individual accuse, taking into account the gravity of the offence." (Deleted in 1954. See Triffterer 1966, p. 77-78.)

[1485] See Art. 3 Draft Code 1996, Comment 7: "It is, in any event, not necessary for an individual to know in advance the precise punishment so long as the actions constitute a crime of extreme gravity for which there will be severe punishment. This is in accord with the precedent of punishment for a crime under customary international law or general principles of law as recognized in the Nürnberg Judgement and in article 15 (2) of the International Covenant on Civil and Political Rights."

[1486] See Boot 2002, p. 319-321; Schabas 2000c, p. 523-524.

lent.[1487] In legal systems based on Islamic law, the courts still have discretion to apply unspecified penalties for a particular category of offenses (*Ta'azir*) whereas for other categories the penalties are fixed.[1488] Yet, most States, including common law systems,[1489] today take the view that not only the crime but also the applicable penalties require definition in law. The ECtHR has held unambiguously that, as a general rule, penalties must be defined by law.[1490] The IACtHR, on the other hand, has suggested that a broad indication of the punishment to be incurred might suffice.[1491]

For the core crimes, however, the "minimalist" approach finds support in practice until the present day. Several post-WW II prosecutions set aside the penalty requirement.[1492] The Dutch prosecution of *Rauter* (1949), resulting in his death sentence, discarded the *nulla poena* argument because important interests of justice "do not permit that extremely serious violations of generally accepted principles of international law (the criminal character of which was already established beyond doubt at the time they were committed), should not be considered punishable solely on the ground that a previous threat of punishment was absent."[1493] Some more recent national judgments regarding core crimes have likewise dismissed objections based on the *nulla poena* principle.[1494]

[1487] See e.g. U.S., Court of Oyer and Terminer, at Philadelphia, *Respublica v. De Longchamps*, October Sessions, 1784, 1 Dall. 111 at 116 ("Punishments [...] must be such as the laws expressly prescribe; or where no stated or fixed judgment is directed, according to the legal direction of the court;").

[1488] See Baderin 2003, p. 78-79 and Lambert-Abdelgawad 2002, p. 525.

[1489] See e.g. U.S., *Cook v. Commonwealth*, 1995, 20 Va. App. 510 (defendant could not be convicted for second-degree murder because legislator had proscribed conduct but by oversight omitted a corresponding penalty); U.S., *Court of Appeal, State v. LaMaster*, 1991, 811 S.W.2d 837; South-Africa, Transvaal Provincial Division, S v. Theledi, 7 October 1991, [1993] 2 SA 402. But see Zambia, High Court, *Thomas James v. State*, 18 April 1974, 8 The comparative and international law journal of Southern Africa 152 at 154 (finding that a legal provision can amount to a criminalization in the absence of a penalty and that the breach of a prohibition in unambiguous and imperative terms regulating a matter of "public grievance," must be held an offence unless the contrary intention is manifest); U.S., Court of Appeal, *Nunley v. State*, 2001, 26 P.3d 1113.

[1490] See ECtHR, *Coëme and Others v. Belgium*, 22 June 2000, para. 145 ("[O]ffences and the relevant penalties must be clearly defined by law."); ECtHR, *C.R. v. the United Kingdom*, 27 October 1995, para. 33 ("[O]nly the law can [...] prescribe a penalty").

[1491] See IACtHR, *Castillo Petruzzi et al.*, 30 May 1999, para. 121 ("This Court has stated that the principle of penal legality 'means a clear definition of the criminalized conduct, establishing its elements and the factors that distinguish it from behaviors that are either not punishable offences or are punishable but not with imprisonment'.").

[1492] See, p. 469; United Nations War Crimes Commission 1947, Vol. 15, p. 166-169. See also Poland, Voivodship Court of Warsaw, *In re Koch*, 9 March 1959, 30 ILR 496 at 504 ("Hague Convention No. IV of 1907 contains legal rules with penal sanctions and therefore there is no room for objection based on the principle *nulla poena sine lege*." It is, however, unclear from the judgment where the Polish court in this case found these penal sanctions, since the Hague Convention does not contain explicit provisions to that effect.).

[1493] Netherlands, Bijzondere Raad van Cassatie, *In re Rauter*, 12 January 1949, Annual Digest 1949, p. 526, at 543.

[1494] See e.g. Austria, Supreme Court (Oberster Gerichtshof), Cvjetkovic, 13 July 1994, available at http://www.ris.bka.gv.at/ (finding that the acts in question were contrary to humanitarian law, *inter alia*

The ECtHR adhered to the minimalist approach for core crimes in *Naletilic* (2000). As set out above, the ECtHR held that a defendant accused of crimes against humanity and war crimes before the ICTY could not rely on the prohibition of heavier penalties in Art. 7 (1) ECHR.[1495] Instead, the Court held, if the principle of legality in the ECHR applied to this case at all, Art. 7 (2) was the relevant clause. This clause does not contain any requirements about the penalty to be applied. It is noteworthy that the ECtHR has also effectively set aside the *nulla poena* principle in a few cases involving ordinary crimes. In its well-known judgments regarding the ability to punish marital rape in the United Kingdom, the Court focused on the object and purpose of the principle of legality to avoid strict scrutiny of its different elements.[1496] In doing so, it minimized the *nulla poena* principle, concentrating instead on the question of foreseeability.[1497] The ECtHR appealed to the manifest illegality of the conduct in question,[1498] perhaps implying like the Dutch court in *Rauter* that the *nulla poena* principle should be interpreted less strictly for particular serious crimes, like the core crimes, if a strict interpretation would preclude their punishment altogether.

Finally, it has been argued that the *nulla poena* principle does require an indication of the penalty, but that this condition is satisfied for the core crimes by a general principle of international law stating that the most serious crimes deserve the most severe penalties available.[1499] Accordingly, this approach would allow national courts to punish the core crimes on the basis of international criminal law, under application of the strictest penalties available in their national laws. Like the minimalist approach, the appeal to a general principle of the most severe penalties for the gravest crimes can be traced back to post-WW II jurisprudence.[1500] The Norwegian Supreme Court, for example, held in *Klinge* (1946) that according to the laws and customs of war, "war crimes can be punished by the most severe penalties, including the death penalty. In other words, the criminal character of the acts dealt with in the present case as well as the degree of punishment are already laid down in International Law in the rules relating to the laws and customs of war."[1501] This approach still finds support in practice. The ICTY relied on "the

the Geneva Conventions "sodaß – der Beschwerde zuwider – der Grundsatz "nulla poena sine lege" vorliegend gar nicht zutrifft"); Canada, Supreme Court, *R. v. Imre Finta*, 24 March 1994, Cory J., para. 218-227.

[1495] See above, note 1340 and accompanying text.

[1496] See ECtHR, *C.R. v. the United Kingdom*, 27 October 1995, para. 42-43.

[1497] See Schabas 1997, p. 474-475.

[1498] ECtHR, *C.R. v. the United Kingdom*, 27 October 1995, para. 42.

[1499] See e.g. Peyró 2003, p. 83; Schabas 1997, p. 474. But compare Schabas 2003b, p. 62 (stating that the phrase "effective penalties" in the Genocide convention is "hardly enough to respect the principle of legality").

[1500] See United Nations War Crimes Commission 1947, Vol. 15, p. 200 (citing several national prosecutions where the death penalty was imposed for non-homicidal crimes, such as torture and rape, and concluding that "[i]nternational law lays down that a war criminal may be punished with death whatever crime he may have committed.").

[1501] Norway, Supreme Court, Klinge, 27 February 1946, Annual Digest 1946, p. 262 at 263.

general principle of law internationally recognised by the community of nations whereby the most severe penalties may be imposed for crimes against humanity" in *Erdemovic*[1502] and on similar reasoning in *Delalic*.[1503] The ICTR seemed to endorse this approach in more implicit terms in *Akayesu*.[1504]

To sum up, there are strongly divergent interpretations of the *nulla poena* principle. While some regard an indication in law of the specific penalty to be incurred as a *conditio sine qua non* for core crimes prosecutions, others dispute the applicability of this requirement altogether. State practice reflects this divergence also in national legislation regarding the core crimes. A cursory survey reveals that national legal systems differ considerably in the specificity of penalties for the core crimes. Most States determine maximum penalties, many of them set minimum penalties[1505] and they all allow for considerable, if differing degrees of discretion in the judicial determination of the penalty in specific cases.[1506] Some national laws contain very broad penalty provisions.[1507] The Swiss Military Penal Code, for example, provides in Art. 109:

> "Violations of the Laws of War:
> (1) Whoever acts contrary to the provisions of any international agreement governing the laws of war or the protection of persons and property, or whoever acts in violation of any other recognized law or custom of war shall be punished with imprisonment except in cases where other provisions involving more severe sanctions are applicable. For offences of high gravity the penalty is penal servitude.
> (2) For offences of little gravity, the punishment can consist of a disciplinary sanction."[1508]

[1502] ICTY, Trial Chamber I, *Erdemovic* Sentencing Judgment, 29 November 1996, para. 40.

[1503] ICTY, Appeals Chamber, *Delalic et al.,* 20 February 2001, para. 817: "There can be no doubt that the maximum sentence permissible under the Rules ("imprisonment for [...] the remainder of a convicted person's life") for crimes prosecuted before the Tribunal, and any sentence up to this, does not violate the principle of *nulla poena sine lege*. There can be no doubt that the accused must have been aware of the fact that the crimes for which they were indicted are the most serious violations of international humanitarian law, punishable by the most severe penalties."

[1504] ICTR, *Akayesu*, Sentencing Judgment, 2 October 1998 ("Rwanda like all States which have incorporated crimes against humanity or genocide in their domestic legislation has envisaged the most severe penalties in its criminal legislation for these crimes.").

[1505] See on the tension between minimum penalties and human rights law Jayawickrama 2002, p. 340-343.

[1506] See The Punishment of Serious Crimes, 2003, Sieber, Vol. I, p. 90-124.

[1507] See e.g. Art. 127 Egyptian Penal Code (generally understood to cover cases of torture, indicating a penalty of imprisonment of unspecified duration for public officials imposing excessive or unlawful punishment); Art. 20 (2) Bangladesh's International Crimes (Tribunals) Act 1973 (Act No. XIX of 19 July 1973) (providing for a "sentence of death or such other punishment proportionate to the gravity of the crime as appears to the Tribunal to be just and proper." Note, however, that no prosecutions have ever been undertaken on the basis of this act). See on Art. 127 Egyptian Penal Code also Abdelgawad 2002, p. 377.

[1508] Translation taken from Ziegler 1998, note 7.

Obviously, the rather open categorization of offences according to their gravity, with different corresponding penalties and the fact that only the form of punishment is indicated but not the duration, starkly limit the predictability of the punishment to be incurred.[1509]

The same schism as in national legislation is found in the work of the ILC,[1510] and the drafting process of the ICTY Statute, where some States proposed general penalty provisions in line with the minimalist approach, determining for example that "penalties shall be based on 'general principles' of law as they exist in the world's major legal systems" or that the Tribunal would "have the power to sentence convicted persons to imprisonment or other appropriate punishment."[1511] Yet, other States found such general provisions unacceptable and wanted the ICTY to derive the penalties from the criminal law and practice of the Former Yugoslavia.[1512] While a provision to that effect was ultimately included in the Statute, the ICTY in its judgments subsequently relativized the need for and binding character of recourse to national law.

But in the final analysis, State practice suggests that the principle of legality under customary international law does not preclude the prosecution of the core crimes in the absence of specified penalties. When distinguishing the international principle of legality from its stricter national counterparts, it seems that no court has declared punishment of a core crime inadmissible on the basis of the *nulla poena* principle in international law.[1513] Instead, there is ample authority for the proposition that a broad indication of the applicable punishment suffices for the prosecution of core crimes, or that these crimes by definition attract (up to) the highest available penalties. In practice, the result of these two approaches is more or less the same, namely broad sentencing discretion for the courts. Moreover, there also is considerable support for the proposition that core crimes may be punished under recourse to the penalty provisions of relevant ordinary crimes. While various States argue for a stricter approach to the applicable penalties, at present their views seem to be no more than aspirational.[1514]

From a policy perspective, it may be questioned whether a stricter interpretation of the *nulla poena* principle is desirable. After all, the admissibility of prosecutions on the basis of unwritten law[1515] has important consequences for the indication of

---

1509 See Ziegler 1997, p. 580 ("[T]he judge remains free to mete out a penalty from a mere three days of imprisonment to 20 years of penal servitude, according to whether he finds a case of ordinary or high gravity and the mitigating circumstances he establishes.").

1510 See above, note 1486.

1511 See Schabas 1997, p. 473.

1512 See above, note 1474.

1513 One of the dissenting judges of the Argentinean Supreme Court in the extradition proceedings concerning Erich Priebke asserted that the *nulla poena* principle prevented extradition or prosecution under direct application of international criminal law. The majority of the Supreme Court, however, rejected this approach. See Mattarollo 2001, p. 36-37 and above, Chapter II, para. 3.3.m.

1514 See on the limited weight of the provisions of the ICC Statute in this regard above, text preceding note 1362.

1515 See above, para. 5.1.

the penalty. Since international law does not demand a written provision for the prosecution of core crimes, the required precision of the penalty can likewise only be limited. Thus, the characteristics of core crimes law oppose too strict a standard for the provision of penalties. This is not necessarily problematic. If States regard a broad indication of the sort of punishment as sufficient, as in Art. 109 Swiss Military Penal Code and some other national laws, it seems overly formalistic to hold the imposition of imprisonment under customary international law in violation of the principle of legality. While national law generally curtails the discretion of the courts by additional rules and jurisprudence, it often leaves them considerable latitude as well.

On the other hand, the principle that core crimes attract the highest penalties seems unfit for "minor" war crimes. While national laws generally impose the highest penalties for at least homicidal acts that amount to core crimes, this is often not the case for acts that do not involve bodily harm, such as property crimes (pillage) and abuse of internationally protected emblems. Most national laws impose considerably lower sentences than the maximum for such crimes, and some only impose solely a fine rather than imprisonment.[1516] Therefore, complete discretion for national courts to punish such crimes with any penalty up to the maximum seems problematic. Yet this problem may be mitigated to some extent by the possibility for national courts to derive sentencing directions for core crimes from the practice of international and other national courts, and the rules of the ICC.[1517]

Finally, it is submitted here that mandatory resort to penalties attached to relevant ordinary crimes has rightfully been rejected by the *ad hoc* tribunals. This sentencing approach is not only unnecessary, but even harmful for the development of international criminal law as it denies its ability to function independently. Moreover, it is doubtful whether this approach provides an appropriate answer to *nulla poena* concerns. The crimes from which penalties are "borrowed" might be superficially comparable, but ultimately they are different crimes.[1518] This is shown most clearly in cases based on universal jurisdiction, where the ordinary crimes which provide the penalties can simply not apply to the conduct to be punished. If, for example, General Pinochet had been prosecuted in Belgium under application of the penalties of corresponding crimes as suggested, his judges would have had to apply the penalty provisions of either Belgian ordinary crimes that did not apply to conduct in Chile, or Chilean ordinary crimes that could not be prosecuted in Belgium. It can be asked whether such a course furthers either the legal certainty of the individual or the delimitation of State power.

[1516] See e.g. Art. 13 of India's Geneva Conventions Act, 1960.

[1517] See Peglau 2001a. See on the sentencing regulations of the ICC Peglau 2001b.

[1518] See above Chapter V, para. 4.

6. Which Offences are Directly Applicable?

What now remains is a translation of the general international rule into a more specific assessment of core crimes law. In other words, when does international criminalization of the core crimes meet the requirements of the international principle of legality? Since international law does not impose firm conditions for the direct application of its rules in general,[1519] the principle of legality constitutes international law's threshold test for the direct application of core crimes law in national courts.

International law's lack of more general demands for direct application finds illustration in the parallel applicability of international rules and national implementing laws. The fact that the legislature has adopted implementing legislation for a treaty does not rule out its simultaneous direct application through a general rule of reference.[1520] Nor does a domestic implementation clause in a treaty prevent the direct applicability of its provisions.[1521] There are good practical reasons why many treaties specifically call for legislative action by the States Parties, but that does not make domestic legislation a necessary condition for the effectuation of those treaties in national courts. In general, national implementation of a treaty may improve its effectuation, and in various States legislative action is necessary to make the treaty effective. In the particular case of international offences, the provision of specified penalties in national law is not necessary, but certainly desirable. Yet, those practical reasons favoring implementing legislation do not rule out the direct application of international rules in those States whose constitutional framework allows it, neither for public international law in general nor for international criminal law.[1522] Thus, the fact that the Genocide Convention contains a domestic implementation clause in Art. 5 does not rule out the direct application of its criminalization of genocide.[1523]

As concluded above, the principle of legality in international law requires both a sufficiently specific definition of an act and a clear indication that it attracts individual criminal responsibility.[1524] It does, however, neither require a written law nor a specification of the precise penalty to be applied. Where national criminal law contains a specific rule of reference to international core crimes law, these conditions will almost always be met.

The harder question is at what stage international offences are sufficiently developed to form the basis for core crimes prosecutions in the absence of a specific rule of reference in national law (general direct application). The test for answering it is complex and certainly does not lie in a comparison to the classic formulation of

---

[1519] See above, p. 7-8.

[1520] Cf. U.S., *Supreme Court, Sosa v. Alvarez-Machain*, 29 June 2004, 124 S.Ct. 2739 at 2760.

[1521] See Paust 1991, p. 366-367; Iwasawa 1986, p. 660. But see Vandermeersch 2002b, p. 593.

[1522] See Triffterer 1966, p. 68 and 85. Cf. Peyró 2003, p. 22-25.

[1523] See Simma and Paulus 1999, p. 308; Triffterer 1966, p. 65-68. Cf. Iwasawa 1986, p. 660. But see Schmidt 2002, p. 138; Schabas 2000b, p. 350; Wolfrum 1996, p. 242.

[1524] Cf. Triffterer 1966, p. 30-34.

offences in national criminal law. International law can well define an act and make it punishable without explicitly mentioning criminal proceedings, courts or penalties.[1525] On the other hand, not every act that is prohibited under international law attracts individual criminal responsibility. Moreover, one must be careful to distinguish acts that are criminal under international law from those for which international law merely imposes an obligation on States to criminalize them without doing so itself.

For customary international law, one must look to a vast array of material sources.[1526] In particular, one should note that the definition of the act and its criminalization may be contained in separate material sources. An act may be defined in a treaty, while its criminality stems from the fact that it has consistently been prosecuted in national courts or prohibited in military manuals.[1527] At present, the ICC Statute and the corresponding Elements of Crimes provide a catalogue of core crimes under customary international law that is on the whole highly authoritative. Yet these instruments include some offences that are of doubtful customary status and omit others that are well-established.[1528] Thus, the ICC Statute provides important guidance but can not substitute for the broader body of customary international law.

The analysis of whether customary international law attaches individual criminal responsibility to a particular act is complicated and may lead to debatable outcomes. An apt illustration of this point is found in the ICTY case of *Vasiljevic*, a rare example of a succesful *nullum crimen* defense in a core crimes prosecution.[1529] In *Tadic*, the ICTY had found that "the acts proscribed by common Article 3 [Geneva Conventions] constitute criminal offences under international law"[1530] and in *Blaskic* that the offence of violence to life and person, contained in Common Art. 3 Geneva Conventions, "is a broad offence which, at first glance, encompasses murder, mutilation, cruel treatment and torture and which is accordingly defined by the cumulation of the elements of these specific offences."[1531] In *Vasiljevic*, however, the Trial Chamber departed from its earlier holdings and found the offence of violence to life and person to be insufficiently defined under customary international law.[1532] There-

[1525] See ICTY, Trial Chamber, *Tadic, Decision on the Defence Motion on Jurisdiction*, 10 August 1995, para. 70 ("The individual criminal responsibility of the violator need not be explicitly stated in a convention for its provisions to entail individual criminal liability."). See also Cassese 2003a, p. 50.

[1526] See Cassese 2003a, p. 50-53.

[1527] See ICTY, Appeals Chamber, *Tadic, Decision on the Defence Motion for Interlocutory Appeal on Jurisdiction*, 2 October 1995, para. 128-129. See also ICTY, Appeals Chamber, *Delalic et al.*, 20 February 2001, para. 161; Netherlands, Bijzondere Raad van Cassatie, *In re Rauter*, 12 January 1949, Annual Digest 1949, p. 526, p. 542.

[1528] See above, note 56.

[1529] ICTY, Trial Chamber, *Vasiljevic*, 29 November 2002.

[1530] ICTY, Trial Chamber, *Tadic, Decision on the Defence Motion on Jurisdiction*, 10 August 1995, para. 67. See also ICTY, Appeals Chamber, *Tadic, Decision on the Defence Motion for Interlocutory Appeal on Jurisdiction*, 2 October 1995, para. 128-137.

[1531] ICTY, Trial Chamber, *Blaskic*, 3 March 2000, para. 182.

[1532] ICTY, Trial Chamber, *Vasiljevic*, 29 November 2002, para. 193-204.

fore, it could not be charged as a violation of the laws and customs of war under Art. 3 ICTY Statute.

The Trial Chamber noted that "[b]oth 'life' and the 'person' are protected in various ways by international humanitarian law."[1533] Yet, "[I]n the absence of any clear indication in the practice of states as to what the definition of the offence of 'violence to life and person' identified in the Statute may be under customary law, the Trial Chamber is not satisfied that such an offence giving rise to individual criminal responsibility exists under that body of law."[1534] The Trial Chamber did convict the defendant for his acts on charges of persecution as a crime against humanity and murder as a violation of the laws and customs of war.[1535] Thus, it disputed solely the criminality of violence to the life and person under customary international law, not the foreseeability of prosecution for the acts under scrutiny. It should further be noted that *Vasiljevic* is not representative of the case law of the ICTY and has been strongly criticized by several commentators.[1536] Still, the case illustrates the complexities of establishing individual criminal responsibility under customary international law.

If treaty-based criminalization of the core crimes is to be directly applied in its own right, *id est* not as evidence of customary law, it must contain both the definition of the act and an indication of its criminality. If that is the case, no other demands need to be fulfilled. The Genocide Convention, for example, defines genocidal acts (Art. 2 and 3) and declares them to be "crime[s] under international law" (Art. 1) and "punishable" (Art. 3). Of course, national law may well rule out direct application of the Genocide Convention and in practice national courts will more often than not regard it as an inadequate legal basis for prosecution.[1537] To satisfy the international principle of legality, however, a criminalization such as this one suffices, despite the fact that it is not formulated like the provisions found in most national criminal codes.[1538]

The Convention on the Prohibition of the Development, Production, Stockpiling and Use of Chemical Weapons and on their Destruction (1993), on the other hand, provides that each State Party shall "prohibit natural and legal persons anywhere on its territory or in any other place under its jurisdiction as recognized by international law from undertaking any activity prohibited to a State Party under this Convention, including enacting penal legislation with respect to such activity"[1539] as well as "extend its penal legislation enacted under subparagraph (a) to any activity prohibited to a State Party under this Convention undertaken anywhere by natural persons, possessing its nationality, in conformity with international law."[1540] This

[1533] Id., para. 195.
[1534] Id., para. 203.
[1535] Id., para. 307.
[1536] See Cassese 2004b; Weckel and Chaouch Helel 2003, p. 751-759.
[1537] See e.g. above, p. 65 (France) and note 1469 (Rwanda). But compare to p. 73 (Argentina).
[1538] See above, note 1523.
[1539] Art. VII (1) sub a.
[1540] Art. VII (1) sub c.

language does not directly criminalize the use of – and various other acts concerning – chemical weapons, but merely obliges States Parties to do so. The 1993 Convention thus contains a duty to criminalize (*Externe Strafpflicht mit Umsetzungspflicht*), rather than a direct criminalization of such acts under international law.[1541] This does not rule out the direct applicability of the 1993 Convention, for example to furnish the definition of prohibited acts.[1542] However, it means that the 1993 Convention can not form the basis for prosecutions standing alone, but needs the support of customary international law, other treaties or national law to establish individual criminal responsibility.

The line between actual offences and duties to criminalize is not always clear.[1543] The CAT defines torture (Art. 1) and determines that each State Party shall "ensure that all acts of torture are offences under its criminal law" and "make these offences punishable by appropriate penalties which take into account their grave nature."[1544] This formulation raises the question of whether States must ensure that their national laws reflect a criminality of torture established by the treaty, or must establish such criminality themselves in their criminal laws. Several national proceedings clearly opted for the latter scenario,[1545] but again, these do not necessarily reflect the standards of international law. Still, while this question is open to debate,[1546] the language of the CAT on the whole appears to establish a duty to criminalize torture rather than a directly applicable criminalization.

A distinction must also be made between those acts that a treaty criminalizes, and those that it merely prohibits without attaching individual criminal responsibility. Some treaties contain both, as in the case of the Geneva Conventions. The provisions on grave breaches[1547] clearly define the acts in question, and can also be said to criminalize them.[1548] Although the language of these provisions could be more explicit, the declaration that these acts are grave breaches, the establishment of the duty to extradite or prosecute, and the obligation for States Parties to enact effective penal sanctions together reflect the criminalization of the acts in question. In this regard, it is significant that the States Parties are not required to criminalize the grave breaches, as is the case in the Chemical Weapons Convention, but merely to provide effective penal sanctions, which suggests that the acts are already criminal under international law. Moreover, Additional Protocol I of 1977 declares that all grave breaches shall be regarded as war crimes.[1549]

[1541] See on the difference between these two categories Schmidt 2002, p. 27-29 and 131-133. Cf. Simma and Paulus 1999, p. 308.

[1542] See Art. I and II.

[1543] Cf. Schmidt 2002, p. 27-39.

[1544] Art. 4 (1) and (2) respectively.

[1545] See above, Chapter II, para. 3.3.e, 3.3.j and 3.3.k.

[1546] See Delmas-Marty 2002b, p. 623; Ferdinandusse *et al.* 2002, p. 347; Schmidt 2002, p. 145.

[1547] See Art. 49 and 50 GC I, Art. 50 and 51 GC II, Art. 129 and 130 GC III and Art. 146 and 147 GC IV.

[1548] Cf. Triffterer 1966, p. 84-88.

[1549] See Art. 85 (5) AP I ("Without prejudice to the application of the Conventions and of this Protocol, grave breaches of these instruments shall be regarded as war crimes.")

Common Art. 3 of the Geneva Conventions,[1550] on the other hand, prohibits certain acts in the context of an internal armed conflict, but does not indicate their criminalization.[1551] This does not preclude the prosecution of individuals who breach these norms. But individual criminal responsibility in such cases flows from either customary international law[1552] or a rule of national law,[1553] not from the treaty itself. Thus, the Geneva Conventions contain both directly applicable offences as regards the grave breaches, and prohibitions of other acts which are not of a penal nature.

Finally, it may be asked whether offences contained in the statutes of international courts are directly applicable in national courts. One may question to what extent the direct application on the national level of a legal framework drafted for a

---

1550 Common Art. 3:
"In the case of armed conflict not of an international character occurring in the territory of one of the High Contracting Parties, each Party to the conflict shall be bound to apply, as a minimum, the following provisions:
(1) Persons taking no active part in the hostilities, including members of armed forces who have laid down their arms and those placed hors de combat by sickness, wounds, detention, or any other cause, shall in all circumstances be treated humanely, without any adverse distinction founded on race, colour, religion or faith, sex, birth or wealth, or any other similar criteria. To this end, the following acts are and shall remain prohibited at any time and in any place whatsoever with respect to the above-mentioned persons:
(a) violence to life and person, in particular murder of all kinds, mutilation, cruel treatment and torture;
(b) taking of hostages;
(c) outrages upon personal dignity, in particular humiliating and degrading treatment;
(d) the passing of sentences and the carrying out of executions without previous judgment pronounced by a regularly constituted court, affording all the judicial guarantees which are recognized as indispensable by civilized peoples.
[...]."

1551 See Triffterer 1966, p. 181.

1552 See ICTR, Trial Chamber, *Akayesu*, 2 September 1998, para. 608: "It is today clear that the norms of Common Article 3 have acquired the status of customary law in that most States, by their domestic penal codes, have criminalized acts which if committed during internal armed conflict, would constitute violations of Common Article 3."; ICTY, Appeals Chamber, *Tadic, Decision on the Defence Motion for Interlocutory Appeal on Jurisdiction*, 2 October 1995, para. 98.

1553 See Art. 49 GC I, Art. 50 GC II, Art. 129 GC III and Art. 146 GC IV ("Each High Contracting Party shall take measures necessary for the suppression of all acts contrary to the provisions of the present Convention other than the grave breaches..."). See also ICTR, Trial Chamber, *Kayishema and Ruzindana*, 21 May 1999, para. 156-157: "The Trial Chamber is cognisant of the ongoing discussions, in other forums, about whether [Common article 3] should be considered customary international law that imposes criminal liability for their serious breaches. In the present case, such an analysis seems superfluous because the situation is rather clear. Rwanda became a party to the Conventions of 1949 on 5 May 1964 and to Protocol II on 19 November 1984. These instruments, therefore, were in force in the territory of Rwanda at the time when the tragic events took place within its borders. Moreover, all the offences enumerated in Article 4 of the Statute, also constituted crimes under the laws of Rwanda. The other Party to the conflict, the RPF, also had stated to the International Committee of the Red Cross (ICRC) that it was bound by the rules of international humanitarian law. Therefore, there is no doubt that persons responsible for the breaches of these international instruments during the events in the Rwandan territories in 1994 could be subject to prosecution."

specific international context[1554] is compatible with the international principle of legality.

Practice does not provide a coherent picture in this regard. The Colombian Constitutional Court, on the one hand, has quite recently ruled out direct application of the ICC Statute in national prosecutions.[1555] Yet, a 2002 judgment of the Venezuelan Supreme Court appears to take the opposite view, as it states that "[c]riminal responsibility for crimes against humanity (regular crimes) will be determined according to the Constitution of the Bolivarian Republic of Venezuela and the Rome Statute of the International Criminal Court, ratified by Venezuela, in its subject matter; and the Code of Organic Criminal Procedure in procedural matters."[1556] Venezuela had at the time of this judgment, and also at the time of this writing, not yet adopted implementing legislation for the ICC Statute. However, its Constitution does incorporate treaties that relate to human rights[1557] and requires the prosecution of crimes against humanity.[1558] Therefore, it appears that the Venezuelan Supreme Court was referring to general direct application of the ICC Statute,[1559] but its succinct holding provides no further guidance on this issue.

East German, French and Polish courts all directly applied the Nuremberg Statute's provision on crimes against humanity for domestic prosecutions of crimes committed during WW II.[1560] More recently, the French courts refused such direct application for crimes outside this context. Yet, they based this refusal on the narrow wording of the provisions of the Nuremberg Statute, not on their place in the Statute of an international court.[1561] Likewise, the refusal of a Dutch Court of Appeal to apply the Nuremberg Statute in a case concerning alleged crimes against humanity in

---

[1554] Provisions denying immunity to serving State officials, for example, are clearly not transposable. See Art. 27 ICC Statute. See also above, p. 165.

[1555] See Colombia, Corte Constitucional, Sala Plena, *Sentencia C-578 (In re Corte Penal Internacional)*, 30 July 2002, 31 Jurisprudencia y Doctrina 2231 at 2346 (holding that the provisions of the ICC Statute "no reemplazan ni modifican las leyes nacionales de tal manera" and that "el tratado no modifica el derecho interno aplicado por las autoridades judiciales colombianas en ejercicio de las competencias nacionales").

[1556] Venezuela, Tribunal Supremo de Justicia, Sala Constitucional, 9 December 2002,: "La responsabilidad penal en las causas por delitos de lesa humanidad (delitos comunes) se determinará según lo disponen la Constitución de la República Bolivariana de Venezuela y el Estatuto de Roma de la Corte Penal Internacional suscrito por Venezuela, en cuanto a la parte sustantiva; y el Código Orgánico Procesal Penal en cuanto a la parte adjetiva." Translation by Zandra Valenzuela Delgado.

[1557] See Art. 23 Constitution: "Los tratados, pactos y convenciones relativos a derechos humanos, suscritos y ratificados por Venezuela, tienen jerarquía constitucional y prevalecen en el orden interno, en la medida en que contengan normas sobre su goce y ejercicio más favorables a las establecidas por esta Constitución y en las leyes de la República, y son de aplicación inmediata y directa por los tribunales y demás órganos del Poder Público." See also Ambos 2002b, p. 504.

[1558] See Art. 29 Constitution, cited above, note 1162.

[1559] See Ambos and Malarino 2003, p. 564-565.

[1560] See above, Chapter II, para. 3.3.b and 3.3.j; notes 1257-1260.

[1561] See France, Court of Cassation, Aussaresses, 17 June 2003, 108 RGDIP 754 at 756 ("Que les dispositions [...] du Statut du Tribunal militaire international de Nuremberg [...] ne concernent que les faits commis pour le compte des pays européens de l'Axe"); above, Chapter II, para. 3.3.j.

Argentina rested on a lack of universal jurisdiction, not on the character of the Statute.[1562]

From the viewpoint of international law, there seems to be no reason to prevent national courts from directly applying generally phrased offences contained in the Statutes of international courts. After all, the statutes of the different international criminal tribunals all criminalize the core crimes in general language and indicate explicitly that those crimes are to be judged also by national courts.[1563] Thus, the offences of genocide, crimes against humanity and war crimes contained in Art. 6 to 8 of the ICC Statute can possibly provide the basis for future national prosecutions, and also if national law does not specifically refer to those provisions.

Importantly, all international offences must be analyzed not only on their direct applicability in general, but also on the foreseeability of their penal consequences for the defendant in the particular case. The manifest illegality of the core crimes is a pivotal factor for the determination of foreseeability. This explains why direct application of treaty-based offences that are not phrased in clear-cut language does not necessarily run afoul of the principle of legality. It also suggests both that direct application of core crimes law will fail the foreseeability test only in exceptional circumstances and that direct application of international offences can be extended beyond core crimes law only to a limited extent. Some international offences are, like the core crimes, manifestly illegal.[1564] For others, foreseeability will be ensured by publication of a treaty or national legislative action.[1565] Yet, in general the foreseeability test requires strict scrutiny of the law to be applied and creates a certain presumption against direct application of less "obvious" offences.[1566]

7. The National Principle of Legality as an Obstacle to Core Crimes Prosecutions

As is readily apparent from both Chapter II and the preceding paragraphs, national formulations of the principle of legality are generally stricter than the international principle of legality. In many cases, they form a decisive obstacle to the prosecution of international crimes which are not fully implemented in national law, as they

[1562] See Netherlands, Amsterdam Court of Appeals, *In re Zorreguieta et al.*, 25 April 2002, para. 5.5.

[1563] See preamble, para. 6 and 10, and Art. 17 ICC Statute; Art. 8 ICTR Statute; Art. 9 ICTY Statute; Art. 4 and 6 London Agreement 1945 as well as Art. 10 and 11 Nuremberg Statute.

[1564] See U.S., District Court (D.C.), *United States v. Yunis*, 12 February 1988, 681 F.Supp. 896 at 902:

"While it might be too much to expect the average citizen to be familiar with all of the criminal laws of every country, it is not unrealistic to assume that he would realize that committing a terrorist act might subject him to foreign prosecution."

[1565] See Broomhall 1999, p. 461.

[1566] See e.g. Prinssen 2004, p. 48-51 (on the lack of direct application of European Law in penal cases).

block prosecution directly on the basis of international law.[1567] National principles of legality can thus collide with States' international obligations.

In general, States are free to adopt a stricter principle of legality than that under international law, as long as it does not interfere with their duty to criminalize and prosecute the core crimes.[1568] But when they fail in this duty, the stricter national principle becomes problematic. Of course, the State in such a case violates its duties not solely through its national principle of legality but rather through the combination of its lack of implementation and its inability to directly apply international law. It is up to the State to choose the way through which to make the international crimes prosecutable and thereby live up to its duty.

Nevertheless, a strict national principle of legality that is applicable to the core crimes can amount to a "measure which may be prejudicial to the international obligations in regard to the punishment of persons guilty of war crimes and crimes against humanity" from which States should refrain.[1569] So much was recognized by the UN Committee against Torture in 2002 when it called on Indonesia to ensure that its national principle of legality would not apply to international crimes like torture and crimes against humanity.[1570] When in a concrete case the national principle of legality blocks a prosecution that is mandatory under international law, the principle is simply a national impediment that must give way to international law, just like a national amnesty law. While national principles of legality and amnesty laws might be perceived differently in terms of legitimacy, international law treats them alike when they block mandatory prosecutions of the core crimes: as national obstacles which are to be removed.[1571]

[1567] See Bouterse and Nulyarimma, above, Chapter II, para. 3.3.d and 3.3.k. See also Bremer 1999, p. 148, 256, 303-304 and 396 (concluding that the national principles of legality block direct application of customary ICL in Belgium, Germany and Switzerland).

[1568] See above Chapter V, para. 3.3.

[1569] See General Assembly resolution 3074 (XXVIII) of 3 December 1973 on Principles of international co-operation in the detection, arrest, extradition and punishment of persons guilty of war crimes and crimes against humanity, Principle 8: "States shall not take any legislative or other measures which may be prejudicial to the international obligations they have assumed in regard to the detection, arrest, extradition and punishment of persons guilty of war crimes and crimes against humanity."

[1570] See CAT, *Concluding Observations on Indonesia, Doc. A/57/44*, 1 November 2002 at para. 44 and 45:
"44. The Committee...expresses its concern about the following:
[...]
(c) The inadequacy of measures to ensure that the second amendment to the 1945 Constitution, relating to the right not to be prosecuted based on retroactive law, will not apply to offences such as torture and crimes against humanity which under international law are already criminalized;
[...]
45. The Committee recommends that the State party:
[...]
(f) Ensure that crimes under international law such as torture and crimes against humanity committed in the past are investigated and, where appropriate, prosecuted in Indonesian courts."

[1571] See further below, Chapter VII, para. 3.

Yet, it should be acknowledged that the legal framework just sketched does not find adequate reflection in State practice regarding the core crimes. While various judgments have confirmed the subordination of the national principle of legality to international obligations, others have taken a different view or ignored the issue. Why did the national principle of legality prevail over international law in cases like *Nulyarimma* and *Habré*? Do these cases amount to State practice that contradicts the conclusions drawn here or are they simply violations of the law?

Three factors may help to explain why national courts have not left aside the national principle of legality more often in order to allow core crimes prosecutions. First, national courts are generally bound by rather restrictive national rules regarding their ability to give effect to international law. Some courts, like the Argentinean and Hungarian ones, have showed themselves willing to go to considerable lengths to give effect to international law. Others have been more hesitant. Yet, even if arriving at a different result, these more conservative decisions do not deny the requirements of international law. None of them asserts that the *international* principle of legality blocks direct application in core crimes prosecutions. Rather, they refer exclusively to *national* principles of legality. Thus, these courts effectively declare themselves unable to adhere to their international obligations because of conflicting national law. As set out before, such practice does not oppose or modify the relevant international obligations.[1572]

Second, for a variety of reasons, national courts generally approach the prosecution of core crimes in a minimalistic and selective way.[1573] This attitude explains why courts often do not interpret or overrule the national principle of legality even where national law allows it and international law requires it. For example, in the Senegalese prosecution of Habré, it was open to the courts to prioritize the duty to extradite or prosecute under the CAT over the national principle of legality. In fact, it was even required under the Senegalese Constitution.[1574] Yet, it was also clearly unwanted by the government. In this situation, the courts came up with different legal innovations (exception for direct application of international criminal law and exception for direct application of non-self-executing treaty law) to avoid the required prosecution. Significantly, however, the Senegalese courts ignored the international obligations rather than confronted them.

Third, in some high profile cases dealing with the core crimes, there was no clear duty to prosecute. In cases involving crimes committed abroad while the foreign suspect is not present in the country, such as *Bouterse*, it is generally assumed that international law does not impose a duty to prosecute.[1575] It should also be noted that broader recognition of the duty to prosecute under general human rights law is a relatively recent phenomenon. It is not common knowledge and may therefore be disregarded by the courts if not argued convincingly. Yet again, unlike de-

[1572] See above, note 1180.
[1573] See above, Chapter III, para. 2.
[1574] See above, Chapter II, para. 3.3.e.
[1575] See above, Chapter V, para. 3.3.a and d.

nial, sheer ignorance of international obligations does not amount to contrary State practice.

These three factors, it is submitted, largely explain why the outcomes of various national prosecutions do not reflect the rules of international law.

As the principle of legality is an important human rights guarantee, it may be questioned whether the bypassing of the national principle in core crimes prosecutions is desirable. For the legal certainty of the individual, bypassing the national principle is not fundamentally problematic, since the international principle that remains in place safeguards the core requirement of foreseeability. If the international principle of legality suffices to safeguard the individual's legal certainty in international prosecutions, there is no reason why it would not suffice for national prosecutions of the same crimes. Moreover, national principles are generally geared to regulating prosecutions of crimes which are not comparable to the core crimes in terms of foreseeability.

Applying the international rather than the national principle of legality is appropriate if one accepts that the foreseeability of core crimes should be judged first and foremost on the international level.[1576] After all, the relevance of national implementing laws is ultimately limited. For national law can only inform the individual about one particular system of enforcement among many (the legal regimes of national and international courts). Also, national prosecutions for these crimes are regularly held on the basis of universal jurisdiction against foreigners, who are not familiar with the national legal system and may not even speak the language. In such cases especially, it is only appropriate to look to international rather than national law.

Meanwhile, considerations of legal certainty should be a strong incentive for caution in the interpretation and development of core crimes. But where the criminality of an act under international law is well-established, the need for effective enforcement of ICL must be taken into account. Given the characteristics of the international law-making process, it is clear that ICL can satisfy only minimal *nullum crimen* requirements if it is to be effective.[1577] The basic tension between international sources and the requirements of criminal law is something that needs to be acknowledged.[1578] It can be alleviated by a more direct form of law-making, for example through treaties that unequivocally criminalize certain acts and determine the applicable penalties, but it will remain a structural feature of ICL. Custom will

---

[1576] See Swart 2002b, p. 585.

[1577] Cf. Rodley 1999, p. 77 ("a juridical definition cannot depend upon a catalogue of horrific practices; for it to do so would simply provide a challenge to the ingenuity of the torturers, not a viable legal prohibition."). Cited approvingly in ICTY, Trial Chamber, *Delalic et al.,* 16 November 1998, para. 469.

[1578] See Ambos 2002a, p. 370-371. See also Canada, Supreme Court, *R. v. Imre Finta*, 24 March 1994, La Forest J. (dissenting), para. 338: "The nature of a decentralized international system is such that international law cannot be conveniently codified in some sort of transnational code. Its differing sources may alarm some strict legal positivists, but almost all international lawyers now recognize that such a crude analogy to the requirements of a domestic law system is simplistic."

always be a necessary part of ICL[1579] and treaties will always be weakened by the need to compromise.[1580] If one believes this makes its norms unsuitable for adjudication, one limits the reach of ICL to a set of commands for States and denies it the status of a self-sufficient system of criminal law. This, however, is not something States are willing to do. Therefore, bypassing the national principle of legality may be a necessary and logical step for the effective enforcement of ICL.

8. Conclusion

The international principle of legality finds its source both in treaties and customary law. It requires foreseeability: the criminality of core crimes must have been apparent at the time of their commission. Therefore, their character as a crime must have a clear legal basis. Yet, this criminal character can be derived from a diffuse set of material sources, both written and unwritten. Instead of demanding one comprehensive criminalization, one must look to the totality of the law. Accessibility of the law is not an independent requirement, but merely a step in assessing foreseeability. For most core crimes, their manifest illegality and/or the legal knowledge that may be expected of individuals in official positions is a more important factor in this analysis. No precise indication of the penalty is required, as long as it is clear that the act will be punished. If a penalty has been set out in law, however, it may not be increased.

National law often contains stricter demands. In particular, many States require written provisions and precise penalties. Numerous States make additional matters such as statutes of limitations and rules of jurisdiction subject to the principle of legality where international law does not. Such additional demands under national law can not be invoked, however, to avoid compliance with international obligations regarding core crimes prosecutions. International law requires States to give priority to the duty to criminalize the core crimes and prosecute them, at the expense of national law. National courts can comply with this obligation through consistent interpretation or, where possible, overruling of the national principle of legality.

Where international law allows but not requires core crimes prosecutions, States are free to adhere to a stricter national principle of legality and refuse prosecution. While there are good policy reasons to apply the international rather than the national principle of legality to all core crimes prosecutions in national courts, including voluntary ones, there is no rule of international law requiring States to do so.

In general, the drawbacks of core crimes as to their accessibility and foreseeability pose no decisive obstacles for their application. Yet, they are not to be dismissed

[1579] After all, "it takes only a small minority of sympathetic nations to thwart the most carefully planned attempts at international law-making," which inhibits in particular law-making through treaties. Komarow 1980, p. 35. See likewise Meron 1998, p. 27.

[1580] See Fischer *et al.* 2001, part I (on the many compromises in the drafting of the ICC Statute).

out of hand. Judging core crimes by the standards of national criminal law may lead to a view that is overly restrictive and unnecessarily impedes the enforcement of core crimes. On the other hand, emphasizing their fundamental character can lead us to dismiss some real problems too easily. Discussion of the application of core crimes in light of the principle of legality is too often confined to these two extremes. This is basically the conflict between the view of the national criminal lawyer, used to standards of legality that are unattainable for international criminal law, and the international lawyer, for whom every appeal to problems of accessibility and foreseeability represents a threat to the international system.

Chapter VII
SYNTHESIS

1. Introduction

This study has set out to describe the present state of the international legal framework governing direct application of the international criminalization of genocide, crimes against humanity and war crimes (the core crimes) in national courts. Direct application in the context of this study means that a national court applies an international rule, without it being transformed into a rule of national law, because it is binding law for the court.[1581] It thus includes cases where national courts apply international norms on the basis of a rule of reference (*renvoi*) in national law. The previous chapters have analyzed the practice of selected States in this regard, the underlying considerations shaping that practice, and the international rules that govern it. This Chapter aims to bring all strands together and to give a concise appraisal of international law's regulation of direct application of core crimes law, as well as an assessment of the prospects of direct application and its relevance for international law in general. It will address four principal questions. First, does international law as a general rule prohibit, allow or impose direct application of core crimes law? Second, how does international law require national courts to handle the aggregate of national and international rules that govern direct application of core crimes law? Third, what are the prospects and limits of direct application of core crimes law for the future? Fourth, what are its broader implications for international criminal law and public international law in general?

2. The International Rules on Direct Application

International law allows national courts to directly apply international law for core crimes prosecutions. As described in Chapter VI, the principle of legality in international law, unlike many national formulations of the principle, does not exclude customary international law or even general principles as a basis for criminality. Neither does the international principle of legality demand a specific penalty provision for core crimes. Thus, the international offences of genocide, crimes against humanity and war crimes, whether contained in treaty or custom, can constitute a legal basis for prosecutions in national courts in conformity with international law.

In principle, direct application is voluntary rather than mandatory. There is a certain tendency to subject international law of a humanitarian character or *jus*

[1581] See above, p. 8.

cogens status, thus including at least part of core crimes law, to a more stringent regime of implementation. At this stage, however, practice does not allow the inference of a firm international rule to that effect. The language of some national judgments suggests more narrowly that core crimes law is subject to a specific regime that is largely independent from national law, and should be applied more or less parallel to it.[1582] However, such suggestions are not matched by corresponding practice. Even those judgments themselves by and large follow the normal constitutional rules governing the position of international law in the national legal order. Hence, international law allows, but does not as a general rule require national courts to directly apply international core crimes law.

3. Reconciling National and International Law

In practice, as set out in Chapter II, national courts demonstrate widely divergent attitudes towards direct application of core crimes law. While they all sanction direct application where national law contains a specific rule of reference to international offences, they differ considerably on its acceptability in the absence of such a specific rule (general direct application). Some courts accept general direct application for treaties but not for custom, others for custom but not treaties, for both, or for neither of the two. Yet even in legal systems that in principle accept general direct application of core crimes law, national courts are hesitant to rely on it. Actual prosecutions of genocide, crimes against humanity or war crimes directly on the basis of international law in the absence of a specific rule of reference in national law are rare.

In determining their position, national courts mainly look towards national law, in particular the constitutional framework for the implementation of international law and the principle of legality. Refusals of direct application generally result from a limiting role of national law. It may therefore be asked how international law requires national courts to handle the variety of national and international rules governing direct application of core crimes law and to resolve conflicts between them.

The fact that international law does not prescribe direct application of core crimes law as a general rule does not mean it leaves the matter entirely to the discretion of national courts. As described in Chapter V, States have extensive obligations under international law with regard to core crimes prosecutions. First, they have a duty to criminalize: an obligation to ensure that most core crimes can be punished under their national law. Second, they have a duty to prosecute at least all core crimes committed within their jurisdiction as well as those for which prosecution is required under specific treaties or the law of State responsibility.

International law requires national courts to take these international obligations into account, regardless of their implementation in national law, or lack thereof.

[1582] See above, notes 1226-1227 and 1265-1271.

The principle of consistent interpretation imposes an obligation on national courts to interpret national law in conformity with relevant international obligations.[1583] This has far-reaching consequences for core crimes prosecutions that various national courts have so far disregarded.

First, when national courts are faced with the question of direct application of core crimes law while national criminal law lacks a specific provision on the crime in question, their answer determines whether or not the State complies with its obligation to ensure that the crime can be punished in the national legal order. The principle of consistent interpretation therefore obliges them to endorse direct application in order to effectuate the international duty to criminalize unless national law unambiguously rules it out.[1584] To find that the crime of genocide is not punishable under national law, that the permissibility of direct application of the customary international criminalization of genocide is a policy issue left open by national law and then decline such direct application, as one of the judges did in *Nulyarimma*,[1585] is an open violation of the principle of consistent interpretation. The principle of consistent interpretation requires courts to accept general direct application of core crimes law if that is the only possible basis of criminalization.

Second, national courts must take the duty to prosecute core crimes into account. This duty imposes additional demands, independent from the duty to legislate. It may be the case that the State has fulfilled its duty to legislate in a general sense, and yet national criminal law fails to provide a legal basis for a particular core crimes prosecution. A national limitation like an amnesty law may provide an obstacle. Direct application can then provide an alternative basis for prosecution. If the prosecution in question is mandatory under international law, national courts must take into account the duty to prosecute core crimes and interpret national law in conformity with it.

Importantly, the principle of consistent interpretation extends to all aspects of national law that impede the effectuation of the duty to legislate on and prosecute the core crimes. Thus, national courts must interpret national provisions on jurisdiction, specific crimes, forms of participation and also the principle of legality in such a way as to enable the unimpeded effectuation of the different international obligations. The courts of various States have demonstrated that such consistent interpretation is a powerful and effective tool that can indeed be applied to a variety of national provisions.

Practice shows in particular, as set out in Chapter VI, that there are various ways to interpret the national principle of legality in such a way as to allow direct application of core crimes law. Where national law requires fixed penalties that are absent, courts can either interpret the *nulla poena* principle as allowing the most severe

[1583] See above, Chapter IV, para. 5.2.

[1584] Of course, if the principle of consistent interpretation can provide no solution, breaches of a duty to criminalize will result in State responsibility.

[1585] See above, note 1277.

penalties for core crimes or resort to penalties for relevant ordinary crimes.[1586] Where the national principle of legality requires conduct to be criminalized in "law," courts can interpret "law" as including international law, in conformity with Art. 7 ECHR and Art. 15 ICCPR. Finally, courts can interpret the national principle of legality as covering only the prosecution of ordinary crimes and not extending to the core crimes at all.

Perhaps an unexpected implication for the principle of consistent interpretation is its effect on the doctrine of self-executing treaties. As described above, this doctrine is a limitation on the direct applicability of treaty provisions imposed by national, not international law.[1587] Thus, like other impediments under national law, it must be interpreted in conformity with relevant international obligations. In other words, if the choice between declaring treaties like the Genocide Convention self-executing or non-self-executing determines whether a State will live up to its obligations to legislate for and prosecute the core crimes, and national law leaves a margin of discretion, courts must hold these treaties to be self-executing.

Of course, the principle of consistent interpretation has its limits. While various national courts have taken it beyond its normal meaning to effectively set aside unambiguous national law, the international principle requires no more than interpretation of national law in light of relevant international obligations. The line between proper and *contra legem* interpretation is thin, disputed and impossible to describe in general terms. What seems like permissible consistent interpretation to one, may well be impermissible judicial activism to the other. But in any case, where national law clearly rules out direct application of core crimes law, the principle does not normally provide a remedy for that situation.

Yet, it is by no means certain that the duties to legislate and prosecute have to go unvindicated where consistent interpretation provides no solution. The broad legal basis of the duties ensures that they are cognizable in almost every national legal system. They flow equally from customary law and treaties. As set forth in Chapter V, they have a basis in human rights law as well as international criminal law. The duty to prosecute has an additional basis in the law of State responsibility. Most States have incorporated one or more of the relevant treaties, or parallel customary obligations, into their national legal order. General human rights treaties like the ECHR and the ICCPR are an especially relevant source of the duties, since numerous States have granted those treaties constitutional status.[1588] Decisions of international courts can provide an additional imperative to recognize overriding international obligations.

Therefore, the duty to prosecute may well override national obstacles to direct application where consistent interpretation can not reconcile the two. For the national principle of legality, however, that chance is limited, since the legality prin-

[1586] But see for criticism of the practice to "borrow" penalties from ordinary criminal law above, p. 256.

[1587] See above, note 825.

[1588] See above, note 984.

ciple often has constitutional status itself. Thus, as can be seen in practice, there are certainly cases where obstacles in national law preclude direct application of international core crimes law and neither the principle of consistent interpretation nor international norms with a superior rank in the national legal system provide a solution. In such cases, the State will most likely violate its international obligations and only the, often unsatisfactory, remedies on the international plane remain to remedy that situation.

4. The Future of Direct Application of Core Crimes Law

The relevance of direct application of international core crimes law is, however, not limited to those instances where international law imposes it. Direct application of core crimes law has important functions which should be taken into account when assessing its feasibility in future cases. First, it provides a means to remedy the lacunae and incongruities of national laws. As described in Chapters II and III, most if not all national legal orders fail to regulate core crimes in full accordance with international law. Irregularities range from minor linguistic adaptations, which can still have significant consequences, to the omission of entire crimes. Where national law does not meet the terms of international law, direct application enables core crimes prosecutions that could not otherwise take place, or at least not in the correct fashion.

Second, direct application both effectuates and emphasizes international criminal law's principled autonomy from national law. An eminent scholar wrote in 1944 that "[o]nce it is realized that the offenders are being prosecuted, in substance, for breaches of international law, then any doubts due to inadequacy of the municipal law of any given State determined to punish war crimes recedes into the background."[1589] This observation has not lost its cogency, but it leaves unsaid the other side of the medal. If it is indeed international law that ultimately governs core crimes prosecutions, then the inadequacies of that law should be solved on the international level. The mediating and "repairing" role of national law can only provide a second-best solution. This is most apparent in prosecutions on the basis of universal jurisdiction, where defendants of core crimes generally have no knowledge of the national law of the forum State whatsoever.

Thus, national courts have good reason to consider direct application of international core crimes law also where it is not mandatory. Conversely, there are grounds to be sceptical about the role of national law as a basis for core crimes prosecutions. In particular the widespread practice of charging core crimes as ordinary crimes such as murder and rape has serious disadvantages. It appears that international law allows this practice, and there may be cases where national courts lack the means and expertise to choose a different course. In general though, it should be noted that the discrepancies between ordinary criminal law and the core crimes lead to numer-

[1589] Lauterpacht 1944, p. 67.

ous practical complications. Moreover, such prosecutions fail to capture the full extent of the acts in question and often do not reflect the international character of both the crimes committed and the legal response thereto.

Specific criminalization of genocide, crimes against humanity and war crimes in national law is more acceptable. Yet, in practice these offences also often diverge from the demands of international law. This may be seen as an acceptable form of State practice, even necessary for the development of customary core crimes law. However, such divergences can also be impediments to the effectuation of the international norms, to be circumvented through direct application of those international norms themselves.

Still, national courts are reticent about the direct application of core crimes law and in part they have legitimate reasons to be cautious. Core crimes law is imperfect, complex and its proper application requires expertise and time, both of which are not always available in national courts. But courts are driven also by other motives, including political considerations and a hesitation to venture beyond the familiarity of their national criminal codes. However one judges its legitimacy, the hesitation of national courts to directly apply international offences is a reality that will not change anytime soon. While the influence of the *ad hoc* tribunals and the ICC, particularly through the resulting implementing legislation in many States, has enhanced the position of core crimes law in the national legal order, it will not dispel all hesitations that currently inhibit national courts.

Therefore, mandatory direct application might one day be a suitable outcome of the development of core crimes law, but not in the foreseeable future. Until that time, national courts should be more vigorous in their enforcement of core crimes law, including through its general direct application where necessary to remedy the deficiencies of national criminal law. They might be encouraged to do so by the realization that direct application has received the sanction of many national legislatures through explicit rules of reference and has also been accepted by the courts of different States in the absence of such rules. The increasing familiarity of national actors with international criminal law as well as that law's growing specificity should provide another incentive for national courts to lose some of their reticence about direct application.

5. Implications of Direct Application of Core Crimes Law

Direct application of international core crimes law in national courts is a topic rooted not only in international criminal law, but also in the fields of public international law and criminal law more generally. Accordingly, various of the specific topics treated here have a broader relevance for international or criminal law. The legal framework for the implementation of international obligations, set forth in Chapter IV, is obviously relevant for international law in general. The principle of consistent interpretation constitutes an important safeguard for the effectuation of those international obligations that have not been properly implemented in national legislation also for other international norms than those concerning core crimes. Similarly, that the principle of legality is not as stringent and absolute as doctrine often portrays it to be, as demonstrated in Chapter VI, has implications for criminal law more generally.

That the topic of this study lies at the crossroads of international and criminal law also explains to a considerable extent why it encounters such diametrically opposed reactions both in practice and doctrine. The viewpoint of (national) criminal law on the direct application of international offences differs fundamentally from that of international law. In fact, the different outcomes of national proceedings reflect different underlying assumptions about both the proper role of national courts in the enforcement of international law, and the current state and proper role of core crimes law.

First, direct application provides something of a yardstick to measure the development of core crimes law. The reticence of national courts is a clear sign that this development still has a long way to go. On the other hand, the fact that direct application actually takes place shows that this development occurs not only in international but also in national courts, and that core crimes law has passed its most rudimentary stage.

Second, the question of direct application of core crimes law provides a vivid illustration of an enduring schism in national courts' appraisal of their proper role in the enforcement of international law in general. While some scholars assert that national courts should act as organs of the international community in their enforcement of international law, others emphatically reject this view.[1590] The practice of national courts regarding the direct application of core crimes law demonstrates that these opposing viewpoints are not merely of theoretical interest, but have a considerable bearing on the outcome of national proceedings. Those courts that conceptualize their role as being an organ of the international community reach markedly "internationalist" results, ensuring diligent adherence to international obligations.[1591] By contrast, courts that explicitly reject this notion focus predominantly on national rather than international law.[1592]

[1590] The most famous conceptualization of national courts as organs of the international community is found in George Scelle's famous theory of *dédoublement fonctionnel*. See for a concise description of this theory and further references Cassese 1990. See in the particular context of international criminal law Burke-White 2002, p. 14 and 16-17 and Wolfrum 1996, p. 236 and 250. See for notable criticism ICJ, International Court of Justice, *Case concerning the Arrest Warrant of 11 April 2000 (Democratic Republic of the Congo v. Belgium)*, 14 February 2002, Separate Opinion of President Guillaume, para. 15 ("[To confer universal jurisdiction *in absentia* on national courts would] be to encourage the arbitrary for the benefit of the powerful, purportedly acting as agent for an ill-defined "international community.").

[1591] See Argentina, Judge Gabriel Cavallo of the Buenos Aires Federal Court, *Julio Simon (Case no. 8686/2000, "Simon, Julio, Del Cerro, Juan Antonio s/sustracción de menores de 10 años")*, 6 March 2001, 2000/B Nueva Doctrina Penal 527, para. III (J): "[E]l estado que tome intervención en el juzgamiento de una persona acusada de haber cometido un crimen contra el derecho de gentes, estará actuando en interés de toda la comunidad internacional. ";
Hungary, Constitutional Court, *Decision No. 53/1993, On War Crimes and Crimes against Humanity,*

Finally, the conditions required for direct application provide a valuable indication of the role we assign to international criminal law in general. Is international criminal law merely a centralized counterpart to national criminal law, formulated at the international level but otherwise subject to similar conditions for its enforcement? Or does the fight against the most serious crimes committed with State involvement require an international criminal law that must be restricted in its subject matter but more flexible in the conditions of its enforcement? It is submitted here that the latter view must prevail. Therefore, the attempt to enhance the foreseeability and quality of international criminal law enforcement, while in itself legitimate and important, should not result in the undifferentiated adoption of national criminal law standards, for that will ultimately undermine international criminal law's effectiveness and even its very rationale.

---

13 October 1993, English translation in Sólyom/Brunner 2000, p. 273-283 at 278: "[T]he state which prosecutes and punishes crimes against humanity and war crimes, acts upon the mandate given to it by the community of nations, according to the conditions imposed by international law."

[1592] See Netherlands, Attorney-General to the Supreme Court, *Voordracht en vordering tot cassatie in het belang der wet door de Procureur-Generaal (Petition for Cassation in re Bouterse)*, 8 May 2001, NJ 2002/559, para. 6: "Treedt de Nederlandse rechter [bij de bestraffing van een internationaal misdrijf op basis van universele jurisdictie] op als internationale of als nationale rechter? Bij het opstellen van de middelen is van dat laatste standpunt uitgegaan.";
U.K., House of Lords, *R. v. Bow Street Metropolitan Stipendiary Magistrate & Others, Ex Parte Pinochet Ugarte (No. 1)*, 25 November 1998, [2000] 1 A.C. 61 at 103: "We apply customary international law as part of the common law, and we give effect to our international obligations so far as they are incorporated in our statute law; but we are not an international court."

TABLE OF CASES

I. International

AfrComHPR
- *Commission Nationale des Droits de l'Homme et des Libertés v. Chad*, October, 1995, Communication No. 74/92

Committee on Economic, Social and Cultural Rights
- *General comment 9*, 3 December 1998, UN Doc E/C.12/1998/24

Committee against Torture
- *Concluding Observations on Indonesia*, 1 November 2002, A/57/44

ECJ
- *Kolpinghuis Nijmegen BV*, 8 October 1987, Case 80/86, 1987 European Court reports 03969

EComHR
- *X. v. Federal Republic of Germany*, 6 July 1976, Application/Requete No. 6946/75
- *S.W. v. the United Kingdom*, 27 June 1994

ECtHR
- *Swedish Engine Drivers' Union v. Sweden*, 6 February 1976
- *Ireland v. UK*, 13 December 1977
- *Ireland v. UK*, 18 January 1978
- *Marckx v. Belgium*, 13 June 1979, 00006833/74
- *Sunday Times v. UK*, 26 April 1979, Series A., No. 30
- *Silver and others v. United Kingdom*, 25 February 1983, Serie A No 61
- *X and Y v. The Netherlands*, 27 February 1985
- *Leander v. Sweden*, 25 February 1987, Serie A No 116
- *Vermeire v. Belgium*, 29 November 1991, 00012849/87
- *Kokkinakis v. Greece*, 25 May 1993, Series A, No. 260-A
- *C.R. v. the United Kingdom*, 27 October 1995
- *G v. France*, 27 September 1995, Series A, No. 325-B, 21 EHRR 288
- *Loizidou v. Turkey, Preliminary Objections*, 23 March 1995
- *Tolstoy Miloslavsky v. the United Kingdom*, 13 July 1995, Series A No. 316-B
- *Cantoni v. France*, 15 November 1996
- *Assenov and Others v. Bulgaria*, 28 October 1998
- *Coëme and Others v. Belgium*, 22 June 2000
- *Kiliç v. Turkey*, 28 March 2000
- *Naletilic v. Croatia, Admissibility decision*, 4 May 2000, 2000 – V Eur. Ct. H.R. 489, Appl. No. 51891/99
- *Al-Adsani v. United Kingdom*, 21 November 2001
- *Bankovic and others v. Belgium and others*, 12 December 2001

- *Hugh Jordan v. the United Kingdom*, 4 May 2001
- *K. – H. W. v. Germany*, 22 March 2001, Application No. 37201/97
- *Krenz et al. v. Germany*, 22 March 2001
- *Kalogeropoulou v. Greece and Germany, Decision on Admissibility*, 12 December 2002
- *McShane v. the United Kingdom*, 28 May 2002
- *Aktas v. Turkey*, 24 April 2003
- *M.C. v. Bulgaria*, 4 December 2003
- *Ilascu and Others v. Moldova and Russia*, 7 May 2004
- *Mutimura v. France*, 8 June 2004
- *Nachova and others v. Bulgaria*, 26 February 2004

Eritrea–Ethiopia Claims Commission
- *Partial Awards on Prisoners of War between the State of Eritrea and the Federal Democratic Republic of Ethiopia*, 1 July 2003

HRC
- *General Comment 3 (Article 2: Implementation at the national level)*, 29 July 1981
- *Concluding Observations on Iceland*, Doc. CCPR/C/79/Add.26, 3 November 1993
- *Concluding Observations on Ireland*, Doc. CCPR/C/79/Add.21, 3 August 1993
- *Thomas v. Jamaica*, 1993, Doc. CCPR/C/49/D/321/1988
- *Concluding Observations on Nepal*, Doc. CCPR/C/79/Add.41, 10 November 1994
- *Bautista de Arellana v. Colombia*, 27 October 1995, Doc. CCPR/C/55/D/563/1993
- *Comments on Paraguay*, Doc. CCPR/C/79/Add. 48, 1995
- *Concluding Observations on the United Kingdom of Great Britain and Northern Ireland, Doc. CCPR/C/79/Add.55*, 21 July 1995
- *Concluding Observations on Denmark*, Doc. CCPR/C/79/Add.68, 18 November 1996
- *Concluding Observations on Gabon*, Doc. CCPR/C/79/Add.71, 18 November 1996
- *Concluding Observations on Portugal*, 5 May 1997, Doc. CCPR/C/79/Add.77
- *General Comment 26 (Continuity of obligations)*, 8 December 1997, contained in document A/53/40, annex VII
- *A. v. Australia*, 30 April 1997, CCPR/C/59/D/560/1993
- *Comments on Cambodia*, Doc. CCPR/C/79/Add.108, 1999
- *Concluding Observations on Portugal (Macau)*, 4 November 1999, Doc. CCPR/C/79/Add.108
- *Comments on Peru*, Doc. CCPR/CO/70/PER
- *Concluding Observations on Guatemala*, 27 August 2001, Doc. CCPR/CO/72/GTM

IAComHR
- *Mendoza et al. v. Uruguay*, 2 Oct. 1992, Report No. 29/92, 82nd session, OEA/LV/11.82Doc.25
- *Lincoleo v. Chile*, 16 April 2001, Report No. 61/01

IACtHR
- *Certain Attributes of the Inter-American Commission on Human Rights (Arts. 41, 42, 44, 46, 47, 50 and 51 of the American Convention on Human Rights)*, 16 July 1993, Advisory Opinion OC-13/93 (Ser. A) No. 13
- *The Effect of Reservations on the Entry Into Force of the American Convention on Human Rights (Arts. 74 and 75)*, 24 September 1982, Advisory Opinion OC-2/82 (Ser. A) No. 2

- *Proposed Amendments of the Naturalization Provisions of the Constitution of Costa Rica*, 19 January 1984, Advisory Opinion OC-4/84 (Ser. A) No. 4
- *Velasquez Rodriguez*, 29 July 1988, Series C No. 4 and 95 I.L.R. 232
- *Godínez Cruz, Compensatory Damages*, 21 July 1989, Ser. C, No. 8 (1990)
- *Castillo Petruzzi et al.*, 30 May 1999, Series C No. 52
- *Giraldo Cardona, Order of the Court of September 30, 1999*, 30 September 1999, Ser. E, No. 2
- *Barrios Altos Case (Chimbipuma Aguierre v. Peru), Merits*, 14 May 2001 (Ser. C) No. 75 (2001) and 41 ILM 93 (2002)
- *Bulacio v. Argentina*, 18 September 2003

ICJ

- *Reservations to the Convention on the Prevention and Punishment of Genocide (Advisory Opinion)*, 1951, 1951 ICJ 23
- *Case concerning the application of the Convention of 1902 governing the Guardianship of Infants (Netherlands v. Sweden)*, 28 November 1958, 1958 ICJ 55
- *Nuclear Tests (Australia v. France)*, 20 December 1974
- *Case Concerning Military and Paramilitary Activities in and against Nicaragua (Nicaragua v. United States of America)*, 27 June 1986, 1986 ICJ 135
- *Border and Transborder Armed Actions (Nicaragua v. Honduras), Jurisdiction and Admissibility*, 1988, 1988 ICJ 69
- *Lockerbie Case (Libya v. United Kingdom), Provisional Measures, Joint Declaration of Judges Evensen, Tarassov, Guillaume and Aguilar*, 9 April 1992, 1992 ICJ 24
- *Case Concerning Application of the Convention on the Prevention and Punishment of the Crime of Genocide (Bosnia-Herzegovina v. Yugoslavia), preliminary objections*, 11 July 1996, 1996 ICJ 595
- *Legality of the Threat or Use of Nuclear Weapons, Advisory Opinion*, 8 July 1996
- *Germany v. United States (LaGrand case)*, 27 June 2001
- International Court of Justice, *Case concerning the Arrest Warrant of 11 April 2000 (Democratic Republic of the Congo v. Belgium)*, 14 February 2002
- *Oil Platforms (Islamic Republic of Iran v. United States of America)*, 6 November 2003
- *Legal Consequences of the Construction of a Wall in the Occupied Palestinian Territory, Advisory Opinion*, 9 July 2004

ICTR

- Trial Chamber, *Akayesu*, 2 September 1998
- Trial Chamber, *Akayesu, Sentencing Judgment*, 2 October 1998
- Trial Chamber, *Kayishema and Ruzindana*, 21 May 1999
- Appeals Chamber, *Semanza, Decision*, 31 May 2000
- Trial Chamber, *Niyitegeka*, 16 May 2003

ICTY

- Appeals Chamber, *Tadic, Decision on the Defence Motion for Interlocutory Appeal on Jurisdiction*, 2 October 1995
- Trial Chamber, *Tadic, Decision on the Defence Motion on Jurisdiction*, 10 August 1995
- Trial Chamber, *Tadic, Decision on the Prosecutor's Motion Requesting Protective Measures for Victims and Witnesses*, 10 August 1995
- Trial Chamber, *Erdemovic, Sentencing Judgment*, 29 November 1996
- Appeals Chamber, *Erdemovic*, 7 October 1997

- Trial Chamber, *Tadic*, 7 May 1997
- Trial Chamber, *Delalic et al.*, 16 November 1998
- Trial Chamber, *Furundzija*, 10 December 1998
- Appeals Chamber, *Kovacevic*, 2 July 1998
- Trial Chamber, *Jelisic*, 14 December 1999
- Appeals Chamber, *Aleksovski*, 24 March 2000
- Trial Chamber, *Blaskic*, 3 March 2000
- Trial Chamber, *Kupreskic*, 14 January 2000
- Appeals Chamber, *Delalic et al.*, 20 February 2001
- Trial Chamber, *Kunarac, Kovac and Vukovic*, 22 February 2001
- Appeals Chamber, *Mucic et al.*, 20 February 2001
- Trial Chamber, *Sikirica et al.*, 3 September 2001
- Trial Chamber, *Vasiljevic*, 29 November 2002

PCIJ

- *Consistency of Certain Danzig Legislative Decrees with the Constitution of the Free City, Advisory Opinion*, 1935, Series A/B, No. 65, 3

II. Internationalized

East-Timor

- Court of Appeal, *Armando dos Santos, Applicable Subsidiary Law decision*, 15 July 2003, Court-Authorised English Language translation available at http://www.jsmp.minihub.org/courtmonitoring/spsccaseinformation2001.htm (Case No. 16/2001)
- Special Panel for Serious Crimes, *Domingos Mendonca, Decision on the defense motion for the Court to order the Public Prosecutor to amend the indictment*, 24 July 2003, available at http://www.jsmp.minihub.org/courtmonitoring/spsccaseinformation2000.htm (Case No. 18a/2001)

Special Court for Sierra Leone

- Appeals Chamber, *Prosecutor against Kallon and Kamara, Decision on Challenge to Jurisdiction (Lomé Accord Amnesty)*, 13 March 2004, Case No. SCSL-04-15-AR72(E) and SCSL-04-16-AR72(E)
- Trial Chamber, *Majority Decision on the Prosecution's Application for Leave to File an Interlocutory Appeal against the Decision's Request for Leave to Amend the Indictment against Samuel Hinga Norman, Moinini Fofana and Allieu Kondewa*, 2 August 2004, Case No. SCSL-04-14-T

III. National

Argentina

- Federal Court of La Plata, *Extradition Josef Franz Leo Schwammberger*, 30 August 1989, unreported
- Supreme Court, *Extradition Josef Franz Leo Schwammberger*, 20 March 1990, 313 Fallos de la Corte Suprema de Justicia de la Nacion 256
- Supreme Court, *Ekmekdjian v. Sofovich*, 7 July 1992, Case No. E. 64. XXIII
- Supreme Court, *Extradition of Erich Priebke*, 2 November 1995, 1996 – I Jurisprudencia Argentina 324
- Supreme Court, 23 December 1997, CODICES ARG-1998-1-002

- Federal Court of Buenos Aires, *In re Massera s/ Excepciones*, 9 September 1999, available at http://www.derechos.org/nizkor/arg/ley/massera.html
- Federal Court of Buenos Aires, *Videla, Ruling on Pre-trial Detention*, 9 September 1999, unreported
- Federal Court of Buenos Aires, *Julio Simon (Case No. 8686/2000, "Simon, Julio, Del Cerro, Juan Antonio s/sustracción de menores de 10 años")*, 6 March 2001, 2000/B Nueva Doctrina Penal 527, also available at http://www.nuncamas.org/juicios/argentin/cavallo_060301_1.htm
- Federal Chamber of Appeals, *Incidente de Apelacion de Julio Simon*, 9 November 2001, unreported
- Supreme Court, *Arancibia Clavel, Enrique Lautaro s/ homicidio calificado y asociación ilícita y otros*, 24 August 2004, Causa n° 259, available at http://www.derechos.org/nizkor/arg/doc/arancibia1.html
- Supreme Court, *Julio Simon*, 14 June 2005, available at http://www.clarin.com/diario/2005/06/14/um/fallopuntofinal.doc

Australia

- High Court, *Polyukhovich v. The Commonwealth of Australia and Another*, 14 August 1991, 172 CLR 501
- High Court, *Horta v. The Commonwealth*, 18 August 1994, 181 CLR 183
- High Court, *Minister for Immigration and Ethnic Affairs v. Teoh*, 7 April 1995, 183 CLR 273
- High Court, *Newcrest Mining (WA) Ltd v. The Commonwealth*, 14 August 1997, 190 CLR 513
- Federal Court, *Nulyarimma v. Thompson*, 1 September 1999, [1999] FCA 1192

Austria

- Supreme Court (Oberster Gerichtshof), *Cvjetkovic*, 13 July 1994, available at http://www.ris.bka.gv.at/

Belgium

- Court of Cassation, *In re Köppelmann*, 27 November 1950, partial English translation in ILR 1950, No. 126
- Court of Cassation, *Van Beggelaer v. Belgian State*, 27 March 1950, partial English translation in ILR 1950, No. 142
- Court of Cassation, 2 June 1993, available at http://www.cass.be (No. RC93621_2)
- Court of Cassation, *Publication of Treaties Case (Belgium)*, 25 November 1993, available at http://www.cass.be (No. RC93BP3_2)
- Tribunal of First Instance (District of Brussels), *In re Pinochet Ugarte*, 6 November 1998, 79 Revue de droit pénal et de criminologie 278, English translation in 2 YIHL 475-485 (1999) and 93 AJIL 700-703 (1999)
- Law for the punishment of Genocide, Report of the Justice Commission, Belgian Senate, 1998–1999
- Court of Arbitration, 10 July 2002, available in CODICES (No. BEL-2002-2-007)
- Tribunal of First Instance Brussels (Kamer van Inbeschuldigingstelling), *In re Sharon and Yaron*, 26 June 2002, reproduced in Wouters and Panken 2003, p. 323–339
- Court of Cassation, *In re Sharon and Yaron*, 12 February 2003, No. P.02.1139.F/1, unofficial English translation available at http://www.indictsharon.net/12feb2003dectrans.pdf

Bolivia
- Tribunal Constitucional, *Resolución 1190/2001 – R (Trujillo Oroza)*, 12 November 2001, available at www.tribunalconstitucional.gov.bo

Botswana
- Court of Appeal, *Unity Dow v. Attorney-General of Botswana*, 3 July 1992, 1994 (6) Butterworths Constitutional Law Reports 1, also available at www.law- lib.utoronto.ca/diana/cases.htm

Canada
- Supreme Court, *R. v. Imre Finta*, 24 March 1994, 28 C.R. (4th) 265 (1994)
- Supreme Court, *R. v. Imre Finta*, 24 March 1994, 28 C.R. (4th) 265 (1994)
- Supreme Court, *Suresh v. Canada (Minister of Citizenship and Immigration)*, 22 May 2002, 2002 SCC 1

Chile
- Court of Appeals (Santiago), *In re Fernando Laureani Maturana y Miguel Krassnoff Marchenko*, 5 January 2004, available at http://www.derechos.org/nizkor/chile
- Supreme Court, *In re Miguel Angel Sandoval Rodríguez*, 17 November 2004, available at http://www.derechos.org/nizkor/chile/doc/krassnoff.html

Colombia
- Corte Constitucional, Sala Plena, *Genocidio, Sentencia C-177*, 14 February 2001, 30 Jurisprudencia y Doctrina 707
- Corte Constitucional, Sala Plena, *Sentencia C-578 (in re Corte Penal Internacional)*, 30 July 2002, 31 Jurisprudencia y Doctrina 2231

Congo (the)
- Supreme Court, *Projet de loi portant définition et répression des crimes contre l'Humanite*, 24 March 1998 (N° 007/CS/98), available at http://www.icrc.org/ihl-nat

Costa Rica
- Supreme Court of Justice (Constitutional Chamber), *Advisory Opinion on the constitutionality of the draft law of approbation of the Rome Statute on the International Criminal Court*, 1 November 2000, available at http://www.icrc.org/ihl-nat, with English summary

Denmark
- Eastern Division of High Court (Third Chamber), *The Prosecution v. Saric*, 25 November 1994, available at http://www.icrc.org/ihl-nat

Ethiopia
- Central High Court, *Indictment of Mengistu and 72 others*, October 1994, Unofficial translation on file with the author
- Central High Court, *Asbete et al.*, 24 March 2002 (Ethiopian Calendar 15-7-1995), judgment and unofficial translation by Gebil Gebremdhin on file with the author

France

- Court of Cassation, *Touvier (No. 1)*, 6 February 1975, Bull. crim., No. 42
- Court of Cassation, *Glaeser*, 30 June 1976, Bull. crim., No. 236, No. 75-93.296
- Court of Cassation, *Barbie (No. 1)*, 6 October 1983, Bull. crim., No. 239; 78 ILR 125
- Court de Cassation, *Barbie (No. 2)*, 26 January 1984, Bull. crim., No. 34; 78 ILR 132
- Court of Cassation, *Barbie (No. 3)*, 3 June 1988, Bull. crim., No. 246; 100 ILR 330
- Court of Appeals of Paris, *Touvier*, 13 April 1992, 100 ILR 337
- Court of Cassation, *Touvier (No. 2)*, 27 November 1992, Bull. crim. 1992, 1082; 100 ILR 358
- Court de Cassation, *Boudarel*, 1 April 1993, Bull. crim., No. 143
- Court of Cassation, *Touvier (No. 3)*, 21 October 1993, Bull. crim., No. 307
- Tribunal de Grande Instance de Paris, Juge d'Instruction, *In re Javor, Ordonnance*, 6 May 1994, on file with the author
- Court of Cassation, *MC Ruby*, 3 May 1995, Bull. crim., No. 161
- Paris Court of Appeals (Cour d'appel de Paris), *Reporters sans Frontières v. Mille Collines*, 6 November 1995, on file with the author
- Tribunal de Grande Instance de Paris, Juge d'Instruction, *Reporters sans Frontières v. Mille Collines, Ordonnance*, 9 February 1995, on file with the author
- Court of Cassation, *Touvier*, 1 June 1995, Bull. crim., No. 202
- Court of Cassation, *In re Javor*, 26 March 1996, Bull. crim., No. 132
- Court of Cassation, *Papon*, 23 January 1997, Bull. crim., No. 32
- Conseil Constitutionnel, *Traité portant statut de la Cour pénale internationale*, 22 January 1999, available at http://www.conseil-constitutionnel.fr
- Court of Cassation, 2 June 2000, available at http://courdecassation.fr (No. 99-60.274)
- Paris Court of Appeals (Cour d'appel de Paris), *In re Gadaffi*, 20 October 2000, 105 RGDIP 475-476
- Court of Cassation, *In re Gadaffi*, 13 March 2001, 105 RGDIP 473–474
- Cour de Cassation, *Ely Ould Dha*, 23 October 2002, Bull. crim., No. 195
- Court of Cassation, *Aussaresses*, 17 June 2003, 108 RGDIP 754, Bull. crim., No. 122

Germany

a) German Democratic Republic

- Oberster Gerichtshof, *Globke*, 23 July 1963, reproduced in DDR-Justiz und NS-Verbrechen: Sammlung ostdeutscher Strafurteile wegen nationalsozialistischer Tötungsverbrechen (Demps et al., ed.), Vol. III, p. 182–183
- Oberster Gerichtshof, *Fischer*, 25 March 1966, reproduced in DDR-Justiz und NS-Verbrechen: Sammlung ostdeutscher Strafurteile wegen nationalsozialistischer Tötungsverbrechen (Demps *et al.*, ed.), Vol. II, p. 713–714

b) Germany

- Reichsgericht in Strafsachen, *Publication of Treaties Case (Germany)*, 25 September 1920, Partial translation in English in Annual Digest 1919–1922, No. 234
- Reichsgericht in Strafsachen, *The Llandovery Castle*, 16 July 1921, Partial translation in English in Annual Digest 1923–24, No. 235
- Bavarian Higher Court (BayObLG), *Djajic*, 23 May 1997, 3 St 20/06, in 51 NJW (1998), 392–395, also reported by Safferling, International Decision: *Public Prosecutor v. Djajic*, in 92 AJIL 528–532 (1998)
- OLG Düsseldorf, *Jorgic*, 26 September 1997, 2 StE 8/96
- Supreme Court (BGH), *Jorgic*, 30 March 1999, 3 StR 215/98, in 19 NStZ (1999), 396–404; BGHSt 45, 64–91

- BayObLG, *Kusljic*, 15 December 1999, 6 St 1/99
- OLG Düsseldorf, *Sokolovic*, 29 November 1999, 2 StE 6/97
- Constitutional Court (BVerfG), *Jorgic*, 12 December 2000, 2 BvR 1290/99, in 54 NJW 2001, 1848–1853
- BGH, *Kusljic*, 21 February 2001, 3 StR 244/00, in 54 NJW (2001), 2732–2734
- BGH, *Sokolovic*, 21 February 2001, 3 StR 372/00; BGHSt 46, 292–307; 54 NJW, 2728–2732
- Bundesgerichtshof, *Distomo Massacre Case*, 26 June 2003, BGH – III ZR 245/98
- Bundesverfassungsgericht, *In re G.*, 14 October 2004, 2 BvR 1481/04

Haiti
- Juge d'Instruction Jean Senat Fleury of the Gonaïves Tribunal of First Instance, *Ordonnance Raboteau Massacre*, 27 August 1999, on file with the author
- Gonaïves Tribunal of First Instance, *Raboteau*, 9 November 2000, reported in Concannon 2001

Hungary
- Constitutional Court, *Decision No. 11/1992, On retroactive criminal legislation*, 5 March 1992, English translation in Sólyom/Brunner 2000, p. 214–228
- Constitutional Court, *Decision No. 53/1993, On War Crimes and Crimes against Humanity*, 13 October 1993, English translation in Sólyom/Brunner 2000, p. 273–283, and on http://www.icrc.org/ihl-nat
- Constitutional Court, *Decision No. 36/1996*, 4 November 1996, Official Journal 1996/75, pp. 4674–4675 (Part. II: par. 2), French translation on http://www.icrc.org/ihl-nat

India
- Supreme Court, *Apparel Export Promotion Council v. A. K. Chopra*, 1999 (1999) A.I.R. 625
- Supreme Court, *Vishaka v. State of Rajasthan*, 13 August 1997 (1999) Butterworths H.R.C. 261, also available at www.judis.nic.in/sc/qrydisp.asp?tfnm=13856

Indonesia
- Ad Hoc Human Rights Tribunal at the Human Rights Court of Justice of Central Jakarta, *Abilio Soares*, 14 August 2002, No. 01/PID.HAM/AD.Hoc/2002/ph.JKT.PST, available at http://socrates.berkeley.edu/%7Ewarcrime/

Israel
- Supreme Court, *Attorney General of Israel v. Eichmann*, 29 May 1962, 36 ILR 277
- Supreme Court, *Oubeid and al., Dirani v. Minister of Defence et al.*, 23 August 2001, excerpted in 32 Israel YBHR 351 and 4 YIHL 553
- Supreme Court, *Society of Physicians for Human Rights v. IDF Commander in the West Bank*, 8 April 2002, excerpted in 32 Israel YBHR 360

Italy
- Tribunale Supremo Militare, *General Wagener and others*, 13 March 1950, Rivista Penale, 1059-II, 745–764
- Court of Cassation, *Ministero Finanze v. Societa Compagnia di Navigazione Marsud*, 20 October 1976, 3 Italian Yearbook of International Law 361

Jamaica

- Privy Council, *Lewis v. Attorney General* (2001) 2 AC 50

Japan

- Tokyo District Court, *Shimoda et al. v. The State*, 7 December 1963, English translation available at http://www.icrc.org/ihl-nat

Luxembourg

- Court of Appeal, *Pinochet*, 11 February 1999, 119 ILR 360

Mexico

- Supreme Court, *In re Cavallo (Amparo en Revision 140/2002)*, 10 June 2002, 42 ILM 884 (2003)

Netherlands

- HR, 3 December 1856, Weekblad van het Regt, No. 1878
- Bijzondere Raad van Cassatie (Special Court of Cassation), *Ahlbrecht I*, 17 February 1947, NJ 1947/87; Partial English translation in Annual Digest 1947, No. 92
- Bijzondere Raad van Cassatie, *Ahlbrecht II*, 11 April 1949, NJ 1949/425; Partial English translation in Annual Digest 1949, No. 141
- Bijzondere Raad van Cassatie, *In re Rauter*, 12 January 1949, Annual Digest 1949, p. 526, NJ 1949/87
- HR, *Nuygat*, 6 March 1959, NJ 1962/2
- Amsterdam Court of Appeals, *In re Pinochet*, 4 January 1995, 28 NYIL 363 (1997)
- Arnhem District Court, Military Division (Chambers), *Knezevic*, 21 February 1996, NJ 1998/463, 30 NYIL 315 (1999)
- Supreme Court, *Knezevic I*, 22 October 1996, NJ 1998/462
- Supreme Court, *Knezevic II*, 11 November 1997, NJ 1998/463
- Amsterdam Court of Appeals, *Bouterse 2000*, 20 November 2000, NYIL
- Amsterdam Court of Appeals, *In re Bouterse*, 3 March 2000, NJ 2000/266
- HR, *In re Bouterse*, 18 September 2001, NJ 2002/559, English translation in 32 NYIL 282-296 (2001)
- Attorney-General to the Supreme Court, *Voordracht en vordering tot cassatie in het belang der wet door de Procureur-Generaal (Petition for Cassation in re Bouterse)*, 8 May 2001, NJ 2002/559
- The Hague District Court, 11 July 2002
- Amsterdam Court of Appeals, *In re Zorreguieta et al.*, 25 April 2002, unreported, on file with the author
- The Hague District Court, 29 August 2003, available at www.rechtspraak.nl (LJN No. AN8981)
- HR, *In re Kesbir*, 7 May 2004, available at www.rechtspraak.nl (LJN No. AF6988)
- Rotterdam District Court, *Nzapali*, 7 April 2004, available at www.rechtspraak.nl (LJN No. AO7178)

New-Zealand

- Court of Appeals, *Tavita v. Minister of Immigration*, 17 December 1993, [1994] 2 NZLR 257

Nigeria
- Supreme Court, *Pius Nwaoga v. The State*, 52 ILR 494-497

Norway
- Supreme Court, *Klinge*, 27 February 1946, Annual Digest 1946, p. 262

Peru
- Consejo Supremo de Justicio Militar, *In re Barrios Altos*, 4 June 2001, Case No. 494-V-94, on file with the author

Pakistan
- Court of Appeal, *Ata-Ur-Rehman v. State*, 30 October 2002, 36 Pakistan Criminal Law Journal 923
- Court of Appeal, *Mir Zaman v. Zubair*, 14 January 2003, 36 Pakistan Criminal Law Journal 1086

Poland
- Voivodship Court of Warsaw, *In re Koch*, 9 March 1959, 30 ILR 496
- Supreme Court, *In re Koch*, 10 November 1959, 30 ILR 509
- Constitutional Tribunal, *Case of 6 July 1999*, 6 July 1999, CODICES (No. POL-1999-2-024, Translation in English)

Scotland
- High Court of Justiciary Appeal Court, *Angela Zelter v. Bodil Ulla Roder, Ellen Moxley*, 30 March 2001, unreported, available in Westlaw at 2001 WL 272884

Slovenia
- Constitutional Court, *U-I-6/93*, 13 January 1994, Uradni list RS (Official Gazette), 23/94; Odlocbe in sklepi ustavnega sodisca (Official digest), 1994, 135; CODICES (SLO-1994-2-008, translation in English)
- Constitutional Court, *U-I-248/96*, 30 September 1998, CODICES (SLO-1998-3-009, translation in English)

South Africa
- Transvaal Provincial Division, *S v. Theledi*, 7 October 1991, [1993] 2 SA 402
- South African Constitutional Court, *Azanian Peoples Organization (AZAPO) and Others v. President of the Republic of South Africa and Others*, 25 July 1996 (4) SA 671 (CC)

Spain
- Audiencia Nacional, *Argentinean Genocide Case*, 4 November 1998, unreported, available at http://www.derechos.org/nizkor/arg/espana/audi.html
- Audiencia Nacional, *Chilean Genocide Case*, 5 November 1998, unreported, available at http://www.derechos.org/nizkor/chile/juicio/audi.html
- Tribunal Supremo, *Guatemalan Genocide Case*, 25 February 2003, 42 ILM 686

Russia
- Constitutional Court, *On the constitutionality of Presidential Decree No. 2137 of 30 November 1994*, 31 July 1995, Sobranie zakonodatelstva Rossiyskoy Federatsii, 1995, No. 33, Art. 3424; available at http://www.icrc.org/ihl-nat

Senegal

- *Plainte avec Constitution de Partie Civile Contre Hissène Habré, Présenté au Juge d'Instruction du Tribunal Régional hors classe de Dakar*, 1999, on file with the author
- Cour d'appel de Dakar, Chambre d'accusation, *Ministère Public et François Diouf Contre Hissène Habré, Arrêt No. 135*, 4 July 2000, on file with the author
- Cour de Cassation, *Souleymane Guengueng et autres Contre Hissène Habré, Arrêt No. 14*, 20 March 2001, on file with the author

Switzerland

- Tribunal militaire, Division 1, Lausanne (Military Tribunal), *In re G.*, 18 April 1997, available at http://www.icrc.org/ihl-nat
- Tribunal militaire, Division 2, Lausanne, *In re N.*, 30 April 1999, unreported
- Military Court of Appeal, *In re N.*, 26 May 2000, available at http://www.icrc.org/ihl-nat
- Military Court of Cassation, *In re N.*, 27 April 2001, available at http://www.icrc.org/ihl-nat

Trinidad and Tobago

- Privy Council, *Briggs v. Baptiste*, 28 October 1999, [2000] 2 AC 40
- Privy Council, *Thomas and Hilaire v. Baptiste*, 23 March 1999 (1999) 3 W.L.R. 249

United Kingdom

- *Le Louis*, 1817, 2 Dods. 210
- Privy Council, *In Re Piracy Jure Gentium*, 26 July 1934, [1934] A.C. 586
- Courts-Martial Appeal Court, *Regina v. Page*, 10 November 1953, [1954] 1 QB 170
- *Blackburn v. Attorney-General*, 1971, 2 All ER 1380, 1 WLR 1037, 52 ILR 414
- House of Lords, *Attorney General v. British Broadcasting Corporation*, 12 June 1980, 3 All E.R. 161 (1981) AC 303
- Court of Appeal, *Schering Chemicals Ltd v. Falkman Ltd*, 27 January 1981, [1982] QB 1
- House of Lords, *Derbyshire County Council v. Times Newspapers Limited*, 1992 (1992) 1 QB 770
- Family Division, *In re N. (Child Abduction: Jurisdiction)*, 31 August 1994, [1995] Fam 96
- Court of Appeal, *Al-Adsani v. Al-Sabah and Kuwait*, 12 March 1996
- Queens Bench Division, *Hipperson v. DPP*, 3 July 1996, [1996] C.L.Y. 1445
- House of Lords, *R. v. Bow Street Metropolitan Stipendiary Magistrate & Others, Ex Parte Pinochet Ugarte (No. 1)*, 25 November 1998, [2000] 1 A.C. 61
- House of Lords, *R. v. Bow Street Metropolitan Stipendiary Magistrate & Others, Ex Parte Pinochet Ugarte (No. 3)*, 24 March 1999, [2000] 1 A.C. 147
- Court of Appeal, *R. v. Anthony Sawoniuk*, 10 February 2000, [2000] 2 Cr. App. R. 220
- Court of Appeal (Civil Division), *R. v. Secretary of State ex parte Thring*, 20 July 2000, ICRC website
- High Court of Justice Queen's Bench Division, *Ken Lukowiak v. Unidad Editorial SA*, 6 July 2001, unreported, available in Westlaw as 2001 WL 720373
- Family Division, *In re C. (Abduction: Interim Directions: Accomodation by Local Authority)*, 12 December 2003, [2003] EWHC 3065 (Fam), [2004] 1 FLR 653
- Chancery Division, *NEC Semi-Conductors Ltd and other test claimants v. Inland Revenue Commissioners*, 24 November 2003, [2003] EWHC 2813 (Ch), [2004] STC 489
- Court of Appeal, *A, B, C, D, E, F, G, H, Mahmoud Abu Rideh, Jamal Ajouaou v. Secretary of State*, 11 August 2004, unreported, available in westlaw as 2004 WL 1640297

– Court of Appeal, *Jones & Milling, Olditch & Pritchard, Richards v. Gloucestershire Crown Prosecution Service*, 21 July 2004, [2004] EWCA Crim 1981

United States of America

– Court of Oyer and Terminer, at Philadelphia, *Respublica v. De Longchamps*, October Sessions, 1784, 1 Dall. 111
– Supreme Court, *Chisholm v. Georgia*, February Term, 1793, 2 U.S. 419
– Circuit Court, D. Pennsylvania, *Henfield's Case*, 22 May 1793, 11 F.Cas. 1099
– Supreme Court, *Murray v. The Schooner Charming Betsy*, 1804, 6 U.S. (2 Cranch) 64
– Supreme Court, *United States v. Hudson & Goodwin*, 13 February 1812, 11 U.S. 32 (Mem)
– Supreme Court of Pennsylvania, *Commonwealth v. Kosloff*, 1820, 5 Serg. & Rawle 545
– Supreme Court, *United States v. Klintock*, 1820, 18 U.S. 144 (Mem), 5 L.Ed. 55, 5 Wheat. 144
– Supreme Court, *United States v. Smith*, 1820, 18 U.S. 153
– Supreme Court, *The Antelope*, 1825, 23 U.S. 66, 6 L.Ed. 268, 10 Wheat. 66
– Supreme Court, *Foster & Elam vs. Neilson*, January Term, 1829, 27 U.S. (2 Pet.) 253
– Supreme Judicial Court of Massachusetts, *Commonwealth v. Tilton*, October Term, 1844, 49 Mass. 232
– Supreme Court, *Rainey v. United States*, 1914, 232 U.S. 310
– Supreme Court, *United States v. Bowman*, 1922, 260 U.S. 94
– United States Court for China, *U.S. v. Kearny*, 8 October 1923, in Lobingier, Extraterritorial Cases, Vol. II (1928), p. 665-686
– District Court (New York), *The Pictonian*, 26 Novemeber 1924, 3 F.2d 145
– District Court (Connecticut), *The Over the Top (Schroeder v. Bissell)*, 26 February 1925, 5 F. 2d 838
– Supreme Court, *Cook v. United States*, 23 January 1933, 288 U.S. 102
– Supreme Court, *Ex Parte Quirin*, 1943, 317 U.S. 1
– Supreme Court, *Yamashita v. Styer*, 1946, 327 U.S. 1
– Military Tribunal at Nuremberg, *United States v. Altstötter et al. (Justice case)*, 3-4 December 1947, III Trials of War Criminals Before the Nuremberg Military Tribunals Under Control Council Law No. 10, 1946-1949, also available at www.mazal.org
– Military Tribunal at Nuremberg, *United States v. Von List et al. (Hostages case)*, 1948, Annual Digest 1948, No. 215
– Supreme Court, *Reid v. Covert*, 10 June 1957, 354 U.S. 1
– Supreme Court, *Mitchell v. United States*, 20 March 1967, 87 S.Ct. 1162 (Mem), 386 U.S. 972
– Supreme Court, *Parker v. Levy*, 19 June 1974, 417 U.S. 733
– Court of Appeals (First Cir.), *Sabatier v. Dabrowski*, 15 November 1978, 586 F.2d 866
– Court of Appeals (Fifth Circuit), *United States v. Columba-Colella*, 604 F.2d 356
– Court of Appeals (2d Cir.), *Filartiga v. Pena-Irala*, 1980, 630 F.2d 876
– Court of Appeals, *Hopson v. Kreps*, 14 July 1980, 622 F.2d 1375
– Court of Appeals (Fifth Circuit), *Spiess v. C. Itoh & Co. (America)*, 1981, 643 F.2d 355
– District Court (Cal.), *U. S. v. Layton*, 6 March 1981, 509 F.Supp. 212
– Circuit Court (D.C.Cir.), *Tel-Oren v. Libyan Arab Republic*, 1984, 726 F.2d 774
– Court of Appeals (6th Cir.), *Demjanjuk v. Petrovsky*, 1985, 776 F.2d 571
– District Court, *Handel v. Artukovic*, 31 January 1985, 601 F.Supp. 1421
– Supreme Court, *Tennessee v. Garner*, 27 March 1985, 105 S.Ct. 1694
– Court of Appeals, D.C.Cir., *Demjanjuk v. Meese*, 27 February 1986, 784 F.2d 1114

- Court of Appeals (D.C. Circuit), *Finzer v. Barry*, 1986, 798 F.2d 1450
- District Court (Cal.), *Matter of Extradition of Artukovic*, 6 February 1986, 628 F.Supp. 1370
- Court of Appeals, 9th Cir.(Cal.), *Quinn v. Robinson*, 26 August 1997, 783 F.2d 776
- District Court (New York), *United States v. Palestine Liberation Organization*, 1988, 695 F.Supp. 1456
- District Court (D.C.), *United States v. Yunis*, 12 February 1988, 681 F.Supp. 896
- Court of Appeal, *State v. LaMaster*, 1991, 811 S.W.2d 837
- Court of Appeals (9th Cir.), *Siderman de Blake v. Argentina*, 22 May 1992, 965 F.2d 699
- Court of Appeals (Fifth Circuit), *Brothers v. Klevenhagen*, 1 August 1994, 28 F.3d 452
- Court of Appeals (9th Cir.), *U.S. v. Vasquez-Velasco*, 25 January 1994, 15 F.3d 833
- *Cook v. Commonwealth*, 1995, 20 Va. App. 510
- Court of Appeals (Second Circuit), *Kadic v. Karadzic*, 13 October 1995, 70 F.3d 232
- Court of Appeals (Ninth Circuit), *U.S. v. Matta-Ballesteros*, 1 December 1995, 71 F.3d 754
- Supreme Court, *Breard v. Greene*, 14 April 1998, 523 U.S. 371
- Court of Appeals (Ninth Circ.), *Alvarez-Machain v.* – 11 June 2001, 331 F.3d 604
- Court of Appeal, *Nunley v. State*, 2001, 26 P.3d 1113
- District Court, *Mehinovic et al. v. Vuckovic*, 2 May 2002, 198 F.Supp.2d 1322
- District Court (Cal.), *Sarei v. Rio Tinto PLC*, 9 July 2002, 221 F.Supp.2d 1116
- United States Court of International Trade, *The Timken Company v.* – 5 September 2002, 240 F.Supp.2d 1228
- Court of Appeals (Fourth Circuit), *Hamdi v. Rumsfeld*, 8 January 2003, 316 F.3d 450
- Supreme Court, *Hamdi v. Rumsfeld*, 28 June 2004, 124 S.Ct. 2633
- Supreme Court, *Sosa v. Alvarez-Machain*, 29 June 2004, 124 S.Ct. 2739

Ukraine
- Constitutional Court, *Conformity of the Constitution of Ukraine to the Rome Statute of the International Criminal Court (the Rome Statute case)*, 11 July 2001, Ophitsiynyi Visnyk Ukrayiny (Official Gazette), 28/2001; CODICES (No. UKR-2001-2-006), with English summary; English translation available at http://www.icrc.org/ihl-nat

Venezuela
- Tribunal Supremo de Justicia, Sala de Casación Penal, 21 November 2000, available at http://www.tsj.gov.ve/jurisprudencia/jurisprudencia.asp
- Tribunal Supremo de Justicia, Sala Constitucional, 9 december 2002, available at http://www.tsj.gov.ve/jurisprudencia/jurisprudencia.asp

Zambia
- High Court, *Thomas James v. State*, 18 April 1974, 8 The comparative and international law journal of Southern Africa 152
- High Court, *The People v. Davies Mumeno, No HPR/79*, 10 July 1990, 1990-1992 Zambia Law Reports 13

Zimbabwe
- Supreme Court, *S v. Mharapara*, 17 October 1985, 1986 (1) SA 556

CITED LITERATURE

Abdelgawad, W., 'Droit égyptien', in: Cassese and Delmas-Marty 2002, 367-398

Abi-Saab, G., 'The Specificities of Humanitarian Law', in: C. Swinarski (ed.) *Studies and Essays on International Humanitarian Law: In Honour of Jean Pictet* (Geneva / The Hague: Martinus Nijhoff, 1984), 265-280

Abi-Saab, G., 'The Proper Role of Universal Jurisdiction', 1 JICJ 596 (2003)

Aceves, W.J., 'Liberalism and International Legal Scholarship: The Pinochet Case and the Move Toward a Universal System of Transnational Law Litigation', 41 Harv. Int. Law J. 129 (2000)

Akkermans, P.W.C. and A.K. Koekkoek, *De grondwet, een artikelsgewijs commentaar* (Zwolle: W.E.J. Tjeenk Willink, 1992)

Aldana-Pindell, R., 'In Vindication of Justiciable Victims' Rights to Truth and Justice for State-Sponsored Crimes', 35 Vand. J. Transnat'l L. 1399 (2002)

Alexidze, L., 'Legal nature of Jus cogens in contemporary international law', 172 RdC 219 (1981)

Alford, R.P., 'Federal courts, international tribunals, and the continuum of deference', 43 Va. J. Int'l L. 675 (2003)

Allain, J. and J.R.W.D. Jones, 'A Patchwork of Norms: A Commentary on the 1996 Draft Code of Crimes against the Peace and Security of Mankind', 8 EJIL 100 (1997)

Allen, R.J. *et al.*, *Constitutional criminal procedure: an examination of the Fourth, Fifth, and Sixth Amendments, and related areas* (Boston: Little Brown, 1995)

Alvarez, A.E. *et al.*, 'Droit argentin', in: Cassese and Delmas-Marty 2002, 299-332

Ambos, K., 'Völkerrechtliche Bestrafungspflichten bei schweren Menschenrechtsverletzungen', 37 AVR 318 (1999)

Ambos, K., *Der Allgemeine Teil des Völkerstrafrechts Ansätze einer Dogmatisierung* (Berlin: Duncker & Humblot, 2002a)

Ambos, K., 'Les pays d'Amerique latine', in: A. Cassese and M. Delmas-Marty (eds.), *Juridictions nationales et crimes internationaux* (Paris: Presses universitaires de France, 2002b), 479-520

Ambos, K., 'On the Rationale of Punishment at the Domestic and International Level', in: M. Henzelin and R. Roth (eds.), *Le droit pénal à l'épreuve de l'internationalisation* (Paris, Bruxelles, Geneve: L.G.D.J, Bruylant, Georg, 2002c), 305-323

Ambos, K., 'Implementación del estatuto de Roma en la legislación nacional', in: K. Ambos and E. Malarino (eds.), *Persecución penal de crímenes internacionales en América Latina y España* (Montevideo: 2003), 25-31

Ambos, K. and E. Malarino (eds.), Persecución penal de crímenes internacionales en América Latina y España (Montevideo: 2003)

Ambos, K. and M. Othmann (eds.), New Approaches in International Criminal Justice: Kosovo, East Timor, Sierra Leone & Cambodia (Freiburg im Breisgau: Max-Planck-Institut für Ausländisches und Internationales Strafrecht, 2003)

Ambos, K. and S. Wirth, 'Genocide and War Crimes in the Former Yugoslavia Before German Criminal Courts', in: H. Fischer, *et al.* (eds.), *International and national prosecution of crimes under international law: current developments* (Berlin: Spitz, 2001), 769-798

Antonopolous, C., 'Whatever happened to crimes against peace?' 6 Journal of Conflict and Security Law 33 (2001)

Arangio-Ruiz, G., 'Dualism revisited: international law and interindividual law', 86 Rivista di diritto internazionale 909 (2003)
Arbour, L., 'Will the ICC have an Impact on Universal Jurisdiction?', 1 JICJ 585 (2003)
Arendt, H., *Eichmann in Jerusalem: a report on the banality of evil* (New York: Viking Press, 1963)
Arnold, J. *et al.*, 'The German Border Guard Cases before the European Court of Human Rights', 11 Eur. J Crime, Crim. L & Crim. Jus 67 (2003)
Arnold, J. and E. Weigend, 'Strafrecht, politischer Systemwechsel und Vergangenheitsaufarbeitung in Polen und Deutschland: Versuch einer Bestandsaufnahme', 41 Recht in Ost und West: Zeitschrift für Ostrecht und Rechtsvergleichung 81 (1997)
Artucio, A., 'Augusto Pinochet Ugarte before the Court of Chilean Justice', Review of the International Commission of Jurists, iss. 62-63, 47-61 (2001)
Aubert, B., *Le droit international devant la chambre criminelle: cinquante ans de jurisprudence* (Paris: Presses universitaires de France, 2000)
Aust, A., *Modern treaty law and practice* (New York: CUP, 2000)
Ayat, M., 'Droit marocain', in: Cassese and Delmas-Marty 2002, 419-436
Baderin, M.A., *International human rights and Islamic law* (Oxford: OUP, 2003)
Bahdi, R., 'Globalization of Judgment: Transjudicialism and the Five Faces of International Law in Domestic Courts', 34 Geo. Wash. J. Int'l L. & Econ. 555 (2002)
Ballard, L.A., 'The Recognition and Enforcement of International Criminal Court Judgments in U.S. Courts', 29 Colum. Hum. Rts. L. Rev. 143 (1997)
Bantekas, I. *et al.*, *International criminal law* (London: Cavendish, 2001)
Barak-Erez, D., 'The International law of human rights and constitutional law: a case study of an expanding dialogue', 2 International Journal of Constitutional Law 611 (2004)
Barboza, J., 'International criminal law', 278 RdC 9 (2000)
Barreto, I.C., 'La jurisprudence de la nouvelle Cour européenne des droits de l'homme sur l'article 7 de la Convention européenne des droits de l'homme', in: A. Donatsch and others (eds.), *Strafrecht, Strafprozessrecht und Menschenrechte. Festschrift für Stefan Trechsel zum 65. Geburtstag* (Zürich: Schulthess, 2002), 3-16
Barrett, N., 'Holding individual leaders responsible for violations of customary international law: the U.S. bombardment of Cambodia and Laos', 32 Colum. Hum. Rts. L. Rev. 429 (2001)
Bassiouni, M.C. *et al.*, 'Remarks: Genocide: The Convention, Domestic Laws, and State Responsibility', 83 Proceedings of the American Society of International Law 314 (1989)
Bassiouni, M.C., *Commentaries on the International Law Commission's 1991 Draft Code of Crimes Against the Peace and Security of Mankind* (Toulouse: Editions Erès, 1993)
Bassiouni, M.C., 'International crimes: Jus cogens and obligatio erga omnes', 59 Law Contemp. Probl. 63 (1996)
Bassiouni, M.C., 'International crimes: Jus cogens and obligatio erga omnes', 14 Nouvelles Études Pénales 133 (1998)
Bassiouni, M.C., *Crimes against humanity in international criminal law* (The Hague; Boston, MA: Kluwer Law International, 1999a)
Bassiouni, M.C., 'The sources and content of international criminal law: a theoretical framework', in: M. C. Bassiouni (ed.) *International criminal law* (Ardsley, N.Y.: Transnational Publishers, 1999b), 3-126
Bassiouni, M.C. and P. Manikas, *The law of the International Criminal Tribunal for the Former Yugoslavia* (Irvington-on Hudson, N.Y.: Transnational Publishers, 1996)
Bassiouni, M.C. and E.M. Wise, *Aut dedere aut judicare: the duty to extradite or prosecute in international law* (Dordrecht; Boston: M. Nijhoff, 1995)

Baxter, R.R., 'The Municipal and International Law Basis of Jurisdiction over War Crimes', in: M. C. Bassiouni and V. P. Nanda (eds.), *A treatise on international criminal law, Vol. II* (Springfield, IL: Thomas, 1973), 65-86

Beigzadeh, E. and A.-H. Nadjafi, 'Droit iranien', in: Cassese and Delmas-Marty 2002, 399-418

Bemmelen, J.M. v. *et al.*, *Ons strafrecht* (Arnhem: Gouda Quint, 1995)

Benillouche, M., 'Droit français', in: Cassese and Delmas-Marty 2002, 159-192

Benvenisti, E., 'Judicial Misgivings Regarding the Application of International Law: An Analysis of Attitudes of National Courts', 4 EJIL 159 (1993)

Benvenisti, E., 'Judges and Foreign Affairs: A Comment on the Institut de Droit International's Resolution on 'The Activities of National Courts and the International Relations of their State'', 5 EJIL 423 (1994)

Benvenisti, E., 'Margin of appreciation, consensus, and universal standards', 31 N.Y.U. J. Int'l L. & Pol. 843 (1999)

Benvenuti, P., 'Italy, Implementation of the ICC Statute in National Legislation, Constitutional Aspects', in: Kress and Lattanzi 2000, 123-137

Bergen, J.G., 'Princz v. The Federal Republic of German: Why the Courts should Find that Violating Jus Cogens Norms Constitutes and Implied Waver of Immunity', 14 Connecticut Journal of International Law 169 (1999)

Bernhardt, R., 'Völkerrechtskonforme Auslegung der Verfassung? Verfassungskonforme Auslegung völkerrechtlicher Verträge?', in: H.-J. Cremer and H. Steinberger (eds.), *Tradition und Weltoffenheit des Rechts: Festschrift für Helmut Steinberger* (Berlin: Springer, 2002), 392-400

Bertodano, S.D., 'Current Developments in Internationalized Courts', 1 JICJ 226 (2003)

Bertodano, S.D., 'Current Developments in Internationalized Courts – East Timor – Justice Denied', 2 JICJ 910 (2004)

Bertossa, B. *et al.*, *La lutte contre l'impunité en droit suisse* (Genève: TRIAL, 1993)

Betlem, G. and A. Nollkaemper, 'Giving Effect to Public International Law and European Community Law before Domestic Courts. A Comparative Analysis of the Practice of Consistent Interpretation', 14 EJIL 569 (2003)

Boas, G., 'An Overview of Implementation by Australia of the Statute of the International Criminal Court', 2 JICJ 179 (2004)

Bohlander, M., 'The Direct Application of International Criminal Law in Kosovo', 1 Kosovo Legal Studies 7 (2001)

Boot, M., *Genocide, crimes against humanity, war crimes: nullum crimen sine lege and the subject matter jurisdiction of the international criminal court* (Antwerpen; New York: Intersentia, 2002)

Bossuyt, M.J., *Guide to the "travaux préparatoires" of the International Covenant on Civil and Political Rights* (Dordrecht; Boston: M. Nijhoff, 1987)

Bothe, M., 'War crimes in non-international armed conflicts', 24 Israel YBHR 241 (1995)

Bothe, M., 'War Crimes in Non-International Armed Conflicts', in: Y. Dinstein and M. Tabory (eds.), *War crimes in international law* (The Hague: Nijhoff, 1996), 293-305

Bothe, M., 'War Crimes', in: A. Cassese, *et al.* (eds.), *International criminal law: a commentary on the Rome Statute for an International Criminal Court* (Oxford: OUP, 2001), 379-426

Bowett, D.W., 'Jurisdiction: changing patterns of authority over activities and resources', 53 BYIL 1 (1982)

Bradley, C.A., 'The Charming Betsy Canon and separation of powers: Rethinking the interpretive role of international law', 86 Geo. L.J. 479 (1998)

Bradley, C.A., 'Breard, our dualist constitution, and the internationalist conception', 51 Stan. L. Rev. 529 (1999a)

Bradley, C.A., 'International Law and United States Law', 93 AJIL 757 (1999b)

Bradley, C.A. and J.L. Goldsmith, 'Customary international law as federal common law: A critique of the modern position', 110 Harvard LR 815 (1997)

Bradley, C.A. and J.L. Goldsmith, 'Federal courts and the incorporation of international law', 111 Harvard LR 2260 (1998)

Bremer, K., *Nationale Strafverfolgung internationaler Verbrechen gegen das humanitäre Völkerrecht: am Beispiel einer Rechtsvergleichung Deutschlands, der Schweiz, Belgiens und Großbritanniens* (Frankfurt am Main: Peter Lang, 1999)

Bridge, J.W., 'The Case for an International Court of Criminal Justice and the Formulation of International Criminal Law', 13 ICLQ 1255 (1964)

Brierly, J.L., 'Do We Need an International Criminal Court?' 8 BYIL 81 (1927)

Brody, R. and H. Duffy, 'Prosecuting Torture Universally: Hissène Habré, Africa's Pinochet?', in: H. Fischer, *et al.* (eds.), *International and national prosecution of crimes under international law: current developments* (Berlin: Spitz, 2001), 817-842

Broomhall, B., 'Nullum crimen sine lege: article 22', in: O. Triffterer and K. Ambos (eds.), *Commentary on the Rome Statute of the International Criminal Court: observers' notes, article by article* (Baden-Baden: Nomos, 1999), 447-462

Brouwer, J.G., *Verdragsrecht in Nederland: een studie naar de verhouding tussen internationaal en nationaal recht in een historisch perspectief* (Zwolle: W.E.J. Tjeenk Willink, 1992)

Brown, A.S., 'Adiós Amnesty: Prosecutorial Discretion and Military Trials in Argentina', 37 Texas I.L.J. 203 (2002)

Brunner, G. and G. Halmai, 'Die juristische Bewältigung des kommunistischen Unrechts in Ungarn', in: G. Brunner (ed.) *Juristische Bewältigung des kommunistischen Unrechts in Osteuropa und Deutschland* (Berlin: Berlin Verlag Arno Spitz, 1995), 9-40

Buck, V., 'Droit espagnol', in: Cassese and Delmas-Marty 2002, 121-158

Buergenthal, T., 'The Advisory Practice of the Inter-American Human Rights Court', 79 AJIL 1 (1985)

Buergenthal, T., 'Self-Executing and Non-Self-Executing Treaties in National and International Law', 235 RdC 303 (1992)

Buergenthal, T., 'International tribunals and national courts: the internationalization of domestic adjudication', *Recht zwischen Umbruch und Bewahrung: Festschrift für Rudolf Bernhardt* (Berlin: Springer-Verlag, 1995), 687-703

Buergenthal, T., 'Modern constitutions and human rights treaties', 36 Columbia J. Transnatl. Law 211 (1997)

Burchell, J., 'Deadly Force and Fugitive Justice in the Balance: The Old and New Face of Section 49 of the Criminal Procedure Act', 13 SACJ 200 (2000)

Burke-White, W.W., 'A community of courts: toward a system of international criminal law enforcement', 24 Michigan journal of international law 1 (2002)

Burmester, H., 'The determination of customary international law in Australian courts', 4 Non-State Actors and International Law 39 (2004)

Cartuyvels, Y., 'Le droit pénal et l'Etat: des frontieres "naturelles" en question', in: M. Henzelin and R. Roth (eds.), *Le droit pénal à l'épreuve de l'internationalisation* (Paris, Bruxelles, Geneve: L.G.D.J, Bruylant, Georg, 2002), 3-28

Cassel, D., 'The ICC's new legal landscape: the need to expand U.S. domestic jurisdiction to prosecute genocide, war crimes, and crimes against humanity', 23 Fordham international law journal 378 (1999)

Cassel, D., 'Empowering United States Courts to Hear Crimes within the Jurisdiction of the International Criminal Court', 35 New England Law Review 421 (2001)

Cassese, A., 'Modern Constitutions and International Law', 192 RdC 331 (1985)

Cassese, A., 'Remarks on Scelle's Theory of "Role Splitting" (dédoublement fonctionnel)', 1 EJIL 210 (1990)

Cassese, A., 'The Statute of the International Criminal Court: some preliminary reflections', 10 EJIL 144 (1999)

Cassese, A., 'Crimes against Humanity', in: A. Cassese, *et al.* (eds.), *International criminal law: a commentary on the Rome Statute for an International Criminal Court* (Oxford: OUP, 2001a), 353-378

Cassese, A., 'Genocide', in: A. Cassese, *et al.* (eds.), *International criminal law: a commentary on the Rome Statute for an International Criminal Court* (Oxford: OUP, 2001b), 335-351

Cassese, A., *International law* (Oxford; New York: OUP, 2001c)

Cassese, A., 'L'incidence du droit international sur le droit interne', in: Cassese and Delmas-Marty 2002, 555-566

Cassese, A., *International criminal law* (Oxford; New York: OUP, 2003a)

Cassese, A., 'Is the Bell Tolling for Universality? A Plea for a Sensible Notion of Universal Jurisdiction', 1 JICJ 589 (2003b)

Cassese, A., 'Are International Human Rights Treaties and Customary Rules on Torture Binding upon U.S. Troops in Iraq?', 2 JICJ 872 (2004a)

Cassese, A., 'Black Letter Lawyering v. Constructive Interpretation', 2 JICJ 265 (2004b)

Cassese, A. and M. Delmas-Marty (eds.), Juridictions nationales et crimes internationaux (Paris: Presses universitaires de France, 2002)

Cerna, C.M., 'Inter-American Court of Human Rights: Barrios Altos Case (Chumbipuma Aguirre Et Al. v. Peru) – Introductory Note', 41 ILM 91 (2002)

Charney, J.I., 'Progress in international criminal law?' 93 AJIL 452 (1999)

Chiavario, M., 'Victim's Right of access to criminal courts: The Case law of the European Court of Human Rights', in: N. Courakis (ed.) *Criminal Sciences in the 21st Century* (Athens: Komotini, 2001), 261-268

Chinkin, C., 'Feminist reflections on international criminal law', in: A. Zimmermann and U. E. Heinz (eds.), *International criminal law and the current development of public international law: proceedings of an international symposium of the Kiel Walther Schücking Institute of International Law: May 30-June 2, 2002* (Berlin: Duncker & Humblot, 2003), 125-160

Choukr, F.H., 'Droit brésilien', in: Cassese and Delmas-Marty 2002, 333-344

Cissé, A., 'Droit sénégalais', in: Cassese and Delmas-Marty 2002, 437-447

Cohen, S., 'State Crimes of Previous Regimes: Knowledge, Accountability, and the Policing of the Past', 20 Law & Soc. Inquiry 7 (1995)

Collins, L., 'Foreign relations and the judiciary', 51 ICLQ 485 (2002)

Concannon, B., 'Beyond Complementarity: The International Criminal Court and National Prosecutions, A View from Haiti', 32 Colum. Hum. Rts. L. Rev. 201 (2000)

Concannon, B., 'Justice for Haiti: The Raboteau Trial', 35 International Lawyer 641 (2001)

Conforti, B., *International law and the role of domestic legal systems* (Dordrecht; Boston: Martinus Nijhoff, 1993)

Conforti, B., 'National courts and the international law of human rights', in: B. Conforti and F. Francioni (eds.), *Enforcing international human rights in domestic courts* (The Hague; Boston: M. Nijhoff, 1997), 3-14

Conforti, B., 'Notes on the relationship between International and National Law', 3 International Law FORUM 18 (2001)

Consigli, J.A., 'The Priebke extradition case before the Argentine Supreme Court', 1 YIHL 341 (1998)

Coomans, F. and M.T. Kamminga (eds.), Extraterritorial application of human rights treaties (Antwerpen: Intersentia, 2004)

Coria, D.C.C., 'Peru', in: K. Ambos and E. Malarino (eds.), *Persecución penal de crímenes internacionales en América Latina y España* (Montevideo: 2003), 447-493

Correa, R.P., 'Developments, Chile', 1 International Journal of Constitutional Law 130 (2003)

Cotler, I., 'Regina v. Finta: Canadian Supreme Court war crimes decision', 90 AJIL 460 (1996)

Cottier, M., 'The Case of Switzerland', in: C. Kreß and F. Lattanzi (eds.), *The Rome Statute and domestic legal orders* (Baden Baden, Ripa di Fagnano Alto: Nomos, Sirente, 2000), 219-246

Cottier, M., 'Did NATO Forces Commit War Crimes During the Kosovo Conflict? Reflections on the Prosecutor's Report of 13 June 2000', in: H. Fischer, *et al.* (eds.), *International and national prosecution of crimes under international law: current developments* (Berlin: Spitz, 2001), 505-538

Craven, M., 'Legal differentiation and the concept of the human rights treaty in international law', 11 EJIL 489 (2000)

Crawford, J., 'The work of the International Law Commission', in: A. Cassese, *et al.* (eds.), *International criminal law: a commentary on the Rome Statute for an International Criminal Court* (Oxford: OUP, 2001), 23-34

Criddle, E., 'The Vienna Convention on the Law of Treaties in U.S. Treaty Interpretation', 44 Va. J. Int'l L. 431 (2004)

Crocker, D., 'Reckoning with Past Wrongs: A Normative Framework', 13 Ethics and International Affairs 43 (1999)

Cumes, G., 'Murder as a Crime against Humanity in International Law: Choice of Law and Prosecution of Murder in East Timor', 11 Eur. J Crime, Crim. L & Crim. Jus 40 (2003)

Daglish, K., 'The crime of genocide: Nulyarimma v. Thompson', 50 ICLQ 404 (2001)

D'Amato, A., 'The President and International Law: A Missing Dimension', 81 AJIL 375 (1987)

D'Amato, A., 'It's a bird, it's a plane, it's jus cogens', 6 Connecticut Journal of International Law 1 (1990)

Danilenko, G.M., 'Implementation of International Law in CIS States: Theory and Practice', 10 EJIL 51 (1999)

David, E., *Principes de droit des conflits armés* (Bruxelles: Bruylant, 2002)

Delmas-Marty, M., 'Global crime calls for global justice', 10 Eur. J Crime, Crim. L & Crim. Jus 286 (2002a)

Delmas-Marty, M., 'La responsabilité pénale en échec (prescription, amnestie, immunités)', in: A. Cassese and M. Delmas-Marty (eds.), *Juridictions nationales et crimes internationaux* (Paris: Presses universitaires de France, 2002b), 613-652

Delmas-Marty, M., 'The contribution of comparative law to a pluralist conception of international criminal law', 1 JICJ 13 (2003)

Dembour, M.-B. and E. Haslam, 'Silencing Hearings? Victim-Witnesses at War Crimes Trials', 15 EJIL 151 (2004)

Denza, E., 'The relationship between international and national law', in: M. D. Evans (ed.) *International law* (Oxford; New York: OUP, 2003), 415-472

Dickinson, L.A., 'The Promise of Hybrid Courts', 97 AJIL 295 (2003)

Dijk, P. v. and B.G. Tahzib, 'Parliamentary Participation in the Treaty-making Process of the Netherlands', 67 Chi.-Kent. L. Rev. 413 (1991)

Dinstein, Y., 'The distinction between unlawful combatants and war criminals', in: Y. Dinstein and M. Tabory (eds.), *International law at a time of perplexity: essays in honour of Shabtai Rosenne* (Dordrecht: Nijhoff, 1989), 103-116

Dinstein, Y., *The conduct of hostilities under the law of international armed conflict* (Cambridge, UK; New York: CUP, 2004)

Discalopoulou-Livada, P., 'The Implementation of the ICC Statute in Greece: Some Thoughts', in: Kress and Lattanzi 2000, 113-121

Dixon, R. *et al.*, *Archbold, international criminal courts: practice, procedure, and evidence* (London: Sweet & Maxwell, 2003)

Dolinger, J., 'Brazilian Supreme Court Solutions for Conflicts between Domestic and International Law: An Exercise in Eclecticism', 22 Capital University Law Review 1041 (1993)

Dörmann, K., 'War Crimes in the Elements of Crimes', in: H. Fischer, *et al.* (eds.), *International and national prosecution of crimes under international law: current developments* (Berlin: Spitz, 2001), 95-139

Dressler, J., *Understanding criminal law* (New York: Matthew Bender/Irwin, 1995)

Duffy, H., 'National Constitutional Compatibility and the International Criminal Court', 11 Duke journal of comparative & international law 5 (2001)

Dugard, J., 'International Law and the South African Constitution', 8 EJIL 77 (1997)

Dugard, J., 'Dealing with Crimes of a Past Regime. Is Amnesty Still an Option?' 12 LJIL 1001 (1999)

Dugard, J., *International law: a South African perspective* (Kenwyn: Juta & Co, 2000)

Dugard, J., 'Possible Conflicts of Jurisdiction with Truth Commissions', in: A. Cassese, *et al.* (eds.), *International criminal law: a commentary on the Rome Statute for an International Criminal Court* (Oxford: OUP, 2001), 693-704

Dupuy, P.-M., 'Les "considérations élémentaires d'humanité" dans la jurisprudence de la Cour Internationale de Justice', in: R. J. Dupuy and L.-A. Sicilianos (eds.), *Mélanges en l'honneur de Nicolas Valticos: droit et justice* (Paris: Pedone, 1999), 117-130

Dupuy, P.-M., 'Normes internationales pénales et droit impératif (*jus cogens*)', in: A. Pellet (ed.) *Droit international pénal* (Paris: Pedone, 2000), 71-80

Dutertre, G., *Key case-law extracts: European Court of Human Rights* (Strasbourg: Council of Europe Publishing, 2003)

Eftekhari, S., 'France and the Algerian War: From a Policy of "Forgetting" to a Framework for Accountability', 34 Colum. Hum. Rts. L. Rev. 413 (2003)

El Zeidy, M.M., 'The Principle of Complementarity: A New Machinery to Implement International Criminal Law', 23 Michigan Journal of International Law 869 (2002)

El Zeidy, M.M., 'Universal Jurisdiction *In Absentia*: Is it a Legal Valid Option for Repressing Heinous Crimes?', 37 The International Lawyer 835 (2003)

El Zeidy, M.M., *The principle of complementarity in international criminal law* (National University of Ireland (Galway): PhD thesis, forthcoming 2005)

Elliott, C., *French Criminal Law* (Willan Publishing, 2001)

Elst, R.v., 'De zaak Darco Knezevic: rechtsmacht over Joegoslavische en andere buitenlandse oorlogsmisdadigers', 73 NJB 1587 (1998)

Elst, R.v., 'Implementing universal jurisdiction over grave breaches of the Geneva Conventions', 13 LJIL 815 (2000)

Elst, R.v., 'Universele rechtsmacht over foltering: Bouterse en de Decembermoorden', 27 NJCM-bulletin: Nederlands tijdschrift voor de mensenrechten 208 (2002)

Engelschiøn, T.S., 'Prosecution of war crimes and violations of human rights in Ethiopia', 8 Jahrbuch für afrikanisches Recht 41 (1994)

Engelschiøn, T.S., 'Ethiopia: war crimes and violations of human rights', 34 RDMDG 9 (1995)

Erades, L. *et al.*, *Interactions between international and municipal law: a comparative case law study* (Hague: T.M.C. Asser Instituut, 1993)

Erasmus, G. and G. Kemp, 'The application of international criminal law before domestic courts in the light of recent developments in international and constitutional law', 27 South African YIL 65 (2002)

Escarameia, P., 'Notes on the Implementation of the Rome Statute in Portugal', in: Kress and Lattanzi 2000, 151-168

Ferdinandusse, W.N., 'Verdragsrechtelijke strafbaarstellingen in de Nederlandse rechtsorde, Over directe werking en het strafrechtelijk legaliteitsbeginsel', 162 Rechtsgeleerd Magazijn Themis 275 (2001)

Ferdinandusse, W.N., 'Out of the Black-box? The International Obligation of State Organs', 29 Brooklyn Journal of International Law 45 (2003)

Ferdinandusse, W.N., 'The interaction of national and international approaches in the repression of international crimes', 15 EJIL 1041 (2004)

Ferdinandusse, W.N. *et al.*, 'Origineel of reproductie? Internationale strafbaarstellingen in de Nederlandse rechtsorde', 77 NJB 341 (2002)

Fichet-Boyle, I. and M. Mossé, 'L'obligation de prendre des mesures internes nécessaires a la prévention et a la répression des infractions', in: A. Pellet (ed.) *Droit international pénal* (Paris: Pedone, 2000), 871-885

Fife, R.E., 'Non-prejudice to national application of penalties and national laws: article 80', in: O. Triffterer and K. Ambos (eds.), *Commentary on the Rome Statute of the International Criminal Court: observers' notes, article by article* (Baden-Baden: Nomos, 1999), 1009-1114

Fischer, H., 'The jurisdiction of the International Criminal Court for War Crimes: some observations concerning differences between the statute of the Court and war crimes provisions in other treaties', in: K. Ipsen, *et al.* (eds.), *Brücken bauen und begehen: Festschrift für Knut Ipsen zum 65. Geburtstag* (München: C.H. Beck, 2000), 77-101

Fischer, H. *et al.* (eds.), International and national prosecution of crimes under international law: current developments (Berlin: Spitz, 2001)

Fitzmaurice, G., 'The general principles of international law considered from the standpoint of the rule of law', 92 RdC 1 (1958)

Flaherty, M.S., 'History right?: Historical scholarship, original understanding, and treaties as "supreme law of the land"', 99 Colum. L. Rev. 2095 (1999)

Fletcher, G., 'Trois modèles de compétence universelle', in: Cassese and Delmas-Marty 2002, 451-460

Fletcher, G.P., *Basic concepts of criminal law* (New York, NY: OUP, 1998)

Fleuren, J.W.A., *Een ieder verbindende bepalingen van verdragen* (Den Haag: Boom Juridische Uitgevers, 2004)

Francisco, F.M.I., *Aspects of implementing the culpability principle both under international and national criminal law* (Nijmegen: Wolf Legal Publishers, 2003)

Franck, T.M. and G.H. Fox (eds.), International law decisions in national courts (Irvington-on-Hudson, NY: Transnational, 1996)

Frände, D., 'Finnland', in: A. Eser and H. Kreicker (eds.), *Nationale Strafverfolgung völkerrechtlicher Verbrechen – National Prosecution of International Crimes. Finnland, Polen, Schweden* (Freiburg i. Br.: 2003), 21-75

Fugard, M.T., 'Implementation of international humanitarian law at the national level with special reference to developments of modern warfare: general report', 28 RDMDG 37 (1989)

Gaja, G., 'Jus cogens beyond the Vienna convention', 172 RdC 271 (1981)

Gaja, G., 'Dualism in modern international law', paper in the serie Seminars on Theoretical Approaches to The Relationship between International and National Law (available at http://www1.jur.uva.nl/acil/pionier/Seminars_on_theoretical_approaches_to_the.htm) (2003)

Gardocki, L., 'Legal Problems Emerging from the Implementation of International Crimes in Domestic Criminal Law', 60 RIDP 91 (1989)

Gartner, I., 'Implementation of the ICC Statute in Austria', in: Kress and Lattanzi 2000, 51-63

Gattini, A., 'To What Extent are State Immunity and Non-Justiciability Major Hurdles to Individuals' Claims for War Damages?', 1 JICJ 348 (2003)

Gattini, A., 'Kelsen's Contribution to International Criminal Law', 2 JICJ 795 (2004)

Gil Gil, A., *Derecho penal internacional. Especial consideración del delito de Genocidio* (Madrid: Editorial Tecnos, 1999)

Gilbert, G., '*Crimes sans frontieres*: jurisdictional problems in English law', 63 BYIL 415 (1993)

Gitti, A., 'Impunity under national law and accountability under international human rights law: has the time of a duty to prosecute come?' 9 Italian YIL 64 (1999)

Gourevitch, P., *We wish to inform you that tomorrow we will be killed with our families: stories from Rwanda* (New York: Farrar Straus and Giroux, 1998)

Gouttes, R. de, 'Un exemple de poursuites de crimes contre l'humanité devant les juridictions nationales: le proces des criminels de l'ancien rigime du colonel Menghistu en Ethiopie', 53 RSC 697 (1998)

Gowlland Debbas, V. and D.L. Tehindrazanarivelo, *National implementation of United Nations sanctions a comparative study* (Leiden: Nijhoff, 2004)

Gowlland-Debbas, V., 'The Domestic Implementation of UN Sanctions', in: E. de Wet and A. Nollkaemper (eds.), *Review of the Security Council by member states* (Antwerpen: Intersentia, 2003), 63-76

Green, L.C., *The contemporary law of armed conflict* (Yonkers, NY / Manchester: Juris Publishing / Manchester University Press, 2000)

Greenwood, C.J., 'Belligerent Reprisals in the Jurisprudence of the International Criminal Tribunal for the Former Yugoslavia', in: H. Fischer, *et al.* (eds.), *International and national prosecution of crimes under international law: current developments* (Berlin: Spitz, 2001), 539-558

Gropp, W., 'Naturrecht oder Rückwirkungsverbot? – Zur Strafbarkeit der Berliner "Mauerschutzen"', in: K. Schmoller and O. Triffterer (eds.), *Festschrift für Otto Triffterer zum 65. Geburtstag* (Wien: Springer, 1996), 103-121

Gulmann, C., 'Denmark', in: F. G. Jacobs and S. Roberts (eds.), *The Effect of treaties in domestic law* (London: Sweet & Maxwell, 1987), 29-37

Haak, W.E., 'Nederlandse Rijnvaartovertredingen onder de Akte van Mannheim', in: G.J.M. Corstens and M.S. Groenhuijsen (eds.), *Rede en recht, Liber Amicorum Nico Keijzer* (Deventer: Gouda Quint, 2000), XII, 407 p

Haile, D., *Accountability for crimes of the past and the challenges of criminal procecutions: the case of Ethiopia* (Leuven: Leuven University Press, 2000)

Halmai, G. and K.L. Scheppele, 'Living Well is the Best revenge: The Hungarian Approach to Judging the Past', in: A.J. McAdams (ed.) *Transitional Justice in New Democracies* (Notre Dame: Notre Dame University Press, 1996), 155-184

Hammel, F.A., *Innerstaatliche Amnestien: Grundlagen und Grenzen aufgrund des internationalen Rechts* (Frankfurt am Main: Lang, 1993)

Handmaker, J., 'Seeking Justice, Guaranteeing Protection and Ensuring Due Process: Addressing the Tensions Between Exclusion from Refugee Protection and the Principle of Universal Jurisdiction', 21 NQHR 677 (2003)

Hankel, G., *Die Leipziger Prozesse Deutsche Kriegsverbrechen und ihre strafrechtliche Verfolgung nach dem Ersten Weltkrieg* (Hamburg: Hamburger Edition, 2003)

Hannikainen, L., *Peremptory norms (jus cogens) in international law: historical development, criteria, present status* (Helsinki: Finnish Lawyers' Pub. Co., 1988)

Harris, D.J. *et al.*, *Law of the European Convention on human rights* (London: Butterworths, 1995)

Hassemer, W., 'Naturrecht im Verfassungsrecht', in: A. Donatsch and others (eds.), *Strafrecht, Strafprozessrecht und Menschenrechte. Festschrift für Stefan Trechsel zum 65. Geburtstag* (Zürich: Schulthess, 2002), 135-150

Haveman, R., 'The Principle of Legality', in: R. Haveman and O. Kavran (eds.), *Supranational criminal law a system sui generis* (Antwerp: Intersentia, 2003a), 39-77

Haveman, R., 'Rape and fair trial in supranational criminal law', 9 Maastricht journal of European and comparative law 263 (2003b)

Haveman, R. and O. Kavran (eds.), Supranational criminal law: a system sui generis (Antwerp: Intersentia, 2003)

Hay, J., 'Implementing the ICC Statute in New Zealand', 2 JICJ 191 (2004)

Heinegg, W.H. v., 'Criminal international law and customary international law', in: A. Zimmermann and U.E. Heinz (eds.), *International criminal law and the current development of public international law: proceedings of an international symposium of the Kiel Walther Schücking Institute of International Law: May 30-June 2, 2002* (Berlin: Duncker & Humblot, 2003), 27-47

Heintze, H.-J., 'Zur durchsetzung der UN-Völkermordkonvention', 13 HuV 225 (2000)

Heiskanen, V., *International legal topics* (Helsinki: Lakimiesliiton Kustannus Finnish Lawyers' Publishing Company, 1992)

Helfer, L.R. and A.-M. Slaughter, 'Toward a Theory of Effective Supranational Adjudication', 107 Yale Law J. 273 (1997)

Henckaerts, J.-M., 'Self-Executing Treaties and the Impact of International Law on National Legal Systems: A Research Guide', 26 International journal of legal information 56 (1998)

Henckaerts, J.-M. *et al.* (eds.), Customary International Humanitarian Law (Cambridge: CUP, 2005)

Henkin, L., 'International law as law in the United States', 82 Michigan law review 1555 (1984)

Henkin, L., 'The Constitution and United States Sovereignty: A Century of "Chinese Exclusion" and its Progeny', 100 Harvard LR 853 (1987)

Henkin, L. (ed.) International law: cases and materials (St. Paul, Minn.: West Pub., 1993)

Henkin, L., 'An Agenda for the Next Century: The Myth and Mantra of State Sovereignty', 35 Va. J. Int'l L. 115 (1994)

Henkin, L., *Foreign affairs and the United States Constitution* (Oxford: Clarendon Press, 1996)

Henkin, L., 'Provisional measures, U.S. treaty obligations, and the States', 92 AJIL 679 (1998)

Henkin, L., 'That "S" word: sovereignty, and globalization, and human rights, et cetera', 68 Fordham Law Rev. 1 (1999)

Henzelin, M., *Le principe de l'universalite en droit penal international: droit et obligation pour les Etats de poursuivre et juger selon le principe de l'universalite* (Bale; Geneve; Munich Helbing & Lichtenhahn; Bruxelles Bruylant: 2000)

Henzelin, M., 'Droit international pénal et droits pénaux étatiques. Le choc des cultures', in: M. Henzelin and R. Roth (eds.), *Le droit pénal à l'épreuve de l'internationalisation* (Paris, Bruxelles, Geneve: L.G.D.J, Bruylant, Georg, 2002), 69-118

Heringa, A.W., *Sociale grondrechten: hun plaats in de gereedschapskist van de rechter* (The Hague: T.M.C. Asser Instituut, 1989)

Hettinger, G., *Die Völkerrechtliche Verpflichtung der Staaten zur Bestrafung Einzelner und das materielle Strafrecht der Bundesrepublik Deutschland* (München: Schön, 1965)

Higgins, R., 'Dualism in the Face of a Changing Legal Culture', in: G. S. Slynn of Hadley, *et al.* (eds.), *Judicial review in international perspective, Liber amicorum in honour of Lord Slynn of Hadley* (The Hague; Boston: Kluwer Law International, 2000), 9-22

Higgins, R., 'The Concept of "the State": Variable Geometry and Dualist Perceptions', in: G. Abi-Saab, *et al.* (eds.), *The international legal system in quest of equity and universality: liber amicorum Georges Abi-Saab* (The Hague; Boston, Mass.: Martinus Nijhoff Publishers, 2001), 547-561

Holdgaard Bukh, M., 'Prosecution before Danish Courts of foreigners suspected of serious violations of human rights or humanitarian law', 6 Revue Européenne de Droit Public 339 (1994)

Hollán, M., 'Globalisation and Conceptualisation in the Sphere of International Criminal Law', 41 Acta Jur. Hung. 225 (2000)

Hoogh, A.de, *Obligations erga omnes and international crimes: a theoretical inquiry into the implementation and enforcement of the international responsibility of states* (The Hague; Boston: Kluwer International Law, 1996)

Hope, D., 'Torture', 53 ICLQ 807 (2004)

Hullu, J.d., 'Internationale invloeden op het materiële strafrecht', in: M.S. Groenhuijsen and G.J.M. Corstens (eds.), *Rede en recht, Bundel opstellen aangeboden aan Nico Keijzer* (Deventer: 2000), 323-341

Hutchinson, M.R., 'The margin of appreciation doctrine in the European Court of Human Rights', 48 ICLQ 638 (1999)

Hyde, C.C., 'Comment: Aspects of the Saboteur Cases', 37 AJIL 88 (1943)

Ingelse, C. and H. v.d. Wilt, 'De Zaak Pinochet. Over Universele Rechtsmacht en Hollandse Benepenheid', 71 NJB 280 (1996)

Iwasawa, Y., 'The doctrine of self-executing treaties in the United States: a critical analysis', 26 Va. J. Int'l L. 627 (1986)

Iwasawa, Y., *International law, human rights, and Japanese law: the impact of international law on Japanese law* (Oxford / New York: Clarendon Press / OUP, 1998)

Jackson, J.H., 'Status of treaties in domestic legal systems: A policy analysis', 86 AJIL 310 (1992)

Jackson, J.H., 'The WTO dispute settlement understanding: misunderstanding on the nature of legal obligation', 91 AJIL 60 (1997)

Jackson, J.H., 'International law status of WTO dispute settlement reports: obligation to comply or option to "buy out"', 98 AJIL 109 (2004)

Jacobs, F.G., 'Introduction', in: F.G. Jacobs and S. Roberts (eds.), *The Effect of treaties in domestic law* (London: Sweet & Maxwell, 1987), xxiii-xxxi

Jäger, H., 'Makroverbrechen als Gegenstand des Völkerstrafrechts – Kriminalpolitisch-kriminologische Aspekte', in: G. Hankel and G. Stuby (eds.), *Strafgerichte gegen Menschheitsverbrechen* (Hamburg: 1995), 325-354

Jayawickrama, N., *The judicial application of human rights law: national, regional and international jurisprudence* (Cambridge: CUP, 2002)

Jessberger, F., 'Prosecuting international crimes in domestic courts: a look back ahead', 12 The Finnish yearbook of international law 281 (2003)

Jessberger, F. and C. Powell, 'Prosecuting Pinochets in South Africa: implementing the Rome Statute of the International Criminal Court', 14 SACJ 344 (2002)

Johnson, K.M., 'The case of General Augusto Pinochet: a legal research guide', 27 Brooklyn journal of international law 519 (2002)

Jones, J.R.W.D., 'Droit anglais', in: Cassese and Delmas-Marty 2002, 31-68

Jones, J.R.W.D. and S. Powles, *International criminal practice* (Ardsley, NY; Oxford: Transnational; OUP, 2003)

Jørgensen, N.H.B., *The responsibility of states for international crimes* (Oxford [England]; New York: OUP, 2000)

Josipovic, I. *et al.*, *The Rome statute and its implementation. Papers written for the Regional Conference "International Criminal Court and the Implementation of the Rome Statute in the Stability Pact Countries*, on file with the author (2001)

Kälin, W., 'Implementing Treaties in Domestic Law: from "Pacta Sunt Servanda" to "Anything Goes"?' in: V. Gowlland-Debbas, *et al.* (eds.), *Multilateral treaty-making: the current status of challenges to and reforms needed in the international legislative process: papers presented at the Forum Geneva held in Geneva, Switzerland, May 16, 1998* (The Hague; Boston, Mass.: Martinus Nijhoff Publishers, 2000)

Kamanga, K., 'The Rwandan conflict and the Genocide Convention: implications for Tanzania', 5 African YIL 63 (1998)

Kamminga, M.T., 'First Report on the Exercise of Universal Jurisdiction in Respect of Gross Human Rights Offences', in: International Law Association (ed.) *Report of the 68th Conference* (London: 1998), 563-583

Kareklás, S.E. and C. Papacharalambous, *Strafrecht in Reaktion auf Systemunrecht: Griechenland* (Freiburg im Breisgau: Ed. Iuscrim, 2001)

Keijzer, N., 'Terrorisme een 'core crime'?' in: M.M. Dolman (ed.) *Terrorisme, Europa en strafrecht* (Amsterdam: Vossiuspers UvA, 2003), 94

Kelsen, H., *Reine Rechtslehre: Einleitung in die rechtswissenschaftliche Problematik* (Leipzig: F. Deuticke, 1934)

Kelsen, H., *Law and Peace in International Relations* (Cambridge, Massachusetts: Harvard University Press, 1942)

Kidane, W.L., 'The Ethiopian "Red Terror" Trials', in: M. C. Bassiouni (ed.) *Post-Conflict Justice* (Ardsley: Transnational Publishers, 2003), 667-694

Kinley, D. and P. Martin, 'International human rights law at home: addressing the politics of denial', 26 Melbourne University Law Review 466 (2002)

Kirby, M., 'Criminal Law – The Global Dimension', available at http://www.lawfoundation.net.au/resources/kirby/papers/19950311_tempo.html (1995)

Kirby, M., 'The growing rapprochement between international law and national law', in: A. Anghie and G. Sturgess (eds.), *Legal visions of the 21st century: essays in honour of judge Christopher Weeramantry* (1998), 333-354

Kirby, M., 'Universal jurisdiction and judicial reluctance: a new "fourteen points"', in: S. Macedo (ed.) *Universal jurisdiction national courts and the prosecution of serious crimes under international law* (Philadelphia, PA: Un. of Pennsylvania Press, 2004), 240-259

Kittichaisaree, K., *International criminal law* (Oxford; New York: OUP, 2001)

Klabbers, J., 'How to defeat a treaty's object and purpose pending entry into force: toward manifest intent', 34 Vand. J. Transnat'l L. 283 (2001a)

Klabbers, J., 'Just Revenge? The Deterrence Argument in International Criminal Law', 12 Finnish YIL 249 (2001b)

Klabbers, J., 'The spectre of international criminal justice: third states and the ICC', in: A. Zimmermann and U.E. Heinz (eds.), *International criminal law and the current development of public international law: proceedings of an international symposium of the Kiel Walther Schücking Institute of International Law: May 30-June 2, 2002* (Berlin: Duncker & Humblot, 2003), 49-72

Kleffner, J., 'Conflict related crimes – legal obligations to prosecute?', unpublished paper, on file with the author (2000)

Kleffner, J., 'Droit néerlandais', in: Cassese and Delmas-Marty 2002, 217-258

Kleffner, J.K., 'The impact of complementarity on national implementation of substantive international criminal law', 1 JICJ 86 (2003)

Kleffner, J.K., *The principle of complementarity in the Rome Statute of the International Criminal Court and its implications for national repression of core crimes* (University of Amsterdam: PhD thesis, forthcoming 2005)

Kleffner, J.K. and A. Nollkaemper, 'The Relationship between Internationalized Courts and National Courts', in: C.P.R. Romano, *et al.* (eds.), *Internationalized Criminal Courts: Sierra Leone, East Timor, Kosovo and Cambodia* (Oxford: OUP, 2004), 359-378

Knoops, G.G.J., 'De semi-monistische invloed van het Statuut van het Internationaal Strafhof op nationaalrechtelijke vervolging van internationale misdrijven', 53 Ars aequi 729 (2004)

Knop, K., 'Here and There: International Law in Domestic Courts', 32 N.Y.U. J. Int'l L. & Pol. 501 (2000)

Kobrick, E.S., 'The Ex Post Facto Prohibition and the Exercise of Universal Jurisdiction over International Crimes', 87 Colum. L. Rev. 1515 (1987)

Koering-Joulin, R., 'L'affaire du MC Ruby et la compétence internationale des jurisdictions répressives françaises', in: C.N. Robert and B. Sträuli (eds.), *Procédure pénale, droit pénal international, entraide pénale: études en l'honneur de Dominique Poncet* (Chêne-Bourg, Suisse: Georg Éditeur, 1997), 143-154

Koh, H.H., 'Is international law really state law?', 111 Harvard LR 1824 (1998)

Komarow, G., 'Individual responsibility under international law: the Nuremberg principles in domestic legal systems', 29 ICLQ 21 (1980)

Konjecic, E., 'Friedenssicherung durch Amnestie?: Überlegungen anhand des kroatische Amnestiegesetzes von 1996', 40 WGO: die wichtigsten Gesetzgebungsakte in den Ländern Ost-, Südosteuropas und in den ostasiatischen Volksdemokratien 349 (1998)

Koskenniemi, M., *From apology to utopia: the structure of international legal argument* (Helsinki: Lakimiesliiton Kustannu, 1989)

Koskenniemi, M., 'The Pull of the Mainstream', 88 Michigan Law Review 1946 (1990)

Koskenniemi, M., 'Lauterpacht: The Victorian Tradition in International Law', 8 EJIL 215 (1997)

Koskenniemi, M., 'Between impunity and show trials', 6 MPYUNL 1 (2002)

Koskenniemi, M., 'What is international law for?' in: M. D. Evans (ed.) *International law* (Oxford; New York: OUP, 2003), 89-144

Kress, C., 'War crimes committed in non-international armed conflict and the emerging system of international criminal justice', 30 Israel YBHR 103 (2001)

Kress, C., 'The German Chief Federal Prosecutor's Decision Not to Investigate the Alleged Crime of Preparing Aggression against Iraq', 2 JICJ 245 (2004)

Kress, C. and F. Lattanzi (eds.), The Rome Statute and domestic legal orders (Baden Baden/ Ripa di Fagnano Alto: Nomos/Sirente, 2000)

Kriangsak, K., *International criminal law* (Oxford; New York: Oxford University Press, 2001)

Kritz, N.J., *Transitional justice: How emerging democracies reckon with former regimes* (Washington, DC: United States Institute of Peace Press, 1995)

Kritz, N.J., 'Coming to terms with atrocities: a review of accountability mechanisms for mass violations of human rights', 59 Law Contemp. Probl. 127 (1996)

Kunz, J.L., 'The Meaning and the Range of the Norm Pacta Sunt Servanda', 39 AJIL 180 (1945)

Küpper, H., 'Völkerrecht, Verfassung und Außenpolitik in Ungarn', 58 ZaöRV 239 (1998)

Labrin, J.B. and H.-D. Bosly, 'Case Note to In re Pinochet Ugarte 1998', 79 RDPC 291 (1999)

Lamb, S., 'Nullum Crimen, Nulla Poena Sine Lege in International Criminal Law', in: A. Cassese, *et al.* (eds.), *International criminal law: a commentary on the Rome Statute for an International Criminal Court* (Oxford: OUP, 2001), 733-766

Lambert-Abdelgawad, É., 'Les pays d'islam', in: Cassese and Delmas-Marty 2002, 521-552

Lambert-Abdelgawad, É., 'Cour pénale internationale et adaptations constitutionnelles comparées', 55 RIDC 539 (2003)

Latcham, A.M., 'Duty to Punish: International Law and the Human Rights Policy of Argentina', 7 B.U. Int'l L. J. 355 (1989)

Lattanzi, F., 'Crimes Against Humanity in the Jurisprudence of the International Criminal Tribunals for the Former Yugoslavia and Rwanda', in: H. Fischer, *et al.* (eds.), *International and national prosecution of crimes under international law: current developments* (Berlin: Spitz, 2001), 473-504

Lauterpacht, E., 'The Contemporary Practice of the United Kingdom in the Field of International Law', 7 ICLQ 92 (1958)

Lauterpacht, E., 'Sovereignty – Myth or reality?' 73 International Affairs 137 (1997)

Lauterpacht, H., 'Decisions of Municipal Courts as a Source of International Law', 10 BYIL 65 (1929)

Lauterpacht, H., 'Law of Nations and Punishment of War Crimes', 21 BYIL 58 (1944)

Lauterpacht, H., *International law, being the collected papers of Hersch Lauterpacht: Volume I – The General Works* (Cambridge [Eng.]: University Press, 1970)

Lavranos, N., *Decisions of International Organizations in the European and Domestic Legal Orders of Selected EU Member States* (Groningen: Europa Law Publishing, 2004)

Lee, K.I., 'Les États-Unis d'Amerique et le Canada', in: Cassese and Delmas-Marty 2002, 461-478

Lelieur-Fischer, J., 'Prosecuting the Crimes against Humanity Committed during the Algerian War: an Impossible Endeavour?', 2 JICJ 231 (2004)

Lenzerini, F., 'Italian Practice on Slavery: The Application of International Obligations Prohibiting Slavery by Italian Courts', 10 Italian YIL 273 (2000)

Lijnzaad, L., *Reservations to UN-human rights treaties: ratify and ruin?* (Dordrecht: Nijhoff, 1995)

Lippman, M., 'Prosecutions of Nazi War Criminals before Post-World War II Domestic Tribunals', 8 University of Miami International and Comparative Law Review 1 (1999)

Lobel, J., 'The limits of constitutional power: conflicts between foreign policy and international law', 71 Va. L. Rev. 1071 (1985)

Lockwood, G.H., 'Report on the Trial of Mercenaries: Luanda, Angola, June 1976', 7 Manitoba Law Journal 183 (1977)

Lukashuk, I.I., 'Contemporary international criminal law: concept and general features', in: G. Ginsburgs, *et al.* (eds.), *International and national law in Russia and Eastern Europe: essays in honor of George Ginsburgs* (The Hague; Boston: M. Nijhoff Publishers, 2001), 261-275

Maison, R., 'Les premiers cas d'application des dispositions pénales des Conventions de Genève par les juridictions internes', 6 EJIL 260 (1995)

Malarino, E., 'Argentina', in: K. Ambos and E. Malarino (eds.), *Persecución penal de crímenes internacionales en América Latina y España* (Montevideo: 2003), 35-81

Malaysia, Privy Council, *Public Prosecutor v. Koi*, 4 December 1967, [1968] A.C. 829

Mantovani, F., 'The general principles of international criminal law: the viewpoint of a national criminal lawyer', 1 JICJ 26 (2003)

Maqungo, S.S., 'Implementing the ICC Statute in South Africa', in: Kress and Lattanzi 2000, 183-195

Marie-Schwartzenberg, N., 'Droit russe', in: Cassese and Delmas-Marty 2002, 259-274

Massé, M., 'Droit pénal international: L'affaire du prêtre rwandais (suite)', RSC 837 (1998)

Mattarollo, R., 'Recent Argentine jurisprudence in the matter of crimes against humanity', Review of the International Commission of Jurists 11 (2001)

Mayfield, J.V., 'The prosecution of war crimes and respect for human rights: Ethiopia's balancing act', 9 Emory international law review 553 (1995)

McCarthy, A.C., 'Torture: Thinking About the Unthinkable – What international and American law rightly forbids, dire circumstances sometimes demand', 118 Commentary 17 (2004)

McFadden, P.M., 'Provincialism in United States Courts', 81 Cornell L. Rev. 4 (1995)

Meijers, H., 'Ongeschreven volkenrecht in de Nederlandse rechtspraak', *Mededelingen van de Nederlandse Vereniging voor Internationaal Recht* (Deventer: Kluwer, 1985), 57-159

Mendelson, M., 'The effect of customary international law on domestic law: An overview', 4 Non-State Actors and International Law 75 (2004)

Meron, T., 'On a hierarchy of international human rights', 80 AJIL 1 (1986)

Meron, T., *Human rights and humanitarian norms as customary law* (Oxford / New York: Clarendon Press / OUP, 1989)

Meron, T., 'The Continuing Role of Custom in the Formation of International Humanitarian Law', 90 AJIL 238 (1996)

Meron, T., 'Is International Law Moving towards Criminalization?' 9 EJIL 18 (1998)

Meyer, M.A., 'Liability of prisoners of war for offences committed prior to capture: the Astiz affair', 32 ICLQ 848 (1983)

Millett, L., 'The Pinochet case: some personal reflections', in: M.D. Evans (ed.) *International law* (Oxford; New York: OUP, 2003), 7-10

Mitchell, A.D., 'Genocide, human rights implementation and the relationship between international and domestic law: Nulyarimma v. Thompson', 24 Melbourne University Law Review 15 (2000)

Modolell González, J.L., 'Venezuela', in: K. Ambos and E. Malarino (eds.), *Persecución penal de crímenes internacionales en América Latina y España* (Montevideo: 2003), 535-576

Mohácsi, P. and P. Polt, 'Estimation of war crimes and crimes against humanity according to the decision of the Constitutional Court of Hungary', 67 RIDP 333 (1996)

Moir, L., *The law of internal armed conflict* (Cambridge, England; New York: CUP, 2002)

Morgenstern, F., 'Judicial Practice and the Supremacy of International Law', 27 BYIL 42 (1950)

Morris, M., 'The disturbing democratic defect of the International Criminal Court', 12 Finnish YIL 109 (2001)

Morris, V. and M.P. Scharf, *The International Criminal Tribunal for Rwanda* (Irvington-on-Hudson, N.Y.: Transnational Publishers, 1998)

Mowbray, A., 'Duties of Investigation Under the European Convention on Human Rights', 51 ICLQ 437 (2002)

Müller-Schieke, I.K., 'Defining the Crime of Aggression Under the Statute of the International Criminal Court', 14 LJIL 409 (2001)

Mundis, D., 'The United States of America and International Justice', 2 JICJ 2 (2004)

Murphy, S.D., 'Contemporary practice of the United States relating to international law', 98 AJIL 591 (2004)

Murray, R., *The African Commission on Human and People's Rights and international law* (Oxford; Portland, Or.: Hart Pub., 2000)

Nemitz, J.C., 'Sentencing in the Jurisprudence of the International Criminal Tribunals for the Former Yugoslavia and Rwanda', in: Fischer/Kreß/Lüder (eds.) *International and National Prosecution of Crimes Under International Law: Current Developments* (Berlin: Berlin Verlag, 2001), 605-625

Neuner, M., *National legislation incorporating international crimes approaches of civil and common law countries* (Berlin: BWV Berliner Wissenschafts-Verlag GmbH, 2003)

Nieto-Navia, R., 'International peremptory norms ("jus cogens") and international humanitarian law', in: A. Cassese and L. C. Vohrah (eds.), *Man's inhumanity to man: essays on international law in honour of Antonio Cassese* (The Hague; New York: Kluwer Law International, 2003), 595-640

Nollkaemper, P.A., *De dialectiek tussen individuele en collectieve aansprakelijkheid in het volkenrecht* (Amsterdam: Vossiuspers AUP, 2000)

Nollkaemper, P.A., 'The Direct Effect of Public International Law', in: J.M. Prinssen and A. Schrauwen (eds.), *Direct effect: rethinking a classic of EC legal doctrine* (Groningen: Europa Law Publishing, 2002), 157-180

Nollkaemper, P.A., 'Concurrence between Individual Responsibility and State Responsibility in International Law', 52 ICLQ 615 (2003a)

Nollkaemper, P.A., 'Decisions of National Courts as Sources of International Law: An Analysis of the Practice of the ICTY', in: G. Boas and W. A. Schabas (eds.), *International and Criminal Law Developments in the Case Law of the ICTY* (Leiden/Boston: Brill, 2003b), 277-296

Nollkaemper, P.A. and L. Zegveld, 'Aleksovski, Commentary', in: A. Klip and G. Sluiter (eds.), *Annotated leading cases of international criminal tribunals, Vol. IV* (Antwerp: Intersentia, 2002), 411-418

Nsereko, D.D.N., 'Implementing the ICC Statute within the Southern African Region (SADC)', in: Kress and Lattanzi 2000, 169-182

Oellers-Frahm, K., 'Die Beachtung völkerrechtlicher Verpflichtungen in Frankreich', in: H.-J. Cremer and H. Steinberger (eds.), *Tradition und Weltoffenheit des Rechts: Festschrift für Helmut Steinberger* (Berlin: Springer, 2002), 865-898

O'Keefe, R., 'Customary international crimes in English courts', 72 BYIL 293 (2002)

O'Keefe, R., 'Universal Jurisdiction – Clarifying the Basic Concept', 2 JICJ 735 (2004)

O'Shea, A., *Amnesty for crime in international law and practice* (The Hague: Kluwer Law International, 2002)

Osiel, M., *Obeying orders: atrocity, military discipline & the law of war* (New Brunswick, NJ: Transaction Publishers, 1999)

Osofsky, H.M., 'Domesticating international criminal law: bringing human rights violators to justice', 107 Yale Law J. 191 (1997)

Panhuys, H.F. v., 'The Netherlands Constitution and International Law', 47 AJIL 537 (1953)

Panhuys, H.F. v., 'The Netherlands Constitution and International Law: A Decade of Experience', 58 AJIL 88 (1964)

Panken, H., 'Individuele strafrechtelijke aansprakelijkheid naar internationaal recht voor ernstige schendingen van mensenrechten', in: J. Wouters and H. Panken (eds.), *De Genocidewet in internationaal perspectief* (2003), 361-364

Panken, H. *et al.*, 'Het arrest Sharon van het Hof van Cassatie: bouwstenen voor de verdere rol van universele jurisdictie, internationale immuniteiten en de doorwerking van het internationaal gewoonterecht', working paper, available at http://www.law.kuleuven.ac.be/iir/nl/wp/WP61n.pdf (2004)

Partsch, K.J., 'International Law and Municipal Law', in: R. Bernhardt (ed.) *Encyclopedia of public international law* (Amsterdam; New York: MPI, 1992), 238-257

Pasqualucci, J.M., *The practice and procedure of the Inter-American Court of Human Rights* (Cambridge: CUP, 2003)

Paust, J.J., 'After My Lai: The Case for War Crime Jurisdiction Over Civilians in Federal District Courts', 50 Texas law review 6 (1971)

Paust, J.J., 'Federal jurisdiction over extraterritorial acts of terrorism and immunity for foreign violaters of international law under the FSIA and the act of state doctrine', 23 Va. J. Int'l L. 191 (1983)

Paust, J.J., 'Self-Executing Treaties', 82 AJIL 760 (1988)

Paust, J.J., 'Suing Saddam: Private Remedies for War Crimes and Hostage-Taking', 31 Va. J. Int'l L. 351 (1991)

Paust, J.J., 'Avoiding Fraudulent Executive Policy: Analysis of Non-Self-Execution of the Covenant on Civil and Political Rights', 42 DePaul L. Rev. 1257 (1993)

Paust, J.J., *International criminal law: cases and materials* (Durham, N.C.: Carolina Academic Press, 2000)

Paust, J.J., 'Abuse of Iraqi Detainees at Abu Ghraib: Will Prosecution and Cashiering of a Few Soldiers Comply With International Law?', available at http://jurist.law.pitt.edu/forum/paust1.php (2004)

Paust, J.J., 'It's no defense: nullum crimen, international crime and the gingerbread man', 60 Albany Law Review 657 (1997a)

Paust, J.J., 'Nullum crimen and related claims', 25 Denver j. int. law policy 321 (1997b)

Paust, J.J. and A.P. Blaustein, 'War Crimes Jurisdiction and Due Process: The Bangladesh Experience', 11 Van. J. Transnat'l. L. 1 (1978)

Pedain, A., 'The emergence of state duties to prosecute perpetrators of gross human rights violations in international law: a jurisprudential perspective', 13 Kings College Law Journal 53 (2002)

Peglau, J., 'Die Vorschriften zu Strafen und Strafzumessung für den Internationalen Strafgerichtshof und ihre Bedeutung für das nationale Strafrecht', 14 HuV 247 (2001a)

Peglau, J., 'Penalties and the Determination of the Sentence in the Rules of Procedure and Evidence', in: H. Fischer, *et al.* (eds.), *International and national prosecution of crimes under international law: current developments* (Berlin: Spitz, 2001b), 141-154

Pellet, A., 'The new draft articles of the International Law Commission on the responsibility of States for internationally wrongful acts: a requiem for State's crimes?', 32 NYIL (2001)

Pellet, A., 'Applicable Law', in: A. Cassese, *et al.* (eds.), *International criminal law: a commentary on the Rome Statute for an International Criminal Court* (Oxford: OUP, 2002), 1051-1084

Pellet, A., 'Les articles de la C. D. I. sur la responsabilité de l'État pour fait internationalement illicite suite – et fin', 48 Annuaire francais de droit international 1 (2003)

Penrose, M.M., 'Impunity – Inertia, Inaction, and Invalidity: A Literature Review', 17 B.U. Int'l L. J. 269 (1999)

Perkins, J.A., 'The changing foundations of international law: from state consent to state responsibility', 15 B.U. Int'l L. J. 433 (1997)

Pescatore, P., 'Conclusion', in: F. G. Jacobs, *et al.* (eds.), *The effect of treaties in domestic law* (London: Sweet & Maxwell, 1987), 273-283

Peyró, L.A., *La compétence universelle en matière de crimes contre l'humanité* (Bruxelles: Bruylant, 2003)

Pictet, J.S. *et al.*, *The Geneva Conventions of 12 August 1949 commentary* (Geneva: International Committee of the Red Cross, 1960)

Pieroth, B. and H.D. Jarass, *Grundgesetz für die Bundesrepublik Deutschland, Kommentar* (München: C. H. Beck'sche Verlagsbuchhandlung, 1995)

Pilloud, C. *et al.*, *Commentary on the additional protocols of 8 June 1977 to the Geneva Conventions of 12 August 1949* (Geneva/Norwell, MA: International Committee of the Red Cross: M. Nijhoff Publishers, 1987)

Polakiewicz, J., 'Die innerstaatliche Durchsetzung der Urteile des Europäischen Gerichtshof für Menschenrechte: Gleichzeitig eine Anmerkung zum Vermeire-Urteil des Europäischen Gerichtshofs für Menschenrechte vom 29. November 1991', 52 ZaöRV 149 (1991)

Politi, M., *The International Criminal Court and the crime of aggression* (Aldershot: Ashgate, 2004)

Pomorski, S., 'International law in the Polish municipal legal order: a historical overview and the current constitutional status', in: G. Ginsburgs, *et al.* (eds.), *International and national law in Russia and Eastern Europe: essays in honor of George Ginsburgs* (The Hague; Boston: M. Nijhoff Publishers, 2001), 295-317

Posner, M.H., ' Response to Harold Koh's Childress Lecture: a United States human rights policy for the 21st century', 46 Saint Louis University Law Journal 411 (2002)

Poutiers, M., 'L'extradition des auteurs d'infractions internationales', in: H. Ascensio, *et al.* (eds.), *Droit international pénal* (Paris: Pedone, 2000), 933-950

Prinssen, J.M., *Doorwerking van Europees recht: de verhouding tussen directe werking, conforme interpretatie en overheidsaansprakelijkheid* (Deventer: Kluwer, 2004)

Provost, R., 'Reciprocity in human rights and humanitarian law', 65 BYIL 383 (1995)

Provost, R., *International human rights and humanitarian law* (Cambridge: CUP, 2002)

Rack, R., *Das Völkerrecht im staatlichen Recht: Transformation und Adoption* (Wien: Manz, 1979)

Raimondo, F., 'The Implementation of the Rome Statute of the International Criminal Court in Latin America: The Case of Argentina', 4 Griffin's View on International and Comparative Law 117 (2003)

Rasulov, A., 'Revisiting state succession to humanitarian treaties: is there a case for automaticity', 14 EJIL 141 (2003)

Ratner, S.R. and J.S. Abrams, *Accountability for human rights atrocities in international law: beyond the Nuremberg legacy* (Oxford: OUP, 2001)

Rawls, J., *The law of peoples* (Cambridge, Mass.: Harvard University Press, 1999)

Redae, M., 'Revisiting the Ethiopian "Genocide" Trial: Problems and Proposals', Paper on file with the author (1999)

Redgwell, C., 'US reservations to human rights treaties: all for one and none for all?' in: M. Byers and G. Nolte (eds.), *United States hegemony and the foundations of international law* (Cambridge, UK; New York: CUP, 2003), 392-415

Reisman, W.M., 'An international farce: the sad case of the PLO Mission', 14 Yale J. Int'l L. 412 (1989)

Reydams, L., 'Universal Jurisdiction over Atrocities in Rwanda: Theory and Practice', 4 Eur. J Crime, Crim. L & Crim. Jus 18 (1996)

Reydams, L., 'Niyonteze v. Public Prosecutor', 96 AJIL 231 (2002)

Reydams, L., *Universal jurisdiction: international and municipal legal perspectives* (Oxford: OUP, 2003)

Riesenfeld, S.A., 'The Doctrine of Self-Executing Treaties and U.S. v. Postal: Win at Any Price?', 74 AJIL 892 (1980)

Roberts, A.E., 'Traditional and Modern Approaches to Customary International Law: A Reconciliation', 95 AJIL 757 (2001)

Robinson, D., 'Serving The Interests Of Justice: Amnesties, Truth Commissions And The International Criminal Court', 14 EJIL 481 (2003)

Robinson, D. and H.v. Hebel, 'War crimes in internal conflicts: Article 8 of the ICC Statute', 2 YIHL 193 (1999)

Robledo, A.G., 'Le ius cogens international: sa genese, sa nature, ses fonctions', 172 RdC 9 (1981)

Rodley, N.S., *The treatment of prisoners under international law* (Oxford: Clarendon Press, 1999)

Rogall, K., 'Bewältigung von Systemkriminalität', in: C.-W. Canaris (ed.) *50 Jahre Bundesgerichtshof: Festgabe aus der Wissenschaft* (München: Verlag C.H. Beck, 2000), 383-438

Rogers, J.M., '"Intensional Contexts" and the Rule that Statutes Should be Interpreted as Consistent with International law', 73 Notre Dame Law Review 637 (1998)

Rogers, J.M., *International law and United States law* (Aldershot, Hants, England; Brookfield, Vt., USA: Ashgate/Dartmouth, 1999)

Roht-Arriaza, N., 'State Responsibility to Investigate and Prosecute Grave Human Rights Violations in International Law', 78 California Law Review 449 (1990)

Roht-Arriaza, N. (ed.) Impunity and Human Rights in International Law and Practice (New York: OUP, 1995)

Röling, B.V.A., 'Supranational criminal law in Netherlands theory and practice', in: H.F. van Panhuys *et al.* (ed.) *International law in the Netherlands* (Alphen aan den Rijn: Sijthoff & Noordhoff, 1979), 161-201

Romano, C.P.R. *et al.* (eds.), Internationalized Criminal Courts: Sierra Leone, East Timor, Kosovo and Cambodia (Oxford: OUP, 2004)

Rosenkrantz, C.F., 'Against borrowings and other nonauthoritative uses of foreign law', 1 International Journal of Constitutional Law 269 (2003)

Rosenne, S., *Developments in the law of treaties, 1945-1986* (Cambridge [Cambridgeshire]; New York: CUP, 1989)

Rosenne, S., 'State responsibility and international crimes: further reflections on Article 19 of the Draft Articles on State Responsibility', 30 N.Y.U. J. Int'l L. & Pol. 145 (1998)

Roth, R. and Y. Jeanneret, 'Droit allemand', in: A. Cassese and M. Delmas-Marty (eds.), *Juridictions nationales et crimes internationaux* (Paris: Presses universitaires de France, 2002a), 7-30

Roth, R. and Y. Jeanneret, 'Droit suisse', in: A. Cassese and M. Delmas-Marty (eds.), *Juridictions nationales et crimes internationaux* (Paris: Presses universitaires de France, 2002b), 275-298

Rowe, P., 'Murder and the Law of War', 42 Northern Ireland Legal Quarterly 216 (1991)

Rowe, P. and M.A. Meyer, 'The Geneva Conventions (Amendment) Act 1995: A Generally Minimalist Approach', 45 ICLQ 476 (1996)

Rubenfeld, J., 'What Good is International Law? The Two World Orders', 27 Wilson quarterly 22 (2003)

Rubin, A.P., *The law of piracy* (Irvington-on-Hudson, N.Y.: Transnational Publishers, 1998)

Rückert, W. and G. Witschel, 'Genocide and Crimes against Humanity in the Elements of Crimes', in: H. Fischer, *et al.* (eds.), *International and national prosecution of crimes under international law: current developments* (Berlin: Spitz, 2001), 59-94

Rüter, C.F., *Enkele aspecten van de strafrechtelijke reactie op oorlogsmisdrijven en misdrijven tegen de menselijkheid* (Amsterdam: University Press, 1973)

Rytter, J.E., 'No punishment without guilt: the case concerning German prosecution of a former GDR border guard', 21 NQHR 39 (2003)

Saar, J. and J. Sootak, 'Estland', in: A. Eser and J. Arnold (eds.), *Strafrecht in Reaktion auf Systemunrecht: Rußland, Weißrußland, Georgien, Estland, Litauen* (Freiburg im Breisgau: Ed. Iuscrim, 2003), 168-180 and 261-278

Sadat, L.N., 'International criminal law and alternative modes of redress', in: A. Zimmermann and U. E. Heinz (eds.), *International criminal law and the current development of public international law: proceedings of an international symposium of the Kiel Walther Schücking Institute of International Law: May 30-June 2, 2002* (Berlin: Duncker & Humblot, 2003), 161-194

Sadat, L.N., 'Universal jurisdiction, national amnesties and truth commissions: reconciling the irreconcilable', in: S. Macedo (ed.) *Universal jurisdiction national courts and the prosecution of serious crimes under international law* (Philadelphia, PA: University of Pennsylvania Press, 2004), 193-213

Sadat Wexler, L., 'The Interpretation of the Nuremberg Principles by the French Court of Cassation: From Touvier to Barbie and Back Again', 32 Columbia J. Transnatl. Law 289 (1994)

Safferling, C.J.M., *Towards an international criminal procedure* (Oxford: OUP, 2001)

Salcedo, J.A.C., 'Reflections on the Existence of a Hierarchy of Norms in International Law', 8 EJIL 583 (1997)

Sancinetti, M.A. and M. Ferrante, *El derecho penal en la proteccion de los derechos humanos* (Buenos Aires: Hammurabi, 1999)

Sancinetti, M.A. and M. Ferrante, *Strafrecht in Reaktion auf Systemunrecht: Argentinien* (Freiburg im Breisgau: Ed. Iuscrim, 2002)

Sands, P., 'International Law Transformed? From Pinochet to Congo...?', 16 LJIL 37 (2003)

Santalla Vargas, E., 'Bolivia', in: K. Ambos and E. Malarino (eds.), *Persecución penal de crímenes internacionales en América Latina y España* (Montevideo: 2003), 83-118

Santulli, C., *Le statut international de l'ordre juridique étatique: étude du traitement du droit interne par le droit international* (Paris: Pedone, 2001)

Sassoli, M., 'Droit international pénal et droit interne: le cas des territoires se trouvant sous administration internationale', in: M. Henzelin and R. Roth (eds.), *Le droit pénal à l'épreuve de l'internationalisation* (Paris, Bruxelles, Geneve: L.G.D.J, Bruylant, Georg, 2002), 119-149

Sassòli, M. and A.A. Bouvier, *How does law protect in war? Cases, documents, and teaching materials on contemporary practice in international humanitarian law* (Geneva: International Committee of the Red Cross, 1999)

Sassòli, M. *et al.*, *Un droit dans la guerre?* (Genève: Comité International de la Croix-Rouge, 2003)

Schaack, B.V., 'The Crime of Political Genocide: Repairing the Genocide Convention's Blind Spot', 106 Yale Law J. 2259 (1997)

Schaack, B.V., 'In Defense of Civil Redress: The Domestic Enforcement of Human Rights Norms in the Context of the Proposed Hague Judgments Convention', 42 Harv. Int. Law J. 141 (2001)

Schabas, W., 'Mugesera v. Minister of Citizenship and Immigration', 93 AJIL 529 (1999)

Schabas, W., 'Akayesu, Commentary', in: A. Klip and G. Sluiter (eds.), *Annotated leading cases of international criminal tribunals Vol. II: The International Criminal Tribunal for Rwanda 1994-1999* (Groningen: Intersentia, 2000a), 539-554

Schabas, W., *Genocide in international law: the crimes of crimes* (New York: CUP, 2000b)

Schabas, W., 'Droit pénal international et droit international des droits de l'homme: faux freres?' in: R. Roth (ed.) *Le droit pénal à l'épreuve de l'internationalisation* (Paris, Bruxelles, Geneve: L.G.D.J, Bruylant, Georg, 2002a), 165-181

Schabas, W., 'Is Terrorism a Crime Against Humanity?' 8 International Peacekeeping 255 (2002b)

Schabas, W., 'Canadian implementing Legislation for the Rome Statute: Jurisdiction and Defences', in: M. Neuner (ed.) *National legislation incorporating international crimes approaches of civil and common law countries* (Berlin: BWV Berliner Wissenschafts-Verlag GmbH, 2003a), 35-43

Schabas, W.A., 'Sentencing by international tribunals: a human rights approach', 7 Duke journal of comparative & international law 461 (1997)

Schabas, W.A., 'Perverse effects of the nulla poena principle: national practice and the ad hoc tribunals', 11 EJIL 521 (2000c)

Schabas, W.A., 'The Crime of Genocide in the Jurisprudence of the International Criminal Tribunals for the Former Yugoslavia and Rwanda', in: H. Fischer, *et al.* (eds.), *International and national prosecution of crimes under international law: current developments* (Berlin: Spitz, 2001), 447

Schabas, W.A., 'National courts finally begin to prosecute genocide, the "crime of crimes"', 1 JICJ 39 (2003b)

Scharf, M.P., 'The Letter of the Law: The Scope of the International Legal Obligation to Prosecute Human Rights Crimes, in: Law and Contemporary Problems', 59 Law Contemp. Probl. 41 (1996a)

Scharf, M.P., 'Swapping Amnesty For Peace: Was There a Duty to Prosecute International Crimes in Haiti?' 31 Texas I.L.J. 1 (1996b)

Schiffrin, L., 'De Eichmann a Schwammberger, de Priebke a Videla: la evolución de la idea de imprescriptibilidad de los delitos de lesa humanidad en el derecho argentino', in: O. Balaban and A. Megged (eds.), *Impunidad y derechos humanos en América latina* (La Plata: Al Margen, 2003), 131-152

Schilling, T., 'Ungeschriebene Strafpflichten: eine wertende Bestandsaufnahme des Völker-, Gemeinschafts-, und (deutschen) Verfassungsrechts', 54 Zeitschrift für öffentliches Recht 357 (1999)

Schmidt, M., *Externe Strafpflichten Völkerstrafrecht und seine Wirkungen im deutschen Strafrecht* (Frankfurt am Main: Peter Lang, 2002)

Scholler, H., 'Die neue äthiopische Verfassung und der Schutz der Menschenrechte', 30 Verfassung und Recht in Übersee 166 (1997)
Schwarzenberger, G., 'The Problem of an International Criminal Law', 3 Current legal problems 263 (1950)
Scott, G.L. and C.L. Carr, 'Multilateral treaties and the formation of customary international law', 25 Denver j. int. law policy 71 (1996)
Segall, A., 'Punishment of War Crimes at the National Level: Obligations under International Humanitarian Law and the Complementarity Principle established by the International Criminal Court', in: M. Neuner (ed.) *National legislation incorporating international crimes approaches of civil and common law countries* (Berlin: BWV Berliner Wissenschafts-Verlag GmbH, 2003), 257-271
Seibert-Fohr, A., 'Domestic implementation of the International Covenant on Civil and Political Rights pursuant to its article 2 para.2', 5 MPYUNL 399 (2001)
Seibert-Fohr, A., 'The fight against impunity under the International Covenant on Civil and Political Rights', 6 MPYUNL 301 (2002a)
Seibert-Fohr, A., 'Neue internationale Anforderungen an die Überführung von Menschenrechtsabkommen in nationales Recht: das Verhältnis des Internationalen Pakts über bürgerliche und politische Rechte zu nationalem Recht', 62 ZaöRV 391 (2002b)
Seibert-Fohr, A., 'The Relevance of the Rome Statute of the International Criminal Court for Amnesties and Truth Commissions', 7 MPYUNL 553 (2003)
Seiderman, I.D., *Hierarchy in international law: the human rights dimension* (Antwerpen: Intersentia, 2001)
Seidl-Hohenveldern, I., 'Transformation or Adoption of International Law into Municipal Law', 12 ICLQ 88 (1963)
Shahabuddeen, M., 'Does the Principle of Legality Stand in the Way of Progressive Development of Law?', 2 JICJ 1007 (2004)
Sharp, D.N., 'Prosecutions, development, and justice: the trial of Hissein Habré', 16 Harv. Hum. Rts. J. 147 (2003)
Shaw, M.N., *International law* (Cambridge, UK; New York, NY: CUP, 2003)
Shirey, K., 'The duty to compensate victims of torture under customary international law', 14 International Legal Perspectives 30 (2004)
Sieber, U., *The punishment of serious crimes, a comparative analysis of sentencing law and practice* (Freiburg/Breisgau: Ed. Iuscrim, 2004)
Simma, B., 'The Contribution of Alfred Verdross to the Theory of International Law', 6 EJIL 33 (1995)
Simma, B. and A. Paulus, 'The Responsibility of Individuals for Human Rights Abuses in Internal Conflicts: A Positivist View', 93 AJIL 302 (1999)
Simma, B. and A. Paulus, 'Le rôle relatif des différentes sources du droit international pénal: dont les principes généraux de droit', in: H. Ascensio, *et al.* (eds.), *Droit international pénal* (Paris: Pedone, 2000), 55-69
Sinclair, I., 'The Vienna Convention on the Law of Treaties: The Consequences of Participation and Nonparticipation', 78 Am. Soc'y Int'l Proc. 271 (1984)
Slaughter, A.M., 'Court to court', 92 AJIL 708 (1998)
Slaughter, A.-M., 'A typology of transjudicial communication', 29 U. Rich. L. Rev. 99 (1994)
Slaughter, A.-M., 'International Law in a World of Liberal States', 6 EJIL 503 (1995)
Sliedregt, E. v., *The criminal responsibility of individuals for violations of international humanitarian law* (The Hague: T.M.C. Asser Press, 2003)
Sloss, D., 'The domestication of international human rights: non-self-executing Declarations and human rights treaties', 24 Yale j. int. law 129 (1998)

Sluiter, G., 'Implementation of the ICC Statute in the Dutch Legal Order', 2 JICJ 158 (2004)
Smet, L. and F. Naert, 'Het toepassingsgebied van de Genocidewet', in: J. Wouters and H. Panken (eds.), *De Genocidewet in internationaal perspectief* (2003), 39-63
Solf, W.A. and E.R. Cummings, 'A Survey of Penal Sanctions Under Protocol I to the Geneva Conventions of August 12, 1949', 9 Case Western Reserve Journal of International Law 205 (1977)
Sólyom, L. and G. Brunner, *Constitutional judiciary in a new democracy: the Hungarian Constitutional Court* (Ann Arbor, Mich: University of Michigan Press, 2000)
Sonnevend, P., 'Verjährung und völkerrechtliche Verbrechen in der Rechtsprechung des ungarischen Verfassungsgerichts', 57 ZaöRV 195 (1997)
Spirakos, D., *Folter als Problem des Strafrechts kriminologische, kriminalsoziologische und (straf-)rechtsdogmatische Aspekte unter besonderer Berücksichtigung der Folterschutzkonvention und der Pönalisierung der Folter in Griechenland* (Frankfurt am Main: Lang, 1990)
Stahn, C., 'Die Umsetzung des Rom-Statuts in nationales Recht: ein erster rechtsvergleichender Überblick zugleich ein Ergebnisbericht der ICLS Konferenz "Rom-Statut – was folgt: Ansätze des In- und Auslandes zur Umsetzung des Völkerrechts in nationales Recht"', 13 HuV 200 (2000)
Steiger, H., 'The Relationship of German National Law with Public International Law and with European Community Law', in: T.A.J.A. Vandamme and J. H. Reestman (eds.), *Ambiguity in the rule of law: the interface between national and international legal systems* (Groningen: Europa Law Publishing, 2001), 63-82
Stein, E., 'International Law in Internal Law: Toward Internationalization of Central-Eastern European Constitutions?', 88 AJIL 427 (1994)
Steiner, H.J. and P. Alston, *International human rights in context: law, politics, morals: text and materials* (Oxford: OUP, 2000)
Steinhardt, R.G., 'International Humanitarian Law in the Courts of the United States: Yamashita, Filartiga, and 911', 36 The George Washington international law review 1 (2004)
Stern, B., 'International decisions: In re Javor and In re Munyeshyaka', 93 AJIL 525 (1999)
Steven, L.A., 'Genocide and the duty to extradite or prosecute: why the United States is in breach of its international obligations', 39 Va. J. Int'l L. 425 (1999)
Stirling-Zanda, S., *L'application judiciaire du droit international coutumier: étude comparée de la pratique européenne* (Zürich: Schulthess, 2000)
Stirling-Zanda, S., 'The individual criminal responsibility of judicial organs in international law in the light of international practice', 48 NILR 67 (2001)
Stirling-Zanda, S., 'The determination of customary international law in European courts (France, Germany, Italy, The Netherlands, Spain, Switzerland)', 4 Non-State Actors and International Law 3 (2004)
Strijards, G.A.M., 'Neerlands dualisme en zijn strafmacht', 75 NJB 2113 (2000)
Stuby, G., 'Internationale Strafgerichtsbarkeit und staatliche Souveränität', in: G. Hankel and G. Stuby (eds.), *Strafgerichte gegen Menschheitsverbrechen* (Hamburg: 1995), 429-464
Stuckenberg, C.-F., 'Multiplicity of Offences: Concursus Delictorum', in: H. Fischer, *et al.* (eds.), *International and national prosecution of crimes under international law: current developments* (Berlin: Spitz, 2001), 559-604
Sunga, L.S., *The emerging system of international criminal law: developments in codification and implementation* (The Hague; Boston: Kluwer Law International, 1997)
Swart, A.H.J., *De berechting van internationale misdrijven* (Deventer: Gouda Quint, 1996)

Swart, A.H.J. and A.H. Klip (eds.), International criminal law in the Netherlands (Freiburg im Breisgau: Edition iuscrim, 1997)

Swart, A.H.J., 'Pinochet, volkenrechtelijk gewoonterecht en (dubbele) strafbaarheid', in: M.S. Groenhuijsen and G.J.M. Corstens (eds.), *Rede en recht, Bundel opstellen aangeboden aan Nico Keijzer* (Deventer: 2000), 191-204

Swart, A.H.J., 'International Crimes: Present Situation and Future Developments', Revised version of a paper submitted to Siracusa Conference 2002, on file with the author (2002a)

Swart, A.H.J., 'Le place des critères traditionnels de compétence dans la poursuite des crimes internationaux', in: A. Cassese and M. Delmas-Marty (eds.), *Juridictions nationales et crimes internationaux* (Presses Universitaires de France, 2002b), 567-587

Swart, A.H.J., 'Universaliteit', in: M. Wladimiroff and T. Spronken (eds.), *Iets bijzonders. Liber Amicorum Mischa Wladimiroff* (Den Haag: SDU Uitgevers, 2002c), 243-262

Tanaka, T., 'Implementation of international criminal law: reconsideration from the perspective of Japanese law', 38 The Japanese annual of international law 65 (1995)

Thürer, D., 'Verfassungsrecht und Völkerrecht', in: D. Thürer, *et al.* (eds.), *Verfassungsrecht der Schweiz: Droit constitutionnel suisse* (Zürich: Schultess, 2001), 179-206

Todres, J., 'Emerging Limitations on the Rights of the Child: The UN Convention on the Rights of the Child and Its Early Case Law', 30 Colum. Hum. Rts. L. Rev. 159 (1998)

Tomuschat, C., 'International law: ensuring the survival of mankind on the eve of a new century: general course on public international law', 281 RdC 9 (2001)

Tomuschat, C., 'The duty to prosecute international crimes committed by individuals', in: H.-J. Cremer and H. Steinberger (eds.), *Tradition und Weltoffenheit des Rechts: Festschrift für Helmut Steinberger* (Berlin: Springer, 2002), 315-349

Tournaye, C., 'Genocidal intent before the ICTY', 52 ICLQ 447 (2003)

Trang, D.V., 'The historical justice debate: international law and its impact on rights in Hungary', 36 Acta Jur. Hung. 79 (1994)

Trang, D.V., 'Beyond the historical justice debate: the incorporation of international law and the impact on constitutional structures and rights in Hungary', 28 Vand. J. Transnat'l L. 1 (1995)

Triffterer, O., *Dogmatische Untersuchungen zur Entwicklung des materiellen Völkerstrafrechts seit Nürnberg* (Frieburg i. Br.: E. Albert, 1966)

Triffterer, O., 'Efforts to recognize and Codify International Crimes', 60 RIDP 31 (1989)

Turns, D., 'Aspects of national implementation of the Rome Statute: the United Kingdom and selected other states', in: D. McGoldrick, *et al.* (eds.), *The permanent international criminal court: legal and policy issues* (Oxford; Portland, Or.: Hart Pub., 2004), 337-387

Udvaros, J., 'Ungarn', in: A. Eser and J. Arnold (eds.), *Strafrecht in Reaktion auf Systemunrecht: Polen, Ungarn* (Freiburg im Breisgau: Ed. Iuscrim, 2002), 151-357

Vandermeersch, D., 'Droit belge', in: A. Cassese and M. Delmas-Marty (eds.), *Juridictions nationales et crimes internationaux* (Paris: Presses universitaires de France, 2002a), 69-120

Vandermeersch, D., 'La compétence universelle', in: A. Cassese and M. Delmas-Marty (eds.), *Juridictions nationales et crimes internationaux* (Paris: Presses universitaires de France, 2002b), 589-612

Vandermeersch, D., 'The ICC Statute and Belgian Law', 2 JICJ 133 (2004)

Vazquez, C.M., 'The four doctrines of self-executing treaties', 89 AJIL 695 (1995)

Vázquez, C.M., 'Laughing at treaties', 99 Colum. L. Rev. 2154 (1999)

Verdross, A. and B. Simma, *Universelles Völkerrecht: Theorie und Praxis* (Berlin: Duncker und Humblot, 1984)

Vereshchetin, V.S., 'New Constitutions and the Old Problem of the Relationship between International Law and National Law', 7 EJIL 29 (1996)

Vest, H., 'Zum Handlungsbedarf auf dem Gebiet des Völkerstrafrechts – Elemente eines Gesetzgebungsvorschlags', 121 Schweizerische Zeitschrift für Strafrecht 46 (2003)

Vyver, J.D. v.d., 'Prosecution and punishment of the crime of genocide', 23 Fordham international law journal 286 (1999)

Wagner, J.M., 'U.S. Prosecution of Past and Future War Criminals and Criminals against Humanity: Proposals for Reform Based on the Canadian and Australian Experience', 29 Va. J. Int'l L. 887 (1989)

Wakjira, G., 'National prosecution: the Ethiopian experience', in: C.C. Joyner and M.C. Bassiouni (eds.), *Reining in impunity for international crimes and serious violations of fundamental human rights proceedings of the Siracusa conference, 17-21 September 1998* (Toulouse: Érès, 1998), 189-191

Wasilkowski, A., 'Monism and dualism at present', in: J. Makarczyk (ed.) *Theory of international law at the threshold of the 21st century: essays in honour of Krzysztof Skubiszewski* (The Hague: Kluwer, 1996, 1996), 323-336

Waters, T.W., 'Unexploded bomb: voice, silence, and consequence at the Hague Tribunals: a legal and rhetorical critique', 35 N.Y.U. J. Int'l L. & Pol. 1015 (2003)

Weckel, P. and A. Chaouch Helel, 'Chronique de jurisprudence internationale', 107 RGDIP 741 (2003)

Weigend, E., 'Polen', in: H. Kreicker (ed.) *Nationale Strafverfolgung völkerrechtlicher Verbrechen – National Prosecution of International Crimes. Finnland, Polen, Schweden* (Freiburg i. Br.: 2003), 77-181

Weigend, E. and A. Zoll, 'Polen', in: A. Eser and J. Arnold (eds.), *Strafrecht in Reaktion auf Systemunrecht: Polen, Ungarn* (Freiburg im Breisgau: Ed. Iuscrim, 2002), 27-150

Weil, P., 'Towards Relative Normativity in International Law?', 77 AJIL 413 (1983)

Weisburd, A.M., 'The emptiness of the concept of Jus Cogens, as illustrated by the war in Bosnia-Herzegovina', 17 Michigan journal of international law 1 (1995)

Weissbrodt, D.S., *The right to a fair trial under the Universal Declaration of Human Rights and the International Covenant on Civil and Political Rights* (The Hague; Boston, Mass.: Martinus Nijhoff Publishers, 2001)

Werle, G., *Völkerstrafrecht* (Tübingen: Mohr Siebeck, 2003)

Wet, E. de, 'The Prohibition of Torture as an International Norm of Jus Cogens and Its Implications for National and Customary Law', 15 EJIL 97 (2004)

White III, R.R., 'Brothers v. Klevenhagen: The Fifth Circuit gives its imprimatur to the indicriminate use of deadly force against escaping pretrial detainees', 69 Tulane law review 1051 (1995)

Wible, B., '"De-jeopardizing justice": domestic prosecutions for international crimes and the need for transnational convergence', 31 Denver j. int. law policy 265 (2002)

Wieland, G., 'Die Ahndung von NS-Verbrechen in Ostdeutschland', in: C.F. Rüter (ed.) *DDR-Justiz und NS-Verbrechen, Verfahrensregister* (Amsterdam: Amsterdam University Press, 2002), 13-94

Wiener, I.A., 'Constitution and criminal law', 38 Acta Jur. Hung. 19 (1997)

Wildhaber, L., 'Bemerkungen zum Fall Schubert Betreffend das Verhaltnis von Volkerrecht und Landesrecht', 30 Annuaire suisse de droit international 195 (1974)

Wilson, R.J., 'Prosecuting Pinochet: International Crimes in Spanish Domestic Law', 21 HRQ 927 (1999)

Wilt, H.v.d., 'Een Internationaal Straftribunaal voor ex-Joegoslavië: de spanning tussen legaliteit en effectiviteit', 20 Recht en kritiek 8 (1994)

Wilt, H. v.d., 'The International Criminal Court and Domestic Jurisdictions: Competition or Concerted Action?' in: T.C. v. Boven and F. Coomans (eds.), *Rendering justice to the vulnerable: liber amicorum in honour of Theo van Boven* (The Hague; Boston, Mass.: Kluwer Law International, 2000), 323-338

Wilt, H.v.d., 'Het terroristische oogmerk', in: M.M. Dolman (ed.) *Terrorisme, Europa en strafrecht* (Amsterdam: Vossiuspers UvA, 2003), 55-81

Wise, E.M., 'International crimes and domestic criminal law', 38 DePaul Law Review 923 (1989)

Woetzel, R.K., *The Nuremberg trials in international law* (London / New York: Stevens / Praeger, 1960)

Wolfrum, R., 'The decentralized prosecution of international offences through national courts', in: Y. Dinstein and M. Tabory (eds.), *War crimes in international law* (The Hague [etc.]: Nijhoff, 1996), 233-251

Woodhouse, D., *The Pinochet case a legal and constitutional analysis* (Oxford: Hart, 2000)

Wouters, J., 'Customary international law before national courts: Some reflections from a continental European perspective', 4 Non-State Actors and International Law 25 (2004)

Wouters, J. and D.v. Eeckhoutte, 'Giving Effect to Customary International Law through European Community Law', in: J.M. Prinssen and A. Schrauwen (eds.), *Direct effect: rethinking a classic of EC legal doctrine* (Groningen: Europa Law Publishing, 2002), 181-234

Wouters, J. and H. Panken, 'De Genocidewet in internationaal perspectief: van nu en straks', in: J. Wouters and H. Panken (eds.), *De Genocidewet in internationaal perspectief* (2003), 1-38

Wright, Q., *The enforcement of international law through municipal law in the United States* Urbana, 1916)

Wyler, E., 'From 'state crime' to responsibility for 'serious breaches of obligations under peremptory norms of general international law'', 13 EJIL 1147 (2002)

Wyngaert, C.v.d., 'De toepassing van de strafwet in de ruimte', in: F. Dumon and R. Bützler (eds.), *Liber amicorum Frédéric Dumon* (Antwerpen: Kluwer Rechtswetenschappen, 1983), 501-525

Wyngaert, C. v.d., *Strafrecht, strafprocesrecht & internationaal strafrecht in hoofdlijnen* (Antwerpen: Maklu, 2003)

Wyngaert, C. v.d. and T. Ongena, '*Ne bis in idem* Principle, Including the Issue of Amnesty', in: J.R.W.D. Jones (ed.) *International criminal law: a commentary on the Rome Statute for an International Criminal Court* (Oxford: Oxford University Press, 2001), 705-729

Wyrozumska, A., 'Direct application of the Polish Constitution and international treaties to private conduct', 25 Polish YIL 5 (2001)

Yánez-Barnuevo, J.A. and Á. Roldán, 'Spain and the Rome Statute of the International Criminal Court', in: Kress and Lattanzi 2000, 197-217

Yoo, J.C., 'Globalism and the Constitution: treaties, non-self-execution, and the original understanding', 99 Colum. L. Rev. 1955 (1999a)

Yoo, J.C., 'Treaties and public lawmaking: a textual and structural defense of non-self-execution', 99 Colum. L. Rev. 2218 (1999b)

Young, E.A., 'Sorting out the debate over customary international law', 42 Va. J. Int'l L. 365 (2002)

Yourow, H.C., *The margin of appreciation doctrine in the dynamics of European human rights jurisprudence* (Dordrecht; Boston: M. Nijhoff, 1995)

Yuan, L. and L. Jianping, 'Droit chinois', in: Cassese and Delmas-Marty 2002, 345-366

Zakaria, F., *The future of freedom: illiberal democracy at home and abroad* (New York: W.W. Norton & Co., 2003)

Zappala, S., 'Droit italien', in: Cassese and Delmas-Marty 2002, 193-216

Zegveld, L., *Armed opposition groups in international law the quest for accountability* (Rotterdam: PhD thesis, 2000)

Zegveld, L., 'Kritische beschouwing van artikel 1(F) Vluchtelingenverdrag en het ACV-advies in het licht van het internationaal recht', Nieuwsbrief Asiel- en Vluchtelingenrecht 4 (2001)

Zegveld, L., *Accountability of armed opposition groups in international law* (Cambridge: CUP, 2002a)

Zegveld, L., 'The Bouterse case', 32 NYIL 97 (2002b)

Zemanek, K., 'The legal foundations of the international system: general course on public international law', 266 RdC 9 (1998)

Ziegler, A.R., 'Domestic prosecution and international cooperation with regard to violations of international humanitarian law: the case of Switzerland', 7 Schweizerische Zeitschrift für internationales und europäisches Recht 561 (1997)

Ziegler, A.R., 'In Re G. Military Tribunal, Division 1, Lausanne, Switzerland, April 18, 1997', 92 AJIL 78 (1998)

Zimmermann, S., *Strafrechtliche Vergangenheitsaufarbeitung und Verjährung: rechtsdogmatische und -politische Analyse mit vergleichenden Ausblicken nach Tschechien, Ungarn und Frankreich* (Freiburg im Breisgau: Edition Iuscrim, 1997)

Zoller, E. and I.A. Reshetov, 'International Criminal Responsibility of Individuals for International Crimes', in: G. Ginsburgs and V. N. Kudriavtsev (eds.), *The Nuremberg trial and international law* (Dordrecht; Boston: M. Nijhoff, 1990), 99-120

Note

'The International Judicial Dialogue: When Domestic Constitutional Courts Join the Conversation', 114 Harvard LR 2049 (2001)

TABLE OF DOCUMENTS

I. International Reports

- Amnesty International, *Report on Universal jurisdiction*, 2001
- International Law Association, *Rapport final sur la succession en matière de traités*, April 2002
- Human Rights Watch, Justice at Risk: War Crimes Trials in Croatia, Bosnia and Herzegovina, and Serbia and Montenegro, 2004
- Working Group of the International Law Commission, *Report on Jurisdictional Immunities of States and their Property*, 1999
- United Nations Committee against Torture and L. Holmström, *Conclusions and recommendations of the UN Committee against Torture: eleventh to twenty-second sessions (1993–1999)* (The Hague; Boston: Martinus Nijhoff Publishers, 2000)
- United Nations War Crimes Commission, *Law reports of trials of war criminals* (London: Pub. for the United Nations War Crimes Commission by H. M. Stationery Off., 1947)

II. National Reports

Canada
- Deschenes, J., Report of the Canadian Commission of Inquiry on War Criminals, 1986

Chile
- *Periodic Report of Chile to the HRC*, 3 December 1998, Doc. CCPR/C/95/Add.11

Guatemala
- *Periodic Report of Guatemala to the HRC*, 5 April 2000, Doc. CCPR/C/GTM/99/2

Hungary
- *Report to the Committee against Torture*, 17 June 1998, CAT/C/34/Add.10
- *Report to the Human Rights Committee*, 13 March 2001, CCPR/C/HUN/2000/4
- *Report to the Committee on the Elimination of Racial Discrimination*, 17 May 2002, CERD/C/431/Add.1

Paraguay
- *Reply to the Inter-American Commission of Human Rights*, March 2002

United Kingdom
- Hetherington, S.T. and W. Chalmers, *Report of the War Crimes Inquiry* (United Kingdom: Cm 744, 1989)

United States of America
- Restatement, *Restatement of the law, third, The foreign relations law of the United States as adopted and promulgated ... May 14, 1986* (St. Paul, Minn.: American Law Institute, 1987)

INDEX